Gender

A sociological reader

This reader offers students an informed overview of some of the most significant sociological work on gender produced over the last three decades. The text is informed by an understanding of gender as both a structural social division and a set of everyday social practices. The readings cover both theoretical and empirical work representing a range of perspectives, and each section addresses the intersection of gender with differences of 'race', class and sexuality. Fifty readings are organised into six parts:

- Gender and knowledge
- Class, gender and the labour market
- Paid and unpaid work
- Marriage and intimate relationships
- Becoming gendered
- Gendered embodiment

In order to guide students through the issues, the book has a substantial critical introduction exploring the history of sociological analyses of gender, as well as introductions to each section and editorial commentary on the readings themselves. Suggestions for further reading and questions for discussion are also included in each section.

Stevi Jackson is Professor and Director of The Centre for Women's Studies at The University of York. **Sue Scott** is Professor of Sociology at The University of Durham.

Routledge Student Readers

Series Editor: Chris Jenks, Professor of Sociology,
Goldsmiths College, University of London

Already in this series:

Theories of Race and Racism: A Reader
Edited by Les Back and John Solomos

Gender

A sociological reader

Edited by

Stevi Jackson and Sue Scott

 Routledge
Taylor & Francis Group

LONDON AND NEW YORK

First published 2002
by Routledge
2 Park Square, Milton Park, Abingdon, Oxon OX14 4RN

Simultaneously published in the USA and Canada
by Routledge
270 Madison Ave, New York, NY 10016

Reprinted 2003, 2005, 2006 (twice)

Routledge is an imprint of the Taylor & Francis Group, an informa business

Typeset in Perpetua and Bell Gothic by
Florence Production Ltd, Stoodleigh, Devon

British Library Cataloguing in Publication Data
A catalogue record for this book is available from the British Library

Library of Congress Cataloging in Publication Data
  Gender: a sociological reader / edited by Stevi Jackson and Sue Scott.
    p. cm. – (Routledge student readers)
  Includes bibliographical references and index.
  1. Sex role.   2. Sex – Social aspects.   3. Feminism.   I. Jackson, Stevi.
  II. Scott, Sue.   III. Series.
  HQ1075 .G426 2001
  305.3–dc21   2001032590

ISBN10: 0–415–20179–9 (hbk)
ISBN10: 0–415–20180–2 (pbk)

ISBN13: 978–0–415–20179–7 (hbk)
ISBN13: 978–0–415–20180–3 (pbk)

Contents

Series Editor's Preface

I AM DELIGHTED TO WELCOME this volume on *Gender* as the second major contribution to our series of Routledge Student Readers in Sociology. The topic, gender, is a complex one and, as the Introduction makes clear, one with a history. Although it may be argued that gender is perhaps the oldest the most enduring source of social differentiation, it is one that has claimed critical address only within the last century and only within some segments of Western society. Within the academy the conceptualisation and re-conceptualisation of gender, as an idea and as a set of practices, has occurred during only the last three decades, which surely reveals the deeply political character of the issues that it raises. Sociology might rightly express some embarrassment at the tardy and often reluctant manner through which it came to cast its attention upon such a universal grounding of social stratification and power. However, through the sustained efforts and militant voice of (largely) one gender group the concept has now been prised free from the stifling, and all too convenient, grip of the natural world and released into the realm of the social and the cultural. Gender is thus amenable to our analysis and deconstruction. Gender is now one of the sociology's central concepts but this does not speak of success and completion. When any idea becomes 'centralised' or 'mainstreamed', there is a danger of new forms of 'normalisation' and 'taken-for-grantedness'. A routine acknowledgement of important forms of differentiation can lead to tokenism, and policies established to handle such differentiation could lead to complacency and a dulling of our critical appreciation.

There is no such danger in the work assembled here. This volume, in common with other books in this series, seeks not to establish an orthodoxy or even a common denominator for its discipline or sub-discipline, nor even to espouse an established set of topics for teaching and learning within this area of study. Rather the work seeks to engage with the student reader, to offer them a series of debates, oppositions, contradictions and dilemmas that have preoccupied sociological thought over the years. Critically, the books in this series are organised in the form of readers but readers assembled thematically to combine both ancient and modern (traditional and fashionable) at a conceptual level. Students of our discipline need to be advised, and reminded, that the sociological tradition is neither a museum nor a petrified forest requiring guides to show us around. Sociology is a living tradition and an emergent dialogue. The multitude of perspectives, thinkers and schools through which it is comprised do not stand in isolation, disconnected through heroic epistemological breaks. Through both continuity and conflict there is engagement. Students of sociology also need to know that some of the contemporary giants like Foucault for example, achieve originality and make sense because of the problems set by earlier thinkers like Durkheim and Marx. Similarly, the nihilism and lack of truth-value in post-modernism acquires its vitality and 'newness' in response to the formalism and certainty of modernity. Finally we have to remember that modernity and science are, and continue to be, the major human achievements that control and organise our world – but despite the sweeping claims of globalisation theory, human experience varies place by place and strata by strata. Gender is a primary variable in that shaping of experience.

Welcome to this important contribution to the series, Routledge Student Readers, and I hope that your experience as a reader of this work matches up to our aspirations in compiling the series. Following in the wake of the highly successful opening volume on *Race and Racism* I am sure that this book will very rapidly establish itself as a most significant and well regarded landmark in this particular area of concern. *Gender* has the singular advantage of having been meticulously compiled by Stevi Jackson and Sue Scott, both leading feminist figures and leading contributors to the sociology of sex and gender. Both of these editors have achieved professorial status within the latter part of the historical process of assimilation and recognition of gender issues that they describe in their Introduction. However, their achievement and the forging of their academic careers through this period of consciousness raising is, like the arrival of a woman Prime Minister, not necessarily a sign that a condition of egalitarianism has emerged. Universities employ fewer women academics than men, promote fewer women senior lecturers and professors (proportionately) than men and even where women professors are in office they tend to be relatively less well paid than their male counterparts. If you are wondering in an age of equal opportunities and in such an enlightened environment how these differentials can possibly exist – read on!

Chris Jenks, Professor of Sociology
Goldsmiths College, University of London

Acknowledgements

We would like to thank those who helped to bring this book into being, in particular our supportive and patient editor at Routledge, Mari Shullaw. We are also
grateful to John Hughes and Heloise Brown for help with the mundane tasks of
photocopying, cutting and pasting and permissions chasing. Heloise undertook the
greater burden of these chores, especially in the later stages. We owe a great deal
to her hard work, attention to detail and tenacious detective work in tracking
down elusive copyright holders.

The publishers would like to thank the following for their permission to reprint
their material:

Allen & Unwin for permission to reprint 'Hegemonic masculinity', from Bob
   Connell, *Gender and Power*, 1996.

The American Sociological Association for permission to reprint Chrys Ingraham,
   'The heterosexual imaginary: feminist sociology and theories of gender', from
   Sociological Theory, July 1994.

Blackwell Publishers for permission to reprint 'Hegemonic masculinity', from Bob
   Connell, *Gender and Power*, 1996; 'The variety of work done by wives' from
   Christine Delphy and Diana Leonard, *Familiar Exploitation: A New Analysis of
   Marriage in Contemporary Western Society*, 1992.

Cambridge University Press for permission to reprint material from Lynne
   Jamieson, 'Intimacy transformed', *Sociology* 33:4, 1999; Jan Pahl, 'Household
   spending and the control of money in marriage' from *Sociology* 24:1, 1990;
   and Anne Witz, 'Patriarchy and the professions: the gendered politics of
   occupational closure', *Sociology* 24:4, 1990.

Columbia University Press for permission to reprint 'Lovers through the looking glass', from Kath Weston, *Families we Choose*, 1991.

Bronwyn Davies for permission to reprint extracts from *Frogs and Snails and Feminist Tales*, Allen & Unwin (Sydney), 1989.

Elsevier Science Ltd for permission to reprint Christine Delphy, 'Rethinking sex and gender', from *Women's Studies International Forum*, 16:1, 1993.

Heinemann for permission to reprint Linda Imray and Audrey Middleton, 'Public and private: marking the boundaries' from E. Gamarnikow *et al.* (eds), *The Public and the Private*.

Suzanne Kessler, *Lessons from the Intersexed*, copyright © 1998 by Susan Kessler; reprinted by permission of Rutgers University Press.

Macmillan Press Ltd for permission to reprint 'Resisting Equal Opportunities: the issue of maternity', from Cynthia Cockburn, *In the Way of Women*; Jean Dunncombe and Dennis Marsden, 'Whose orgasm is this anyway?' from J. Weeks and J. Holland (eds), *Sexual Cultures*, 1996; 'Lesbians in manual jobs', from Gillian Dunne, *Lesbian Lifestyles*, 1996; Brian Heaphy, Catherine Donovan and Jeffery Weeks, 'Sex, money and the kitchen sink', from J. Seymour and P. Bagguley (eds), *Relating Intimacy*, 1996.

Open University Press for permission to reproduce 'Sexual servicing and the labour market' from Lisa Adkins, *Gendered Work*, 1995; 'From objectified body to embodied subject', from S. Wilkinson (ed.), '*Feminist Social Psychologies*', 1996; 'Do boys and girls have different cultures?' from Barrie Thorne, *Gender Play*, 1993; Janet Holland, Caroline Ramazanoglu and Rachel Thomson, 'In the same boat the gendered inexperience of first heterosex', from Diane Richardson (ed.) *Theorizing Heterosexuality*, 1996.

Pluto Press for permission to reprint 'Women working worldwide' from Swasti Mitter, *Common Fate, Common Bond*, 1985; 'Manly aesthetics' from Emmanuel Reynaud *Holy Virility*, 1983; and 'Domestic labourers: or Stand by your man – while he sits down and has a cup of tea', from Sallie Westwood, *All Day, Every Day*, 1984.

Routledge for permission to reprint Sue Baxter and Geoff Raw, 'Fast food, fettered work: Chinese women in the ethnic catering industry', from S. Westwood and P. Bhachu (eds), *Enterprising Women*, 1988; 'Performative subversions' from Judith Butler, *Gender Trouble*, 1990; Richard Ekins, 'The career path of the male femaler', from R. Ekins and D. King, *Blending Genders: Social Aspects of Cross-dressing and Sex Changing*, 1996; 'But he said he loved me', from Wendy Langford, *Revolutions of the Heart: Gender, Power and the Delusions of Love*, 1999; Sophie Laws, 'Who needs PMT?' in S. Laws, V. Hey and A. Eagan (eds), *Seeing Red: The Politics of Premenstrual Tension*; Liz Stanley and Sue Wise, *Breaking Out*, 1983; Alan Mansfield and Barbara McGinn, 'Pumping irony', from, Sue Scott and David Morgan (eds), *Body Matters*, 1993; 'Redefining Black womanhood' from Heidi Mirza, *Young, Female and Black*, 1991; David Morgan, 'You too can have a body like mine' from Sue Scott and David Morgan (eds), *Body Matters* (1993); Gemma Tang Nain, 'Black women, sexism and racism,' from *The Journal of Ethnic and Migration Studies*, 15:2, 1989; Annie Phizacklea, 'A single or segregated market? Gender and racialised divisions', from Heleh Afshar and Mary Maynard (eds) *The Dynamics of 'Race' and Gender*, 1994; 'Full wages and component wages' from Janet Siltanen, *Locating Gender: Occupational Segregation. Wages and Domestic Responsibilities*, 1994; 'The sexualisation of love' from Steven Seidman, *Romantic Longings: Love in America*, 1991; Liz Stanley, 'Should "Sex" Really be "Gender" or "Gender" Really be "Sex"?', from R. Anderson and W. Sharrock (eds), *Applied Sociology*, 1984; Vera Whisman 'Choosing a story', from *Queer by Choice*, 1996.

Sage Publications for permission to reprint 'Ambivalent femininities' from Beverley Skeggs, *Formations of Class and Gender*, 1997; Candace West and Don H. Zimmerman, 'Doing Gender', from Judith Lonber and Susan A. Farrell (eds), *The Social Construction of Gender*, 1991.

Barry Thorne, *Gender Play: Girls and Boys in School*, © 1993 by Barrie Thorne; Reprinted by permission of Rutgers University Press.

The University of California Press for permission to reprint 'Emotional Labour' from Arlie Hochschild, *The Managed Heart: Commercialization of Human Feeling*, 1983; Patricia Hill-Collins, 'Learning from the outsider within: the socio-logical significance of Black feminist thought, from *Social Problems*, 33:6, 1996.

The University of Chicago Press for permission to reprint Joan Acker, 'Women and stratification: a case of intellectual sexism', from the *American Journal of Sociology*, 78:4, 1973; Sander Gilman, 'Black bodies, White bodies', from W. L. Gates Jnr (ed.), *Race, Writing and Difference*, 1985; Heidi Hartmann, 'Capitalism, patriarchy and job segregation by sex', from *Signs*, 1, 1976; Emily Martin, 'The egg and the sperm, from *Signs*, 16:3, 1991; and Esther Newton, 'Drag and camp', from *Mother Camp: Female Impersonators in America*, 1972.

The University of Texas for permission to reprint Dorothy Smith, 'Women's perspective as a radical critique of sociology', from *Sociological Inquiry*, 44: 1, pp. 7–13. © 1974 by the University of Texas Press. All rights reserved.

The University of Toronto Press for permission to reprint 'Lesbians in manual jobs', from Gillian Dunne, *Lesbian Lifestyles*, 1996.

Sylvia Walby for permission to reprint 'Gender, class and stratification: towards a new approach', from R. Crompton and M. Mann (eds) *Gender and Stratification*, Polity Press, 1986.

Yale University Press for permission to reprint 'The husband's marriage and the wife's marriage', from Jessie Bernard, *The Future of Marriage*, 1972.

The publishers have made every effort to contact authors and copyright holders of works reprinted in *Gender: A Sociological Reader*. It has not been possible in every case, however, and we would welcome correspondence from individuals or companies we have been unable to trace.

Introduction:
The gendering of sociology

■ Stevi Jackson and Sue Scott

SINCE ENTERING SOCIOLOGY'S LEXICON in the early 1970s gender has become one of its key concepts. This centrality is entirely appropriate; what is surprising is the length of time it took for gender to find its rightful place within sociological thinking. It is now so taken for granted that all aspects of social life are gendered, that it may be difficult for newcomers to the social sciences to appreciate the extent to which recognising gender divisions once went against the grain of mainstream sociology. While there had been work on 'sex roles' prior to the 1970s, this was marginal to sociology's core concerns. For the most part sociologists studied the world of men as if men constituted the whole of society. This not only rendered women invisible, but also concealed the gendered characteristics of men's social locations, activities and identities. Even where women were included in sociological thinking, their place in society was frequently regarded as a 'natural' given or, at best, thought of in terms of 'roles' which were social but nonetheless unproblematic.

The resurgence of feminism in the 1970s changed this state of affairs, challenging the androcentric view of the world which had prevailed for so long. It was central to the feminist project to counter the assumption that existing differences between women and men were ordained by nature. The concept of gender was adopted in order to emphasise the social construction of masculinity and femininity and the social ordering of relations between women and men. Since not everyone defines and uses the term 'gender' in exactly the same way, we should make it clear from the outset how we are using it here. Gender as we define it denotes a hierarchical division between women and men embedded in both social institutions and social practices. Gender is thus a social structural phenomenon but is also produced, negotiated and sustained at the level of everyday interaction. The world we inhabit is always already ordered by gender, yet gender is also embodied and lived by men and women, in local, specific, biographical contexts and is experienced as central to individual identities. Gender thus encompasses the social division and cultural distinction between women and men as well as the characteristics commonly associated with femininity and masculinity. It should be remembered, however, that gender cannot be abstracted from the wider social relations with which it is enmeshed, that gender intersects other social divisions and inequalities, such as class, 'race' and sexuality, and that the meanings of masculinity and femininity vary within, as well as between, societies.

In this introduction we will chart the development and elaboration of the concept of gender within sociological theory and research. We will begin from the 'prehistory' of gender, the ways in which sociologists thought about relations between women and men prior to the 1970s. We will then assess the impact of feminist thinking on sociology and the incorporation of gender into the discipline's analytical toolkit. Finally we will consider recent controversies around gender demonstrating that, although the concept has come to be widely accepted, it nevertheless continues to be contested.

The ghosts of sociology past

The origins of sociology are conventionally traced back to the nineteenth century, when a number of thinkers sought to make sense of the rapid social changes brought about by the rise of industrial capitalism. That these thinkers are collectively known as the founding *fathers* says something about gender. Not only were they men, but they paid little attention to issues of gender and sexuality, despite the fact that the social transformations which preoccupied them entailed major shifts in family life, in relations between men and women and in conceptualisations of masculinity and femininity (Seidman 1997). Many of the ideas about gender we now regard as 'traditional', along with the practices associated with them, were established at this time. For example, the separation of the workplace from domestic space was accompanied by the notion that women and men were suited to separate spheres and that a woman's place was in the home (Hall 1992; Davidoff and Hall 1987).[1] The changes in domestic and working life this entailed were products of the economic and social changes accompanying the rise of industrial capitalism, but the founding fathers of sociology had little to say about them. Yet there was much debate in the nineteenth century and early twentieth century about 'the woman question', and both male and female writers, such as J. S. Mill, Cicely Hamilton and Charlotte Perkins Gilman, challenged the confinement of women to the domestic sphere. These ideas, however, did not find their way into what was becoming established as mainstream sociology.

The work of the founding fathers did subsequently have some impact on sociological thinking about gender relations. Hence it is worth saying a little about the underlying assumptions about gender which informed their work and the influence they had on later sociological and feminist analysis. Moreover, even when gender does not figure centrally in sociological work, certain hidden, taken-for-granted assumptions about it tend nevertheless to inform sociologists' conclusions about social relations. This gendered subtext of sociology has been evident from the beginnings of the discipline; one of the contributions of more recent work on gender is that it has brought critical reflection to bear on these subterranean assumptions.

Marx and Engels

Of the major nineteenth century thinkers, it is Karl Marx who has had the greatest impact on feminist work, although he himself had little to say about women and gender. Marx was concerned exclusively with class, with the exploitation of the proletariat (the working class) by the bourgeoisie (the capitalist class). Although these classes were theoretically asexual, in fact Marx treated both workers and capitalists as men (without seeing their gender as in any way significant). Women were thus rendered invisible: 'they are absent from the analysis of the labour market on the one hand, and their domestic work and its exploitation is taken as given on the other' (Delphy 1984: 160). The way in which Marx took women's domestic work for granted is evident, for example, in his discussion of the reproduction of labour power in the first volume of *Capital*.

His argument was as follows. Since capitalism requires a constant supply of labour, it must be 'reproduced' in two senses. First the worker must be kept fit enough to work each day and thus must be fed, clothed and sheltered; second, the working class must reproduce itself over time through producing and rearing the next generation of workers. In the former sense the working class is reproduced through the workers' consumption of food, clothing and so on through which 'the means of subsistence given by capital' (i.e. wages) are converted into 'fresh labour power'. What Marx ignores is that this process itself requires labour, the cooking of meals and washing of shirts done by the male proletarian's wife. Marx claimed that, aside from providing wages, capital could leave the reproduction of labour power to 'the worker's drive for self-preservation and propagation' (1976: 717–18). Thus he makes it seem that male workers could even accomplish biological reproduction without the involvement of women!

While Marx only occasionally acknowledged women's existence, his collaborator, Friedrich Engels, had rather more to say about the position of women in society. Nonetheless Engels, like Marx, took the division of labour between women and men for granted. In *The Origins of the Family, Private Property and the State*, Engels starts from the assumption that at some time in prehistory women and men were equal – if different. He assumed that the division of labour between men (breadwinners) and women (domesticated wives and mothers) had always existed (an assumption we now know, from the perspective of both anthropology and archaeology, to be false). He thought, however, that the contributions of women and men to the social group had, in prehistoric times, been equally valued. He also assumed that the original human societies had traced descent through the female line (what he called 'mother right') and that fathers, therefore, had no rights in their offspring (another assumption now recognised as flawed). He argued

that 'the world historic defeat of the female sex' came about with the development of private property, which led men to seek control over women's sexual and
reproductive capacity in order to pass their worldly goods on to their own offspring.
This led to the overthrow of 'mother right' in favour of 'father right', to monogamous marriage and the subordination of women within the family. Hence Engels
questioned the universality of women's subordination, but nonetheless assumed that
gender divisions were entirely natural.

Both Marx and Engels influenced later discussion of women and the family
(see, for example, Zaretsky 1976). In the 1970s many Marxist feminists tried to
bring gender into Marxism by focusing on the ways in which women's domestic
labour contributed to the reproduction of labour power and thus to the maintenance of capitalism (for summaries see Kaluzynska 1980; Rushton 1979). Others
followed Engels in discussing the 'relations of reproduction' through which women
were subordinated within families (e.g. McDonough and Harrison 1978). While
these later writings made women more visible within Marxism, they did not really
confront the problem of *gender*: the assumption of a 'natural' distinction between
women and men remained, and the division of labour between them was not fully
explained. It was not possible, within conventional Marxism, to ask why it should
be *women* who occupied particular social positions as domestic labourers or repro-
ducers of labour power. It was all too easy to conclude that women were placed
in this situation simply because they gave birth to babies.

Weber

Max Weber's contribution to the study of gender is the concept of patriarchy.
For Weber patriarchal authority was the oldest form of socially legitimated
power. In traditional, pre-capitalist societies, the power traditionally vested in male
heads of households gave them authority not only over women and children but
also over younger men, servants, slaves and any other household dependants.
Weber saw this arrangement as the template for other forms of traditional authority
such as the feudal system where every man owed allegiance to an overlord, from
whom he gained his right to land or a livelihood, thus creating a hierarchical
chain of social relations up to the ultimate overlord, the monarch. This form
of patriarchal society was structured rather like a series of nested boxes in which
each household, with its own internal authority structure, was subsumed by those
further up the social hierarchy and in turn subsumed those of lower status.
Within each of these 'boxes' women were subordinate to men. Like Marx and
Engels, Weber did not question the basic division between men and women. He
considered the mother/child unit to be natural and therefore not sociologically
significant. He saw men as linking the mother/child relationship into the wider
society, thus 'it is fathers that civilize the relationship' (Sydie 1987: 63). Here
he did anticipate some feminist discussion of the relationship between public and
private spheres, particularly the idea that women and children inhabit a private
sphere separate from but subsumed by the male-dominated public sphere (Rosaldo
1974).

Weber's work has had a limited impact on modern approaches to gender. Only a few modern feminist writers, such as Roberta Hamilton (1978), have developed an explicitly Weberian analysis of patriarchy. While others use the term 'patriarchy', they do not necessarily trace it back to Weber, although some have considered the term to be most appropriate to those forms of social structure Weber described, or at least to those societies where kinship is the fundamental organising principle (Barrett 1980). Some sociologists have brought a gender dimension to Weberian analyses of class, focusing on the ways in which women and men are differentially distributed within the occupational hierarchy (Britten and Heath 1983; Roberts 1993; Witz 1990, chapter 14 in this book). However, more traditional Weberians, as we shall see later, still resist the incorporation of gender into class analysis (Goldthorpe 1983; 1984).

Durkheim

Of the three main 'founding fathers' Emile Durkheim is the least appealing to modern feminists largely because of his view of society as a neatly integrated functioning whole in which everyone had their place – and women's place was in the home. Durkheim argued that the division of labour became more elaborated as societies progressed. At the same time men's and women's roles became increasingly specialised and the differences between them more marked: 'among cultivated people, the woman leads a completely different existence from that of a man' (1964: 60). Durkheim saw this sexual difference as fundamental to the conjugal bond, making men and women dependent on each other in a complementary relationship in which 'one of the sexes takes care of the affective functions and the other of intellectual functions' (1964: 60). (No prizes for guessing which is which.) Durkheim came closest to recognising the social subordination of women in showing that married women were more likely to commit suicide than either married men or single women. He concluded that men benefited more from marriage than women, although some of the reasons he posited for this are not likely to appeal to modern feminists. He believed, for example, that monogamous marriage beneficially restrained men's sexuality, affording them security, tranquillity and mental calmness. Women did not need this calming influence, because their sexual life, he thought, was less intellectual and more tied to biological imperatives. He did, however, recognise that the double standard of morality imposed monogamy more powerfully on women than on men (1966: 270–5). While Durkheim did, therefore take gender into account as a variable, he simply reported what he saw as an effect of an inevitable 'civilised' division of labour superimposed upon an assumed 'natural' biological difference.

Simmel

Georg Simmel, a more neglected figure among the founders of sociology, shared the common preconception of his time that differences between men and women were natural. Although he took it for granted that men's orientation to the public world and women's to the private domestic sphere reflected natural masculine and feminine proclivities, he was acutely aware of the imbalance of power between women and men. Very insightfully for a man of his time, he was sensitive to the ways in which masculinity was treated as the human norm and femininity as a deviation from it. It is worth quoting him at length:

> The fact that the male sex is not only considered relatively superior to the female, but that it is taken as the universal human norm . . . is, in many different ways, based on the power position of the male. If we express the historical relation between the sexes crudely in terms of master and slave, it is part of the master's privileges not to have to think continuously of the fact that he is the master, while the position of the slave carries with it the constant reminder of his [sic] being a slave. It cannot be overlooked that the woman forgets far less often the fact of being a woman than the man of being a man. . . . This fact is evident in the extremely frequent phenomenon that certain judgements, institutions, aims, or interests which we men, naively so to speak, consider purely objective, are felt by women to be thoroughly and characteristically masculine.
>
> (Simmel 1911, quoted in Klein 1946: 82–3)

This perceptive statement presages much modern feminist thinking about the ways in which men are able to represent themselves as ungendered and pass off knowledge as objective when it is, in fact, constructed from a masculine perspective.

Sex roles and sociology

Mainstream sociology continued, well into the twentieth century, to produce knowledge from an unquestioned masculine standpoint – even when dealing explicitly with gender. Hence it was the more conservative ideas of the 'founding fathers' which held sway. The prime example is the functionalist analysis of the family put forward in the 1950s by Talcott Parsons. Echoing Durkheim's analysis, Parsons believed that there was a complementary division of labour between husbands and wives which stabilised the family and integrated it into the wider society. The potential strain between the instrumental ethos of industrial society and the emotional orientation of family life was minimised by men who worked outside the home specialising in instrumental (goal-oriented) roles and domestically oriented women specialising in affective (emotional) roles (Parsons and Bales 1956).

More critical analyses of sex roles, however, were beginning to emerge, challenging the dominant perspectives of the era. One of the earliest was Margaret Mead's (1935) questioning of naturalistic assumptions about sex differences in her anthropological study of three New Guinea societies, which she saw as representing very different ideas about the temperament of each sex. The first of these societies, the Arapesh, she characterised as relatively androgynous in temperament, with both men and women exhibiting the nurturtant, caring qualities which, in Western cultures, are regarded as feminine. The second society, the Mundugamor, were equally androgynous, but here, by Western standards, both men and women were 'masculine' in that both were very aggressive. Mead claimed that the third society which she studied, the Tchambuli, reversed our ideas about masculinity and femininity, with the women being the practical doers and the men being largely preoccupied with idle gossip and self-adornment. Mead sought to establish that feminine and masculine attributes and roles were largely cultural rather than natural. In her later work she suggests that, despite the diversity in the human organisation of sex-differentiated activities, what is deemed masculine is always and universally deemed also to be superior:

> Men may cook or weave or dress dolls or hunt humming-birds, but if such activities are the appropriate occupation of men, then the whole society, men and women alike, votes them as important. When the same occupations are performed by women, they are regarded as less impor-tant. In a great number of human societies men's sureness of their sex role is tied up with their right, or ability, to practice some activity that women are not allowed to practice.
>
> (Mead 1950/1962: 157–8)

Despite her concern to establish the cultural specificity of ideas about sex and temperament Mead nonetheless judged other societies through the lens of Western gender stereotypes (see Errington and Gewertz 1987). Moreover, she assumed a fixed pool of human potential which was the same in all societies but which was divided by gender in varied ways within different societies. She presupposed that the two sexes were fixed, but that the qualities attributed to each varied, along with the tasks allotted to them. Although flawed, Mead's pioneering work did provide useful ideas and data for a later generation of sociologists and was widely drawn upon to demonstrate the cultural malleability of gender and thus illustrate its disconnection from biological sex.

Contemporaneously with Mead's anthropology, some sociologists, such as Viola Klein in Britain and Mirra Kimarovsky in the United States, also began to ques-tion the social ordering of 'sex roles' and to critique the inequities they produced. In 1946 Viola Klein published her ground-breaking book *The Feminine Character*. Subtitled *A History of an Ideology*, this work exposes the androcentric biases underlying supposedly 'objective' social science and argues that 'femininity' is constructed rather than given. Moreover, Klein also points out that, despite the prevailing belief in 'real' differences between men and women, there is very little agreement among 'experts' or the general population about what constitutes 'femi-ninity': 'there are almost as many opinions as there are minds, and it is hard to find even two essential characteristics on which the common man [sic] or the majority of experts would agree' (1946: 163). Klein suggests that feminine traits are sociologically rather than biologically given. A key determinant is women's domestic responsibilities, which absorb 'a preponderating part of women's energy' (1946: 181).

Klein, in association with Alva Myrdal, conducted one of the first studies of women's strategies in combining paid work with domestic work. At a time when mainstream sociologists of the family assumed that women were primarily 'house-wives' Myrdal and Klein were alert to the increasing participation of women in the post-war labour force and the double burden this imposed upon them. Myrdal and Klein saw the integration of women into the labour force as potentially eman-cipating. Challenging the Parsonian view of contented full-time housewives, they suggested that women at home experienced social isolation and boredom exacer-bated by the financial dependence being a housewife entailed and the low esteem in which the role was held. In many respects *Women's Two Roles* (1956) antici-pates later feminist research into the inequities of the gendered division of labour (e.g. Hochschild 1989; Yeandle 1984; Westwood 1984) and women's dissatis-faction with housework (Gavron 1966; Oakley 1974).

Mirra Komarovsky is best known for her in-depth study *Blue Collar Marriage* (1962), which revealed the divergences between men's and women's expectations and experience of married life. While the women generally accepted an inequitable division of domestic labour, many expressed dissatisfaction with the lack of emotional intimacy and companionship in their marriages – a finding that presaged more recent studies (see, for example, Mansfield and Collard 1988). Like Mead and Klein, Komarovsky was aware of the ways in which social change was impinging on women, often subjecting them to contradictory expectations. In an earlier study of women college students, she explored the tensions between the pursuit of educa-tional success and the demands of sexually desirable femininity. The college women, she found, admitted to 'playing dumb' in male company, allowing their boyfriends to explain things they already understood – often better than the young men who displayed their supposed intellectual superiority – in order to flatter the young men's egos and preserve their own 'femininity' (Komarovsky 1946).

These early anthropological and sociological studies of sex roles began to mark out the terrain and establish some of the conditions for the later conceptualisa-tion of gender. First, they called into question social scientists' assumptions about the naturalness of sex differences. Second, they cast doubt on the idea of an unproblematic complementarity between men's and women's 'roles'. Third, they began to establish that sex roles were not merely indicators of differences between women and men, but marked a key social division and, importantly, a hierarchical one. Thus the stage was set for the more explicitly feminist analyses that were to emerge in the 1970s.

Feminism and its effects

The rise of 'second wave' feminism in the late 1960s and early 1970s inspired many young sociologists to look for more critical approaches to the study of men's and women's social lives. More emphasis was placed on the inequalities between women and men, and the language of 'sex roles' began to be replaced by new concepts, in particular 'gender' and 'patriarchy'. This new generation of scholars drew on earlier sociological research and also on existing feminist work. A key influence was the French writer and philosopher, Simone de Beauvoir. In her classic *The Second Sex*, first published in 1949, de Beauvoir laid the foundations for a feminist analysis of gender. Her famous assertion that 'one is not born, but rather becomes, a woman' emphasised the social character of womanhood as distinct from biological femaleness. According to de Beauvoir bodily differences between women and men may be 'inescapable' but 'in themselves they have no significance', since they depend for their meaning on the 'whole context' in which actual women and men live their lives (1949/1972: 66–7). Here she anticipates the distinction between biological sex and socio-cultural gender which English-speaking feminists adopted in the 1970s.

One of the first to elaborate this distinction was the British sociologist Ann Oakley (1972). Oakley borrowed the terminology of sex and gender from Robert Stoller (1968), a US psychiatrist and psychoanalyst who worked with individuals whose biological sex was defined as ambiguous or whose sense of themselves conflicted with their assigned sex. He found the distinction between sex and gender useful In describing the situation of those people whose biological sex was found to differ from the gender category in which they had been placed or in which they located themselves. Following Stoller, Oakley defined sex as the anatomical and physiological characteristics which signify biological maleness and femaleness and gender as socially constructed masculinity and femininity. Masculinity and femininity are products not of biology but of the social, cultural and psychological attributes acquired through the process of becoming a man or a woman in a particular society at a particular time. Gender is thus a social characteristic, not a direct product of biological sex.

A few years later, in the United States, Gayle Rubin (1975) wrote another account of gender which was to become highly influential. Whereas Oakley distinguished gender from biological sex, Rubin related gender to reproductive sexuality, encompassing the two in the concept of the 'sex/gender system'. According to Rubin, each society 'has a sex/gender system – a set of arrangements by which the biological raw material of human sex and procreation is shaped by human, social intervention' (1975: 165). These arrangements vary from one society and culture to another and serve as conventional means of organising human sexual relations, especially through the structuring of kinship and marriage. Gender, for Rubin, is 'a socially imposed division of the sexes' and 'a product of the social relations of sexuality' (1975: 179).

What these two formulations have in common is that they see gender as distinct from, but related to, the biological bases of male/female relations. This subsequently gave rise to further debate, which we will return to later, but at this point we should emphasise what had been achieved by the introduction of the concept of gender. Most important, the concept of gender enabled us to think of masculinity and femininity as historically and culturally variable rather than fixed by nature. Moreover, what it means to be a woman or a man can also vary within any given society at any one time, often reflecting other differences and inequalities such as those of class and 'race'. It may be argued, for example, that the dominant ideal of femininity is that of the white middle classes. This was certainly true in the nineteenth century, when the ideal of women as fragile, innocent creatures requiring the protection of chivalrous virile men could be achieved only by the socially privileged. This ideal of womanhood was directly contested by the Black ex-slave and suffrage campaigner, Sojourner Truth, in a speech delivered at a women's rights convention in Akron, Ohio, in 1852:

> That man over there says women need to be helped into carriages and over ditches and to have the best places. No one ever helped me into carriages or over ditches or gave me the best place − and ain't I a woman? Look at me! Look at my arm . . . I have ploughed, and I have planted, and gathered into barns and no man could head me − and ain't I a woman? I could work as much as any man . . . and bear the lash as well and ain't I a woman?
>
> (Quoted in Carby 1982: 214−15)

If gender is social rather than natural, change and variability are always possible. Hence continuities also require a social explanation. One important continuity is the hierarchical relationship between women and men, which has persisted despite many changes in the meaning of femininity and masculinity and in the social activities of women and men. While male dominance can and does change in form and degree, it seems that gender hierarchy can coexist with a wide variety of beliefs about gender and with differing divisions of labour between women and men. Gender thus denotes a hierarchical relationship between women and men, not merely differences between them. If gender is understood to be social, this hierarchical relationship needs to be explained as a product of social arrangements.

Some theorists found the concept of patriarchy useful as a means of emphasising that male dominance was both systematic and pervasive. However, patriarchy proved to be a more contentious concept than gender and was not as widely accepted. Patriarchy literally means the rule of fathers, and in its original usage, derived from Weber, it referred to a traditional form of authority vested in men as heads of families. Some feminists argued for a wider definition of patriarchy as any form of systematic male domination; others worried that this produced an ahistorical conceptualisation. Some argued that the term should be reserved for the rule of the father within those societies ordered through kinship, but was not applicable to modern Western societies (Rubin 1975). Some sought to challenge the charge of ahistoricity by defining more closely the form of patriarchal domination prevalent in contemporary society (Delphy 1984) while others sought to explore the ways in which it had changed over time (Walby 1986). Some theorised patriarchy as an autonomous social system separate from, though articulating with, capitalism (Delphy 1984; Hartmann 1981; Walby, 1986; 1990) while others argued that there could be no separate social order outside capitalism (Barrett 1980). Some saw it as too monolithic a concept, disguising differences of class, 'race' and sexuality among women and among men (Beechey 1979; Carby 1982). In particular there were debates on whether the concept of patriarchy effectively encapsulated the experience of Black women and whether Black men enjoyed the patriarchal privileges accorded to White men (Bhavnani and Coulson 1986; hooks 1982; Nain 1991). There were disagreements among those who did use the concept of patriarchy concerning where its roots were located, whether it was founded on the exploitation of women's labour or on the appropriation of their sexuality and reproductive capacities or whether it was primarily sustained ideologically (see Jackson 1998).

These disagreements were never resolved, with the result that the term 'patriarchy' is used less frequently than gender, although its value continues to be debated (Bottero 1998; Pollert 1996). If we bear in mind that 'gender' describes an asymmetrical, hierarchical division between men and women, which is ubiquitous and enduring, some of the issues feminists sought to raise through the concept of patriarchy remain in view. Certainly, the research and theory relating to gender which have accumulated since the 1970s, and which are represented in this book, have amply demonstrated the inequalities that still exist between women and men. These gender inequalities, of course, must always be understood as intersecting other social divisions, distinctions and hierarchies such as those of class, 'race' and sexuality.

The gendering of sociology

Although these debates firmly established the centrality of the concept of gender within feminist scholarship they by no means guaranteed that its importance would be recognised within sociology. The prevailing view within British sociology in the 1970s was that class was the only significant form of stratification. Gender, or rather 'sex', did, however, receive some attention in the work of those American sociologists who took a multidimensional approach to stratification, which included any and all forms of inequality in income, status and power (e.g. Lenski 1966). This view assumed a meritocratic society of individuals who might be ranked high on some indicators while occupying more lowly status on others: for example, a low-paid worker might gain prestige from being an active local politician. Here men and women could be seen as occupying different positions as a result of the status distinction between them. The problem with this approach was that the analysis assumed a relatively open society and tended to treat all forms of inequality as equally salient, ignoring the ways in which some forms of inequality are far more significant than others. Moreover, the unit of analysis tended to be the individual, leading to failure to recognise the ways in which systematic inequalities tend to produce distinct social divisions between groups, rather than a hierarchy of individuals.

British sociologists were critical of this individualistic perspective and focused far more on social class, seen as the most fundamental form of stratification. Frank Parkin (1972) argued that 'sex' could not be regarded as an 'important dimension of stratification', since the 'disabilities attaching to female status' did not override those of class. Like other British sociologists, Parkin took class as an indicator and a predictor of a wide range of social attitudes and attributes as well as of lifestyle and life chances. Social class was assumed to be defined for all members of a household by the occupation of the male breadwinner – indeed, it was common for major studies of social class to include only men in the sample and thus only households headed by men (Glass 1954; Goldthorpe *et al.* 1980). It was assumed that women were defined first by their father's social class and then on marriage by that of their husband. Although sociologists had long been aware that there was a division of labour between women and men within families, they nonetheless analysed the social world as if wives occupied exactly the same social location as their husbands. Parkin argued explicitly that the family was the main unit of stratification, that women's position in society was determined far more by their membership of their kin group. Feminists had got it wrong because women did not have 'interests in opposition to their male kin'. On these grounds he argued that 'inequalities between different members of the family . . . cannot really be said to provide the basis of a distinct form of social stratification' (1972: 15). Feminist work unsettled these assumptions in two ways. First by analysing, in more detail than ever before, sources of inequality within families and households and second, by analysing the ways in which the labour market itself was segregated by gender (see Parts Two and Three). However, some sociologists refused to take gender seriously as an analytical category, which led to heated debates between feminists and mainstream stratification theorists (see Goldthorpe 1983, 1984; Stanworth 1984; Roberts 1993). Nonetheless a great deal of progress has been made here, resulting in a reorientation of sociological understanding of class (see, for example, Crompton 1997).

Paradoxically the barriers to taking gender seriously were also the potential gateways to its integration. When class was considered to be the only significant form of inequality, gender was rendered invisible and male dominance could be ignored. Yet precisely because sociology's core concerns were social divisions and inequalities, once gender was rendered visible there was a strong case for its centrality. Thus sociologists who accepted the importance of gender began to see the whole of the social world from a new angle. Sociologists have also questioned commonsense understandings of social arrangements as 'natural' and social problems as individual. As C. Wright Mills put it, the 'sociological imagination' transforms 'personal troubles' into 'public issues' (1970: 14–17). This had long been accepted in relation to poverty and unemployment, for example, but was also clearly applicable to issues relating to the subordination of women, such as low wages, domestic labour and sexual violence. Thus a connection was forged between sociological thinking and the feminist dictum that the personal was also political.

This is not to imply that it was always easy to persuade sociologists to take gender seriously or that all areas of sociology have been equally transformed through engagement with feminism. It has, however, been easier to make headway within sociology than within many other disciplines. Whereas feminists in other disciplines often had to make their colleagues look at the world from a completely different angle in order to 'see' gender, we had to persuade them to shift their

focus in order to sharpen their perception of what was already within the sociological field of vision.

The study of gender became established fairly quickly in such core areas of
the discipline as the sociology of the family and the sociology of work. It was not
simply that gender was added as a variable, but that its inclusion radically altered
the ways in which these fields developed. For example, families came to be seen
less as undifferentiated units or the locus of a harmonious integration of complementary roles than as forms of social organisation structured around hierarchies
of gender and generation (see Parts Three and Four). Once it was recognised that
gender played a key role in structuring the labour market and the workplace, it
was no longer possible to analyse occupational hierarchy or workplace culture
without also analysing the gendering of jobs and places of work (see Parts Two
and Three). Moreover, it became possible to rethink the relationship between the
'public' sphere of work and the 'private' sphere of the home, to recognise relationships between them and the extent to which an unproblematic acceptance of
the public/private divide had masked similar social processes operating in both
spheres. The classic example of this was that housework came to be seen as work,
carried on within a hierarchical relationship within which women serviced men's
needs and at the same time contributed to the economy through preparing their
husbands, and themselves, for work in the labour market. Conversely, women's
paid work and the skills deemed to be 'feminine' often mirrored the tasks women
were expected to undertake in the home, such as caring, cooking, cleaning and
sewing or, in the case of the secretary, becoming an 'office wife', supporting her
boss in all his [sic] endeavours (Pringle 1989).

Not only did the study of gender reorientate established fields of sociological
investigation, it also opened up new areas to the sociological gaze, such as sexuality, the body and violence against women and children. Here, however, the process
of transformation took longer, since it was easier to introduce gender into studies
of social institutions and social structure than to get sociologists to look at interpersonal interaction, especially intimate behaviour. In part this was a product of
the perspectives that dominated sociology in the 1970s. While micro-sociological
perspectives focusing on everyday interaction and social processes had enjoyed a
period of popularity in the late 1960s and early 1970s, especially in fields such
as deviance and health and illness, these gave way to other approaches, most
notably structural Marxism, which was seen as having more critical edge. The
study of work, whether waged or unwaged, and debates about the position of
women in the social structure fitted into this frame far more easily than issues
which seemed more personal – and potentially far more threatening to the privileges enjoyed by male academic sociologists.

The realm of the personal and interpersonal was more often seen as the
preserve of psychology, the study of individual idiosyncrasies rather than as
patterned, social conduct. Even where specific gendered patterns of interaction
were seen as social, they were often accepted uncritically as normal features of
given cultural contexts. For example, violence against women was seen either as
a manifestation of individual pathology best studied by psychologists or as simply

part of everyday life in certain working class communities – a classic example of the latter approach being *Coal is our Life* (Dennis et al. 1956), which portrayed wife-beating as an acceptable and accepted part of life in mining villages. However, the feminist insistence that the personal is political and therefore social eventually made it possible to question whether the private, in this instance and others, was merely personal. In making the connection between violence and power it became possible to see domestic violence as neither merely cultural nor merely personal but as symptomatic of the power relations underpinning the marriage contract, and by the mid-1970s this was becoming an accepted view among sociologists. Hence, for example, Colin Bell and Howard Newby depicted authority in marriage as underpinned by 'the power of the hand and the power of the purse' (1976: 164).

Extending this insight to areas which had not previously been of sociological concern at all was even more problematic. One such area was sexuality, which had been addressed by sociologists only in relation to marriage or demographics, and was seen as a 'natural' human capacity regulated through moral codes and social institutions, but not as a sphere of social life in its own right. This may now seem absurd, given that two people engaged in sex with each other are clearly involved in social interaction, but in the 1970s most sociologists either had not noticed this or considered it too frivolous to be worth serious sociological investigation.[2] There had been pioneering sociological work on sexuality during the 1960s and early 1970s (Gagnon and Simon 1974; McIntosh 1968), but it was not until gender had become much more established as a sociological concept that sexuality came to be more widely seen as amenable to sociological investigation (see Jackson 1999). However, in introducing the concept of gender, and extending the study of it to areas such as sexuality and the body, the ultimate result was a widening of the scope of sociological inquiry, bringing a wider range of phenomena within its ambit.

Sexuality itself came to be seen as another axis of inequality, in that heterosexuality is the institutionalised norm, routinely privileged over lesbian and gay sexualities (Jackson 1999; Jackson and Scott 2000; Chapter 7 below). The binary divide of heterosexuality and homosexuality clearly mirrors, and is interrelated with, that of gender, but also produces inequalities within gender categories. Thus, while gay men may enjoy certain privileges as men, their status as men is not altogether secure; they have frequently been regarded as less than 'real men', subjected to discrimination, ridicule and even violence. Lesbians are similarly seen as less than 'real women' and can also be victimised for departing from normative femininity. However, while gay men lose out on the status accorded to straight men, lesbians are doubly disadvantaged as women and as lesbians . Both lesbians and gay men threaten to destabilise the gender hierarchy by their refusal to live within the confines of compulsory heterosexuality, rejecting the tie between sex and reproduction and refusing the legitimisation of gender difference as the basis of emotional and sexual attraction.

It has also become apparent that gender and sexuality intersect other forms of inequality such as those based on class and racism. These intersections are too complex to be understood simply as distinct and discrete variables. For example, if 'race' and gender are treated as entirely separate dimensions of social inequality we are in danger of missing the specificity of black women's lives, and of gendered forms of racism and racialised forms of sexism. There are, however, still sociologists who are unwilling even to treat gender as more than an additional variable and who are reluctant to take it seriously where it would entail fundamental rethinking of key conceptual categories. A good example is class analysis, where those who hold to more traditional measures of class based on the occupation of male heads of household have fought a sustained rearguard action against those who take gender more seriously (see, for example, Goldthorpe 1983, 1984; Erikson 1984; Erikson and Goldthorpe 1988).

We would not, then, want to give the impression that sociology has been thoroughly transformed. There are still fields where there is considerable resistance to recognising the significance of gender and areas of sociology that remain relatively untouched by gender, particularly mainstream social theory (Maynard 1990). While feminists engage routinely with the work of male theorists, the compliment is only rarely reciprocated – and then most often by men working specifically on gender (see, for example, Connell 1986; Seidman 1997). It has therefore been left largely to feminists to further the conceptualisation of gender itself.

Sex and gender reconsidered

One of the problems created by the distinction between sex and gender was that it left biological 'sex' untheorised, treated as simply given. Thus, while gender was treated as socially constructed, it was assumed to rest on an existing 'natural' division (see Stanley 1984; Nicholson 1994; Hawkesworth 1997). The assumptions underpinning the sex/gender distinction have, therefore, increasingly been called into question.

One current within feminism has always been more interested in revalorising the feminine or bringing woman's radical alterity, her difference, into being (Fouque, in Duchen 1987; Irigaray 1985). These 'sexual difference' feminists have resisted the dissociation of gender from sex on the grounds that the concept of gender is insufficient to capture the interplay between the specificity of women's embodiment and the social and cultural definition of woman as devalued other (Braidotti 1991, 1994). These theorists, however, pitch their arguments at an abstract philosophical level which rarely connects with the everyday social practices and material social relations[3] and also posit the existence of some form of essential, extra-social femininity. What is more interesting from a sociological perspective is the opposing view: that the sex/gender distinction did not go far enough, that it assumed a fixed biological root on to which socio-cultural gender was grafted. Questioning sex as well as gender enables us to arrive at a more fully social understanding of the distinction between women and men.

There are three strands of theorising which have influenced this radical questioning: ethnomethodology, materialist feminism and poststructuralism/postmodernism. The first is distinctly sociological, the second was developed initially by a group of French feminists, most of whom were sociologists or anthropologists, and the third originated outside sociology but has since become a significant current within it. Of these it is the first, ethnomethodology, which is the most neglected in recent discussion of gender, although it was the perspective from which the earliest challenge was mounted to the idea of a natural binary divide between males and females.

That challenge dates back to Garfinkel's (1967) case study of Agnes, a male-to-female transsexual (see Chapter 2). Garfinkel had no discernible feminist sympathies: Agnes simply provided him with a means of explicating his ethnomethodological approach to the social order, in which 'members' (of society) are conceptualised as constantly making sense of social reality and, in the process, constructing it. In focusing on the ways in which Agnes 'passes' as a 'real woman' despite having male genitals (pre-operatively), and later 'artificial' female genitals, Garfinkel calls biological sex itself into question and treats our sexed being as an achievement. 'Passing', for Agnes, entails a carefully managed 'performance' of femininity through which gender is accomplished. Garfinkel's point (over two decades before Butler 1990) is that the production of a sexed persona is *always* a performance. Agnes simply makes visible what is usually invisible and her practices teach us how the normally sexed make sexuality – or what we would now call gender – happen (p. 180).[4] This requires not only a performance of gender but a reading of that performance through which we attribute gender to others. In the process we make certain assumptions – for example, that everyone belongs to one of two gender categories. It is because of this that Agnes is able to pass, since she can rely on others to take her feminine appearance, dress and demeanour as undoubtedly that of a normal woman.

The first fully developed ethnomethodological account of gender was provided by Kessler and McKenna in 1978, by which time the sex/gender distinction had become established in much sociological and feminist theorising. Whereas Garfinkel used the pre-feminist terminology of sex and sexuality, Kessler and McKenna preferred to use gender in order to underline the social origins of differences between women and men – even when referring to differences assumed to be biological. Like Garfinkel before them, they refused to accept that gender was founded on a fixed pre-social reality. Their central question was 'How is a social reality where there are two, and only two, genders constructed?' (1978: 3). They suggest that the recognition of gender differences is always a social act, whether that recognition is part of scientific procedure or everyday interaction. Hence they are critical of those formulations, such as Gayle Rubin's (1975) sex/gender system, which are underpinned by naturalistic assumptions. Rubin's account, as they point out, is 'still grounded in, and takes for granted, the objective reality of two biological sexes' and therefore 'does not question the facticity of two genders' (Kessler and McKenna 1978: 163).

Kessler and McKenna stress the primacy of gender attribution over all other aspects of gender: it is only because we make a gender distinction in the first place that we are able to talk about masculine or feminine characteristics or activities. The existence of a gendered social order depends upon the division or distinction of gender itself. Hence it is impossible to rid ourselves of gender 'roles' or gender inequalities without ridding ourselves of gender itself. Like Garfinkel, they see gender attribution as an interactive process involving both a performance of gender and a reading of that performance. Where they go further is in suggesting that the process is androcentric. They point out that the categories 'male' and 'female' are defined in relation to each other; to be classified as the former is to be excluded from the latter. But these two categories, while mutually constitutive, are not equally significant, since to be male is the socially defined norm: to be female is to be not male.

Despite this radical challenge to the residual biological foundationalism of the sex/gender distinction, most feminists continued to assume a basic, natural sex distinction underlying gender. Hence some years later Liz Stanley (1984) found it necessary to point out that most feminists challenged biological essentialism without questioning the biological reductionism entailed in accepting the idea of pre-given sex differences (see Chapter 1). The ethnomethodological case was also restated by Candace West and Don Zimmerman (Chapter 2) and influenced some of those writing from other perspectives, such as Bronwyn Davies's poststructuralist account of children's constructions of gender (Chapter 35).[5] However, ethnomethodologists were not the only theorists questioning the sex/gender distinction in the late 1970s and early 1980s: this was also a feature of a quite different theoretical perspective, materialist feminism. Whereas ethnomethodologists were concerned with everyday interactive processes and practices, with *how* gender is done, materialist feminists began from questions of social structure, with *why* women are subordinate.

Materialist feminism developed in France in the 1970s in opposition to 'sexual difference' feminism. Materialist feminists were radical feminists but used a Marxist method of analysis. In the first issue of their journal *Questions féministes*, the collective established the critique of naturalistic explanations of sexual difference as a basic tenet of their radical feminist stance. They refuse any notion of 'woman' that is unrelated to social context.

> The corollary of this refusal is our effort to deconstruct the notion of 'sex differences' which gives a shape and a base to the concept of 'woman' and is an integral part of naturalist ideology. The social mode of being of men and of women is in no way linked to their nature as males and females nor with the shape of their sex organs.
>
> (1977/1981: 214–15)

Just as class struggle seeks to do away with classes, so feminist struggle should aim to do away with sex differences. In a non-patriarchal society there would be no social distinctions between men and women. This does not mean women becoming like men, since 'men' as we know them would no longer exist: 'for at the same time as we destroy the idea of the generic "Woman" we also destroy the idea of "Man"' (1981: 215).

Their position on gender follows from a conceptualisation of men and women as existing in a class-like relationship. Rather than seeing male domination as based upon pre-existing sex differences, they argued that gender exists only as a social division because of patriarchal domination. As Delphy and Leonard later put it:

> For us 'men' and 'women' are not two naturally given groups who at some time fell into a hierarchical relationship. Rather the reason the two groups are distinguished socially is because one dominates the other.
>
> (Delphy and Leonard, 1992: 258)

This argument is in keeping with a Marxist method of analysis. For Marxists classes exist only in relation to one another: conceptually and empirically there can be no bourgeoisie without the proletariat, and vice versa. Similarly 'men' and 'women' exist as socially significant categories because of the exploitative relationship which both binds them together and sets them apart from each other. Conceptually there could be no 'women' without the opposing category 'men', and vice versa. As Monique Wittig says, 'there are no slaves without masters' (1992: 15).

The materialist feminist perspective thus treats 'sex' – in the sense of biological 'sex differences' – as itself the product of society and culture. This is clearest in the work of Christine Delphy, who is unusual among the French materialist feminists in using the term 'gender'. Delphy reversed the usual logic of the sex/gender distinction, suggesting that, rather than gender being built upon the foundation of biological sex difference, 'sex has become a pertinent fact, hence a perceived category, because of the existence of gender' (1984: 144). Gender creates anatomical sex 'in the sense that the hierarchical division of humanity into two transforms an anatomical difference (which is itself devoid of social implications) into a relevant distinction for social practice' (1984: 144). These ideas were further elaborated in her more recent work (Chapter 4).

These ideas look superficially similar to those developed by some postmodern feminists, notably Judith Butler (1990). The link between Delphy's and Butler's positions is provided by Monique Wittig, a French materialist feminist whom Butler draws on extensively. However, Butler does not interpret Wittig within a materialist frame of analysis, but in one deriving from a more culturally based poststructuralist and postmodernist tradition. This also had roots in the late 1970s and was another means by which feminists called the category 'woman' into question. The foundations of this form of feminism were laid by writers influenced by structural anthropology, linguistics and psychoanalysis, such as those involved in the British journal *m/f*, for whom the question of how women are produced as a category was central (see Adams *et al.* 1978). Gayle Rubin had also suggested that 'men' and 'women' are social, rather than natural, categories, products of systems of marriage and kinship (1975: 179) but, as we have seen, left the reproductive underpinnings of this view unquestioned. This residual essentialism persisted within this perspective for a while, but by the 1980s was being modified as the emphasis shifted from cultural and linguistic structures to a more fluid notion of the discursive constitution of subjects deriving from the work of Foucault and the deconstructive analytical strategies of Derrida. This shift began to be evident in historical work which deconstructed not just the singular 'woman' but 'women'. Denise Riley (1988), for example, argued that women came to be understood as radically other than men (as opposed to merely an inferior version of them) only at the turn of the eighteenth and nineteenth centuries and that the categories of 'sex', as we understand them, have a history. What came to be a central issue for poststructuralist and postmodern theorists was the binary divide of gender.

Judith Butler's deconstruction of sex and gender represents the most comprehensive and influential analysis from this perspective. In *Gender Trouble* Butler points out that if gender does not follow automatically from sex there is no reason to believe that there are inevitably only two genders. As soon as we begin to question this belief we must also begin to ask whether sex itself is simply a fact of nature. Once the immutability of sex is contested it becomes apparent that 'this construct called "sex" is as culturally constructed as gender; indeed perhaps it was always already gender' (Butler 1990: 7). If sex, as well as gender, is a construct it follows that the body does not have a pre-given essential sex. Rather bodies are rendered intelligible through gender and 'cannot be said to have a signifiable existence prior to the mark of their gender' (Butler 1990: 8). Bodies become gendered through the continual performance of gender. Hence gender, rather than being part of our inner essence, is performative; to be feminine is to perform femininity. A central means through which Butler explains this is through her analysis of drag (see Chapter 3).

In conceptualising gender as performative, she is not saying that gender is something you 'put on' in the morning and discard at will (see Butler 1993: x). In response to those critics who accuse her of denying the materiality of the body, Butler argues that materiality is an effect of power and that sexed bodies are forcibly materialised through time.[6] Rather than thinking of the 'performative' as a performance, in *Bodies that Matter* (1993) Butler turns to a notion of 'performativity' deriving from linguistics. Linguistic performatives are forms of speech which, by their utterance, bring what they name into being – for example, when a priest or registry office official says, 'I pronounce you man and wife.'

Performativity works because it is 'citational': it entails citing past practices, referring to existing conventions, reiterating known norms. For example, saying 'It's a girl' at a baby's birth brings a girl into being, begins the process, as Butler puts it, of 'girling the girl'. The process is effective because the phrase 'It's a girl' cites the norms of sex, draws on the authority of the conventions that establish what a girl is. Sex is materialised, according to Butler, through a complex of such citational practices, which are both normative and regulative. However, as Caroline Ramazanoglu points out, the question of where these norms come from or why they 'so often produce "heterosexual hegemony", male dominance, or any other imbalance of power does not appear to be an appropriate question to be asked within the logic of her theory' (1995: 37).

Unlike materialist feminists Butler does not consider social structures. Hence she does not address the question of *why* gender is hierarchical. Even though her account of gender as a performance echoes that of Garfinkel and Kessler and McKenna she nevertheless fails to ask *how* it is possible to sustain it in ordinary everyday interaction. Where Butler has made a useful contribution is in reinforcing the critique of the sex/gender distinction which ethnomethodologists and materialist feminists had already developed. If it is the case that 'sex' is as much a construction as 'gender', this raises the question of which term should be used. Some, in declaring the sex/gender distinction redundant, have suggested that we should return to using the term 'sex' (Wittig 1992; Grosz 1995). While we agree that the distinction between sex and gender is problematic, we would argue strongly for the retention of 'gender' rather than 'sex' to denote the division between men and women. There are two sets of reasons for this.

First, gender is a sociological concept: it focuses attention on men and women as *social* rather than natural categories and emerged out of debates which sought to challenge the 'naturalness' of differences between men and women (Lindemann 1997). While gender is now often used in an unsociological sense, it remains the best analytical tool we have, given that it is difficult to divest the term 'sex' of its naturalistic connotations. Moreover, gender is also sociological in that it focuses our attention on the *division* between women and men and the hierarchical relationship between them (Delphy 1993).

A second reason for retaining the word 'gender' is that the term 'sex' is so much more ambiguous. 'Sex' can refer both to differences between women and men and to specifically sexual (erotic) relations and practices. This ambiguity is itself sociologically interesting in that it is part of the naturalistic construction which links our genitals with our social position (as women or men) and with our sexual identities and practices, which defines femininity and masculinity as 'natural' and privileges heterosexuality as the only 'normal' and therefore legitimate form of sexuality. Theoretically we need to challenge assumptions that bind anatomy into gender and sexuality. Conceptually we need to know what we are talking about, and the ambiguity of the term 'sex' often clouds the issue. If we speak of 'gender relations' we know we refer to all aspects of social life; 'sexual relations' is more often understood as the specifically physical/erotic interaction. (Indeed, it can sometimes be even more specific, as in US President Bill Clinton's infamous claim that he 'did not have sexual relations with that woman'.)

Gender and sexuality are, of course, empirically interrelated: sexuality is gendered in fundamental ways and gender divisions sustain, and are sustained by, normative heterosexuality. Nonetheless it is important to maintain an analytical distinction between them. If they are conflated, there is a danger of reducing the entirety of gender to sexuality, of ignoring the aspects of gender which are not about sexuality. This is what tends to happen when 'sex' is used instead of gender. For example, in declaring gender redundant Elizabeth Grosz defines 'sex' as referring to bodily sexual differences and sexuality as sexual impulses, desires, pleasures, practices and so on. Gender is redundant because everything it designates can be described in terms of the interplay between sex and sexuality (see Grosz 1995:

213). Thus the entire field of gender, as sociologists would understand it – encompassing paid and unpaid work and so on – is erased.

The conflation of gender and sexuality which results from designating the former as sex is also evident in psychoanalytical thought, which explicitly ties our existence as sexed (gendered) subjects to our sexual being. Hence what we are designating gender has often been referred to as sexuality. (For example, Rosalind Coward's *Female Desire*, 1982, which purported to be about female sexuality, actually contained very little about sexuality as such.) The intersections of gender and sexuality should be a matter for investigation, and should not be decided in advance by definitional fiat. Indeed, this question has received a great deal of attention, with both feminists and queer theorists considering how the binary division of gender and the binary divide of heterosexuality and homosexuality sustain each other (see, for example, Butler 1990; Fuss 1991; Seidman 1997; Richardson 1996; Jackson 1999).

Gender categories are not homogeneous. Gender is lived and experienced differently depending on one's class, ethnicity, nationality and sexuality. Whereas cultural perspectives tend to conceptualise differences among women and among men simply as differences of culture or identity, sociologists are more concerned with patterned inequalities. The most significant differences which cut across those of gender, in terms of their impact on individuals' lives, are founded on inequalities: for example, the effects of class divisions, racism and normative heterosexuality. The complex intersections of these various social hierarchies are reflected in some of the readings we have chosen here (for example, Chapters 7, 8, 12, 13, 16, 17). These intersecting inequalities impact not only on the material conditions of our lives, but on our identities and sense of self. To be a man or a woman may, therefore, have differing meanings inflected by one's identity as Black or White, straight or gay, working class or middle class (see Chapters 37, 38, 40, 45, 49). A sociological understanding of self and identity must, however, go beyond merely recognising differences and consider the social contexts in which identities are forged through interaction with others and through reflexively constructed biographies (see Part Five).

It has been argued that sociological analysis of gender lost ground to cultural analysis in the 1980s and 1990s because of sociology's apparent inability to handle such complexities (Barrett 1992; Walby 1992). It is not the case that sociology is inherently unsuited to the analysis of differences within gender categories. However, in order to address this issue sociology must do more than treat gender as just another variable that can be added to the list of class, race and so on. As sociologists we need to understand the ways in which these various social divisions are interlaced with each other such that, for example, class and race are always gendered and conversely the experience and consequences of gender are always mediated through class and race. Hence it is not possible simply to add gender and stir! What is needed is not just a sociology of gender, but rather a gendered sociology. On the other hand it is not acceptable to disembed gender from its social context or to forget that gendered lives are lived within material constraints. For example, global and local divisions of labour and distributions of wealth and other resources impact on both women's and men's lives at least as much as the cultural practices through which identities are constructed. Sociology is uniquely placed to understand gender both as a form of structural inequality and as it is lived in everyday social settings.

About this book

We have chosen readings which, in our view, contribute to the process of bringing sociological and feminist analysis of gender together. We have arranged the readings in six parts. These are not meant to be exhaustive or definitive of the field: since all areas of social life are gendered, there are inevitably many areas which are not directly addressed. Obvious examples which we would have liked to include are studies of violence and health. Within the constraints of space we have sought to represent areas in which some of the most significant advances in the socio-logical analysis of gender have occurred and have chosen work from a variety of perspectives. We have included both empirical and theoretical readings in order to display the range of contributions which sociology has made to understanding how gender both structures, and is structured by, social processes, practices and institutions. Each part has a short introduction guiding the reader through the chapters and locating them within wider debates; each chapter is prefaced by a brief editorial comment setting it in its immediate context. We have also made some suggestions for further reading for each part, but we would also like to encourage students to read in full the texts from which we have taken the extracts reprinted here. This book, then, should not be taken to represent all there is to be said about the sociology of gender; instead it should be treated as a starting point for further exploration of the issues it raises.

Notes

1   This affected middle class and working class women in different ways. Middle class women, who had once played key roles in economic life, were largely excluded from business and commerce during the first few decades of the nine-teenth century. Meanwhile working class women were increasingly relegated to a narrow range of unskilled jobs and, by the second half of the century, skilled working men were aspiring to a 'family wage' enabling them to keep a wife at home (Walby 1986).

2   Each of us, quite independently, embarked on studies of sexuality during the 1970s and received similar comments from more established academics to the effect that this was not 'proper sociology', that it was trivial or would lead us away from sociology and towards 'psychological reductionsim'.

3   One exception is the legal theorist Drucilla Cornell, who is concerned with the ways in which sexual difference may be incorporated into advancing the cause of freedom for women (see Cornell 1998).

4   Note that Garfinkel here is using the terms 'sex' and 'sexuality' not in the sense of erotic practices and identities, but to refer to gender division and gender identity.

5   McKenna and Kessler (1997), themselves, have restated their case more recently and Kessler (1998) has applied their perspective to her study of intersexuality.

6   In her shift of focus to the materialisation of sexed bodies, gender as a social division is displaced from centre stage (see Hughes and Witz 1997).

References

Adams, Parveen, Brown, Beverly and Cowie, Elizabeth (1978) 'Editorial', *m/f*, 1: 3–5.

Barrett, Michèle (1980) *Women's Oppression Today*. London: Verso.

Barrett, M. (1992) 'Words and things: materialism and method in contemporary feminist analysis', in M. Barrett and A. Phillips (eds), *Destabilizing Theory: Contemporary Feminist Debates*. Cambridge: Polity pp. 201–19.

Beauvoir, S. de (1972) *The Second Sex*, trans. H. M. Parshley. Harmondsworth: Penguin.

Beechey, Veronica (1979) 'On patriarchy', *Feminist Review*, 3: 66–82.

Bell, C. and Newby, H. (1976) 'Husbands and wives: the dynamics of the deferential dialectic', in D. Leonard Barker and S. Allen (eds) *Dependence and Exploitation in Work and Marriage*. London: Longman.

Bhavnani, K-K. and Coulson, M. (1986) 'Transforming socialist feminism: the challenge of racism', *Feminist Review*, 23: 81–92.

Bottero, W. (1998) 'Clinging to the wreckage', *Sociology*, 32 (3): 469–90.

Braidotti, Rosi (1991) *Patterns of Dissonance*. Cambridge: Polity.

Braidotti, Rosi (1994) 'Feminism by any other name' (interview), *differences*, 6 (2/3): 27–61.

Britten, N. and Heath, A. (1983) 'Women, men and social class', in E. Gamarnikow, D. Morgan, J. Purvis and D. Taylorson (eds) *Gender, Class and Work*. London: Heinemann.

Butler, Judith (1990) *Gender Trouble: Feminism and the Subversion of Identity*. New York: Routledge.

Butler, Judith (1993) *Bodies that Matter*. New York: Routledge.

Carby, Hazel (1982) 'White women listen' in Centre for Contemporary Cultural Studies (eds) *The Empire Strikes Back*. London: Hutchinson.

Connell, R. W. (1987) *Gender and Power*. Cambridge: Polity.

Cornell, D. (1998) *At the Heart of Freedom: Feminism, Sex and Equality*, New Brunswick NJ: Rutgers University Press.

Coward (1982) *Female Desire*. London: Paladin.

Crompton, R. (1997) *Women and Work in Modern Britain*. Oxford: Oxford University Press.

Davidoff, L. and Hall, C. (1987) *Family Fortunes*. London: Hutchinson.

Davies, Bronwyn (1989) *Frogs and Snails and Feminist Tales*. Sydney: Allen and Unwin.

Delphy, Christine (1984) *Close to Home: A Materialist Analysis of Women's Oppression*. London: Hutchinson.

Delphy, Christine (1993) 'Rethinking sex and gender', *Women's Studies International Forum*, 16 (1): 1–9.

Delphy, Christine and Leonard, Diana (1992) *Familiar Exploitation: A New Analysis of Marriage in Contemporary Western Societies.* Cambridge: Polity.

Dennis, N., Henriques, F. and Slaughter, C. (1956) *Coal is our Life.* London: Eyre and Spottiswoode.

C. Duchen (ed.) (1987) *French Connections.* London: Hutchinson.

Durkheim. E. (1964) *The Division of Labour in Society.* New York: Free Press.

Durkheim. E. (1966) *Suicide.* New York: Free Press.

Erikson, R. (1984) 'Social class of men, women and families', *Sociology*, 18 (4): 500–14.

Erikson, R. and Goldthorpe, J. H. (1988) 'Women at class crossroads: a critical note', *Sociology*, 22: 545–53.

Errington, F. and Gewertz, D. (1987) *Cultural Alternatives and a Feminist Anthropology.* Cambridge: Cambridge University Press.

Fuss, Diana (1991) *Inside/Out: Lesbian Theories, Gay Theories.* New York: Routledge.

Gagnon, John and Simon, William (1974) *Sexual Conduct.* London: Hutchinson.

Garfinkel, H. (1967) *Studies in Ethnomethodology.* Englewood Cliffs NJ: Prentice-Hall.

Gavron, H. (1966) *The Captive Wife.* London: Penguin.

Glass, D. (1954) *Social Mobility in Britain.* London: Routledge.

Goldthorpe, J. (1980) *Social Mobility and the Class Structure in Modern Britain.* Oxford: Clarendon Press.

Goldthorpe, J. H. (1983) 'Women and class analysis: in defense of the conventional view', *Sociology*, 17 (4): 445–58

Goldthorpe, J. H. (1984) 'Women and class analysis: a reply to the replies', *Sociology*, 18 (4): 491–99.

Grosz, E. (1995) 'Experimental desire: rethinking queer subjectivity' in her *Space, Time and Perversion.* New York: Routledge.

Hall, C. (1992) *White, Male and Middle Class: Explorations in Feminism and History.* Cambridge: Polity.

Hamilton, R. (1978) *The Liberation of Women: A Study of Patriarchy and Capitalism.* London: Allen and Unwin.

Hartmann, Heidi (1981) 'The unhappy marriage of Marxism and feminism: towards a more progressive union', in L. Sargent (ed.) *Women and Revolution: the Unhappy Marriage of Marxism and Feminism,* London: Pluto.

Hawkesworth, M. (1997) 'Confounding gender', *Signs* 22 (3): 649–87.

Hochschild, A. (1989) *The Second Shift.* London: Piatkus.

hooks, b. (1982) *Ain't I a Woman?* London: Pluto Press.

Hughes, A. and Witz, A. (1997) 'Feminism and the matter of bodies: from de Beauvoir to Butler', *Body and Society*, 3 (1): 47–60

Irigaray, L. (1985) *This Sex which is not One.* Ithaca NY: Cornell University Press.

Jackson, S. (1998) 'Feminist social theory', in S. Jackson and J. Jones (eds) *Contemporary Feminist Theories.* Edinburgh: Edinburgh University Press.

Jackson, S. (1999) *Heterosexuality in Question.* London: Sage.

Jackson, S. and Scott, S. (2000) 'Sexuality', in G. Payne (ed.) *Social Divisions.* London: Macmillan.

Kaluzynska, Eva (1980) 'Wiping the floor with theory: a survey of writings on house-work', *Feminist Review*, 6: 27–54.

Kessler, S. J. (1998) *Lessons from the Intersexed*, New Brunswick NJ: Rutgers University Press.

Kessler, S. J. and McKenna, W. (1978) *Gender: An Ethnomethodological Approach*. New York: Wiley.

Klein, V. (1946) *The Feminine Character*. London: Routledge.

Komarovsky, M. (1946) 'Cultural contradictions and sex roles', *American Journal of Sociology*. 52: 184–9.

Komarovsky, M. (1962) *Blue Collar Marriage*. New York: Random House.

Lenski, G. (1966) *Power and Privilege*. New York: McGraw-Hill.

Lindemann, G. (1997) 'The body of gender difference', in K. Davis (ed.) *Embodied Practices: Feminist Perspectives on the Body*. London: Sage.

McDonough, Roisin and Harrison, Rachel (1978) 'Patriarchy and relations of produc-tion', in A. Kuhn and A. M. Wolpe (eds) *Feminism and Materialism*. London: Routledge.

McIntosh, M. (1968) 'The homosexual role', *Social Problems*, 16 (2): 182–92.

McKenna, W., and Kesler, S. J. (1997) 'Comment on Hawkesworth's "Confounding gender". Who needs gender theory?' *Signs*, 22: 3.

MacKinnon, C. (1982) 'Feminism, Marxism, method and the state: an agenda for theory', *Signs*, 7 (2): 515–44.

Mansfield, P. and Collard, J. (1988) *The Beginning of the Rest of your Life: A Portrait of Newly-wed Marriage*. London: Macmillan

Marx, Karl (1976) *Capital Volume 1*. Harmondsworth: Penguin.

Maynard. M. (1990) 'The reshaping of sociology? Trends in the study of gender', *Sociology*, 24 (2): 269–90.

Mead, Margaret (1935) *Sex and Temperament in Three Primitive Societies*. London: Routledge: New York; William Morrow.

Mead, Margaret (1950/1962) *Male and Female*. London: Penguin.

Mead, George Herbert (1934) *Mind, Self and Society*. Chicago: University of Chicago Press.

Mills, C. Wright (1970) *The Sociological Imagination*. Harmondsworth: Penguin.

Myrdal, A. and Klein, V. (1956) *Women's Two Roles: Home and Work*. London: Routledge.

Nain, G. T. (1991) 'Black women, sexism and racism', *Feminist Review*, 37: 1–22.

Nicholson, Linda (1994) 'Interpreting *gender*', *Signs*, 20 (1): 79–105.

Nouvelles questions féministes Collective (1984) 'A movement for all women' (extracts from editorial to *Nouvelles questions féministes*, 1), trans. Sophie Laws, *Trouble and Strife*, 2: 33–4.

Oakley, Anne (1972) *Sex, Gender and Society*, London: Temple Smith.

Oakley, Anne (1974) *The Sociology of Housework*. Oxford: Martin Robertson.

Parkin, F. (1972) *Class, Inequality and Political Order*. London: Paladin.

Parsons, T. and Bales, R. (eds) (1956) *Family: Socialization and Interaction Process*. London: Routledge.

Pollert, A. (1996) 'Gender and class revisited; or, The poverty of "patriarchy"', *Sociology*, 30: 639–59.

Pringle, R. (1989) *Secretaries Talk*. London: Verso.

Questions féministes Collective (1981) 'Variations on a common theme', in E. Marks and I. de Courtivron (eds) *New French Feminisms*. Brighton: Harvester.

Ramazanoğlu, Caroline (1995) 'Back to basics: heterosexuality, biology and why men stay on top', in M. Maynard and J. Purvis (eds) *(Hetero)sexual Politics*. London: Taylor and Francis.

Richardson, Diane (1996) *Theorizing Heterosexuality: Telling it Straight*. Buckingham: Open University Press.

Riley, Denise (1988) *I am that Name: Feminism and the Category of 'Women' in History*. London: Macmillan.

Roberts, H. (1993) 'The women and class debates', in L. Stanley and D. H. J. Morgan (eds) *Debates in Sociology*. Manchester: Manchester University Press.

Rosaldo, M. Z. (1974) 'Women, culture and society: a theoretical overview', in M. Z. Roslado and L. Lamohere (eds) *Women, Culture and Society*. Stanford CA: Stanford University Press.

Rubin, Gayle (1975) 'The traffic in women: notes on the "political economy" of sex', in R. Reiter (ed.) *Toward an Anthropology of Women*. New York: *Monthly Review* Press.

Rushton, P. (1979) 'Marxism, domestic labour and the capitalist economy: a note on recent debates', in C. C. Harris *et al. The Sociology of the Family: New Directions for Britain*. *Sociological Review,* Monograph No. 28, University of Keele.

Seidman, S. (1997) *Difference Troubles: Queering Social Theory and Sexual Politics*. Cambridge: Cambridge University Press.

Stanley, L. (1984) 'Should "sex" really be "gender" or "gender" really be "sex"?', in R. Anderson and W. Sharrock (eds) *Applied Sociology*. London: Allen and Unwin.

Stanworth, M. (1984) 'Women and class analysis: a reply to John Goldthorpe', *Sociology*, 18 (2): 159–70.

Stoller, R. (1968) *Sex and Gender*. New York: Aronson.

Sydie, R. (1987) *Natural Women, Cultured Men*. Milton Keynes: Open University Press.

Walby, Sylvia (1986) *Patriarchy at Work*. Cambridge: Polity.

Walby, Sylvia (1990) *Theorizing Patriarchy*. Oxford: Blackwell.

Walby, Sylvia (1992) 'Post-postmodernism? Theorizing social complexity', in M. Barrett and A. Phillips (eds) *Destabilizing Theory: Contemporary Feminist Debates*. Cambridge: Polity.

Westwood, S. (1984) *All Day, Every Day: Factory and Family in the Making of Women's Lives*. London: Pluto.

Wittig, Monique (1992) *The Straight Mind and other Essays*. Hemel Hempstead: Harvester Wheatsheaf.

Witz, A. (1990) 'Patriarchy and the professions: the gendered politics of occupational closure', *Sociology*. 24 (4): 675–90.

Yeandle, S. (1984) *Women's Working Lives*. London: Tavistock.

Zarektsky, E. (1976) *Capitalism, the Family and Personal Life*. London: Pluto.

PART ONE

Gender and knowledge

INTRODUCTION

PART ONE IS CONCERNED with the concept of gender and the gendering of knowledge. A key theme is the need to question what is taken for granted in relation to both gender itself and what passes for truth in a gendered social world.

As we have explained in the introduction, the concept of gender has been much debated over the last three decades of the twentieth century. As the debate progressed, the distinction between biological sex and social gender was questioned. It became clear that a fully sociological understanding of gender disrupted the notion that biological difference is a simple, given fact. The readings we have selected on this issue, particularly Chapters 1–4, contribute to an understanding of gender as a social and cultural construction. The authors represented here, however, address slightly different questions from varied points of view, including West and Zimmerman's ethnomethodology (Chapter 2), Butler's postmodern stance (Chapter 3) and Delphy's materialist feminism (Chapter 4). The social division between women and men does, however, have material effects, as will become clear in later parts.

The idea of gender as a social division and cultural distinction raises questions about how it impacts on our being as men or as women. The ways in which we become gendered are discussed in Part Five, but in reading Part One it is important to be aware that there is no single mode of being a man or being a women. Although men are the dominant group within the hierarchy of gender, there are nevertheless differences among them. In Chapter 5 Bob Connell introduces the influential concept of 'hegemonic masculinity', an idealised form of masculinity premised on assumptions of men's greater physical and mental prowess.

Although many, perhaps most, men do not fit this stereotype, men and women often behave as if it represented reality and it is used as a yardstick to judge some men (for example, Black men) as inferior, or, as in the case of gay men, as not 'real men' at all. Similarly standards of femininity are based primarily on white middle class heterosexual womanhood.

One aspect of hegemonic masculinity is the idea of rational man, and this has underpinned Western thinking on science and knowledge since the eighteenth century Enlightenment. This in turn has affected the construction and production of knowledge, what can be known and who decides what counts as legitimate knowledge. Knowledge has been thought of as more or less objective 'truth' existing out there in the world waiting to be discovered or known. Social scientists, however, have long been aware that knowledge is a human product, forged in particular social contexts. They were nonetheless reluctant to see that both knowledge and those who produce it were gendered. Hence research and theory generated by men and privileging a masculine standpoint could be thought of as neutral, as representing a view of the world that would make sense to anyone whatever their gender. Sociologists described, investigated and analysed many facets of social life only through the experience of men – for example, studies of work were studies of male workers and studies of crime concentrated on male criminals. Only in areas such as the sociology of the family did women make more than a fleeting appearance. Sociologies of public life represented largely and sometimes exclusively the world of men, relegating women to the private and local spheres of family and community.

Women were absent not only from sociological research but also from the contexts in which such research was undertaken. Thirty years ago women constituted a tiny minority of professional social scientists (one of us was not taught by a woman during the whole of her undergraduate and postgraduate education). The lack of women in the profession at that time helps to explain why women's views on social life were so seldom heard. It was not simply that sociologists studied mainly men, but that they thought as men without even being aware that they were doing so. Hence men's ways of knowing seemed to be the only ways of knowing. The first sustained analysis and critique of this situation was produced by Dorothy Smith (Chapter 6). She points out that men are able to produce the kinds of knowledge they do because of their privileged social position. Women, on the other hand, produce knowledge from a different standpoint. Women's ways of knowing diverge from men's not because of any innate difference between them, but as a result of their location within and experience of gendered divisions of labour.

Once gender divisions in the production of knowledge are recognised, it should become apparent that other social divisions may affect ways of knowing. Knowledge produced from a woman's standpoint may, for example, include some categories of women and exclude others. Patricia Hill-Collins (Chapter 7) demonstrates the ways in which a Black feminist standpoint may have a particular contribution to make to sociology. Even when gender is under scrutiny the presumption of heterosexuality may remain unexamined. Chrys Ingraham (Chapter 8) takes feminists to task for failing to notice the ways in which the regulation of gender is enmeshed with the institutionalisation of heterosexuality. In so doing she also revisits the central questions raised in the first few chapters and posits that gender is structured through heterosexuality.

FURTHER READING

Allen, S. and Leonard, D. (1996) 'From sexual divisions to sexualities: changing sociological agendas', in J. Weeks and J. Holland (eds) *Sexual Cultures*. Basingstoke: Macmillan.

Fausto-Sterling, Anne (1992) *Myths of Gender*, second edition. New York: Basic Books.

Haraway, Donna (1991) '"Gender" for a Marxist dictionary: the sexual politics of a word', in D. Haraway, *Simians, Cyborgs and Women*. London: Free Association Books.

Harding, S. (1986) *The Science Question in Feminism*. Milton Keynes: Open University Press.

Hawksworth, M. (1997) 'Confounding gender', *Signs* 22 (3): 649–87.

Jackson, S. (1998) 'Theorising gender and sexuality', in S. Jackson and J. Jones (eds) *Contemporary Feminist Theories*. Edinburgh: Edinburgh University Press.

Jackson, S. (2000) 'For a sociological feminism', in J. Eldridge, J. McInnes, S. Scott, S. Warhurst and A. Witz, *For Sociology*. Durham: sociologypress.

Maynard, M., and Purvis, J. (eds) (1994) *Researching Women's Lives from a Feminist Perspective*. London: Taylor and Francis.

Nicholson, Linda (1994) 'Interpreting *gender*', *Signs*, 20 (1): 79–105.

Young, Iris Marion (1994) 'Gender as seriality: thinking about women as a social collective', *Signs*, 19 (3): 713–38.

KEY QUESTIONS

- What are the implications of arguing that 'sex' as well as gender is socially constructed?
- How do the perspectives on gender in Part One differ and what assumptions do they share? How, for example, do they define gender? How do they conceptualise its social construction?
- On what basis can it be argued that knowledge has traditionally been constructed from a White, male and heterosexual perspective? What are the consequences of this argument?

Chapter 1

Liz Stanley

SHOULD 'SEX' REALLY BE 'GENDER' – OR 'GENDER' REALLY BE 'SEX'

This was one of the earliest challenges to the sex-gender distinction, arguing that treating biological sex as unproblematic limited the scope of social constructionist critique.

From R. Anderson and W. Sharrock (eds) *Applied Sociology*, London: Allen & Unwin (1984).

The social construction of biology

The argument

THE BASIC ARGUMENT IS whether 'sex' (our 'maleness' or 'female-ness', the biological basis of sex differentiation) causes 'gender' (culturally ascribed notions about 'femininity' and 'masculinity'), or whether and to what extent 'gender' is a social construction. Two polarised positions on this can be described as 'biological essentialism' and 'social constructionism'. Paradoxically, it has more often been natural scientists working on these questions who have taken an unequivocally social constructionist line, while most academic feminists have occupied the so-called 'middle ground' of arguing for social constructionism which takes place on a biological base.

'Biological essentialism', then, argues that the social roles and psychological attributes of females and males in relation to a whole range of behaviours and personality traits are biological reductionism', for the essentialist view is that what exists now is a *direct* product of biological factors still operative, while the reductionist view says they are the *indirect* product of biological factors no longer operative.

The feminist response has identified biological essentialism in the social and natural sciences as importantly involved in the maintenance of 'biology is destiny' ideas within commonsense views on this topic. It is, however, equally possible and equally likely that scientific views are the product of commonsense ones rather than the other way around. The feminist response has thus gone about dismantling what has been seen as 'popular ignorance' with an attack on scientific conservatism and prejudice, through the use of a very wide body of evidence drawn from various disciplines; these main kinds of evidence are now outlined.

The evidence

Previously reference has been made to the fact that fifteen years or so of feminist activity in the social sciences and elsewhere has resulted in a huge amount of work of various kinds. Again, because of this it is impossible fully to account for all the research involved. And so, instead of this, brief overviews are presented of this work under three headings. These are variations between cultures, variations in one culture over time, and variations in one culture at one point in time.

1. *Variations between cultures*. Here the main body of work is anthropological in origin and concerns a very wide range of different cultures indeed. This evidence suggests that 'sex' forms a universal categorisation in all known societies; and in all known societies it also involves a hierarchy in which it is men and men's activities and attributes which are the more highly valued. Earlier work which had claimed the existence of totally non-stratified societies to a large extent now recants this view and accepts that within it the anthropologist had been 'blind to sex', in the sense of simply 'overlooking' women's inequality.

In addition, anthropological work has pointed out the fascinating and, for feminist theories of women's oppression, crucial fact that within this what is believed to constitute maleness and femaleness is subject to seemingly endless variation. Some of the best examples of this come from the work of Margaret Mead and in particular her *Sex and Temperament in Three Primitive Societies* (1935), where she describes three cultures, all existing in close proximity to each other but which nevertheless have very different constructions of 'gender'.

In addition, there is now an increasing amount of anthropological work which focuses on the different, and not so different, meanings attached to various behaviours in other cultures, which can be used to illustrate similar ones in our own. One example of this is in the work of Yolanda and Robert Murphy among the Mundurucu, where group rape is an explicit and widely used means of controlling women's behaviour (Murphy and Murphy 1974). Another is in the work of Margery Wolf in rural Taiwan, which examines the role that gossip plays among seemingly powerless women in order to gain power (Wolf 1974). Both of these examples concern sex-related behaviours which occur in our own culture, but which may be seen and understood very differently in others; and it is precisely from both the similarities *and* the differences that we can learn.

The overall import of this kind of research is that 'gender' is a lot more complex than it at first may appear; that it is variously constructed; and that even the 'same' behaviours may be seen and understood very differently in different cultures. Because of this it has formed a very important plank in feminist writings concerned with 'gender'.

2. *Variations in one culture over time*. The key discipline involved here is history, and in particular both economic and social history. Within work here two different, and sometimes opposing, strands can be discerned. Perhaps the more significant, certainly in terms of the volume of work available, is that which is concerned with the changes brought about by capitalism in the economic and social roles of women and men.

Sheila Rowbotham's *Hidden from History* deals with the hidden history of women, hidden because mainstream history has not seen women's lives as either significant or interesting (Rowbotham 1974). It examines changes brought about by capitalist development but also by developments within capitalism. In some ways it exemplifies the central Marxist tenet that in a sense 'gender' as a hierarchy of social value is a product of capitalism. However, in some other respects it just as clearly shows some of the differences between Marxist and Marxist-feminist analysis. For one thing, it is centrally concerned with women's place both in history (and the discipline of history) and in Marxist theory itself. And for another, it is written in a very different style. It deliberately sets out to make its own arguments and even 'facts' redundant, in the sense that it necessarily skims over the surface of the things it discusses; for the failings of history as a discipline have ensured that all that exists, with regard to women's lives, *is* surface.

Rowbotham's work has been superseded as more research has been done on the vast number of issues, problems and very wide time-period touched on in her book. Nevertheless, in a sense its central argument remains alive and flourishing, for whether men and women were different but not 'genders' before capitalism has not been satisfactorily 'answered'. Indeed, the second strand in historical writings illustrates fairly clearly the fact that it is unanswerable in any final sense, for neither question nor 'answer' is to be seen as theory-free. This second strand addresses itself, in a direct sense, to the question of women's and men's situation in pre-capitalist and capitalist periods.

Alan Macfarlane's *The Origins of English Individualism* rejects various of the key Marxist arguments about the nature and origin of capitalism on the basis of very detailed historical researches (Macfarlane 1978). Macfarlane points out that most of the characteristics associated with 'capitalism' existed in England certainly as far back as the fourteenth century; and therefore that work which dates it as a seventeenth and eighteenth-century phenomenon in fact results from theoretical imperialism rather than close attention to historical fact. It also deals with, among other things, women's situation in the geographical locations he is concerned with; and emphasises that in the 'pre-capitalist' period women were controlled and the subject of discrimination, but also that they could and did inherit, run businesses, and the like. In other words, their situation was complex, much more complex than Marxist and Marxist-feminist theory usually recognises.

In a quite different vein, Dale Spender's *Women of Ideas* points out that, as far back historically as one cares to research, women's resistance to various aspects of their situation can be found (Spender 1982). Concerned with finding 'feminist writings', that is, those of women who offered a conscious critique of women's situation as a systematic phenomenon, she establishes that as far back as her research went (the early seventeenth century) organised groups of women were concerned with analysing women's situation as the result of discrimination, exploitation and oppression.

Different again, *The Diaries of Hannah Cullwick*, a Victorian maidservant, show that the stereotype of the Victorian woman is precisely a stereotype of the Victorian woman is precisely a stereotype, and a class-based one at that (Stanley 1984). Hannah Cullwick was almost entirely 'unwomanly', in the sense that she was immensely strong and went freely about the roughest parts of Victorian London without molestation, but also cherished herself as a worker and resisted all attempts to confine her in terms of 'feminine' dress, behaviours and attitudes. Moreover, these diaries make it clear that she was by no means atypical in doing so; and that vast numbers of other Victorian working women lived their lives in a very similar fashion.

The first strand in historical work outlined here stresses uniformity, both within pre-capitalist periods and then within capitalist ones. The second is in seemingly marked contrast, with its stress on variation within any particular period. However, it is useful to note that a tension can be perceived within the first strand, a tension between the empirical material used and the theoretical framework in relation to which this is used. Out of this seems to be coming a 'new generation' of Marxist and Marxist-feminist historical work, which utilises a rather different notion of 'theory' and which is much more dialectical in its approach.

3. *Variations in one culture at one point in time*. There are obvious points of connection between the second of the two strands in historical writings and work which is specific is specific to 'now' in our culture, because in both is to be found evidence of, simply, *variation*. 'Gender' may vary between cultures and over time – but that it varies in the here and now too is the overall conclusion which can be drawn from this body of work.

The idea that there is a sharp biological demarcation of males from females with an associated and automatic segregation of behaviour patterns has come into question as research has revealed that such boundaries are somewhat less sharp and determinate than has been imagined. Women and men are not always nor emphatically distinguished from one another either biologically or psychologically, though social structures may treat people as though they must be distinguished from one another in sharp and discontinuous ways. 'Intersexuality' is a case in point.

There are various different forms of 'intersexuality' or cases where the sex of someone's upbringing and one or more of their biological sex characteristics do not match. The interlinked characteristics which constitute 'biological sex' are: chromosomal constitution, gonadal structure (whether ovaries or testes), morphology of external genitalia, morphology of genital ducts (whether Mullerian or fallopian tubes and uterus, or Wolffian or vas and prostate), and, sometimes included, hormonal status (preponderance of oestrogens over androgens, or androgens over oestrogens). All these five characteristics are organic; however, hormonal status by itself is an insufficient indicator of intersexuality as there is an enormous range in relative distributions of oestrogens and androgens throughout the population.

At least fifteen different forms of intersexuality exist. However, the best known are probably 'Kleinfelter's syndrome' and 'Turner's syndrome'. Kleinfelter's syndrome involves chromosomally XXy males with undescended testes, vaginal openings which are blind-ended and a normal 'male' hormonal status although the androgens are interpreted in the brain as though they were oestrogens; and people with this syndrome function as normal although infertile and period-less females. Turner's syndrome involves chromosomally XO people, brought up as ordinary but 'slow' females but who in fact do not have a 'true' chromosomal sex as 50 per cent of the genetic sex material is absent.

Cases of intersexuality, particularly Kleinfelter's syndrome and other cases involving perfectly ordinarily functioning 'males' and 'females', have come to the attention of the medical profession primarily because of infertility, lack of menstrual periods, or more general 'sex problems' such as the experience of discomfort during heterosexual intercourse for people with Kleinfelter's. Clinics dealing with such cases are the 'practice' of which medical cytogenetics (research into the genetic structure of cells) is the 'theory'. In the early days of counselling, intersexed people were sometimes told that they were 'really' a different sex from that they experienced themselves as. Reactions to this included nervous breakdown and suicide. Since then counselling has changed and now it is likely that careful questioning will try to elicit whether 'patients' are happy members of their 'sex' of upbringing. If they are then they will often not be told that they are 'really' another 'sex' but instead that they are infertile for physiological reasons of various kinds. For the last fifteen years or so medical cytogenetics textbooks too have made it perfectly clear that for these natural scientists 'gender', social sex and psychological sex, are all entirely matters of upbringing. And this happened at a time, it should be remembered, when even to hint as much in the social sciences was to be seen as 'unscientific'.

The implications of this natural science research/practice are perfectly clear – that 'sex' is important, but not as important as social factors. However, exactly how 'gender' is produced is still a matter for great conjecture. The kind of natural science work just outlined filtered through to the social sciences only comparatively recently and disputes still rage between people who differently interpret its meaning.

In particular, whether and to what extent psychological sex differences are a product of biological sex differences in the functioning of the brain has been one site of dispute. Corinne Hutt, a physiological psychologist, has argued that the evidence both of cytogenetics and of intersexuality instead shows the deterministic result of biological sex (Hutt 1972). Thus it can be seen that Hutt interprets the same evidence very differently from the view of it outlined above and that current among practitioners. However, it is worth noting that her argument tends to focus on androgenised females (that is, organically normal females who have been subject to large doses of androgens while in the womb) and uses as a control a group of Turner's syndrome females, themselves decidedly atypical, 'passive' and super-stereotypically 'feminine'.

A key feature of Hutt's argument is that the brain is itself sex differentiated and it is this which gives rise to many differences in psychological and so social functioning. However, Hutt takes as a given the existence of a wide range of psychological sex differences, a 'fact' disputed in other work. Of particular importance here has been the work of Maccoby and Jacklin, which has reviewed the then-existing psychological sex research literature (Maccoby and Jacklin 1975). Many interesting points are made by Maccoby and Jacklin concerning the quality and focus of much of the research, but also about the main overall conclusions to be drawn from it. Generally, they suggest, almost all the popularly supposed sex differences in psychological functioning could not be demonstrated in research, which often tried very hard indeed to find them. They argue that the only psychological sex differences which research supports the existence of are four in number. First, females have greater verbal abilities than males. However, this difference begins to show only at around the age of eleven; and so its often assumed biological basis must be doubted. Secondly, males have greater visual-spatial abilities than females. However, this difference begins to show only at around the age of thirteen; and so the often assumed biological basis of this too must be doubted. Thirdly, males have greater mathematical abilities than females. This too only manifests itself at around the age of twelve; and its biological basis is again in doubt. Fourthly, males are more aggressive than females. This difference begins to manifest itself at around the age of three, when social play begins.

Maccoby and Jacklin are willing to consider the possibility that this last psychological difference between males and females may have a biological basis. However, they also note that its existence neither means that all males are more aggressive than all females nor that male aggression is immutable. In other words, they suggest that although biology may be important it can be changed, modified and indeed completely overturned in particular societies or particular groups within a larger society (an example might be men who are Quakers and women who are political terrorists in our own society).

Some conclusions?

Both biological essentialists and social constructionists claim that the weight of evidence is on *their* side; and this highlights something of the practical difficulties involved in the operations of science within the social sciences. That is, it is most certainly easy to find evidence which categorically supports the essentialist position but it is just as easy to find categorical rejections of it; and similarly so with the constructionist position.

That being said, it seems that the general trend has been towards a much greater acceptance of constructionist ideas about biological sex. Paradoxically, constructionism is found more within certain of the natural sciences involved in research and counselling in this area of practice than within the social sciences. And interestingly, a large number of academic feminists have eschewed constructionism in favour of the 'middle ground' of arguing that social construction takes place, but on a given biological base of physiologically determined traits, attributes, and so forth. This is a variation within the position earlier referred to as 'biological reductionism'. Nevertheless, the overall trend is still that 'sex' should really be considered as, to a large extent, 'gender'. Perhaps ideas about 'normal science' and what is and is not thought to be professionally acceptable in the social sciences play a part here, for while much of academic feminism is to be found in this middle ground, feminists outside academic life are to a large extent constructionists.

Since the differentiation between females and males is seen as something socially sustained, much research concerned with explaining this has emphasised the 'coercive' aspect of socialisation, the extent to which gender identities are *imposed* upon people, through internalisation by the child during primary socialisation and reinforcement by social control mechanisms. Power certainly operates in the construction and allocation of sexual identities, but the next section suggests that such an interpretation of it is not only too crude but also sets up a particular reading of the nature of interconnection between 'gender', 'sex' and 'biology' which can be similarly characterised.

'Biology', rationality and 'sex' as a 'natural order'

Scientific and everyday rationalities

In the last section some of the now vast body of evidence which has been used in debates concerning the 'sex/gender controversy' has been outlined; and the general tenor of conclusions to be drawn from this were summarised as an increasing acceptance that 'sex' should really be construed as 'gender'. However, 'gender' is conceptualised in much social science theory and research as a set of 'internalised' traits, attributes, behaviours, and so forth. Much recent work on 'socialisation', whether by feminists or not, has focused on what is known as 'primary socialisation' (sometimes referred to as 'sex role socialisation'); and is concerned with the period from birth until the age of about four or five, during which, it is assumed, 'gender' is somehow 'laid down' through the pattern of interaction between the child and its social and physical environment. Much of this work has been located within psychology or a sociology very heavily influenced by psychology. There is, however, another sociological way of understanding 'gender' and around which some extremely interesting work has been carried out. Some of this will be outlined later; and around this an alternative way of understanding the persistence of biological considerations will be discussed.

Within the general movement of social scientific opinion towards various versions of social constructionism there has been a sometimes implicit and sometimes explicit judgement of 'popular opinion', with its continued support of essentialism. Essentially this support is depicted as irrational or perhaps 'prescientific', for it is seen to fly in the face of scientific facts of the kind earlier outlined. However, such assessments of 'popular' as against 'scientific' not only treat both as having the same purposes and goals but also treat the realm of the scientific as by definition more advanced in its understandings, modes of procedure, and so forth.

Instead of seeing everyday and scientific theorising as competing forms of explanation, the philosopher Schutz prefers to see them as different attitudes, each with different purposes, procedures and desired outcomes (Schutz 1967). In everyday life, our 'commonsense knowledge' is practical and contingent on what Schutz calls 'projects', our concern with various features of the here and now rather than the pursuit of 'truth'. In this sense scientific knowledge is not 'practical' at all because it is not dependent on everyday knowledge and standards but those specific to 'science'. Behaving in a 'scientific' way in everyday life, unless acknowledged and licensed as such through the recognition that this is indeed 'science', can lead to behaviour being seen as odd, eccentric, or even as a kind of madness.

An alternative way of seeing and understanding the persistence of biological invocations in relation to 'sex' and 'gender' is to see these as part of everyday theorising and thus as practical, contingent, purposeful and rational, rather than as the result of ignorance and confusion which will dissolve on receipt of 'scientific fact'. 'Gender' is conceptualised in psychological, rather than sociological, terms in most of the relevant literature. That is, 'gender' is seen as internalised behaviours, traits and the like which are then later 'released' into various social situations.

This can be seen as a kind of 'psychological essentialism', which may not be biologically determined but is certainly deterministic. However, sociology sees social life as *inter*subjective, as the result of negotiation and interaction, and not as the release of something 'inside'. It argues that the social world is one shared in common between us and to be seen as a human social construction rather than as a multiplicity of inner worlds. Thus the way into an alternative understanding of biological invocations is through reconceptualising 'gender' in more sociological terms.

'Gender' in sociological terms

In *Gender Advertisements* Erving Goffman examines various features by which 'gender' is pictorially constructed in a range of media advertisements (Goffman 1976). However, as well as demonstrating the very stark way in which 'gender' and 'power' overlay each other in these, Goffman also emphasises that advertisements deal with an obviously unreal world, unreal in various ways. One feature of its unreality is the starkness of 'gender advertisements'; and Goffman argues two things out of this. One is that 'gender' in this form is an atypical feature of social interaction; most everyday behaviours are equivocal, and stark and unequivocal instances of 'gender' and of other forms of behaviour are rare. The other is that the atypicality of 'gender' does not mean its unimportance; indeed rather the reverse. By presenting images which stand out in the way that these do, gender advertisements mark out 'ideals' and these feed back into the construction of 'gender' in everyday life.

A discussion of male/female, and parent/child, conversational interactions by Candice West and Don Zimmerman in 'Women's place in everyday talk' (West and Zimmerman 1977) notes both the interactional construction of 'gender' and also its close similarity to other forms of power. West and Zimmerman note in particular that men in conversation with women, and adults in conversation with children, 'do power' in comparable ways through interruptions and other ways of disturbing turn-taking sequences in conversational structure.

Both Goffman and West and Zimmerman stress the interactional construction of 'gender' rather than its release into social situations and that the specific mechanisms by which this occurs can be analysed by close attention to detailed pieces of recorded interaction. Harold Garfinkel's work concerned with 'Agnes', an apparently intersexed person, is ostensibly in a different vein (Garfinkel 1967). One of

Garfinkel's concerns is with the role that 'passing', or achieving and security . . . rights to live as a normal, natural female', plays in Agnes's life. However, an implication of Goffman's and West and Zimmerman's work is that 'passing', with its attendant possibility of failure, is a feature of 'gender' for 'normal' males and females also, although the 'taken-for-grantedness' of interactional response some- what differs, along with the specific consequences of failure.

Garfinkel treats Agnes as an intersexed person concerned with the manage- ment of what she perceives to be her natural, original, real 'sex', and only residually as someone who might be actually involved in the production (through the use of hormones) of her 'real sex' attributes; and indeed this possibility becomes more residual over time. However, an appendix deals with Agnes's disclosure to Garfinkel's medical collaborator that she was in fact not intersexed. In essentials, as Garfinkel notes, the practical accomplishment by Agnes of her intersexuality was achieved in a specific setting through the establishment of a determinate account of 'Agnes and her past', whereby alternative accounts are ruled out.

In this work, the usually symbiotic relationship of 'sex' and 'gender' (and whatever the culturally specific content of 'gender') is demonstrated. By estab- lishing claims to her 'real sex', Agnes also achieves a determinate reading by others of her behaviours as 'gender' (and this in its turn reinforces the claims to her 'real sex') rather than 'effeminacy' or other terms which deny a correspondence between them and 'real sex'. In a sense, then, 'gender' 'works' because of the assumption of various links, most importantly between 'gender' and 'sex', and between 'sex' and ideas about 'natural orders'.

'Sex as a natural order'

The idea of a 'natural order' is one which includes the notion that what is 'natural' is also given, fixed, determined and non-volitional, and is thus *not* socially con- structed, changing and volitional. 'Sex' construed as a natural order is thus concep- tualised in ways which cut out the possibility of conceptualising it as 'really' 'gender', really socially constructed and so mutable. Moreover, implicit within ideas about 'natural orders' is a way of treating and understanding alternative, non-natural, con- ceptualisations. These are indeed seen as 'non-natural', as unnatural in the sense that they fly in the face of what is self-evidently fixed, given, and so forth.

'Sex' as a natural order includes more than ideas about our 'biological selves' and our social behaviours and attributes. It also importantly includes ideas about people as sexual beings in the sense of 'doing sex', 'having sex'. That is, the 'natu- ralness' of 'sex' extends to, indeed crucially includes, sex as innately heterosexual reproductive behaviours. 'Sex' in the strictly biological sense is thereby not only an outcome of 'doing sex' but also what this is naturally 'for'; and a number of interesting pieces of work have taken up this idea and explored it by looking at sexual behaviours and 'sexual roles' and their relationship to 'gender'.

At this point it becomes possible to return to the question of the persistence of biological invocations in the explanation of sex differences and sex inequalities; and to examine this around the ideas briefly summarised above.

Biological invocations persist because these are rooted in a supremely rational way of interpreting and constructing what it is to be a man or a woman in our society. Commonsensically 'gender' is instead seen as 'sex' because in a practical sense this explains a great deal more, and is much more useful, than the other way around. Ordinarily, normally, typically, 'sex' has a great deal more explicatory power, for it is linked in with ideas about 'sexual orientation' and thus into 'doing sex' as reproductive behaviour. This 'correspondence theory', as it is known, states that ordinarily a correspondence is assumed between 'sex', 'gender', 'sexual orientation' and 'reproductively sexual behaviour' with, standing behind these constituent elements, the notion that these constitute a 'natural order'. In a sense these form an 'impermeable theory', one not amenable to modification through, for example, new evidence. It constitutes an internally consistent self-fulfilling prophecy in which 'contrary evidence' is instead treated as a confirmation of the theory because its very existence demonstrates its own unnaturalness and thus irrationality.

Here it is instructive to consider that, very frequently, feminists are construed as failed 'real women', who hate men and want to castrate them, and who deny not only biology as related to 'sex' but also as related to the assumed ideas that 'doing sex' is necessarily penetrational and that childbirth and child care are necessarily central in women's lives. In this can be seen the implicit argument that feminists deny the natural order of 'sex' and are thus not only unnatural in doing so, but unnatural in themselves. 'Sex' as a natural order is also an order involving *power* and its distribution; and feminists and feminism threaten the present distribution of power within this order. Responding to the message of feminism in terms already set within the notion of a 'natural order', however, removes this threat because one consequence is that the debate opened up by feminism is thereby depoliticised by being taken out of the realm of the social and mutable and back into the realm of the natural and immutable.

The recent growth of interest in the social position of women is obviously, from what has been said above, connected with the rise of the feminist movement; and it is feminists who have made much of the running in attempting to explain the persistence of sexual differences and their associated inequalities. . . .

References

Garfinkel, H. (1967) *Studies in Ethnomethodology*. Englewood Cliffs NJ: Prentice-Hall.

Goffman, E. (1976) *Gender Advertisements*. London: Macmillan.

Hutt, C. (1972) *Males and Females*. Harmondsworth: Penguin.

Maccoby, E. and Jacklin, C. (1975) *The Psychology of Sex Differences*. London: Oxford University Press.

Macfarlane, A. (1978) *The Origins of English Individualism*. Oxford: Blackwell.

Mead, M. (1935) *Sex and Temperament in Three Primitive Societies*. London: Routledge.

Murphy, Y. and Murphy, R. (1974) *Women of the Forest*. New York: Columbia University Press.

Rowbotham, S. (1974) *Hidden from History*. London: Pluto.

Schutz, A. (1967) *Collected Papers* I, *The Problem of Social Reality*. The Hague: Nijhoff.

Spender, D. (1982) *Women of Ideas*. London: Routledge.

Stanley, L. (1984) *The Diaries of Hannah Cullwick*. London: Virago.

West, C. and Zimmerman, D. (1977) 'Women's place in everyday talk'. *Social Problems*, 24: 521–44.

Wolf, M. (1974) *Women and the Family in Rural Taiwan*. Stanford CA: Stanford University Press.

Chapter 2

Candace West and
Don H. Zimmerman

DOING GENDER

This piece elaborates the ethnomethodological perspective on gender developed by Garfinkel and Kessler and McKenna (see introduction), revisiting Garfinkel's classic study of Agnes.

From J. Lorber and S. Farrell (eds) *The Social Construction of Gender,* London: Sage (1991). Originally published in *Gender and Society,* 1 (2) 1987: 125–51.

OUR PURPOSE IN THIS CHAPTER is to propose an ethnomethodologically informed, and therefore distinctively sociological, understanding of gender as a routine, methodical, and recurring accomplishment. We contend that the 'doing' of gender is undertaken by women and men whose competence as members of society is hostage to its production. Doing gender involves a complex of socially guided perceptual, interactional, and micropolitical activities that cast particular pursuits as expressions of masculine and feminine 'natures'.

When we view gender as an accomplishment, an achieved property of situated conduct, our attention shifts from matters internal to the individual and focuses on interactional and, ultimately, institutional arenas. In one sense, of course, it is individuals who 'do' gender. But it is a situated doing, carried out in the virtual or real presence of others who are presumed to be oriented to its production. Rather than as a property of individuals, we conceive of gender as an emergent feature of social situations: as both an outcome of and a rationale for various social arrangements and as a means of legitimating one of the most fundamental divisions of society. . . .

To elaborate our proposal, we suggest at the outset that important but often overlooked distinctions should be observed among *sex, sex category,* and *gender. Sex* is a determination made through the application of socially agreed upon biological criteria for classifying persons as females or males.[1] The criteria for classification can be genitalia at birth or chromosomal typing before birth, and they do not necessarily agree with one another. Placement in a *sex category* is achieved through application of the sex criteria, but in everyday life, categorization is established and sustained by the socially required identificatory displays that proclaim one's membership in one or the other category. In this sense, one's sex category presumes one's sex and stands as proxy for it in many situations, but sex and sex category can vary independently; that is, it is possible to claim membership in a sex category even when the sex criteria are lacking. *Gender*, in contrast, is the activity of managing situated conduct in light of normative conceptions of attitudes and activities appropriate for one's sex category. Gender activities emerge from and bolster claims to membership in a sex category.

We contend that recognition of the analytical independence of sex, sex category, and gender is essential for understanding the relationships among these elements and the interactional work involved in 'being' a gendered person in society. . . .

Sex, sex category, and gender

Garfinkel's (1967: 118–40) case study of Agnes, a transsexual raised as a boy who adopted a female identity at age seventeen and underwent a sex reassignment operation several years later, demonstrates how gender is created through interaction and at the same time structures interaction. Agnes, whom Garfinkel characterized as a 'practical methodologist', developed a number of procedures for passing as a 'normal, natural female' both prior to and after her surgery. She had the practical task of managing the facts that she possessed male genitalia and that she lacked the social resources a girl's biography would presumably provide in everyday interaction. In short, she needed to display herself as a woman, simultaneously learning what it was to be a woman. Of necessity, this full-time pursuit took place at a time in her life when most people's gender would be well accredited and routinized. Agnes had to consciously contrive what the vast majority of women do without thinking. She was not faking what real women do naturally. She was obliged to analyze and figure out how to act within socially structured circumstances and conceptions of femininity that women born with appropriate biological credentials take for granted early on. As in the case of others who must 'pass', such as transvestites, Kabuki actors, or Dustin Hoffman's 'Tootsie', Agnes's case makes visible what culture has made invisible – the accomplishment of gender.

Garfinkel's (1967) discussion of Agnes does not explicitly separate three analytically distinct, although empirically overlapping, concepts – sex, sex category, and gender.

Sex

Agnes did not possess the socially agreed upon biological criteria for classification as a member of the female *sex*. Still, Agnes regarded herself as a female, albeit a female with a penis, which a woman ought not to possess. The penis, she insisted, was a 'mistake' in need of remedy (Garfinkel 1967: 126–7, 131–2). Like other competent members of our culture, Agnes honored the notion that there are essential biological criteria that unequivocally distinguish females from males. However, if we move away from the commonsense viewpoint, we discover that the reliability of these criteria is not beyond question. . . .

More central to our argument is Kessler and McKenna's (1978: 1–6) point that genitalia are conventionally hidden from public inspection in everyday life; yet we continue through our social rounds to 'observe' a world of two naturally, normally sexed persons. It is the *presumption* that essential criteria exist, and would or should be there if looked for, that provides the basis for sex categorization. Drawing on Garfinkel, Kessler and McKenna argued that 'female' and 'male' are cultural events – products of what they term the 'gender attribution process' – rather than some collection of traits, behaviors, or even physical attributes. Illustratively, they cite the child who, viewing a picture of someone clad in a suit and a tie, contends, 'It's a man, because he has a pee-pee' (Kessler and McKenna 1978: 154). Translation: 'He must have a pee-pee [an essential characteristic] because I see the *insignia* of a suit and tie.' Neither initial sex assignment (pronouncement at birth as a female or male) nor the actual existence of essential criteria for that assignment (possession of a clitoris and vagina or penis and testicles) has much – if anything – to do with the identification of sex category in everyday life. There, Kessler and McKenna note, we operate with a moral certainty of a world of two sexes. We do not think, 'Most persons with penises are men, but some may not be' or 'Most persons with penises are men, but some may not be' or 'Most persons who dress as men have penises.' Rather, we take it for granted that sex and sex category are congruent – that knowing the latter, we can deduce the rest.

Sex categorization

Agnes's claim to the categorical status of female, which she sustained by appropriate identificatory displays and other characteristics, could be discredited before her transsexual operation if her possession of a penis became known and after by her surgically constructed genitalia (see Raymond 1979: 37–138). In this regard, Agnes had to be continually alert to actual or potential threats to the security of her sex category. Her problem was not so much living up to some prototype of essential femininity but preserving her categorization as female. This task was made easy for her by a very powerful resource, namely, the process of commonsense categorization in everyday life.

The categorization of members of society into indigenous categories, such as girl or boy, or woman or man, operates in a distinctively social way. The act of categorization does not involve a positive test, in the sense of a well defined set of criteria that must be explicitly satisfied prior to making an identification. Rather, the application of membership categories relies on an 'if-can' test in everyday interaction (Sacks 1972: 332–5). This test stipulates that *if* people *can be seen* as members of relevant categories, *then categorize them that way*. That is, use the category that seems appropriate, except in the presence of discrepant information or obvious features that would rule out its use. This procedure is quite in keeping with the attitude of everyday life, in which we take appearances at face value unless we have special reason to doubt them (Bernstein 1986; Garfinkel 1967: 272–7; Schutz 1943).[2] . . .

Agnes's initial resource was the predisposition of those she encountered to take her appearance (her figure, clothing, hair style, and so on) as the undoubted appearance of a normal female. Her further resource was our cultural perspective on the properties of 'natural, normally sexed persons'. Garfinkel (1967: 122–8) notes that in everyday life, we live in a world of two – and only two – sexes. This arrangement has a moral status in that we include ourselves and others in it as 'essentially, originally, in the first place, always have been, always will be once and for all, in the final analysis, either "male" or "female"' (Garfinkel 1967, p. 122). . . .

Gender

Agnes attempted to be '120 per cent female' (Garfinkel 1967: 129), that is, unquestionably in all ways and at all times feminine. She thought she could protect herself from disclosure before and after surgical intervention by comporting herself in a feminine manner, but she also could have given herself away by overdoing her performance. Sex categorization and the accomplishment of gender are not the same. Agnes's categorization could be secure or suspect, but did not depend on whether or not she lived up to some ideal conception of femininity. Women can be seen as unfeminine, but that does not make them 'unfemale'. Agnes faced an ongoing task of *being* a woman – something beyond style of dress (an identificatory display) or allowing men to light her cigarette (a gender display). Her problem was to produce configurations of behavior that would be seen by others as normative gender behavior.

Agnes's strategy of 'secret apprenticeship', through which she learned expected feminine decorum by carefully attending to her fiancé's criticisms of other women, was one means of masking incompetencies and simultaneously acquiring the needed skills (Garfinkel 1967: 146–7). It was through her fiancé that Agnes learned that sunbathing on the lawn in front of her apartment was 'offensive' (because it put her on display to other men). She also learned from his critiques of other women that she should not insist on having things her way and that she should not offer her opinions or claim equality with men (Garfinkel 1967: 147–8). (Like other women in our society Agnes learned something about power in the course of her 'education').

Popular culture abounds with books and magazines that compile idealized depictions of relations between women and men. Those focused on the etiquette of dating or prevailing standards of feminine comportment are meant to be of practical help in these matters. . . .

Agnes could perhaps have used such sources as manuals, but, we contend, doing gender is not so easily regimented (Mithers 1982; Morris 1974). Such sources may list and describe the sorts of behaviors that mark or display gender, but they are necessarily incomplete (Garfinkel 1967: 66–75; Wieder 1974: 183–214; Zimmerman and Wieder 1970: 285–98). To be successful, marking or displaying gender must be finely fitted to situations and modified or transformed as the occasion demands. Doing gender consists of managing such occasions so that, what-ever the particulars, the outcome is seen and seeable in context as gender-appropriate or purposefully gender-inappropriate, that is, *accountable*.

Gender and accountability

As Heritage (1984: 136–7) notes, members of society regularly engage in 'descrip-tive accountings of states of affairs to one another', and such accounts are both serious and consequential. These descriptions name, characterize, formulate, excuse, excoriate, or merely take notice of some circumstance or activity and thus place it within some social framework (locating it relative to other activities, like and unlike).

Such descriptions are themselves accountable, and societal members orient to the fact that their activities are subject to comment. Actions are often designed with an eye to their accountability, that is, how they might look and how they might be characterized. The notion of accountability also encompasses those actions undertaken so that they are specifically unremarkable and thus not worthy of more than a passing remark, because they are seen to be in accord with culturally approved standards.

Heritage (1984: 179) observes that the process of rendering something account-able is interactional in character:

> [This] permits actors to design their actions in relation to their circum-stances so as to permit others, by methodically taking account of circumstances, to recognize the action for what it is.

The key word here is *circumstances*. One circumstance that attends virtually all actions is the sex category of the actor. As Garfinkel (1967: 118) comments:

> [T]he work and socially structured occasions of sexual passing were obstinately unyielding to [Agnes's] attempts to routinize the grounds of daily activities. This obstinacy points to the *omnirelevance* of sexual status to affairs of daily life as an invariant but unnoticed background in the texture of relevances that compose the changing actual scenes of everyday life. (emphasis added)

If sex category is omnirelevant (or even approaches being so), then a person engaged in virtually any activity may be held accountable for performance of that activity *as a woman or a man*, and their incumbency in one or the other sex category can be used to legitimate or discredit their other activities (Berger *et al.* 1972; Berger *et al.* 1974; Berger *et al.* 1977; Humphreys and Berger 1981). Accordingly, virtu-ally any activity can be assessed as to its womanly or manly nature. And note, to 'do' gender is not always to live up to normative conceptions of femininity or masculinity; it is to engage in behavior *at the risk of gender assessment*. Although it is individuals who do gender, the enterprise is fundamentally interactional and institutional in character, because accountability is a feature of social relationships and its idiom is drawn from the institutional arena in which those relationships are enacted. If this is the case can we ever *not* do gender? Insofar as a society is partitioned by 'essential' differences between women and men and placement in a sex category is both relevant and enforced, doing gender is unavoidable.

Notes

1   This definition understates many complexities involved in the relationship between biology and culture (Jaggar 1983: 106–13). However, our point is that the determination of an individual's sex classification is a *social* process through and through.
2   Bernstein (1986) reports an unusual case of espionage in which a man passing as a woman convinced a lover that he/she had given birth to 'their' child, who, the lover, thought, 'looked like' him.

References

Berger, J., Cohen, B. P., and Zelditch, M. Jr (1972) 'Status characteristics and social interaction', *American Sociological Review*, 37: 241–55.
Berger, J., Conner, T. I., and Hamit Fisek, M. (eds) (1974) *Expectation States Theory: A Theoretical Research Program*. Cambridge MA: Winthrop.
Berger, J., Hamit Fisek, M., Norman, R. Z., and Zelditch, M. Jr (1977) *Status Characteristics and Social Interaction: An Expectation States Approach*. New York: Elsevier.
Bernstein, R. (1986) 'France jails two in odd case of espionage', *New York Times*, 11 May.
Garfinkel, H. (1967) *Studies in Ethnomethodology*. Englewood Cliffs NJ: Prentice-Hall.
Heritage, J. (1984) *Garfinkel and Ethnomethodology*. Cambridge: Polity.
Jaggar, A. M. (1983) *Feminist Politics and Human Nature*. Totawa NJ: Rowman & Allanheld.
Kessler, S. J. and McKenna, W. (1978) *Gender: An Ethnomethodological Approach*. New York: Wiley.
Mithers, C. L. (1982) 'My life as a man', *Village Voice*, 27 (5 October): 1 ff.
Morris, J. (1974) *Conundrum*. New York: Harcourt Brace Jovanovich.
Raymond, J. G. (1979) *The Transsexual Empire*. Boston MA: Beacon.
Sacks, H. (1972) 'On the analyzability of stories by children', J. J. Gumperz and D. Hymes (eds) *Directions in Sociolinguistics*. New York: Holt Rinehart & Winston.
Schutz, A. (1943) 'The problem of rationality in the social world', *Economics*, 10: 130–49.
Wieder, D. L. (1974) *Language and Social Reality: The Case of Telling the Convict Code*. The Hague: Mouton.
Zimmerman, D. H. and Wieder, D. L. (1970) 'Ethnomethodology and the problem of order: comment on Denzin', in N. J. Denzin (ed.) *Understanding Everyday Life*. Hawthorne NY: Aldine.

Chapter 3

Judith Butler

PERFORMATIVE SUBVERSIONS

In these extracts from Judith Butler's influential *Gender Trouble*, she explores the ways in which certain transgressive performances may subvert the binary logic of gender, the rigid division between masculine and feminine. In focusing on those performances that parody aspects of femininity and masculinity she suggests that gender cannot be thought of as having some essential basis; there is no original 'authentic' femininity or masculinity located in male and female bodies or in our inner selves.

From *Gender Trouble: Feminism and the Subversion of Identity*, London: Routledge (1990).

. . .

THE TERMS QUEENS, BUTCHES, *femmes, girls*, even the parodic reappropriation of *dyke, queer*, and *fag* redeploy and destabilize the categories of sex and the originally derogatory categories for homosexual identity. All of these terms might be understood as symptomatic of 'the straight mind', modes of identifying with the oppressor's version of the identity of the oppressed. On the other hand, *lesbian* has surely been partially reclaimed from it historical meanings, and parodic categories serve the purposes of denaturalizing sex itself. When the neighborhood gay restaurant closes for vacation, the owners put out a sign, explaining that 'she's overworked and needs a rest'. This very gay appropriation of the feminine works to multiply possible sites of application of the term, to reveal the arbitrary relation between the signifier and the signified, and to desta-bilize and mobilize the sign. Is this a colonizing 'appropriation' of the feminine?

My sense is no. That accusation assumes that the feminine belongs to women, an assumption surely suspect.

Within lesbian contexts, the 'identification' with masculinity that appears as butch identity is not a simple assimilation of lesbianism back into the terms of heterosexuality. As one lesbian femme explained, she likes her boys to be girls, meaning that 'being a girl' contextualizes and resignifies 'masculinity' in a butch identity. As a result, that masculinity, if that it can be called, is always brought into relief against a culturally intelligible 'female body'. It is precisely this dissonant juxtaposition and the sexual tension that its transgression generates that constitute the object of desire. In other words, the object [and clearly, there is not just one] of lesbian-femme desire is neither some decontextualized female body nor a discrete yet superimposed masculine identity, but the destabilization of both terms as they come into erotic interplay. Similarly, some heterosexual or bisexual women may well prefer that the relation of 'figure' to 'ground' work in the opposite direction – that is, they may prefer that their girls be boys. In that case, the perception of 'feminine' identity would be juxtaposed on the 'male body' as ground, but both terms would, through the juxtaposition, lose their internal stability and distinctness from each other. Clearly, this way of thinking about gendered exchanges of desire admits of much greater complexity, for the play of masculine and feminine, as well as the inversion of ground to figure can constitute a highly complex and structured production of desire. Significantly, both the sexed body as 'ground' and the butch or femme identity as 'figure' can shift, invert, and create erotic havoc of various sorts. Neither can lay claim to 'the real', although either can qualify as an object of belief, depending on the dynamic of the sexual exchange. The idea that butch and femme are in some sense 'replicas' or 'copies' of heterosexual exchange underestimates the erotic significance of these identities as internally dissonant and complex in their resignification of the hegemonic categories by which they are enabled. Lesbian femmes may recall the heterosexual scene, as it were, but also displace it at the same time. In both butch and femme identities, the very notion of an original or natural identity is put into question; indeed, it is precisely that question as it is embodied in these identities that becomes one source of their erotic significance. . . .

The notion of an original or primary gender identity is often parodied within the cultural practices of drag, cross-dressing, and the sexual stylization of butch/femme identities. Within feminist theory, such parodic identities have been understood to be either degrading to women, in the case of drag and cross-dressing, or an uncritical appropriation of sex-role stereotyping from within the practice of heterosexuality, especially in the case of butch/femme lesbian identities. But the relation between the 'imitation' and the 'original' is, I think, more complicated than that critique generally allows. Moreover, it gives us a clue to the way in which the relationship between primary identification – that is, the original meanings accorded to gender – and subsequent gender experience might be re-framed. The performance of drag plays upon the distinction between the anatomy of the performer and the gender that is being performed. But we are actually in the presence of three contingent dimensions of significant corporeality: anatomical sex, gender identity, and gender performance. If the anatomy of the performer is already distinct from the gender of the performer, and both of those are distinct from the gender of the performance, then the performance suggests a dissonance not only between sex and performance, but sex and gender, and gender and performance. As much as drag creates a unified picture of 'woman' (what its critics often oppose), it also reveals the distinctness of those aspects of gendered experience which are falsely naturalized as a unity through the regulatory fiction of heterosexual coherence. *In imitating gender, drag implicitly reveals the imitative structure of gender itself – as well as its contingency.* Indeed, part of the pleasure, the giddiness of the performance is in the recognition of a radical contingency in the relation between sex and gender in the face of cultural configurations of causal unities that are regularly assumed to be natural and necessary. In the place of the law of heterosexual coherence, we see sex and gender denaturalized by means of a performance which avows their distinctness and dramatizes the cultural mechanism of their fabricated unity.

the notion of gender parody defended here does not assume that there is an original which such parodic identities imitate. Indeed, the parody is *of* the very notion of an original; just as the psychoanalytic notion of gender identification is constituted by a fantasy of a fantasy, the transfiguration of an Other who is always already a 'figure' in that double sense, so gender parody reveals that the original identity after which gender fashion itself is an imitation without an origin. To be more precise, it is a production which, in effect – that is, in its effect – postures as an imitation. This perpetual displacement constitutes a fluidity of identities that suggests an openness to resignification and recontextualization; parodic proliferation deprives hegemonic culture and its critics of the claim to naturalized or essentialist gender identities. Although the gender meanings taken up in these parodic styles are clearly part of hegemonic, misogynist culture, they are nevertheless denaturalized and mobilized through their parodic recontextualization. As imitations which effectively displace the meaning of the original, they imitate the myth of originality itself. In the place of an original identification which serves as a determining cause, gender identity might be reconceived as a personal/cultural history of received meanings subject to a set of imitative practices which refer laterally to other imitations and which, jointly, construct the illusion of a primary and interior gendered self or parody the mechanism of that construction.

Chapter 4

Christine Delphy

RETHINKING SEX AND GENDER

Despite further elaboration of the concept of gender its relationship to sex remained problematic. Arguing from a materialist feminist perspective, Delphy seeks to establish the priority of gender over sex. Having charted the emergence of the concept of gender, she goes on, in the extract reprinted here, to explain why the concept has not yet been fully exploited and to suggest ways of furthering the social analysis of gender.

From *Women's Studies International Forum* 16 (1) 1993: 1–9.

Sex and gender

WITH THE ARRIVAL OF the concept of gender, three things became possible (which does not mean they have happened):

1   All the differences between the sexes which appeared to be social and arbitrary, whether they actually varied from one society to another or were merely held to be susceptible to change, were gathered together in one concept.
2   The use of the singular ('gender' as opposed to 'genders') allowed the accent to be moved from the two divided parts to the principle of partition itself.
3   The idea of hierarchy was firmly anchored in the concept. This should, at least in theory, have allowed the relationship between the divided parts to be considered from another angle.

As studies have accumulated showing the arbitrariness of sex roles and the lack of foundation for stereotypes in one area after another, the idea that gender is independent of sex has progressed. Or rather, since it is a question of the content, the idea that both genders are independent of both sexes has progressed, and the aspects of 'sex roles' and sexual situations which are recognised to be socially constructed rather than biologically determined has grown. . . .

What is problematic, however, is that the ongoing discussion around this question has presumed epistemological and methodological paradigms which should actually have been questioned. We have continued to think of gender in terms of sex: to see it as a social dichotomy determined by a natural dichotomy. We now see gender as the *content* with sex as the *container*. The content may vary, and some consider it *must* vary, but the container is considered to be invariable because it is part of nature, and nature, 'does not change'. Moreover, part of the nature of sex itself is seen to be its *tendency to have a social content*/to vary culturally.

What should have happened, however, is that recognising the independence of the genders from the sexes should have led us to question whether gender is in fact independent of sex. But this question has not been asked. . . . Even the neutral question 'We have here two variables, two distributions, which coincide totally. How can we explain this covariance?' does not get considered.

The response is always: sex comes first, chronologically and hence logically – although it is never explained why this should be so. . . . [S]uggesting or admitting the precedence of sex, even implicitly, leads to one being located, objectively, in a theory where sex causes, or explains, gender. And the theory that sex causes gender, even if it does not determine the exact forms gender divisions take, can derive from only two logical lines of argument.

1   In the first line of argument, biological sex, and particularly the different functions in procreation between males and females which it provokes, necessarily gives rise to a minimal division of labour.
      I would include in this line of argument, with its naturalist premises, most contemporary anthropological accounts, feminist as well as patriarchal, from George Murdock (1949) to Martha Moia (1981) by way of Gayle Rubin (1975) [with just a few notable exceptions, such as Mathieu (1991) and Tabet (1982)]. It fails to explain satisfactorily: (a) the nature and the natural reason for this first division of labour; and (b) the reasons it is extended into all fields of activity, that is, why it is not limited to the domain of procreation. It therefore fails to explain gender other than by suppositions which reintroduce upstream one or more of the elements it is supposed to explain downstream.
2   The second line of argument sees biological sex as a physical trait which is not only suitable, but destined by its intrinsic 'salience' (in psycho-cognitive terms) to be a receptacle for classifications.
      Here it is postulated that human beings have a universal need to establish classifications, independently of and prior to any social organisation; and that they also need to establish these classifications on the basis of physical traits, independently of any social practice.[1] But, these two human needs are neither justified nor proven. They are simply asserted. We are not shown *why* sex is more prominent than other physical traits, which are equally distinguishable, but which do not give birth to classifications which are (i) dichotomous and (ii) imply social roles which are not just distinct but hierarchical.

I call this latter line of argument 'cognitivist', not because it is particularly held by the 'Cognitivists', but because it presumes certain 'prerequisites' of human cognition The best-known academic version of such theories is that of Lévi-Strauss, who, while not a psychologist, bases all his analyses of kinship and (by extension) human societies on an irrepressible and presocial (hence psychological) need of human beings to divide everything in two (and then in multiples of two). Lévi-Strauss (1969) was very much influenced by linguistics, in particular by Saussure's phonology (1959), and he devised by analogous construction what the social sciences call 'structuralism'.

A rather more recent version of this thesis has been presented by Derrida (1976) and his followers, who say that things can only be distinguished by opposition to other things. However, while Saussure is concerned purely with linguistic structures, Derrida and his clones want to draw philosophical conclusions about the importance of 'différence'.

. . . We may agree things are only known by distinction and hence by differentiation, but these differentiations can be, and often are, multiple. Alongside cabbages and carrots, which are not 'opposites' of each other, there are courgettes, melons, and potatoes. Moreover, distinctions are not necessarily hierarchical: vegetables are not placed on a scale of value. Indeed, they are often used as a warning against any attempt to hierarchisation: we are told not to compare (or to try to add) cabbages and carrots. They are incommensurable. They do not have a common measure. Therefore, they cannot be evaluated in terms of being more or less, or better or worse than one another.

Those who adhere to Derrida's thesis thus fail to distinguish between the differences on which language is based and differences in social structures. The characteristics of cognition, in so far as they can be reduced to the characteristics of language, cannot account for social hierarchy. This is external to them. They therefore cannot account for gender – or they can do so only at the expense of dropping hierarchy as a constitutive element of gender.

Hence, neither of the two lines of argument which might justify a causal link from sex to gender is satisfactory. The presupposition that there *is* such a causal link remains, therefore, just that: a presupposition.

But if we are to think about gender, or to think about anything at all, we must leave the domain of presuppositions. To think about gender we must rethink the question of its relationship to sex, and to think about this we must first actually ask the question. We must abandon the notion that we already know the answer. We must not only admit, but also explore, two other hypotheses:

1   That the statistical coincidence between sex and gender is just that, a coincidence. The correlation is due to chance. This hypothesis is, however, untenable, because the distribution is such that the coincidence between so-called biological sex and gender . . . is stronger than any correlation could be which is due to chance.

2   That *gender* precedes sex: that sex itself simply marks a social division; that it serves to allow social recognition and identification of those who are dominants and those who are dominated. That is, that sex is a sign, but that since it does not distinguish just any old thing from anything else, and does not

distinguish equivalent things but rather important and unequal things it has historically acquired a symbolic value. . . .

Since society locates the sign which marks out the dominants from the dominated within the zone of physical traits, two further remarks need to be made:

1   The marker is not found in pure state, all ready for use.
        As Hurtig and Pichevin (1986) have shown, biologists see sex as made up of several indicators which are more or less correlated one with another, and the majority are continuous variables (occurring in varying degrees). So in order for sex to be used as a dichotomous classification, the indicators have to be reduced to just one. And as Hurtig and Pichevin (1985) also say, this reduction 'is a social act'.
2   The presence or absence of a penis[2] is a strong predictor of gender (by definition one might say). However, having or not having a penis correlates only weakly with procreational functional differences between individuals. It does not distinguish tidily between people who can bear children and those who cannot. It distinguishes, in fact, just some of those who cannot. Lots of those who do not have penises also cannot bear children, either because of constitutional sterility or due to age.

It is worth pausing here, because the 'cognitivists' think sex is a 'prominent trait' because they think physical sex is strongly correlated with functional differences, and because they assume that the rest of humanity shares this 'knowledge'. But they only think biological sex is a 'spontaneous perception' of humanity because they themselves are convinced that it is a natural trait that no one could ignore. To them, it is self-evident that there are two, and only two, sexes, and that this dichotomy exactly cross-checks with the division between potential bearers and non-bearers of children.

To try to question these 'facts' is indeed to try to crack one of the toughest nuts in our perception of the world.

We must therefore add to the hypothesis that gender precedes sex the following question: when we connect gender and sex, are we comparing something social with something natural, or are we comparing something social with something natural, or are we comparing something social with something which is *also* social (in this case, the way a given society represents 'biology' to itself)?

One would think that this would logically have been one of the first questions to be asked, and it is doubtless the reason why some feminists in France (e.g. Guillaumin, 1982, 1985; Mathieu 1980; and Wittig, 1992) are opposed to using the term 'gender'. They believe it reinforces the idea that 'sex' itself is purely natural. However, not using the concept of gender does not mean one thereby directly questions the natural character of sex. So economising on the concept of gender does not seem to me the best way to progress.

'Sex' denotes and connotes something natural. It is therefore not possible to question 'sex' head on, all at once . . . We must first define and lay claim to a territory for the social, having a different conceptual location from that of sex but tied to the traditional sense of the word 'sex', in order to be able, from this strategic location, to challenge the traditional meaning of 'sex'.

To end this section, I would say that we can only make advances in our knowledge if we initially increase the unknown: if we extend the areas which are cloudy and indeterminate. To advance, we must first renounce some truths. These 'truths' make us feel comfortable, as do all certainties, but they stop us asking questions – and asking questions is the surest, if not the only way of getting answers.

Divisions, differences, and classifications

The debate on gender and its relationship to sex covers much the same ground as the debate on the priority of the two elements – division and hierarchy – which constitute gender. These are empirically indissolubly united, but they need to be distinguished analytically. If it is accepted that there is a line of demarcation between 'natural' and socially constructed differences, and that at least some differences are socially constructed, then there is a framework for conceptualising gender. This means, or should mean, recognising that hierarchy forms the foundation for differences – for all differences, not just gender.

However, even when this is accepted as an explanation, it is not accepted as a politics nor as a vision of the future, by feminists. It is not their Utopia. All feminists reject the sex/gender hierarchy, but very few are ready to admit that the logical consequence of this rejection is a refusal of sex roles, and the disappearance of gender. Feminists seem to want to abolish hierarchy and even sex roles, but not difference itself. They want to abolish the contents but not the container. They all want to keep some elements of gender. Some want to keep more, others less, but at the very least they want to maintain the classification. Very few indeed are happy to contemplate there being simple anatomical sexual differences which are not given any social significance or symbolic value. . . .

This is especially clear in the debate on values. Feminist (and many other!) theorists generally accept that values are socially constructed and historically acquired, but they seem to think they must nonetheless be preserved. There are two typical variants on this position: One says, we must distribute masculine and feminine values through the whole of humanity; the other says that masculine and feminine values must each be maintained in their original group. The latter view is currently especially common among women who do not want to share feminine values with men. . . . [W]e might well ask how women who are 'nurturant' and proud of it are going to become the equals of unchanged men – who are going to continue to drain these women's time? This is not a minor contradiction. It shows, rather, that if intellectual confusion produces political confusion, it is also possible to wonder, in a mood of despair, if there is not a deep and unacknowledged desire *not* to change anything at work behind the intellectual haze.

In any case, both variants of the debate show an implicit interpretation of the present situation which contradicts the problematic of gender:

1   On the one hand, there is a desire to retain a system of classification, even though (it is said) it has outlived its function of *establishing* a hierarchy between

individuals – which would seem to indicate that people do not *really* think that gender is a social classification.

2   On the other, there is a vision of values . . . which can be summarised as: All human potentialities are already actually represented, but they are divided up between men and women. 'Masculine' plus 'feminine' subcultures, in fact culture itself, is not the product of a hierarchical society. It is independent of the social structure. The latter is simply superimposed upon it.

Hierarchy as necessarily prior to division

This last view is contrary to everything we know about the relationship between social structure and culture. In the Marxist tradition, and more generally in contemporary sociology whether Marxist or not, it is held that the social structure is primary. This implies, as far as values are concerned, that they are, and cannot but be, appropriate to the structure of the society in question. Our society is hierarchical, and consequently its values are also hierarchically arranged. But this is not the only consequence. . . .

Rather, if we accept that values are appropriate to social structures, then we must accept that values are *hierarchical* in general, and that those of the dominated are no less hierarchical than those of the dominants. According to this hypothesis, we must also accept that masculinity and femininity are not just, or rather not at all, what they were in Mead's (1935) model – a division of the traits which are (i) present in a potential form in both sexes, or (ii) present in all forms of possible and imaginable societies. According to the 'appropriateness' paradigm (i.e. the social construction of values), masculinity and femininity are the cultural creations of a society based on a gender hierarchy (as well, of course, as on other hierarchies). This means not only that they are linked to one another in a relationship of complementarity and opposition, but also that this structure determines the *content of each of these categories* and not just their relationship. It may be that together they cover the totality of human traits *which exist today*, but we cannot presume that even together they cover the whole spectrum of human potentialities. If we follow the 'appropriateness' paradigm, changing the respective statuses of the groups would lead to neither an alignment of all individuals on a single model, nor a happy hybrid of the two models.

Both the other sorts of conjecture presuppose, however, that these 'models' (i.e. the 'feminine' and the 'masculine') exist *sui generis*, and both imply a projection into a changed future of traits and values which exist now, prior to the change in the social structure.

To entrust oneself to this sort of guesswork, which moreover is totally implicit, requires a quite untenable, static view of culture. Even if it was progressive when Margaret Mead (1935) was writing just to admit that cultures varied and that values were arbitrarily divided between groups, this view is no longer tenable because it assumes the invariability of a universal human subject, and this has been invalidated by historians' studies of 'mentalities', and by the social constructionist approaches inspired (even if generally unwittingly) by the Marxist principles discussed above.

This vision of culture as static is, however, fundamental to all the variants of the notion of positive complementarity between men and women . . .

. . . The fear that a generalised sameness, or absence of differentiation, would be provoked by the disappearance of what is apparently the only kind of difference that we know (for this view point ignores all other sorts of variance)[3] is, of course, not new; though currently the fear that the world will align on a single model often takes the more specific form that the single model will be the current masculine model. This (it is said) will be the price we shall have to pay for equality; and (it is said) it is (perhaps) too high a price. However this fear is groundless since it is based on a static, hence essentialist, vision of women and men, which is a corollary to the belief that hierarchy was in some way added on to an essential dichotomy.

Within a gender framework such fears are simply incomprehensible. If women were the equals of men, men would no longer equal themselves. Why then should women resemble what men would have ceased to be? If we define men within a gender framework, they are first and foremost dominants with characteristics which enable them to remain dominants. To be like them would be also to be dominants, but this is a contradiction in terms. . . . [T]o be dominant one must have someone to dominate. One can no more conceive of a society where everyone is 'dominant' than of one where everyone is 'richer'.

It is also not possible to imagine the values of a future egalitarian society as being the sum, or a combination, of existing masculine and feminine values, for these values were created in and by hierarchy. So how could they survive the end of hierarchy?

This vision of a society where values existed as 'entities', prior to their being organised into a hierarchy is, as I have said, static and ultimately naturalist. But it is also not an isolated idea. It is part of a whole ensemble of ideas which includes:

1   commonsense and academic theories of sexuality which involve a double confusion: a confusion of anatomical sex with sexuality, and sexuality with procreation; and
2   a deep cultural theme to which these theories themselves refer back: viz. that each individual is essentially incomplete in so far as he or she is sexed. Emotional resistance and intellectual obstacles to thinking about gender both originate from this: from the individual and collective consciousness.

This is what I earlier called 'a set of confused representations turning around a belief in the necessity of close and permanent relations between most males and most females' (Delphy 1980). I wanted to call this *set* (or representations) 'heterosexuality', but it has been suggested it would be better called 'complementarity'. Its emblem is the image of heterosexual intercourse, and this gives it a social meaning and an emotional charge which is explicable only by its symbolic value. It could therefore equally be called a set of representations of 'fitting together'.
. . .

Imagination and knowledge

We do not know what the values, individual personality traits, and culture of a nonhierarchical society would be like, and we have great difficulty in imagining it. But to imagine it we must think that it is possible. And it *is* possible. Practices produce values; other practices produce other values.

Perhaps it is our difficulty in getting beyond the present, tied to our fear of the unknown, which curbs us in our utopian flights, as also in our progress at the level of knowledge – since the two are necessary to one another. To construct another future we obviously need an analysis of the present, but what is less recognised is that having a utopian vision is one of the indispensable staging-posts in the scientific process – in *all* scientific work. We can only analyse what *does* exist by imagining what does *not* exist, because to understand what is, we must ask how it came about. . . .

In conclusion, I would say that perhaps we shall only really be able to think about gender on the day when we can imagine nongender. . . .

Notes

1   See, for example, Archer and Lloyd (1985), who say gender will continue because it is a 'practical way of classifying people'.
2   This is 'the final arbiter' of the dichotomous sex classification for the state, according to Money and Ehrhardt (1972, quoted by Hurtig and Pichevin 1985).
3   This would mean that I would only talk to a male baker since I would no longer be able to distinguish a female baker from myself.

References

Archer, John and Lloyd, Barbara (1985) *Sex and Gender*, revised edition. Cambridge: Cambridge University Press.

Delphy, Christine (1980) 'A materialist feminism is possible', *Feminist Review*, 4.

Derrida, Jacques (1976) *Of Grammatology*, trans. Gayatri Spivak. Baltimore MD: Johns Hopkins University Press.

Guillaumin, Colette (1982) 'The question of difference', *Feminist Issues*, 2(2).

Guillaumin, Colette (1985) 'The masculine: denotations/connotations', *Feminist Issues*, 5(1).

Hurtig, Marie-Claude and Pichevin, Marie-France (1985) 'La variable sexe en psychologie: donne ou construit?' *Cahiers de psychologie cognitive*, 5(2) 187–228.

Hurtig, Marie-Claude and Pichevin, Marie-France (1986) *La Différence des sexes*. Paris: Tierce.

Komarovsky, Mirra (1950) 'Functional analysis of sex roles', *American Sociological Review*, 15(4).

Lévi-Strauss, Claude (1969) *The Elementary Structures of Kinship*. London: Eyre & Spottiswoode.

Mathieu, Nicole-Claude (1980) 'Masculinity/femininity', *Feminist Issues*, 1(1).

Mathieu, Nicole-Claude (1991) *L'Anatomie politique : categorisations et ideologies du sexe*. Paris: Côté-femmes.

Mead, Margaret (1935) *Sex and Temperament in three Primitive Societies*. New York: Morrow.

Moia, Martha (1981) *La Saumone*. Paris: Mercure de France.

Money, John and Ehrhardt, Anke A. (1972) *Man and Woman, Boy and Girl*. Baltimore MD: Johns Hopkins University Press.

Murdock, George (1949) *Social Structure*. New York: Macmillan.

Rubin, Gayle (1975) 'The traffic in women: notes on the political economy of sex' in Rayna Rapp Reiter (ed.) *Towards an Anthropology of Women*. New York: *Monthly Review* Press.

Saussure, Ferdinand de (1959) *Course in General Linguistics*, trans. W. Baskin, London: Philosophical Library.

Tabet, Paula (1982) 'Hands, tools, weapons', *Feminist Issues*, 2(2).

Wittig, Monique (1992) *The Straight Mind and other Essays*. Boston MA: Beacon Press; Hemel Hempstead: Harvester Wheatsheaf.

Chapter 5

Bob Connell

HEGEMONIC MASCULINITY

Bob Connell argues that there is no single form of masculinity of femininity in Western societies, only different ways of being a man or a woman. However, there are culturally dominant forms of gendered being, which he characterises as hegemonic masculinity and emphasised femininity. Here he explains the former.

From *Gender and Power*, Cambridge: Polity (1987).

. . .

IN THE CONCEPT OF hegemonic masculinity, 'hegemony' means (as in Gramsci's analysis of class relations in Italy from which the term is borrowed) a social ascendancy achieved in a play into the organization of private life and cultural processes. Ascendancy of one group of men over another achieved at the point of a gun, or by the threat of unemployment, is not hegemony. Ascendancy which is embedded in religious doctrine and practice, mass media content, wage structures, the design of housing, welfare/taxation policies, and so forth, is.

Two common misunderstandings of the concept should be cleared up immediately. First, though 'hegemony' does not refer to ascendancy based on force, it is not incompatible with ascendancy based on force. Indeed, it is common for the two to go together. Physical or economic violence backs up a dominant cultural pattern (for example, beating up 'perverts'), or ideologies justify the holders of physical power ('law and order'). The connection between hegemonic masculinity and patriarchal violence is close, though not simple.

Second, 'hegemony' does not mean total cultural dominance, the obliteration of alternatives. It means ascendancy achieved within a balance of forces, that is, a state of play. Other patterns and groups are subordinated rather than eliminated.

If we do not recognize this it would be impossible to account for the everyday contestation that actually occurs in social life, let alone for historical changes in definitions of gender patterns on the grand scale.

Hegemonic masculinity, then, is very different from the notion of a general masculinity, then, is very different from the notion of a general 'male sex role' . . . First, the cultural ideal (or ideals) of masculinity need not correspond at all closely to the actual personalities of the majority of men. Indeed, the winning of hegemony often involves the creation of models of masculinity which are quite specifically fantasy figures, such as the film characters played by Humphrey Bogart, John Wayne and Sylvester Stallone. Or real models may be publicized who are so remote from everyday achievement that they have the effect of an unattainable ideal, like the Australian Rules footballer Ron Barassi or the boxer Muhammed Ali.

As we move from face-to-face settings to structures involving millions of people, the easily symbolized aspects of interaction become more prominent. Hegemonic masculinity is very public. In a society of mass communications it is tempting to think that it exists only as publicity. Hence the focus on media images and media discussions of masculinity in the 'Books About Men' of the 1970s and 1980s, from Warren Farrell's *The Liberated Man* to Barbara Ehrenreich's *The Hearts of Men*.

To focus on the media images alone would be a mistake. They need not correspond to the actual characters of the men who hold most social power – in contemporary societies the corporate and state elites. Indeed a ruling class may allow a good deal of sexual dissent. A minor but dramatic instance is the tolerance for homosexuality that the British diplomat Guy Burgess could assume from other men of his class during his career as a Soviet spy. The public face of hegemonic masculinity is not necessarily what powerful men are, but what sustains their power and what large numbers of men are motivated to support. The notion of 'hegemony' generally implies a large measure of consent. Few men are Bogarts or Stallones, many collaborate in sustaining those images.

There are various reasons for complicity, and a thorough study of them would go far to illuminate the whole system of sexual politics. Fantasy gratification is one – nicely satirized in Woody Allen's Bogart take-off, *Play It Again, Sam*. Displaced aggression might be another – and the popularity of very violent movies from *Dirty Harry* to *Rambo* suggest that a great deal of this is floating around. But it seems likely that the major reason is that most men benefit from the subordination of women, and hegemonic masculinity is the cultural expression of this ascendancy.

This needs careful formulation. It does not imply that hegemonic masculinity means being particularly nasty to women. Women may feel as oppressed by non-hegemonic masculinities, may even find the hegemonic pattern more familiar and manageable. There is likely to be a kind of 'fit' between hegemonic masculinity and emphasized femininity. What it does imply is the maintenance of practices that institutionalize men's dominance over women. In this sense hegemonic masculinity must embody a successful collective strategy in relation to women. Given the complexity of gender relations, no simple or uniform strategy is possible: a 'mix' is necessary. So hegemonic masculinity can contain at the same time, quite consistently, openings towards domesticity and openings towards violence, towards misogyny and towards heterosexual attraction.

Hegemonic masculinity is constructed in relation to women and to subordinated masculinities. These other masculinities need not be as clearly defined – indeed, achieving hegemony may consist precisely in preventing alternatives gaining cultural definition and recognition as alternatives, confining them to ghettoes, to privacy, to unconsciousness.

The most important feature of contemporary hegemonic masculinity is that it is heterosexual, being closely connected to the institution of marriage; and a key form of subordinated masculinity is homosexual. This subordination involves both direct interactions and a kind of ideological warfare. Some of the interactions . . . [include] police and legal harassment, street violence, economic discrimination. These transactions are tied together by the contempt for homosexuality and homosexual men that is part of the ideological package of hegemonic masculinity. The AIDS scare has been marked less by sympathy for gays as its main victims than by hostility to them as the bearers of a new threat. The key point of media concern is whether the 'gay plague' will spread to 'innocent', i.e. straight, victims.

In other cases of subordinated masculinity the condition is temporary. Cynthia Cockburn's splendid study of printing workers in London portrays a version of hegemonic masculinity that involved ascendancy over young men as well as over women. The workers recalled their apprenticeships in terms of drudgery and humiliation, a ritual of induction into trade and masculinity at the same time. But once they were in, they were 'brothers'. . . .

Chapter 6

Dorothy E. Smith

WOMEN'S PERSPECTIVE
AS A RADICAL CRITIQUE
OF SOCIOLOGY

Here we have a pioneering critique of the androcentric assumptions underpinning mainstream sociology and an exploration of how sociology might be reconfigured from women's perspective. Smith's argument was crucial to the development of what was to become known, in debates on epistemology, as the feminist standpoint.

From *Sociological Inquiry*, 44 (1) 1974: 70–13. © 1974 University of Texas Press.

THE WOMEN'S MOVEMENT HAS given us a sense of our right to have women's interests represented in sociology, rather than just receiving as authoritative the interests traditionally represented in a sociology put together by men. What can we make of this access to a social reality that was previously unavailable, was indeed repressed? What happens as we begin to relate to it in the terms of our discipline? We can of course think as many do merely of the addition of courses to the existing repertoire. . . . But thinking more boldly or perhaps just thinking the whole thing through a little further might bring us to ask first how a sociology might look if it began from the point of view of women's traditional place in it and what happens to a sociology which attempts to deal seriously with that. Following this line of thought, I have found, has consequences larger than they seem at first.

From the point of view of 'women's place' the values assigned to different aspects of the world are changed. Some come into prominence while other standard sociological enterprises diminish. . . .

But it is not enough to supplement an established sociology by addressing ourselves to what has been left out, overlooked, or by making sociological issues of the relevances of the world of women. That merely extends the authority of the existing sociological procedures and makes of a women's sociology an addendum. We cannot rest at that because it does not account for the separation between the two worlds and it does not account for or analyze for us the relation between them. . . .

The sociologist enters the conceptually ordered society when he goes to work. He enters it as a member and he enters it also as the mode in which he investigates it. He observes, analyzes, explains and examines as if there were no problem in how that world becomes observable to him. He moves among the doings of organizations, governmental processes, bureaucracies, etc., as a person who is at home in that medium. The nature of that world itself, how it is known to him and the conditions of its existence or his relation to it are not called into question. His methods of observation and inquiry extend into it as procedures which are essentially of the same order as those which bring about the phenomena with which he is concerned, or which he is concerned to bring under the jurisdiction of that order. His perspectives and interests may differ, the substance is the same. He works with facts and information which have been worked up from actualities and appear in the form of documents which are themselves the product of organizational processes, whether his own or administered by him, or of some other agency. He fits that information back into a framework of entities and organizational processes which he takes for granted as known, without asking how it is that he knows them or what are the social processes by which the phenomena which correspond to or provide the empirical events, acts, decisions, etc., of that world, may be recognized. He passes beyond the particular and immediate setting in which he is always located in the body (the office he writes in, the libraries he consults, the streets he travels, the home he returns to) without any sense of having made a transition. He works in the same medium as he studies.

But like everyone else he also exists in the body in the place in which it is. This is also then the place of his sensory organization of immediate experience, the place where his co-ordinates of here and now before and after are organized around himself as centre; the place where he confronts people face to face in the physical mode in which he expresses himself to them and they to him as more and other than either can speak. It is in this place that things smell. The irrelevant birds fly away in front of the window. Here he has indigestion. It is a place he dies in. Into this space must come as actual material events, whether as the sounds of speech, the scratchings on the surface of paper which he constitutes as document, or directly anything he knows of the world. It has to happen here somehow if he is to experience it at all.

Entering the governing mode of our kind of society lifts the actor out of the immediate local and particular place in which he is in the body. He uses what becomes present to him in this place as a means to pass beyond it to the conceptual order. This mode of action creates then a bifurcation of consciousness, a bifurcation of course which is there for all those who participate in this mode of action. It establishes two modes of knowing and experiencing and doing, one located in the body and in the space which it occupies and moves into, the other, which passes beyond it. Sociology is written in and aims at this second mode. *Vide* Bierstedt (1966):

Sociology can liberate the mind from time and space themselves and remove it to a new and transcendental realm where it no longer depends upon these Aristotelian categories.

Even observational work aims at its description in the categories and hence conceptual forms of the 'transcendental realm'.

Women are outside and subservient to this structure. They have a very specific relation to it which anchors them into the local and particular phase of the bifurcated world. For both traditionally and as a matter of occupational practices in our society, the governing conceptual mode is appropriated by men and the world organized in the natural attitude, the home, is appropriated by (or assigned to) women (Smith 1973).

It is a condition of a man's being able to enter and become absorbed in the conceptual mode that he does not have to focus his activities and interests upon his bodily existence. If he is to participate fully in the abstract mode of action, then he must be liberated also from having to attend to his needs, etc., in the concrete and particular. The organization of work and expectations in managerial and professional circles both constitutes and depends upon the alienation of man from his bodily and local existence. The structure of work and the structure of career take for granted that these matters are provided for in such a way that they will not interfere with his action and participation in that world. Providing for the liberation from the Aristotelian categories of which Bierstedt speaks, is a woman who keeps house for him, bears and cares for his children, washes his clothes, looks after him when he is sick and generally provides for the logistics of his bodily existence.

The place of women then in relation to this mode of action is that where the work is done to create conditions which facilitate his occupation of the conceptual mode of consciousness. The meeting of a man's physical needs, the organization of his daily life, even the consistency of expressive background, are made maximally congruent with his commitment. A similar relation exists for women who work in and around the professional and managerial scene. They do those things which give concrete form to the conceptual activities. They do the clerical work, the computer programming, the interviewing for the survey, the nursing, the secretarial work. At almost every point women mediate for men the relation between the conceptual mode of action and the actual concrete forms in which it is and must be realized, and the actual material conditions upon which it depends.

Marx's concept of alienation is applicable here in a modified form. The simplest formulation of alienation posits a relation between the work an individual does and an external order which oppresses her, such that the harder she works the more she strengthens the order which oppresses her. This is the situation of women in this relation. The more successful women are in mediating the world of concrete particulars so that men do not have to become engaged with (and therefore conscious of) that world as a condition to their abstract activities, the more complete man's absorption in it, the more effective the authority of that world and the more total women's subservience to it. And also the more complete the dichotomy between the two worlds, and the estrangement between them.

Women sociologists stand at the centre of a contradiction in the relation of our discipline to our experience of the world. Transcending that contradiction means setting up a different kind of relation than that which we discover in the routine practice of our worlds.

The theories, concepts and methods of our discipline claim to account for, or to be capable of accounting for and analyzing the same world as that which we experience directly. But these theories, concepts and methods have been organized around and built up out of a way of knowing the world which takes for granted the boundaries of an experience in the same medium in which it is constituted. It therefore takes for granted and subsumes without examining the conditions of its existence. It is not capable of analyzing its own relation to its conditions because the sociologist as actual person in an actual concrete setting has been cancelled in the procedures which objectify and separate him from his knowledge. Thus the linkage which points back to its conditions is lacking.

For women those conditions are central as a direct practical matter, to be somehow solved in the decision to take up a sociological career. The relation between ourselves as practising sociologists and ourselves as working women is continually visible to us, a central feature of experience of the world, so that the bifurcation of consciousness becomes for us a daily chasm which is to be crossed, on the one side of which is this special conceptual activity of thought, research, teaching, administration and on the other the world of concrete practical activities in keeping things clean, managing somehow the house and household and the children a world in which the particularities of persons in their full organic immediacy (cleaning up the vomit, changing the diapers, as well as feeding) are inescapable. Even if we don't have that as a direct contingency in our lives, we are aware of that as something that our becoming may be inserted into as a possible predicate.

It is also present for us to discover that the discipline is not one which we enter and occupy on the same terms as men enter and occupy it. We do not fully appropriate its authority, i.e. the right to author and authorize the acts and knowing and thinking which are the acts and knowing and thinking of the discipline as it is thought. We cannot therefore command the inner principles of our action. That remains lodged outside us. The frames of reference which order the terms upon which inquiry and discussion are conducted originate with men. The subjects of sociological sentences (if they have a subject) are male. The sociologist is 'he'. And even before we become conscious of our sex as the basis of an exclusion (*they are not talking about us*), we nonetheless do not fully enter ourselves as the subjects of its statements, since we must suspend our sex, and suspend our knowledge of who we are as well as who it is that in fact is speaking and of whom. Therefore we do not fully participate in the declarations and formulations of its mode of consciousness. The externalization of sociology as a profession which I have described above becomes for women a double estrangement.

There is then for women a basic organization of their experience which displays for them the structure of the bifurcated consciousness. At the same time it attenuates their commitment to a sociology which aims at an externalized body of knowledge based on an organization of experience which excludes theirs and excludes them except in a subordinate relation.

. . . Women's perspective, as I have analyzed it here, discredits sociology's claim to constitute an objective knowledge independent of the sociologist's situation. Its conceptual procedures, methods and relevances are seen to organize its subject matter from a determinate position in society. This critical disclosure becomes then the basis for an alternative way of thinking sociology. If sociology cannot avoid being situated, then sociology should take that as its beginning and build it into its methodological and theoretical strategies. As it is now, these separate a sociologically constructed world from that which is known in direct experience and it is precisely that separation which must be undone.

I am not proposing an immediate and radical transformation of the subject matter and methods of the discipline nor the junking of everything that has gone before. What I am suggesting is more in the nature of a reorganization which changes the relation of the sociologist to the object of her knowledge and changes also her problematic. This reorganization involves first placing the sociologist where she is actually situated, namely at the beginning of those acts by which she knows or will come to know; and second, making her direct experience of the everyday world the primary ground of her knowledge. . . .

The only way of knowing a socially constructed world is knowing it from within. We can never stand outside it. A relation in which sociological phenomena are objectified and presented as external to and independent of the observer is itself a special social practice also known from within. The relation of observer and object of observation, of sociologist to 'subject', is a specialized social relationship. Even to be a stranger is to enter a world constituted from within as strange. The strangeness itself is the mode in which it is experienced.

. . . An alternative sociology must be reflexive (Gouldner 1971), i.e. one that preserves in it the presence, concerns and experience of the sociologist as knower and discoverer.

To begin from direct experience and to return to it as a constraint or 'test' of the adequacy of a systematic knowledge is to begin from where we are located bodily. The actualities of our everyday world are already socially organized. Settings, equipment, 'environment', schedules, occasions, etc., as well as the enterprises and routines of actors are socially produced and concretely and symbolically organized prior to our practice. By beginning from her original and immediate knowledge of her world, sociology offers a way of making its socially organized properties first observable and then problematic.

Let me make it clear that when I speak of 'experience' I do not use the term as a synonym for 'perspective'. Nor, in proposing a sociology grounded in the sociologist's actual experience, an I recommending the self-indulgence of inner exploration or any other enterprise with self as sole focus and object. Such subjectivist interpretations of 'experience' are themselves an aspect of that organization of consciousness which bifurcates it and transports us into mind country while stashing away the concrete conditions and practices upon which it depends. We can never escape the circles of our own heads if we accept that as our territory. Rather the sociologist's investigation of our directly experienced world as a problem is a mode of discovering or rediscovering the society from within. She begins from her own original but tacit knowledge and from within the acts by which she brings it into her grasp in making it observable and in understanding how it works.

She aims not at a reiteration of what she already (tacitly) knows, but at an exploration through that of what passes beyond it and is deeply implicated in how it is. . . .

Women's situation in sociology discloses to her a typical bifurcate structure with the abstracted conceptual practices on the one hand and the concrete realizations, the maintenance routines, etc., on the other. Taking each for granted depends upon being fully situated in one or the other so that the other does not appear in contradiction to it. Women's direct experience places her a step back where we can recognize the uneasiness that comes in sociology from its claim to be about the world we live in and its failure to account for or even describe its actual features as we find them in living them. The aim of an alternative sociology would be to develop precisely that capacity from that beginning so that it might be a means to anyone of understanding how the world comes about for her and how it is organized so that it happens to her as it does in her experience.

Though such a sociology would not be exclusively for or done by women it does begin from the analysis and critique originating in their situation. Its elaboration therefore depends upon a grasp of that which is prior to and fuller than its formulation. It is a little like the problem of making a formal description of the grammar of a language. The linguist depends and always refers back to the competent speakers' sense of what is correct usage, what makes sense, etc. In her own language she depends to a large extent upon her own competence. Women are native speakers of this situation and in explicating it or its implications, and realizing them conceptually, they have that relation to it of knowing it before it has been said.

The incomprehensibility of the determinations of our immediate local world is for women a particularly striking metaphor. It recovers an inner organization in common with their typical relation to the world. For women's activities and existence are determined outside them and beyond the world which is their 'place'. They are oriented by their training and by the daily practices which confirm it, towards the demands and initiations and authority of others. But more than that, the very organization of the world which has been assigned to them as the primary locus of their being is determined by and subordinate to the corporate organization of society (Smith 1973). Thus as I have expressed her relation to sociology, its logic lies elsewhere. She lacks the inner principle of her own activity. She does not grasp how it is put together because it is determined elsewhere than where she is. As a sociologist then the grasp and exploration of her own experience as a method of discovering society restores to her a centre which in this enterprise at least is wholly hers.

References

Bierstedt, Robert (1966) 'Sociology and general education', in Charles H. Page (ed.), *Sociology and Contemporary Education*. New York: Random House.

Gouldner, Alvin (1971) *The Coming Crisis in Western Sociology*. London: Heinemann.

Smith, Dorothy E. (1973) 'Women, the family and corporate capitalism', in M. L. Stephenson (ed.), *Women in Canada*. Toronto: Newpress.

Chapter 7

Patricia Hill-Collins

LEARNING FROM THE OUTSIDER WITHIN

The sociological significance of Black feminist thought

Taking a feminist standpoint may serve to privilege particular women's perspectives at the expense of others. Here Patricia Hill-Collins challenges not only
androcentrism but also ethnocentrism, exploring the particular forms of knowledge
that black feminist thought can offer to sociology.

From *Social Problems*, 93 (6) 1986: 14–32.

A FRO-AMERICAN WOMEN HAVE long been privy to some of the
most intimate secrets of white society. Countless numbers of Black women
have ridden buses to their white 'families', where they not only cooked, cleaned,
and executed other domestic duties, but where they also nurtured their 'other'
children, shrewdly offered guidance to their employers, and frequently, became
honorary members of their white 'families'. These women have seen white elites,
both actual and aspiring, from perspectives largely obscured from their Black
spouses and from these groups themselves.[1]

On one level, this 'insider' relationship has been satisfying to all involved. The
memoirs of affluent whites often mention their love for their Black 'mothers',
while accounts of Black domestic workers stress the sense of self-affirmation they
experienced at seeing white power demystified – of knowing that it was not the
intellect, talent, or humanity of their employers that supported their superior
status, but largely just the advantages of facism.[2] But on another level, these same
Black women knew they could never belong to their white 'families'. In spite of
their involvement, they remained 'outsiders'.[3]

This 'outsider within' status has provided a special standpoint on self, family,
and society for Afro-American women.[4] A careful review of the emerging Black
feminist literature reveals that many Black intellectuals, especially those in touch

with their marginality in academic settings, tap this standpoint in producing distinctive analyses of race, class, and gender. . . .

In spite of the obstacles that can confront outsiders within, such individuals can benefit from this status. Simmel's (1921) essay on the sociological significance of what he called the 'stranger' offers a helpful starting point for understanding the largely unexplored area of Black female outsider within status and the usefulness of the standpoint it might produce. Some of the potential benefits of outsider within status include: (1) Simmel's definition of 'objectivity' as 'a peculiar composition of nearness and remoteness, concern and indifference'; (2) the tendency for people to confide in a 'stranger' in ways they never would with each other; and (3) the ability of the 'stranger' to see patterns that may be more difficult for those immersed in the situation to see. Mannheim (1936) labels the 'strangers' in academia 'marginal intellectuals' and argues that the critical posture such individuals bring to academic endeavours may be essential to the creative development of academic disciplines themselves. Finally, in assessing the potentially positive qualities of social difference, specifically marginality, Lee notes, 'for a time this marginality can be a most stimulating, albeit often a painful, experience. For some, it is debilitating . . . for others, it is an excitement to creativity' (1973: 64).[5] . . .

Black feminist thought consists of ideas produced by Black women that clarify a standpoint of and for Black women. Several assumptions underlie this working definition. First, the definition suggests that it is impossible to separate the structure and thematic content of thought from the historical and material conditions shaping the lives of its producers (Berger and Luckmann 1966; Mannheim 1936). Therefore, while Black feminist thought may be recorded by others, it is produced by Black women. Second, the definition assumes that Black women possess a unique standpoint on, or perspective of, their experiences and that there will be certain commonalities of perception shared by Black women as a group. Third, while living life as Black women may produce certain commonalities of outlook, the diversity of class, region, age, and sexual orientation shaping individual Black women's lives has resulted in different expressions of these common themes. Thus, universal themes included in the Black women's standpoint may be experienced and expressed differently by distinct groups of Afro-American women. Finally, the definition assumes that, while a Black women's standpoint exists, its contours may not be clear to Black women themselves. Therefore, one role for Black female intellectuals is to produce facts and theories about the Black female experience that will clarify a Black woman's standpoint for Black women. In other words, Black feminist thought contains observations and interpretations about Afro-American womanhood that describe and explain different expressions of common themes. . . .

The sociological significance of Black feminist thought

Taken together, the three key themes in Black feminist thought – the meaning of self-definition and self-valuation, the interlocking nature of oppression, and the importance of redefining culture – have made significant contributions to the task of clarifying a Black women's standpoint of and for Black women. While this accomplishment is important in and of itself, Black feminist thought has potential contributions to make to the diverse disciplines housing its practitioners.

The sociological significance of Black feminist thought lies in two areas. First, the content of Black women's ideas has been influenced by and contributes to on-going dialogues in a variety of sociological specialities. While this area merits attention, it is not my primary concern in this section. Instead, I investigate a second area of sociological significance: the process by which these specific ideas were produced by this specific group of individuals. In other words, I examine the influence of Black women's outsider within status in academia on the actual thought produced. . . . In this section, I spell out exactly what form the relationship between the three key themes in Black feminist thought and Black women's outsider within status might take for women scholars generally, with special attention to Black female sociologists.

First, I briefly summarize the role sociological paradigms play in shaping the facts and theories used by sociologists. Second, I explain how Black women's outsider within status might encourage Black women to have a distinctive stand-point *vis-à-vis* sociology's paradigmatic facts and theories. I argue that the thematic content of Black feminist thought described above represents elements of just such a standpoint and give examples of how the combination of sociology's paradigms and Black women's outsider within status as sociologists directed their attention to specific areas of sociological inquiry.

Two elements of sociological paradigms

Kuhn defines a paradigm as the 'entire constellation of beliefs, values, techniques, and so on shared by the members of a given community' (1962: 175). As such, a paradigm consists of two fundamental elements: the thought itself and its producers and practitioners.[6] In this sense, the discipline of sociology is itself a paradigm – it consists of a system of knowledge shared by sociologists – and simul-taneously consists of a plurality of paradigms (e.g. functionalism, Marxist sociology, feminist sociology, existential sociology), each produced by its own practitioners.

Two dimensions of thought itself are of special interest to this discussion. First, systems of knowledge are never complete. Rather, they represent guidelines for 'thinking as usual'. Kuhn (1962) refers to these guidelines as 'maps', while Schutz (1944) describes them as 'recipes'. As Schutz points out, while 'thinking as usual' is actually only partially organized and partially clear, and may contain contradic-tions, to its practitioners it provides sufficient coherence, clarity, and consistency. Second, while thought itself contains diverse elements, I will focus mainly on the important fact/theory relationship. As Kuhn (1962) suggests, facts or observations become meaningful in the context of theories of interpretations of those observa-tions. Conversely, theories 'fit the facts' by transforming previously accessible observations into facts. According to Mulkay, 'observation is not separate from interpretation; rather these are two facets of a single process' (1979: 49).

Several dimensions of the second element of sociological paradigms – the community formed by a paradigm's practitioners – are of special interest to this discussion. First, group insiders have similar worldviews, acquired through similar educational and professional training, that separate them from everyone else. Insider worldviews may be especially alike if group members have similar social class, gender, and racial backgrounds. Schutz describes the insider worldview as the 'cultural pattern of group life' – namely, all the values and behaviors which characterize the social group at a given moment in its history. In brief, insiders have undergone similar experiences, possess a common history, and share taken-for-granted knowledge that characterizes 'thinking as usual'.

A second dimension of the community of practitioners involves the process of becoming an insider. How does one know when an individual is really an insider and not an outsider in disguise? Merton suggests that socialization into the life of a group is a lengthy process of being immersed in group life, because only then can 'one understand the fine-grained meanings of behavior, feeling, and values . . . and decipher the unwritten grammar of conduct and nuances of cultural idiom' (1972: 15). The process is analogous to immersion in a foreign culture in order to learn its ways and its language (Merton 1972; Schutz 1944). One becomes an insider by translating a theory or worldview into one's own language until, one day, the individual converts to thinking and acting according to that worldview.

A final dimension of the community of practitioners concerns the process of remaining an insider. A sociologist typically does this by furthering the discipline in ways described as appropriate by sociology generally, and by areas of specialization particularly. Normal foci for scientific sociological investigation include: (1) determining significant facts; (2) matching facts with existing theoretical interpretations to 'test' the paradigm's ability to predict facts; and (3) resolving ambiguities in the paradigm itself by articulating and clarifying theory (Kuhn 1962).

Black women and the outsider within status

Black women may encounter much less of a fit between their personal and cultural experiences and both elements of sociological paradigms than that facing other sociologists. On the one hand, Black women who undergo sociology's lengthy socialization process, who immerse themselves in the cultural pattern of sociology's group life, certainly wish to acquire the insider skills of thinking in and acting according to a sociological worldview. But on the other hand, Black women's experienced realities, both prior to contact and after initiation, may provide them with 'special perspectives and insights . . . available to that category of outsiders who have been systematically frustrated by the social system' (Merton 1972: 29). In brief, their outsider allegiances may militate against their choosing full insider status, and they may be more apt to remain outsiders within.[7]

In essence, to become sociological insiders, Black women must assimilate a standpoint that is quite different than their own. White males have long been the dominant group in sociology, and the sociological worldview understandably reflects the concerns of this group of practitioners. As Merton observes, 'white male insiderism in American sociology during the past generations has largely been of the tacit or *de facto* . . . variety. It has simply taken the form of patterned expectations about the appropriate . . . problems for investigation' (1972: 12). In contrast, a good deal of the Black female experience has been spent coping with avoiding, subverting, and challenging the workings of this same white male insiderism. It should come as no surprise that Black women's efforts in dealing with the effects of interlocking systems of oppression might produce a standpoint quite distinct from, and in many ways opposed to, that of white male insiders.

Seen from this perspective, Black women's socialization into sociology represents a more intense case of the normal challenges facing sociology graduate students and junior professionals in the discipline. Black women become, to use Simmel's (1921) and Schutz's terminology, penultimate 'strangers'.

> The stranger . . . does not share the basic assumptions of the group. He becomes essentially the man who has to place in question everything that seems to be unquestionable to the members of the approached group. . . . To him the cultural patterns of the approached group do not have the authority of a tested system of recipes . . . because he does not partake in the vivid historical tradition by which it has been formed.
>
> (Schutz 1944: 502)

Like everyone else, Black women may see sociological 'thinking as usual' as partially organized, partially clear, and contradictory, and may question these existing recipes. However, for them, this questioning process may be more acute, for the material that they encounter – white male insider-influenced observations and interpretations about human society – places white male subjectivity at the center of analysis and assigns Afro-American womanhood a position on the margins.

In spite of a lengthy socialization process, it may also be more difficult for Afro-American women to experience conversion and begin totally to think in and act according to a sociological worldview. Indeed, since past generations of white male insiderism have shaped a sociological worldview reflecting this group's concerns, it may be self-destructive for Black women to embrace that worldview. For example, Black women would have to accept certain fundamental and self-devaluing assumptions: (1) white males are more worthy of study because they are more fully human than everyone else; and (2) dichotomous oppositional thinking is natural and normal. More importantly, Black women would have to act in accordance with their place in a white male worldview. This involves accepting one's own subordination or regretting the accident of not being born white and male. In short, it may be extremely difficult for Black women to accept a worldview predicated upon Black female inferiority.

Remaining in sociology by doing normal scientific investigation may also be less complicated for traditional sociologists than for Afro-American women. Unlike Black women, learners from backgrounds where the insider information and expenses of sociology are more familiar may be less likely to see the taken-for-granted assumptions of sociology and may be more prone to apply their creativity to 'normal science'. In other words, the transition from student status to that of a practitioner engaged in finding significant facts that sociological paradigms deem important, matching facts with existing theories, and furthering paradigmatic development itself may proceed more smoothly for white middle-class males than for working-class Black females. The latter group is much more inclined to be struck by the mismatch of its own experiences and the paradigms of sociology itself. Moreover, those Black women with a strong foundation in Black women's culture (e.g. those that recognize the value of self-definition and self-valuation, and that have a concrete understanding of sisterhood and motherhood) may be more apt to take a critical posture toward the entire sociological enterprise. In brief, where traditional sociologists may see sociology as 'normal' and define their role as furthering knowledge about a normal world with taken-for-granted assumptions, outsiders within are liable to see anomalies.

The types of anomalies typically seen by Black female academicians grow directly from Black women's outsider within status and appear central in shaping the direction Black feminist thought has taken thus far. Two types of anomalies are characteristically noted by Black female scholars. First, Black female sociologists typically report the omission of facts or observations about Afro-American women in the sociological paradigms they encounter. As Scott points out, 'from reading the literature, one might easily develop the impression that Black women have never played any role in this society' (1982: 85). Where white males may take it as perfectly normal to generalize findings from studies of white males to other groups, Black women are more likely to see such a practice as problematic, as an anomaly. Similarly, when white feminists produce generalizations about 'women', Black feminists routinely ask, 'Which women do you mean?' In the same way that Rollins (1985) felt invisible in her employer's kitchen, Afro-American female scholars are repeatedly struck by their own invisibility, both as full human subjects included in sociological fats and observations, and as practitioners in the discipline itself. It should come as no surprise that much of Black feminist thought aims to counter this invisibility by presenting sociological analyses of Black women as fully human subjects. For example, the growing research describing Black women's historical and contemporary behavior as mothers, community workers, church leaders, teachers, and employed workers, and Black women's ideas about themselves and their opportunities, reflects an effort to respond to the omission of facts about Afro-American women.

A second type of anomaly typically noted by Black female scholars concerns distortions of facts and observations about Black women. Afro-American women in academia are frequently struck by the difference between their own experiences and sociological descriptions of the same phenomena. For example, while Black women have and are themselves mothers, they encounter distorted versions of themselves and their mothers under the mantle of the Black matriarchy thesis. Similarly, for those Black women who confront racial and sexual discrimination and know that their mothers and grandmothers certainly did, explanations of Black women's poverty that stress low achievement motivation and the lack of Black female 'human capital' are less likely to ring true. The response to these perceived distortions has been one of redefining distorted images – for example, debunking the Sapphire and Mammy myths.

Since facts or observations become meaningful in the context of a theory, this emphasis on producing accurate descriptions of Black women's lives has also refocused attention on major omissions and distortions in sociological theories themselves. By drawing on the strengths of sociology's plurality of subdisciplines, yet taking a critical posture toward them, the work of Black feminist scholars taps some fundamental questions facing all sociologists. One such question concerns the fundamental elements of society that should be studied. Black feminist researchers' response has been to move Black women's voices to the center of the analysis, to study people, and by doing so, to reaffirm human subjectivity and intentionality. They point to the dangers of omission and distortion that can occur if sociological concepts are studied at the expense of human subjectivity. For example, there is a distinct difference between conducting a statistical analysis of Black women's work, where Afro-American women are studied as a reconstituted amalgam of researcher-defined variables (e.g. race, sex, years of education, and father's occupation), and examining Black women's self-definitions and self-valuations of themselves as workers in oppressive jobs. While both approaches can further sociological knowledge about the concept of work, the former runs the risk of objectifying Black women, of reproducing constructs of dichotomous oppositional difference, and of producing distorted findings about the nature of work itself.

A second question facing sociologists concerns the adequacy of current interpretations of key sociological concepts. For example, few sociologists would question that work and family are two fundamental concepts for sociology. However, bringing Black feminist thought into the center of conceptual analysis raises issues of how comprehensive current sociological interpretations of these two concepts really are. For example, labor theories that relegate Afro-American women's work experiences to the fringe of analysis miss the critical theme of the interlocking nature of Black women as female workers (e.g. Black women's unpaid domestic labor) and Black women as radically oppressed workers (e.g. Black women's unpaid slave labor and exploited wage labor). Examining the extreme case offered by Afro-American women's unpaid and paid work experiences raises questions about the adequacy of generalizations about work itself. For example, Black feminists' emphasis on the simultaneity of oppression redefines the economic system itself as problematic. From this perspective, all generalizations about the normal workings of labor markets, organizational structure, occupational mobility, and income differences that do not explicitly see oppression as problematic become suspect. In short, Black feminists suggest that all generalizations about groups of employed and unemployed workers (e.g. managers, welfare mothers, union members, secretaries, Black teenagers) that do not account for interlocking structures of group placement and oppression in an economy as simply less complete than those that do.

Similarly sociological generalizations about families that do not account for Black women's experience will fail to see how the public/private split shaping household composition varies across social and class groupings, how racial/ethnic family members are differentially integrated into wage labor, and how families alter their household structure in response to changing political economies (e.g. adding more people and becoming extended, fragmenting and becoming female-headed, and migrating to locate better opportunities). Black women's family experiences represent a clear case of the workings of race, gender, and class oppression in shaping family life. Bringing undistorted observations of Afro-American women's family experiences into the center of analysis again raises the question of how other families are affected by these same forces.

While Black women who stand outside academia may be familiar with omissions and distortions of the Black female experience, as outsiders to sociology, they lack legitimated professional authority to challenge the sociological anomalies. Similarly, traditional sociological insiders, whether white males or their nonwhite and/or female disciples, are certainly in no position to notice the specific anomalies apparent to Afro-American women, because these same sociological insiders produced them. In contrast, those Black women who remain rooted in their own experiences as Black women – and who master sociological paradigms yet retain a critical posture toward them – are in a better position to bring a special perspective not only to the study of Black women, but to some of the fundamental issues facing sociology itself.

Toward synthesis: outsiders within sociology

Black women are not the only outsiders within sociology. As an extreme case of outsiders moving into a community that historically excluded them, Black women's experiences highlight the tension experienced by any group of less powerful outsiders encountering the paradigmatic thought of a more powerful insider community. In this sense, a variety of individuals can learn from Black women's experiences as outsiders within: Black men, working-class individuals, white women, other people of color, religious and sexual minorities, and all individuals who, while from social strata that provided them with the benefits of white male insiderism, have never felt comfortable with its taken-for-granted assumptions.

Outsider within status is bound to generate tension, for people who become outsiders within are forever changed by their new status. Learning the subject matter of sociology stimulates a reexamination of one's own personal and cultural experiences; and, yet these same experiences paradoxically help to illuminate sociology's anomalies. Outsiders within occupy a special place – they become different people, and their difference sensitizes them to patterns that may be more difficult for established sociological insiders to see. Some outsiders within try to resolve the tension generated by their new status by leaving sociology and remaining sociological outsiders. Others choose to suppress their difference by striving to become bonafide, 'thinking as usual' sociological insiders. Both choices rob sociology of diversity and ultimately weaken the discipline.

A third alternative is to conserve the creative tension of outsider within status by encouraging and institutionalizing outsider within ways of seeing. This alternative has merit not only for actual outsiders within, but also for other sociologists as well. The approach suggested by the experiences of outsiders within is one where intellectuals learn to trust their own personal and cultural biographies as significant sources of knowledge. In contrast to approaches that require submerging these dimensions of self in the process of becoming an allegedly unbiased, objective social scientist, outsiders within bring these ways of knowing back into the research process. At its best, outsider within status seems of offer its occupants a powerful balance between the strengths of their sociological training and the offerings of their personal and cultural experiences. Neither is subordinated to the other. Rather, experienced reality is used as a valid source of knowledge for critiquing sociological facts and theories, while sociological thought offers new ways of seeing that experienced reality.

What many Black feminists appear to be doing is embracing the creative potential of their outsider within status and using it wisely. In doing so, they move
themselves and their disciplines closer to the humanist vision implicit in their work
– namely, the freedom both to be different and part of the solidarity of humanity.

Notes

1   In 1940, almost 60 per cent of employed Afro-American women were domestics.
     The 1970 census was the first time this category of work did not contain the
     largest segment of the Black female labor force. See Rollins (1985) for a discus-
     sion of Black domestic work.
2   For example, in *Of Women Born: Motherhood as Experience and Institution*, Adrienne
     Rich has fond memories of her Black 'mother', a young, unstereotypically slim
     Black woman she loved. Similarly, Dill's (1980) study of Black domestic workers
     reveals Black women's sense of affirmation at knowing that they were better
     mothers than their employers, and that they frequently had to teach their
     employers the basics about children and interaction in general. Even though the
     Black domestic workers were officially subordinates, they gained a sense of self-
     worth at knowing they were good at things that they felt mattered.
3   For example, in spite of Rich's warm memories of her Black 'mother', she had
     all but forgotten her until beginning research for her book. Similarly, the Black
     domestic workers in both Dill's (1980) and Rollins' (1985) studies discussed the
     limitations that their subordinate roles placed on them.
4   For a discussion of the notion of a special standpoint or point of view of oppressed
     groups, see Harsock (1983). See Merton's (1972) analysis of the potential contri-
     butions of insider and outsider perspectives to sociology. For a related discussion
     of outsider within status, see his section 'Insiders as "Outsiders"' (1972: 29–30).
5   By stressing the potentially positive features of outsider within status, I in no
     way want to deny the very real problem this social status has for large numbers
     of Black women. American sociology has long identified marginal status as prob-
     lematic. However, my sense of the 'problems' diverges from those espoused by
     traditional sociologists. For example, Robert Park states, 'the marginal man
     . . . is one whom fate has condemned to live in two societies and in two, not
     merely different but antagonistic cultures, (1950: 373). From Park's perspec-
     tive, marginality and difference themselves were problems. This perspective
     quite rationally led to the social policy solution of assimilation, one aimed at
     eliminating difference, or if that didn't work, pretending it was not important.
     In contrast, I argue that it is the meaning attached to difference that is the
     problem. See Lorde (1984: 114–23 and *passim*) for a Black feminist perspective
     on difference.
6   In this sense, sociology is a special case of the more generalized process discussed
     by Mannheim (1936). Also, see Berman (1981) for a discussion of Western
     thought as a paradigm, Mulkay (1979) for a sociology of knowledge analysis of
     the natural sciences, and Berger and Luckmann (1966) for a generalized discus-
     sion of how everyday knowledge is socially constructed.
7   Jackson (1974) reports that twenty-one of the 145 Black sociologists receiving
     doctoral degrees between 1945 and 1972 were women. Kulis *et al.* (1986) report
     that Blacks comprised 5.7 per cent of all sociology faculties in 1984. These data

suggest that, historically, Black females have not been sociological insiders, and currently, Black women as a group comprise a small portion of sociologists in the United States.

References

Berger, Peter L. and Luckmann, Thomas (1966) *The Social Construction of Reality*. New York: Doubleday.

Berman, Morris (1981) *The Reenchantment of the World*. New York: Bantam.

Dill, Bonnie Thornton (1980) '"The means to put my children through": child-rearing goals and strategies among Black female domestic servants', in LaFrances Rodgers-Rose (ed.) *The Black Woman*. Beverley Hills CA: Sage.

Harstock, Nancy M. (1983) 'The feminist standpoint: developing the ground for a specifically feminist historical materialism', in Sandra Harding and Merrill Hintikka (eds) *Discovering Reality*. Boston MA: Reidel.

Jackson, Jacquelyn (1974) 'Black female sociologists', in James E. Blackwell and Morris Janowitz (eds) *Black Sociologists*. Chicago: University of Chicago Press.

Kuhn, Thomas S. (1962, 1970) *The Structure of Scientific Revolutions*, second edition. Chicago: University of Chicago Press.

Kulis, Stephen, Miller, Karen A., Axelrod, Morris and Gordon, Leonard (1986) 'Minority representation of US departments', *ASA Footnotes*, 14: 3.

Lee, Alfred McClung (1973) *Toward Humanist Sociology*. Englewood Cliffs NJ: Prentice-Hall.

Lorde, Audre (1984) *Sister Outsider*. Trumansburg NY: Crossing Press.

Mannheim, Karl (1936, 1954) *Ideology and Utopia: An Introduction to the Sociology of Knowledge*. New York: Harcourt Brace.

Merton, Robert K. (1972) 'Insiders and outsiders: a chapter in the sociology of knowledge', *American Journal of Sociology*, 78: 9–47.

Mulkay, Michael (1979) *Science and the Sociology of Knowledge*. Boston MA: Allen & Unwin.

Park, Robert E. (1950) *Race and Culture*. Glencoe IL: Free Press.

Rich, Adrienne (1976) *Of Women Born: Motherhood as Experience and Institution*. New York: Norton.

Rollins, Judith (1985) *Between Women, Domestics and their Employers*. Philadelphia PA: Temple University Press.

Schutz, Alfred (1944) 'The stranger: an essay in social psychology', *American Journal of Sociology*, 49: 499–507.

Scott, Patricia Bell (1982) 'Debunking sapphire: toward a non-racist and non-sexist social science', in Gloria T. Hull, Patricia Bell Scott, and Barbara Smith (eds) *But Some of us are Brave*. Old Westbury NY: Feminist Press.

Simmel, Georg (1921) 'The sociological significance of the "stranger"', in Robert E. Park and Ernest W. Burgess (eds) *Introduction to the Science of Sociology*. Chicago: University of Chicago Press.

Chapter 8

Chrys Ingraham

THE HETEROSEXUAL IMAGINARY

Critiques of gender have often failed to question heterosexuality. Chrys Ingraham here develops the concept of the 'heterosexual imaginary' in order to challenge some of our assumptions and to explore the ways in which gender hierarchy interconnects with the institutionalisation of heterosexuality.

From *Sociological Theory*, 12 (2) 1994: 203–19.

. . .

IN THIS ESSAY I MAKE the argument that feminist sociological understandings of gender need to be reexamined for the ways in which they participate in the reproduction of what I call 'the heterosexual imaginary'. The 'imaginary' is a Lacanian term borrowed by Louis Althusser for his theory of ideology . . . Althusser (1971) argues that the imaginary is that image or representation of reality which masks the historical and material conditions of life. The heterosexual imaginary is that way of thinking which conceals the operation of heterosexuality in structuring gender and closes off any critical analysis of heterosexuality as an organizing institution. The effect of this depiction of reality is that heterosexuality circulates as taken for granted, naturally occurring, and unquestioned, while gender is understood as socially constructed and central to the organization of everyday life. Feminist studies of marriage, family, and sexual violence (which might seem to cover this ground) invariably depend upon the heterosexual imaginary deployed in a variety of heternormative assumptions. Heteronormativity – the view that institutionalized heterosexuality constitutes the standard for legitimate and prescriptive sociosexual arrangements – represents one of the main premises not only of feminist sociology but of the discipline in general. As such, it underlies and defines the direction taken by feminist sociology and by gender studies in particular.

If this is to change, feminist sociology must develop a critique of institutionalized heterosexuality which does not participate in the heterosexual imaginary. To interrupt the ways in which the heterosexual imaginary naturalizes heterosexuality and conceals its constructedness in the illusion of universality requires a systemic analysis of the ways in which it is historically imbricated in the distribution of economic resources, cultural power, and social control.

It will be the work of this essay to call for a reconsideration of gender as the key organizing concept of feminist sociology. The main argument of this article is that the material conditions of capitalist patriarchal societies are more centrally linked to institutionalized heterosexuality than to gender and, moreover, that gender (under the patriarchal arrangements prevailing now) is inextricably bound up with heterosexuality. Rearticulating some of the critical strategies of early feminist sociology within a materialist feminist framework, it is possible to both redress and disrupt the heterosexual imaginary circulating in contemporary gender theory.

Gender, or what I would call 'heterogenders', is the asymmetrical stratification of the sexes in relation to the historically varying institutions of patriarchal heterosexuality. Reframing gender as heterogender foregrounds the relation between heterosexuality and gender. Heterogender confronts the equation of heterosexuality with *the natural* and of gender with the cultural, and suggests that both are socially constructed, open to other configurations (not only opposites and binary), and open to change. As a materialist feminist concept, heterogender denaturalizes the 'sexual' as the starting point for understanding heterosexuality, and connects institutionalized heterosexuality with the gender division of labor and the patriarchal relations of production. . . .

Feminist sociology and the heterosexual imaginary

. . . A particularly important patter . . . in feminist sociology is the contestation of the andronormative starting point of sociological inquiry, which relegates all other knowledges to the margins and thereby reinforces patriarchal authority and value. For example, studies of mothering, teaching, child care, caregiving, and other aspects of the 'domestic sphere' have been either ignored or devalued by mainstream sociology. Patriarchy, however, is not only andronormative; it is also heteronormative. Those aspects of the division of labor which are trivialized and neglected in sociological research and theory are also those practices which count as 'women's work' in heterogendered social arrangements. By shifting the focus from gender to heterogender as the primary unit of analysis, institutionalized heterosexuality becomes visible as central to the organization of the division of labor. This shift also reveals the ways in which the heterosexual imaginary depends on an abject 'other', which is regulated as deviant. This 'other' consists of any sexual practice which does not participate in dominant heterogender arrangements and therefore does not count as legitimate or normal.

When I say that the critical insights of feminist sociologists can be employed to interrogate the heterocentrism of feminist sociology, I am not talking only about the marginalization of lesbian/gay/bisexual knowledges from sociological inquiry, but also about the way in which heteronormative assumptions organize many conceptual and professional practices. For instance, many social science surveys ask respondents to check off their marital status as either married, divorced, separated, widowed, single, or (in some cases) never married. Not only are these categories presented as significant indexes of social identity; they are offered as the only options, implying that their organization of identity in relation to marriage is universal and not in need of explanation. Questions concerning marital status appear on most surveys regardless of relevance, in some cases as 'warm-up' questions. The heteronormative assumption of this practice is rarely, if every, called into question; when it is questioned, the response is generally dismissive. Heteronormativity works in this instance to naturalize the institution of heterosexuality. . . .

Heteronormative sociology, then, plays its part in what Dorothy Smith has conceptualized as textually mediated social practice.

> Such textual surfaces presuppose an organization of power as the concerting of people's activities and the uses of organization to enforce processes producing a version of the world that is peculiarly one-sided, that is known only from within the modes of ruling, and that defines the objects of its power.
>
> (1990: 84)

To not answer such seemingly innocent or descriptive questions is to become deviant according to sociology's enactment of modes of ruling, which signal to respondents in a variety of ways – from theory to surveys – what counts as normal. Under these conditions, sociology is a political field of study, invested in the reproduction of a heteronormative social order, and closed off to struggles over the construction of sexuality and to the exploration of social relations in *all* their layered and complex configurations. . . .

Critiquing heteronormative gender theory

. . . Recent works within areas of inquiry covered by the sociology of sex and gender[1] generally assume a level of agreement on what gender is, how to study it, and why it is important. Gender, family, and introductory sociology textbooks, journal articles, and conference presentations in recent years show little variation in definitions of sex and gender.

A sampling of gender texts within sociology reveals the presence of a dominant framework in gender theory. Sex is typically defined as 'the biological identity of the person and is meant to signify the fact that one is either male or female'. Gender is described as 'the socially learned behaviors and expectations that are associated with the two sexes' (Andersen 1993: 31). . . .

. . . [T]he biological/cultural differentiation of sex and gender has become 'normalized' in sociology generally and among feminist sociologists in particular. Although inclusion of gender studies in 'legitimate' sociology may be cause for celebration for some, the lack of debate over such a crucial concept as gender – not to mention its companion concept, sex – should be grounds for concern among feminists. Acquiescence to an unexamined gender concept goes against the grain of two of feminist sociology's founding principles – to keep a critical eye on the disciplining of knowledge and on forms of gender bias.

Consider some of the contradictions present in the acceptance of these theories of sex and gender. As Maria Mies (1986) points out, separating sex from gender reinforces the nature/culture binary, opening the study of sex to the domain of science and closing off consideration of how biology is linked to culture. Sex, as a biological category, escapes the realm of construction or achieved status, even though it is 'defined' or 'constructed'. Because we are always engaged in giving meaning to the natural world, how we do that and to what end are questions of major significance. Sex as a category of analysis can never exist outside prevailing frames of intelligibility. It is a concept that is related to ways of making sense of the body, often by those – sociologists and biologists – who have a great deal of authority in the creation of knowledges. As a socially constructed category, sex must be scrutinized in relation to the interests that its definition furthers. That is, as sociologists we need to ask what ends are served by constructing sex as 'the division of humanity into biological categories of female and male' (Macionis 1993: 350). . . .

Contemporary sex/gender ideology provides limited options for how we organize sexuality, but expanding these options is not simply a matter of attending to marginalized sexualities. Instead, it seems to me that we need to question our assumptions about sex and gender as to how they organize difference, regulate investigation, and preserve particular power relations, especially those linked to institutionalized heterosexuality.

All of the institutions involved in the production of sex as a biological category defined as male or female, where each is distinct and opposite from the other, are participating in reproducing lines of power. Claims that XX is female and XY is male are just that: scientific *claims* about the natural world, authorized by the ruling order and processed through organizing structures which assign meanings based on frames of intelligibility already circulating in the culture at large. What counts as normal and natural or as 'fact' comes out of ways of making sense already ideologically invested in the existing social order. Often it closes off our ability to imagine otherwise. . . .

. . . At the present, the dominant notion of sex in feminist sociology depends upon a heterosexual assumption that the only possible configuration of sex is male or female as 'opposite sexes', which, like other aspects of the physical world (e.g. magnetic fields), are naturally attracted to each other. Masking the historical relation of sex to history and to heterosexuality is guaranteed by what I have defined as the heterosexual imaginary.

Gender, as the cultural side of the sex/gender binary, is frequently defined by sociologists as either achieved or constructed through a process of 'socialization', whereby males and females become men and women attaining opposite and distinct traits based on sex. In addition to appearing in prominent texts and articles on gender, this understanding of gender circulates in introductory sociology texts. For instance, Hess et al.'s *Sociology* asserts that gender is made up of 'femininity and masculinity as *achieved* characteristics' but that maleness and femaleness are 'ascribed traits' (1989: 193). Although this particular text makes reference to gender as variable cross-culturally and historically, its reliance on an unsaid hetero-sexual dualism implies a static or normative understanding of gender. In addition, this definition of gender illustrates the need for the concept of heterogender as a more appropriate description of the relation between sex and gender. Finally, this explanation does not account for the 'necessity' of gender. This theory of gender as an 'achieved' status does not address to what ends gender is acquired. Nor does it account of the interests served by ascribing or assigning characteristics based on sex. In other words, this text, as well as many others, does not examine what historical and material arrangements organize or are organized by gender. By fore-grounding gender as dependent on the male/female binary, the heterosexual assumption remains unaddressed and unquestioned. . . .

Evident in most conceptualizations of gender is an assumption of heteronor-mativity. In other words, to become gendered is to learn the proper way to be a woman in relation to a man, or feminine in relation to the masculine. For instance, consider Mary Maynard's argument that 'a significant factor in understanding the organisation of society is women's socially constructed difference from men' (1990: 281). Patricia Lengermann and Ruth Wallace state that 'exploring the gender insti-tution means looking at the identity of females in relation to male and vice versa . . . in the context of a two-gender social reality' (1985: 3). As Margaret Andersen explains, 'Gender refers to the complex social, political, economic, and psycho-logical relations between women and men in society' (1993: 34). These are just a few examples among many that identify gender as a cultural binary organizing relations *between* the sexes. Ask students how they learned to be heterosexual, and they will consistently respond with stories about how they learned to be boys or girls, women or men, through the various social institutions in their lives. Heterosexuality serves as the unexamined organizing institution and ideology (the heterosexual imaginary) for gender.

Most important in these theories is the absence of any concept of heterosex-uality as an institutional organizing structure or social totality. The cultural production of behaviors and expectations as 'socially learned' involves all social institutions from family, church, and education to the Department of Defense. Without institutionalized heterosexuality – that is, the ideological and organiza-tional regulation of relations between men and women – would gender even exist? If we make sense of gender and sex as historically and institutionally bound to heterosexuality, then we shift gender studies from localized examinations of indi-vidual behaviors and group practices to critical analyses of heterosexuality as an organizing institution. By doing so, we denaturalize heterosexuality as a taken-for-granted biological entity; we begin the work of unmasking its operations and meaning-making processes and its links to large historical and material conditions. Although feminist sociologists have made important contributions to the analysis of the intersection of gender and social institutions, they have not examined the relation of gender to the institution of heterosexuality. By altering the starting point of feminist sociology from gender to heterosexuality, or heterogender, as I have defined it, we focus on one of the primary roots of exploitation and oppres-sion rather than on one of the symptoms.

Notes

1   These areas include marriage and family, human sexuality, homosexuality, and any other category which makes use of sex or gender for its secondary level of analysis.

References

Althusser, Louis (1971) *Lenin and Philosophy and other Essays*. London: *Monthly Review Press*.

Andersen, Margaret (1993) *Thinking about Women*. New York: St Martin's Press.

Hess, Beth, Markson, E., and Stein, P. (1989) *Sociology*. New York: Macmillan.

Lengermann, Patricia, and Wallace, Ruth A. (1985) *Gender in America*. Englewood Cliffs NJ: Prentice-Hall.

Macionis, John J. (1993) *Sociology*. Englewood Cliffs NJ: Prentice-Hall.

Maynard, Mary (1990) 'The reshaping of sociology? Trends in the study of gender', *Sociology*, 24 (2): 269–90.

Mies, Maria (1986) *Patriarchy and Accumulation on a World Scale*. London: Zed Books.

PART TWO

Class, gender and the labour market

INTRODUCTION

PARTS TWO AND THREE are both concerned, in different ways, with the world of work. We are leaving discussion of the conditions under which women work until Part Three in order to concentrate first on the wider context: gender divisions in the labour market and how they relate to forms of social stratification. The relative positions of women and men within occupational divisions of labour are fundamental to debates on the relationship between class and gender.

In the introduction we drew attention to the reluctance of sociologists to recognise anything other than class as a significant social division. We also pointed out that analyses of class were based almost entirely on studies of men's location within the class structure. While feminist sociologists have made it clear that class is not the only significant form of social stratification, its importance is still nevertheless widely accepted. Hence it is necessary to include women in analyses of class and to consider how women and men are differentially placed in the class system. Moreover class and gender intersect ethnic divisions within local, national and global labour markets, producing complex patterns of social advantage and disadvantage.

The first two chapters in Part Two deal specifically with class as a form of stratification. Early feminist contributions to debates on this issue exposed the biases inherent in basing class analysis entirely on male workers. Joan Acker's argument (Chapter 9) exemplifies this form of critique. These challenges to conventional stratification theory gave rise to a number of related concerns and debates (see Roberts 1993). For example, excluding women could produce a distorted picture of the occupational hierarchy, since job niches filled almost exclusively by women, such as low grade clerical work, were rendered invisible. Second, the tendency to treat the family as the unit of stratification, based entirely on the position of the male head of the household, ignored the contribution women's earnings and occupational status made to the family's standard of living, social location and the educational opportunities of the children. In this respect there was also concern about the anomalous situation of so-called 'cross-class families' where a woman's occupational position was higher than that of her husband (see Britten and Heath 1983). For example, if a male plumber were married to a female neurosurgeon conventional measures would define their household as working class – hardly likely to be an accurate representation.

There was a further, even more intractable, problem in attempts to incorporate women into class analysis: how to place wives who did not have a paid occupation. The usual solution was to define them by their husband's occupation; they were thus treated as not having a class position of their own at all but were subsumed into the person of their husband. The issue of what to do with these non-holders of class positions led some sociologists to investigate the specific position of wives (see Delphy 1984 and Delphy and Leonard 1986). This is the issue taken up by Sylvia Walby in Chapter 10.

Women's position in the labour market and as unpaid workers in the home also figured in wider feminist debates about the relationship between capitalism and patriarchy. During the 1970s and early 1980s considerable argument revolved around the degree to which capital's exploitation of labour and the patriarchal domination of women were related. One strategy was to investigate them historically as Heidi Hartmann does. Her analysis of the means by which men marginalized women in the labour market (Chapter 11) formed the basis of her later argument (1981) that patriarchy and capitalism are mutually reinforcing. Women's disadvantage in the labour market is compounded by their position in the domestic sphere, trapping them in a vicious circle. Because women are pushed into low paid jobs, they cannot earn enough to keep themselves and thus become dependent on men; as dependants women exchange domestic services for maintenance from their husbands or partners; because they have taken on these domestic responsibilities they are further disadvantaged in the labour market.

The development of capitalism was also historically bound up with imperialism, with the economic exploitation of colonised peoples. The legacy of this history remains in the post-colonial era – creating a global division of labour in which the poorer nations continue to provide a pool of cheap labour for transnational capital. In the widening gulf between rich and poor, women are particularly disadvantaged, as Swasti Mitter demonstrates (Chapter 12). Another legacy of imperialism is the persistence of racism within the wealthy 'Western' nations. The history of slavery, and of forced and voluntary migrations of various kinds, has created a racially stratified society. Different forms of stratification – class, 'race', and gender – impact on each other so that gender cannot be assumed to operate independently of other factors influencing women's position in the labour market. From the late 1970s Black feminist writings have made us take racism more seriously. Gemma Tang Nain (Chapter 13) responds to these early debates and demonstrates the dual effects of race and gender on occupational hierarchies.

During the 1980s and 1990s feminist sociologists began to look in more detail at the ways in which labour markets were structured and segmented along gendered lines. A number of theories were put forward to explain both the development and the effects of gendered labour markets (see Walby 1986: chapters 1–4). More recently these issues have been investigated empirically. Some feminist scholars explored historically the ways in which particular occupations had come to be male or female preserves and under what conditions this situation could be challenged and changed. Anne Witz's (1992) study of the medical profession is a classic example of such work (see Chapter 14). A key aspect of labour market segregation is the unequal distribution of rewards, with jobs defined as women's work being lower paid than men's jobs. In her study of postal workers and telephonists Janet Siltanen (Chapter 15) develops the concepts of 'full wages' and 'component wages' as a means of exploring men's ability to earn enough to sustain a household and women's work bringing in less than a subsistence wage.

Gillian Dunne (Chapter 16) draws on Siltanen's concepts in discussing lesbians' participation in the labour market. Lesbians do not have the option of being financially dependent on a man and must therefore find a means of earning a 'full wage'. For those with the benefit of good educational qualifications this is less of a problem, since they have access to middle class occupations which pay a living wage. For working class lesbians, however, choices are more restricted, since most working class women's jobs are low paid, which leads these women to seek routes into traditional male trades and jobs. Here class can be seen to intersect both gender and sexuality.

Of all traditionally female forms of employment home working provides the lowest remuneration. It is important to differentiate the largely menial tasks encompassed by the term 'home working' from the increased flexibility granted to middle class professionals freed from the office by new technology. The home workers studied by Phizacklea and Wolkowitz (1994) in Coventry were often engaged in low grade assembly tasks (finishing lingerie and making Christmas crackers) and paid on piece rates (i.e. per completed item). Although some were engaged in non-manual occupations, or in jobs such as child care, most were relatively low paid. Significantly the Asian women in their sample were all employed in the more menial jobs and were earning even less than the White home workers undertaking similar tasks. Phizacklea (Chapter 17) relates these findings to wider features of the labour market and the existence of racialised divisions of labour in Britain and Europe. In the supposedly single European labour market gendered and racialised divisions persist.

REFERENCES AND FURTHER READING

Britten, N. and Heath, A. (1983) 'Women, men and social class', in E. Gamarnikow *et al.* (eds) *Gender, Class and Work*. London: Heinemann.

Crompton, R. (1997) *Women and Work in Modern Britain*. Oxford: Oxford University Press.

Delphy, C. (1984) 'Women in stratification theory', in her *Close to Home*. London:
  Hutchinson.
Delphy, C. and Leonard, D. (1986) 'Class analysis, gender analysis and the family',
  in R. Crompton and M. Mann (eds) *Gender and Stratification*. Cambridge: Polity.
Glucksman, M. (2000) *Cottons and Casuals: Gendered Organisation of Labour in Time
  and Space*. Durham: sociologypress.
Hartmann, Heidi (1981) 'The unhappy marriage of Marxism and feminism: towards
  a more progressive union', in L. Sargent (ed.), *Women and Revolution: the
  Unhappy Marriage of Marxism and Feminism*. London: Pluto.
Phizacklea, A. and Wolkowitz, C. (1994) *Working at Home*. London: Sage.
Roberts, H. (1993) 'The women and class debates', in L. Stanley and D. H. J. Morgan
  (eds) *Debates in Sociology*. Manchester: Manchester University Press.
Walby, S. (1986) *Patriarchy at Work*. Cambridge: Polity.
Witz, A. (1992) *Patriarchy and the Professions*. London: Routledge.

KEY QUESTIONS

- How might including women in studies of social class change our view of
  the class structure of society?
- Consider the position of your family and friends in the labour market and
  think how it may have been affected by the intersection of class, racial,
  gender and sexual inequalities. (Remember that being middle class, White,
  male and heterosexual has as much effect as being working class, Black,
  female and lesbian.)
- How are gender and racially segregated labour markets maintained at local,
  national and global levels?

Chapter 9

Joan Acker

WOMEN AND SOCIAL STRATIFICATION
A case of intellectual sexism

In this, the first, classic critique of male bias in stratification studies, Joan Acker questions the assumptions about women underpinning sociological work in this area.

From *American Journal of Sociology*, 78 (4) 1973: 936–45.

. . .

IN STRATIFICATION LITERATURE, six assumptions are made, sometimes explicitly and sometimes implicitly, about the social position of women. These are most clearly stated by the functionalists but are present also in the work of nonfunctionalists and Marxists.[1] These assumptions are:

1   The family is the unit in the stratification system.
2   The social position of the family is determined by the status of the male head of the household.
3   Females live in families; therefore, their status is determined by that of the males to whom they are attached.
4   The female's status is equal to that of her man, at least in terms of her position in the class structure, because the family is a unit of equivalent evaluation (Watson and Barth 1964).
5   Women determine their own social status only when they are not attached to a man.
6   Women are unequal to men in many ways, are differentially evaluated on the basis of sex, but this is irrelevant to the structure of stratification systems.

The first assumption, that the family is the unit in stratification, is basic to the other five. Together, these assumptions neatly dispense with the necessity for considering the position of women in studies of social stratification or considering the salience of sex as a dimension of stratification.[2] To put it another way, the fate of the female in the class system is determined by the fate of the male. Therefore, it is only necessary to study males.

How adequate are these assumptions? There are, I believe, deficiencies of both logic and validity which I will discuss briefly.

1. *The family is the unit in the stratification system.* The choice of the family as the unit may be based on the belief that all persons live in families. This is obviously not true, since 11 per cent of the population over age eighteen is categorized as unattached individuals in 1970 data.[3] This assumption also rests on the validity of the other five assumptions, which I examine in the following paragraphs.

2. *The social position of the family is determined by the status of the male head of the household.* This is a researchable question which has been little researched. Instead, empirical researchers often imply an answer to this question in their choice of indicators of class or status position. Thus, if family income is chosen as an indicator, there is an implication that total family resources determine standing. If class placement is measured by occupation alone or an index including occupation, the occupation of the male head of household is invariably used, implying that his position does decide that of the family.[4]

There is one situation in which the second assumption is clearly invalid. The position of the family cannot be determined by the male head if there is no male head of the household. This is the case in a substantial proportion of American families. On the basis of the 1960 census, Watson and Barth (1964) estimated that approximately two-fifths of the households in the United States do not have a male head, in the sense implied by the traditional model of the small nuclear family. They found that two-fifths of the households were either 'females or female headed households or husband–wife families in which the husband is retired or otherwise not in the labor force, is unemployed, or is working only part time'.

3. *Females live in families; therefore, their status is determined by that of the males to whom they are attached.* This assumption may be challenged on the grounds that all females do not live in families. Further, the assumption that a woman's status is determined by that of the man to whom she is attached implies that women have no status resources of their own. In a society in which women, as well as men, have resources of education, occupation, and income, it is obviously not true that women have no basis for determining their own status. If women do have such resources, why do we assume that they are inoperative if the woman is married? It is inconsistent to rank an unmarried woman on the basis of her education and occupation and then maintain that these factors are of no importance to her social status or class placement after she gets married the next day.[5] However, such an abrupt alteration of the criteria of class placement at the time of a shift in marital status is necessary if we are to accept the assumption that only women without men determine their own social status.

4. *The female's status is equal to that of her man.* Once we question the assumption that the woman's status is determined by the man, we must also question the

assumption that the status of the female is equal to that of her male. Of course, wife and husband may be equal, but equivalent evaluation can no longer be assumed.

Even if all females had no independent, status-creating resources, the equality of their status with that of their husbands would still be in question. Equality can be assessed on numerous dimensions. Prestige in the community, style of life, privileges, opportunities, association with social groups, income, education, occupation, and power might all be considered in evaluating the equality of husband and wife in the class structure. Occupation, equated by the functionalists with a full-time, functionally important social role, is often used as the indicator of position for men. However, the full-time occupation of many women, that of housewife-mother, is never considered as a ranking criterion in stratification studies. Are we to conclude that this role is either not functionally important or not a full-time activity, or are we to conclude that only those activities which are directly rewarded financially can bestow status upon the individual or the family? Perhaps this is another question which could be explored through empirical research. There is some research evidence to suggest that housewives whose husbands work in a given occupation have less prestige than women who themselves are employed in the same occupation (Haavio-Mannila 1969). However, the evidence to support or refute the assumption of equal status in regard to the class structure is unfortunately sparse.

5. *Women determine their own social status only when they are not attached to a man.* This assumption can be interpreted as a way of coping with the inconvenient fact that some women are not married or living in the household of a male relative.

6. *Women are at a disadvantage in hierarchies of wealth, power, and prestige, but this fact is irrelevant to the study of stratification systems.* This assumption is implicit in the stratification literature. I draw this conclusion from, on the one hand, the scant attention to the situation of women in the stratification literature, and, on the other hand, the existence of ample evidence that women are excluded from the higher positions of power, that they earn less than men, and that they are present in very small proportions in the more prestigious occupations.

But, perhaps, the position of women is irrelevant to the structure of the larger system. I don't think so. For example, female-headed households account for almost 40 per cent of those below the poverty line (Ferriss 1970). This statistic suggests that the economic and social disadvantages of being female may have an impact on class differentials in family structure. When stratification theorists talk about some classes, they are talking about women to a large extent. It is possible that some of the differences they discuss are sex rather than class differences. These differences may, for example, have an effect upon mobility patterns and the permeability of class boundaries, thus affecting the larger system in complex ways.

In sum, it is not adequate or useful to assume that females have no relevant role in stratification processes independent of their family roles and their ties to particular men. . . .

Notes

1   See, e.g., two recent studies of class structure in Poland and Czechoslovakia (Machonin 1970; Wesolowski and Slomczyński 1968) which explicitly make the assumptions outlined here.

2   Lenski (1966) makes the same point: 'This neglect [of women] has been due in large measure to the tendency of sociologists to treat families, rather than individuals, as the basic unit in systems of stratification' (p. 402).

3   Calculated from table 6, 8, and table 44, p. 36, *Statistical Abstract of the United States, 1971* (US Bureau of the Census 1971).

4   Hofstetter (1970) explores this problem. She concludes that class self-placement by college student respondents may be determined by the combined resources of father and mother, rather than by those of father alone.

5   Many of these points have also been made by Watson and Barth in a penetrating critique of some assumptions in stratification theory and research published in 1964.

References

Ferriss, Abbott L. (1970) *Indicators of Change in the American Family*. New York: Russell Sage.

Haavio-Mannila, E. (1969) 'Some consequences of women's emancipation', *Journal of Marriage and the Family*, 31: 123–34.

Hofstetter, Heather N. (1970) 'The Problem of Family Status Arrangements in Stratification Analysis', unpublished dissertation, Eugene OR: University of Oregon.

Lenski, Gerhard (1966) *Power and Privilege*. New York: McGraw-Hill.

Machonin, Pavel (1970) 'Social stratification in contemporary Czechoslovakia', *American Journal of Sociology*, 75: 725–41.

US Bureau of the Census (1971) *Statistical Abstract of the United States, 1971*. Washington DC: Government Printing Office.

Watson, Walter B. and Barth, Ernest A. (1964) 'Questionable assumptions in the theory of social stratification', *Pacific Sociological Review*, 7: 10–16.

Wesolowski, Wlodzimierz, and Slomczyński, Kazimierz (1968) 'Social stratification in Polish cities', in J. A. Jackson (ed.) *Social Stratification*, Cambridge: Cambridge University Press.

Chapter 10

Sylvia Walby

GENDER, CLASS AND STRATIFICATION
Towards a new approach

Sylvia Walby argues that critics of androcentric approaches to stratification have often not gone far enough, that simply adding women into measures of occupational hierarchy ignores the specific social location of wives. She suggests that, while women as a whole do not constitute a class, housewives do.

From R. Crompton and M. Mann (eds) *Gender and Stratification*, Cambridge, Polity (1986).

Housewives, husbands and class

. . .

I AM GOING TO ARGUE that housewives and husbands can be conceptualized as classes, when class is defined in terms of a distinctive work and market position, but that gender should not be reduced to class. That is, while husbands and housewives are classes, women and men are not. The distinctive material position of housewives is the major determinant of gender relations, but not the only one, and the extent of this determination should be considered an empirical question in need of exploration. Other relevant sets of patriarchal relations include those at the workplace, in the state, in sexuality and in male violence.

I do wish to argue that the sexual division of labour is crucial to patterns of gender relations, but not that the two can be simply equated.

I shall, in the ensuing discussion of housewives and husbands as classes, utilize a definition of class as a set of positions with a common work and market situation. This is because I wish to operate with a conceptual distinction between material position and consciousness and action, so as to facilitate asking the question of the relationship (if any) between the two. Hence I would reject, for my project, the concept of class which embodies notions of consciousness and action around a common set of interests, in the grounds that it is heuristically confusing.

The starting point for my approach is a recognition that housework is a distinctive form of work. It is hard work and the fact that it does not receive a wage should not be held to disqualify it from the status of work (Gershuny 1983; Gilman 1966; Oakley 1974; Schreiner 1911; Seccombe 1974). The domestic labour of the housewife comprises the production of the labour power of the husband, herself and children and other dependants (if any). However, I would argue that it is a mistake to identify the distinctiveness of domestic labour in the nature of the tasks (for instance, O'Brien 1981); rather this should be seen to reside in the distinctive nature of the relations of production under which the housewife labours (Delphy 1977). The content of housework changes over time and varies according to the income and wealth of the household, yet the essential nature of the relations of production hold constant despite this. For example, two centuries ago a housewife in Britain would include many of the stages of the making of clothing among her tasks while today this is unusual (Schreiner 1911; Pinchbeck 1981), but changes in the content of the tasks have little effect on the underlying relations of production. These movements of task from the household economy to the market economy (and sometimes back again) are common (Gershuny 1983; Schreiner 1911). Yet whatever the precise nature of her tasks the housewife is involved in an unequal exchange relationship in which she receives maintenance for her labour – which is most unlike exchange relationships under capitalist relations of production.

. . . [I]t is not just the quantity of work which is important here. More significant is the distinctive social relations under which the work is performed by the woman. It is neither exchanged in a calculated bargain for a wage which varies in proportion to the effort expended, nor with an employer who may be changed easily; rather the exchange is indirect, although nonetheless present (since a wife who refused to perform domestic services of various sorts is liable to be divorced), and changing the employer (the husband) is much more difficult than for a wage labourer. The social relations which induce a wife to part with her labour for less return than her husband are again distinctive to the patriarchal household. The circumstances in which the labour contract under marriage and under waged labour are made and broken, and the implications of this for the nature of the labour contract itself, serve to differentiate significantly the social relations of production under which these forms of labour are performed.

It is sometimes argued that the differences between housewives are too great for them to be included in the same class (e.g. Molyneux 1979). However, this is merely a quantitative difference in the standard of living and does not effect the position of housewives in the relations of production in which they are engaged. The housewife married to a middle-class man is still engaging in the same relations of production as that married to a working-class one; each exchanges her labour with him indirectly for her maintenance. Even a woman with servants is still working under patriarchal relations of production, since she is still dependent upon her husband for maintenance in return for her efforts at household management. This is not to deny that there is reason to distinguish between housewives according to the class position of their husbands, merely that it is not sufficient to deny their common subordination to patriarchal relations of production in the household.

The position of the husband should be taken into account when issues such as the standards of living, access to resources and sources of political influence are considered, but this is not the same as suggesting that married women should take the same class position as their husbands.

Thus I would argue that housewives (both full-time and part-time) are a class exploited by their husbands, who also constitute a class. This is not, however, a sufficient characterization of the class position of women. I do not believe that it is appropriate to designate all women as a class. Not all women are housewives, and thus not all women have a class position in the patriarchal mode of production. This applies only to those women who perform unpaid domestic labour for a husband (or father)[3] in a household and not all women are in this position. It is not appropriate to accord to all women a common class position on the basis that most women will expect, at some point in their lives, to be housewives (as does Delphy 1977). . . . [C]lass location is dependent solely upon an individual's direct work and market situation.

However, while all women do not constitute a class, they do nevertheless have some features of their social situation which are common to all women. Women share a large variety of economic and non-economic circumstances. For instance, sexual choices are affected crucially by gender divisions; gender is the first characteristic to be taken into account in the process of selecting a sexual partner. Further, significant forms of violence and harassment are organized socially by gender in that all women are vulnerable to male attack in the form of rape and other forms of sexual molestation in ways which affect the conduct of women significantly. Again, forms of discrimination in the workplace affect all women, regardless of their actual marital status. Still further, access to rights of citizenship such as suffrage, and some legal rights, have often, historically, been withheld from all women on the basis of their sex alone. Thus there are many illustrations of the ways in which gender is a significant organizing principle in society.

Nevertheless, I would argue that it is not consistent with the principles of class analysis to suggest that women rather than housewives form a class, since these common statuses do not follow directly from a shared economic position. Rather they have a certain degree of autonomy from the economic. I would suggest that in Weberian terminology this would mean that while housewives and husbands are classes, women and men are status groups.

A further important issue in the class location of women is that many women also have a class position deriving from their participation in waged labour. Thus many women have a dual class position. Many women are engaged in two distinct sets of relations of production, and to try to conflate these or ignore one of them by emphasizing the primacy of the other (cf. Goldthorpe 1983; Stanworth 1984) is, in my opinion, a serious mistake for social theory. Sometimes this dual class location will be contradictory, sometimes in harmony: there are no *a priori* conclusions to be drawn here. . . .

References

Delphy, C. (1977) *The Main Enemy*. London: Women's Research and Resources Centre.

Gershuny, J. K. (1983) *Social Innovation and the Division of Labour*. Oxford: Oxford University Press.

Gilman, C. P. (1966) *Women and Economics*. New York: Harper & Row.

Goldthorpe, J. H. (1983) 'Women and class analysis: in defence of the conventional view', *Sociology*, 18 (4).

Molyneux, M. (1979) 'Beyond the domestic labour debate', *New Left Review*, 116.

Oakley, A. (1974) *The Sociology of Housework*. Oxford: Martin Robertson.

O'Brien, M. (1981) *The Politics of Reproduction*. London: Routledge.

Pinchbeck, I. (1981) *Women Workers and the Industrial Revolution, 1750–1850*. London: Virago.

Schreiner, O. (1911) *Woman and Labour*. London: Unwin.

Seccombe, W. (1973) 'The housewife and her labour under capitalism', *New Left Review,* 83: 3–24.

Stanworth, M. (1984) 'Women and class analysis: a reply to John Goldthorpe', *Sociology*, 18 (2).

Chapter 11

Heidi Hartmann

CAPITALISM, PATRIARCHY AND JOB SEGREGATION BY SEX

In a foundational theoretical statement on patriarchal segregation in the labour market, Heidi Hartmann argues that organised male labour actively worked to confine women to low paid unskilled jobs or to unpaid work in the home. Using historical data from the nineteenth century onwards, she argues that job segregation by sex is the root of women's low status in the labour market.

From *Signs*, 1, 1976: 137–68.

THE DIVISION OF LABOR by sex appears to have been universal throughout human history. In our society the sexual division of labor is hierarchical, with men on top and women on the bottom. Anthropology and history suggest, however, that this division was not always a hierarchical one. The development and importance of a sex-ordered division of labor is the subject of this paper. It is my contention that the roots of women's present social status lie in this sex-ordered division of labor. It is my belief that not only must the hierarchical nature of the division of labor between the sexes be eliminated, but the very division of labor between the sexes itself must be eliminated if women are to attain equal social status with men and if women and men are to attain the full development of their human potentials.

The primary questions of investigation would seem to be, then, first, how a more sexually egalitarian division became a less egalitarian one, and second, how this hierarchical division of labor became extended to wage labor in the modern period. . . .

I want to argue that, before capitalism, a patriarchal system was established in which men controlled the labor of women and children in the family, and that in so doing men learned the techniques of hierarchical organization and control. With the advent of public/private separations such as those created by the emergence of state apparatus and economic systems based on wider exchange and larger production units, the problem for men became one of maintaining their control over the labor power of women. In other words, a direct personal system of control was translated into an indirect, impersonal system of control, mediated by society-wide institutions. The mechanisms available to men were (1) the traditional division of labor between the sexes, and (2) techniques of hierarchical organization and control. These mechanisms were crucial in the second process, the extension of a sex-ordered division of labor to the wage-labor system, during the period of the emergence of capitalism in Western Europe and the United States.

The emergence of capitalism in the fifteenth to eighteenth centuries threatened patriarchal control based on institutional authority as it destroyed many old institutions and created new ones, such as a 'free' market in labor. It threatened to bring all women and children into the labor force and hence to destroy the family and the basis of the power of men over women (i.e. the control over their labor power in the family).[1] If the theoretical tendency of pure capitalism would have been to eradicate all arbitrary differences of status among laborers, to make all laborers equal in the market place, why are women still in an inferior position to men in the labor market? The possible answers are legion; they range from neoclassical views that the process is not complete or is hampered by market imperfections to the radical view that production requires hierarchy even if the market nominally requires 'equality'.[2] All of these explanations, it seems to me, ignore the role of men – ordinary men, men as men, men as workers – in maintaining women's inferiority in the labor market. The radical view, in particular, emphasizes the role of men as capitalists in creating hierarchies in the production process in order to maintain their power. Capitalists do this by segmenting the labor market (along race, sex, and ethnic lines among others) and playing workers off against each other. In this paper I argue that male workers have played and continue to play a crucial role in maintaining sexual divisions in the labor process.

Job segregation by sex, I will argue, is the primary mechanism in capitalist society that maintains the superiority of men over women, because it enforces lower wages for women in the labor market. Low wages keep women dependent on men because they encourage women to marry. Married women must perform domestic chores for their husbands. Men benefit, then, from both higher wages and the domestic division of labor. This domestic division of labor, in turn, acts to weaken women's position in the labor market. Thus, the hierarchical domestic division of labor is perpetuated by the labor market, and vice versa. This process is the present outcome of the continuing interaction of two interlocking systems, capitalism and patriarchy. Patriarchy, far from being vanquished by capitalism, is still very virile; it shapes the form modern capitalism takes, just as the development of capitalism has transformed patriarchal institutions. The resulting mutual accommodation between patriarchy and capitalism has created a vicious circle for women. . . .

The emergence of capitalism and the industrial revolution in England and the United States

. . . The creation of a wage-labor force and the increase in the scale of production that occurred with the emergence of capitalism had in some ways a more severe impact on women than on men. To understand this impact let us look at the work of women before this transition occurred and the changes which took place as it occurred.[3] In the 1500s and 1600s, agriculture, woolen textiles (carried on as a by-industry of agriculture), and the various crafts and trades in the towns were the major sources of livelihood for the English population. In the rural areas men worked in the fields on small farms they owned or rented and women tended the household plots, small gardens and orchards, animals, and dairies. The women also spun and wove. A portion of these products were sold in small markets to supply the villages, towns, and cities, and in this way women supplied a considerable proportion of their families' cash income, as well as their subsistence in kind. In addition to the tenants and farmers, there was a small wage-earning class of men and women who worked on the larger farms. Occasionally tenants and their wives worked for wages as well, the men more often than the women.[4] As small farmers and cottagers were displaced by larger farmers in the seventeenth and eighteenth centuries, their wives lost their main sources of support, while the men were able to continue as wage laborers to some extent. Thus women, deprived of these essential household plots, suffered relatively greater unemployment, and the families as a whole were deprived of a large part of their subsistence.[5]

In the 1700s, the demand for cotton textiles grew, and English merchants found they could utilize the labor of the English agricultural population, who were already familiar with the arts of spinning and weaving. The merchants distributed materials to be spun and woven, creating a domestic industrial system which occupied many displaced farm families. This putting-out system, however, proved inadequate. The complexities of distribution and collection and, perhaps more important, the control the workers had over the production process (they could take time off, work intermittently, steal materials) prevented an increase in the supply of textiles sufficient to meet the merchant's needs. To solve these problems first spinning, in the late 1700s, and then weaving, in the early 1800s, were organized into factories. The textile factories were located in the rural areas, at first, in order both to take advantage of the labor of children and women, by escaping the restrictions of the guilds in the cities, and to utilize water power. When spinning was industrialized, women spinners at home suffered greater unemployment, while the demand for male handloom weavers increased. When weaving was mechanized, the need for handloom weavers fell off as well.[6]

In this way, domestic industry, created by emerging capitalism, was later superseded and destroyed by the progress of capitalist industrialization. In the process, women, children, and men in the rural areas all suffered dislocation and disruption, but they experienced this in different ways. Women, forced into unemployment by the capitalization of agriculture more frequently than men, were more available to labor, both in the domestic putting-out system and in the early factories. It is often argued both that men resisted going into the factories because they did not want to lose their independence and that women and children were more docile and malleable. If this was in fact the case, it would appear that these 'character traits' of women and men were already established before the advent of the capitalistic organization of industry, and that they would have grown out of the authority structure prevailing in the previous period of small-scale, family agriculture. Many historians suggest that within the family men were the heads of households, and women, even though they contributed a large part of their families' subsistence, were subordinate.[7] . . .

In the seventeenth and eighteenth centuries the family industry system and the guilds began to break down in the face of the demand for larger output. Capitalists began to organize production on a larger scale, and production became separated from the home as the size of establishments grew. Women were excluded from participation in the industries in which they had assisted men as they no longer took place at home, where married women apparently tended to remain to carry on their domestic work. Yet many women out of necessity sought work in capitalistically organized industry as wage labor they appear to have been at a disadvantage relative to men. First, as in agriculture, there was already a tradition of lower wages for women (in the previously limited area of wage work). Second, women appear to have been less well trained than men and obtained less desirable jobs. And third, they appear to have been less well organized than men.

Because I think the ability of men to organize themselves played a crucial role in limiting women's participation in the wage-labor market, I want to offer, first, some evidence to support the assertion that men were better organized and, second, some plausible reasons for their superiority in this area. I am not arguing that men had greater organizational abilities at all times and all places, or in all areas or types of organization, but am arguing here that it is plausible that they did in England during this period, particularly in the area of economic production. As evidence of their superiority, we have the guilds themselves, which were better organized among men's trades than women's, and in which, in joint trades, men had superior positions – women were seldom admitted to the hierarchical ladder of progression. Second, we have the evidence of the rise of male professions and the elimination of female ones during the sixteenth and seventeenth centuries. The medical profession, male from its inception, established itself through hierarchical organization, the monopolization of new, 'scientific' skills, and the assistance of the state. Midwifery was virtually wiped out by the men. Brewing provides another example. Male brewers organized a fellowship, petitioned the king for monopoly rights (in exchange for a tax on every quart they brewed), and succeeded in forcing the numerous small-scale brewsters to buy from them.[8] Third, throughout the formative period of industrial capitalism, men appear to have been better able to organize themselves as wage workers. And as we shall see below, as factory production became established men used their labor organizations to limit women's place in the labor market.

As to why men might have had superior organizational ability during this transnational period, I think we must consider the development of patriarchal social relations in the nuclear family, as reinforced by the state and religion, a process briefly described above for Anglo-Saxon England. Since men's superior position was reinforced by the state, and men acted in the political arena as heads of households and in the households as heads of production units, it seems likely that men would develop more organizational structures beyond their households. Women, in an inferior position at home and without the support of the state, would be less likely to be able to do this. men's organizational knowledge, then, grew out of their position in the family and in the division of labor. Clearly, further investigation of organizations before and during the transition period is necessary to establish the mechanisms by which men came to control this public sphere.

Thus, the capitalistic organization of industry, in removing work from the home, served to increase the subordination of women, since it served to increase the relative importance of the area of men's domination. But it is important to remember that men's domination was already established and that it clearly influenced the direction and shape that capitalist development took. As Clark has argued, with the separation of work from the home men became less dependent on women for industrial production, while women became more dependent on men economically. From a position much like that of African women . . . , English married women, who had supported themselves and their children, became the domestic servants of their husbands. Men increased their control over technology, production, and marketing, as they excluded women from industry, education, and political organization.[9]

When women participated in the wage-labor market, they did so in a position as clearly limited by patriarchy as it was by capitalism. Men's control over women's labor was altered by the wage-labor system, but it was not eliminated. In the labor market the dominant position of men was maintained by sex-ordered job segregation. Women's jobs were lower paid, considered less skilled, and often involved less exercise of authority or control.[10] Men acted to enforce job segregation in the labor market; they utilized trade union associations and strengthened the domestic division of labor, which required women to do housework, child care, and related chores. Women's subordinate position in the labor market reinforced their subordinate position in the family, and that in turn reinforced their labor-marked position.

The process of industrialization and the establishment of the factory system, particularly in the textile industry, illustrate the role played by men's trade union associations. Textile factories employed children at first, but as they expanded they began to utilize the labor of adult women and of whole families. While the number of married women working has been greatly exaggerated,[11] apparently enough married women had followed their work into the factories to cause both their husbands and the upper classes concern about home life and the care of children. Smelser has argued that in the early factories the family industry system and male control could often be maintained. For example, adult male spinners often hired their own or related children as helpers, and whole families were often employed by the same factory for the same length of working day.[12] Technological change, however, increasingly made this difficult, and factory legislation which limited the hours of children, but not of adults, further exacerbated the difficulties of the 'family factory system'.

The demands of the factory laborers in the 1820s and 1830s had been designed to maintain the family factory system,[13] but by 1840 male factory operatives were calling for limitations on the hours of work of children between nine and thirteen to eight a day, and forbidding the employment of younger children. According to

Smelser this caused parents difficulty in training and supervising their children, and to remedy it male workers and the middle and upper classes began to recommend that women, too, be removed from the factories.[14]

The upper classes of the Victorian Age, the age that elevated women to their pedestals, seem to have been motivated by moral outrage and concern for the future of the English race (and for the reproduction of the working class): 'In the male,' said Lord Shaftesbury, 'the moral effects of the system are very sad, but in the female they are infinitely worse, not alone upon themselves, but upon their families, upon society, and, I may add, upon the country itself. It is bad enough if you corrupt the man, but if you corrupt the woman, you poison the waters of life at the very fountain.'[15] Engels, too, appears to have been outraged for similar reasons: '. . . we find here precisely the same features reappearing which the Factories Report presented, – the work of women up to the hour of confinement, incapacity as housekeepers, neglect of home and children, indifference, actual dislike to family life, and demoralization; further the crowding out of men from employment, the constant improvement of machinery, early emancipation of children, husbands supported by their wives and children, etc., etc.'[16] Here, Engels has touched upon the reasons for the opposition of the male workers to the situation. Engels was apparently ambivalent about whose side he was on, for, while he often seems to sharer the attitudes of the men and of the upper classes, he also referred to the trade unions as elite organizations of grown-up men who achieved benefits for themselves but not for the unskilled, women, or children.[17]

That male workers viewed the employment of women as a threat to their jobs is not surprising, given an economic system where competition among workers was characteristic. That women were paid lower wages exacerbated the threat. But why their response was to attempt to exclude women rather than to organize them is explained, not by capitalism, but by patriarchal relations between men and women: men wanted to assure that women would continue to perform the appropriate tasks at home. . . . Hostility to the competition of young females, almost certainly less well trained and lower paid, was common enough. But if anything, the wage work of married women was thought even less excusable.

In 1846 the *Ten Hours' Advocate* stated clearly that they hoped for the day when such threats would be removed altogether: '. . . It is needless for us to say, that all attempts to improve the morals and physical condition of female factory workers will be abortive, unless their hours are materially reduced. Indeed we may go so far as to say, that married females would be much better occupied in performing the domestic duties of the household, than following the never-tiring motion of machinery. We therefore hope the day is not distant, when the husband will be able to provide for his wife and family, without sending the former to endure the drudgery of a cotton mill.'[18] Eventually, male trade unionists realized that women could not be removed altogether, but their attitude was still ambivalent. One local wrote to the Women's Trade Union League, organized in 1889 to encourage unionization among women workers: "Please send an organizer to this town as we have decided that if the women here cannot be organized they must be exterminated."[19] . . .

The main explanation the English literature offers for lower wages is job segregation by sex, and for both lower wages and the existence of job segregation it offers several interdependent explanations: (1) the exclusionary policies of male unions, (2) the financial responsibility of men for their families, (3) the willingness of women to work for less (and their inability to get more) because of subsidies or a lower standard of living, and (4) women's lack of training and skills. The English historical literature strongly suggests that job segregation by sex is patriarchal in origin, rather longstanding, and difficult to eradicate. Men's ability to organize in labor unions – stemming perhaps from a greater knowledge of the technique of hierarchical organization – appears to be key in their ability to maintain job segregation and the domestic division of labor.

Turning to the United States experience provides an opportunity, first, to explore shifts in the sex composition of jobs, and, second, to consider further the role of unions, particularly in establishing protective legislation. The American literature, especially the works of Abbott and Baker,[20] emphasizes sex shifts in jobs and, in contrast to the English literature, relies more heavily on technology as an explanatory phenomenon.

Conditions in the United States differed from those in England. First, the division of labor within colonial farm families was probably more rigid, with men in the fields and women producing manufactured articles as home. Second, the early textile factories employed young single women from the farms of New England; a conscious effort was made, probably out of necessity, to avoid the creation of a family labor system and to preserve the labor of men for agriculture.[21] This changed, however, with the eventual dominance of manufacture over agriculture as the leading sector in the economy and with immigration. Third, the shortage of labor and dire necessity in colonial and frontier America perhaps created more opportunities for women in nontraditional pursuits outside the family; colonial women were engaged in a wide variety of occupations.[22] Fourth, shortages of labor continued to operate in women's favor at various points throughout the nineteenth and twentieth centuries. Fifth, the constant arrival of new groups of immigrants created an extremely heterogeneous labor force, with varying skill levels and organizational development and rampant antagonisms.[23]

Major shifts in the sex composition of employment occurred in boot and shoe manufacture, textile manufacture, teaching, cigar making, and clerical work.[24] In all of these, except textiles, the shift was toward more women. New occupations opened up for both men and women, but men seemed to dominate in most of them, even though there were exceptions. Telephone operating and typing, for example, became women's jobs. . . .

Cigar making offers ample opportunity to illustrate both the opposition of male unionists to impending sex changes in labor-force composition in their industries and the form that opposition took: protective legislation.[25] Cigar making was a home industry before 1800, when women on farms in Connecticut and elsewhere made rather rough cigars and traded them at village stores. Early factories employed women, but they were soon replaced by skilled male immigrants whose products could compete with fancy European cigars. By 1860, women were only 9 per cent of the employed in cigar making. This switch to men was followed by one to women, but not without opposition from the men. In 1869, the wooden mold was introduced, and so were Bohemian immigrant women (who had been skilled workers in cigar factories in Austria-Hungary).[26] The Bohemian women, established by tobacco companies in tenements, perfected a division of labor in which young girls (and later their husbands)[27] could use the molds. Beginning in 1873 the Cigarmakers International Union agitated vociferously against home work, which was eventually restricted (for example, in New York in 1894). In the late 1880s machinery was introduced into the factories, and women were used as strike-breakers. The union turned to protective legislation.

The attitude of the Cigarmakers International Union toward women was ambivalent at best. The union excluded women in 1864, but admitted them in 1867. In 1875 it prohibited locals from excluding women, but apparently never imposed sanctions on offending locals.[28] In 1878 a Baltimore local wrote Adolph Strasser, the union president: 'We have combatted from its incipiency the move-ment of the introduction of female labor in any capacity whatever, be it bunch maker, roller, or what not.'[29] Lest these ambiguities be interpreted as national/local conflicts, let Strasser speak for himself (1879): 'We cannot drive the females out of the trade, but we can restrict their daily quota of labor through factory laws. No girl under 18 should be employed more than eight hours per day; all over-work should be prohibited. . . .'[30]

Because women are unskilled workers, it may be erroneous to interpret this as animosity to women *per se*. Rather it is the fear of the skilled for the unskilled. Yet male unions denied women skills, while they offered them to young boys. This is quite clear in the case of printing.[31]

Women had been engaged as typesetters in printing from colonial times. It was a skilled trade, but required no heavy work. Abbott attributed the jealousy of the men in the trade to the fact that it was a trade 'suited' to women. In any case, male unions seem to have been hostile to the employment of women from the beginning. In 1854 the National Typographical Union resolved not to 'encourage by its act the employment of female compositors.'[32] Baker suggests that the unions discouraged girls from learning the trade, and so women learned what they could in non-union shops or as strikebreakers.[33] In 1869, at the annual convention of the National Labor Union, of which the National Typographical Union was a member, a strug-gle occurred over the seating of Susan B. Anthony, because she had allegedly used women compositors as strikebreakers. She had, she admitted, because they could learn the trade no other way.[34] in 1870 the Typographical Union charted a women's local in New York City. Its president, Augusta Lewis, who was also corresponding secretary of the National Typographical Union, did not think the women's union could hold out for very long, because, although the union women supported the union men, the union men did not support the union women: 'It is the general opinion of female compositors that they are more justly treated by what is termed "rat" foremen, printers, and employers than they are by union men.'[35] The women's local eventually folded in 1878.

Apparently, the general lack of support was successful from the men's point of view, for, in 1910, Abbott claimed that: 'Officers of other trade unions frequently refer to the policy of the printers as an example of the way in which trade union control may be successful in checking or preventing the employment of women.'[36] The Typographical Union strongly backed equal pay for equal work as a way to protect the men's wage scale, not to encourage women. Women who had fewer skills could not demand, and expect to receive, equal wages.[37]

Unions excluded women in many ways,[38] not the least among them protective legislation. In this the unions were aided by the prevailing social sentiment about work for women, especially married women, which was seen as a social evil which ideally should be wiped out,[39] and by a strong concern on the part of 'social feminists'[40] and others that women workers were severely exploited because they were unorganized. The social feminists did not intend to exclude women from desirable occupations but their strategy paved the way for this exclusion, because, to get protection for working women – which they felt was so desperately needed – they argued that women, as a sex, were weaker than men and more in need of protection.[41] Their strategy was successful in 1908 in Muller v. Oregon, when the Supreme Court upheld maximum hours laws for women, saying: 'The two sexes differ in structure of body, in the capacity for long-continued labor particularly when done standing, the influence of vigorous health upon the future well-being of the race, the self-reliance which enables one to assert full rights, and in the capacity to maintain the struggle for subsistence. This difference justifies a difference in legislation and upholds that which is designed to compensate for some of the burdens which rest upon her.'[42]

In 1916 in Bunting v. Oregon Brandeis uses virtually the same data on the ill effects of long hours of work to argue successfully for maximum hours laws for men as well as women. Bunting was not, however, followed by a spate of maximum hours law for men, the way Muller had been followed by laws for women, in general, unions did not support protective legislation for men, although they continued to do so for women. Protective legislation, rather than organization, was the preferred strategy only for women.[43] . ,

Historically, male workers have been instrumental in limiting the participation of women in the labor market. Male unions have carried out the policies and attitudes of the earlier guilds, and they have continued to reap benefits for male workers. Capitalists inherited job segregation by sex, but they have quite often been able to use it to their own advantage. If they can supersede experienced men with cheaper women, so much the better; if they can weaken labor by threatening to do so, that's good, too; or if, failing that, they can use those status differences to reward men, and buy their allegiance to capitalism with patriarchal benefits, that's okay too.[44]

. . . Perhaps the relative importance of capitalists and male workers in instituting and maintaining job segregation by sex has varied in different periods. Capitalists during the transition to capitalism, for example, seemed quite able to change the sex composition of jobs – when weaving was shifted to factories equipped with power looms women wove, even though most handloom weavers had been men, and mule spinning was introduced with male operators even though women had used the earlier spinning jennies and water frames. As industrialization progressed and conditions stabilized somewhat, male unions gained in strength and were often able to preserve or extend male arenas. Nevertheless, in times of overwhelming social or economic necessity, occasioned by vast increases in the demand for labor, such as in teaching or clerical work, male capitalists were capable of overpowering male workers. Thus, in periods of economic change, capitalists' actions may be more instrumental in instituting or changing a sex-segregated labor force – while workers fight a defensive battle. In other periods male workers may be more important in maintaining sex-segregated jobs; they may be able to prevent the encroachment of, or even to drive out, cheaper female labor, thus increasing the benefits to their sex.[45]

Conclusion

The present status of women in the labor market and the current arrangement of sex-segregated jobs is the result of a long process of interaction between patriarchy and capitalism. I have emphasized the actions of male workers throughout this process because I believe that emphasis to be correct. Men will have to be forced to give up their favored positions in the division of labor – in the labor market and at home – both if women's subordination is to end and if men are to begin to escape class oppression and exploitation.[46] Capitalists have indeed used women as unskilled, underpaid labor to undercut male workers, yet this is only a case of the chickens coming home to roost – a case of men's co-optation by and support for patriarchal society, with its hierarchy among men, being turned back on themselves with a vengeance. Capitalism grew on top of patriarchy; patriarchal capitalism is stratified society *par excellence*. If non-ruling-class men are to be free they will have to recognize their co-optation by patriarchal capitalism and relinquish their patriarchal benefits. If women are to be free, they must fight against both patriarchal power and capitalist organization of society.

Because both the sexual division of labor and male domination are so long-standing, it will be very difficult to eradicate them and impossible to eradicate the latter without the former. The two are now so inextricably intertwined that it is necessary to eradicate the sexual division of labor itself in order to end male domination.[47] Very basic changes at all levels of society and culture are required to liberate women. In this paper, I have argued that the maintenance of job segregation by sex is a key root of women's status, and I have relied on the operation of society-wide institutions to explain the maintenance of job segregation by sex. But the consequences of that division of labor go very deep, down to the level of the subconscious. The subconscious influences behavior patterns, which form the micro-underpinnings (or complements) of social institutions and are in turn reinforced by those social institutions. . . .

In attacking both patriarchy and capitalism we will have to find ways to change both society-wide institutions and our most deeply ingrained habits. It will be a long, hard struggle.

Notes

1   Marx and Engels perceived the progress of capitalism in this way, that it would bring women and children into the labor market and thus erode the family. yet despite Engel's acknowledgement in *The Origin of the Family, Private Property, and the State* (New York: International Publishers, 1972) that men oppress women in the family, he did not see that oppression as based on the control of women's labor, and, if anything, he seems to lament the passing of the male-controlled

family (see his *The Condition of the Working Class in England*, Stanford CA: Stanford University Press. 1968, especially pp. 161–4).

2   See Richard C. Edwards, David M. Gordon, and Michael Reich, 'Labor Market Segmentation in American Capitalism,' draft essay, and the book they edited, *Labor Market Segmentation* (Lexington KY: Lexington Books, 1976) for an explication of this view.

3   This account relies primarily on that of Alice Clark, *The Working Life of Women in the Seventeenth Century* (New York: Harcourt Brace & Howe, 1920). Her account is supported by many others, such as B. L. Hutchins, *Women in Modern Industry* (London: G. Bell & Sons, 1915): Georgiana Hill, *Women in English Life from Medieval to Modern Times*, two volumes (London: Richard Bentley & Son, 1896); F. W. Tickner, *Women in English Economic History* (New York: E. P. Dutton & Co., 1923); Ivy Pinchbeck, *Women Workers and the Industrial Revolution, 1750–1850* (London; 1930; reprinted Frank Cass & Co., 1969).

4   Women and men in England had been employed as agriculture laborers for several centuries. Clark found that by the seventeenth century the wages of men were higher than women's and the tasks done were different, though similar in skill and strength requirements (Clark 1920, p. 60). Wages for agricultural (and other work) were often set by local authorities. These wage differentials reflected the relative social status of men and women and the social norms of the time. Women were considered to require lower wages because they ate less, for example, and were expected to have fewer luxuries, such as tobacco (see Clark and Pinchbeck throughout for substantiation of women's lower standard of living). Laura Oren has substantiated this for English women during the period 1860–1950. . . .

5   The problem of female unemployment in the countryside was a generally recognized one which figured prominently in the debate about poor-law reform, for example. As a remedy, it was suggested that rural families be allowed to retain small household plots, that women be used more in agricultural wage labor and also in the putting-out system, and that men's wages be adjusted upward (see Ivy Pinchbeck, *Women Workers and the Industrial Revolution, 1750–1850*, pp. 69–84).

6   See Stephen Marglin, 'What do bosses do? The origins and functions of hierarchy in capitalist production', *Review of Radical Political Economics* 6, no. 2 (1974): 60–112, for a discussion of the transition from putting out to factories. The sexual division of labor changed several times in the textile industry. Hutchins writes that the further back one goes in history, the more was the industry controlled by women. By the seventeenth century, though, men had become professional handloom weavers, and it was often claimed that men had superior strength or skill – which was required for certain types of weaves or fabrics. Thus, the increase in demand for handloom weavers in the late 1700s brought increased employment for men. When weaving was mechanized in the factories women operated the power looms, and male handloom weavers became unemployed. When jenny and waterframe spinning were replaced by mule spinning, supposedly requiring more strength, men took that over and displaced women spinners. A similar transition occurred in the United States. It is important to keep in mind that as a by-industry, both men and women engaged in various processes of textile manufacture, and this was intensified under putting out (see Pinchbeck 1969, chapters 6–9).

7   See Clark; Pinchbeck; E. P. Thompson, *The Making of the English Working Class* (New York: Vintage Books, 1963).

8   See Clark, pp. 221–31, for the brewers, and pp. 242–84, for the medical profession.

9   Ibid., chapter 7. Eli Zaretsky ('Capitalism, the family, and personal life', *Socialist Revolution*, nos. 13, 14, 1973), follows a similar interpretation of history and offers different conclusions. Capitalism exacerbated the sexual division of labor and created the *appearance* that women work for their husbands; in reality, women who did domestic work at home were working for capital. Thus according to Zaretsky the present situation has its roots more in capitalism than in patriarchy. Although capitalism may have increased the consequence for women of the domestic division of labor, surely patriarchy tells us more about why men didn't stay home. That women worked for men in the home, as well as for capital, is also a reality.

10   William Lazonick argues in his dissertation, 'Marxian Theory and the Development of the Labor Force in England' (Ph.D., Harvard University, 1975), that the degree of authority required of the worker was often decisive in determining the sex of the worker. Thus handloom weavers in cottage industry were men because this allowed them to control the production process and the labor of the female spinners. In the spinning factories, mule spinners were men because mule spinners were required to supervise the labor of piecers, usually young boys. Men's position as head of the family established their position as heads of production units, and vice versa. While this is certainly plausible, I think it requires further investigation. Lazonick's work in this area (see chapter 4, 'Segments of the labour force: women, children, and Irish') is very valuable.

11   Perhaps 25 per cent of female textile factory workers were married women (see Pinchbeck, p. 198; Margaret Hewitt, *Wives and Mothers in Victorian Industry*. London: Rockliff, 1958, pp. 14 ff.). It is important to remember also that factory employment was far from the dominant employment of women. Most women worked as domestic servants.

12   Neil Smelser, *Social Change and the Industrial Revolution* (Chicago: University of Chicago Press, 1959), chapters 9–11. Other researchers have also established that in some cases there was a considerable degree of familial control over some aspects of the work process. See Tamara Hareven's research on mills in New Hampshire, e.g. 'Family time and industrial time: the interaction between family and work in a planned corporation town, 1900–1924', *Journal of urban History* 1, no. 3 (1975): 365–89. Michael Anderson, *Family Structure in Nineteenth Century Lancashire* (Cambridge: Cambridge University Press, 1971), argues, based on demographic data, that the 'practice of allowing operatives to employ assistants, though widespread, can at no period have resulted in a predominantly parent–child pattern of employment' (p. 116). Also see Amy Hirsch's treatment of this question in her 'Capitalism and the Working Class Family in British Textile Industries during the Industrial Revolution', mimeographed (New York: New School for Social Research, 1975).

13   '[The factory operatives'] agitation in the 1820s and 1830s was one avenue taken to protect the traditional relationship between adult and child, to perpetuate the structure of wages, to limit the recruitment of labourers into industry, and to maintain the father's economic authority' (Smelser, p. 265). Lazonick argues that the workers' main interest were not in maintaining their familial dominance

in industry but in maintaining their family life outside industry. According to Smelser, agitation before 1840 sought to establish equal length days for all workers, which would tend to maintain the family in the factory, whereas after 1840 male workers came to accept the notion that married women and children should stay at home.

14   The question of the motives of the various groups involved in passing the factory acts as indeed a thorny one. Women workers themselves may have favored the legislation as an improvement in their working conditions, but some undoubtedly needed the incomes longer hours enabled. Most women working in the mills were young, single women who perhaps benefited from the protection. Single women, though 'liberated' by the mills from direct domination in their families (about which there was much discussion in the 1800s), were nevertheless kept in their place by the conditions facing them in the labor market. Because of their age and sex, job segregation and lower wages assured their inability to be completely self-sufficient. Ruling-class men, especially those associated with the larger firms, may have had an interest in factory legislation in order to eliminate unfair competition. Working-class and ruling-class men may have co-operated to maintain men's dominant position in the labor market and in the family.

15   From Mary Merryweather, *Factory Life*, cited in *Women in English Life from Medieval to Modern Times*, 2: 200. The original is recorded in *Hansard Parliamentary Debates*, third series, House of Commons, 7 June 1842.

16   Frederick Engels, *The Condition of the Working Class in England in 1844* (London: Allen & Unwin, 1892), p. 199.

17   Ibid., p. xv.

18   Smelser, p. 301. Similarly, Pinchbeck quotes from a deputation of the West Riding Short Time Committee which demands 'the gradual withdrawal of all females from the factories' because 'home, its cares, its employments, is woman's true sphere'. Gladstone thought this a good suggestion, easily implemented by appropriate laws, e.g. 'forbidding a female to work in a factory after her marriage and during the lifetime of her husband' (Pinchbeck, p. 200, n. 3, from the *Manchester and Salford Advertiser*, 8, 15 January 1842).

19   Quoted in G. D. H. Cole and Raymond Postgate, *The Common People, 1746–1946*, fourth edition (London: Methuen, 1949), p. 432.

20   Edith Abbott, *Women in Industry* (New York: Arno Press, 1969): Elizabeth F. Baker, *Technology and Woman's Work* (New York: Columbia University Press, 1964).

21   See Abbott, especially chapter 4.

22   Ibid., chapter 2.

23   These antagonisms were often increased by employers. During a cigar makers' strike in New York City in 1877 employers brought in unskilled native American girls. By printing on the boxes 'These cigars were made by American girls,' they sold many more boxes of the imperfect cigars than they had expected to Abbott, p. 207).

24   This summary is based on Abbott and is substantiated by both Baker and Helen L. Sumner, *History of Women in Industry in the United States, 1910*, US Bureau of Labor, *Report on Condition of Women and Child Wage Earners in the United States* (Washington DC: Government Printing Office, 1911), vol. 9.

25   This account is based primarily on Abbott, chapter 9, and Baker, pp. 31–6.

26   According to Abbott, Samuel Gompers claimed the Bohemian women were brought in for the express purpose of strikebreaking (p. 197, n.).

27   Bohemian women came to America first, leaving their husbands behind to work on the fields. Their husbands, who were unskilled at the cigar trade, came over later (ibid., p. 199).

28   In 1877 a Cincinnati local struck to exclude women and was apparently successful. The *Cincinnati Inquirer* said: 'The men say the women are killing the industry. It would seem that they hope to retaliate by killing the women' (ibid., p. 207).

29   Baker, p. 34.

30   John B. Andrews and W. D. P. Bliss, *History of Women in Trade Unions* in *Report on Condition of Woman and Child Wage Earners in the United States*, vol. 10. Although the proportion of women in cigar making did increase eventually, in many other manufacturing industries the proportion of women decreased over time. Textiles and clothing are the outstanding examples (see Abbott, p. 320, and her 'The history of industrial employment of women in the United Sates', *Journal of Political Economy* 14, 1906: 461–501). Sumner, cited in US Bureau of Labor Statistics, Bulletin 175, concluded that men had taken over the skilled jobs in women's traditional fields, and women had to take unskilled work wherever they could find it (p. 28).

31   This account is based primarily on Abbott and Baker. The hostility to training women seems generalizable. The International Molders Union resolved: 'Any member, honorary or active, who devotes his time in whole or in part to the instruction of female help in the foundry, or in any branch of the trade shall be expelled from the Union' (Gail Falk, 'Women and Unions: A Historical View', mimeographed, New haven CT: Yale Law School, 1970. Published in somewhat shortened form in *Women's Rights Law Reporter* 1, 1973: 54–65).

32   Abbott, pp. 252–3.

33   Baker, pp. 39–40.

34   See Falk.

35   Eleanor Flexner, *Century of Struggle* (New York: Atheneum Publishers, 1970), p. 136.

36   Abbott, p. 260.

37   Baker observed that the testimony on the Equal Pay Act in 1963 was about evenly divided between those emphasizing women's needs and those emphasizing the protection of men (p. 419).

38   Falk noted that unions used constitutional exclusion, exclusion from apprenticeship, limitation of women to helper categories or nonladder apprenticeships, limitation of proportion of union members who could be women, i.e. quotas, and excessively high fees. Moreover, the craft unions of this period, pre-1930, had a general hostility toward organizing the unskilled, even those attached to their crafts.

39   Such a diverse group as Caroll Wright, first US Labor Commissioner (Baker, p. 84), Samuel Gompers and Mother Mary Jones, traditional and radical labor organizers, respectively (Falk), James L. Davis, US Secretary of Labor, 1922 (Baker, p. 400), Florence Kelley, head of the National Consumers League (Hill), all held views which were variations of this theme. (Hill is Ann C. Hill, 'Protective Labor Legislation for Women: Its Origin and Effect', mimeographed, New Haven CT: Yale Law School, 1970, parts of which have been published in Barbara A.

Babcock, Ann E. Freedman, Eleanor H. Norton, and Susan C. Ross, *Sex Discrimination and the Law: Causes and Remedies*, Boston MA: Little Brown & Co., 1975, a law text which provides an excellent analysis of protective legislation, discrimination against women, etc.)

40   William O'Neill characterized those women who participated in various reform movements in the late nineteenth and early twentieth centuries 'social feminists' to distinguish them from earlier feminists like Stanton and Anthony. The social feminists came to support women's rights because they thought it would help advance the cause of their reforms; they were not primarily interested in advancing the cause of women's rights (*Everyone was Brave*, Chicago: Quadrangle Books, 1969, especially chapter 3). William H. Chafe, *The American Woman* (New York: Oxford University Press, 1972), also provides an excellent discussion of the debate around protective laws.

41   What was achievable, from the legislatures and the courts, was what the social feminists aimed for. Because in Ritchie *v*. People (155 Ill. 98 [1895]), the court had held that sex alone was not a valid basis for a legislature to abridge the right of an adult to contract for work and, thus, struck down a maximum hours law for women, and because a maximum hours law for baking employees had been struck down by the US Supreme Court (Lockner), advocates of protective labor legislation believed their task would be difficult. The famous 'Brandeis Brief' compiled hundreds of pages on the harmful effects of long hours of work and argued that women needed 'especially protection' (see Babcock *et al*.).

42   Ibid., p. 32.

43   In 1914 the AFL voted to abandon the legislative road to reform (see Ann C. Hill).

44   Capitalists are not always able to use patriarchy to their advantage. Men's ability to retain as much of women's labor in the home as they have may hamper capitalist development during expansive phases. Men's resistance to female workers whom capitalists want to utilize also undoubtedly slows down capitalist advance.

45   David Gordon suggested to me this 'cyclical model' of the relative strengths of employer and workers.

46   Most Marxist-feminist attempts to deal with the problems in Marxist analysis raised by the social position of women seem to ignore these basic conflicts between the sexes, apparently in the interest of stressing the underlying class solidarity that should obtain among women and men workers. . . . A few months ago a friend (female) said, 'We are much more likely to be able to get Thieu out of Vietnam that we are to get men to do the dishes.' She was right.

47   In our society, women's jobs are synonymous with low-status, low-paying jobs: '. . . we may replace the familiar statement that women earn less because they are in low paying occupations with the statement that women earn less because they are in *women's jobs*. . . . As long as the labor market is divided on the basis of sex, it is likely that the tasks allocated to women will be ranked as less prestigious or important, reflecting women's lower social status in the society at large' (Francine Blau [Weisskoff], 'Women's place in the labor market', *American Economic Review*, 62 4, 161).

Chapter 12

Swasti Mitter

WOMEN WORKING
WORLDWIDE

Gender divisions in the labour market increasingly need to be understood in the context of a global economy. Here Swasti Mitter demonstrates that, on a world scale, women continue to be doubly disadvantaged, undertaking the lowest paid, most marginal paid work while also being responsible for unpaid domestic labour.

From *Common Fate, Common Bond*, London: Pluto Press (1985).

No farewell to the working class

A SIGNIFICANT YET GROSSLY underemphasized aspect of the current global restructuring is, as we have seen, the emergence of an acutely polarized labour market. In such a market, increasingly, a small number of core workers is going to coexist with a vast array of peripheral workers. There are many names for these peripheral workers: flexible workers, casual workers, or, as in the context of Free Trades Zones, temporary or part-time proletariat. All these terms have the same or similar connotations, and conjure up invariably the image of a worker who is a woman, and whose status as a wage-earner does not necessarily carry with it an automatic prospect of career progression. Nor does the image imply job security or other employment-related benefits such as a core worker enjoys.

Who are these peripheral of casual workers? They work for small subcontracting firms, or are young recruits in the Free Trade Zone areas, where hiring and firing are easy. In larger companies, they provide services on a contract basis to meet sudden or seasonal upturns in demand. These predominantly female workers are called casual not because of a lack of commitment or experience on their part, but simply because their conditions of work have been deliberately casualized. They provide the base of a growing 'shoeshine' economy even in the affluent West.

Equally striking is the creation of a small but highly privileged and multi-skilled elite of workers in corporate organizations. With a well defined career path in a secure job, such workers are likely to identify themselves more with company ethics and corporate management than with casual workers. Significantly, the majority of core workers are men, and the trade unions still maintain commitment to their cause.

The division of labour along these lines is influenced by the Japanese system of management; in fact, the system is an extension of the principle used by Japanese companies for a successful method of stock control. It is known as the 'kan ban' system, and implies having materials 'just in time' rather than 'just in case'. The principle is applied equally effectively by management to the problem of recruiting labour at the lowest possible cost.

This approach to manpower planning, novel in the West, has begun to change the composition of the working class. This change is becoming more pronounced with the growth of home-based work. Increasingly the self-employed and the hidden workers of the 'sweatshop economy' complement the flexible workers of the 'shoeshine economy'. Unfortunately, in spite of their growing numbers, they remain, like the flexi-workers on the factory floor, at the margin of the mainstream labour movement.

These changes imply that the working class no longer consists mainly of white male workers; instead, the concept 'working class' increasingly covers blacks, women, and in many sectors black women workers. This new working class is largely ignored not only by the mainstream labour movement but by most writers on economic and political issues. Whereas literally thousands of articles have been written on the labour-replacing aspect of new technology, only a handful have been written on the casualization of work, and these mostly by committed women scholars. . . . Concerned philosophers attempt to alter our world-view in order to help us come to terms with the changed material conditions of production. In his thought-provoking book *Farewell to the Working Class*, André Gorz, for example, looks forward longingly to the abolition of most kinds of work, which will usher in the 'non-class of non-workers', who are not conditioned to believe in the sacredness of work. His non-class, unlike the outmoded Marxist concept of the working class, is not 'social subject': 'It has no transcendent unity or mission . . . it has no prophetic aura. Instead, it reminds individuals of the need to save themselves and define a social order compatible with their goals and autonomous existence.'[1] Striving towards this new social order would involve, according to Gorz, a coherent 'polity of time', which would involve reduction of working hours, and sharing of jobs. But most of all it would entail learning to appreciate the pleasures of unpaid jobs and being prepared to relinquish the right to paid jobs.[2]

This scenario does not appear plausible at present, when the major impact of new technology seems to be in the intensification of the work process through massive subcontracting and casualization of employment. Moreover, to strive for a future of this kind may not seem so attractive either, especially to millions of women workers. In fact, the 'labour of love' or 'unpaid work' is not a new experience to women. Society's expectation that women will provide such labour at home does not disappear even when they are in paid jobs. As a result, in market-oriented as well as in socialist countries, increased wage employment for women in the post-war years has almost invariably meant burdening women with two jobs.

'Labour of love'

'Have you many children?' the doctor asked.

'God has not been good to me. Of fifteen born, only nine live,' he answered.

'Does your wife work?'

'No, she stays at home.'

'I see. How does she spend her day?'

'Well, she gets up at four in the morning, fetches water and wood, makes the fire and cooks breakfast. Then she goes to the river and washes clothes. After that she goes to town to get corn ground and buys what we need in the market. Then she cooks the midday meal.'

'You come home at midday?'

'No, no, she brings the meal to me in the fields — about three kilometres from home.'

'And after that?'

'Well, she takes care of the hens and pigs and of course she looks after the children all day . . . then she prepares the supper so it is ready when I come home.'

'Does she go to bed after supper?'

'No, I do. She has things to do around the house until about nine o'clock.'

'But of course you say your wife doesn't work?'

'Of course she doesn't work. I told you, she stays at home.'

Source: International Labour Organisation (1977).

In spite of the burden of a double day, however, most women would welcome the opportunity of going out to work, as only this gives credibility to their status as worker. The limited achievement of such credibility that women have gained in the last two decades has in fact been entirely due to the expansion of paid work outside the home, however exploitative. Nor surprisingly, therefore, in a trade-off between the oppression of family life and the drudgery of ill-paid work, most women prefer the latter.

Ironically, it is the access to paid outside work which has given many women a chance to reclaim dignity for themselves in the domain of their own family lives. Unwaged hours of work, by general consensus, are seen as an extra-economic activity, however essential they may be for the productive sphere of a society. The hidden labour of women becomes unrecognized labour, and there is always a pressure not to subject this labor to the cool calculations of economic accounting. As André Gorz writes: 'Raising children, looking after and decorating a house, repairing or making things, cooking good meals . . . none of these activities is carried out for economic ends or for consumption.'[3]

Much to the chagrin of romantic visionaries, however, women's movements have adopted the strategy of demanding wages for housework. Alternatively, they demand greater social provision of care facilities for children and the old. This is because only by bringing some of these occupations out of the private sphere into the social domain have women in the West achieved some power in the political system. it is power of this kind that could be used effectively for an equitable distribution of work and leisure in tomorrow's society.

Indeed one looks with some trepidation at the glorification of the family, not only by the moral majority in America and the Thatcherites in the UK, but also by an iconoclast of the radical world such as Ivan Illich. He sees the sexual division of labour in and outside the home ad based on 'vernacular gender', that is, on a natural complementarity which he claims is clearly visible in pre-industrial societies. To question it leads him to 'the conclusion that the struggle to create economic equality between genderless humans of two different sexes resembles the efforts made to square the circle with ruler and straight edge'.[4]

In Father Illich's natural order, it is the women who are to contribute most of the unpaid work, 'shadow work' as he calls it. For this type of work, women ought not to ask for remuneration, because 'the best they can hope for is not a shadow price but a consolation prize'.[5] In his bitter critique of the women's movement, Illich concludes that the demand to end sex discrimination is an idle luxury of elite women who have benefited somehow from economic growth:

> . . . the Mexican woman with the two-car garage leaves the house in charge of a domestic when she escapes to a feminist gathering . . . Her experience is totally beyond that of her distant cousin, who lives with the tooth puller in the village . . . The tooth puller's concubine still knows by magic and gossip how to keep men in their place. The bourgeois latina has traded both for the servant plus car, and the right to flirt with feminist rhetoric.[6]

A priest's vision of a womanly woman in her natural habitat is a far cry form the vernacular women I know of, who frantically search for paid employment to escape poverty, the oppression of family life and bride-burning. In a world where one in three families is headed by a woman, and where the number of such families is increasing at an alarming rate, the idealized image of a woman immersed contendedly in her 'shadow work', while her vernacular hunter man brings the bacon home, ought to be confined only to a romantic's dream. It is the woman's urgency and desire to work outside the home that have created a new working class.

Notes

1   André Gorz, *Farewell to the Working Class: An Essay on Post-industrial Socialism*, London: Pluto Press (1982), pp. 10–11.
2   Ibid., p. 143.
3   Ibid., p. 82.
4   Ivan Illich, *Gender*, London: Marion Boyers (1983), p. 66.
5   Ibid., p. 57.
6   Ibid., p. 60.

Chapter 13

Gemma Tang Nain

BLACK WOMEN, SEXISM AND RACISM

Differences among women complicate the picture of gender segregation in the labour market. While some have held that racialised inequalities can override those based on gender, Gemma Tang Nain's analysis of data from the 1980s suggests that it is gender inequalities that have the greater impact on Black women's labour market position.

From *Feminist Review* 37, 1991.

Black women and the working of patriarchy

PARALLELING ITS CONTROVERSY within mainstream feminism, it is the concept of patriarchy which has provoked the greatest antagonism from black feminists. They have argued that, however understood, patriarchy cannot be used in an unqualified way within the context of a racist society.

For Amos and Parmar (1984: 9), 'it is a denial of racism and its relationship to patriarchy to posit patriarchal relations as if they were non-contradictory'. Gloria Joseph goes even further. She states that, with respect to the United States, the term patriarchy can only be applicable to white male dominance since '*all* white women have ultimate power over Black men' on account of the racist nature of the executive, legislative and judicial systems (Joseph 1981: 100, my emphasis).

But before beginning the discussion about patriarchy's relevance, I wish to clarify the distinction between patriarchy and sexism. For, while some writers use these terms interchangeably, they are not being used here in that way. In this article, Heidi Hartmann's definition of patriarchy is being employed. This refers to a set of hierarchical social relations between men which allows for control of women's labour power (Hartmann 1981). In other words, patriarchy is operationalized through the gendered division of labour in social production, in both its vertical and horizontal manifestations. Sexism, on the other hand, refers to an ideology which assumes women's inferiority, and which legitimizes discrimination against them on the basis of their sex and feminine gender. Let us, therefore, first address the issue of sexism.

While black women in Britain and the United States acknowledge the sexism of both white and black men, Gloria Joseph (1981) 'learned' (by implication from white men) to dominate black women, a statement which implies that these men, prior to their arrival in the United States as slaves, did not do so. A related point has been made by some black women in Britain who stated that: 'We don't alienate [black] men because they put down black women, because we recognise that the source of that is white imperialist culture' (Bryan *et al.* 1985: 173). But such claims are fundamentally refuted by Lauretta Ngcobo when she says: 'In considering the relations between the sexes in the Black community, it would be self-delusion to pretend that our problems are entirely due to slavery and racism' (1988: 28). For her, many of the attitudes of black men to black women were formed in Africa, in spite of the fact that some women did enjoy positions of power in precolonial times, and it was these attitudes that were taken to the Caribbean and elsewhere, albeit having been diluted by slavery. This attitude is clearly borne out by Stokely Carmichael's famous phrase that the only position for women in the black movement is prone (Haralambos 1980), and by the following comment attributed to Amiri Baraka, another prominent proponent of black resistance in the United States. Paraphrasing Jim Brown, he noted that 'there are black men and white men, then there are women [and the] battle is really between white men and black men' (cited in hooks 1982: 97).

Some people have argued, however, that the sexism of black men in both Britain and the United States is different from the sexism of white men in those societies. 'The oppressive white man and the oppressed Black man [*sic*] may both exhibit sexist behaviour, but the former does so from a position of power, the latter from a position of powerlessness' (Ngcobo 1988: 31) While this may be true, I would challenge the usefulness of such a distinction. One can in fact take a similar position regarding the racism of white women and the racism of white men, and Sandra Harding (1981) alludes to this, but do these distinctions change the nature of institutionalized sexism and racism? Does the fact that there are unequal power relationships among members of the dominant sex/gender, and among members of the dominant race, really make a difference to the victims of sexist and racist oppression respectively? I think not, and there are times when shared racism among white people can override sexism and when shared sexism among men can override racism.[1]

Having addressed the issue of sexism, let us now turn our attention to patriarchy.

If one is to determine whether the lives of black women are affected by patriarchy in societies which are considered racist, and whether black men participate in it, one will have to show that the labour power of black women is controlled in such a way as to limit their access to income through a gendered division of labour in employment, and to show that the labour power of black men is not controlled in the same way. In order to address these issues, the United States will be used as an example of such a society. The use of the United States is related to access to information and is not intended to suggest that conclusions can be extrapolated to Britain or any other country, nor is such extrapolation necessary. It is simply intended to demonstrate the relevance (or otherwise) of patriarchy to the lives of black women within the context of a society that is assumed to be racist.

While recognizing the inherent inadequacies in the use of statistics, I will attempt to demonstrate the existence of patriarchy through use of income levels, employment distribution, years of schooling completed, and income relative to educational qualifications. (It is factual to state that statistics do not provide a total picture of reality. For instance, statistics of income levels do not indicate how many hours of work correspond to a particular income. Also, while statistics on employment distribution clearly show the gendered division of labour along occupational lines, they do not adequately reveal what kinds of jobs are done, for example, by black women vis-à-vis white women in clerical and service work. Bruegel (1989) highlights some of these difficulties in respect of black and white women in the British labour market.)

Even before the reforms to the US system became operationalized following the emergence of the black power movement in the 1960s, black men were earning more than black women (Lewis 1977).[2] Figures for 1963 reveal that the year-round median earnings for full-time black male workers were $4,019, compared to $2,280 for full-time black female workers. In fact, the earnings of black men also surpassed [those] of white women whose comparable earnings for 1963 were $3,687. By 1974, the earnings of black male workers had reached $8,705, compared with $6,371 for black women and $7,021 for white women. For white male workers their earnings moved from $6,245 in 1963 to $12,434 in 1974 (Lewis 1977).

What is revealed by these figures, then, is that although white men are by far the highest earners, black men do constitute the second-highest earning group. In fact, while the income gap between black and white women closed during the period 1963–74, the gap between women (black and white) and black men widened. These findings are even more startling when it is recognized that black women had completed more years of schooling than black men, and white women more years than white men, during that period. Figures for 1966 indicate that the median years of school completed by black women were 10.1, compared with 9.4 for black men. For white women the figure was 12.2 compared with 12.0 for white men. (Murray 1970) These figures reveal that black men, even with the least schooling of the four groups, managed to achieve the second-highest earnings.

In terms of employment distribution, data for 1974 showed the greatest concentration of black women in service work (26 per cent), closely followed by clerical work (25 per cent). For white women the figures were 36 per cent in clerical work followed by 17 per cent in service work. On the other hand, the greatest concentration of black men was in transport (26 per cent), followed by craft and kindred work (16 per cent), while for white men the comparable figures were 18 per cent in transport, and 21 per cent in craft and kindred work. The data given here for black women and men is inclusive of other non-white groups, although 'blacks' accounted for almost 90 per cent of this non-white population

(Lewis 1977). Clearly, then, there was greater homogeneity in employment along sex lines than along race lines. These findings also lend support to the observation of Floya Anthias and Nira Yuval-Davis that 'within Western societies, gender divisions are more important for women than ethnic divisions in terms of labour market subordination. In employment terms, migrant or ethnic women are usually closer to the female population as a whole than to ethnic men in the type of wage-labour performed' (Anthias and Yuval-Davis 1983: 69).

Finally, an interesting picture is provided by a breakdown of earnings according to educational levels for the year 1979. For persons with qualifications under a high-school diploma, white males earned $9,625, black males $6,823, white females $3,961 and black females $8,618. For persons with a Bachelor's degree, white males earned $19,783, black males $14,131, white females $9,134 and black females $10,692 (King 1988: 49). At the latter level of education, *the income of black females actually surpassed that of white females*, though all women lag behind black men, who in turn lag behind white men. It is noted by Deborah King (1988), in reference to comments made by P. M. Palmer, that white women are better off than black women due to their access to the higher earnings of white men. While this is no doubt true, it simply reinforces white female dependency and subordination, and leaves patriarchy intact. In fact, the existence of patriarchy ensures that white women have an interest in the retention of racism and the higher incomes it offers to white men.

It seems obvious, then, that while racism is a significant factor in the differences between white and black men's earnings, it is sexism and the operationalization of patriarchy which crucially affect the earnings of all women in the United States. Further, the above information does demonstrate the participation of black men in these patriarchal relations. In fact, although Hartmann's (1981) definition implies that these relations which restrict women's access to productive resources would have only intra-group applicability, i.e. that women within a particular group would be subordinate, economically, to the men of that group, the evidence for the United States contradicts this implication since white women, as well as black women, earn less than black men. Therefore, while it is true that racism in the United States ensures that the hierarchy within patriarchy is steeper than it would normally be (between classes for instance), it does not negate patriarchy's existence.[3] This evidence also refutes Joseph's (1981) claim that all white women have power over black men. For, while it can be conceded that economic power is not the only source of power, it is in fact an important source. . . .

Notes

1   An example of sexism overriding racism is provided by the granting of the franchise to black male ex-slaves at the end of the Civil War in the United States and its denial to all women. Davis's (1981) interpretation of this decision as simply the desire of the Republicans to acquire two million black votes appears overly simplistic. Surely the vote to women would have ensured them of much more. For hooks, on the other hand, the extension of the franchise to black men and not

to women demonstrated that both black and white men were able to ally themselves to each other 'on the basis of shared sexism' (hooks 1982: 90).

2   With respect to the reforms, mention is made of the Civil Rights Act of 1964
     and the Voting Rights Act of 1965 which had repercussions in various American
     institutions. 'Education, direct political participation, and jobs began to become
     more accessible to "upwardly mobile" blacks' (Lewis 1977: 349).

3   Unemployment has not been dealt with since I was addressing the specific issue
     of the operation of patriarchy through the gendered division of labour in employ-
     ment. In any event, while it is common knowledge that black men suffer higher
     rates of unemployment than white men in both Britain and the United States,
     it is also true that unemployment rates for all women tend to be underestimated.

References

Amos, Valerie and Parmar, Pratibha (1984) 'Challenging imperialist feminism', *Feminist Review* 17, 'Many Voices, One Chant: Black Feminist Perspectives'.

Anthias, Floya and Yuval-Davis, Nira (1983) 'Contextualizing feminism – gender, ethnic and class divisions', *Feminist Review* 15.

Bruegel, Irene (1989) 'Sex and race in the labour market', *Feminist Review* 32.

Bryan, Beverly, Dadzie, Stella and Scafe, Suzanne (1985) *The Heart of the Race: Black Women's Lives in Britain*. London: Virago.

Davis, Angela (1981) *Women, Race and Class*. London: Women's Press.

Haralambos, Michael, with Robin Heald (1980) *Sociology: Themes and Perspectives*. Slough: University Tutorial Press.

Harding, Sandra (1981) 'What is the real material base of patriarchy and capital?' in L. Sargent (ed.) *Women and Revolution*. London: Pluto.

Hartmann, Heidi (1981) 'The unhappy marriage of Marxism and feminism: towards a more progressive union', in L. Sargent (ed.) *Women and Revolution*. London: Pluto.

hooks, bell (1982) *Ain't I a Woman! Black Women and Feminism*. London: Pluto.

Joseph, Gloria (1981) 'The incompatible *ménage à trois*: Marxism, feminism and racism', in L. Sargent (ed.) *Women and Revolution*. London: Pluto.

King, Deborah K. (1988) 'Multiple jeopardy, multiple consciousness: the context of a Black feminist ideology', *Signs*, Vol. 14, No. 1.

Lewis, Diane K. (1977) 'A response to inequality: Black women, racism, and sexism', *Signs* vol. 3, No. 2.

Murray, Pauli (1970) 'The liberation of Black women', in Mary Lou Thompson (ed.) *Voices of the New Feminism*. Boston MA: Beacon.

Ngcobo, Lauretta (1988) editor, *Let it be Told: Essays by Black Women in Britain*. London: Virago.

Chapter 14

Anne Witz

PATRIARCHY AND THE PROFESSIONS
The gendered politics of occupational closure

The sociology of the professions, like many other areas, has suffered from gender blindness. Here Anne Witz uses the Weberian concept of occupational closure in order to explain the processes whereby professions become gendered. Taking the example of health care professions, she explores the marginalisation of women and the strategies women have employed to gain entry to medicine and to raise the status of nursing.

Others have developed Weber's idea of occupational closure, the way in which particular occupational groups seek to control entry to a trade or profession in order to preserve, defend or promote its status and interests. Whereas traditionally this was analysed without reference to gender, feminist sociologists have explored the strategies men have used to exclude women from prestigious occupations and the counter-strategies women have deployed to contest such exclusion.

From *Sociology*, 24 (4) 1990.

Professional projects and patriarchal structures

. . .

THE FIRST STEP ON the way to purging analyses of professions of their androcentric bias is to abandon any generic concept of professions of their androcentric bias is to abandon any generic concept of profession and redefine the sociology of professions as the sociological history of occupations as individual, empirical and above all historical cases rather than as specimens of a more general, fixed concept (cf. Freidson 1983). The term 'professional projects' serves to establish the concrete, historically bounded character of the profession as 'an empirical entity about which there is little ground for generalising' (Freidson 1983: 33).

Professional projects are essentially labour market strategies which aim for an occupational monopoly over the provision of certain skills and competencies in a market for services. They consist of strategic courses of action which take the form of occupational closure strategies and which employ distinctive tactical means in pursuit of the strategic aim or goal of closure. . . . But closure concepts as they are currently applied to professionalisation strategies fail to capture their gendered dimensions. They are primarily designed to illuminate the class dynamics of professionalisation as a strategy for social closure and collective mobility (cf. Parry and Parry 1976). We need a more finely tuned model of the variety of closure strategies which may be employed by occupational groups engaged in professional projects and one which captures their specifically gendered dimensions.

The first step in charting out the possibility of a less androcentric sociology of professions is, then, to treat professional projects as concrete, individual and historically located projects, whilst the second step is to conceptualise these projects as strategies of occupational closure. The third step is to gender the agents of professional projects, addressing the possibility that the agents of such projects are positioned not only within class relations but also within gender relations of dominance and subordination. The remaining step is to ground these gendered professional projects of closure within the structural and historical parameters of patriarchal capitalism. . . .

An analysis of the gendered dynamics of professional projects as strategies of occupational closure must also locate these within patriarchal structures which constitute the facilitating or constraining parameters of such strategies. This raises the issue of the relation between strategic action and structural constraints, an issue which is highlighted as a particularly problematic aspect of the use of the concept of strategy in sociology generally by Crow (1989). The term 'strategy' heavily connotes *process* and, whilst this is one of its strengths, it is also one of its potential weaknesses in so far as structures threaten to dissolve into infinitely malleable processes. It is therefore essential to keep in view the interplay between strategy and structure, between actions and resources for action. . . . By referring to gendered strategies and patriarchal structures, I am establishing that gendered actors engaged in professional projects as strategic courses of action will have differential access to the tactical means of achieving their aims in a patriarchal society within which male power is institutionalised and organised. There are *resources* of (male) power to which women are denied access, and are unable to mobilise.

I shall endeavour to keep in view the interplay between strategy and structure by distinguishing between strategic courses of action, which are gendered, and facilitating or constraining structures, which are patriarchal. Gendered strategies and patriarchal structures are mediated through the institutionalisation and organisation of male power within different sites of social, economic and political relations, within which the tactical means of strategic action are mobilised. . . .

Gender, closure and professional projects

. . . Frank Parkin (1974, 1979), one of the major protagonists of neo-Weberian closure theory, offers a baseline definition of modes of closure as different means of mobilising power in order to stake claims to resources and opportunities. A conceptual model of the specifically gendered dimensions of occupational closure is concerned with how occupational closure strategies provide the means of mobilising male power in order to stake claims to resources and opportunities distributed *via* the mechanism of the labour market. The bare conceptual bones of a model of the various occupational closure strategies that may be utilised within the context of professional projects is set out in Figure 1. This model turns upon a fourfold distinction between strategies of exclusionary, inclusionary, demarcationary and dual closure.

Both exclusionary and demarcationary strategies are engaged in by a dominant social or occupational group in the hierarchy of closure, whilst inclusionary and dual closure strategies describe the responses of subordinate social or occupational groups. The distinction between exclusionary and demarcationary strategies of closure is suggested by Freidson's discussion of the Janus-headed nature of the professional power of doctors, who enjoy not only an occupational monopoly but also a position of dominance *vis-à-vis* related and adjacent occupations in the medical division of labour. This is a distinction between, on the one hand, exclusionary strategies which aim for intra-occupational control over the internal affairs of and access to the ranks of a particular occupational group and, on the other hand, demarcationary strategies which aim for inter-occupational control over the affairs of related or adjacent occupations in a division of labour.

The distinction between inclusionary and dual closure strategies is one between the different countervailing responses of groups who are subject to either exclusion or demarcation. Inclusion describes the upwards, countervailing exercise of

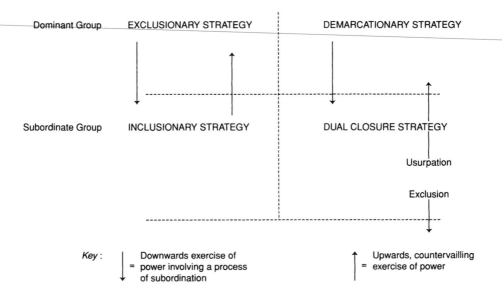

Figure 1 Strategies of occupational closure: a conceptual model

power by a social group which is hit by exclusionary strategies, but which seeks inclusion within the structure of positions from which they are collectively debarred. dual closure strategies, but the strategic aim is not to be included in the ranks of the occupational group engaged in demarcationary closure. Dual closure strategies are conceptually and empirically far more complex than this. They entail the upwards countervailing exercise of power in the form of resistance on the part of subordinate occupational groups to the demarcationary strategies of dominant groups, but who also in their turn seek to consolidate their own position within a division of labour by employing exclusionary strategies.

Let me now elaborate and illustrate each of these strategies in turn by using this fourfold distinction between exclusionary, inclusionary, demarcationary and dual closure strategies in an analysis of the struggles of gendered occupational groups in the emerging medical division of labour. Medical men engaged in an exclusionary strategy of closure, concerned with restricting access to medical practice, as well as in demarcationary strategies, which were concerned with policing and controlling the boundaries between the occupation of medicine and related occupations in the medical division of labour. But medical men were met with countervailing strategic responses from aspiring medical women, who challenged medical men's exclusionary strategy by engaging in a strategy of inclusion, as well as from midwives and nurses, who engaged in dual closure strategies as they both resisted medical men's demarcationary strategies and strove themselves to secure a degree of exclusionary closure in the occupations of midwifery and nursing. Midwives and nurses were engaged in female professional projects, and it is the concept of a dual closure strategy which best describes these projects.

Gendered strategies of exclusion and inclusion

Parkin (1979) defines exclusionary strategies of closure as involving the downwards exercise of power in a process of subordination as a social group seeks to secure, maintain or enhance privileged access to rewards and opportunities. Parkin also introduces the term 'usurpationary closure' to describe the upwards exercise of power whereby excluded groups engage in forms of countervailing action and resistance to exclusion. Exclusionary strategies are exercised by dominant social collectivities; usurpationary strategies by subordinate social groups. . . . It would seem to me . . . that the term 'usurpation' is best used in the minimal sense of the upwards, countervailing exercise of power, whilst the term 'inclusion' describes the strategic aim of a usurpationary struggle.

This leads me to propose a distinction between two forms of occupational strategy, which provides the starting point for the development of a model of the gendered dimensions of occupational closure. This is a distinction between gendered strategies of exclusionary closure and inclusionary usurpation. The first, a gendered strategy of exclusionary closure is one which is exercised by a dominant social collectivity, men, and which serves to create women as a class of ineligibles. It secures for men privileged access to rewards and opportunities in the occupational labour market. This strategy employs gendered collectivist criteria of exclusion vis-à-vis women and gendered individualist criteria of inclusion vis-à-vis men. The second, a gendered strategy of inclusionary usurpation, describes the ways whereby women, who are hit by gendered strategies of exclusion, do not simply acquiesce in the face of patriarchal closure in an occupational labour market, but challenge a male monopoly over competence by seeking to be included in a structure of occupational positions from which they are excluded on account of their gender. The essence of the usurpationary struggle is that it is a countervailing strategy, in tension with an exclusionary strategy. It is an inclusionary strategy of usurpation because it seeks to replace gendered collectivist criteria of exclusion with non-gendered individualist criteria of inclusion.

The case of the medical profession in the mid-nineteenth century demonstrates the utility of the twin concepts of gendered strategies of exclusion and inclusion. The 1858 Medical Act in effect set up a male monopoly over legitimate medical practice. I say 'in effect' because rules of sexual exclusion were not explicitly codified into the Act itself, but operated in the context of the universities, medical corporations and teaching hospitals which made up the nineteen portals of entry onto the medical register. These were state-approved routes to registered medical practice as a 'legally or duly qualified medical practitioner'. So an important plank of exclusionary closure in modern medicine was the operation of gendered collectivist criteria of exclusion *vis-à-vis* women. Crucially, these exclusionary mechanisms were embedded in the institutional spheres of civil society, operating in the modern university and the professional corporations. They were only indirectly reinforced within the institutional arena of the state. Thus, in the case of gendered exclusionary closure strategies operating within the context of a male professional project, it is the sphere of civil society within which male power is organised and institutionalised and where gendered exclusionary strategies operate to sustain patriarchal modes of occupational closure. This suggests, interestingly, that although legalistic tactics in the form of state-sponsored registration have been central to modern professional projects (cf. MacDonald 1985), patriarchal closure has been primarily sustained through credentialist tactics by controlling access to education and accreditation.

But the exclusive male prerogative over legitimate medical practice was immediately challenged by aspiring women doctors, who engaged in a protracted usurpationary struggle to gain admission to medical education and examination, and thereby to the medical register and the legitimate practice of medicine. This usurpationary struggle began with the isolated attempt by Elizabeth Garrett in the 1860s (cf. Manton 1965), and continued at Edinburgh University, where, between 1869 and 1873, a group of women attempted to receive medical lectures and present themselves for medical degrees. It culminated in the attempts between 1874 and 1876 to secure women's access to medical education and examination, and thereby to the medical register, by means of Act of Parliament (cf. Jex-Blake 1886, Thorne 1915, Bell 1953, Stansfeld 1877). This challenge to the male monopoly over medical practice sustained by gendered strategies of exclusion took the form of a gendered strategy of inclusion, as women attempted to gain entry to a structure of positions from which they were excluded by replacing gendered collectivist criteria of exclusion with non-gendered criteria of inclusion.

. . . Women's usurpationary struggle initially concentrated on countervailing credentialist tactics as they sought access to medical education and training in the universities and teaching hospitals, and to present themselves for examination by universities and the medical corporations, such as the Royal Colleges of Physicians and Surgeons, and the Society of Apothecaries. But the universities and corporations proved remarkably resilient to women's usurpationary claims when these centred on countervailing credentialists tactics. It was for this reason that aspiring women doctors eventually concentrated their attention on legalistic tactics, seeking to gain entry to medical education and practice by parliamentary means. It was this second, legalistic tactic of usurpation which was eventually successful, culminating in the passage of the 1876 Enabling Bill, which established that universities and medical corporations could not use their existing powers to exclude women, but neither could they be forced to include them. This suggests that the resources of male power were most effectively institutionalised within the modern university and professional corporations or associations, whilst the nineteenth century patriarchal capitalist state was the weaker link in the chain of patriarchal closure in medicine. . . .

Gendered strategies of demarcation and dual closure

The twin concepts of exclusionary closure and inclusionary usurpation only capture some of the complex and varied processes of occupational closure in the emerging medical division of labour. This leads me to propose a further set of occupational closure strategies, which are gendered strategies of demarcationary closure and of dual closure. Strategies of demarcation relate to processes of inter-occupational rather than to processes of intra-occupational control. . . . The concept of a demarcationary strategy of closure is designed to capture what Larkin (1983) refers to as 'occupational imperialism'. The concept of a dual closure strategy is designed to capture the countervailing response of occupational groups hit by the demarcationary strategies of a dominant social and occupational group. . . .

Gendered strategies of demarcationary closure . . . describe processes of inter-occupational control concerned with the creation and control of boundaries between gendered occupations in a division of labour. They turn not upon the exclusion, but upon the encirclement of women within a related but distinct sphere of competence in an occupational division of labour and, in addition, their possible subordination to male-dominated occupations. The concept of a gendered strategy of demarcationary closure directs attention to the possibility that the creation and control of occupational boundaries and inter-occupational relations may be crucially mediated by patriarchal power relations. It also establishes that the gender of occupational groups embroiled in inter-occupational, demarcationary struggles, both as architects and as targets of demarcationary practices, is not a fortuitous or contingent, but a necessary factor in explaining both the form and the outcome of such strategies. . . .

The paradigmatic case of gendered strategies of demarcationary closure in the emerging medical division of labour may be found in the troubled inter-occupational relations between medical men and midwives in the latter half of the nineteenth century (cf. Donnison 1977; Verluysen 1980; Witz 1987, 1985). Medical men's demarcationary strategies in relation to midwives describe their interventions in the affairs of midwives, an adjacent but unregulated occupation in the provision of medical services. The protracted debate about the desirability or otherwise of a system of state-sponsored registration for midwives reveals that medical men were intimately concerned with defining and controlling the inter-occupational boundaries between medical and midwifery practice. Without going into a detailed account of this whole debate, I simply want to establish how an analysis of the inter-occupational relations between doctors and midwives demonstrate the need for a concept of demarcationary as distinct from exclusionary closure.

By the mid-nineteenth century the occupational boundaries between midwifery and medical practice had been constructed around a division between assistance in the process of 'normal' labour, constructed as a natural process and remaining within the sphere of the midwife, and intervention (frequently with instruments such as forceps) in the process of 'abnormal' labour, which was the exclusive prerogative of medical men. Medical men's demarcationary strategies were essentially concerned to police the boundaries between midwifery and medical practice particularly in view of the fact that it was the midwife who, whilst attending an ostensibly normal case of labour, had to decide when it became necessary to call on the assistance of a doctor. One solution advocated by medical men was to abolish the independent midwifery practitioner and to establish an exclusive medical prerogative over the provision of all midwifery services. However, this demarcationary strategy was unsuccessful, largely because it was simply inexpedient, as doctors could not possible have met the total demand for midwifery services. The alternative demarcationary strategy was to segment the market according to the social class of the client and the gender of the practitioners. Female midwives would meet the demand for routine midwifery services from the poor, whilst medical men would supply midwifery services to the rich, and deal with all cases of abnormal labour. This de-skilling strategy of demarcation preserved the independent midwifery practitioner, although limited her to a narrowly and rigidly prescribed sphere of competence determined by medical men. It also entailed the monitoring and controlling of midwifery practice by medical men, who sought to ensure that they defined the knowledge base of midwifery by providing the only legitimate educational route to registered midwifery practice and that medical men were in a majority on the Central Midwives Board, established under the terms of the midwives Act in 1902, thus effectively controlling the occupational infrastructure of midwifery.

Finally, the concept of a dual closure strategy remains to be elaborated. A dual closure strategy involves a two-way exercise of power, in an upwards direction as a form of usurpation and in a downwards direction as the form of exclusion (Parkin 1979). But whereas the gendered strategies of inclusionary usurpation of aspiring medical women described the manner in which women contest exclusion, gendered strategies of dual closure describe the manner in which women may contest demarcation. Most importantly, they capture the form typically assumed by female professional projects – such as, for example, the campaigns for state-sponsored systems of registration waged by midwives and nurses (cf. Donnison 1977; Baly 1980; Abel-Smith 1960; Dingwall et al. 1988).

Both conceptually and empirically, dual closure strategies are complex and varied. Along their usurpationary dimensions, they do not have the same inclusionary aims as usurpationary responses to exclusion, which involve members of an excluded group seeking inclusion in a structure of positions, as we have seen in the case of women's challenge to the male monopoly over legitimate medical practice. Nurses and midwives did not aspire to become fully qualified medical practitioners. Dual closure strategies are usurpationary in the minimal sense of entailing the countervailing exercise of power. Nonetheless, the usurpationary dimensions of midwives' and nurses' responses to the demarcationary strategies of medical men varied in the extent to which nurses and midwives either resisted or concurred with these demarcation strategies.

A closer and more detailed examination of nurses' and midwives' responses to medical men's demaractionary strategies suggests a further distinction between revolutionary and accommodating dimensions of usurpation within the context of a dual closure strategy. The stance adopted by different groups of midwifes provides an exemplary case for this distinction. The usurpationary response of a group of radical midwives in the 1860s to medical men's demarcationary strategy of de-skilling was revolutionary in the sense that it directly challenged medical men's vision of a de-skilled and inferior midwifery role in the medical division of labour. It advocated instead that midwives should stand alongside medical men as re-skilled obstetric specialists, thoroughly educated in obstetrics (including obstetric surgery) and holding a licence in midwifery on a par with the medical license. The idea, it was said, was not to make midwives the servants of medical men, but to place them in a position analogous to the dentist who did not call the doctor to pull out a tooth (Select Committee on Midwives Registration 1892).

But compare this with the later usurpationary response of another group of midwives associated with the Midwives Institute in the 1890s. This was far more accommodating, conceding to medical men's restrictive definition of the midwife's sphere of competence, as well as concurring with the limited knowledge base and programme of training set down and provided by doctors for midwives. Midwives of the Midwives Institute also accepted that the Central Midwives Board, their statutory controlling body, would be overwhelmingly composed of medical men, and that midwives would have neither majority nor direct representation on that board, relying instead upon a few lay members to represent their interests. Clearly a more accommodating response. . . .

It is essential to recognise that the stances adopted by the female occupational groups of midwives and nurses in the face of medical men's demarcationary strategies were not purely usurpationary. They were strategies of dual closure precisely because they also contained exclusionary dimensions. Both nurses and midwives waged long campaigns for state-sponsored systems of registration and aimed to regulate entry into nursing and midwifery by legitimating the practice of accredited nurses and midwives who had undergone a system of training and examination set down and monitored by a statutory regulatory body. Such a body would admit only accredited nurses on to a register of practitioners and would also have disciplinary powers to strike malpractitioners off that register. To regulate entry is to control supply by including some and excluding others. To seek a state-sponsored system of registration is to utilise a key exclusionary tactic, registration. To call for a uniform system of education, training and examination is to use yet another exclusionary tactic, that of credentialism. In addition, both nurses' and midwives' campaigns were spearheaded by elite groups of trained, middle class practitioners (Vicinus 1985; Cowell and Wainwright 1981) whose aims to regulate the practice of nursing and midwifery were articulated as a quest for professional status, with its associated material and symbolic rewards. There were, then, prestige goals attached together with a vision of restructuring the class base of nursing and midwifery. It was hoped that a state-sponsored system of registration would transform these occupations into occupations suitable for 'educated refined gentlewomen' (*Nursing Notes*, 1888: 11) or for 'cultured women' (*British Journal of Nursing*, 1904: 492).

It is precisely because these campaigns contained what can only be described as exclusionary elements that we may speak of female professional projects. The concept of a dual closure strategy captures the two-way exercise of power that characterises these female professional projects. Finally, I wish to develop further the notion of a female professional project by analysing the nurses' campaign for a state-sponsored system of registration using the concept of a dual closure strategy to sociologically unpick the aims and objectives of this campaign.

The campaign for nurse registration: a female professional project of dual closure

The long and bitter campaign for a state-sponsored system of nurse registration spanned the years between 1888, when the British Nurses Association [was] formed with the aim of obtaining the legal status of a profession, and 1919, when the Nurse Registration Act was passed . . . It was a female professional project, a strategy of dual closure with strongly usurpationary and strongly exclusionary aims, employing both legalistic and credentialist tactics.

Pro-registrationist nurses looked to the state to sponsor their professional project and provide nurses with the machinery of self-government, thereby granting nurses the autonomy to determine the standard and duration of nurse education, to control entry into the ranks of nurses, and to improve their pay and conditions. The pro-registrationist nurses' demand for 'self-government' was the nub of their strategy of professionalisation, and it was posed as an alternative to the 'subjugation' of nurses.

Along its usurpationary dimensions this campaign posed a strong challenge to three sets of power relations. The first of these was the employment relation between hospitals and nurses within which hospitals controlled both the standard and length of nurse training, as well as the pay and conditions of nursing labour (cf. Davies 1982). The second of these was inter-occupational relations of control between medical men and nurses, particularly the power of elite medical corporations such as the Royal Colleges of Physicians and of Surgeons to gain a controlling foothold in any statutory nursing body. . . . And the third set of power relations which were contested were gender relations as Mrs Bedford-Fenwick's advocacy of 'self-government' for nurses was linked to her broader commitment to the autonomous organisation of women in the labour market.

Nurses' professional project also contained exclusionary aims. These were threefold. First, to set up a centralised means of control over the occupational infrastructure of nursing (cf. Bellaby and Oribabor 1980). This would be a Central Board or Council of Nurses, a statutory body set up by Act of Parliament, and would provide the institutional means of regulating the supply of nursing labour, thereby creating an occupational monopoly. But it would not necessarily follow that this would be under the control of nurses themselves. And so the second key exclusionary dimension of nurses' professional project was the demand of self-government for nurses, which meant majority and direct representation of nurses on any central body set up to control the affairs of the nursing profession. . . . The third exclusionary dimension was the demand for a one-portal system of entry into nursing. The one-portal system of entry into nursing hinged around centralised control over the curriculum of nurse education as well as over the length and standard of nurse education and training. That one portal was to be 'the uniform examination of the Central Council' (*British Journal of Nursing*, 1905: 252).

What was remarkable about the nurses' professional project, in view of the fact that nurses were so tightly constrained within the three sets of power relations set out above – i.e. within institutional relations of control between hospitals and nurses, inter-occupational relations of control between doctors and nurses, and gender relations of control – was that it did contain such strongly usurpationary and exclusionary dimensions. It makes a compelling case for the recognition of female professional projects as strategic responses on the part of women in the face of structural constraints that were as much to do with patriarchy as with capitalism. The notion of a female professional project directs our attention to the fact that there is nothing inevitable about the relative positioning of women within sets of capitalist and patriarchal relations, and more specifically within gendered occupational divisions of labour, but that relations of dominance and subordination are contested relations. . . .

References

Bell, F. M. (1953) *Storming the Citadel: The Rise of the Woman Doctor*. London: Constable.

Bellaby, P. and Oribabor, P. (1980) '"History of the present" – Contradiction and struggle in nursing', in C. Davies (ed.) *Rewriting Nursing History*. London: Croom Helm.

Cowell, B. and Wainwright, D. (1981) *Behind the Blue Door: The History of the Royal College of Midwives, 1881–1981*. London: Routledge.

Crow, G. (1980) 'The use of the concept of "strategy" in recent sociological literature', *Sociology*, 23: 1–24.

Davies, C. (1982) 'The regulation of nursing work: an historical comparison of Britain and the USA', *Research in the Sociology of Health Care*, 2: 121–60.

Dingwall, R., Rafferty, A. M. and Webster, C. (1988) *An Introduction to the Social History of Nursing*. London: Routledge.

Donnison, J. (1977) *Midwives and Medical Men*. London: Heinemann.

Freidson, E. (1983) 'The theory of professions: state of the art', in R. Dingwall and P. Lewis (eds) *The Sociology of the Professions*. London: Macmillan.

Jex-Blake, S. (1886) *Medical Women: A Thesis and a History*. Edinburgh: Oliphant Andersen & Ferrier.

Larkin, G. (1983) *Occupational Monopoly and Modern Medicine*. London: Tavistock.

MacDonald, K. M. (1985) 'Social closure and occupational registration', *Sociology* 19: 541–56.

Manton, J. (1965) *Elizabeth Garrett Anderson*. London: Methuen.

Parkin, F. (1974) 'Strategies of social closure in class formation', in F. Parkin (ed.) *The Social Analysis of Class Structure*. London: Tavistock.

Parkin, F. (1979) *Marxism and Class Theory: A Bourgeois Critique*. London: Tavistock.

Parry, N. and Parry, J. (1976) *The Rise of the Medical Profession*. London: Croom Helm.

Stansfeld, J. (1877) 'Medical women', *Nineteenth Century*, 1: 889–901.

Thorne, I. (1915) *Sketch of the Foundation and Development of the London School of Medicine for Women*. London: Women's Printing Society.

Verluysen, M. (1980) 'Old wives' tales? Women healers in English history', in C. Davies (ed.) *Rewriting Nursing History*. London: Croom Helm.

Vicinus, M. (1985) *Independent Women: Work and Community for Single Women, 1880–1920*. London: Virago.

Witz, A. (1985) *Midwifery and the Medical Profession: Sexual Divisions and the Process of Professionalisation*. Lancaster Regionalism Group Working Paper No. 13, Lancaster: University of Lancaster.

Witz, A. (1987) '"The Spider Legislating for the Fly": Patriarchy and Occupational Closure in the Medical Division of Labour, 1858–1940'. Unpublished Ph.D. thesis, University of Lancaster.

Chapter 15

Janet Siltanen

FULL WAGES AND COMPONENT WAGES

Janet Siltanen analyses occupational segregation in relation to full wages (those sufficient to maintain an independent household) and component wages (those insufficient to support an independent household). Drawing on a study of postal workers and telephonists, she shows that women can earn enough to support themselves and their dependants only if they are able to undertake jobs which have traditionally been the preserve of men.

From *Locating Gender: Occupational Segregation, Wages and Domestic Responsibilities*, London: UCL Press (1994).

. . .

A FULL-WAGE JOB ENABLES its incumbents to take sole responsibility for maintaining an independent household, a responsibility that in some cases includes financial maintenance of other household members not in waged work. A component-wage job does not enable incumbents to be wholly responsible for the financial maintenance of a household. In other words, people in component-wage jobs contribute to the financial maintenance of households but do not have the resources to maintain an independent household single-handedly.

Three points should be clear from the outset. First, the designations full-wage and component-wage refer to the form of social relations enabled by the level of wages received. The full-wage designation implies the ability of incumbents to assume full responsibility as sole wage earners in their household. The standard of living at which they are able to do so is a separate issue, as full-wages could range from those just sufficient to support an independent household of a single adult to those more than sufficient for a household composed of a number of dependants.

In principle it is possible, and it would certainly be desirable, further to differentiate types of full-wages. . . . Secondly, as indicated above, some jobs may be more marginal as full-wage and component-wage jobs than others. This is certainly the case for the jobs considered here. The night telephonist and postal jobs were full-wage jobs only to the extent that extensive overtime was a regular component of earnings. Similarly, . . . the earnings of day telephonists were towards the upper end of component-wages. Some of the contrasts to be drawn between the circumstances of incumbents in full-wage and component-wage jobs are slightly subdued as a consequence of the marginal nature of the full-wage and component-wage jobs in this study. Nevertheless, differences in the domestic profile of incumbents are substantial enough to justify and illustrate the full-wage and component-wage designations. Thirdly, current relations to household financing and domestic circumstances, as well as an individual's position on recruitment, are taken as indicators of the full-wage or component-wage status of a job. . . .

The characterization of the day telephonist job as a component-wage job and the night telephonist and postal jobs as full-wage jobs is justified in that a sizeable proportion of night telephonists and postal workers were maintaining dependants and households as the sole wage earner, whereas the proportion doing so in the day telephonist job was substantially less. One in every two incumbents of the full-waged jobs was providing the only wage coming in to his or her household – 56 per cent of the women and 48 per cent of the men. In addition, one-third of these women and over half of the men were the sole providers for households containing dependent children. In contrast, a considerably lower proportion (approximately one in four) of women and men in the component-wage job was solely responsible for the financial maintenance of a households contained dependent children. As sole wage earners, people in the component-wage job are typically supporting themselves only, often as boarders in rented accommodation. They were not, in other words, fully responsible for the maintenance of even a one person household. The majority of component-wage earners contributed to more substantial households along with other wage earners. . . .

Domestic circumstances and the distribution of people to jobs

In examining variations in the domestic circumstances of the labour force in component-wage and full-wage jobs, patterns of experience will come into sharper focus. The women and men recruited to component-wage and full-wage jobs were in different stages of family life cycles and domestic circumstances. Further, the women and men in the two types of jobs stood in a contrasting position in relation to standard employment patterns associated with the female and male labour force. Women and men in the jobs typical for their sex had a domestic profile in relation to employment that was similar to the standard pattern in the general female and male labour force. Women and men in the jobs atypical for their sex were in very particular domestic circumstances. . . .

Underlying the distribution of men in full-wage and component-wage jobs is primarily a differentiation by marital status. Men who had ever been married were in full-wage jobs and they had relations to household maintenance that were representative of the range of circumstances in the households of the general male labour force. The distribution of single men to the two types of jobs is differentiated by age – older single men constituted a greater proportion of single men employed in full-wage jobs and younger single men predominated in the component-wage job.

Underlying the distribution of women in the full-wage and component-wage jobs is, in the first place, a differentiation between white and black women in terms of typical patterns in employment experience, and, in the second place, marital breakdown among white women. All of the ever married black women were in full-wage jobs, and a large proportion of them were supporting dependent children. Typically, black women were recruited to the full-wage jobs in their thirties, that is, at a time when many white married women had withdrawn from the labour force. There is a dramatic difference in the type of job held by married and previously married white women. For white women, it was the termination of a marriage that was related to employment in a full-wage job. Previously married white women, many of whom were lone parents, were usually recruited to full-wage jobs around their fortieth birthday Most married white women were in the component-wage job, along with younger single women. The distribution of white women's age at recruitment to the component-wage job forms a bi-modal pattern similar to the profile of employment activity in the general female population.

Instead of a stark gender distinction as the general characteristic of occupational segregation, the above patterns suggest greater complexity in the structuring of employment distributions. Gender distinctions are significant, but they are located within a more general process – a process encompassing contrasting relations to household maintenance between the (male and female) incumbents of full-wage and component-wage jobs. Overall, those who were in employment typical for their sex (the full-wage men and the component-wage women) had a standard gendered pattern of employment in relation to domestic circumstances. The reverse is true for those in employment atypical for their sex. The particular nature of the domestic circumstances of men in the component-wage job, and of women in the full-wage jobs, is of major importance in explaining their position in jobs where their gender was in the minority.

Chapter 16

Gillian Dunne

LESBIANS IN MANUAL JOBS

Gill Dunne's data, taken from a qualitative study of lesbians' employment strategies, reveals that their orientation to work differs from that of heterosexual women. Since they are not economically dependent on men these women need to earn sufficient to support themselves. For those without education qualifications this means finding a way into male-dominated manual jobs. The experiences of some of these women are discussed in the following extract.

From *Lesbian Lifestyles,* London: Macmillan (1996).

Respondents' experience in male-dominated manual occupations

ON EXAMINATION OF THE sample's work histories, at least fifteen had some experience of male-dominated manual work. These were unconventional women because they had expanded their occupational choices to include working-class jobs which their fathers and brothers, rather than their mothers and sisters, might have considered. Within these occupations, respondents' movement up the hierarchies was often slow and plagued by difficulties, but most found the experience rewarding, both intrinsically and extrinsically. The armed forces were viewed by some respondents as a useful entry point to traditional male occupations.

The armed forces

In all, five respondents, including two Black women, entered the armed forces, while many others spoke of having had the desire to do so. The armed forces provided four respondents with the opportunity to develop 'male' technical and/ or craft skills, and a fifth to gain a nursing qualification. They were particularly appealing to women from less privileged social backgrounds, who did not have the opportunity to stay on at school to study 'A' levels. Given the limited job opportunities they felt were available to them, entering the forces clearly represented a career with prospects for advancement and job security. Furthermore, it was seen to offer a chance to travel and an opportunity to keep up their sporting interests. Thelma explains her reasons for entering the forces. She has spent most of her working life in male-dominated occupations, using the skills that she had developed while in the forces:

> [*Where there any other aspects that appealed about going into the Forces?*] The security, the availability of travel, also the different types of sports that you could do. I would never have been able to have afforded to learn [these sports] . . . The girls were doing the same sports as the boys . . . I could do everything that a man could do. [*Why did you go for driving in the Forces?*] To be able to learn the mechanics of a car. I would have liked to have been a fully fledged mechanic, but they didn't actually have mechanics in the [Women's Corps]. Doing this I was affiliated to the Mechanics Corps and could go and learn from the boys, and I learnt as much as the mechanics did. I had the ability, when I came out, to maintain my own car.
>
> (43*I*)

As with women interviewed in Faderman's (1992: 150) detailed history of twentieth-century lesbian life in America, the military appealed to respondents for a range of important reasons. These respondents tended to be fairly ambitious and achievement-oriented and they all wanted to learn a trade. Further, most wished to develop more technical and mechanical skills, and the forces were perceived as being a more 'equal opportunities' environment where occupational gender boundaries were more blurred. They could perform jobs that were physically demanding, which were freer from the constraints of physical confinement that they associated with clerical and factory work. Verity expresses these sentiments:

> I don't want to be a typist, that's the last thing, that's another reason why I joined the forces. I didn't want to go into an office, I didn't want to be a clerk, secretary, etc. . . . I wanted to be out and about, I wanted to do something different, I didn't want to do what the girls did. I am not saying I wanted to do what the boys wanted, or did . . . The driving suited me down to the ground: I was outside, I was learning something, I was doing something different, I wasn't doing what all the girls used to do, and I excelled in it . . . The forces, they do try their best to make you one of the team; you have the same rank as the blokes. If you have a bloke soldier to give him orders, you have to give him orders whether you are female or male, and I take orders from males or females, and they have to accept what a woman tells them.
>
> (29*M*)

Respondents who were keen on entering the forces had usually been questioning their sexuality. They saw the forces as providing an environment where they might come into contact with lesbians and clarify the possibilities. All the respondents who had been in the forces spoke of the existence of tightly knit lesbian networks. In some cases exposure to this community raised questions in the minds of respondents regarding their own sexuality; lesbianism could be seen as a feasible option. Furthermore, this community was always reported as being highly achievement-oriented and career-minded. Wendy is typical of the rest in her description of her lesbian colleagues' approaches to their jobs:

> The gay girls were certainly the stronger . . . and wanted to get on more than the straights . . . Not physical strength, it's as people, they were always the harder workers. Why they were doing it or what they were doing it for I don't know, but certainly . . . the girls that had the boyfriends didn't want to work the longer hours anyway, because they wanted to meet their boyfriends at night. Whereas the gay girls – I wouldn't say they didn't want to meet their women – put their work first somehow. There was no extra money, you got paid the same as someone that didn't want to do it. I just used to love the job, so I didn't mind how many hours I did anyway.
>
> (34M)

The tendency to put career first seemed to affect their approaches to relationships. As marriage was never an option for them, frequent postings meant that long-term relationships were hard to maintain. Consequently, relationships were described as being entered on the understanding that they would probably be short-lived.

Lesbians, however, appear to hold a very ambiguous position in the forces. One respondent remarked that the Women's Corps would probably be unable to function without the competent input of the lesbians, yet the level of official homophobia was particularly high.[1] Purges were commonplace and respondents lived under the continual threat of exposure. Ali originally intended joining the Military Police. However, her experience of their behaviour towards lesbians made her reconsider:

> When I got in and saw how the military operated I thought no way [am I going to join the Military Police]. They were just a bunch of animals. I couldn't relate to that; the women were as bad as the men. They would have your bunk ripped apart, the mattresses off, looking for letters . . . Because being gay is illegal in the army and they used to have these purges . . . What would happen is, the young girls coming in would get frightened of what was going on [high level of lesbian visibility] and freak, and would hand in a list of names to whoever, to the CO even, and they would have to act on it, and there would be this purge, and all the names on the list were investigated. The young girls coming in were very dangerous one way or another, which is why I kept really low-key about things.
>
> (35M)

One respondent fell victim of a purge and was discharged. This had serious repercussions, as she lost her opportunity to train in medicine. Furthermore, the knowledge that the forces are intolerant of homosexuality deterred some respondents who would have really liked to join up. For these respondents fear of building a career and then being exposed as a lesbian influenced their decision against entry. Moreover, I was unable to interview any serving military women, as those who had been approached were worried about the possibility of being identified.

The four women who developed more 'male' mechanical and technical skills in the forces utilized them when they re-entered civilian life. One entered higher education to develop her technical skills further, and the others entered driving or motor-trade occupations. Several remarked that they found civilian life, in terms of employment opportunities, far more gender-segregated than was their experience in the forces. They also commented on the difficulty in reaching the relatively high levels of pay and perks which they had experienced in the forces.

Making a career in male-dominated manual occupations

Three respondents were currently employed in traditionally 'male' manual occupations at the point of interview. A further four had moved up from male-dominated manual occupations to low-level management. All these seven women were from intermediate or manual backgrounds. Interestingly, these women tended to be older: their median age was thirty-six, and two women were in their forties. In the case of the older women, their earlier unconventional employment choices were very much perceived as being made in the context of an extreme polarity between women's and men's work. For them, women's work offered little in the way of job security, pay or prospects; in contrast, men's work represented the possibility of developing skills and establishing a career.

Occupations which involved driving were popular with many of the fifteen respondents who had had some experience of male manual occupations. . . . Some had previously been in factory and shop work, which they found highly regimented; they spoke of disliking the constant surveillance of supervisors and of having to clock in and clock out. In contrast, driving occupations represented greater freedom and the ability to exercise greater control. They enjoyed being able to organize their daily work routines, setting their own pace, and being out and about. Tamsin explains why she chose to enter a job in transport. She enjoys this work, although she sometimes has to put up with the sexist attitudes of male co-workers.

> It's been a very successful move for me. There are other women that do driving and they have a very good work record . . . The customers we deal with always ask for us back. [*How have you found the job as a woman?*] It's quite interesting; you get these blokes: 'Here you go, we have a woman trying to do a man's job,' that sort of attitude thrown at you. That's not what I am trying to do. I'm trying to earn a decent wage, that's all. I don't want to be a secretary, so I want to be a driver instead . . . They [men] do find it quite a novelty, really, especially [with me being] in the big trucks, because they do find that quite hard.
>
> (29M)

Others found the sexist hostility from male co-workers more enduring. Their experience highlights the important role played by sexist male workplace culture in 'policing' the boundaries of traditionally male occupations.[2] In the case of some respondents, their interest in particular occupations was dampened by the sexism and homophobia that prevailed. Consequently, they were propelled out of jobs that they found challenging into jobs where the working environment was more pleasant. This was the case for Christine, who went to work backstage in a theatre in the Midlands. She was involved in carpentry and painting. Although she loved the actual job, she found having to defend herself from the sexist attitudes of her male co-workers too great a strain. She left the job after a year and is now self-employed:

> I found it very hard going because of the sexism involved. It was very sexist, and I thought all theatres would be like that. It was also very homophobic. It's a total double standard, a lot of homosexuality in the theatre, but the sort of butch attitude with the people who shifted the scenery was quite horrible. . . .

Many of the respondents in male-dominated areas of employment found that male co-workers were initially hostile to new female co-workers. However, those respondents who have remained in such occupations found that, once they had proved themselves competent, they seemed to have good working relationships with their colleagues.

Respondents who have made long-term careers in male manual occupations usually worked themselves up to low-level management. Typically, they started their careers in driving or garage work. However, initial entry into male occupations had been fairly difficult for respondents as school leavers. Lenora talks of the sexist attitudes of an employer in her first job interview after leaving school. She had seen an advertisement for an apprenticeship with a sign-writing company and thought it would be a good craft to learn:

> They advertised for an apprentice. I got an interview – don't know why they bothered to interview me – and then got told, 'We're looking for a lad.' They had no intention of employing me. I told them I wasn't going to rush off and marry – I couldn't' say, 'Look, pal, I'm queer!' What can you say?
>
> (38)

Very unequal treatment in gaining access to training in male craft skills was common for respondents now in their late thirties and forties. They saw themselves as early pioneers in their chosen occupations. Three were semi-skilled mechanics, none had trained formally on apprenticeship schemes. They learnt their skills on the job, picking up information from their male colleagues. Lenora . . . eventually learnt her trade, after working in a garage as a petrol pump attendant . . .

. . . For several respondents, entry into male occupations was facilitated by fathers. Carol's father helped establish her in a career in mechanical parts:

I followed in my father's footsteps [into the motor trade] – selling parts, everything to do with looking after parts, selling them, ordering them. . . .

However, achieving equal pay proved much more difficult for her:

[The job isn't well paid] until you start getting up through the ranks. It took me about ten years to rise up and command a decent wage, but then that wasn't the same as the men were getting. . . .

Fighting against this kind of discrimination was common amongst respondents in male-dominated occupations. Jackie talks of the problem of being taken seriously by employers. She had been delivering parts for a company. She had an interest in mechanics, was ambitious and wanted to move into a better paid, more demanding job. She spent any free time at work with the parts store-man learning the trade. A chance came up to join the sales team:

[I] ended up mainly in the stores, because I knew a bit about cars and parts; . . . knew more than the storeman did . . . There again I came up against the male bit. We had about five reps on the road, selling the parts. If one was off sick or on holiday I got his job to go and do his round, and I was as good as he was on that . . . I said to the manager, thinking on promotion lines, 'If one of the reps leaves, do I get a chance of his job if I work hard and prove I can do it?' They said, 'No, no chance! It's always men that are reps.' I thought, no, I am not going to be a toerag just because I am female.

(39)

Jackie left this company; she later achieved a management position in transport, and eventually did well enough to set up her own business.

Like Jackie, respondents usually persevered until they were taken seriously by their bosses. Jessy managed to move up from 'male' manual work to a management position in garage:

It was very difficult to get into the actual management position. [My company] was a very old-fashioned firm and there weren't any women in management positions. The manager went on holiday and I used to cover for him . . . No one [else] wanted to cover; no one wanted to know about [it]. It was a very difficult [area of work] to get into. It's a hell of a responsibility. They said no, so someone said, 'What about [Jessy]' and they said, 'She's a woman!' They said it really wouldn't hurt covering, and I covered. I got quite good at it and I did enjoy it.

(34)

It was not until she became frustrated with her manual job, and decided to leave, that she was seriously considered for promotion. Her employers were unwilling to let her go, she refused to stay unless she was given a permanent management position and finally they agreed to give her the job. . . .

Promotion for these women came as the result of this actively putting them-selves forward. They had not been considered 'natural' promotion candidates by their bosses, and attention had to be drawn to their merits. It seemed that they often had the support and encouragement of male co-workers who had perhaps greater awareness of their individual competences . . .

Respondents in male occupants tended to enjoy their work. It provided variety and challenge. They also recognised that they had to be very good at their jobs to earn the respect of the men that they worked with. They knew that, if they made mistakes, this would be understood in gender terms by their male co-workers. Consequently, they were very aware of the need to work doubly hard to earn the respect of male colleagues. As one respondent put it, 'You have to be twice as good as the men.'

Notes

1   For a very entertaining discussion of the central role played by lesbians in the military see Faderman (1992: chapters 5–6) and Miller (1995). For information on brutal and underhand tactics used in catching lesbians see Faderman (1992).
2   See, for example, Adkins (1995), Cockburn (1991) and Stanko (1998) for a discussion of the implications of the sexual harassment of women by men in maintaining gender separation.

References

Adkins, L. (1995) *Gendered Work: Sexuality, Family and the Labour Market*. Buckingham: Open University Press.
Cockburn, C. (1991) *In the Way of Women: Men's Resistance to Sex Equality in Organizations*. Basingstoke: Macmillan.
Faderman, L. (1992) *Odd Girls and Twilight Lovers: a History of Lesbian Life in Twentieth-century America*. London: Penguin.
Miller, N. (1995) *Out of the Past: Gay and Lesbian History from 1869 to the Present*. London: Vintage.
Stanko, E. (1988) 'Keeping women in and out of line: sexual harassment and occu-pational segregation', in S. Walby (ed.) *Gender Separation at Work*. Milton Keynes: Open University Press.

Chapter 17

Annie Phizacklea

A SINGLE OR SEGREGATED MARKET?
Gendered and racialised divisions

Using comparative data from the UK, France and Germany, Annie Phizacklea argues that labour markets are both gendered and racialised. Taking a case study of women home workers, she shows that even in this traditionally female sector of the economy White women do better than their Asian counterparts.

From H. Afshar and M. Maynard (eds) *The Dynamics of 'Race' and Gender*, London: Taylor & Francis (1994).

Introduction

ORIGINALLY THEORIES OF occupational segregation were developed to explain why both women and black people generally were crowded into certain sectors of the labour market and not others. Not surprisingly these blanket theories were not very satisfactory because the processes of gendering and racialization may have similar outcomes but they have their own histories and their own dynamics. So the debates diverged, leaving the question of black and ethnic minority women outside the theoretical boundaries.

Certainly in Britain and the United States there is a lively academic and political debate about the continued gendering of jobs and the real cost of that to women in their wage packets. My long-term concern has been to make those debates sensitive to the impact of racialization and suggest how such a sensitivity can help us bring together both the demand and supply side factors in understanding occupational segregation. Towards that end I began, in the early 1980s, to look at national employment statistics, stratified by ethnic/nationality grouping, in Britain, France and what was then West Germany, and also to carry out micro-level research which aimed to paint a fuller picture than aggregate data can provide (see, for example, Phizacklea, 1983, 1987, 1988, 1990). Those early researches led me to the conclusion that the subordinate position of minority women within some Western European labour markets introduced another layer of occupational segregation within the narrow band of jobs into which women were already crowded (Phizacklea 1983). In 1992 I re-examined the same national data sets and, as we shall see . . . in Britain and France, at least, there appeared to have been some bridging of the gap between majority and ethnic minority women's employment levels. Nevertheless, I go on to suggest a number of factors which may make this seeming improvement illusory. In the final section I use the case of home-based work in Coventry to illustrate how these factors operate to produce and reproduce racialized disadvantage and occupational segregation. . . .

Minority women in Britain, Germany and France ten years on

Before considering any figures on occupational segregation and the representation of majority and minority women within the labour force, it is necessary to emphasize some of the many problems which beset such a comparative exercise. Unlike Britain, other European countries do not use the category 'ethnic minority' statistically. Rather, aggregate data refers to 'foreigners'. Thus the category 'foreigner' does not include persons who belong to ethnic minorities but who hold the citizenship of the member country. This is further complicated by the fact that data for Britain is now presented in two ways. The categories 'white' and 'ethnic minority group' are retained for domestic consumption (for instance, Labour Force Surveys), but for the purposes of European-wide statistics anyone who does not possess British citizenship becomes classified as a 'foreigner', in line with the other member states (see SOPEMI 1990: 91). Despite these and many more problems of comparability, one can discern certain trends in the three countries over the last decade.

For Britain, Labour Force Surveys indicate that in 1987–88 ethnic minorities constituted 4.7 per cent of the population of working age. A glance at aggregate data suggests that the gap in job levels between black and white women is much less than between black and white men and in the last ten years that gap has been further bridged. But this interpretation of the trends needs to be qualified in the following ways: during recessionary periods black women are far more likely to become unemployed than white women and even in a period, such as 1987–88, which was not regarded as an employment 'trough', 16 per cent of black women were unemployed compared to 9 per cent of white women (for men the figures were 17 per cent and 10 per cent respectively). The marked differences in unemployment levels led analysts at the Policy Studies Institute to argue, as early as 1982, that the bridging of the gap is largely illusory, much of the change being due to the fact that black women in the poorest jobs have become unemployed and those in the better jobs have become a larger proportion of all those in employment (Brown 1984: 179).

Another factor, which is important in comparing black and white women's job levels, is that black women are much more likely to work full-time (40 per cent compared to 27 per cent of white women). As we shall see in the home-based work case study this can be explained with reference to household finances and the greater dependency that the black households have on the mother's earnings. The 1982 PSI report provides evidence to show that in all types of household the earned income per person is lower among Caribbeans than among whites and is particularly low in Asian households (Brown 1984: 231). In addition it has been argued that, while full-time work lifts many white women out of low-pay ghettoes, this is far less true for black women (GLC 1986: 114).

The final point that needs to be made is that large categories, such as 'professional and managerial', hide more than they reveal. For instance, if we unpack this category we find that close to half the Caribbean women within it are working in the Health Service in nursing grades, while white women are more likely to be represented in administrative grades. Thus, while Caribbean women remain over-represented in the Health Service, Asian women are overrepresented in the clothing industry (and national figures underestimate their involvement in clothing manufacture), in both cases ethnic 'niches' within traditional sectors of 'women's work'.

In France 'foreign' women are still more likely to be found in manufacturing than French women, twice as likely to be unemployed and less likely to be found in the more 'desirable' sectors of 'women's work. Nevertheless, the gap between French and 'foreign' women's job levels has, at an aggregate level, shrunk over the last decade (INSEE 1989).

There is less evidence to suggest that the gap is shrinking in Germany, though the trends over the decade are interesting. In the early 1980s there was clear evidence that 'foreign' women were taking the brunt of manufacturing job losses, thus acting as a 'buffer' to German women. Data for 1990 indicates a rise in employment for German and 'foreign' women across all sectors of the economy, though 'foreign' women are still more likely to be located in manufacturing industry (42 per cent) than German women (24 per cent) and more likely to be located in the manual sectors of 'women's work' (Sonderdruck. Sozialversicherungspflichtig Beschäftigte 1990).

To reiterate, if we interpret the trends at face value there is some evidence to suggest that the large gap in job levels apparent ten years ago between majority and minority women has to some extent been bridged in Britain and France. But this is aggregate data relating to employment in the formal economy and needs to be treated with a good deal of caution. Moving our level of analysis down in scale we uncover a rather different picture, and this is what my colleague Carol Wolkowitz and I found in Coventry in the first phase of a research project that we carried out on home-based work.

Racialized divisions at home

The first in-depth phase of our 1990 research on home-based work was designed to uncover what, if any, ethnic differences exist amongst Coventry home-based workers. A full account of the research methodology and findings as a whole can be found in our book *Working at Home* (1994). Our findings suggest that, within the shared constraints that all women with children experience, there are ethnic differences in levels of employment that force families into a situation where inadequate benefits have to be supplemented by low-waged home-based work. Unlike white women, Asian women in Coventry were not represented at all in the better-paid, less onerous clerical home-based work available in the city.

For the manual workers in the sample, the issues which arise out of ethnic segregation are not only differences in hourly earnings but also differences in hours, regularity and the intensity of work. This is particularly acute in the Coventry clothing industry, a major employer of Asian women, because of the extent to which employers are themselves in a 'master/servant' relationship in the subcontracting chain of production.

All nineteen Asian women that we interviewed in Coventry were manual workers, fifteen of whom were involved in clothing assembly, most earning well below the Wages Council minimum. The work of the other Asian home workers was even more poorly paid. Two assembled Christmas crackers and were earning, in 1990, between 8p and 16p an hour. Another was packing nappies for 53p an hour and one was a childminder charging only 33p per hour per child. This was far less than white childminders were charging. The Asian childminder was not registered and she explained she could not register because at the rates her clients could afford she had to care for more children than registered childminders are permitted in order to make it financially viable for herself.

Amongst the thirty white home workers interviewed nine were clerical workers. The latter earned more for less hours and had a fair amount of control over their work flow. While homeworking wages generally are low by any standard, there was a difference between Asian and White women in Coventry, with two-thirds of the Asian women earning between 75p and £1.50 an hour, compared to white home workers' earnings of £2.00 an hour or more.

The Coventry homeworking labour force reproduced the occupational segregation that is evident in the external labour market. The impact of racialization and ethnicity on the working lives of Asian women is demonstrated by their concentration in a narrower band of jobs and their exclusion from the better-paid and less onerous clerical work available in the city. If they have sewing skills their hourly earnings are low. If not they are usually thrown into even more poorly paid assembly work.

Equally important are differences in the place of home work in the women's lives and its role in the household economy. The very long hours worked by the Asian women reflect economic need. Sixty per cent worked forty-five hours or more and a third over sixty hours a week. Twelve of the Asian households but only three of the white ones depended on Income Support and the Asian households had more children to support. In fact, the only advantage that some Asian women could see in home working was that they could bring some money into the household in order to supplement their inadequate benefits. As one Asian woman explained,

> My husband is unemployed. We cannot manage on the Income Support we receive. The children constantly need some form of clothing or shoes. My husband has gone for an interview today.

One of the questions we asked was whether the respondent was happier working at home or whether she would prefer to go out to work 'if that were possible'. The answers showed a clear difference between Asian and White women. Slightly over half the white women said that they preferred to work at home as against only two of the Asian women. The other Asian women responded that they were neither happier nor unhappier working at home, which suggests that they felt that they had no choice.

We also asked the respondents if working at home 'made for an easy-going day'. While three-quarters of the white clerical workers responded that it did, none of the Asian women agreed. As one explained:

> work is always there to be done, housework, homework – I shout at the children most of the time, I lose my temper quickly. I don't have as much time for the children as I would like. The homework is messy and this creates more work for me

While there is a good deal in common between the working conditions of the Asian and white home workers, the Asian women were much more likely to be dependent on benefit or trying to manage on a very low income. As a consequence they were being thrown into home work that was so badly paid that they had to work very long hours. So why are Asian women not getting access to the better-paid forms of home work in Coventry? Part of the explanation is the informal recruitment processes so typical of home working. Contrary to popular belief, none of the Asian women in our sample acquired their jobs through relatives. Rather, where it exists, the recruitment of kin can discriminate against minority women. For instance, the better-paid electronics home work carried out by white women in Coventry was brought home by husbands who worked in the factory. The better-paid clerical homework was acquired through word of mouth, as was the bow making. Some years ago the Council for Racial Equality investigated recruitment practices at the Massey-Ferguson plant in Coventry and uncovered a similar process of indirect racial discrimination reproduced through informal recruitment practices. In addition, some of the ethnic differences in earnings and the intensity of work reflect the position of the suppliers of home work in the economy. For instance, the clothing industry in Coventry is dominated by Asian entrepreneurs who occupy a subordinate position in the subcontracting production chain for low-value-added product where labour costs constitute a high proportion of total costs (Phizacklea 1990).

Employment segregation and the impact of immigration policy

Supply-side explanations for occupational segregation by sex have emphasized women's 'domestic responsibilities' as the key to their disadvantaged and occupationally crowded position in the labour market. For minority women their supposed 'language deficiencies' and 'lack of skills' are routinely added and trotted out as explanations for their doubly disadvantaged position. There is little doubt that employers take advantage of these gendered and racialized ideologies (see Phizacklea 1983). While language can constitute a problem for some women, the last Policy Studies Institute study of racial disadvantage at work indicated that this is far less of a problem than is commonly thought (Brown 1984).

What is often overlooked is the role of the state in shaping job status through immigration policy. Obviously this is formally the case with specific recruitment policies and work permit allocations but state intervention is apparent in less direct forms in the case of family reunion. Since the early 1970s and the banning of new worker entries throughout the European Community the major migration flows have been related to family reunion, asylum seekers and refugees.

In the case of family reunion the entry of spouses and dependants is only allowed if a sponsor can provide evidence that he or she can support and accommodate them without recourse to 'public funds' (particularly benefits). Not only is the family then forced to settle without state support, there are also residence conditions for non-contributory benefit claims and in some countries a waiting period before access to the labour market is granted. All of these factors push families who are struggling to reconstruct their lives in the migration setting into poverty and often women into work in the informal economy.

Conclusions

Aggregate data on the occupational distribution of majority and minority women in Britain, France and Germany might at face value provide grounds for cautious optimism in so far as the large gap in job levels that existed ten years ago appears to have been bridged slightly in Britain and France at least. My own view is that one would need to be very wary of coming to such a conclusion.

The aggregate data on employment tells us nothing about the much higher rates of unemployment amongst minority men and women, about the hours that they work, about their pay, about the formation of 'ethnic niches' within national labour markets nor about the overall level of household income, all factors which we need to consider if we are going to gain a more complete picture of what is really going on.

What really is a priority on the policy front is a radical change in EC member states' attitudes to tackling racial discrimination combined with an aggressive commitment to the pursuit of equal opportunities. Without this there is a little that can be regarded as beneficial in the single market for Europe's ethnic minorities.

References

Brown, C. (1984) *Black and White Britain: The Third PSI Survey*. London: Heinemanm.

Greater London Council (1986) *The London Labour Plan*. London: GLC.

INSEE (1989) *Enquête emploi*.

Phizacklea, A. (ed.) (1983) *One Way Ticket: Migration and Female Labour*. London: Routledge.

Phizacklea, A. (1987) 'Minority women and economic restructuring: the case of Britain and the Federal Republic of Germany', *Work, Employment and Society*, 1 (3): 309–25.

Phizacklea, A. (1988) 'Entrepreneurship, ethnicity and gender', in S. Westwood and P. Bhachu (eds) *Enterprising Women*. London: Routledge.

Phizacklea, A. (1990) *Unpacking the Fashion Industry: Gender, Racism and Class in Production*. London: Routledge.

Phizacklea, A. and Wolkowitz, C. (1994) *Working at Home*. London: Sage.

Sonderdruck. Sozialversicherungspflichtig Beschäftigte (1990) Bundesanstalt für Arbeit, Nuremberg.

SOPEMI (1990) *Continuous Reporting Systems on Migration*. Paris: OECD 1991.

PART THREE

Paid and unpaid work

INTRODUCTION

WHEREAS PART TWO WAS concerned with the structure of the labour market, Part Three deals with the gendered experience of paid and unpaid work. Until the 1970s work, for sociologists, meant paid work in the public domain. Women's unpaid, domestic labour thus did not figure as work at all and was more likely to be described as a 'role' or, at best, a set of 'responsibilities'. Pioneering work in the 1970s, such as Oakley (1974), began to challenge the idea that work was defined by whether it was paid or where it was carried out. Anne Oakley applied concepts and methods derived from the sociology of work to housework in order to demonstrate that its content and process could be analysed just like any other job. At the same time Marxist feminist theorists were debating the extent to which women's domestic labour contributed to capitalist production through servicing the labour force and rearing the next generation of workers (see Kaluzynska 1980; Rushton 1979). Others concentrated on the ways in which men benefited from domestic labour and the extent to which it could be understood as taking place within patriarchal relations of production (Delphy 1984).

Since that time domestic work has been taken more seriously as work, and more attention has been given to the relationship between women's paid and unpaid labour. Unpaid work in the home forms a constant backdrop to whatever else women do; recent research suggests that, while men do more in the home than they did in the past, women continue to do most of the domestic work and to take responsibility for organising it. Men are not only not doing their share, they have their share done for them. Men have more leisure than women and their leisure can create yet more unpaid work for women, as Linda Imray and Audrey Middleton's description of a village cricket match demonstrates (Chapter 18).

Given their domestic commitments and the fact that most women are now also engaged in paid work outside the home, they inevitably work longer hours than men. This means that for many women their daily lives revolve around managing the demands of paid and unpaid work. This entails not only organising their own lives, but also facilitating others' work and education – getting adult men off to work, taking children to school and preparing everyone's evening meal. The sort of burden this imposes is graphically portrayed by Sallie Westwood (Chapter 19).

Women's work within families is by no means confined to housework. If they are involved in a family business they may also work unpaid in this context, once more working for men, for husbands or fathers (see Chapter 20). This pattern is particularly common among some ethnic minorities because running a family business is an attractive alternative to the poor opportunities existing within a racialised labour market. It is not only among ethnic minorities, however, that it occurs. Women make contributions to their husbands' occupations in a variety of contexts: wives of small independent tradesmen frequently contribute free labour, answering the phone or doing the books, while the wife of a high-flying businessman can put many hours of labour into organising a dinner party for his colleagues or clients. Indeed, many wives are 'married to the job' (Finch 1983). One specific aspect of women's work as wives is that it is a personal service with no fixed job description or hours; hence a wife may undertake a variety of tasks depending on her husband's position, requirements or preferences (see Chapter 21).

Women's domestic work may affect paid work in the public sphere in a number of ways. Women contribute to the paid work of others through the sorts of direct contribution to men's work discussed above, but also through maintaining the home, cooking the meals and so on. Because women are constrained by the juggling of paid and unpaid work, this may limit their choices about where they work and the hours they work. Once they enter the work force they frequently encounter assumptions about the effect of domestic responsibilities on their commitment to paid work which further limit their opportunities. Cynthia Cockburn's study reveals considerable resistance to the full implementation of Equal Opportunities policies (Chapter 22). Women were often seen as less reliable as colleagues and employees because of their domestic responsibilities, yet when policies were put in place to make it easier to combine, for example, work and motherhood it was seen as giving women an unfair advantage. What rarely occurred to the men was that if they took on an equal share of domestic work and childcare many of the problems would not exist.

There are other respects, too, in which assumptions about domesticity affect women's paid work. It has long been noted that many traditional 'women's jobs' – for example, in nursing, teaching and catering – mirror the tasks women perform unpaid in the home and utilize similar skills. More recently, however, the expanding service sector has called upon less tangible 'feminine' attributes in its reliance on emotional and sexualised labour. The concept of emotional labour was originally developed by Arlie Hochschild (Chapter 23) in analysing the means by which airline cabin crews kept passengers happy and maintained a calm, serene and smiling demeanour regardless of how they felt or how passengers treated them. Although men now undertake this work, it has neither the status nor the pay and conditions of traditional men's work. This is also the case where men have entered other female occupations such as nursing – another job requiring the input of emotional as well as physical labour. Emotional labour can be extended to sexualised labour, where women workers are expected to look sexually attractive, where making male customers feel good shades into the assumption that they are both heterosexual and available. We refer here not to prostitution or any other form of sex work but to ordinary jobs in the leisure industry where being 'sexy' is a covert part of the job description (Chapter 24).

The conditions under which women work, the tasks they undertake and the expectations of them as workers are all highly gendered, defining them as women first and workers second. The paradigmatic 'normal' worker remains a male worker.

REFERENCES AND FURTHER READING

Delphy, C. (1984) *Close to Home*. London: Hutchinson.

Finch, J. (1983) *Married to the Job*. London: Allen & Unwin.

Glucksman, M. (1990) *Women Assemble: Women Workers and the 'New Industries' in Inter-war Britain*. London: Routledge.

Hearn, J. and Parkin W. (1987) *Sex at Work*. Brighton: Wheatsheaf.

Hochschild, A. R. and Maching, A. (1990) *The Second Shift: Working Parents and the Revolution at Home*. London: Piatkus.

Kaluzynska, E. (1980) 'Wiping the floor with theory: a survey of writings on housework', *Feminist Review*, 6: 27–54.

Oakley, A. (1974) *The Sociology of Housework*. Oxford: Martin Robertson.

Pahl, R. (1904) *Divisions of Labour*. London: Routledge.

Pringle, R. (1989) *Secretaries Talk: Sexuality, Power and Work*. London: Verso.

Rushton, P. (1979) 'Marxism, domestic labour and the capitalist economy: a note on recent debates', in C. C. Harris *et al.*, *The Sociology of the Family: New Directions for Britain*, *Sociological Review* Monograph No. 28 Keele: University of Keele.

Savage, M. and Witz, A. (eds) (1992) *Gender and Bureaucracy*. Oxford: Blackwell.

Key questions

- In what ways does housework differ from waged work? How would you account for the differences?
- Why, now that so many women are engaged in paid work, do they still carry the main burden of domestic work?
- How do assumptions and expectations about gender impact on both women and men in the workplace?

Chapter 18

Linda Imray and
Audrey Middleton

PUBLIC AND PRIVATE
Marking the Boundaries

While primarily concerned with the construction of public and private spheres and the gendered use of space and place, this reading also highlights gender divisions of work and leisure. In particular, the organisation of village cricket reveals one context in which women's work facilitates men's leisure.

From E. Gamarnikow, D. Morgan, J. Purvis and D. Taylorson (eds) *The Public and the Private*. London: Heinemann (1983).

. . .

WE WILL ARGUE THAT a model based on the concept of private and public spheres may throw light on the universality of male dominance and show how the boundaries between what is valued and what is not valued change over time and between and within cultures. We hope to demonstrate that an analytical separation of the spheres can clarify the meaning of the activities which take place in concrete social situations. Throughout human societies, what men do is valued above what women do, even if both women and men do the same things in the same places at the same time. The opposition between private and public, then, is not seen as opposed activity, but rather in terms of power relationships which are thrown into sharp relief by rituals that mark these boundaries. . . .

. . . [I]n order to indicate the ubiquity of these boundaries between public and private, we turn now to research being done by one of us (Middleton) in a small Yorkshire village. In this rural community, the reflection of the public and private spheres in geographical space is clear, and Middleton as a member of the private sphere who rejected reclassification as an honorary male found herself trespassing on public space and, as a result, being subjected to a continuum of male control ranging from courtesy, through gossip and ridicule, to violence and its threat (Middleton 1981).

. . . [W]e will concentrate on one activity in the village to illustrate the reflection of public and private spheres in village space. The activity is village cricket. The cricketers are a team of men from both middle and working-class backgrounds whose ages range from fourteen to sixty. They are the 'prima donnas' of the community: other village events are arranged around their fixture list. They give no support to other village activities and yet expect support from the community; they dominate the bar area of the sports and social club; and no other sport is allowed to take part on 'their' pitch – even in the off season.

The cricket pitch is situated in the centre of the village, adjacent to the river. The clubhouse of the village sports and social club was designed so that the verandah overlooks the cricket pitch and not the tennis courts which stand in its shade. And the benches that stand on the clubhouse perimeter of the pitch have their backs fixed so that, sitting on them, one *has* to face the cricket field rather than the tennis courts.[1]

On a fine day when the cricket team is at home it seems as though the whole village turns out to watch. This may be because the cricket field is the best piece of public land in the village and does have access to the river, but the effect is of support for the cricket team. The verandah and steps of the clubhouse are packed with spectators; looking from the cricket field, men sit on the right of the french windows with women on the left.[2] Other spectators sit on benches or on the grass while, outside the token fence which marks the perimeter of the pitch, women push their prams, this evidence of female fecundity framing the purity of the male ritual within. No woman is allowed to set foot on the pitch.

But in the private sphere, women are hard at work producing leisure for men. Besides being responsible for maintaining the 'whites' of the team, there is a rota of women who provide teas for the cricketers. From early afternoon onwards, woman may be seen arriving at the village hall, adjacent to the clubhouse, with plates of sandwiches and cakes which they carry into the kitchen. In the hall itself, they set up trestle tables on to which they load the food they have brought. They are not seen, nor do they see, but they are as vital to this production of a cricket match as are the women listeners outside the Iatmul and Askwẽ-Shavante Men's Houses.

When the men have been playing for a couple of hours, a woman emerges from the kitchen with a tray of drinks which she carries to the edge of the pitch where it is taken from her by a man who carries it to the 'square'.

At five o'clock, the teams leave the field for the village hall where the women serve them the food they have prepared. And after the return of the men to the field, the women clear the tables, dismantle them, wash up and go home where eventually they will be handed the grass-stained 'whites' to prepare for the next match.

After the end of the match, the two teams return to the clubhouse for showers. The corridor in which the men's changing rooms are located is forbidden to women, even though this corridor leads from the bar to the kitchen. Women who want to enter the bar from the kitchen have to walk around the outside of the building. However, most women are not usually to be seen in the bar after the match;

having provided leisure for their men, they are not welcome. Later in the evening some wives do reappear in order to drive home husbands who have had too much to drink. . . .

Once a year, however, women are allowed on to the 'square' on the occasion of the men versus women cricket match. This takes place on a weekday evening so that it does not interfere with the fixture list, and usually lasts between two and three hours. The men field a young, inexperienced side while the women's team comprises the wives of young cricketers plus young women from the village. They wear a 'uniform' of brief badminton skirts, tan-coloured tights, men's cricket sweaters which reach almost to the hemline of their skirts, and plimsolls. They are watched from the club verandah by the established cricketers on the right and their wives on the left.

The play is accompanied throughout by a barrage of obscene comments on the play of the male cricketers from their more experienced colleagues on the balcony. The women, aware of the exposure of their legs, run awkwardly to field the ball to the accompaniment of sexual banter from the male spectators. To Middleton, sitting with one ear tuned in to the comments of the men, it seemed as though there was a *double entendre* a minute.

In this match, right-handed men have to play with their left hands and left-handers with their right, but the men still have enough control of the game to ensure, aided by instructions from the 'elders' on the balcony, that the game comes to its ritual end of the women winning by one run. Long before that point is reached, however, the men on the balcony show their impatience and contempt for their junior colleagues by shouting at them to 'get on with it' so that they can retire to the clubhouse for an evening's drinking.

Once a year, then, members of the private sphere are allowed on to the 'square' where they are encouraged to flaunt their femininity and where inexperienced cricketers are defined as 'women', being beaten by them . . . The Yorkshire village ritual, in which the male cricketers are deliberately made weaker and the women are made to look strong, has the long-term effect of emphasising the strength and permanence of the usual order. . . .

After watching the men versus women's game in 1981, Middleton, as secretary of the sports and social club, decided to try to make some space for women in the village to play seriously as a team. Discreet enquiries in the village elicited the information that some women were keen to play hockey. It was about this time that the cricket club refused to pay an increase in 'rent' which had been imposed on all sections by the sports and social club. Middleton used this dispute to get support from the committee for her suggestion that hockey be played on the outfield of the cricket pitch during the winter. Support was given in the belief that the suggestion of a women's hockey team was merely a stick with which to threaten the cricket team into payment of 'rent' rather than a reality of eleven women wanting actually to play hockey. When this was realised, support was withdrawn. Not, however, before Middleton had had the matter discussed in several meetings, the minutes of which were posted out to committee members and passed from them to members of the cricket team.

Walking into the sports and social club bar one evening, Middleton was greeted with overt hostility – not even disguised as humour. Comments recorded included:

'I've no time for strangers who come into this village and try and change it;' 'Women will never be allowed to play on that field, it's ours by right of usage' and – most tellingly – 'If women are allowed on the cricket pitch, this village will fall apart'. . . .

The issue of a woman's hockey team continues to be put on the agenda of committee meetings at which women are outnumbered fifteen to two. At the time of writing, consideration is being given to letting a hockey team play on the old school playing field, which is unusable: it is adjacent to a busy trunk road, is uneven, gets flooded at certain times each year, and slopes down to the river. The football team has refused to use it as a practice ground, and the children's swings have recently been moved to a safer part of the village. A request for goalposts to the village charitable trust, which owns all the recreation grounds and which provided the cricket team with its roller and scoreboard, has not been acknowledged to date. The message is clear both from the committee of the sports and social club which has withdrawn its support for a women's hockey team now that the cricket team has paid its 'rent' and from the charitable trust which is effectively denying women access to public ground. Women, as a women's team, would be seen as 'matter out of place' (Douglas 1970) on public land in this Yorkshire village.[3] . . .

Our work points to the need to study male institutions in order to uncover the ways in which patriarchal systems operate as well as concentrating on the effect on women of patriarchal domination. Put another way, we must study not only how women are constructed as subordinate but how male structures operate to keep them this way. . . .

Notes

1   Women, of course, are allowed to participate in tennis and thus pollute it so that within the sports and social club it has relatively low status. For an analysis of the concepts of pollution, see Mary Douglas (1970).

2   Herz (1973: 10) writes, 'Society and the whole universe have a side which is sacred, noble and precious and another which is profane and common: a male side, strong and active, and another, female, weak and passive; or, in two words, a right-side and left-side.'

3   Middleton's suggestion that a women's hockey team should play on the outfield of the cricket pitch was greeted with incredulity by some male sociologists when she presented a paper on her work at a BSA Ethnography Study Group meeting in January 1982 (in Lancashire).

References

Douglas, M. (1970) *Purity and Danger*. Harmondsworth: Penguin.

Hertz, R. (1973) 'The pre-eminence of the right hand', in R. Needham (ed.) *Death and the Right Hand*. London: Cohen & West.

Middleton, A. (1981) 'Who pulls the Strings? Male Control of the Ethnographer in a Yorkshire Village', paper presented to the British Sociological Association Sexual Divisions Study Group, University of Bradford, February.

Chapter 19

Sallie Westwood

DOMESTIC LABOURERS
or Stand by your man — while he sits down and has a cup of tea

This reading is taken from an ethnographic study of White and Asian women workers in a stocking factory. In the following extract some of the women talk about combining unpaid housework with their (low) paid factory work and, in the process, reveal something of the meanings of work for them.

From *All Day Every Day*, London: Pluto Press (1984).

THE NOTION THAT WOMEN were the foundation upon which the whole edifice of social and familial life was based was a common view among the women of StitchCo, and they expressed this in the sentence, 'Men, ah, they don't know they're born, they've got no idea,' which was, of course, very convenient for the men generally. Women, we know, are engaged in the double shift; they work outside the home for wages and within the home for 'love'. . . .

The material oppression to which women are subject is carried on in the hidden world of the family and in isolated households. Yet it was made public in the department at StitchCo because the women who came to work brought these concerns with them, into an environment where the definition of woman as wife and mother was elaborated upon by the culture of the shop floor, thereby reinforcing the view the women held of themselves as wives and mothers first. Thus, many women expressed considerable anxiety over the whole area of housework. It was fraught with difficulties because, it seemed, women never had enough time to cook and clean and polish to a standard that they considered acceptable. The emphasis upon cleanliness and order has a long history among large sections of working-class women who tied this to respectability and created a distance between themselves and those families who were poorer, less well organised and labelled 'rough'.[1] . . .

The amount of time women spent on housework was apparent from the discussions that they had in their breaks. Not only did this work consume so many of their waking hours, but housework also became a major subject of conversation. Some of the women from the examining and packing sections were celebrating Mave's birthday by eating cream cakes mid-morning. . . .

SALLIE: How long do you think you spend on housework?
CHORUS: Hours and hours, at least as long as we spend here, and more . . .
FLO: We do two jobs, one here and one in the house. We'd earn a fortune if we ever got paid for both.

The rest of the group agreed and Bridie added: 'I mean house-keeping's for the food and the house, not to pay for washing and cleaning.' Everyone in the group accepted the view that they worked at home unpaid, and that the work that they did had a cash value which they never realised because they were servicing the needs of their families. There was no romance surrounding housework and no illusions about the time and effort involved. Yet this knowledge and understanding never seemed to dim the enthusiasm of the younger generation of brides. It seemed to pass over them until they became wives when, in fact, they looked to the models around them and followed them.

FLO: [continued] Housework is a full-time job, let alone coming here all week. There's so much to do and you don't do half of it when you're working. You've got to have a routine, otherwise if you don't do it one day you've got two jobs the next.

Everyone murmured agreement and nodded as they started to tell me about the routines they followed.[2] What this meant, in effect, was that the discipline and routinisation of factory production was brought into the household as a way, the women said, of getting through the week. This is an interesting and important amendment to our emphasis upon the way in which women workers bring the world of the home into the workplace. It is a two-way process: women not only domesticate production, but take production imperatives away from the factory into the home, recreating aspects of the capitalist labour process in their housework. What some women have learned from this is that there must be time off and so they build into their routine a space for themselves. Consequently, when Flo described her week it included a night off. Flo was a married woman of about 50; she had no children and lived in a flat that she and her husband were buying. Her week went like this:

I always do my washing on Sunday and then Monday it's ironing. Tuesday is my night off and I won't touch a thing. Thursday I do the bathroom and if it's 3.00 a.m. I won't go to bed until it's done. I hoover the bedrooms on Wednesday and all the other rooms Friday. Friday I go up town and pay the bills, do the shopping and get the 4.40 bus home. I get in and make a cup of tea and, while Les sits and has his, I unpack the shopping. Then I hoover the hall, lounge (we're in a flat, so it's a bit easier) while I put the dinner in the oven. Every morning I make the bed and do what's needed for dinner, like cut the potatoes, make the gravy, whatever . . .

Before I had time to interject and marvel at Flo's energy, or ask what was wrong with Les, the other women came in and supported Flo's account of the week. Kath intervened quickly with her own routine. She was a woman who looked older that her forty years; she was frail and had had pleurisy the previous year. This had not stopped her working twenty hours a day for her husband and her children, who were all living at home; one son was working and another son and her daughter were still at school.

I'm the same as you, Flo, 'cept we've got a dog, so I hoover down-stairs every day. I get up first, but not until 8.30 on a Sunday now. I get the tea on for the first lad and give him his breakfast because he has to go at 6.30, then it's me hubby. I make the lad's bed while the tea's brewing, then it's the other two and then I get meself ready while I make our bed, cut the sandwiches and I'm off out the door. I wash about three times a week because me hubby and the lad have overalls. You have to soak them, they can't go straight in the machine, then I put them in. I do all my pressing for the whole week on Sunday after-noon and pick up all the washing for Monday. The whole house gets a clean at the weekend. . . .

. . . With many of the . . . women I often had the greatest difficulty in raising questions about their work load at home. Any faint suggestion that I was critical of what they did sent them springing to the defence of husbands and children. Husbands were 'good' men because they brought their money home regularly, and they didn't get drunk and beat up their wives and children on Friday nights. 'Good' kids were prone to fits of sentimentality on birthdays and at Christmas, which meant they bought huge cards with poems celebrating 'Mum' for her unselfishness and her heart of gold. It was a poor trade for the work the women gave to their husbands and children. The problem for the women was that they had internalised the notion that womanhood was bound to the care of others, espe-cially husbands and children. . . . It was a matter of pride to the women at StitchCo that they cared for their children and their homes as they might have done if they were full-time home makers. Any criticism seemed cruelly out of place and was interpreted as a criticism of them, not of the men and children in their house-holds and the way that domestic labour was organised.

It was all perfectly understandable, but it meant that women colluded in their own oppression by insisting upon their right to manage the home and their duty in working for their family. To them, this was women's work, their *proper* work, which offered them a place at the centre of family life, and, through that, status and power – which work outside the home did not offer. The women were conscious that domestic work was isolated and lonely and few wanted to be on their own all day. It was this that they complained about, not the physical effort involved in wash-ing and cooking and cleaning, nor the fact that it was routine manual labour, as boring as sewing side seams all day. Instead, it was invested with a special status because it was done for love and was part of the way that women cared for their families. Boring, manual work was, therefore, transformed into satisfying, caring work which required both an emotional and an intellectual commitment; that commitment could only be made because the context for this work was the family, with its attendant ideological load. . . .

When discussing their domestic loads, some of the white women in the factory would tell me that they were lucky compared with the Indian women, whom they described as working 'round the clock' – a description which applied equally well to many of them. In fact, it was Indian women who were most vocal in their complaints about the amount of work they had to do. While the white women turned their domestic labours into labours of love, some Indian women looked back to a situation where minions and servants had done the cleaning and washing, shopping and, in some cases, the cooking. Housework carried no mystique for Asha or Pritty, who already knew that there were less arduous, more interesting and pleasant ways to spend their time. They regarded the situation they found themselves in, where they were involved in wage work and housework, as the worst of all worlds. Whenever I went to visit them at home they were working in the kitchen, preparing food for that evening, or the next day for other members of the household to take to work. No concessions were made to the fact that they worked all day at the factory; they were still expected to prepare food and serve their husbands as though they were at home full-time. This meant that their days started early, before everyone else's, and finished late, after the rest of the family had gone to bed. Like all the other women on the double shift, they paid a heavy price in terms of their health and well-being.

Usha, for example, always seemed to be run-down and unwell, complaining of leg aches, back aches and period pain. She had three children – two daughters who were studying at the local polytechnic and a younger son who was still at school. She and Pritty were waiting for some work to arrive when Usha said to me:

> I get so tired because I work here all day and then I go home and cook for all the family. Work, work, it's always the same in England. In Uganda we had servants to do the washing and cleaning and ladies didn't work.

Usha smiled as she remembered what were clearly the good old days.

> My husband had a shop there, now he works in an engineering factory. I have leg pains and back pains a lot so I don't like to stand, and, you know, in Indian cooking you have to make so many things. Sometimes I make this many chapatis. [*Usha demonstrated a pile about 18 in. high*]

Pritty joined in:

[PRITTY:] It's the same for all the Indian ladies; we have so much work in the house. If you are a young wife you have to cook for his family, his parents and brothers. It is like that in my house. All weekend I am doing the washing and cleaning and every day I must cook curry, dal, chapatis for all of them. Indian men don't work in the house.

SALLIE: Do you have any help with shopping?

PRITTY: Yes, but you still have to go because if you say get this and this, they don't know what size to get or what is fresh and good.

USHA: Sometimes my husband comes with me on Saturdays.

Pritty, like some of her friends, didn't look as though she was strong enough to carry the burden of work that fell on her, and on top of her work load there was the worry associated with her husband's unemployment which she kept largely to herself. She confided in me:

> My husband tries and tries to find a job, two years he has been trying but when he phones they say the job has gone. It is so hard for us here, I would like to go back to India. I went to visit two years ago for my marriage and it was so nice. The weather is nice and the people are friendly. Maybe we will go back there, but there's no work in India, either. It's very hard for us wherever we are. Ladies in India don't go to the factory; they are at home, they work in the house, but they have some help from one another and they have time to relax as well. We ladies here, we don't have any time for ourselves. We work at the factory all day and at home all night. I get up very early and make some of the food before I go to work and then I start again when I come home at night.[3]

Pritty's situation was not unusual. She was among the growing number of women who not only carried the burden of domestic work, but also the responsibility for earning the money necessary for the family. Like many other Indian women, she lived in an old terraced house that was badly in need of modernisation; this meant that housework was even more difficult. She, like Taruna and Lata, was trying her best to be a dutiful wife in a house without an inside bathroom, running hot water, or a long-handled broom to help her sweep up. Taruna and Lata polished their old houses and their meagre furniture until it shone and, unlike Pritty, who was tired and unwell, Taruna scrubbed and cleaned, shopped and cooked with tremendous energy and enthusiasm. She redefined the disadvantages in the house into charming, old-fashioned quirks that gave the house character – like the front door that had to be pulled to open, and the kitchen shelves that were far too high for her to reach. The materials with which they built their lives were unpromising; nevertheless, . . . Taruna . . . regarded it all as a part of the adventure of marriage in a situation where she was in charge. This sharply differentiated her from Pritty, who had her parents-in-law to cope with in addition to the lack of money, security and decent housing.

Notes

1   See, for example, Richard Hoggart, *The Uses of Literacy* (Harmondsworth: Penguin, 1957).

2   In the emphasis upon routine the StitchCo women also echoed the Peak Frean's workers of Bermondsey, Pearl Jephcott, *Married Women Working* [London: Allen & Unwin, 1962], p. 125. See also Anna Pollert, *Girls, Wives, Factory Lives*, [London: Macmillan, 1981] pp. 109–26.

3   Indian women do, of course, work outside the home, often doing the most menial, insecure and poorly paid work. Women in this situation are not counted as 'ladies'.

Chapter 20

Sue Baxter and Geoff Raw

FAST FOOD, FETTERED WORK
Chinese women in the ethnic catering industry

One form of women's work that is often neglected is the labour of wives and daughters in family businesses, where they frequently work unpaid or underpaid in enterprises owned and controlled by husbands and fathers. This situation is common among ethnic minorities; faced with racism in the labour market, one means of achieving status and a degree of economic stability is to run a family business. The situation of Chinese women discussed in this reading may, therefore, reflect more widespread practices.

From S. Westwood and P. Bhachu (eds) *Enterprising Women*, London: Routledge (1988).

FOR A QUARTER OF A CENTURY, Chinese restaurants, chip shops, and 'takeaways' have been a common feature of towns and cities throughout the country. Yet although they are the third largest ethnic community in Britain, the Chinese have received relatively little attention from politicians and researchers. . . .

Whilst scarcely any serious literature exists on the Chinese community in general (let alone on Chinese women), what little there is tends to focus exclusively on its cultural features (e.g. Ng 1986; Watson 1977; Baker 1977). This is not to say that such contributions are unimportant. However, because so little is known about the structural factors that to a large extent dictate the lives of Chinese people in the fast food industry, it is necessary to establish a wider explanatory framework within which to understand their specific experiences. In relation to Chinese women, this means first apprehending the way in which gender roles have been and continue to be transformed as a consequence of the erratic development of capitalism in south-east China. Imposed with the expansion of British and other imperial powers, rapid capitalist industrialization entailed the destruction of the local agricultural economy and prompted massive demographic movements which stretched far beyond the borders of China to the developing colonies and to Britain. Second, the lives of Chinese women must be seen not only within the context of racist and sexist immigration laws affecting female workers and dependants but also with a critical appreciation of employment conditions within the fast food industry. From this perspective it is evident that the concentration of Chinese women in an ethnic sub-economy is a direct result of the post-war economic demand for cheap, colonial labour to provide inexpensive, ready-cooked meals. In this sense, Chinese women in the catering trade share a common historical oppression with other women from New Commonwealth countries, despite appearing often to enjoy a petit bourgeois class position. . . .

Chinese women in Britain

> When I came in 1968 I went to live with my husband above his uncle's takeaway shop for a year. We both worked there in the evenings and he gave us free food and never asked for any rent. . . . Oh no, we didn't get paid. Then we rented a fish and chip shop for a couple of years but it didn't do too well, so we moved to Chinese Street. I had two kids by then. In those days, all the Chinese used to live there in the big houses. There were five families in ours – well, one was only a single man. But the rent was only £3 a week, which was all we could afford. Only three families used to cook there – the others ate at work. So things weren't too bad.

Many women (and children) were absorbed into Chinese restaurants as kitchen hands and cleaners, often for no wages at all since it was assumed by employers that their labours were spent in part payment for their accommodation.

> My sister can't speak English, so she just washes dishes in a restaurant. I was the same when I first came to this country. My husband got me the job in the same place as he was learning to be a cook but it's hard work and I didn't get much money.

> I remember when I first came to this country we lived above a Chinese restaurant in Wales. I had to work there on Thursday and Friday nights and every weekend because my parents had to work so hard on those days, they couldn't keep up with the business. Sometimes the boss would give me 50p pocket money for the week but that's nothing, is it?

From the mid-1970s onwards, Chinese restaurants increasingly met with competition from fast food 'chains' such as Kentucky Fried Chicken (introduced to Britain during the 1960s) and McDonald's (first established on this side of the Atlantic as early as 1974) (Jones 1985: 56). The advantage of the fast food chains lay in their heavy investment in cost-cutting technology which obviated the need for labour-intensive production, a saving passed on to customers. Since, by this period, rapidly diminishing new work permits kept wages reasonably stable for Chinese restaurant workers, the relative profitability of restaurants began to decline as economic competition began to bite. Together with the availability of family workers upon which to draw and the total unsuitability of dormitory, tied accommodation to family life, the falling profitability of restaurants transformed the Chinese catering economy into one composed of smaller capital units operating on lower running costs but with a similar rate of profitability to restaurants. In short, the mid- to late 1970s witnessed the simultaneous decline of Chinese restaurants and the rapid spread of Chinese 'takeaway' and fish and chip shops, the majority run as family businesses.

> running a restaurant involves a lot of money. But to open up a takeaway only costs about a third of what it costs to open up a restaurant. The profit margin is about the same – in fact it's more without the heavy outgoings. All you need is one chef in the kitchen and one waiter at the counter.

> Twenty years ago there wasn't any takeaways. It was all restaurants. Me and my husband used to work in one of the big ones in the city centre. He was just learning then, like me. It was no good, though. Then we got a job in this place here for two years. He worked in the kitchen and I worked at the counter. There was another cook as well but he got the sack soon after because business wasn't very good then – not enough customers. After two years, we bought the business. That was ten years ago. The old owner, he's only got one business now. That's where he works with his family. I work seven days a week – but only in the evening, not in the daytime. We don't open for lunch. Some of our friends do, though. We both have to work at night but we can have a rest during the day, although we've still got to prepare the food for five o'clock, when we open. Thursday, Friday and Saturday we work quite hard in the day – cutting the meat, getting it ready, chips, vegetables – things like that. Some of the stuff we get delivered but other stuff we've got to get from the wholesale market. You have to get up early for that. It's very difficult sometimes because we can't go to bed until about two o'clock (a.m.) and the market closes at eleven (a.m.). Weekends, it must be two or three (a.m.) before we're even finished in the kitchen. You have to clean everything after you've closed at night, you know. There's a lot of cleaning.

Whilst it is true that the lives of both Chinese women and men are dictated by the opening hours of the takeaway shops, it is nevertheless women who generally bear the brunt of the social and economic marginality such a living imposes. Time and again the sentiment 'It's his business, he makes the decisions' is reiterated and this is noticeably reflected in community life.

John is a waiter with a dependent wife and three children. A description of how he spends his spare time reveals that he and his wife have little in common socially.

This is my second job. The first is in the casino or down the bookies. I go out with all the others in the restaurant all the time. In this business, there's nothing – nothing. Last weekend I played Mah Jeung for seventy-two hours – seventy-two hours and no sleep but I couldn't stop. We finished at five o'clock in the morning and I got in the car and drove straight back to work. Last night, quarter to four (a.m.) I'd lost £90. By four o'clock I won £230. That's about £300 in fifteen minutes. The other night, we all put money in the kitty – about £50. In four spins we'd made £500. But what happened? We lost it again. Easy come, easy go. If I was in Hong Kong I would save all my money for my children's future and buy my son and his family a house but it's not the same here. When they grow up, they say, 'Bye-bye, Daddy, I'm off.' So what's the point? I might as well enjoy myself – as long as they've got enough to eat.

John's social life contrasts sharply with that of many Chinese women, not least his wife:

There's nothing for me here. That's the truth. Everybody's too busy in England to make real friends. If you want to be friends with the English, you have to make an appointment to see them. Back East you can go and see people any time you like and do anything you like. My husband doesn't feel the same as me. He likes it here. But he's got more friends and he can go out more than me. I've got to look after the kids.

Social isolation is a far more acute problem for Chinese women than for men. John's wife is not alone in her frustration. Whether as dependent wives of workers or themselves working in the family takeaway, the monotony and alienation of life in the Chinese fast food industry for all women is striking. . . .

I used to cry a lot – not really for any particular reason. There was just no one I could really talk to. I've been trying to learn English ever since I came but it's very difficult when you've got nobody to talk to.

For Chinese women the isolation of the family workplace mitigates [sic] against conscious, collective struggle. However, it would be incorrect to conclude that Chinese women are merely the passive recipients of the adversities imposed upon them through migration. Working in a family business where profitability depends as much upon the efforts of the wife as upon those of the husband actually means that there is a material basis for Chinese women to assert a certain degree of control, albeit on an individualized level. Indeed, an increasing minority of women are becoming joint partners in their husbands' businesses and others are running businesses themselves. This is tempered, however, by a growing awareness of the economic and social trap that running an ethnic takeaway shop or restaurant holds in store for future generations of Chinese women. Consequently, it is accompanied often by a desire to see children leave the fast food trade through educational attainment:

I'll tell you one thing, I don't want this life for my daughter. I want better for her. I want her to speak English and get a good job.

This attitude finds resonance with a younger generation of Chinese women and girls: .

A few years ago my Dad kept asking us if we would help him run a take-away and we all said, 'No way.' I don't want to work like a slave. I know what it's like because I've got friends who work in their parents' take-away shops and they have to work like dogs. My Mum saw it from our point of view. She said it would be better for us to carry on at school so we could choose what we wanted to do when we finished. . . .

References

Baker, H. (1977) *The Cultural Background*, report of a conference entitled 'Chinese Children in Britain', April 1977, London: Commonwealth Institute.

Jones, P. (1985) 'Fast food operations in Britain', *Service Industries Journal*, 5 (1): 55–63.

Ng, R. (1986) 'My people: the Chinese community in the north-east', *Multicultural Teaching*, 4 (3): 30–3.

Watson, J. (1977) 'The Chinese: Hong Kong villages in the British catering trade', in J. Watson (ed.) *Between Two Cultures*, Oxford: Blackwell.

Chapter 21

Christine Delphy and
Diana Leonard

THE VARIETY OF WORK DONE
BY WIVES

The unpaid work undertaken by wives can include a wide range of tasks, from working in family businesses, as in the previous reading, to housework and child care. In this reading, taken from their theoretical analysis of marriage, Delphy and Leonard explore the variety of work wives do for their husbands, arguing that the diversity of wives' work results from the social relation of marriage within which it is undertaken. They suggest that wives routinely contribute to their husband's ability to engage in waged work, whether by making direct or indirect contributions to men's jobs or simply by undertaking the routine chores which free men to pursue waged work and enable them to function effectively.

From *Familiar Exploitation*, Cambridge: Polity (1992).

THE VARIATION IN THE WORK women do as wives is rarely commented upon and yet it is one of its most distinctive features. Some of the historical changes in wives' work have been noted, especially those associated with the development of domestic and reproduction technologies; and lifecycle changes are also frequently commented upon – how the hours women work vary with whether or not they have children to care for and (related to this) whether or not they are in full-time or part-time employment. But these are seen as variations in women's roles as mothers as waged workers, not in their role as wives. It seems to be assumed that women's lives as wives are pretty uniform. Each cares for her husband, maintains his household, and has sexual relations and children with him. But the extent to which their choice of husband leads to variation in married women's lives – in the hours they work, and in the productive, emotional, sexual and reproductive tasks they perform – is little recognized.

Commentary on the family, and in particular feminist writing on the family, has indeed so emphasized the labour women perform 'for children' that at times it has virtually excluded the work they do for other family members and specifically for male heads of household. . . . The work which wives do for their husbands' occupations, for men's leisure activities, and for their emotional and sexual well-being, gets completely lost sight of because it is so varied, so personalized and so intimate.

We are therefore going to stress how women's work varies according to the men to whom they are married, and we shall only secondarily consider variations according to the dependants requiring care of 'the household's' need for the wife to earn money, since these are already stressed in the literature. The primacy of wives' work for husbands can, however, be seen from the way in which, during the Second World War, when the men were away in the armed services, children were happily put into nurseries, but the minute the men came home, despite post-war labour shortages, women were put back into the home to service the men. This was their primary role; and immigrant labour was sought to replace them in the labour market. Children were returned to the care of their mothers (or rather white indigenous children were placed full-time with their mothers – migrant women often had to leave their children with kin for many years before they could afford to have them join them) and the wartime nurseries were closed down.

The variation in wives' work according to their husbands' needs depends on both men's occupations and circumstances, and their personal interests and preferences. The occupational differences have to some extent been considered by Janet Finch in her book *Married to the Job* (1983), which uses Delphy's earlier work and collects together information on the effects of men's jobs on their wives in a number of specific occupational categories. That is to say, how men as doctors, dentists, academics, architects, creative writers, lawyers, diplomats, politicians, clergy, members of large corporations, managing directors, middle managers, young men in business administration and marketing, small businessmen and shop-keepers, policemen, army, navy, and prison officers, railway workers, miners, lorry drivers and deep-sea fishermen use their wives' labour.

This is a very useful source, but it . . . is not concerned with all the work wives do for their husbands, . . . only with how husbands' employers benefit from their employees' wives' work. It therefore concentrates on only some wives, those with employed husbands, and describes the wives of small businessmen as 'quite untypical' (p. 104) because they work for a 'team' running a 'joint enterprise'. So . . . farmers' wives . . . fall outside Finch's remit, and so too do women married to men who are either employers themselves or the wives of retired or unemployed men . . . In addition, her approach deals only with the work wives do which passes via their husbands to the men's employers, so she does not consider the work done by the wives of employed men from which the husbands benefit personally. Thus her book does not discuss how a wife's life and work may vary according to, for example, her husband's leisure activities or personal needs and preferences.[1]

Finch thus extends the usual analysis of domestic work considerably . . . But she gives no reason why we should not include as family work a wife preparing a formal tea for her husband's cricket team or for sale in a café which he owns, if we are to include her cooking dinner for people he needs to entertain for his job. Nor does she explain why a wife cooking her husband breakfast to set him up for work should be considered work, whereas a wife cooking her husband particular dishes at odd hours when he comes in from an all-male outing should not. . . . All these tasks are done under the same terms and conditions, whatever the final use the husband (and thence his boss) may have for a wife's products and services.

How wives contribute to their husbands' work and leisure

Wives commonly contribute to their husband's work by actually doing some of it for him or with him, as [is] the case with the farmers' wives . . . Wives also always help indirectly by doing most or all of the household work, which frees men not only for paid work but also for other activities, including voluntary work, sport, hobbies and socializing. Finally, wives give their husbands moral and psychological support which helps them cope not only with their paid employment but also with life in general.

Direct contributions

Husbands' direct use of their wives' work for occupational/direct exchange purposes is especially common and most obvious when the husband is self-employed and runs his own business. 'Many of those currently running their own small business would simply not have made it without their wives – and wives sacrifice as much as their husbands (though their sacrifice is less publicized)' (Scase and Goffee, 1980).

Wives routinely work alongside their husbands and under their direction when men are artisans, such as plumbers, electricians and mechanics, who sell both goods and the services to install them. Such men cannot usually afford a secretary, so their wives put in a full day's work when there is a shop of any kind, while the men go around to see the customers. When there is no shop, the wives work from home, sometimes in addition to having a waged job. They calculate, type and send out estimates and bills to clients. They order spare parts and other equipment from the warehouses, and they either do the books (which an accountant looks at each month) or all the accounts . . .

When husbands are shopkeepers, wives may work from 8.00 a.m. to 8.00 p.m. six days a week at the cash desk, or they may actually run the shop if the man is a baker and produces the goods which are sold, or a greengrocer who has to go to market. They may serve in the family restaurant, work on the market garden, or be the junior partner in his law firm. They may help with office work – opening letters and filing, making appointments, and typing reports. Or they may work in their husband's stead: the wife of a driving instructor will sit in the shop waiting for customers and give instruction on the Highway Code (which is part of the lesson). The wife of a man who runs a health clinic can help not only by sorting out employees' problems and maintaining company morale, but also by giving aerobics classes.

Even when men are employed there are instances where wives do so much work that employers effectively get two employees for the price of one. This is sometimes so routinized and recognized that particular industries only employ marred men, or they agree to pay the wife's expenses, though they do not give her any actual pay or insurance cover or a pension (other than the one normally provided for the dependant of an employee). Such jobs the one normally provided for the dependant of an employee). Such jobs include work in the diplomatic service, the rural police force, and running a pub. The wife works because she is the incumbent's spouse. There is a particular role for a wife, an institutionalized consort position, and particular tasks suited to a (female) spouse, such as being a hostess or cooking meals or looking decorative behind a counter. In such cases, if the holder of the post does not have a wife he may have to provide a woman to fulfil that part of a wife's role or risk losing the job. Breweries in Britain, for example, only give tenancies of pubs to married couples and may take the pub away from a man if he divorces. The same applies to corner grocery shops which are parts of chains in France.

In addition to helping with the work men do to earn money, wives also often give direct help with their husbands' voluntary and leisure activities – which for women are not 'voluntary' and not 'leisure' because they do not choose them and because they have the knock-on effect of more work for them. Wives may be kept busy in summer getting grass stains out of white flannel cricket trousers and in winter cleaning football kits caked in mud; or collecting, preparing and boiling fruit for wine making; or running fund-raising jumble sales for a Boy Scout troop. If a man wants to be elected to the local council, his wife and children will support him on the hustings and help deliver election leaflets. Particular duties can also fall to a wife because of her husband's voluntary activities, for example, if he is active in local politics and becomes mayor she will be expected to accompany him to formal dinners and to provide 'hospitality' for visitors to their home.

Even where a wife does not work full-time for her husband's occupation, she will often work for him occasionally, acting in his stead, as second best, in his absence, in a crisis or when he is busy. Politicians' wives take care of their husbands' constituencies while the men are away in the capital and they may write their speeches on local issues. Academics' wives often type up research reports, make indexes, proof-read books and at a pinch mark students' essays. Diplomats' wives attend minor functions to save their husbands time. Doctors' wives may receive patients when their husbands are out and either give first aid advice or make the decision to refer things on to a hospital. Clergymen's wives give succour and spiritual advice as well as making appointments for weddings and funerals. And farmers' wives . . . take on men's tasks and run the farm in their husbands' absence.

The ability of a wife to step in and act for her husband depends on course on her having certain competences, but men often have the sense to marry appropriate spouses (would-be politicians often marry women interested in politics, academics marry their research students, doctors marry nurses, farmers marry farmers' daughters who have had jobs giving them office skills, and clergy wives are expected to be committed Christians). Alternatively, if the spouse does not have the skills initially, she is expected to acquire them 'over the breakfast table'. . . .

Women get little personal recognition or reward for such work. Doing it well involves staying in the background and an individual must make it clear she is acting only in her capacity as a wife. In addition, even if the business depends upon the wife and/or (as far as the tax officials are concerned) she is paid a salary for working in it, of even if the husband's employer requires that she does the work, she will rarely be paid any money. If a wife is skilled and domestic circumstances permit her to run part of the business in a semi-autonomous fashion, her husband can still take the money she makes as part of the business's profits.

The most common work done by wives, whether or not they also do highly specialized work, for their husbands is as general backup workers. They answer the phone and take messages, or keep certain people away from their husbands, filtering serious from trivial enquiries. They may deal with visitors, clients and sales reps, take in deliveries, run errands, and tidy and clean an office. As Finch says, such work is 'central to the daily performance of a man's work but [it is] routine and non-specialized'. A wife may do it regularly, even on a twenty-four-hour basis, or just occasionally (as in the case of the shop stewards' wives in Bristol who needed to do it only during a strike). In other words a wife is the much sought-after Girl Friday: consistent, reliable and on the spot, who helps constantly or when the work load is heavy or at times of crisis. Her work in many ways parallels that of a personal assistant – as has been noted by writers on secretarial employment.[2]

Such wifely work is especially likely if the husband works at home, full-time or part-time. This includes many professional men, for example, freelance journalists and insurance salesmen, as well as locksmiths and window cleaners. It is also likely if the husband is actively involved in local associations, such as a neighbourhood sports club or a choir or a voluntary organization.

Wives also perform what Finch calls 'peripheral activities' for their husbands: 'things which are not central to day-to-day demands on the husband but which help the smooth conduct of his work and his ultimate success' (Finch 1983: 88). This includes knowing his clients/constituents/informants/patients; and entertaining . . .

Most of these activities can be done even if the wife herself has paid employment, providing it is not too demanding. Both she (indirectly) and her husband and/or his employer (if he has one) unquestionably benefit from the work she does.

But wives' up-front' involvement depends not only on their husbands having an appropriate job or leisure activity, but also upon his wanting her to do it. . . .

Giving moral support

While giving direct support to a husband in his occupation and other activities can perhaps be seen as specific to certain men in certain occupations (though in fact it covers a very large number of men in a wide range of occupations and leisure pursuits), giving moral support and caring for his well-being is more widespread. All wives do this and it involves a lot of caring work. It is not just a case of feeling a general affection towards one's husband, but rather active 'relationship work': observing and moderating his emotions, arranging entertainment and relaxation, and supplying his personal needs.

A good wife enables her husband to talk intimately and confidentially. She is the person to whom he can unburden himself, who will share his anxieties and siphon off his discontents. She is the sounding board against which he can rehearse an argument or an important speech, who will 'reflect him at twice his natural size'. She will tell him not only how clever he is but justify his ambition by saying how important it is that he does well in his job and gets promotion and a higher salary because the family depends on him. A middle class husband may have a personal assistant or secretary who functions in some similar ways, but a wife is a peer in the way a secretary is not, and her loyalty and identity of interests is more guaranteed. It is certainly more guaranteed than that of a mere friend. 'Arthur Koestler's wife, who committed suicide with him when he was terminally ill, was described as his "lover, wife, nurse, housekeeper, cook, mother, daughter and inseparable companion"' (Mikes 1983).[3]

Since men frequently unwind best post-coitally, wives also have an important role as providers of trouble-free sex – which is why employers may encourage men to take their wives with them on jobs abroad. . . .

Wives 'make a house a home'. They manipulate the environment to make it comfortable, warm and undemanding. They do (should) not complain (for example, when a husband works late), or make a fuss (for example, when they have to move house), or engage in controversial activities which could embarrass their husband in the community. In other words, a wife should look after her husband's life so he is free to devote himself to living: to being an efficient worker or entre-preneur, and when he is not doing that, to enjoying his free time. This psychically stabilized, domestically serviced and economically motivated man is recognized as a reliable employee and sought by employers. But this aspect of a wife's work is probably even more important to the self-employed businessman, who may need to cope with heavy stress and financial burdens, and to the unemployed or retired man who needs to overcome depression and a loss of sense of self.

Much of wives' servicing is thus emotional work – as is also, of course, much of the women's paid employment. Women provide emotional care for others while controlling their own emotions. They defer to others and help establish and continue solidary bonds between groups of people. . . .

Micaela di Leonardo's work develops this in one specific area: women's main-taining of kin contact between households, which is an important part of our cultural expectation of satisfying family life.

> Maintaining these contacts, this sense of family, takes time, intention and skill . . . [it is] *work*; and, moreover, it is largely women's work. [It in-volves] the conception, maintenance, and ritual celebration of . . . ties, including visits, letters, telephone calls, presents, and cards to kin; the organization of holiday gatherings; the creation and maintenance of quasi-kin relations; decisions to neglect or to intensify particular ties; the mental reflection about all these activities; and the creation and communication of altering images of family and kin vis-à-vis the images of others.
>
> (Leonardo 1987: 442–3; stress in original)

If there is no adult woman in a household, such work is left undone, and single, widowed and divorced men say how much they miss it.

The creation of alternative images of family life is especially important, Leonardo argues, in ethnic minority cultures, such as the Italian American community in which her research as based. Women are charged with being the 'preservers of the culture' in this as in many other ethnic minority and religious groups. They have to observe the religion more orthodoxly and dress in more traditional clothes than men; they must be able and willing to cook traditional food and to keep festivals; they must generally behave modestly so as to maintain the family's honour; and must hold themselves and the children at a distance from the mainstream culture. . . .

Domestic labour

The comfortable environment provided for a husband by a good wife is based on her taking on most of the household tasks. He is thereby fit for his occupational work and leisure and able to give them his undivided attention. 'A "normal" day's work is that of a person who does not have to do his own domestic work' (Delphy 1976: 81).

Women's 'keeping the home fires burning' allows soldiers to wage wars, senior executives to work twelve hours a day and to fly off abroad at a day's notice, skilled manual workers to be called out to do overtime at short notice, (male) teachers to gain higher qualifications at evening and weekend courses, and trade union officials and local politicians to cope with emergency meetings. Wives' coverage of domestic work also, of course, enables husbands to devote themselves to leisure – it allows sportsmen to go away on rugby tours or to play golf on Sundays.

Women's coverage of domestic work also allows men to do nothing when they are unemployed or retire. French time-budgets in 1985 showed that in couples where both are employed, men did 2 hours 41 minutes of domestic work per day (twenty minutes more than in 1965) and wives 4 hours 38 minutes, but the difference actually increased when men were retired. Women at 65 do three hours' more domestic work a day than their husbands.[4]

The availability of utilities (running water, gas and electricity), domestic appliances (washing machines, vacuum cleaners, food processors) and industrially produced commodities (cook-chilled food, disposable nappies, ready-made easy-care clothes and spray furniture polishes) have not reduced the time spent on household work, although they have reduced some of the hard physical effort involved. Rather they have (1) enabled some tasks formerly contracted out to be taken back and done within the home (for example, laundry); (2) other tasks to be done to higher standards and more frequently (for example, cooking, cleaning, laundry and particularly child care); and (3) middle class housekeeping standards to be maintained despite the departure of servants. Almost all the increased purchasing, transporting and domestic management has fallen to wives. They have taken on not only most of the work formerly done by servants in middle class households, but also, in all households, work formerly done by other members of the household, including husbands.[5]

Time-budget studies show not only that the amount of time women spend on domestic work has not declined this century and that they still do twice as much each day as men in all Western and Eastern Bloc countries even when they have paid employment, but also that women do the more highly organized domestic work (for example, in the morning, from waking to 9.00 a.m., to get everyone off to work and school). When men spend time on housework, it does not involve the same kind of strain.[6]

The fact that husbands may now offer increased help in the home has thus very rarely affected their freedom to take any form of employment or to enjoy leisure outside the home. Men have a 'right' to time off, to some regular leisure time spent away from home and family each week; and they can also be absent from home for long periods, for days or weeks or even months to pursue a whole range of manual, managerial and professional occupations and/or a range of leisure activities.

But of course men do not necessarily have to be away from home for their wives to take charge of housework and child care. On the contrary, as Janet Finch stresses, women's domestic work enables men to work at home while being assured of protection from disturbance – and in fact such men usually do less domestic work and child care than those who work elsewhere . . . She argues that employers benefit from their (male) employees' wives' labour because they can assume that none of their workers has responsibility for the physical care of any dependants or needs to do much domestic work for themselves. But in fact it is men who are self-employed who most rely on their wives – who leave them to do the domestic work single-handedly. And it is not only men's occupational work at home which relies on women's domestic labour – so too does men's ability to spend undisturbed leisure time at home, whether playing with train sets in the attic or reading the paper in the sitting room, and their being able to find 'going out with the wife and kids' a pleasure.

When wives have servants, even part-time cleaners a few days a week, they may appear to do less domestic work, and they are certainly often reviled as lazy parasites when they rely on paid help with child care and housework (even if they are in full-time employment). But women are actually only given servants or au pairs when their work load simply cannot be carried by one person (for example, when they have several small children and no kin living near by) or when their husbands want their time to be shifted elsewhere. For instance, when their husbands prefer them to earn an extra (professional-level) income, and/or to undertake the extra work needed for a higher standard of living and more consumption: buying and maintaining more things (more houses, more rooms, more interior decorating, more suits of more elaborate clothes), more entertaining and more involvement in a particular cultural milieu. Husbands may want their wives to have time to organize frequent, elaborate kin reunions or weekends with friends in their country cottages. Or to do more good works for charity. Or to learn another foreign language, and to visit exhibitions and go to the opera and read the latest books so that they can talk confidently to guests. Or to be conspicuously leisured – showing off the men's wealth by demonstrating they do not need their wives to work and that they can afford for them to play bridge, or keep horses and go hunting, or to play tennis and ski, or to have beauty treatments and buy clothes, or to create an elaborate garden.

However, having servants in itself involves work for women. Servants have to be hired, trained and managed. (Management and training in industry are not usually seen as idleness!) They also require emotional work: helpers have to be listened to, praised, made to feel important, and to have their anxieties soothed, etc. This is especially true of au pairs, who are in many ways yet another member of the family whom the wife looks after, albeit they are family members who contribute labour.

In any case, most women do not have servants. Rather they are themselves, as J. K. Galbraith says (1973), 'crypto-servants'. . . .

Notes

1 We follow the categories developed by Finch to classify wives' work and to consider the ways in which husbands' jobs structure women's lives, but our analysis obviously takes us beyond her particular concerns.

2 These researchers have stressed the personal retainer nature of the relationship between private secretary and boss, and their accounts carry a tone of outrage that a secretary's job should require her to be personally attractive and to do things for her boss's personal life: 'half of their time is taken up with domestic tasks.' See Benet (1972: 74–5) and Vinnicombe (1980). What is equally note-worthy, however, is how much of the work which could legitimately be that of a secretary/PA is routinely done by wives.

3 While not wanting to get entangled in the specific arguments around the Koestler's case, we note the numbers of cases in which men actually do kill their wives before committing suicide (see Dobash and Dobash 1980: 15–17 and Cameron and Frazer 1987: 13 ff.).

4 In a sample from six cities in France (and from Pskov in the USSR) in 1966, employed wives were found to spend an average 5 hours 26 minutes (and 6 hours 55 minutes), and employed husbands 3 hours 19 minutes (and 3 hours 5 minutes) per day on household chores on their 'free' days. See Szalai (1972) and Cullen (1974). For the recent French figures see Grimler and Roy (1987).

5 See Bose (1979) and Game and Pringle (1984).

6 See Berk and Berk (1979).

References

Benet (1972) *Secretary: An Enquiry into a Female Ghetto*. London: Sidgwick & Jackson.

Berk, R. and Berk, S. F. (1979) *Labour and Leisure at Home*. London: Sage.

Bose, C. (1979) 'Technology and changes in the division of labor in the American home', *Women's Studies International Quarterly*, 2: 395–304.

Cameron, D. and Frazer, E. (1987) *The Lust to Kill*. Oxford: Polity.

Cullen (1974) 'A day in the life of . . .', *New Society*, 11 April, pp. 63–5.

Delphy (1976) 'Continuities and discontinuities in marriage and divorce', in D. Leonard Barker and S. Allen (eds) *Sexual Divisions and Society*. London: Tavistock.

Dobash, R. E. and Dobash, R. (1980) *Violence against Wives*. Wells: Open Books.

Finch, J. (1983) *Married to the Job*. London: Allen & Unwin.

Galbraith, J. K. (1973) 'The economics of the American housewife', *Atlantic Monthly*, August.

Game, A. and Pringle, R. (1984) *Gender at Work.* London: Pluto.

Grimler, G. and Roy, C. (1987) *Time Use in France in 1985–1986*, INSEE, Premiers resultants, no. 100, Version anglaise, October.

Leonardo, M. di (1987) 'The female world of cards and holidays: women, families and the work of kinship', *Signs*, 12 (3): 440–53.

Scase, R. and Goffee, R. (1980) *The Real World of the Small Business Owner.* London: Croom Helm.

Szalai, A. (1972) *The Use of Time: Daily Activities of Urban and Suburban Populations in Twelve Countries.* The Hague: Mouton.

Vinnicombe, S. (1980) *Secretaries, Management and Organization.* London: Heinemann.

Chapter 22

Cynthia Cockburn

RESISTING EQUAL OPPORTUNITIES
The issue of maternity

In her study of men's resistance to gender equality in employment, Cynthia Cockburn draws on empirical work in a variety of organisations: a retail chain ('High Street Retail') a civil service department ('the Service'), a local authority and a trade union. In this extract she focuses on this issue of motherhood, exploring how assumptions about maternity inform men's attitudes to women colleagues and employees and the assumptions behind the resentment they express about maternity rights.

From *In the Way of Women: Men's Resistance to Sex Equality in Organizations*, Basingstoke: Macmillan (1991).

W HEN MEN REPRESENT WOMEN as a problem in the workplace, whether as their employees, as professional colleagues or co-labourers, they invoke several criteria. . . . [W]omen's imputed temperament is sometimes hauled into question, particularly with regard to their handling of authority roles. . . . [W]omen's sexuality is always significant for men. Over and again, however, what is problematized is *women's relation to the domestic sphere*. The way women do or do not fit into the schema of paid employment and organizational life is seen primarily as a correlate of their marital status and, more important still, whether they do or do not have children. This is what women *are* to most men (and to most women): people who have domestic ties. Even if the woman in question is celibate or childless she is seen and represented as one of the maternal sex. Much of the argument surrounding Equal Opportunities at work circles about the question: can women *ever* be equal, given their different relation to reproduction?

Pregnancy, childbirth and child rearing are matters on which positive discrimination in favour of women is permitted without any thought that it may be 'unfair to men'. Indeed, to make provision for employed women to carry out these activities is not spoken of as positive discrimination at all. The state routinely provides for maternity benefit, and employers for their part are quite free to extend the amount of leave they offer to women at full or part pay and to ease women's return to work by adapting their hours or terms of engagement. Men of course do not get pregnant or give birth. They could, however, look after their children in their early months and years. Yet there is no *requirement* in the law to offer appropriate facilities to fathers to enable this. Nor do men complain that they are discriminated against on this score. It goes without saying that the practice whereby women as a sex raise the children, keep house and have less economic independence than their husbands is of far-reaching advantage to men as a sex. . . . [T]o sustain this form of family is at the very heart of men's sexual contract with each other.

Most organizations introducing sex equality policies include within their notion of positive action a number of measures designed to make it easier for women to combine paid work with child care and other domestic responsibilities. Where they differ, the relative length of the equality agenda, is in the generosity of the provisions for women, the range of women to whom they are offered and whether appropriate facilities (and positive encouragement to make use of them) are offered to men. . . .

Maternity provision in equality initiatives

Some of the disadvantage women experience at work on grounds of their domesticity is nothing more than prejudice. In assessing women for a job managers think to themselves 'She'll get married and leave,' 'with two children she'll never cope,' or 'Her husband would never let her move to Birmingham.' In both High Street Retail and the Service women were certain that male managers used to think this way before the advent of Equal Opportunity policies. Perhaps they still did. Some men freely admitted that they had once thought this way and that many other men had done so too. 'The first question a woman was always asked in any reporting interview was, if she was single, was she likely to get married; if she was married, when was she going to have children. Those questions were asked every time with no inhibitions whatsoever.' Women today, however, fortified by the equality policy, are fighting back. One, now at last a professional, told me how her reporting manager had said he was not considering her for professional training 'because you're married, you've got a home to run, shopping to do'. She, as it happened, was married to a Service man in the same grade as herself. She replied coolly to her superior, 'I imagine you will be asking those same questions to my husband when you interview him next week.'

This prejudice is often unfounded: in many cases a woman could give as much of her attention to a job as a man. For some women at some times of their lives, however, the truth is that the combining of child care, husband care and housework with a demanding paid job *is* very difficult indeed. A woman professional in the Service described how she had been simply unable to combine the training for the elite corps with the care of two young children. 'Unless you're really brilliant there's no way you can do it without a lot of study at home. That's a lot easier for a man than a woman. He comes home and he's got a wife who puts a meal in front of him, makes sure the children are in bed or kept quiet. If you're a woman you have to come home, stop off for the shopping, see to the children, cook the meal. Obviously you're going to be at a disadvantage. It's structured for men.'

This woman, perhaps most women, *will* put the family first if it comes to the crunch. A woman senior manager in High Street Retail had for some years been held back simply because she would not reassure her managing director that she would invariably put the company before her family:

> I'd always made it clear to him that I was not prepared to up sticks and go anywhere. On a temporary basis, yes, but not on a permanent basis. And the argument I always got from his was, 'Well, if I spoke to a man he'd say his career came first.' And I'd say . . . 'Well, I'm in different circumstances. I'll do a damn good job and I don't feel it's got any relevance whether I'm married or not.' And he always said he's never promote me. But in the end he did.

It is not only the job that is forced to cede to the demands of family in women's lives. Women are often impeded from playing a full part in the trade union. One of my case studies was of a public sector union, three-quarters of whose members were women. They were mainly low-paid manual workers, many of whom worked part-time and whose hours, both at work and at home, were crammed with intensive work. Like some employers, the Union had recently developed an equality policy and a Positive Action strategy for its women members. They had taken steps to improve women's representation in the decision-making structures of the Union, to adapt bargaining priorities and campaign more actively on women's issues.

The shop stewards and branch secretaries who ran the Union at local level were predominantly men. The Women's Committee, a product of the equality measures, had consequently been preoccupied with the question how to increase women members' participation. Union activism may mean a couple of nights a week out, attendance at an occasional weekend educational conference. If a woman has children it means her partner or someone else staying in to mind them. But it also means a woman having a life of her own, 'getting political'. Perhaps even more than taking a job, getting involved in a trade union or other forms of activism signifies entering the public sphere, flouting the sexual contract that reserves public life for the brothers and confines women to domesticity.

Quite apart from the considerable resistance such women meet from men within the union, therefore, they face another impediment in the shape of that 'other man', the husband or partner in the home. A male branch secretary told me, 'A lot of women would be put in a very difficult situation with their husbands at home by wanting to take on the sort of responsibility I carry. . . . I've got to be blunt about this. Some of the women shop stewards in our branch are only allowed a certain amount of time to attend meetings, to be active, by their husbands.' Husbands resent a wife escaping their domain. 'She'll not start that fucking lark. In and out to the clothes line's enough for her,' I was told was one husband's view of the matter.

A man has to tolerate not only his wife's absence but also the intrusion of union business into the home. The phone rings a lot – and it's for *her*. A woman can only succeed in sustaining her activism, I was told, if she succeeds in 'taking *him* along'. Yet 'to have support from their partners for what they do is the exception, rather than the rule'.

The two sets of men – union men and husbands of union women – sometimes act in harmony to sustain patriarchal order, male sex right. One male full-time officer felt it behoved the union to take care not to step on the toes of husbands. 'If you're going to promote women in the organization and if those women have family commitments, you've got to be very careful to ensure she has the support of her family and partner . . . I've perhaps got a rooted sexism myself [he admitted]. If my partner did my job, I'd resent that, I couldn't handle that at home.' 'It'd make you feel put down?' I asked him. 'Absolutely. Absolutely.'

Husbands and partners may impede women becoming active in the union by making it clear they resent their engagement in union life. But they also simply make it impossible by failing to take their share of housework and child care. The Women's Officer and Women's Committee of this union were pressing branches to organize meetings in working hours so that women could more easily attend, to choose convenient and appropriate venues, to offer child care expenses. But of the branches, mainly male-led, few were committed to such positive steps. The Union also, like other unions today with large women memberships and some women activists, was pressing employers to develop equality policies geared to the needs of working women with dependent children (or adults).

High Street Retail and the Service had both improved on statutory maternity provision as part of the equality package. It was the Local Authority however, my fourth case study, that had gone furthest in this respect. This Local Authority is a London borough, well known during the period 1982–87 for its left-wing Labour approach to local politics. Its generous new provision for mothers, taken with other aspects of its positive measures for women, probably put it among the most progressive of British employers in 1989. The policy began with a Code of Safe Working during Pregnancy. The guiding principle was that women who wish and are able to continue working throughout pregnancy be enabled to do so without danger. Advice was available. A woman who did not wish to continue operating a visual display unit for fear of radiation hazard might be transferred to other work. Of course the mandatory provision for time off without loss of pay to enable attendance at antenatal and relaxation classes was taken for granted.

Maternity leave might start, as in the statutory regulations prevailing in 1988, eleven weeks before expected confinement date. The Local Authority differed from the official norm, however, in waiving the two-year qualifying period for eligibility for maternity benefits. All that was necessary was for the woman in question to be a permanent (not casual) employee of the council before the expected week of confinement. . . . Both the length of leave and the level of pay were a considerable improvement on the statutory provision. The first sixteen weeks of absence were paid at full normal salary, deducting the amount received in statutory maternity allowance. Following this, twenty-four weeks' more leave were available to be taken, at the woman's choice, either in their entirety at half-pay, or the first twelve weeks fully paid, the second without pay. The mother might thus remain away from work for a total of forty weeks. Similar provisions applied to parents adopting a child.

The council also provided *paternity* leave of ten days at the birth of a child. This, however, was termed 'nominated carer leave', to reflect a mother's right to choose a relative or friend as substitute for the father. Besides, all employees, regardless of length of service, were entitled to special paid leave for the care of dependants who might be sick, or whose normal care arrangements had broken down. Up to ten working days could be taken in any one period of absence, to a maximum of fifty working days a year. Further extensions were allowable on manager's discretion.

On return from maternity leave the mother had the right to come back to her own or a very similar job on terms and conditions no less favourable than before. She might, however, request to return as a part-timer, or to turn her job into a shared post. Indeed, quite independently of maternity rules, an employee of the council could at any time request to convert from full-time to part-time working, or to turn her or his job into a job-share. There was no job in the council that was ruled out as a possibility for job-sharing, including that of chief executive. Part-time employees of this Local Authority, so long as they worked sixteen or more hours a week, lost none of a fulltimer's rights and benefits. . . .

The women I talked with in the Local Authority appreciated the maternity provision perhaps more than any other aspect of the EO policy. Having more senior women officers visibly pregnant or with young children was encouragement to juniors thinking of combining work with babies. One said, 'The personnel officer who's advising me about my maternity leave is also a pregnant woman who is in the same position as me. That's one of the kinds of things that's kept me in this local authority.'

. . . A problem recognized by women was that of finding temporary cover for the absent woman at a time of critical staff shortages. In these circumstances even women managers admitted they were finding maternity leave difficult to handle.

Things have got so bad from a staff morale point of view, people feel so strained and stressed that they aren't in a position, or able, or want to take on someone else's job [as well as their own], or even a part of it.

. . . However, the characteristic woman manager's point of view was summed up as follows:

I suppose you're involved creatively making Equal Opportunities work. It gives you the extra administrative problem of interviewing and so on, but I don't view it as a problem but as their right. You just get on with it, ad far as I'm concerned. And if people are negative about it, you put them down for it.

Equality policy had certainly strengthened women's arm here.

Accommodating motherhood

The issue of maternity provision highlights a tension between men at the top of the hierarchy, particularly those senior personnel managers with responsibility for labour market strategies and human resource management, and men, particularly line managers, down the line. The former, with the organization's overall competitiveness in mind – and when we are talking of competitiveness in labour markets this applies as much to public sector as private sector employers – are identifying the special value of domestically defined women employees and adapting personnel policy to make better use of them. The hapless line managers have to deal with the contradictions. For them, all this increased maternity provision that arrives in the name of equality of opportunity for women is a bit like a blow to the funny bone, leaving them midway between pain and mirth. On the one hand it is a severe nuisance. It makes practical difficulties for managers, increases the proportion of women in the labour force and brings an unwelcome domestic odour, a whiff of kitchen and nursery, into the workplace. On the other the more women are permitted various kinds of flexibility in relation to work to enable them to cope with motherhood and other domestic responsibilities the more they can be dismissed as 'different', less serious than male employees.

In the Local Authority there were many male managers who were 'fed up to the back teeth' with the continual absences of women for 'one thing or another'. Now it's the clinic, now the baby's due, now here youngest has the measles. One chief officer made it clear he felt he had adapted nobly to all this coming and going as far as his clerical and administrative staff were concerned. Now that women of childbearing propensity, supported by the equality policy, were entering his *professional* team and they too were needing 'cover' for months at a time, that was altogether too much and he felt aggrieved.

Annoyance with the managerial implications of maternity leave and related provisions such as special leave, part-timing and job sharing, seems to be widespread. In High Street Retail too, men were embittered by the disturbance caused, for example, to the orderly ways of the buying department. One manager said he would frankly prefer pregnant women to leave and not return. Others felt confused. Yes, of course 'the girls' ought to be allowed back, provided they gave adequate warning and kept their word on the matter. But how could the department manage in the meantime? You train up a temp and no sooner has she learned the job than the original employee returns. One young man, new to employment and its laws, was simply astonished at the extent of the adaptation called for in a company to meet the needs of pregnant women To him employees had just been undifferentiated people. He had never imagined the *physical* reality of women employees.

In the Service, too, many managers felt maternity leave and flexibility were 'too generous' today, had 'gone far enough', and managers were being 'hemmed in'. Service rates of pay, held down by government policy, were falling behind the private sector. Top managers knew they needed to compete with the private sector for women recruits. 'We're losing them to industry,' they complained. They had to use the only incentive available to them, better terms and conditions. Maternity leave, for instance. Pregnant women, said one personnel manager in a

startling metaphor, 'they've got us over a barrel'. Because provision in local authorities and government departments therefore tended to be more generous than in
companies, 'there is, I regret to say, a tendency for the public service to carry
the can in circumstances of conflict between domestic and work obligations'. If
one spouse worked for a private company, the other for a public service, 'the
chances are it's the public sector that takes the cat to the vet. That's the way it
is. And it's wrong.'

The irritation noticeable in all three sites had been exacerbated by a tendency
for maternity leave to be exploited as an occasion for reducing staff levels, simply
by failing to provide cover for the absent woman. So managers felt the problem
with maternity leave was 'the financial tag attached. How the bloody hell do we
do the job without a replacement?' And colleagues complained 'those who are
constantly here have to bear the burden for those that aren't. Top men are called
on to impose the new flexibilities on middle managers below them. It is the latter
who pay the price in inconvenience and whose complaints ring loudest. A particular source of scandal is women who 'con us' by saying they will come back and
then fail to reappear. They 'hold us to ransom while they are away'. There is a
deep-rooted feeling among many men at all levels that pregnant women and new
mothers are 'cheating', 'taking us for a ride' or generally 'messing the organization around'. Yet sick leave, which is more frequent and less predictable than
maternity leave (Daniel 1980) does not incur the same blame.

Underlying some of the resentment against the maternity provisions is a widespread view that mothers of young children morally ought to stay at home with
them, should not attempt to 'have their cake and eat it too'. 'If you want to have
babies, go and have babies. If you want to work, work.' Several men in the Service,
for instance, had wives who, they were happy to say, had 'chosen their priorities', had dedicated themselves to their families because 'they felt it was important'.
'I find it a bit surprising,' one such man remarked, 'the rather *detached* attitude
some ladies have to farming children out.' Having made the housewife/bread-
winner decision for themselves and sacrificed that second salary, some resented
the better standard of living of some of their colleagues whose wives had remained
in employment.

Men are experiencing disturbance in two spheres simultaneously, provoked by
changes in women's economic and domestic behaviour. As Carole Pateman put it,
'paid employment for wives threatens both the husband's right of command over
the use of their services and the fraternal order of the workplace itself' (Pateman
1988: 139). First, men's wives, mothers of their children, are leaving the home
in increasing numbers for at least part of their day. This is making women, in
men's eyes, more uppity, less ready to accept a husband's authority. We have seen
that a woman who gets involved with the union may be even more troubling. One
who had become a shop steward found 'I can talk to anyone now. It gives me a
wee bit of power.' Being involved outside the home reduces the priority a woman
places on domestic responsibilities. One woman shop steward I interviewed looked
at her watch as it approached 5.00 p.m. and observed,

> If I hadn't been in the union now I'd have been thinking. I'd better
> get home to put the dinner in the oven. Now I'll say I've got other

things to do. You'll have to wait for your dinner. I think my husband's changed too, because I'm in the union. He can't say things as heavy as he used to. He knows I've a mind of my own now. I'd have been just . . . having dinner ready for a certain time and having his shirts done and that. Now I couldn't give a hoot. I do something then I want to do it. I'm not neglecting them [she added], they're just getting something different.

Secondly, at middle levels women are a growing source of competition for men in the workplace. In some cases they spoil the fraternal relations of a formerly all-male work group. They come in trailing evidence of domesticity, for not all women will or can pretend they do not have to hunk plastic bags full of vegetables back from their lunch-hour shopping, lie down for half an hour because of menstrual pain or phone the school about a child's truancy. A top woman manager at High Street Retail reported a curious exchange with a senior male colleague who had been staring at her during meetings, behaving in a way she found unsettling. Eventually she asked him, 'What's the matter?' He said, 'I'm sorry, but I can't help it. Every-time I look at you I see *my wife*.' She answered curtly, 'That's your problem.' But she commented to me on men's confusion in their experience of women in two worlds. 'Men do have difficulty in seeing a woman as anything other than a secretary, a sex object or a wife.'

Men are angry with women who try to be both mothers and employees. They are, however, used to reckoning on women being less of a threat to male career chances because they are held back by pregnancy and child care. They therefore *also* feel angry with women who cheat by remaining single or childless. A male professional in the Service said bitterly, 'To get on in this place you need to have had a divorce and a hysterectomy.' He was referring directly to a woman who had experienced both things and been promoted over him.

If dealing with the interaction of work and motherhood is a source of stress between male managers, it is also a source of division among women. There is some mutual resentment between women who combine care of children with paid work and those who do not. . . .

Ambitious women without children, some of whom are unmarried besides, know full well that having all these 'mother's privileges' serves to confirm men's belief that women as a sex are unreliable employees who have their mind half the time on domestic matters. Though part-timing, job sharing and career-break schemes are now sometimes available to women to help them through the child-rearing years, they know full well that this route is a succession of career impediments. In the Service, for instance, women told me one would be ill advised to go part-time if serious about a career above the clerical grades. The career-break or returner scheme being introduced by all three of these organizations is a particular example of this ambiguity. To many women and men it was a welcome scheme precisely because it enabled women to fulfil their motherly duties by staying with their children for four or five years. For that very reason it was, of all the maternity provisions, the least controversial among men. Yet there were few who really believed that five years away from work would not put paid to their promotion chances. A double standard is clear when men praise the career-break scheme as enabling the progress of women while saying that *men* could not afford to make use of it because to do so would 'damage their careers'.

Domesticating men

As things are, maternity and domesticity are undeniably a hazard dashing women's hopes of equal chances in the hierarchy. Only a few women will slip through the rapids, those who trim their shape by avoiding encumbrances, real or apparent. For the more typical woman, life must involve juggling both domestic and employment responsibilities. . . .

. . . When a woman, a child on either arm, attempts to claim as hers a citizen's place in the public sphere, aspires to be a party to the social contract, she finds her entry ticket is unrecognized. When put to the test, the social contract reveals itself as an understanding between men from which women are excluded. Indeed, it is precisely a compact underpinned by male sex right. it is a silent accord between men to grant each other equal status and independence defined precisely as the rendering of women dependent. Until the symbolic man-as-citizen has his mind on the cooker, his eye on a toddler and a hand on Grandad's wheelchair, no constitution will guarantee social equality.

For women to escape subordination to men the relationship of home to work has to change beyond anything yet envisaged in the name of equality policy. Men have to be domesticated and in the workplace (to use Joan Acker's phrase) the rhythm and timing of work must be adapted to the rhythms of life outside (Acker 1987: 27). For women, getting into the workplace, becoming workers, earning their own money, has proved a necessary but insufficient step towards liberation. A further necessary condition is for men to move the other way, yet into the home, start nurturing, become domestics. For *that* to happen their relationship to work and career has to change. Like women, they must begin to see employment as something you pick up and put down, contingent on the needs of other human beings. There is no room in this scenario for fetishized masculine careers. A requisite of course is that employing organizations make available to fathers too these flexibilities that some are just now offering to mothers. More, however, they have to direct their personnel policies towards the expectation that men will really use them.

I asked men in all three employing organizations whether they would value the extension to men of some of the provisions mainly intended for women. For instance, would they want a week or more of paternity leave at the time of birth or adoption of a child? . . . Secondly, would men value the right to share in the longer maternity leave – to make it truly *parental* leave? . . . Third, I wanted to know whether men would consider using the proposed career-break or returner scheme to enable them to be away from work for longer periods with reinstatement rights. . . .

Most of the men I spoke with, like most men today perhaps, [would] welcome a week or ten days' childbirth leave for fathers. Some, it has to be said, felt 'any excuse for extra days off can't be bad'. Others felt they had done it out of their annual holiday entitlement – so should the rest. The question of sharing in the longer maternity leave was swiftly dismissed by almost all men. The arguments were mainly essentialist: women are the 'natural' child rearers. 'It's biological, it's women's role.' The mother is the 'one the child naturally turns to', 'the paternal link is not so close'. The father's role was to 'assist in all the little jobs when he's around'. As to the career-break scheme, these men showed less enthusiasm still. Except, it must be said, that one or two supposed the provision, if it was to apply equally to men and women, as in all these organizations was the case, should mean a man could take a sabbatical now and then to visit Australia or write a novel.

Some men simply acknowledged that they would not wish to play a more domestic role. They frankly preferred their work, not only for the economic independence it gave them but for the sense of having a place in society, belonging to a men's club. Interruptions to a career 'would have spoilt it'. One said he would never have considered it because of the loss of continuity in his reporting record. You built up a reputation with a reporting officer. They kept looking back at your reports. 'If you get out of that and let someone else go past, you've lost the momentum – and momentum is everything.' The whole idea of such an added career handicap was perverse. 'You are pulling back the man to have the same problems as a woman', said one man in disbelief.

. . . Do senior managers and personnel managers who administer these new rules for their part really intend men to behave like women? I found no evidence of it. A senior man in the Service elite gave a not untypical answer.

> Oh dear me [he sighed]. I haven't really addressed my mind to this at all. And I confess to having a prejudice against it. [His irritation increased as he chewed the matter over.] I can see the case for giving a few days' leave at the time of birth. That would be humane and desirable, and it wouldn't cost much. If you go beyond that – I admit it's irrational, it's prejudice – but I like to see men who give *proper* priority to their job . . . *doing* the job for forty-six weeks in the year with six weeks' leave. A half-hearted commitment whereby he's here part of the time and fulfilling a domestic function the rest doesn't seem to me to show an ideal attitude towards the job on the part of a male employee. But there we are. I accept that's improper, irrational and prejudiced. . . .

Public and private: sources of separation

. . . There is no evidence of men's attachment to paid work modifying in response to married women's entry into paid jobs. Indeed, men in the UK work longer hours in their paid employment (an average of 43.5 per week) than men in any other EEC country, and their commitment of time to paid work actually increased by forty minutes per week between 1984 and 1986 (Central Statistical Office 1990). The sexual division of roles, with men making the economic input, women giving the labour time, intensifies with parenthood. Peter Moss finds that the longest hours are worked by men with young families. They need to compensate by overtime for the loss of their partner's earnings. Married men under thirty with children work four times as much paid overtime as similarly aged but childless husbands. Even among the relatively few men who are single parents, 86 per cent work and most full-time. Their average weekly stint of forty-one hours is only one hour less than that of fathers in married couples (Moss 1980: 48). Later British studies confirm such findings (Sharpe 1984; Martin and Roberts 1984). Nor does being unemployed appear to drive men to the kitchen sink (McKee and Bell 1985).

Political context seems to make little difference to the likelihood of men becoming more domesticated. In social democratic Sweden only one in five fathers uses parental leave and those who do on average take only forty-one days to care for their baby (Svenska Institutet 1987). This is in spite of the fact that a proportion of the leave is forfeit if the father does not take it. In Norway men reduced their paid work time by five hours a week – but increased their household work by only twelve minutes per day. The rest became increased leisure time (Lingsom and Ellingsaeter 1983). . . .

. . . [M]en continue, with verve but scant imagination, to assert their right, legitimated by appeal to nature and to history, to a woman who will attend both to their own domestic needs and the rearing of their children. They continue to express themselves as uneasy with the emergence of those women from the private realm into the economic and political world of men. They play their lives as the deft administration of the sexual contract, maintaining the proper gender relationship of its domestic clause on the one hand, its workplace clause on the other. They dedicate their creativeness to the public sphere, to production, politics, governance.

Many men feel a sadness and an anxiety over their alienation from women and domestic concerns. They regret their dependence on women to bear their children and link them to reproduction, to the species. They suffer from the increased independence of women and the growing volatility of marriage, which often removes their children from them. Increasingly too men are recognizing the costs they pay, tied to the rat race to earn their breadwinner wage. Yet the gap between themselves and women is not easily closed. If they are to come closer, really share our lives, contribute their own labour of love (as opposed to their money) to child rearing, to the care of the ill and elderly, to the sustenance of life, men will have to renounce their male sex right and with it their masculine identity as it is currently constituted. Some men know this. A few are willing to do it, but individual voluntarism is not enough. More and more will be forced to think about it. The dilemma for men is intensifying as women – with advances in contraceptive technology, access to a salary, backed by this pervasive ideology of 'equality' and with feminist ideas always within reach – become new people.

Meanwhile, however, 'mothers' privileges' are highly contradictory for women. It is not surprising that any opposition to them from men is muted. They are beneficial in bridging the gap between work and home. But they benefit only some women and for a relatively short span of their working lives. If they are not extended to men and used by men, so that men too come to lead more 'womanly' lives, increased support for women's domestic role could drive women even more firmly into a distinct, domestically defined, place in the labour market. What in the long run has to change is the pattern of men's lives. A forty-five-hour week, a forty-eight-week year and a fifty-year wage-earning life cannot be sustained by both sexes. It should be worked by neither.

References

Acker, J. (1987) 'Hierarchies, Jobs and Bodies: An Outline for a Theory of Gendered Organisations', paper presented to the annual meeting of the American Sociological Association, Chicago, August.

Central Statistical Office (1990) *Social Trends* No 20. London: HMSO.

Daniel, W. W. (1980) *Maternity Rights: The Experience of Women*. London: Policy Studies Institute.

Lingsom, S. and Ellingsaeter, A. L. (1983) *Arbeid, fritid og samvaer*. Oslo: Central Bureau of Statistics SA 49.

Martins, J. and Roberts, C. (1984) *Women and Employment: A Lifetime Perspective*. London: Department of Employment and OPCS.

McKee, L. and Bell, C. (1986) 'His unemployment, her problem: the domestic and marital consequences of male unemployment', in S. Allen, K. Purcell, S. Wood and A. Watton (eds) *The Experience of Unemployment*. London: Macmillan.

Moss, P. (1980) 'Parents and work', in P. Moss and N. Fonda (eds) *Work and the Family*. London: Temple Smith.

Patemen, C. (1988) *The Sexual Contract*. Cambridge: Polity Press.

Sharpe, Sue (1984) *Double Identity: The Lives of Working Mothers*. Harmondsworth: Penguin.

Svenska Institutet (1987) Fact Sheet on Sweden. Stockholm: Svenska Institutet.

Chapter 23

Arlie Hochschild

EMOTIONAL LABOUR

Work is usually thought of as physical or mental labour. Arlie Hochschild coined the term 'emotional labour' to describe a process entailed in particular forms of caring work often, but not exclusively, associated with traditionally female occupations. The original formulation of the concept occurred in the context of a study of airline cabin crews. Here, and in similar occupations, workers must manage their own emotions in order to create a particular ambience for the clients or customers. In this extract Hochschild explains what is entailed in emotional labour.

From *The Managed Heart*, Berkeley CA and Los Angeles: University of California Press (1983).

IN A SECTION IN *Das Kapital* entitled 'The Working Day', Karl Marx examines depositions submitted in 1863 to the Children's Employment Commission in England. One deposition was given by the mother of a child laborer in a wallpaper factory: 'When he was seven years old I used to carry him [to work] on my back to and fro through the snow, and he used to work sixteen hours a day. . . . I have often knelt down to feed him, as he stood by the machine, for he could not leave it or stop.' Fed meals as he worked, as a steam engine is fed coal and water, this child was 'an instrument of labor.'[1] Marx questioned how many hours a day it was fair to use a human being as an instrument, and how much pay for being an instrument was fair, considering the profits that factory owners made. But he was also concerned with something he thought more fundamental: the human cost of becoming an 'instrument of labor' at all.

On another continent 117 years later, a twenty-year-old flight attendant trainee sat with 122 others listening to a pilot speak in the auditorium of the Delta Airlines Stewardess Training Center. Even by modern American standards, and certainly by standards for women's work, she had landed an excellent job. The 1980 pay scale began at $850 a month for the first six months and would increase within seven years to about $20,000 a year. Health and accident insurance is provided, and the hours are good.[2]

The young trainee sitting next to me wrote on her notepad, 'Important to smile. Don't forget smile.' The admonition came from the speaker in the front of the room, a crew-cut pilot in his early fifties, speaking in a southern drawl: 'Now, girls, I want you to go out there and really *smile*. Your smile is your biggest *asset*. I want you to go out there and use it. Smile. *Really* smile. Really *lay it on*.'

The pilot spoke of the smile as the *flight attendant's* asset. But as novices like the one next to me move through training, the value of a personal smile is groomed to reflect the company's disposition – its confidence that its planes will not crash, its reassurance that departures and arrivals will be on time, its welcome and its invitation to return. Trainers take it as their job to attach to the trainee's smile an attitude, a viewpoint, a rhythm of feeling that is, as they often say, 'professional'. This deeper extension of the professional smile is not always easy to retract at the end of the workday, as one worker in her first year at World Airways noted: 'Sometimes I come off a long trip in state of utter exhaustion, but I find I can't relax. I giggle a lot, I chatter, I call friends. It's as if I can't release myself from an artificially created elation that kept me "up" on the trip. I hope to be able to come down from it better as I get better at the job.'

As the PSA jingle says, 'Our smiles are not just painted on.' Our flight atttendants' smiles, the company emphasizes, will be more human than the phony smiles you're resigned to seeing on people who are paid to smile. There is a smile-like strip of paint on the nose of each PSA plane. Indeed, the plane and the flight attendant advertise each other. The radio advertisement goes on to promise not just smiles and service but a travel experience of real happiness and calm. Seen in one way, this is no more than delivering a service. Seen in another, it estranges workers from their own smiles and convinces customers that on-the-job behavior is calculated. Now that advertisements, training, notions of professionalism, and dollar bills have intervened between the smiler and the smiled upon, it takes an extra effort to imagine that spontaneous warmth can exist in uniform – because companies now advertise spontaneous warmth, too.

As first glance, it might seem that the circumstances of the nineteenth-century factory child and the twentieth-century flight attendant could not be more different. To the boy's mother, to Marx, to the members of the Children's Employment Commission, perhaps to the manager of the wallpaper factory, and almost certainly to the contemporary reader, the boy was a victim, even a symbol, of the brutalizing conditions of his time. We might imagine that he had an emotional half-life, conscious of little more than fatigue, hunger, and boredom. On the other hand, the flight attendant enjoys the upper-class freedom to travel, and she participates in the glamour she creates for others. She is the envy of clerks in duller, less well paid jobs.

But a close examination of the differences between the two can lead us to some unexpected common ground. On the surface there is a difference in how we know what labor actually produces. How could the worker in the wallpaper factory tell when his job was done? Count the rolls of wallpaper; a good has been produced. How can the flight attendant tell when her job is done? A service has been produced; the customer seems content. In the case of the flight attendant, the *emotional style of offering the service is part of the service itself*, in a way that loving or hating wallpaper is not a part of producing wallpaper. Seeming to 'love the job' becomes part of the job; and actually trying to love it, and to enjoy the customers, helps the worker in this effort. . . .

The work done by the boy in the wallpaper factory called for a co-ordination of mind and arm, mind and finger, and mind and shoulder. We refer to it simply as physical labor. The flight attendant does physical labor when she pushes heavy meal carts through the aisles, and she does mental work when she prepares for and actually organizes emergency landings and evacuations. But in the course of doing this physical and mental labor, she is also doing something more, something I define as *emotional labor*.[3] This labor requires one to induce or suppress feeling in order to sustain the outward countenance that produces the proper state of mind in others – in this case, the sense of being cared for in a convivial and safe place. This kind of labor calls for a co-ordination of mind and feeling, and it some-times draws on a source of self that we honor as deep and integral to our individuality.

Beneath the difference between physical and emotional labor there lies a simi-larity in the possible cost of doing the work: the worker can become estranged or alienated from an aspect of self – either the body or the margins of the soul – that is *used* to do the work. The factory boy's arm functioned like a piece of machinery used to produce wallpaper. His employer, regarding that arm as an instrument, claimed control over its speed and motions. In this situation, what was the relation between the boy's arm and his mind? Was his arm in any mean-ingful sense his *own*?[4]

This is an old issue, but as the comparison with airline attendants suggests, it is still very much alive. If we can become alienated from goods in a goods-producing society, we can become alienated from service in a service-producing society. . . .

When she came off the job, what relation had the flight attendant to the 'arti-ficial elation' she had induced on the job? In what sense was it her *own* elation on the job? The company lays claim not simply to her physical motions – how she handles food trays – but to her emotional actions and the way they show in the ease of a smile. The workers I talked to often spoke of their smiles as being *on* them but not *of* them. They were seen as an extension of the make-up, the uniform, the recorded music, the soothing pastel colors of the airplane décor, and the daytime drinks, which taken together orchestrate the mood of the passengers. The final commodity is not a certain number of smiles to be counted like rolls of wall-paper. For the flight attendant, the smiles are a *part of her work*, a part that requires her to co-ordinate self and feeling so that the work seems to be effortless. To show that the enjoyment takes effort is to do the job poorly. Similarly, part of the job is to disguise fatigue and irritation, for otherwise the labor would show in an unseemly way, and the product – passenger contentment – would be damaged.[5] Because it is easier to disguise fatigue and irritation if they can be banished alto-gether, at least for brief periods, this feat calls for emotional labor.

The reason for comparing these dissimilar jobs is that the modern assembly-line worker has for some time been an outmoded symbol of modern industrial labor; fewer than 6 per cent of workers now work on assembly lines. Another kind of labor has now come into symbolic prominence – the voice-to-voice or face-to-face delivery of service – and the flight attendant is an appropriate model for it. There have always been public-service jobs, of course; what is new is that they are now socially engineered and thoroughly organized from the top. Though the flight attendant's job is no worse and in many ways better than other service jobs, it makes the worker more vulnerable to the social engineering of her emotional labor and reduces her control over that labor. Her problems, therefore, may be a sign of what is to come in other such jobs.

Emotional labor is potentially good. No customer wants to deal with a surly waitress, a crabby bank clerk, or a flight attendant who avoids eye contact in order to avoid getting a request. Lapses in courtesy by those paid to be courteous are very real and fairly common. What they show us is how fragile public civility really is. We are brought back to the question of what the social carpet actually consists of and what it requires of those who are supposed to keep it beautiful. The laggards and sluff-offs of emotional labor? What do we do when we manage emotion? What, in fact, is emotion? What are the costs and benefits of managing emotion, in private life and at work? . . .

. . . The secretary who creates a cheerful office that announces her company as 'friendly and dependable' and her boss as 'up-and-coming', the waitress or waiter who creates an 'atmosphere of pleasant dining', the tour guide or hotel receptionist who makes us feel welcome, the social worker whose look of solicitous concern makes the client feel cared for the salesman who creates the sense of a 'hot commodity', the bill collector who inspires fear, the funeral parlor director who makes the bereaved feel understood, the minister who creates a sense of protective outreach but evenhanded warmth – all of them must confront in some way or another the requirements of *emotional labor*.

Emotional labor does not observe conventional distinctions between types of jobs. By my estimate, roughly one-third of American workers today have jobs that subject them to substantial demands for emotional labor. Moreover, of all *women* working, roughly one-half have jobs that call for emotional labor. . . . Thus this inquiry has special relevance for women, and it probably also describes more of their experience. As traditionally more accomplished managers of feeling in private life, women more than men have put emotional labor on the market, and they know more about its personal costs. . . .

Notes

1   Marx, *Capital* (1977), pp. 356–7, 358.
2   For stylistic convenience, I shall use the pronoun 'she' when referring to a flight attendant, except when a specific male flight attendant is being discussed. Otherwise I shall try to avoid verbally excluding either gender.
3   I use the term *emotional labor* to mean the management of feeling to create a publicly observable facial and bodily display; emotional labor is sold for a wage and therefore has *exchange value*. I use the synonymous terms *emotion work* or *emotion management* to refer to these same acts done in a private context where they have *use value*.

4   Marx, in his *Economic and Philosophic Manuscripts* (Tucker 1972), may have provided the last really basic idea on alienation. Among recent useful works on the subject are Blaunder (1964), Etzioni (1968), Kohn 1976) and Seeman (1967).

5   Like a commodity, service that calls for emotional labor is subject to the laws of supply and demand. Recently the demand for this labor has increased and the supply of it drastically decreased. The airline industry speed-up since the 1970s has been followed by a worker slowdown. The slowdown reveals how much emotional labor the job required all along. It suggests what costs even happy workers under normal conditions pay for this labor without a name. The speed-up has sharpened the ambivalence many workers feel about how much of oneself to give over to the role and how much of oneself to protect from it.

References

Blauner, Robert (1964) *Alienation and Freedom*. Chicago: University of Chicago Press.

Etzioni, Amitai (1968) 'Basic human needs, alienation and inauthenticity' *American Sociological Review* 33: 870–85.

Kohn, Melvin (1976) 'Occupational structure and alienation', *American Journal of Sociology* 82: 111–30.

Marx, Karl (1977) *Capital* I, trans. Ben Fowkes. New York: Vintage.

Seeman, Melvin (1967) 'On the personal consequences of alienation in work', *American Sociological Review* 32: 273–85.

Tucker, Robert (1972) *The Marx–Engels Reader*. New York: Norton.

Chapter 24

Lisa Adkins

SEXUAL SERVICING AND
THE LABOUR MARKET

In an empirical study of gendered work in a hotel and a leisure park, Lisa Adkins considers how women's labour is routinely sexualised in the tourist industry. The persistent sexualisation of women's labour — the use of women as display, the particularities of dress codes, the expectation that coping with sexual harassment from customers was 'part of the job' — was far from incidental. This 'heterosexualisation' was coded into the gendered division of labour: it was a covert aspect of the 'person specification' for particular jobs and the everyday practices of recruitment and work discipline. She is thus able to argue that sexuality may play a much larger part in the structuring of gendered labour markets than is usually assumed.

From *Gendered Work: Sexuality, Family and the Labour Market*, Buckingham: Open University Press (1995).

. . .

M Y WORK ON TOURISM looked at the gendered structure and the dynamics of work in two tourist organizations — a hotel and a leisure park — in order to explore the relationship between sexuality and the gendered organization of employment relations.[1] The fieldwork itself took place over a six-month period, from April to September 1989. Numerous visits to the two establishments were made and my activities ranged from watching and listening, to carrying out a series of in-depth interviews and attending staff training sessions. I also collected a range of documentary evidence from personnel records and various in-house and company-wide publications. The interviewees included general managers of the establishments, various departmental managers (sometimes up to three or four interviews with just one individual) and women and men workers. In addition, a series of interviews were held with various representatives from the parent companies of both the leisure park and the hotel. . . .

The sexualization of women by men co-workers

. . . [W]ithin the catering department at Fun Land the catering manager devoted a lot of time to ensuring her catering assistants maintained the 'right' appearance. The 1989 season was a 'very good one' in that the majority of the women catering assistants 'had very high [appearance] standards'. But although 1989 was a 'good' year from women workers, it was no different from previous years for the catering manager as regards the 'disgusting behaviour' of the men operatives. During their breaks, the men operatives used the restaurant facilities at Fun Land, and at such times the women catering assistants and the catering manager herself were subject to 'constant abuse'.

This abuse included the men constantly trying to chat up the women and making comments regarding aspects of their appearance, with clear sexual innuendoes. One woman catering assistant, for example, said that the operatives were 'always hassling us [the women workers], eyeing us up, trying to get us to go out with them and stuff like that . . . and they were always making comments out loud about things like our sex lives . . . whether or not they thought we'd be good in bed'. Another woman catering assistant went on, 'but if we ignored them it seemed to make them worse . . . they'd get even worse, and wouldn't stop'. Such forms of behaviour on the part of the operatives [were] a daily occurrence. All the women catering assistants interviewed spoke of this behaviour as unwanted, and although some said they would sometimes try to 'laugh it off', it was so routine that many of them said it was difficult to maintain this approach.

Although the forms the men operatives' behaviour took varied, it was always sexualizing behaviour. It was all a form of unwanted sexual attention, or sexual harassment. This routine sexual harassment by the men operatives of the women catering assistants caused the women workers and the catering manager great distress – not least because, as the catering manager said, 'there was nothing we could do about it . . . I constantly complained to the parks manager, but he didn't do anything. He even used to laugh about it. And I complained to the general manager and he didn't do anything either . . . and [the operatives] never took any notice of me. If I tried to stop them, it would just make them worse. They'd make out it was all a laugh . . . they even did it to me.'

When they reflected on the forms and degree of harassment to which they were subjected, both the catering manager and the women catering assistants shared remarkably similar sentiments about why the operatives engaged in these practices. The catering manager said: 'They seem to think it's part of their job to do it to us, and to the customers.' Similarly, one of the women catering assistants commented: 'It's like they think it's their right, because they work on the park. That's why they hate it when we don't like it because they just think they should be able to.' . . .

The women who worked in the bars were also subject to regular sexual attention from the bars manager, who was 'always ready to try something on'. These women were particularly disturbed by the uniform requirement in their depart-ment. The bars manager insisted they wear their dresses pulled down 'off the shoulder', claiming that this was the correct way to wear them. The women were distressed by this requirement, as they felt it was degrading and that it was used by the manager to 'try to turn us into sex toys or something'. They were equally concerned about the way in which this uniform requirement was aggressively enforced by the bars manager. He would often pull their dresses down into this position. On one occasion, a woman operative reported that she entered the bar at a moment when the bars manager was trying to pull a woman's dress down over her shoulders and the woman in question 'just turned round and screamed at him "I'm not a fucking prostitute, I'm here to serve drinks"'. . . .

Both the catering manager and the women catering assistants were also subject to forms of sexual attention from men customers on a daily basis. This attention again included verbal harassment, for example sexual teasing, jokes and pressure for sexual favours, and also some physical forms of sexual attention, including deliberate touching of breasts and also rubbing their bodies against the women. But the most common forms were chatting up and 'eyeing up'. The latter involves sexual objectification – treating a person as if they were an object which the observer has a right to gaze at for as long as, and in whatever way, pleases him. It frequently includes focusing upon a particular part of the body, but in a way which attempts to get the person objectified to agree to the process and to be flat-tered by it – to accept it as an expression of sexual interest.

One woman catering assistant reported these forms of behaviour as being directed at her by men customers on a regular basis. The men customers 'were always eyeing us up' and often 'saying things about our appearance', commenting on 'the way we looked in our uniforms . . . how they liked the way we looked in them'. Another woman catering assistant said men customers would often try to chat up the women workers: 'they were always trying to get us to meet them in the bar after work'. The women frequently found some of the things men customers said and did highly offensive. For example, when they were serving them, the men would say things like 'a plate of chips and a blow job please', or 'rubbing themselves against us when we were clearing the tables, and making out it was accidental'. The women catering assistants said these forms of sexual atten-tion made them feel as if they were primarily defined as sex objects: 'They [the men customers] just seem to think we are on display for them, that we were there just for their benefit.'

But despite the fact that these forms of sexual attention from customers were similar to those from operatives, the catering manager made a distinction between them. She 'expected' women workers to be able to cope with sexual behaviour and attention from men customers as 'part of the job'. She said that if 'the women catering assistants complain, or say things like they can't cope, I tell them it happens all the time and not to worry about it . . . it's part of the job . . . if they can't handle it then they're not up to working here'.

Although they often found sexual attention from men customers as problem-atic as that from men workers, in particular the way its routine nature consistently undermined and denied their status as employees, the women catering assistants also made a distinction between the two. . . .

The ways in which the women spoke of such behaviour from men customers was entirely different from the way they spoke of it from men workers. They were often angry and outraged by the latter, but there was a level of acceptance of customers. Indeed, they were blasé about it and somewhat surprised that I was even bothering to ask questions about this part of their work. This seemed to be connected to the ways in which they viewed (and indeed experienced) this aspect of their work as routine and normal. Dealing with such behaviour by men customers was inevitable and knowing how to deal with it was a skill they quickly developed.

The women staff dealt with being sexualized by men customers by 'laughing it off', or 'playing along with it'. They said the worst thing they could do was to 'get annoyed with [the men], or to 'look angry', or 'not respond' – even if they were feeling annoyed or threatened. To do this would mean the men would just 'carry on bothering us . . . If you play along with it they think they've got what they wanted, so they go.' The strategy these women use to cope with forms of sexualization from men customers is thus to 'enter into' a form of sexual 'exchange', to respond to some extent to sexual jokes, comments and being chatted up. These responses are, for the women, 'part of the job'. . . .

. . . The routine sexualization for the majority of women workers at Fun Land provides some very important indicators as to the dynamics of the production of many of the gendered characteristics of work. . . . Perhaps the most significant is in the manner in which women workers expected and coped with all manner of forms of sexual behaviour from men customers. . . .

The question therefore arises as to why women workers had to cope with sexualization to the extent that it was recognized to be part of their job? What is then striking is that the various forms of sexualization of women by both men customers *and men workers* is that they were explicitly related to the forms of internal workplace regulation which operate specifically in relation to women.

For example, in the case of the women bar staff, the bars manager consistently harassed them while requiring them to wear their uniforms 'off the shoulder'. But the wearing of uniforms constituted a condition of employment, and staff had to wear their uniforms in the 'correct' manner or face dismissal. Moreover, Fun Land's departmental managers had the power to decide the form of uniforms for their seasonal workers, including decisions regarding the 'correct' manner in which the uniforms should be worn. So, clearly, it was the bars manager himself who decided that the women bar staff should wear gingham dresses, and that the correct way to wear them was 'off the shoulder'. Here, the controls and regulations to which workers are subject and the sexualization of women converge. The 'correct' wearing of their uniforms was a requirement which sexualized the women bar staff. . . . It made them feel that they were being defined primarily through the sexualization that the uniform produced, that they were being turned 'into sex toys'. The uniform requirement thus acted to sexually commodify women workers: to turn them into commercial sex objects.

This was also evident elsewhere than the bar. Men customers also made comments/innuendoes about how women catering assistants looked sexually attractive in their uniforms. Here again, the form of the uniform – which the women have no choice but to wear – turned them into objects of sexual attention for men. The uniform, and behind that, the requirement to wear the uniform, sexually commodified women.

The links between sexualization and forms of control and regulation of women workers extend far beyond uniforms, however, for most forms of sexualization of women relate to their general personal appearance and men customers and workers made routine comments about the appearance of women workers with clear sexual innuendoes. For instance, men operatives would openly 'judge' whether or not women would be good in bed on the basis of their appearance, and they were always 'eyeing up' women. Women workers' appearance was also the object of attention when they were hassled walking through the park. . . . Men customers also routinely visually objectified women and made reference to their appearance in sexual innuendoes/comments/jokes, to the extent that the women felt 'we were on display for them'.

However, apart from the women operatives, all the women workers at Fun Land required the 'right' appearance to work there. It was a condition of their recruitment and continued employment, and at its centre was visual attractiveness. It was precisely this 'attractive', 'right' appearance which was subject to constant sexual attention from men (both customers and workers). As with the case of uniforms, the conditions and controls which operated in relation to the 'right' appearance for women workers served to produce a sexually commodified female work force. This process of commodification took place through 'attractiveness' being systematically prioritized above all other 'requirements' of women workers: they had to fulfil this criterion above all else. This prioritization of sexual attractiveness was embodied in the general manager's comment that women employees 'ideally . . . should be like Raquel Welch'. Sexual attractiveness was thus part of what was 'sold' to employers by women in 'exchange' for employment.

. . . Being sexually attractive was a condition of both entry into the workplace, and of remaining there. Failure to be sexually attractive (to be a sexual commodity) led to dismissal, but it meant that the work they did and their skills went largely unnoticed. . . .

. . . [O]ne of women's main roles in customer relations work is the sexual servicing of men customers.

This work is done by women for men customers, and for men customers alone, and yet the language used in relation to customer relations at Fun Land was gender-neutral. . . . But in fact this role in customer relations was both gender-specific in terms of employees (it is women who carried it out) and gender-specific in terms of customers (it was done for men customers). Women's role in customer relations was, in other words, not straightforwardly to do with the production of profit, but also to do with the (re)production of gendered power relations.

This set of connections gains further weight when we consider the few women who were employed as operatives. These were women who had the 'wrong' appearance to work in the occupations in which the majority of women were clustered. They were 'too butch' and 'too manly'; they did not fulfil the criteria of being (hetero)sexually attractive. In conditions of labour shortage (as during the 1989 season), such women were employed in the children's park, where men customers did not spend much time: 'It's mostly mums and grannies.' Because these women did not meet the requirements of feminine attractiveness, they were employed in a capacity where this 'failure' to meet the criteria was relatively insignificant, that is where they had minimal contact with men customers. . . . They did not have to carry out the sexual work which other women had to do routinely, but they were also, though differently, sexually harassed . . . and in conditions of abundant labour they might not have been employed at all. . . .

The suggestion that women are routinely compelled to carry out forms of sexual labour in the context of employment raises all sorts of issues regarding the gendering of the labour market, and in particular for our understandings of service work. Hence, the gendered structuring of work relations identified at Fun Land . . . uncovers a number of issues for the feminist analyses of the gendering of the labour market. . . .

Note

1   Rather than focusing on one particular occupation or set of occupations, and changes over time and across different work sites – as has been typical of recent empirical work on the gendered operations of the labour market (e.g. Bradley 1989; Crompton and Sanderson 1990) – it was decided to carry out fieldwork on the whole range of different occupations to be found within individual workplaces. That is, in-depth fieldwork within specific leisure operations was to form the basis of the research. This allowed exploration of both the general hypothesis that sexuality may structure gendered work relations within employment, and the specific research questions formulated through the existing literature. Various factors and workplace processes, which might potentially act to shape work relations between men and women, could then be explored – from control of workers to the role of customers.

References

Bradley, H. (1989) *Men's Work, Women's Work*. Cambridge: Polity.
Crompton, R., and Sanderson, K. (1990) *Gendered Jobs and Social Change*. London: Unwin Hyman.

PART FOUR

Marriage and intimate relationships

INTRODUCTION

MARRIAGE TODAY IS USUALLY thought of as a relationship between two equal partners based on love, intimacy and companionship. Over several decades, however, sociological research has accumulated which demonstrates that marital relations do not always live up to this ideal, that gender inequalities pervade the most personal of relationships and that what happens within the private life of each couple cannot be understood as separable from the wider social inequalities and cultural *mores* in which it is embedded. There has also been increasing awareness of the diversity of family and household forms and the complexity of marital and non-marital couplings and uncouplings (Smart and Neal 1999). Marriage has been by definition a heterosexual institution; this was once taken for granted, but now some lesbians and gay men are contesting it and campaigning for their relationships to be given the same recognition – despite the fact that one in three heterosexual marriages now ends in divorce. Meanwhile lesbian and gay relationships are receiving more attention from sociological researchers and there is greater recognition of the ways in which marriage is bound up with the reinforcement of normative heterosexuality.

Jessie Bernard's classic study (first published in 1972), was one of the first sustained critiques of marriage (Chapter 25). Drawing on existing research, she argues that the husband's marriage and the wife's marriage are not identical, that structurally and experientially they differ, so that the accounts each partner gives of the 'reality' of their marriage are commonly discrepant. This is a question not merely of differences, but of profound inequalities. Since then an ever increasing body of research has continued to demonstrate that marriage is rarely an equal partnership. Neither the division of labour (as we have seen in Part Three) nor the distribution of resources between husband and wife is likely to be equitable. Jan Pahl's research, for example, indicates that women generally contribute a higher proportion of their income to the household budget, and spend less on themselves, than do their partners (Chapter 26).

Marriages tend to be not only financially and organisationally unequal, but also emotionally asymmetrical. Love is commonly assumed to form the basis of a mutual, caring bond created by romance and sexual attraction and cemented through physical and emotional intimacy. These ideals and the expectations to which they give rise have changed over time. For example, sexual desire and satisfaction would not have been regarded as so necessary to a successful marriage a century ago (see Chapter 27). The process of 'falling in love' is premised on overwhelming attraction to, and mutual absorption in, each other. This can mask, at least temporarily, inequalities and differences. Most couples at the beginning of their relationship do experience a strong sense of 'togetherness' and intimacy, but once the first flush of love has faded women commonly report a loss of emotional closeness. This has emerged in a number of studies since the 1950s (e.g. Komarovsky 1962; Rubin 1983; Mansfield and Collard 1988). Wendy Langford (2000 and Chapter 28) reported on the women's accounts of the passage of love, from its hopeful beginnings to its destructive end, as they struggled to retain some vestige of intimacy with their increasingly distant male partners. There are a number of studies which suggest that women put a great deal more emotional labour into heterosexual relationships than men (see, for example, Lewis et al. 1992). This extends to coping with the disappointment they frequently experience in the specifically sexual aspects of their relationship so that conjugal sex becomes work rather than pleasure (Chapter 29).

Among the dominant white population of Western societies, then, marriage is usually thought of as a relationship between the two people involved, entered into on the basis of mutual love. This is not a universal view. In many cultures marriage is a relationship in which wider kin are involved, as is the case in the British Pakistani community described by Haleh Afshar (Chapter 30). Here marriage, while founding a relationship between the two parties, is also a means of securing kin and community ties beyond the couple. Under such circumstances marriages are often arranged by the couple's relatives but this does not inevitably entail a lack of choice on the part of the spouses. Love is expected to develop and mature after marriage rather than precipitating couples into matrimony.

Not only are there different forms of kinship and marriage among heterosexuals, but increasing attention has been paid to the ways in which lesbians and gays construct their own families of choice, forming couples, engaging in parenting and creatively constructing kin networks (see Chapters 31–2). The analysis of kinship and intimacy was once founded on the assumption of heterosexuality, with heterosexual marriage taken as the adult norm and 'natural' ties of procreation forming the basis of kinship. However, in the light of ever more sophisticated options for assisted conception and reproduction, some of these assumptions are being called into question by heterosexuals as well as by lesbians and gay men.

Debate about the future of marriage and the family has produced rather different accounts of the extent of social change. Anthony Giddens (1992) has argued that we are moving away from lifelong commitments to serial 'pure' relationships based on choice and lasting only as long as they are mutually rewarding. On the other hand Lynne Jamieson (Chapter 33) takes issue with this analysis, arguing that for many, if not most, people choices are too constrained to risk indulging in the fleeting pleasures of the 'pure relationship'. Marriage is as popular as ever, with many people marrying more than once. There is little evidence, however, that marriage is entered into on the assumption that it is temporary and contingent. Romantic love continues to produce expectations of lifelong conjugal bliss, but such hopes are frequently dashed when couples face the mundane realities of married life. Being aware of this should perhaps make us less judgemental about alternatives, such as arranged marriages, stable gay and lesbian relationships or non-monogamy.

REFERENCES AND FURTHER READING

Giddens, A. (1992) *The Transformation of Intimacy*. Cambridge: Polity.

Ingraham, C. (1999) *White Weddings*. New York: Routledge.

Jackson, S. (1993) 'Even sociologists fall in love: an exploration in the sociology of emotions', *Sociology*, 27 (2): 201–20.

Jackson, S. and Moores, S. (eds) (1995) *The Politics of Domestic Consumption*. Hemel Hempstead: Prentice-Hall/Harvester Wheatsheaf.

Jamieson, L. (1998) *Intimacy*. Cambridge: Polity.

Komarovsky, M. (1962) *Blue Collar Marriage*. New York: Norton.

Langford, W. (2000) *Revolutions of the Heart*. London: Routledge

Leonard, D. (1980) *Gender and Generation*. London: Tavistock.

Lewis, J. Clark, D. and Morgan, D. H. J. (1992) *Whom God hath Joined Together: The Work of Marriage Guidance*. London: Routledge.

Mansfield and Collard (1988) *The Beginning of the Rest of your Life: A Portrait of Newlywed Marriage*. London: Macmillan.

Pahl, J. (1989) *Money and Marriage*. London: Macmillan.

Rubin, L. (1983). *Intimate Strangers*. New York: Harper and Row.

Smart, C. and Neale, B. (1999) *Family Fragments*. Cambridge: Polity.

VanEvery, J. (1995) *Heterosexual Women Changing the Family: Refusing to be a Wife*. London: Taylor & Francis.

KEY QUESTIONS

- Can love conquer all?
- Consider how the institution of marriage may perpetuate both gender inequality and the dominance of normative heterosexuality. How might hetero-

sexual women, lesbians and gay men challenge this? What might they seek to change?

- To what extent can changes in heterosexual, lesbian and gay relationships be understood in terms of a transformation of intimacy? How else may we make sense of the varied patterns of intimate and domestic life in late modern societies?

Chapter 25

Jessie Bernard

THE HUSBAND'S MARRIAGE AND
THE WIFE'S MARRIAGE

As Jessie Barnard says, there are 'two marriages . . . in every marital union, his and hers' and his 'is better than hers' (1972: 14). Writing at a time when most women were married by their early twenties, and most married women were full-time housewives, she goes on to document the evidence on the advantages of marriage for men and, at greater length, its disadvantages for women.

From *The Future of Marriage*, second edition, New Haven CT: Yale University Press (1982).

The husband's marriage

. . .

FOR CENTURIES MEN HAVE been told – by other men – that marriage is: no bed of roses, a necessary evil, a noose, a desperate thing, a field of battle, a curse, a school of sincere pretense. . . .

Men . . . have been railing against marriage for centuries. If marriage were actually as bad for men as it has been painted by them, it would long since have lost any future it may ever have had. In the face of all the attacks against it, the vitality of marriage has been quite stupendous. Men have cursed it, aimed barbed witticisms at it, denigrated it, bemoaned it – and never ceased to want and need it or to profit from it.

The male clichés could hardly have been more wrong. . . . For, contrary to all the charges leveled against it, the husbands' marriage, whether they like it or not (and they do), is awfully good for them.

Marriage is good for men

There are few findings more consistent, less equivocal, more convincing than the sometimes spectacular and always impressive superiority on almost every index — demographic, psychological, or social — of married over never-married men. Despite all the jokes about marriage in which men indulge, all the complaints they lodge against it, it is one of the greatest boons of their sex. Employers, bankers, and insurance companies have long since known this. And whether they know it or not, men need marriage more than women do. As Samuel Johnson said, marriage is, indeed 'the best state for man in general; and every man is a worse man in proportion as he is unfit for the married state.'

The research evidence is overwhelmingly convincing. . . . Although the physical health of married men is no better than that of never-married men until middle age, their mental health is far better, fewer show serious symptoms of psychological distress, and fewer of them suffer mental health impairments. . . . Blau and Duncan, Melita Odin, and William H. Whyte have shown that marriage is an asset in a man's career, including his earning power. The value of marriage for sheer male survival is itself remarkable. It does, indeed, pay men to be married. 'Most men,' Paul C. Glick notes, 'profit greatly from having a wife to help them to take care of their health.' . . .

Marriage is so demonstrably good for men that when social scientists were asked to come up with a set of social indicators that would tell us how our society was operating, one such index proposed by Paul C. Glick as a favourable sign was the proportion of adult males who were married. The statistical underpinning for this rationale was convincing. Compared with never-married men, the lot of married men is a providential one.

. . . and they know it

The actions of men with respect to marriage speak far louder than words; they speak, in fact, with a deafening roar. Once men have known marriage, they can hardly live without it. Most divorced and widowed men remarry. At every age, the marriage rate for both divorced and widowed men is higher than the rate for single men. Half of all divorced white men who remarry do so within three years after divorce. Indeed, it might not be far-fetched to conclude that the verbal assaults on marriage indulged in by men are a kind of compensatory reaction to their dependence on it. . . .

The wife's marriage

Because we are so accustomed to the way in which marriage is structured in our society, it is hard for us to see how different the wife's marriage really is from the husband's, and how much worse. But, in fact, it is. There is a very considerable research literature reaching back over a generation which shows that: more wives than husbands report marital frustration and dissatisfaction; more report negative feelings; more wives than husbands report marital problems; more wives than husbands report marital problems; more wives than husbands consider their marriages unhappy, have considered separation or divorce, have regretted their marriages; and fewer report positive companionship. Only about half as many wives (25 per cent) as husbands (45 per cent) say that there is nothing about their marriage that is not as nice as they would like. And twice as many wives (about a fourth) as husbands (about 12 per cent) in a Canadian sample say that they would not remarry the same partner or have doubts about it. Understandably, therefore, more wives than husbands seek marriage counseling; and more wives than husbands initiate divorce proceedings.

In a population of couples undergoing counseling, the wives were found by Emile McMillan to be more

> discontent than the husbands. More of the wives than of the husbands related themselves as unhappy during the first year of marriage, and also during the next several years. The wives saw the problems as having started sooner and lasting longer. . . . They saw a greater density of problem areas. . . . They showed less desire to save their marriage, and gave more negative reasons and fewer positive reasons for saving their marriage.

Even among happily married couples, Harvey J. Locke found, fewer wives than husbands report agreement on such family problems as finances, recreation, religion, affection, friends, sex, in-laws, time together, and life aims and goals; and more report serious marital difficulties. The proportions were not great in most cases, but the proportion of these happily married wives who reported no difficulties at all was considerably lower than the proportion of happily married men who reported none. The wives reported problems in more than twice as many areas as did husbands.

The evidence for the destructive nature of the wife's marriage does not, however, rest on his bill of particulars, impressive as it is. For, despite the dissatisfactions catalogued above, a very large proportion of married women, inconsistently enough, consider themselves and their marriages to be happy, a paradox to be commented on in greater detail below. It is not, therefore, the complaints of wives that demonstrate how bad the wife's marriage is, but rather the poor mental and emotional health of married women as compared not only to married men's but also to unmarried women's.

Husbands and wives

Although the physical health of married women, as measured by absence of chronic conditions or restricted activity, is as good as, and in the ages beyond sixty-five even better than, that of married men, they suffer far greater mental health hazards and present a far worse clinical picture. Gurin et al., for example, found that more married women than married men have felt they were about to have a nervous breakdown; more experience psychological and physical anxiety; more have feelings of inadequacy in their marriages and blame themselves for their own lack of general adjustment. Other studies report that more married women than married men show phobic reactions, depression, and passivity; greater than expected frequency of symptoms of psychological distress; and mental health impairment.

Although marriage protects both marital partners against suicide as compared with single men and women, it protects husbands more than wives. Only about half as many white married as single men commit suicide; almost three-fourths as many married as single women do. And although women in general live longer than men, marriage is relatively better for men than it is for women in terms of sheer survival, quite aside from suicide. That is, the difference in death rates between married and unmarried women is less than that between married and unmarried men (30 per cent as compared to 48 per cent). . . .

The psychological costs of marriage, in brief, seem to be considerably greater for wives than for husbands and the benefits considerably fewer.

Merely a sex difference?

If the mental and emotional health of wives – anxious, depressed, psychologically distressed – is so dismal, perhaps we are dealing with a sex difference quite unrelated to marriage. Perhaps, that is, what we find are not husband/wife but male/female differences. Perhaps the mental and emotional health of wives shows up so poorly simply because they are women? . . .

. . . This is an answerable question, and the answer is no. For the mental health picture of wives shows up just as unfavourably when compared with unmarried women. Thus, for example, a study by R. R. Willoughby a generation ago found that married more than unmarried women were troubled by ideas that people were watching them on the street, were fearful of falling when on high places, had their feelings easily hurt, were happy and sad by turns without apparent reason, regretted impulsive statements, cried easily, felt hurt by criticism, sometimes felt miserable, found it hard to make up their minds, sometimes felt grouchy, were burdened by a sense of remorse, worried over possible misfortune, changed interests quickly, were bothered when people watched them perform a task, would cross the street to avoid meeting people, were upset when people crowded ahead of them in line, would rather stand than take a front seat when late, were self-conscious about their appearance, and felt prevented from giving help at the scene of an accident. Moreover, more recent studies, tend to confirm such differences. Genevieve Knupfer found that more married than unmarried women tend to be bothered by feelings of depression, unhappy most of the time, disliking their present jobs, sometimes feeling they are about to go to pieces, afraid of death, terrified by windstorms, worried about catching diseases, sometimes thinking of things too bad to talk about, and bothered by pains and ailments in different parts of the body. Overall, more of the wives than of the single women she found to be passive, phobic, and depressed; and although the total number who showed severe neurotic symptoms was small, these were evident in almost three times as many married as single women. . . .

So far, we have held marital status constant and varied sex, as they say in laboratory experiments, and then we have held sex constant and varied marital status. Now again we hold marital status constant and vary sex by comparing single men and women. The sex differences that show up in this 'design' are enormous – but quite opposite to those that show up when we compare married men and women. Now it is the women who show up well and the men poorly. Unless one has actually examined the evidence it is hard to realize what a poor showing unmarried men make and what a good showing the unmarried women make.

In Manhattan, for example, about twice as many never-married men as never-married women show mental health impairments. Single women in this country, Gurin *et al.* report, experience 'less discomfort than do single men: they report greater happiness, are more active in . . . working through the problems they face, and appear in most ways stronger in meeting the challenges of their positions than men'. Single women show far less than expected frequency of symptoms of psychological distress as compared with single men. And, as though further corroboration were necessary, single women suffer far less than single men from neurotic and antisocial tendencies. More single men than single women are depressed and passive. In 1960, about 10 per cent of the never-married men thirty-five years of age and over, as compared with only half that proportion of single women thirty years of age and over 'resided involuntarily in institutions', and over half were in mental institutions.

Like almost everyone else who researches this seemingly anomalous situation, even seasoned psychologists like Gerald Gurin, Joseph Veroff, and Sheila Feld were surprised to find results so 'contrary to the popular stereotypes of the frustrated old maid and the free and unencumbered bachelor life'. Now it is the superiority, not the inferiority, of the women that has to be explained. . . .

Education, occupation, and income all tell the same story of the relative superiority of unmarried women over unmarried men. At every age level, the average single women surpass the average single men. At the earlier ages, say twenty-five to thirty-four, the single men and women are not very different in education, occupation, or income; the marriageables are still mixed in with the nonmarriageables. But as the marriageable men drop out of the single population, those who are left show up worse and worse as compared with their feminine counterparts, so that twenty years later, at ages forty-five to fifty-four, the gap between them is a veritable chasm. The single women are more educated, have higher average incomes, and are in higher occupations.[1]

When, finally, we vary both marital status and sex, by comparing married men and unmarried women, we find relatively little overall difference so far as mental health is concerned, superiorities and inferiorities tending to cancel out. But the women are spectacularly better off so far as psychological distress symptoms are concerned, suggesting that women start out with an initial advantage which marriage reverses. . . .

It is not necessarily the magnitude of the statistical differences between the mental health of married and single women or between married men and married women that is so convincing; it is, rather, the consistency of the differences. No one difference or even set of differences by itself would be definitive; but the cumulative effect of so many is. The poor mental health of wives is like a low-grade infection that shows itself in a number of scattered symptoms, no one of which is critical enough to cause an acute episode. And so, therefore, it is easy to ignore. Or to dismiss. Or to blame on women themselves. There must be something wrong with them if they are psychologically so distressed.

But even those who blame women themselves for their psychological malaise and see it as an inability on their part to cope with the demands of marriage or to come to terms with their destiny finally have to concede that the way the social world is organized may have something to do with their plight.

A shock theory of marriage

A generation ago, I propounded what I then called a shock theory of marriage. In simple form, it stated that marriage introduced such profound discontinuities into the lives of women as to constitute genuine emotional health hazards.

There are some standardized 'shocks' that are almost taken for granted. Mirra Komarovsky, for example, has analyzed the conflict the bride experienced between her attachment to her parental family and her attachment to her husband. There is, too, the end of the romantic idealization that terminates the 'honeymoon', known in the research literature as 'disenchantment'. The transition from the always-on-good-behaviour presentation of the self during courtship to the daily lack of privacy in marriage, symbolized in the media by hair curlers and the unshaved face, presents its own kind of shock. So also does the change that occurs when the wife ceases to be the catered-to and becomes the caterer-to. These and related discontinuities have to go with redefinition of the self, with the assumption of new role obligations. . . .

Some of the shocks that marriage may produce have to do with the lowering of status that it brings to women. For, despite all of the clichés about the high status of marriage, it is for women a downward status step. The legal status of wives, for example, is lower not only than that of husbands but also than that of unmarried women. A women, Diane Schulder reminds us, loses a considerable number of legal rights when she marries. But that is relatively minor compared to other forms of status loss, to be documented presently, as Congreve's Mrs Millamant in *The Way of the World* so well knew when she spoke of 'dwindling' into a wife. Even after she had bargained with Mirabel to preserve at least some of her prerogatives in marriage, she said, 'these articles subscribed, if I continue to endure you a little longer, I may by degrees dwindle into a wife.' And Mirabel recognized that his status would be enhanced: 'Well, have I liberty to offer conditions, that when you are dwindled into a wife I may not be beyond measure enlarged into a husband?'

The Pygmalion effect

'Dwindling' into a wife takes time. It involves a redefinition of the self and an active reshaping of the personality to conform to the wishes or needs or demands of husbands. Roland G. Tharp, a psychologist, concludes, from a summary of the research literature, that wives 'conform more to husbands' expectations than husbands do to wives''. This tendency of wives to shape themselves to conform to their husbands has been documented in recent research in some detail. Among freshman women who were the top 1 per cent of their class at Michigan State University, for example, Dorothy Robinson Ross found that those who married lost independence and 'impulse expression'; after marriage they became more submissive and conservative. . . .

We do not have to imagine a man enforcing conformity with a whip or clenched fists or even a sculptor lovingly shaping the woman of his dreams to account for the Pygmalion effect. The conditions of marriage itself as now structured lead to this result. Women who are quite able to take care of themselves before marriage may become helpless after fifteen or twenty years of marriage. Genevieve Knupfer describes a woman who had managed a travel agency before marriage, for example, who when widowed at the age of fifty-five had to ask friends how to get a passport. No wonder the self-image of wives becomes more negative with age. No wonder Alice Rossi warns us that 'the possibility must be faced . . . that women lose ground in personal development and self-esteem during the early and middle years of adulthood, whereas men gain ground in these respects during the same years'. For it is the husband's role – not necessarily his own wishes, desires, or demands – that proves to be the key to the marriage and requires the wife to be more accommodating.

Wives make more adjustments

This Pygmalion effect tallies with the finding generally reported that wives make more of the adjustments called for in marriage than do husbands. Understandably so. Because the wife has put so many eggs into the one basket of marriage, to the exclusion of almost every other, she has more at stake in making a go of it. If anything happens to that one basket, she losses everything; she has no fallback position. She tends, therefore, to have to make more of the concessions called for by it. Thus, when a sample of husbands and wives were asked by Burgess and Wallin three to five years after marriage who had made the greater adjustment in marriage, 'the preponderance of replies . . . was that the wives had made the greater adjustment'. The husband upon marriage maintains his old life routines, with no thought or expectation of changing them to suit his wife's wishes. 'Often the submits without voicing a protest,' Burgess and Wallin found. 'In other cases the wife may put up a contest, although she generally loses.' Both wives and husbands in this study agreed that the wives had made the greater adjustment. Sometimes, when the wife concedes that the husband has made more adjustments, he reports himself to be quite unaware of making any; they were probably too trivial for him even to notice.

One of the most poignant adjustments that wives have to make is in the pattern of emotional expression between themselves and their husbands. Almost invariably, they mind the let-down in emotional expression that comes when the husband's job takes more out of him, or the original warmth subsides. Lee Rainwater found in marriages between men and women in the lower lower classes that wives tended to adopt their husbands' taciturnity and lack of demonstrativeness rather than insist on winning him over to theirs. They settled for a fairly low emotional diet. 'I support you, don't I?' is a common reply to the question desperate women sometimes ask, 'Do you still love me?' Not a very nutritious one for a starving person. Some women call it dehumanizing. . . .

Occupational change in marriage

One of the basic differences in the wife's and the husband's marriages results from this life style – namely, the almost complete change in work that marriage brings in her life but not in his. Until yesterday, and for most women even today, every wife becomes a *house*wife. And this is not always a congenial role. Militant feminists have argued that this occupational change amounts to the same thing as requiring all men upon marriage to give up their jobs and become janitors, whether they like janitor work or not. Regardless of whether this analogy is fair or not, it is true that interest in the aptitude for housework are not as equally distributed among the female population as is the occupation of housework, wherefore a large number of vocational misfits is almost inevitable. For, as it happens, not all women have an interest in or aptitude for the job of housewife – just as, no doubt, there are many men who do and would prefer it to what they are doing.

'The housewife is a nobody,' says Philip Slater, and almost everyone agrees. Her work is menial labor. Even more status-degrading is the unpaid nature of her job. Few deny the economic as well as the sociological importance of housework and home making. Housework is part of the great infrastructure on which, as David Riesman has reminded us, the entire superstructure of the economy and the government rests. If women did not supply the services of taking care of the living arrangements of workers, industry would have to do so, as in the case of lumber camps, ships, and the military. But housewives are not in the labor force. They are not paid for the services that they perform.

The low status of the wife's work has ramifications all through her marriage. Since her husband's work is not only higher in status but usually competitive, as hers is not, and he has to meet certain clothing and grooming standards or lose his job, his needs have to be catered to. If there has to be a choice, his new suit is more important than hers. This, quite apart from whatever personal or institutional prestige his work confers, tends to put him in a position of status superiority to the wife.[2]

Housework is a dead-end job; there is no chance of promotion. One cannot grow in it. There is a saying that passes as wit to the effect that Washington is full of talented men and the women they married when they were young. The couple who began their marriage at the same stages of their development find themselves far apart in later years. . . .

. . . As life is now organized in small, private living units, housework is isolating. 'The idea of imprisoning each woman alone in a small, self-contained, and architecturally isolating dwelling is a modern invention,' Philip Slater reminds us, 'dependent upon an advanced technology. . . . In our society the housewife may move about freely, but since she has nowhere in particular to go and is not a part of anything her prison needs no walls. This is in striking contrast to her premarital life, especially if she is a college graduate. In college she was typically embedded in an active group life with constant emotional and intellectual stimulation. College life is in this sense an urban life. Marriage typically eliminates much of this way of life for her, and children deliver the *coup de grace*. Her only significant relationships tend to be with her husband, who, however, is absent most of the day. Most of her social and emotional needs must be satisfied by her children, who are hardly adequate to the task.'

Isolation has negative psychological effects on people. It encourages brooding; it leads to erratic judgments, untempered by the leavening effect of contact with others. It renders one more susceptible to psychoses. . . .

The housewife syndrome

That it is being relegated to the role of housewife rather than marriage itself which contributes heavily to the poor mental and emotional health of married women can be demonstrated by comparing housewives, all of whom may be presumed to be married, with working women, three-fifths of whom are also married. Marriage *per se* is thus at least partially ruled out as an explanation of differences between them. The comparison shows that wives who are rescued from the isolation of the household by outside employment show up very well. They may be neurotic, but, as Sharp and Nye have shown, they are less likely than women who are exclusively housewives to be psychotic. And even the allegation of neuroticism can be challenged. For Sheila Feld tells us that 'working mothers are less likely than housewives to complain of pains and ailments in different parts of their body and of not feeling healthy enough to carry out things they would like to do.'[3]

But the truly spectacular evidence for the destructive effects of the occupation of housewife on the mental and emotional health of married women is provided by the relative incidence of the symptoms of psychological distress among housewives and working women. In all except one of twelve such symptoms – having felt an impending nervous breakdown – the working women were overwhelmingly better off than the housewives. Far fewer than expected of the working women and more than expected of the housewives, for example, had actually had a nervous breakdown. Fewer than expected of the working women and more than expected of the housewives suffered from nervousness, inertia, insomnia, trembling hands, nightmares, perspiring hands, fainting, headaches, dizziness, and heart palpitations. The housewife syndrome is far from figment of anyone's imagination. . . . In terms of the number of people involved, the housewife syndrome might well be viewed as Public Health Problem Number One.

Comment

. . . [T]he woman suffering from the housewife syndrome is not likely to elicit much sympathy; she's sitting pretty, and has no cause for complaint. She annoys us if she even mentions any symptoms of psychological distress. They are not worth anyone's attention. . . .

If we were, in fact, epidemiologists and saw bright, promising young people enter a certain occupation and little by little begin to droop and finally succumb, we would be alerted at once and bend all our research efforts to locate the hazards and remove them. But we are complacent when we see what happens to women in marriage. We have, in fact, almost boxed women into a corner. Or, to change the figure of speech, we have primed young fillies to run fast and then put impossible hurdles in their way. We tell young women that they are free to embark on careers, and then make it almost impossible for them to succeed in them. We tell them they may have access to all the privileges and prerogatives of professionals, and then punish them if they accept the challenge. More important still, we put an enormous premium on their getting married, but make them pay an unconscionable price for falling in with our expectations. We then blame them no matter what they do – refuse to run, kick over the traces, run wild, or become inert.

Happiness is . . .?

If the wife's marriage is really so pathogenic, why do women marry at all? They marry for a wide variety of reasons. They want emancipation from the parental home, and marriage is one way to achieve it. They want babies, and marriage is the only sanctioned way – as yet – to get babies in our society. In addition, there is the pressure of social expectations. . . . There are, in fact, few, if any, better alternatives to marriage for young women in their late teens and early twenties. Most of the alternatives are – or, to date, have seemed to be – too awful. If marriage helps young women to achieve any of these goals and to avoid worse alternatives, their stampede into marriage is understandable.

The problem is not why do young women marry, but why, in the face of all the evidence, do more married than unmarried women report themselves as happy? As, in fact, they do. For it is strange to find wives, such a large proportion of whom are filled with fears and anxieties, so many of whom are depressed, reporting themselves as happy. . . .

There are several ways to look at the seeming anomaly involved here. One is that happiness is interpreted in terms of conformity. Wives may, in effect, be judging themselves happy by definition. . . . The pressures to conform are so great that few young women can resist them. Better, as the radical women put it, dead than unwed. Those who do not marry are made to feel inferior, failures. . . .

Such conformity to the norm of marriage does not have to be imposed from the outside. Women have internalized the norms prescribing marriage so completely that the role of wife seems the only acceptable one. And since marriage is set up as the *summum bonum* of life for women, they interpret their achievement of marriage as happiness, no matter how unhappy the marriage itself may be. They have been told that their happiness depends on marriage, so, even if they are miserable, they *are* married, aren't they? They *must* therefore be happy.

Another way to explain the anomaly of depressed, phobic, and psychologically distressed women reporting themselves as happy may be that they are interpreting happiness in terms of adjustment. . . . The married woman has adjusted to the demands of marriage; she is reconciled to them. She interprets her reconciliation as happiness, no matter how much she is paying for it in terms of psychological distress. . . .

The hidden deformities of women

Another way to solve the paradox of depressed wives reporting their marriages as happy is to view the socialization process as one which 'deforms' them in order to fit them for marriage as now structured. We cut the motivational wings of young women or bind their intellectual feet, all the time reassuring them that it is all for their own good. Otherwise, no one would love them or marry them or take care of them. . . .

. . . [W]e are quite remarkably successful. We do not clip wings or bind feet, but we do make girls sick. For to be happy in a relationship which imposes so many impediments on her, as traditional marriage does, a woman must be slightly ill mentally. Women accustomed to expressing themselves freely could not be happy in such a relationship; it would be to confining and too punitive. . . . It may therefore be that married women say they are happy because they are sick rather than sick because they are married.

There are some researchers who believe that this is indeed the case. They note that our standards of mental health for men are quite different from those for women, that if we judged women by the standards which we apply to men they would show up as far from well. A generation ago, Terman could judge women who were conformist, conservative, docile, unaggressive, lacking in decisiveness, cautious, nontolerant to be emotionally stable and well balanced. They were the women who had achieved an adjustment standard of mental health. They fitted the situation they were trained from infancy to fit. They enjoyed conformity to it. They were his 'happily' married women.

But modern clinicians see them in a different light. Inge K. Broverman and her associates, for example, ask whether a constellation of traits which includes 'being more submissive, less independent, less adventurous, more easily influenced, less aggressive, less competitive, more excitable in minor crises, having their feelings more easily hurt, being more emotional, more conceited about their appearance, less objective' – a constellation of traits which a set of clinicians attributed to mature adult women – isn't a strange way of 'describing any mature, healthy individual'. These researchers conclude that we have a double standard of mental health, one for men and one for women. We incorporate into our standards of mental health for women the defects necessary for successful adjustment in marriage.

We do our socializing of girls so well, in fact, that many wives, perhaps most, not only feel that they are fulfilled by marriage but even hotly resent anyone who raises questions about their marital happiness. They have been so completely shaped for their dependency and passivity that the very threat of changes that would force them to greater independence frightens them. They have successfully come to terms with the conditions of their lives. They do not know any other. They do not know that other patterns of living might yield greater satisfactions, or want to know. Their cage can be open. They will stay put.

Notes

1   . . . But the disabilities under which women perform in the labor force are illustrated by the fact that only 1.9 per cent of the single white women who had incomes were in the income bracket of $10,000 and over, as compared with 4 per cent of the single men.

2   Even if a wife is working, a disparity in occupational status between her job and her husband's may make a difference to her. If her occupation is lower in status

than her husband's, she is more likely to show symptoms of anxiety (Sharpe and Nye 1963). When both are on the same occupational level, as among blue-collar and unskilled workers, the status differential does not exist and the anxiety symptoms do not show up.

3   Actually, in the earlier age brackets, twenty-five to forty-four, working women averaged more days of restricted activity or bed disability than housekeeping women, though in the later age brackets the reverse was true. (Data from an unpublished table by the National Center for Health Statistics.)

References

Blau, Peter M., and Duncan, Otis Dudley (1967) *The American Occupational Structure*. New York: John Wiley, 357.

Broverman, Inge K., *et al.* (1970) 'Sex-role stereotypes and clinical judgments of mental health', *Journal of Counseling and Clinical Psychology*, 34: 6–7.

Burgess, E. W., and Willin, Paul (1953) *Engagement and Marriage*. Philadelphia: Lippincott.

Glick, Paul C. (1949) 'First marriages and remarriages', *American Sociological Review*, 14 727.

Glick, Paul C. (1969) 'Marital stability as a social indicator', *Social Biology*, 16: 158–66.

Gurin, Gerald, Veroff, Joseph, and Feld, Sheila (1960) *Americans View their Mental Health*. New York: Basic Books, 42, 72, 190, 110, 234–35.

Knupfer, Genevieve, Clark, Walter, and Room, Robin (1966) 'The mental health of the unmarried', *American Journal of Psychiatry*, 122: 844.

Komarovsky, Mirra (1950) 'Functional analysis of sex roles'. *American Sociological Review*, 15: 508–16.

Locke, Harvey J. (1951) *Predicting Adjustment in Marriage: A Comparison of a Divorced and Happily Married Group*. New York: Holt, 68–9.

McMillan, Emile L. (1969) 'Problem build-up: a description of couples in marriage counseling', *Family Coordinator*, 18: 267.

Odin, Melita, H. (1968) 'The fulfillment of promise: forty-year follow up of the Terman gifted group', *General Psychology Monographs*, 77: 92.

Ross, Dorothy Robinson (1968) 'The Story of the Top One Percent of the Women at Michigan State University', unpublished study.

Rossi, Alice 'Transition to parenthood', *Journal of Marriage and the Family*, 30: 34.

Schulder, Diane B. (1970) 'Does the law oppress women?', in Robin Morgan (ed.) *Sisterhood is Powerful*. New York: Vintage.

Sharp, Lawrence J., and Nye, F. Ivan. (1963) 'Maternal mental health', in F. Ivan Nye and Lois Wladis Hoffman (eds) *The Employed Mother in America*. Chicago: Rand McNally, 309–19.

Slater, Philip. (1970) 'What hath Spock wrought?' *Washington Post*, 1 March.

Terman, Lewis M., and Wallin, Paul (1940) 'Marriage prediction and marital-adjustment tests', *American Sociological Review*, 14: 502.

Tharp, Roland G. (1963) 'Psychological patterning in marriage', *Psychological Review*, 60: 114.

Veroff, Joseph, and Feld, Sheila (1970) *Marriage and Work in America*. New York: Van Nostrand-Reinhold, 30.

Whyte, William H., Jr (1956) *The Organization Man*. New York: Simon & Schuster, 258–63.

Willoughby, Raymond R. (1938) 'The relationship to emotionality of age, sex, and conjugal condition', *American Journal of Sociology*, 43: 920–31.

Chapter 26

Jan Pahl

HOUSEHOLD SPENDING, PERSONAL SPENDING AND THE CONTROL OF MONEY IN MARRIAGE

Drawing on data from a study of household budgets, Pahl discusses the gendered patterns in the financial contribution to 'housekeeping'. She argues for the need to understand not only that money is a fundamental measure of inequality between men and women, but also the social and economic processes involved in households. Her data indicate that women tend to be responsible for the day-to-day management of household money even when they don't have ultimate control over the finances. Also, women contribute a greater proportion of any earnings to the housekeeping than do their partners, at every level of income, and take less for their personal needs. Pahl argues, therefore, that increases in women's income, rather than men's, whether through wages or benefits, will be of greater direct benefit to the household as a whole.

From *Sociology*, 24 (1) 1990: 119–38.

. . .

WHERE A WIFE CONTROLS finances she will usually also be responsible for money management; where a husband controls finances he will usually delegate parts of money management to his wife. Thus where a wife controls finances she will usually be responsible for paying the main bills and for making sure that ends meet, as well as for buying food and day-to-day necessities. Where a husband controls finances he will typically delegate to his wife the responsibility for housekeeping expenses, sometimes giving her a housekeeping allowance for this purpose. Marriages where the wife controls the money and the husband manages it are rare. There were no examples of this pattern in the study sample, nor were there examples of the small number of marriages where the husband both controls and manages the money. Evidence from other studies suggests that in these circumstances there is likely to be extreme inequality between husband and wife and deprivation on the part of the wife and children (Wilson 1987).

Who spends on what?

. . . [P]atterns of spending were differentiated by gender. Wives were likely to pay for food, clothing for themselves and their children, presents, and school expenses such as dinner money. Husbands were likely to be responsible for paying for their own clothing, the car, repairs and decorating, meals taken away from home, and alcohol. Joint responsibilities, paid for by either partner or by both together, included consumer durables, donations to charity and Christmas expenses. . . .

Responsibility for spending varied significantly according to the control of the finances within the household, but only for some items of expenditure. In general the person who controlled the finances, whether or not there was a joint account, was also responsible for the major bills. This applied in the case of the bills for mortgage or rent, rates, fuel, phone and insurance. However, the pattern for consumer goods was rather different: where there was a joint account, whether it was controlled by husband or wife, it was likely that they would both be responsible for buying the washing machine, refrigerator or other household item. However, where there was no joint account, husbands were likely to be responsible for spending on consumer goods.

. . . [W]e shall examine [two] different areas of spending. These are, first, spending on food, since this clearly comes into the category of household spending and represents a major claim on most household budgets. Secondly, we shall consider expenditure on leisure, as an example of an area where spending and consumption are most individualised. . . . In each area we shall explore the extent to which patterns of control and management of money affect patterns of spending.

Spending on food

. . . As household income rose the amount spent on housekeeping increased. However, the ratio between housekeeping and income was not the same at every income level. That is to say, though the average household spent 26 per cent of its income on housekeeping, poorer households spent a higher proportion than this, while richer households spent a lower proportion. The proportion of income spent on housekeeping varied from 48 per cent in a very poor household with numerous children to 14 per cent in an affluent household with low living costs.

. . . At any one income level the housekeeping-to-income ratio varied considerably: some households were spending a much higher proportion of their income on housekeeping than others. Up to this point we have been concerned only with the total income of each household. But the total income was made up of contributions from both husband and wife, coming to them either as wages and salaries, or as Child Benefit or other social security payments. . . .

. . . [T]he amount spent on housekeeping was related both to the level of household income and to the amount contributed by each partner. The . . . analysis suggested that:

(a)   the husband contributed most absolutely to housekeeping since on average his income was four times as great as that of his wife;

(b)   the wife contributed most relatively to housekeeping; this meant that, if the incomes of wife and husband rose by the same amount, 28 per cent of her increase would go to housekeeping compared with 16 per cent of his.

Put simply, if an additional pound entered the household economy through the mother's hands more of it would be spent on food for the family than would be the case if the pound had been brought into the household by the father.

We have seen that the amount spent on housekeeping was likely to differ depending on who earned the money: did it also differ according to who controlled the family's finances? . . . [T]he way in which household finances were organised, and the person who controlled the money, had a powerful influence on the proportion of total income spent as housekeeping. Where wives controlled finances the proportion spent on housekeeping was likely to be higher than in households where husbands controlled finances. Thus at one extreme, in wife-controlled systems, two-thirds of couples spent over a quarter of total household income on housekeeping; at the other extreme, in husband-controlled systems, only two-fifths of couples spent more than a quarter of their total income on housekeeping. This difference was statistically significant.

The conclusion of this analysis is that the amount spent on housekeeping is related, first, to the level of household income, secondly, to the sources of that income and, thirdly, to the control of income within the household. . . .

. . . [T]hough husbands typically contributed more absolutely to housekeeping, wives typically contributed a larger proportion of their income. The implications for policy are [that the] . . . best way to raise the living standards of poor children is to increase the amount of money over which their mothers have control. . . . Giving additional money to mothers, whether in the form of wages or social security payments, is likely to produce bigger increases in family living standards than giving the same sums of money to fathers. . . .

Husbands were more likely to have money for personal spending and for leisure than were wives. Thus twelve husbands said that they had an identified allowance for personal spending, compared with only two wives, and 86 per cent of the men said they spent money on leisure activities compared with 67 per cent of the women. Husbands were also likely to have more money to spend on themselves than wives. Among the 102 couples who took part in the study seven either spent nothing on leisure or had no set amounts for this, while twenty-three couples spent approximately the same amounts. Seventeen wives spent more than their husbands on leisure activities, while fifty-five husbands spent more than their wives. Estimating spending on leisure is difficult because it is often spasmodic, with subscriptions payable yearly, fees for classes payable termly, sports equipment bought when needed and so on. Nevertheless, the problem of estimating the amount spent on leisure applied to both husband and wives, since they were asked identical sets of questions, so it may be assumed that comparisons between the two sets of answers are justified, even if the total amounts spent are likely to be inaccurate. In addition, it is important to remember that drinking and gambling were the most common leisure activities on which men spent money and that sums spent on these are notoriously underestimated. Thus, if anything, men were spending even more on leisure than they admitted to the interviewers.

Typically, husbands overestimated the amounts wives spent on leisure, while wives underestimated how much their husbands spent. They also had rather different attitudes to each others' leisure activities. Both husbands and wives tended to give precedence to the husband's right to leisure: as a nurse said of her milkman husband: 'You can't deny a man when he's earning.' By contrast wives' right to leisure seemed less secure and 'leisure' sometimes involved domestic work. Thus when one husband was asked what leisure activities his wife had, he replied, 'Ironing, sewing, reading.'

Employment status had both financial and ideological implications. Unemployment could drastically alter leisure patterns. One couple said:

HUSBAND: I used to spend money on the garden when I was at work but I can't now. There's a 20 ft greenhouse in the garden and it's empty. No money for seeds or anything like that.
WIFE: I used to play bingo, but we can't afford it. I like to read but now I borrow books from friends. I like a Mills & Boon in bed.

Wives who were earning had more money to spend and more money over which they had a degree of control, and they also felt they had a right to pursue leisure activities of which their husbands disapproved, such as going to the pub with women friends or taking independent holidays. However, the fact that a wife managed or controlled the money did not necessarily give her more to spend on herself. A secretary who had given up paid work to look after their two small children said:

I feel guilty if I buy something for myself. My husband says I shouldn't have to, but I do. As he brings in the money I do need to justify how I spend it.

The ideological construction of the relationship between earner and dependant, which expresses itself in the dependant's defence and subordination, is seen particularly clearly in the case of spending on personal needs and leisure.

What determined the amount of money which each person felt they could spend on leisure and personal needs? . . . Husbands were more likely than wives to take their personal spending money from their earnings, while wives are likely to use the housekeeping money for their personal needs, especially if they were not earning. The source of personal spending money varied according to how the couple organised their finances. Where there was a joint account and money management was shared, both partners tended to get their own spending money from the pool. When money was managed independently both partners took their personal spending money from their earnings. Where there was an allowance system the husband's personal spending money tended to come from his earnings, while the wife's money came from the housekeeping money, a situation which was particularly likely to make a woman feel that she had no right to spend on herself. . . .

. . . In the sample as a whole husbands were likely to spend more than their wives, but this was especially so when there was no joint account. Husbands were particularly likely to spend more on leisure than wives in those households where wives controlled finances, that is, in households with the lowest incomes. A rather unexpected result was found, however, when wife-controlled pooling couples were compared with husband-controlled pooling couples. It was among the latter category that wives who spent more on leisure than their husbands were most commonly found. Of the seventeen women who spent more on leisure than their husbands, ten were found in those households where the husband controlled finances and there was a joint account. Perhaps these were the households where a larger than average income was combined with an ideology of financial sharing? . . .

Conclusion

The evidence presented in this article demonstrates the value of opening up the black box of the household in order to understand the social and economic processes which lie between earning and spending. . . . The amounts spent on leisure activities and on food reflect both the total income of the household and the control of money within it. Thus inequalities in the wider society are translated into inequalities within the household and vice versa. Money, as one of the most fundamental measures of equality, provides a fruitful route to exploring the social and economic processes involved.

Reference

Wilson, G.1987. *Money in the Family*. Aldershot: Avebury.

Chapter 27

Steven Seidman

THE SEXUALISATION
OF LOVE

Steven Seidman's historical study of love charts changing ideals of the relationship between love and sexuality from the 1930s to the 1980s. In the following
passages, taken from the introduction to his book, he outlines his basic thesis.
While the Victorians defined love primarily as a spiritual bond, during the twentieth century love has become more sexualised. This has not only led to a greater
eroticisation of sex, but has had profound implications for heterosexual monogamous marriage and for other forms of intimate relationships.

From *Romantic Longings*, New York: Routledge (1991).

INTIMATE NORMS AND PRACTICES in twentieth-century America
which have valued an expansive notion of sexual choice, diversity and erotic
pleasure are today under assault. The value placed upon sex as a domain of pleasure and self-expression is being held responsible for a variety of contemporary
personal and social ills. Our expanded sexual freedom, it is argued, has eroded
relational commitments; it has created unrealistic expectations for personal happiness; it has uncoupled sex from stable social bonds. The yield of this intimate
culture, some critics contend, has not been sexual and intimate fulfillment but an
anomic and narcissistic culture. AIDS, herpes, escalating rates of divorce, illegiti-
macy and teen pregnancies, loneliness, violence against women, and the
impoverishment and abandonment of our children are claimed as its bitter fruit.
This critique of current sexual trends often carries a nostalgia for an idealized nineteenth-century intimate culture. In this period, it is assumed, sex was firmly
embedded in permanent social bonds and intimacy was not dependent on fleeting
sexual pleasures but anchored in a deep spiritual kinship and a range of social

responsibilities. Although this critique is especially prevalent among conservatives, it has surfaced among liberals and the left, including feminists.

I take issue with this critical perspective on contemporary American intimate culture. . . . The Victorian period cannot serve as a standard to judge contemporary intimate life. Although the myth of the 'repressed Victorian' may have been put to rest, reinventing the Victorians as moderns who successfully integrated desire and affect is no less a simplification. Our contemporary intimate conventions are anchored primarily in twentieth-century developments. In the early decades of this century an intimate culture formed which framed sex as a medium of love. By sexualizing love, this culture encouraged a heightened attention to the body, sensual pleasure and sex technique. One consequence of the 'sexualization of love' was that eroticism was conceived of as a source of romantic bonding. Mutual erotic fulfillment was intended to enhance intimate solidarity in a social context where other unifying forces (e.g. kinship, patriarchy, economic dependency) were losing their power to do so. A second consequence of the development of the erotic aspects of sex was that the pleasurable and expressive qualities of sex gradually acquired legitimacy apart from settings of romantic intimacy. In the post-World War II years, discourses appeared in mainstream culture that constructed sex as having multiple meanings (procreation, love and pleasure) and diverse legitimate social contexts. Although this development has been bewailed by some critics for causing many current ills, it has, in my view, been crucial to the expansion of sexual choice and diversity. In short, there materialized in the twentieth-century United States an intimate culture that framed sex as a sphere of love and romantic bonding as well as a domain of self-expression and sensual happiness.

My aim, however, is not to celebrate the American intimate culture. Discourses and representations promoting the joys and social uses of eroticism have sometimes neglected the dangers of sex; they have not adequately examined the emotional and moral context of sex; they have, at times, overloaded sex with excessive expectations of self-fulfillment. Finally, the culture of eroticism has imbued sex with ambiguous, often conflicting meanings: sex is projected as a sphere of love and romance and, alternatively, as a medium of pleasure and self-expression. . . .

The meanings and purposes we invest in love are, in part, a product of diverse discourses, representations, traditions, and legal and moral customs. These cultural forces construct love as a domain about which we hold a range of beliefs and judgments. These meanings shape the way we imagine and experience love. They define what we expect or hope for from love and how it relates to self-fulfillment as well as the welfare and future of our society. These public representations change over time. . . .

The sexualization of love

The eroticization of sex

. . . Between the early part of the nineteenth century and the later part of the twentieth century, the meaning and place of sex in relation to love, and therefore the meaning of love, underwent important changes. Love changed from having an essentially spiritual meaning to being conceived in a way that made it inseparable from the erotic longings and pleasures of sex. By the early decades of the twentieth century, the desires and pleasures associated with the erotic aspects of sex were imagined as a chief motivation and sustaining source of love. The Victorian language of love as a spiritual communion was either marginalized or fused with the language of desire and joy. I chart a process of the progressive 'sexualization of love' in which the erotic dimensions of sex assume an expanded role in proving and maintaining love.

Paralleling the sexualization of love is an equally momentous dynamic, namely the legitimation of the erotic aspects of sex. To the extent that erotic pleasure was viewed as a medium of love, the pursuit of sensual pleasure received public legitimation. I am suggesting, in other words, an account of the rise in the twentieth century of an intimate culture in which sex was valued for its sensually pleasurable and expressive qualities. It became legitimate to pursue sex for carnal pleasure to the extent that eroticism acquired a higher meaning as a symbol or vehicle of love.

The sexualization of love made possible the legitimation of the erotic aspects of sex. Ironically, while the eroticization of sex was initially accepted only in a context of love, by the post-World War II period the pleasurable and expressive qualities of eroticism acquired value apart from a context of love. This development introduced new possibilities and complexities into America's intimate culture. For example, if sex now carried multiple legitimate meanings, individuals had more opportunities to design their own sexual and intimate lifestyles. Yet expanded sexual choice and the pursuit of erotic pleasure raised fears about negatively impacting on the stability of intimate bonds; concerns were voiced regarding the morality of sexual objectification and the reduction of individuals to vessels of pleasure. Moreover, sex was now invested with conflicting meanings. Despite even the most enthusiastic efforts to deromanticize sex and construct it as merely a domain of pleasure and self-expression, it remains culturally entangled with emotional and moral resonances of love. As both an expression and medium of love and a domain of pleasure and self-expression, sex carried ambiguous meanings and behavioral directives. The possibilities of expanded choice and lifestyle diversity as well as the new dangers and strains presented by these developments define the ambiguous moral meaning of contemporary American intimate culture. . . .

. . . [T]he Victorian period, 1830–1890. In white, middle-class, Victorian culture, a spiritual ideal of love figured prominently. Love referred to a spiritual affinity and spiritual companionship. The Victorians, however, were by no means prudes. They affirmed the power and beneficial qualities of sex. Sex was an expected, obligatory and healthy part of marriage. However, we can discern an antagonism between sex and love in Victorian culture. Love was considered an ideal basis and the essential state of marriage. Yet sex was thought of as an equally vital part of marriage. It is the nature of sex, so many Victorians thought, to incite sensuality, which threatens to destroy the spiritual essence of marriage by engulfing it in a sea of lust. Accordingly, Victorians sought to control the place of sex in marriage. They did this by urging the desexualization of love and the desensualization of sex. At times, Victorians defended the desexualization of marriage itself, but this contradicted their belief in the omnipresence and beneficent power of the sex instinct. Curiously, the desexualization of love and the desensualization of sex made same-sex love more acceptable. Romantic friendships or love between women and, to a lesser extent, love between men was fairly typical and carried no trace of wrongdoing or shame. The antithesis today between a pure and ennobled heterosexuality and an impure and ignoble homosexuality was absent. Love between members of the same sex and [love] between members of the opposite sex were often viewed as complementary not mutually exclusive.

[T]he post-Victorian, 'modern' years from 1890 to 1960. The language of love now intermingles with that of sex. Sexual attraction is taken as a sign of love; the giving and receiving of sexual pleasures are viewed as demonstrations of love; sustained sexual longing and satisfaction is thought to be a condition for maintaining love. It is, moreover, the sensual side of sex that is valued. Sensuality is legitimated as a vehicle of love. Hence, the Victorian antithesis between love and sex and especially between love and sensuality disappears. Of course, love means more than sex. The Victorian ideal of spiritual companionship is transfigured into an idealized solidarity of lovers based upon personal, social and cultural companionship. True love is thought to combine sexual fulfillment and this idealized solidarity. The sexualization of love was paralleled by the exaltation of heterosexual love and the pollution of homosexual love. Under the impact of a scientific-medical discourse of homosexuality, the nineteenth-century paradigm of romantic friendship was replaced by that of homosexual or lesbian love. Heterosexuality and homosexuality were now described as mutually exclusive categories of desire, identity and love.

[T]he contemporary period, 1960–80. [T]he sexualization of love . . . inadvertently led to legitimating the erotic aspects of sex. In the early decades of the twentieth century, sensual pleasures were imbued with a higher value and purpose. Erotic fulfillment sustained, enhanced and revitalized love. This implied a heightened focus and value placed upon erotic technique and fulfillment. Although the value placed on eroticism was legitimated initially only for the purpose of strengthening romantic bonds, by the 1960s the pleasurable and expressive qualities of sex were appealed to as a sufficient justification of sex. Discourses and representations appeared that constructed sex as a domain of pleasure and self-expression requiring no higher purpose so long as the interpersonal context was one of consent and mutuality. Eros was released from the culture of romance that gave birth to it. . . . In the post-World-War II years we can observe a third dramatic change in the meaning of same sex intimacy. The Victorian model of romantic friendship, we recall, gave way to the model of homosexual or lesbian love in the early decades of the twentieth century. In the contemporary period, 'gay love' emerges as a new, positive model of same sex intimacy. . . .

. . . I take issue with critics who relate current disturbances in American intimate culture to the expansion of sexual choice and diversity. Although a liberal intimate culture may occasion excesses or discontents associated with sexual objectification, vulgarity, emotional callousness, even sexual disease, these are acceptable costs for expanded choice and an intimate culture that values erotic pleasure and variety.[1]

Note

1   Obviously, I am not saying that AIDS is an acceptable cost for expanded sexual choice. My claim is that the widespread eradication of HIV requires 'safe sex' practices, not necessarily the restriction of intimate lifestyle options. See Steven Seidman, 'The transfiguring sexual identity: AIDS and the construction of homosexuality', *Social Text* (fall 1988), pp. 19–20.

Chapter 28

Wendy Langford

BUT HE SAID HE LOVED ME

This study of the dynamics of heterosexual love is based on in-depth interviews with fifteen women. All the women describe the positive, transformative effects of being 'in love', during the early phases of their relationships, a stage at which their male partners are sensitive, open and attentive to their needs. As relationships progress, however, men distance themselves more and more from their partners, a distancing exacerbated by women's attempts to repair the relationship, to recover mutual intimacy. Wendy Langford analyses this 'counter-revolutionary' stage of love in terms of Hegel's 'master/slave dialectic' in which the man, assuming the master position, seeks to affirm his selfhood by denying the subjectivity of the other – his lover. The woman, meanwhile, adopts the slave position, seeking recognition from the master through self-denial. Here she discusses the consequences of this pattern of sexual relations.

From *Revolutions of the Heart: Gender, Power and the Delusions of Love*, London Routledge (1999).

. . .

THE OPENNESS AND SENSITIVITY which men exhibited 'in the beginning' all too readily disappeared as they resorted to a 'paternal' power exemplified by the capacity to objectify women and block their attempts at communication. Here we will look at how this behaviour represents a classic manifestation of the 'master' position in Hegel's [master/slave] dialectic. . . .

One area where this was particularly evident was in some women's accounts of sex. Men were commonly portrayed as simply expecting that their partners would, as a matter of course, provide them with sexual pleasure – an expectation not matched by any attempt to ascertain how far women themselves desired sexual intercourse. Indeed, some men appeared determined to 'block out' evidence that was contrary to their own desire. Women described how, if they were resistant to their partners' sexual demands, they would engage in pressurising behaviours such as sulking or 'whingeing'. If she still did not agree to sex, he might be hurt and bad-tempered and the atmosphere of the relationship would become more openly difficult. This is not to suggest that women simply did not want to have a sexual relationship. Rather they said that they only wanted to have sex when they felt recognised and appreciated, and in so far as they did not feel recognised and appreciated they would experience reluctance. However, this situation was not straightforward. Given women's propensities to assume responsibility for 'making the relationship work' and given the central place of sex in ideals of a 'proper' relationship, it is not surprising that women's resistance was weak and ambivalent. Moreover, since a common complaint among women was that the only time their partners expressed affection or interest in them was when they wanted sex, neither is it surprising that women's resistance might also be undermined by their own desire to re-establish intimacy.

In practice, sex in the context of established relationships was often described as being far from intimate and the question of whether it took place at all appeared to become increasingly separate from the question of whether women themselves either desired it or found it pleasurable. As with the more general picture, women expressed anger and disappointment at their partner's selfishness and ineptitude and described their efforts at love-making as 'hopeless' and 'pathetic'. For some women, sex appeared to have become simply one aspect of their 'maternal duties', something they provided on demand which appeared no more welcome or enjoyable than doing all the housework. The following quotes from Mary and Jane are typical:

MARY: I am not really sure that it's me he is having sex with any more, not inside his head. Yes, I feel I am just a useful vehicle.

JANE: Keith has woken me in the night a few times, and you just – it is just not worth the hassle or the row or the argument or the aftermath by saying 'No, sod off.' Erm, so you just go along with it, but you don't enjoy it. But they don't seem to . . . actually *realise* whether you are enjoying it or not.

In such narratives, men appeared at once as greedy and desperate for the comfort afforded by their 'mother's' body, and as assailants who expressed a violent disregard for the well-being of the woman they 'loved'. Where women continued to engage in sexual relationships on these terms, they did so – and indeed could only do so – through 'blocking out' their own experience. In the following extract, for example, Ruth reveals some of what normally remains hidden during the alienated encounters of counter-revolutionary sex:

RUTH: I've often felt quite detached when I've had sex, and I know from talking to other women that that's quite a common thing, you know? Like, er, you start to think like Oh God – you know? – did I iron my shirt for tomorrow or whatever – you know? – that kind of thing – Oh God, I wish this would just be over – you know? – which speaks volumes, doesn't it?

It would be hard to do justice to the question of the distress and harm inflicted upon women by their being reduced to mere instruments of their partner's gratification. I will not try, save to say that tears were shed during some interviews, and to give these two quotes from Sarah and Jean:

SARAH: It's horrible. He doesn't even like me. He doesn't look at me . . . And I feel awful afterwards, because I feel like I have just been used. . . . It is soul-destroying, and I think it just makes me lose all my confidence.

JEAN: After it was over I would sort of just lie there for a while and then come down[stairs] and break my heart, thinking *for God's sake I can't stand this*. I hated it.

Without accounts from men, it is not possible to know how they understood this violence which they exacted upon their partners. Women's accounts suggested that the aim of men's aggression was, paradoxically, to block out all knowledge of the suffering they were inflicting in their hopeless attempt to enforce the fantasy that women actually could, and wanted to, provide them with unconditional gratification. This observation would certainly correspond with the psychology of the 'master'. The master does not aim to inflict suffering for its own sake. Indeed, he might feel extremely guilty were he to allow knowledge of the slave's suffering to come fully into his awareness. The master's ability to exhibit concern or compassion for the slave is overridden, however, by his own existential drama; his aggression is aimed at reassuring himself that he has control over the independent will of the slave, whose recognition he needs to convince himself of his own existence.

Chapter 29

Jean Duncombe and Dennis Marsden

WHOSE ORGASM IS THIS ANYWAY?
'Sex work' in long-term heterosexual
couple relationships

Drawing on interviews with both partners in established heterosexual couples, the authors explore the gendered responses to the expectations about and the practice of sex and intimacy. They develop the concept of 'sex work' to explain how their respondents managed feelings of distaste and disappointment as time progressed, in contrast with earlier feelings of attraction or passion, which had masked any flaws and difficulties. The data indicate that many of the women had never been really happy about the quality of sex with their partners and were relieved to find ways to negotiate a minimal degree of intimacy. The men, on the other hand, tended to regret the decline, and in some cases expected sex as a conjugal right. This study suggests that despite women's greater equality and sexual freedom behind the bedroom door they are not experiencing sexual pleasure and that this is still being blamed on their 'frigidity' rather than their partner's failings.

From Jeffery Weeks and Janet Holland (eds) *Sexual Cultures: Communities and Intimacy*, London: Macmillan (1996).

T O S U S T A I N T H E S E N S E of intimacy in long-term relationships, women often undertake 'emotion work' on their partners and *on themselves* by insisting that 'We're ever so happy, really' and putting up defences against evidence to the contrary. This process may be described as 'living the family myth' (Hochschild 1990) or, as we would say, 'playing the couple game'. . . .

By analogy with emotion work, in doing 'sex work' individuals would 'manage' their emotions according to 'feeling rules' of how sex *ought* to be experienced (Hochschild 1983), to try to attain or simulate (for themselves and/or their part-ners) a sexual fulfilment they would not feel 'spontaneously': for example, to endure sex, Victorian brides-to-be were exhorted to 'lie back and think of England'; and, more recently, women admit they sometimes fake orgasms, and couples (or women) are advised to 'work' on their fading relationships by restaging romance. . . .

In fact, married couples generally experience a long-term decline in sexual activity,[1] which has been attributed to 'habituation', or the 'distractions' of family life and work (Frank and Anderson 1980; Rubin 1991; Weiss 1990). It has been suggested that a companionate 'tenderness' may outweigh any sexual regrets (Frank and Anderson 1980), but Rubin reports how many of her respondents in longer-term relationships 'mourn the passing of . . . passion' (Rubin 1991: 166–71), and occasionally get nostalgic flashbacks and wonder, 'Why can't we make this happen all the time?' (Rubin 1991: 186).

Our study of change in longer-term relationships

Our respondents echoed this puzzlement that they could not recapture earlier passion and romance – apart from the occasional sense of *déja vu* with the aid of wine or the romantic setting of a holiday (Duncombe and Marsden 1995). But the decline of passion and tactile or sensual intimacy seemed somehow inevitable: one wife said, 'We don't have sex so much now, I mean I think you'd have to be pretty energetic to maintain that sort of . . . Sometimes we have a long kiss but not so much now. Not every day. . . . We like being, I mean *I* like being close.'

However, it was surprisingly common for women now to 'confess' that they had *always* 'at some level' found their sexual relationships unfulfilling:

> He didn't really bother with foreplay. But somehow I was so into him that it didn't matter, and I never said anything. I sort of didn't notice, yet I sort of did. . . . I think somehow it doesn't seem important, and you don't want to hurt their feelings. And somehow the sex seemed wonderful even when it went wrong.

Other wives commented on early doubts (about erection failures, or the shape or size of their husband's penis) about which they had reassured their husband or blamed themselves, but which they now consciously recognised *had* mattered 'at some level' even then, and had come to matter more later.

In contrast, men who acknowledged early problems tended to blame what they saw as their wives' low sex drive:

> I really do . . . *try*, but. . . . I think she might be one of those women who just doesn't need sex. . . . I remember a very funny night, we went out to see some friends and the bloke had devised a chart. . . . There were three colours, one where his wife wanted it, one when he wanted it, and one when they both wanted it. . . . But I thought, I wouldn't need . . . the one when Penny wanted it. . . . [But] if I'd sat down and said, 'Look Penny, we've got a problem in our sex life, we need to talk about it,' she would have gone off in a rage, so I just didn't bother.

However, several husbands had recognised their own deficiencies, again initially at some rather deep level:

> We kind of settled into a routine where I liked sex early in the morning . . . but she was sleepy . . . although she'd let me have it (I was a 'dawn raider'!). . . . I can remember . . . 'subliminally' . . . I was frightened of *letting* her get into it . . . because I wouldn't know what to do with it. . . . It made me feel a bit inadequate. . . . [But] it's not all my fault because she never said – she sort of said she got pleasure even if she didn't come – and she would never participate much if I tried anything different.

Discussion was avoided because each partner did not want to hurt the other, but also men feared looking vulnerable while women feared men's anger:

> It was like he knew there had to be foreplay so – a couple of squeezes up here, then a quick rummage about down there and straight in. But he went *berserk* when I tried to say I'd like him to try more in the fore-play bit. . . . I thought he'd hit me.

So couples tended to develop informal strategies and routines – restricting sex to particular nights, or giving coded messages like wearing sexy nighties or bathing at an unusual time – which indicated and regulated sexual availability (and incidentally avoided the need for women openly to show desire). . . .

Sexual experimentation, pornography and masturbation

To overcome boredom or sexual difficulties couples sometimes experimented with the use of pornography or changes of sexual techniques, or they had resorted to more frequent masturbation.[2] Our data suggest differences between the incorporation of pornography during the earlier passionate phase of a relationship, as compared with the attempt to liven up sex that had lost its passion. In either case men tended to be the initiators because they more readily found pornography arousing and hoped it would help overcome women's inhibitions (get them 'worked up'). But pornography was more acceptable to women early in the relationship (when they might also dress up in sexy undies) than later with a partner for whom they had lost their sense of intimacy, when they felt less able to 'allow' themselves to become (and admit to being) sexually aroused.

Some couples had agreed to experiment with the introduction of pornography later in their relationship: as one husband said, 'What else can you do if you've been married for twelve years and you don't want to endanger your relationship by having affairs?' However, this couple were uneasy at how maintaining the boost to their sex life seemed to need more frequent changes and ever 'harder' porn. Then, it was women who began to find pornography distasteful and a 'turn-off'.

In our study, the husbands had often wanted their wives to give them oral sex, although it was not uncommon for wives to refuse even early on. And while a few who had complied sensed a power over men's vulnerability, they sometimes admitted suppressing qualms about smell and taste. However, as intimacy decayed, such feelings increased, as did the sense of coercion, until oral sex ceased.

As a relatively guilt-free and 'functional' safety valve for their marriages, husbands began to resort to more frequent solitary masturbation – not uncommonly at work where pornography was available.

> You have to be quiet, it's funny really. Sometimes I wonder, after-wards, how many other blokes were wanking in the loo!

Although some wives felt released by this from pressures to have sex, over time husbands might become resentful:

> It would be no skin off her nose. . . . Sometimes I just want her to let me put it in and do it. . . . She's broken the contract. Sex is *part* of marriage, and I can't see that anything's changed enough to alter that.

One woman claimed she didn't mind her husband masturbating in the bathroom but she resented the way it joggled her about in bed; but the husband claimed that she aroused his desire, so she should help or at least let him do it in comfort! For a husband deliberately to let his wife know he masturbated could be a delib-erate attempt to induce guilt. . . .

Unlike men, women actually *preferred* to masturbate alone, out of greater shyness but also afraid their husbands would see their behaviour as an insult or a prelude to penetration. Women's masturbation might also be seen as 'functional' for marriage (giving them the orgasm their husband could not). However, (as with men) masturbation could bring the realisation of lack of fulfilment in their relation-ship; and discovering about orgasms (in one instance through contact with a women's group) could sometimes change women's lives more radically:

> I started to think [feeling frigid] wasn't my fault – which actually [my husband] had . . . let me believe. And I started to feel angry . . . I read about [masturbation] so I decided to try it and it made me feel very powerful to learn about my own body.

This wife then discovered she could attain orgasm with other men, and the couple have now negotiated an open relationship. . . .

In conclusion: the pursuit of 'authentic' sex

Overall, we would argue that there is considerable empirical evidence of sex work, both where individuals reveal that influence of ideologies of how they believe sex 'ought' to be and, more explicitly, where they say they have to 'try' or 'work' or 'force' themselves to have sex. We cannot say how far sex work pervades sexual life, but we are not arguing that people live at a constant pitch of sexual disappointment or even desperation – only that we suspect that 'at some level' many long-term couples would recognise the difficulties described here. . . .

Notes

1   In the US and UK, sexual activity and marital satisfaction decline, the latter reaching a low point after fifteen years, although the pattern is by no means simple (Frank and Anderson 1980; evidence summarised in Goodman 1993; Wellings *et al.* 1994).

2   Rubin gives some evidence on pornography and changes in sexual technique, e.g. oral sex is now practised by most younger couples – though not anal sex (Rubin 1991). US surveys indicate that masturbation is relatively common in marriage, men more than women (Aldridge 1983; Goodman, 1993).

References

Aldridge, R. G. (1983) 'Masturbation during marriage', *Correctional and Social Psychology Journal*, 27: 112–14.

Duncombe, J. and Marsden D. (1995) 'Can men love? "Reading", "staging" and "resisting" the romance', in L. Pearce and J. Stacey (eds), *Romance Revisited*. London: Lawrence & Wishart.

Frank, E. and Anderson, C. (1980) 'The sexual stages of marriage', *Family Circle*, February, p. 64.

Goodman, N. (1993), *Marriage and the Family*. New York: HarperCollins.

Hochschild, A. R. (1983) *The Managed Heart*. London: University of California Press.

Hochschild, A. R. with Maching, A. (1990) *The Second Shift*. London: Piatkus.

Rubin, L. B. (1991) *Erotic Wars*. New York: Harper & Row.

Weiss, R. S. (1990) *Staying the Course*. New York: Fawcett Columbine.

Wellings, K., Field, J., Johnson, A. M. and Wadsworth, J. (1994) *Sexual Behaviour in Britain: The National Survey of Sexual Attitudes and Lifestyles*. London: Penguin.

Chapter 30

Haleh Afshar

MARRIAGE AND FAMILY
IN A BRITISH PAKISTANI
COMMUNITY

Based on an on-going study of three generations of Pakistani women living in West Yorkshire, this reading deals with their views on, and experiences of, marriage. While these women see their own patterns of marriage as distinct from White Western ideals, there are also differences among them, reflecting the life experiences and expectations of each generation and their understanding of their place as women in wider kinship networks.

From 'Gender and "the moral economy of kin" among Pakistani women in West Yorkshire', *New Community*, (2) 1989: 221–5.

Marriage

> Having gone through with the marriage and made their commitment, often with considerable foreboding, most young Asians come to feel that their parents' careful choice of a spouse has not been such a bad one and that they have more freedom than expected.
> (Bullard 1979: 124–5).

ALL THE WOMEN I spoke to saw marriage as an inevitable and desirable part of life and all agreed that their parents should have a say in the arrangements. Even those who were born and brought up in England were somewhat sceptical about romantic love and Western-style marriage. On the other hand all the younger generation felt strongly that they should be consulted about the choice of future husbands.

The older generation, who had married without ever meeting their prospective spouses, felt on the whole that the younger generation should be more pliable. Among the second and third generation, however, there was a degree of ambivalence about sight unseen, non-consultative, marriages. In particular, schoolgirls resented any suggestion that they should leave school in order to be married off. All recognised that parents arranged such marriages in order to get rid of troublesome daughters, who were likely to behave in a way that could lead to a loss of face. The parental ruse of transferring the responsibility for guarding the chastity of young daughters to more able and younger men was clearly observed and generally resented (Afshar 1985). At the same time such knowledge did play an important role in the self-policing of younger women, who saw their side of the bargain and accepted it. In practice the acquiescence towards arranged marriages was, for daughters, tinged with the fear of having to part from their families and going back to their husband's home.

There was a marked contrast between the wishes of many mothers born and raised in Pakistan, who wished to send at least one daughter back to the homeland to secure close family ties and a home base for the next generation. But the daughters, though they accepted the institution of patrilocal marriages, sought to move next door rather than to another country. The youngest group all expressed the hope of staying close to their mothers and bringing their future husbands home. By contrasting the older generation of women, who had been reared almost as guests in their homes and who had been prepared for the move to the mother-in-laws' house from the very beginning, felt that their granddaughters were ill prepared for 'real life' and co-operation with future in-laws.

Mothers found it very difficult to find a middle way. Many, particularly the less well off, had come to depend heavily on the domestic services of their eldest daughter and when the time came found it extremely difficult to marry them off. The ideal solution was perceived by many to be a double marriage, marrying a daughter away and bringing in a daughter-in-law at the same time. Amongst women I talked to, one had managed to do just this. But although in terms of practicability this seemed a sensible solution, the entire family felt emotionally torn apart by the departure of the eldest daughter.

There was, however, a wide variation in the way marriages were arranged and the degree of consultation that took place with daughters, and sons for that matter. There was a close correlation with parental background. Those who had the closest ties with the rural areas tended to have the least consultation. Those from urban areas, who also tended to be the more affluent, tended to marry their children off later and allow them a greater degree of choice. The introduction of the latest Nationality Act in 1986 made parental decisions considerably harder and caused much heart-break searching amongst those who had promised their daughters in marriage before the Act and had to go through with the ceremony afterwards in the knowledge that their daughter could not bring her spouse into the country and would have to leave.

Although all the women we talked to approved of the institution of marriage, their views about what it was and the obligations that it entailed varied markedly across the generations. The oldest generation viewed marriage as the beginning of 'real life'. They accepted their mothers-in-law as the real authority in charge of their household and some had had their lives mapped out for them by their future in-laws. One grandmother from a rural background had had her marriage arranged with a young educated urban-dwelling cousin. Her father-in-law had decided that his son needed an educated wife and had arranged for the future daughter-in-law, accompanied by her sister, to be sent off to a boarding school near Delhi to complete her secondary education. The subsequent marriage and life with the in-laws had been, according to this informant, simple and untraumatic. It may be that the passage of time has made the past seem more agreeable, but this lady was convinced that her early married days were as good as anyone's. She had been trained to cook and sew and her mother-in-law taught her to do so in a way that pleased her husband. When her husband moved to Leeds, she had stayed on with her in-laws until he was ready to receive her, and in many ways she found the parting from her mother-in-law more painful than the move to her marital home from the village. She had hoped that her husband would return and had followed him extremely reluctantly. She found the move to Britain a terrible experience for which she had no mental or emotional preparation. This woman had great sympathy for those young girls who were married off to return to Pakistan and felt very strongly that such a move was emotionally unbearable and should not be imposed on anyone. . . .

References

Afshar, H. (1986) 'Khomeini's teachings and their implications for women in Iran', in A. Tabari and N. Yeganeh (eds) *In the Shadow of Islam*, London: Zed Press, pp. 79–96.

Bullard, C. (1979) 'Conflict, continuity and change: second-generation South Asians', in V. Saifullah Khan (ed.) *Minority Families in Britain: Support and Stress*, London: Macmillan, pp. 109–31.

Chapter 31

Kath Weston

LOVERS THROUGH THE
LOOKING GLASS

Whereas heterosexual love and eroticism are conventionally thought of in terms of attraction based on 'difference', lesbian and gay desire is, by definition, founded on same-gender attraction. Kath Weston uses the idea of the looking glass to question these easy assumptions about sameness and difference. Her exploration of the relationship between gender and sexuality in the negotiation of intimacy among lesbians and gay men is part of a larger ethnographic study of lesbians and gay men in the San Francisco Bay area. Her fieldwork, conducted between 1985 and 1987, combined participant observation with in-depth interviews with forty men and forty women.

From *Families we Choose*, New York: Columbia University Press (1991).

WHAT TO MAKE OF the relationships that lesbians and gay men label lovers and claim as kin, erotic ties that bear no intrinsic connection to procreative sexuality or gendered difference?[1] In the United States, where procreation occupies the cultural imagination in its guise as the outcome of differences between women and men, both gender and kinship studies 'begin by taking "difference" from granted and treating it as a presocial fact' (Yanagisako and Collier 1987: 9). When David Schneider (1977: 66) discusses the distinction between erotic and nonerotic love in the United States, for example, he treats erotic love as 'the union of opposites, the other the unity which identities have'.

Viewed against the backdrop of accounts that ground erotic relations in the symbolism of genital and gendered difference, lesbian or gay loves appear 'the same' and therefore incomplete. Looking-glass imagery casts gay couples in the one-dimensional relations of a likeness defined by its opposition to the differences of anatomy and gender understood to configure heterosexual marriage, sexuality, and procreation. To the extent that heterosexuals view lesbian or gay lovers as two like halves that cannot be reconciled to make a whole, gay relationships seem to yield a cultural unit deficient in meaning (which, as any good structuralist knows, must be generated through contrast). Representations that draw on mirror imagery reduce this apparent similarity of gay or lesbian partners to mere replication of the self, a narcissistic relation that creates no greater totality and brings little new into the world.

How can lesbian and gay relationships gain legitimacy as bonds of kinship, shaped within a discourse on families we choose, if they lack this more basic recognition as authentically social ties? More than a bias toward procreative sexuality contributes to the devaluation of gay relationships. In a society that symbolically links procreation to heterosexual intercourse and gendered difference, depicting gay couples exclusively in terms of a gender identity shared by both partners tends to make 'same/same' relationships appear problematic, unworkable, meaningless, even 'unnatural'. Not only one's lover, but features of the cultural construction of heterosexuality, implicitly return to the gay or lesbian self as reflection.

In scholarly analysis of gay relationships as well as in the perceptions of most lesbians and gay men, a focus on gendered continuity has replaced the interpretation that prevailed earlier in the century of homosexuality as a transgender identification. Rather than perpetuating stereotypes of gay men who are universally effeminate and lesbians who 'really' want to be men, contemporary wisdom has it that lesbians are more like heterosexual women than like gay men. Correspondingly, gay men are supposed to have more in common with straight men than with lesbians (Bell and Weinberg 1978; Simon and Gagnon 1967a, b). Typical of this line of reasoning is Denise Cronin's (1975: 277) assertion that 'lesbians are women first and homosexuals second'. From personal narratives and sociological studies to psychoanalytic and literary accounts, too often each member of a gay or lesbian couple appears as the mirror image of the other, based upon a presumption of the overwhelming saliency of gender identity within the relationship. After studying San Francisco's Castro neighborhood, Frances FitzGerald (1986: 7) concluded, 'Liberated gay women . . . turned out to be archetypally women, and gay men in the Castro archetypally men – as if somehow their genders had been squared by isolation from the other sex.' Associated with this shift in scholarly representation as the *de facto* separation of most lesbian and gay male institutions during the 1970s and 1980s. . . .

The sociological conception of a looking-glass self who gains personal awareness in the process of being evaluated by others experiences a sort of turnabout in depictions of gay relationships, within which knowledge of a partner is often supposed to be mediated by knowledge of the self. In his widely read advice manual *Loving Someone Gay*, Don Clark (1977: 51) contends, 'A Gay person often starts the love-search being attracted to people who are opposite or shadows of the self, as if seeking some sort of integration or completion. This phenomenon may have to do with anti-Gay training that taught you to devalue yourself.' His recommendation is to value likeness, taking oneself as the point of departure and comparison. Writing in the gay press, Ken Popert (1982: 73) utilized the language of the looking glass when he described 'the realization that, in turning away from unknown gay men, I was turning away from myself'. Such constructions of gay relationships as relationships of identity implicitly cede the territory of difference and opposition to heterosexual couples. My same-sex partner becomes a reflection of myself, based upon an inferred likeness that in turn depends upon gendered differences defined in the culture at large. 'We're both women,' Rose Ellis insisted, speaking of a lover, 'so we *understand* each other, so to speak.' The contrast between sameness and difference then joins the distinction between biological family and families we choose in patrolling the border that separates gay from straight identity.

Given the widespread influence of imagery that emphasizes gendered continuities between gay partners, it should not be surprising to find that lesbians and gay men in the Bay Area tended to depict one another as approaching relationships from different directions – women from the side of love and men from the side of sex. When they spoke in generalities, most agreed on the terms of the cultural equation: love + sex = a relationship. To call a relationship 'committed' signaled for both men and women not only a mutual intention for it to endure, but often a claim to kinship as well. This ideal combination of emotional with physical unity made gay couples 'about' love and friendship as well as sex, in a manner consistent with twentieth-century ideologies of companionate marriage. But in their coming-out stories, men frequently highlighted the shock of realizing that it could be possible for two men to love, dance, kiss erotically, become jealous, or have on-going relationships rather than a string of sexual encounters. Women, in contrast, were more likely to report originally finding it easy to imagine love between women without recognizing the option of adding an erotic component (cf. Peplau *et al.* 1978: 8). When I asked interview participants if they were currently involved in a relationship, a few were uncertain how to answer. Of those who hesitated, the women wondered whether they should count primary emotional bonds as relationships in the absence of sexual involvement, while the men wondered whether to include routinized sexual relationships that lacked emotional depth and commitment.

Identifying (gay) men with sex and (lesbian) women with love reinforces the appearance of an overwhelming continuity and similarity between partners who share a common gender identity. Significantly, interviews and everyday encounters also turned up plenty of exceptions to such gender-typed generalizations: men whose first same-sex involvement occurred with a best friend, women sexually active with multiple partners since childhood. In a humorous play on conventional understandings of gendered difference, Louise Romero portrayed herself being socialized into the proper way for a lesbian to go about meeting a partner.

> Coffee goes good. Usually coffee first date, and then they go to bed with you, but otherwise forget it. . . . My other friend, Stacey, that I lived with, she said 'Louise, you got to stop going to bed with somebody in one night. You can't just do that. You got to date for a few months, and *then* go to bed with them.' I said, 'Date?' She said, 'That's the only way you get a steady girlfriend. You just can't rush into things.' So I tried it once with this one woman. She came over for dinner. I fixed it real nice, I had the fireplace going and everything. And then I talked to her the next day and stuff. She goes, 'Well, I didn't think

you were interested.' It was like she put it on *me*. She wanted to go to bed that night!

With the advent of AIDS, gay wit pointed out the ironic combination of a 'new romanticism' and more cautious attitude toward sex among gay men with the 'rediscovery' of sex by lesbians. During the 1980s the same gay publications that featured how-to articles on dating for gay men presented lesbians with tongue-in-cheek tips on cruising for a sexual partner. Strip shows, erotic magazines, more candid discussions of sexuality, and debates about controversial practices like s/m captured the attention of many lesbians in the Bay Area during this decade. Within the same time frame, according to a survey conducted by the San Francisco AIDS Foundation, gay men reported having less sex, safe or unsafe (Helquist 1985). Some concluded from such survey results that sex had become less important to gay men, yet what I observed was the development of new forms of camaraderie in the face of the epidemic, accompanied by a redefinition of what qualifies as sex. 'Years ago,' Harold Sanders maintained,

> the way men would treat each other in a sexual context, it would be very covert. Then there might be something like [gruff voice], 'Do you want to suck my cock?' And you knew that what the other persons wanted was the same kind of tenderness and sharing of affection that you wanted, but that you could not possibly exempt [yourself from] that definition of being a man.

In the early 1980s, gay men incorporated miniature teddy bears into the handkerchief color code developed to indicate preferences for various specialized sexual practices. Handkerchiefs of particular colors placed in particular pockets (right or left) coexisted with this novel symbol of the desire to hug or be hugged, to 'share emotion'. A similar move toward integrating love and caring with masculinity and toughness surfaced in the context of AIDS organizing. Pamphlets distributed by a major AIDS organization in San Francisco displayed the title 'A Call to Arms' next to the graphic of a teddy bear, mixing metaphors of militarism (the battle with AIDS) and affection. In the 1986 Gay Pride parade one man had handcuffed a teddy bear to the back of his motor-cycle where a lover might ride, while another dressed in a full set of leathers carried a small bear attached to a picture of his lover and his lover's date of death.[2]

To a degree, then, the identification of sex and emotion with men and women, respectively, would seem to have blurred for gay men and lesbians during the 1980s. Yet this apparent integration of the two domains coincided with a sense of exploring unknown territories that members of the 'opposite gender' would better understand. If a gay man wanted to know about dating and romance, the person to go to for information was a woman; if a lesbian wanted to try picking up someone in a bar, why not ask a gay male friend for advice? Ideologies of gendered contrast and continuity also persisted in the form of the common belief that gay men have difficulty maintaining relationships, whereas lesbian couples suffer from too much intimacy. Among interview participants, the longest same-sex relationships listed by lesbians had endured on average for more years than the longest same-sex relationships listed by gay men. However, based upon this limited sample, the gap appeared to narrow as the number of years together extended. Nearly equal numbers of men and women had partners at the time of the interview, while similar proportions of single women and men claimed they desired a committed relationship . . . Percentages notwithstanding, some gay men considered their relationships especially susceptible to dissolution because they believe men do not learn to 'nurture'. Many lesbians agreed that women are more empathetic and better prepared to keep the home fires burning, but asserted that they encountered a dilemma 'opposite' to that facing gay men: difficulty setting limits to circumvent dependency within relationships. Put two women or two men together, they argued, and a magnification of the gendered traits attributed to each must surely result.

For every instance of a gay man or lesbian following the cultural logic of the looking glass, another portrayal contradicted or inverted its terms. When comparing themselves to straight men, many gay men described themselves as more sensitive or nurturing; in certain contexts, lesbians tended to present self-sufficiency, strength, and independence as characteristically lesbian traits. In the specific context of discourse on lovers, however, notions of gay relationships as relationships of likeness in which partners reflect back to one another their common gender identity shaped the way both lesbians and gay men configured eroticism and commitment.

Another correlate of the mirror metaphor, with its stresses on sameness and the intensification of gender within gay relationships, is the application to couples of normative expectations that have long since been discredited in association with community. Roberta Osabe, like many of her peers, reported an initial anticipation of perfect harmony with her lover based on a shared gender identity.

> When I realized that just because you were a lesbian doesn't mean your relationships with women are cut out − it doesn't mean you'll find happiness − that's when I *really* got depressed 'Cause I thought it was gonna be just like la-la-la, you know − flowers (laughs). Happiness! I'd found the yellow brick road, and it was on the way to the Emerald City. [Then] I realized you still had a shitty job. You still had all your problems. People are still gonna leave you. You're still gonna be alone, basically. And that was a *big* disappointment.

To search for the man or woman in the mirror, the lover at the end of a journey to self-love and self-acceptance, is to fall under the spell of the oversimplified contrasts of likeness and difference implicit in the mirror metaphor. As Paulette Ducharme observed, 'I do definitely think I have a preference for women's bodies over men's bodies. But also [a preference for] beings − there are beings in those bodies, and all women certainly aren't the same.' In addition to idiosyncratic differences such as squeezing toothpaste from different parts of the tube, differences of class, age, race, ethnicity, and a host of other identities that crosscut gender are sufficient to put to rest the notion of a single unified woman's or man's standpoint. The assumption that gender identity will be the primary *subjective* identity for every lesbian or gay man, universally and without respect to context, remains just that: an assumption.

Consider the case of interracial couples. Far from presenting an inherently unproblematic situation of sameness and identification between partners, the interracial aspect of a relationship can become a point of saliency that overwhelms any sense of likeness. For Leroy Campbell, a particular sort of difference, rooted in racist interpretations of the meaning of skin color and leading to painful reversals of situational expectations, became the overriding issue when he talked about trying to meet other men through the bars.

> See, I don't know if you can imagine what it's like seeing somebody walking towards you, or being in a bar and looking at someone, and feeling attracted to them, when there's a possibility that if you walk up to them and talk to them, that they're gonna say, 'I don't like black people.' So you have this perception of being attracted to this person who might *hate* you.

When issues of race and racism came up in her three-year relationship with a white woman, explained Eriko Yoshikawa, who was Japanese, 'it always makes us feel how different we are, and it creates a certain kind of distance.' On another occasion, Eriko's lover cautioned, 'We're careful not to attribute all differences between us to the most obvious difference between us.'

Some lesbians and gay men have extended mirror imagery to race and ethnicity with the argument that getting involved with someone of another race means 'not really facing yourself', or through their expectation that relationships with someone of the same ethnic identification would prove intrinsically easier to negotiate. Yet likeness no more automatically follows from a common racial identity than from a shared gender identity. The challenge is to understand how, why, and in what contexts individuals abstract gender from a range of potential identities, elevating gender identity into *the* axis for defining sameness.

Some of the same individuals who emphasized gendered continuity when discussing their current lovers highlighted divergent racial identities, class backgrounds, or ages to explain recent breakups and describe past relationships. Because people in the United States conventionally attribute separation and divorce to 'irreconcilable differences', here context becomes significant in determining whether the language of the looking glass will come into play. That individuals enjoy considerable interpretive leeway in this regard, however, is evident from a comment made by Kenny Nash as a black gay man: 'It became more a matter of being gay [than being black] if a man I was with was white. . . . It was like, "If you react badly because I'm with this man, it's not because he's white, it's because he's a man."'

Refracting relationships through looking-glass imagery leads discussion toward the catch-all terms of sameness and difference, too often omitting the crucial questions: in what *way* the same, and in what *respect* different (Scott 1988)? Lost in a partner's reflection of the mirrored self are distinctive constructions of likeness and contrast, constructions that have varied through time as well as from couple to couple and between gay men and lesbians. The diversity of gendered relations associated with androgyny, 'Castro clones', butch/fem among lesbians, the eclipse of elements of the campy style of 1950s queens by a 'new masculinity' shared between gay male partners, and the eroticization of symbolic contrasts among gay men elaborated through class imagery, invalidate any attempt to confine lesbian and gay couples within the terms of an abstract gender symmetry.

Notes

1   Many of the gay men and lesbians I met voiced dissatisfaction with the expressions available to describe gay couples. They generally felt that 'lovers' understates commitment to a relationship and 'partners' sounds too much like a business arrangement, while 'boyfriends' or 'girlfriends' minimizes the seriousness, maturity, and kinship status of committed relationships. I have elected to use 'lovers' and 'partners' interchangeably.
2   See Nungesser (1986) for stories of gay men with AIDS who describe learning about intimacy and affection through coping with the disease.

References

Bell, A. P. and Weinberg, M. S. (1978) *Homosexualities. A study of Diversity among Men and Women*. New York: Simon & Schuster.

Clark, D. (1977) *Loving Someone Gay*. Millbrae CA: Celestial Arts.

Cronin, D. (1975) 'Coming out among lesbians', in E. Goode and R. T. Troiden (eds) *Sexual Deviance and Sexual Deviants*. New York: Morrow.

FitzGerald, F. (1986) *Cities on a Hill: A Journey Through Contemporary American Cultures*. New York: Simon & Schuster.

Helquist, M. (1985) 'New behaviour survey released by SF AIDS Fdn', *Coming Up!*, August.

Nungesser, Lon G. (1986) *Epidemic of Courage: Facing AIDS in America*. New York: St Martin's Press.

Peplau, L. A. *et al.* (1978) 'Loving women: attachment and autonomy in lesbian relationships', *Journal of Social Issues*, 34 (3): 7–27.

Popert, K. (1982) 'Neighbourly sentiments', in E. Jackson and S. Persky (eds) *Flaunting It! A Decade of Gay Journalism from The Body Politic*. Vancouver: New Star Books.

Schneider, D. (1977) 'Kinship, nationality and religion in American culture', in J. Dolgin *et al.* (eds) *Symbolic Anthropology*. New York: Columbia University Press.

Scott, J. W. (1988) 'Deconstructing equality-versus-difference: or, the uses of post-structuralist theory for feminism', *Feminist Studies*, 14 (1): 33–50.

Simon, W. and Gagnon, J. (1967a) 'Homosexuality: the formulation of a sociological perspective', *Journal of Health and Social Behaviour*, 8: 177–85.

Simon, W. and Gagnon, J. (1967b) 'The lesbian: a preliminary overview' in J. Gagnon and W. Simon (eds) *Sexual Deviance*. New York: Harper & Row.

Yanagisako, S. and Collier, J. (1987) 'Towards a unified analysis of gender and kinship', in J. Collier and S. Yanagisako (eds) *Gender and Kinship*. Stanford CA: Stanford University Press.

Chapter 32

Brian Heaphy, Catherine Donovan and Jeffrey Weeks

'SEX, MONEY AND THE KITCHEN SINK'

Drawing on research with same-sex couples, the authors question the assumption that these relationships are free from the inequalities and constraints which beset heterosexual couples. The narratives which they discuss indicate that love and power are intertwined regardless of sexual orientation.

From 'Sex, money and the kitchen sink: power in same-sex couple relationships', in J. Seymour and P. Bagguley (eds) *Relating Intimacy: Power and Resistance*. London: Macmillan (1996).

. . .

THE LIMITED RESEARCH AVAILABLE on same-sex relationships emphasizes the *difference* between heterosexual and non-heterosexual relationships . . . In brief, it is suggested that members of same-sex couples are allowed to remain free of the traditional 'entrapments' of feminine/masculine stereotypes, and in the absence of conventions and guidelines are faced with the opportunity and possibility of developing more egalitarian relationships . . .

In this chapter we consider this view by drawing on a exploration of . . . data from . . . in-depth semi-structured interviews with ninety-six non-heterosexuals – a term including the broad self-definitions given in interviews such as lesbian, gay, queer and so on . . . We suggest that non-heterosexuals are actively involved in 'everybody experiments' with regard to the creating and maintaining of relationships, and that such experiments appear to be carried out with reference to an 'egalitarian ideal' (Peplau *et al.* 1996; Dunne, 1997). . . .

It is not, however, that such relationships operate in a power-free zone. Rather, the focus is on 'relative equality' and attempts to achieve an egalitarian ideal. The aim of egalitarian relationships has to be struggled for against other inequalities such as those relating to income, day-to-day commitment, emotional labour, ethnic difference and the like, which present important limits for the operation of equality. . . .

Looking out at heterosexual relationships: 'roles', 'inequality' and 'entrapments'

> So much is somehow assumed in heterosexual relationships, whereas in gay relationships it has to be made somehow more explicit. . . . You can't slide through recognised patterns of relationships. You've got to make a more conscious decision about what you want from each other . . . same-sex couples are much more obliged to be explicit about or think – scrutinise what they want from a relationship – what they're expecting – think about it.
>
> (M25)

The above extract, from an interview with a gay man, touches on three interrelated themes that emerge from our interviewees' accounts of 'looking out' at heterosexual relationships. These relate to questions of difference, the 'irrelevance' of dominant models of relationships for same-sex relationships, and the extent to which non-heterosexuals must be both explicit and reflexive regarding how they want their relationships to be. Implicit in the above quotation is a notion that informed many of our interviewees' accounts of difference: that same-sex relationships involved fashioning in a way that heterosexual forms did not. Such a notion was expressed with regard to the various forms of relationships that non-heterosexuals might have, from family relationships to couple relationships. . . .

. . . [I]n the research on lesbian and gay relationships . . . it is argued that, because their relationships lack institutional supports and cultural guidelines, members of same-sex couples are free to fashion their own modes of relating to each other (Harry and DeVall 1978; Mendola 1980; McWhirter and Mattison 1984; Johnson 1990; also see Peplau *et al.* 1996; Weeks *et al.* 1996). As Blasius (1994) notes, it is not only that hey are 'free' in this regard but may, in many senses, be obliged to do so . . . 'because there are no ready-made cultural or historical models or formulas for erotic same-sex relationships, as there are for different-sex erotic relationships' (Blasius 1994: 191). There are, of course, similarities here with notions of self-invention outlined in the theoretical literature that has emphasized the fluid nature of social possibilities, and the extent to which the present era has been marked by a break with the constraints of traditional institutional patterns (e.g. Giddens 1992; Weeks 1995). In terms of changing patterns of intimacy, recent work has related the necessity of engaging in experiments with regard to everyday life and relationships to both homosexual *and* heterosexual experiences (Giddens 1992; Bech 1992); . . . While this work suggests that there may be overlaps between heterosexuals and non-heterosexuals in this regard . . . amongst many non-heterosexuals there is a sense that the necessity of fashioning oneself and one's relationship is a distinguishing factor of non-heterosexual experience. From our interviews a key perception of difference between same-sex relationships and heterosexual forms emerges in terms of observations that, while some 'changes' may be occurring in the ways that heterosexual relationships operate, they continue to be structured by set patterns, expectations and assumptions:

> I think there's a lot less structure in gay relationships in that heterosexual relationships in my eyes follow a pattern. . . . Whereas a gay relationship, I don't think there's the same kind of 'career structure' as it were . . . there's a lot less 'You do this here, this here and this here.'
>
> (M12)

For many respondents the lack of institutional supports and cultural guidelines implies that same-sex relationships allow for 'freer' relationships, in the sense that they are disembedded or cut of from the dominant models, assumptions and conventions that inform heterosexual relationships. . . .

. . . While there are, of course, many limits placed on freedoms and choices – most often framed by respondents in terms of the extent to which 'homophobia' and 'heterosexism' set important limits on how relationships can be lived – the 'freedoms' available in and through same-sex relationships were often compared with the perceived 'entrapments' of marriage that might work to limit heterosexuals' choices:

> I would like to think that people in gay relationships stay together because they actually want to stay together to a greater extent than heterosexual relationships do . . . it's possible that the expectations of society and the trappings attached to marriage and all that, put more pressure on heterosexuals to stay together against their will than is the case with gay men and lesbians.
>
> (M15)

. . . From our interviews the extent to which our respondents believed that same-sex couple relationships offer unique possibilities for the construction of 'more' egalitarian relationships is striking. The potential offered by same-sex relationships is most widely framed in terms of the extent to which the 'irrelevance' of heterosexual models of relationships allows for the possibility of moving beyond gendered roles. In this sense the lack of cultural or historical models of same-sex relationships may be experienced as being a negative factor with potentially positive effects:

> In a way, not having had any role models, any of us as we grew up – in certain ways that's still very damaging, I think, for lesbians and gay men – but in certain ways it at least means we haven't had so much to throw out. You know – whereas I do think that heterosexual friends who are trying to create more equal relationships are having to be very conscious about it all the time.
>
> (F21)

> I think they're different because they - I think they're more equal than heterosexual relationships. I think they're more equal because I think there is less of a male/female role . . . being able to negotiate, being on an equal level to be able to negotiate in the first place. And I think that's what makes them different.
>
> (M04)

From respondents' accounts it is clear the creation and maintenance of 'more equal' relationships necessitate a considerable amount of labour. Such labour, primarily spoken about in terms of the need for discussion and negotiation, was, however, overwhelmingly compared favourably to the labour that was perceived to be involved in challenging the assumptions and set patterns that informed hetero-sexual relationships. While the work in and on their own relationships tended to be perceived as having potential rewards in terms of 'more equality', the need to engage in challenges and contests to facilitate change in relationships between men and women was often seen as having less potential. Women particularly empha-sized this point . . .

> I think certainly I'm aware that heterosexual friends who are feminists have to work much harder at creating equal relationships than we do, because they're fighting the rest of the world.
>
> (F21)

The 'entrapments' of female/male roles

In 'looking out' at heterosexual relationships, the accounts of our female respon-dents are consistent with those provided in Dunne's (1997) research. Dunne (1997: 181–2) suggests that her interviews highlight two main aspects of heterosexual relationships which were understood to pre-empt an egalitarian outcome. The first of these concerns structural inequalities, which relate to the different material resources available to men and women. In our own research this was most often articulated in the terms of there being 'an essential power imbalance' (F34) between women and men. The second feature concerns gendered assumptions and expec-tations that impact on the operation of heterosexual relationships. Many of the women we interviewed placed a strong emphasis on the unequal expectations and assumptions about the labour women perform in heterosexual relationships and family forms:

> When I look at other people's relationships [heterosexuals], yeah, there's differences. I think they're much more role-defined, although they would like to think that they've moved on a lot from where they were, I don't see it very often. It may be hidden, but it's still very role-defined. I still see the women doing the majority of the house-work and looking after the children and the men going out doing their leisure time.
>
> (F36)

> I just found the family and heterosexuality really oppressive. I con-
> stantly, constantly had battles about my rights to any sort of equal status
> in terms of cleaning, cooking, washing, child care, going out to work,
> having friends, having a life of my own. I think from beginning to end
> it was a struggle and a battle and I hadn't realised that they were battles
> and struggles.
>
> (F28)

Importantly, in some of the women's accounts it was not only individuals who
were located as being implicated in the operation of 'unequal' relationships, but
rather that heterosexuality itself was perceived to be bound up with the disem-
powerment of women. As is evident in the extract above (F28), for some women
with experience of heterosexual relationships, heterosexuality was experienced and
talked about as producing pressures to conform to hegemonic notions of 'appropriate' gender behaviour, but also constraining impulses in terms of 'possibilities
of being'. . . .

> For me, they're [lesbian relationships] based on trying to kind of – find
> some equality between two people and they're based on freedom and
> they're based on not owning a person and not dictating to the person
> what they can do and what they can't do . . . [in heterosexual relation-
> ships] there is a role that is ascribed to the man and a role that is
> ascribed to the woman. And I don't mean roles as in housework and
> breadwinner – I mean roles as in – you know – game-playing, manip-
> ulation, being passive, being victim – whatever.
>
> (F03)

. . . In many of the accounts provided by women regarding their understandings
of the operation of heterosexual relationships the influence of feminist analyses of
power is evident (cf. Dunne 1997). From women's responses it was clear that
feminist discourses – or what Benjamin and Sullivan (1996: 229) term 'the feminist value system' – were often employed as a personal resource in making sense
of 'power' in interpersonal relationships. On the surface this could be said to be
the case for some of the men interviewed, such as M04 earlier. The extract below,
from an interview with a male respondent, brings together many of the themes
addressed above and focuses explicitly on the relationship between heterosexuality, gender roles and hegemonic forms of masculinity and femininity:

> I suppose I would have to relate it to my experience of having been in a
> heterosexual relationship, really. And I mean, it's something to do with
> how I think we're socialised as men and the way that we think we can
> be. . . . I think there is less a sense of possession, or property, in same-
> sex relationships, and more emphasis on . . . emotional bonding . . .
> that's not quite what I mean, but they're less ritualised, really. . . . I
> think that kind of creates a necessity for . . . same-sex relationships to
> find their own identity – whereas I think that heterosexual relationships,
> they can . . . coast more . . . there is more kind of ascribed roles. . . .

> You know, I think the kind of macho male bit is very destructive and
> you know – there's an awful lot of it about, really. As there is the stereo-
> type of the kind of passive, the passive female. But I mean, those are kind
> of stereotypes, but you can see them being acted out.
>
> (M39)

While many male respondents talked of the potential that same-sex relationships
offered in going 'beyond' gendered roles, such potential did not, in the main, refer
to the *structural* differences between men and women or address questions of
unequal labour that women undertake. Rather, the tendency was to emphasize
the 'entrapments' of the male role as they related to the pressure to conform to
hegemonic notions of masculinity (Connell 1987, 1995). While women focused
on the material and the emotional, in men's accounts the primary focus is the
extent to which heterosexuality and heterosexual relationships are bound up
with particular notions of masculinity – and particularly the 'possibilities of being'
in terms of their emotional lives. In this sense responses were often framed in
terms of the extent that homosexuality and the same-sex relationships provided
ways of imagining being men that did not have to conform to notions of 'hegemonic masculinity'. The above extract (M39) points to a key common factor that
was identified by both male and female respondents in terms of the emphasis on
emotional bonding. Related terms that reoccur in the men's accounts are 'honesty'
and 'openness' . . .

. . . For many men, heterosexual relationships were productive of pressures to
conform to hegemonic notions of masculinity – primarily in terms of emotional lives
and worlds. Some respondents' stories of what heterosexual relationships looked
like were bound up with stories of 'unemotional' and 'uncommunicative' men:

> I think it's much easier to have equal relationships if you're the same
> sex. I'm not at all sure how heterosexual men of my age get emotional
> support. I think a lot of them don't. That's a tragedy for them . . . I
> mean, to be a heterosexual former public schoolboy. I mean, can you
> imagine how they cope with life? I mean, I just don't think they know
> who they are or who anybody else is, ever. I don't think they get
> beyond a certain level of knowledge of people.
>
> (M03)

One of the defining elements of hegemonic masculinity, and the entrapments of
male roles, that emerges from accounts such as the above is heterosexual men's
perceived inability to communicate on an emotional level, and an inability to
'know' others (cf. Duncombe and Marsden 1993). In these accounts it was not
women who were located as problematic, but rather the extent to which heterosexual models were implicated in the reproduction of particular 'types' of
masculinity. In this construction, heterosexual men's perceived inability to access
emotional support is located in terms of the lack of mutuality. . . . Equality, in
accounts such as those, is located in reciprocal emotional relationships.

While there are differences between men and women in terms of *how* same-
sex relationships are experienced and articulated as being more equal, there are

also commonalities. Where non-heterosexual women are likely to place a notable emphasis on the unequal divisions of labour within heterosexual relationships, both non-heterosexual men and women emphasize the 'emotional' possibilities opened up in same-sex relationships. While there are differences in terms of how it is articulated, and what is focused on, what emerges is the notion of an 'egalitarian ideal' (Peplau *et al.* 1996; Dunne 1997), where 'equality' is given a central place in narratives of the potentials offered by same-sex relationships. This ideal concerns the desire to exist within, and actively construct, democratic, egalitarian relationships.

Looking in at same-sex relationships: 'power', 'inequality' and 'negotiation'

The notion of an egalitarian ideal is also present in respondents' accounts of 'looking in' at their own relationships. This is particularly evident in the emphasis placed on the negotiation of domestic, emotional and sexual lives. Almost all respondents, however, identified factors that had the *potential* to cause inequality. . . .

. . . There were a broad set of factors identified that could influence, or impact negatively on, the operation of the egalitarian ideal that respondents espoused. The aim of egalitarian relations has to be constantly struggled for against inequalities of income, unequal emotional and physical labour, ethnic and class differences, and so on. Peplau *et al.* (1996: 225–6) note that much of the work on same-sex relationships identifies that greater relationship-defining power can accrue to the partner who has greater personal resources. While this has usually been framed in terms of financial resources and education, we suggest that a broader focus on capital is more apt. Such a focus can allow us to take into account cultural, economic and *social* resources. Our interviews suggest that one important potential source of differential 'relationship-defining power' that has tended to be overlooked is unequal access to *social* capital (see Wan 1995; Weeks 1996). In terms of being lesbian or gay, social capital can relate to questions of 'outness' and the ability to access local or 'lesbian and gay community' knowledge and supports. In this way we can understand comments such as the following, from a gay man who felt that he belonged to strong network of lesbian and gay friends who were a part of a local lesbian and gay community:

> There are a lot of things that potentially make it very imbalanced in terms of power because I'm more experienced in gay life and I'm more comfortable in it than he is. I'm much more secure in my sort of – friendship networks than he is and I have a lot of people to talk about my relationship with James and he doesn't have those people.
>
> (M11)

As was noted earlier, a key issue in accounts of the potential for equality was the extent to which dichotomous gender scripts and 'roles' were not at play in same-sex relationships. When 'looking in' at their own relationships, the notion that couples might organize their own domestic lives in accordance with male/female (or 'butch/femme') roles, or that they might be perceived by others as doing so, was sometimes seen as shocking and almost always refuted by respondents. In the few cases in which respondents themselves suggested that their household division of labour could 'appear' to match such roles, the notion of choice was emphasized:

> I occasionally look and think 'My God! We're a 1950s butch/femme couple' with 'who is doing what round the house', sort of thing. Uhm, there are aspects of that. I'm reasonably comfortable with that – so it's OK. I would worry – in some ways it feels less of a problem in a lesbian relationship than it would in a heterosexual relationship where one would be working harder at getting rid of gendered roles . . . as I've got older I've got easier about the fact that actually I do like cooking and I really don't like hammering nails into fences . . . I'm less bothered because I don't . . . because the fact that two adults of the same gender choose to do different things within the house, doesn't give kids a message that says 'Men are only supposed to do this one' or 'Women are only supposed to do that one'.
>
> (F21)

While our interviewees highlighted that assumptions about the domestic division of labour could not be made in terms of gender difference, some respondents' accounts pointed to the possibility of assumptions being informed by other factors. The extract from one respondent below, who is retired and live with a male partner who is over twenty years younger, highlights that tensions around domestic labour may arise when both members of a relationship are not in paid employment:

> We very rarely get angry with each other. He still complains I don't do enough housework. . . . Well, we didn't have a row, we had a discussion the other day and I said, 'Alright look.' He was busy and he couldn't clean the bathroom for a fortnight and because he hadn't done it he thought that I should have done it. 'Right, we'll sit down and we'll make a list of the jobs that need doing and we'll write a list of who is going to do what and then we're not going to have these misunderstandings' . . . because in a way I feel that I'm . . . this is my retirement when I should have leisure and the time to do things and what not . . . well, I feel as if I don't really benefit very much from being retired . . . and he's got a very exacting job.
>
> (M44)

From the account of the respondent above it is clear that factors such as employment status (and age) can cause conflict in terms of expectations regarding domestic work. While this respondent stressed the negotiated nature of the relationship when first discussing household labour – it is clear from the above that such dilemmas also necessitate on-going reassessment. This example highlights the extent to which power relations within same-sex relationships are not static and stable. Material inequality, for instance, can be influential in informing the extent to which it is felt that the relationship is equal, but does not necessarily remain constant. The extract below from a woman who is temporarily unemployed and who lives with a partner who is in paid employment, highlights both points:

> I think until I'm working and earning the same amount of money that she is, it can never be equal. In, in certain ways and yet it can be. In other ways, But I think as individuals we probably make it difficult to be equal because there's, even if she was perfectly fine, and said, even if we had a joint bank account and, which we don't at the present time, and I could take any of her money whenever I wanted it, or whatever, I wouldn't feel equal. Because I wouldn't feel that I was making an equal contribution. So, I would make myself unequal.
>
> (F43)

. . . From the interview data it is clear that there are many factors that can be in tension with the operation of an egalitarian ideal. However, the emphasis . . . is on the possibilities offered by negotiation an the potential for 'working out' these issues. Indeed, the *more* respondents identified potential power imbalances in their relationship, the more the necessity to 'talk' and 'negotiate' was emphasized. This resonates with the findings in Finch and Mason's (1993) work, where less discussion was equated with a more 'traditional' allocation of caring tasks. . . .

. . . It is clear from the accounts of non-heterosexual women and men that same-sex relationships do not dissolve 'power'. Indeed, one of the striking issues to emerge from respondents' accounts of both heterosexual *and* their own relationships is the *extent* to which non-heterosexuals appear to have stories about power to tell. As the extracts outlined in this section highlight, among our respondents there would appear to be an acute awareness of potential imbalances within their relationships. This is particularly so with regard to differential access to material, cultural and social resources. While the accounts of 'looking out' at heterosexual relationships stress the extent to which assumptions regarding roles and positions within relationships cannot be made in terms of gender, in accounts of 'looking in' at same-sex relationships there is an emphasis on the need for negotiation of the potential inequalities that are influenced by *other* dynamics. Such negotiation is seen to be key to the construction and operation of egalitarian relationships.

. . . [F]ar from an *absence* of cultural guidelines or same-sex relationships, the narratives of power in relationships outlined in the previous sections suggest the existence of emergence of strong 'local' or 'community' guidelines – that emphasize the egalitarian ideal. The literature and respondents' accounts overwhelmingly emphasize the *lack* of cultural guidelines and models for the construction of same-sex relationships. Yet one crucial and central set of 'local' guidelines or knowledges concerning 'possibilities of being' in same-sex relationships emerges that has marked similarities with what Giddens (1992: 58) terms the 'pure relationship': relationships of sexual and emotional equality that are sought and entered into as long as they are mutually fulfilling.

What also emerges is a sense of what Blasius (1994: 206) calls a lesbian and gay ethic: a type of existence that is the consequence of coming out, and which is bound up with a set of knowledges about the possibilities of living as lesbians and gay men. Such knowledges are potentially accessed through 'coming out' of the heterosexual selves that are allocated to individuals, and 'coming out' of the heterosexual selves that are allocated to individuals, and 'coming into' non-hetero-sexual 'communities'. Coming out necessitates re-evaluation and relearning with regard to *how it is possible to live and relate* in a world as lesbians and gay men (cf. Davies 1992). As such it can facilitate an engagement with community knowledges that are informed by various analyses and power – including those influenced by 'feminist value systems' and lesbian and gay politics. . . .

. . . Other important resources are what Plummer (1995) refers to as 'sexual stories'. Such stories circulate in and through developing into pretive communi-ties. In this sense private testimonies, such as those of our respondents, *are*, in part, publicly scripted. It is not that these testimonies simply reproduce particular stories (of equality) – but rather that the stories are themselves *reflexively* produced (Plummer, 1995), as are the analyses of power that are central to them. As noted in the previous section, it is not that the 'egalitarian ideal' dissolves power in same-sex relationships, but that the self-reflexivity that is necessary for the creation and maintenance of same-sex relationships might make 'power' an issue for more *explicit* consideration and negotiation within the relationships themselves. Indeed, our data would suggest that this is the case.

Conclusion

Our discussion of power in same-sex relationships has been based on non-hetero-sexuals' 'stories' of the potential offered for equality, reciprocity, and negotiation in same-sex couples. We would like to conclude with a brief consideration of what these stories reveal about the 'reality' of power in same-sex relationships. In this regard we take seriously Duncombe and Marsden's (1996: 150) point that it is necessary to account for a connection between the narrative of living that is constructed in the interview and 'the life as lived by the subject' . . .

It is not possible to claim that the accounts of non-heterosexuals outlined in this chapter reveal the essential truth about the nature and operation of same-sex relationships. Rather, we suggest that the accounts about couple relationships and power tell us something important about the ways in which these social actors see relationships in both the non-heterosexual and heterosexual worlds, and shape their lives accordingly. These narratives are, in part, publicly scripted, and they bear a striking resemblance to broader narratives (including some of those produced by academics and researchers) of the possibilities offered in same-sex relationships. They are reflexively constructed – as are the relationships they are concerned with. In the end it is not *simply* stories of equality that are at stake, but stories that significantly shape the ways in which non-heterosexuals conceive of the possibili-ties of existing in couple relationships.

References

Beech, H. (1992) 'Report from a rotten state: "marriage" and "homosexuality", in "Denmark"', in K. Plummer (ed.) *Modern Homosexualities: Fragments of Lesbian and Gay Experience*. London: Routledge.

Benjamin, O. and Sullivan, O. (1996) 'The importance of difference: conceptualising increased flexibility in gender relations at home', *Sociological Review*, 44 (2): 225–51.

Blasius, M. (1994) *Gay and Lesbian Politics: Sexuality and the Emergence of a New Ethic*. Philadelphia: Temple University Press.

Connell, R. W. (1987) *Gender and Power*. Cambridge: Polity.

Connell, R. W. (1995) *Masculinities*. Cambridge: Polity.

Davies, P. (1992) 'The role of disclosure in coming out among gay men', in K. Plummer (ed.) *Modern Homosexualities: Fragments of Lesbian and Gay Experience*. London: Routledge.

Dunne, G. A. (1997) *Lesbian Lifestyles: Women's Work and the Politics of Sexuality*. London: Macmillan.

Duncombe, J. and Marsden, D. (1993) 'Love and intimacy: the gender division of emotion and emotion work', *Sociology*, 27 (2): 221–41.

Duncombe, J. and Marsden, D. (1996) 'Can we research the private sphere? Methodological and ethical problems in the study of the role of intimate emotion in personal relationships', in L. Morris and S. Lyons (eds) *Gender Relations in Public and Private: Research Perspectives*. London: Macmillan.

Finch, J. and Mason, J. (1993) *Negotiating Family Responsibilities*. London: Routledge.

Giddens, A. (1992) *The Transformation of Intimacy: Sexuality, Love and Eroticism in Modern Societies*. Cambridge: Polity.

Harry, J. and DeVall, W. B. (1978) *The Social Organisation of Gay Males*. New York: Praeger.

Johnson, S. E. (1990) *Staying Power: Long Term Lesbian Couples*. Tallahassee Fl.: Naiad Press.

McWhirter, D. and Mattison, A. M. (1984) *The Male Couple: How Relationships Develop*. Englewood Cliffs NJ: Prentice-Hall.

Mendola, M. (1980) *The Mendola Report: A New Look at Gay Couples in America*. New York: Crown.

Peplau, L. A., Venigas, R. C. and Miller Campbell, S. (1996) 'Gay and lesbian relationships', in R. C. Savin-Williams and K. M. Cohen (eds) *The Lives of Lesbians, Gays, and Bisexuals*. New York: Harcourt Brace College.

Plummer, K. (1995) *Telling Sexual Stories: Power, Change and Social Worlds*. London: Routledge.

Wan, M. (1995) *Building Social Capital: Self-help in the Twenty-first Century Welfare State*. London: IPPR.

Weeks, J. (1995) *Invented Moralities: Sexual Values in an Age of Uncertainty*. Cambridge: Polity.

Weeks, J. (1996) 'The idea of a sexual community', *Soundings*, 2: 71–83.

Weeks, J., Donovan, C. and Heaphy, B. (1996) *Families of Choice: Patterns of Non-heterosexual relationships. A Literature Review*, Social Science Research Papers No. 2. London: South Bank University.

Chapter 33

Lynne Jamieson

INTIMACY TRANSFORMED?

In this piece (which draws on the argument of her 1998 book, *Intimacy*) Lynne Jamieson offers a critique of Giddens's concepts of the 'pure relationship' and 'plastic sexuality'. She argues that changes in the basis of intimate relationships are neither as a recent nor as transformatory as Giddens suggests.

From *Sociology*, 33 (1) 1999.

I N DESCRIBING LATE TWENTIETH-CENTURY processes of social change, which involve a transformation in a nature of self-identity and intimacy, Giddens talks of the ascendancy of 'confluent love' and 'the pure relationship'. Confluent love is contingent on lovers opening themselves out to each other. The 'pure relationship', like the ideal-typical dyad, has no overarching structure to sustain it. Rather, its key sustaining dynamics are mutual self-disclosure and appreciation of each other's unique qualities.

> A pure relationship is one in which external criteria have become dissolved: the relationship exists solely for whatever rewards that relationship can deliver. In the context of the pure relationship, trust can be mobilised only by a process of mutual disclosure.
>
> (Giddens 1991: 6)

> It [a pure relationship] refers to a situation where a social relation is entered into for its own sake, for what can be derived by each person from a sustained association with another; and which is continued only in so far as it is thought by both parties to deliver enough satisfaction for each individual to stay within it.
>
> (Giddens 1992: 58)

The type of intimacy involved in 'the pure relationship' necessarily requires equality between the parties to the relationship, that is a shared sense of self-disclosure and contributing on an equal footing to the relationship.

Giddens claims that the trend towards 'the pure relationship' is paralleled by the emergence of a more responsive and creative form of sexuality which he calls 'plastic sexuality', referring to a heightened self-awareness of the plasticity of sexuality, a late twentieth-century freedom from any essential pre-given way of being sexual. . . .

. . . For Giddens, a 'revolution in female sexual autonomy', that is, in women finding sexual pleasure in ways which are not dictated by men, and 'the flourishing of homosexuality' (1992: 28) are manifestations of 'plastic sexuality'. In 'confluent love' sexuality and intimacy are tied together 'as never before' (1992: 84).

The underlying causal factors promoting the ascendancy of the pure relationship and plastic sexuality are the uncertainties and new social conditions created by reiterative processes of social change characteristic of late modernity. In combination they heighten the sense that individuals have of their own creativity and their own limitations in the business of producing their selves and their social world. . . .

> Where large areas of a person's life are no longer set by pre-existing patterns and habits, the individual is continually obliged to negotiate life-style options. Moreover – and this is crucial – such choices are not just 'external' or marginal aspects of the individual's attitudes, but define who the individual 'is'. In other words, life-style choices are constitutive of the reflexive narrative of self.
>
> (Giddens 1992: 75)

The phrase 'narrative of the self' emphasises the on-going process of self-construction. In the social conditions of the late twentieth century personal relationships are the key site in which men and women find 'forms of self exploration and moral construction' (Giddens 1992: 144). A successful pure relationship recreates psychological stability by resonating with the ontological security and basic trust of others which is developed in an untraumatised and successful childhood and which derives from the trust placed by children in their 'caretakers' (Giddens 1991: 186). But at the same time, 'pure relationships' necessarily contain the internal tension of attempting to reconcile mutual trust and commitment with the knowledge that the relationship is voluntary and only 'good until further notice'. For Giddens such tension and consequent fragility is an inherent aspect of the more profound potential for openness and intimacy rather than a symptom of general *malaise*. . . .

Critical issues

Giddens presents the trends he is identifying as relatively recent. Yet the idea that how personal life is conducted is more intensely intimate, individualised or personalised than ever before, is a long-running theme. For example, eighteenth-century philosophers of the Scottish Enlightenment saw intimate friendship as a 'modern' pattern emerging in their time (Silver 1997). . . . In more recent sociological writing about marriage and the family, the themes of growing intimacy, privacy and equality date back to at least the 1940s (Burgess and Locke 1945) and are part of the orthodox account of how the 'modern family' developed (Jamieson 1987). . . .

David Morgan (1991, 1992, 1996) has analysed how the twentieth-century story of change in family and marriage 'from institution to relationship', became an ideological simplification of social change particularly promoted by professionals with a vested interest in marital and relationship problems. As Morgan notes, ideological constructions are nevertheless consequential. However, the nature of the fit between the ideological story and everyday relationships is not simple. It is possible, for example, for the discourse of 'relationship experts' to infuse everyday talk while other factors modify the parameters of everyday practice. Such issues are not fully explored in *The Transformation of Intimacy*. Despite reference to the reflexive interrelationship between his work, popular culture and therapeutic discourse, Giddens draws relatively uncritically on therapeutic literature, as documents about and symptoms of personal and social change (Giddens 1992: 86). Not surprisingly, his account of 'the pure relationship' fits well with a therapeutic discourse that assumes the value of self-disclosure in therapy and in the relationships which therapy hopes to cure.

. . . In claiming openness as a constructive process, Giddens interleaves his analysis of late modernity with a rather unpacked psychological theory. It is the ontological security of childhood that provides the self-resources for a subsequent creative process of self-disclosure. The starting premise is that a wide range of social circumstances in childhood, anything more caring than suffering violent, sexually abusive or highly neglectful parents, will create the necessary psychological conditions for 'generalised trust' in others and ontological security. This leaves an under-explained biographical contrast between an easily acquired secure sense of self in childhood and an adult who only just escapes doubts about self-authenticity by working hard on a narrative of the self and fragile personal relationships. Given the emphasis Giddens places on the fragility of personal life in a highly self-reflexive late modernity, the exempting of the parent/child relationship from fragility involves resort to a psychology divorced from his own sociological analysis.

The contribution of therapeutic discourse to damaging gender stereotypes is also unremarked, reflecting a more general underplaying of structures of gender inequality in *The Transformation of Intimacy*. Feminist work has documented how women carrying the burdens of systematic gender inequality have been recast by medical and therapeutic experts as pathological individuals (recent accounts are given by Busfield 1996; Dobash and Dobash 1992). Morgan has recently warned that the continued theoretical focus on the relational character of heterosexual partnerships can obscure persisting and institutionalised gender inequalities (1996: 77–8). While drawing on particular pieces of feminist work, there is no sustained discussion in *The Transformation of Intimacy* of the feminist scholarship that has subjected the interrelationships between 'private' and 'public', 'personal' and 'political' to intensive theorising and empirical exploration over the last decades. Yet debate concerning the resilience of gender inequality is centrally relevant to Giddens's case. . . .

Couple relationships

Giddens intimates potential radical shifts in heterosexual practices. If 'pure rela-tionships' are indeed becoming more common, equalisation in men and women's interest in the experience of sex and intimacy can be anticipated. Similarly the ascendancy of 'plastic sexuality' will mean greater sexual experimentation and hence an increase in the diversity of sexual practice.

There has undoubtedly been a significant shift in public discourse about sex and sexuality that appears to acknowledge gender equality and show grater toler-ance of diversity in sexual practices (Weeks 1995). Greater acceptance of gender equality is typified by the shift in magazines aimed at women and girls. Where once their content retained a coy silence on sex and a strong emphasis on romance, readers now receive acceptance or encouragement of active sexuality and sexual desire (McRobbie 1991, 1994, 1996). However, as Jackson and Scott note, the messages of public discourse remain mixed, reasserting as often as challenging the boundaries of conventional femininity. Incitements to active female sexuality have not undermined the dominant view of 'real sex' as coitus ending in ejaculation. Moreover, 'women and girls are positioned as sexual carers who do the emotional work and police their own emotions to ensure that they do not place excessive demands on men' (Jackson and Scott 1997: 567).

Sexual behaviours, their meanings and significance are notoriously difficult to investigate. Only partial insight can be gleaned from the behavioural measures which surveys offer, such as incidence of 'mutual orgasm'. However, relevant indi-cators can be found in recent large-scale surveys published in Britain and the United States (Wellings et al. 1994; Layman et al. 1994). There is modest evidence of departures from conventional forms of sexual activity and of the more varied sexual repertoire implied by 'plastic sexuality'. The British survey found high levels of 'non-penetrative' sex and the US survey of 'oral sex', although it is not possible to know about the meanings and interpersonal dynamics behind these activities. However, there was no clear evidence of gender convergence in sexual behaviour but rather a rediscovery of patterns of gender difference, which appear to have only modestly moderated since Kinsey (1958, 1953). On all measures of sexual activity investigated, ranging from questions on thinking about sex and mastur-bating (asking only in the United States) to questions on number and type of partners and forms of sexual activity engaged in with them, more men are sexu-ally active than women. The US survey revealed that men are still more likely to experience orgasm during sex than women and the British survey that men think orgasm is more essential to sexual satisfaction than women. Nevertheless, there is some evidence of gender convergence in expectations and ideas about sex. When responding to attitude questions in surveys men and women often say very similar things about the meaning and significance of sexual behaviour in a couple rela-tionship. For example, in the British survey, most men and women think that 'companionship and affection are more important than sex in a marriage'.

However, in-depth interview studies continue to uncover a persistent, tena-cious and phallocentric view of heterosexual sex as something that men do to women. It is conclusively documented that the early sexual experiences of most young people involve neither the negotiation of mutual pleasure nor a fusion of sex and emotional intimacy (Holland *et al.* 1991, 1993, 1994, 1998; Thomson and Scott 1991; Tolman 1994; Wight 1994, 1996). Evidence of mutual sexual plea-sure, equality and deep intimacy among older heterosexuals is outweighed by sex and gender trouble. In their study of long-term couples, Jean Duncombe and Dennis Marsden (1993, 1995, 1996) find women complaining about lack of intimacy and men about lack of sex. It seems that men are more emotionally withdrawn from the relationship than women and men derive more pleasure from sex in the relationship (see also Mansfield and Collard 1988; Thompson and Walker 1989). . . .

The *Transformation of Intimacy* raises the possibility of equality and intimacy in personal life democratising gender relationships more generally. However, empir-ical work on heterosexual couples routinely continues to find that men exercise more power than women in the partnerships: for example, having more choice concerning opting in and out of domestic work and child care (Brannen and Moss 1991), and exercising more control of money (Morris 1990; Pahl 1989; Vogler 1994). But at the same time, research continues to find couples exhibiting such inequalities who collaboratively generate a sense of caring, intimate, equal rela-tionships. This was eloquently demonstrated by Kathryn Backett (1982) in the 1970s and her findings continue to be echoed in much more recent work. Couples' carefully constructed sense of each other as good, mutually caring partners, despite unequal sacrifice for their common good, diverges considerably from the 'pure relationship'.

Research suggests that the ways in which couples generate a sense of them-selves and their partners as mutually caring often reproduce gender inequality – the creativity and intimacy of couples is not yet typically harnessed to gender trans-formation. Many couples refer to gendering (i.e. underpinning gender difference) structural factors – the vagaries of employment including men and women's different earnings and prospects in the labour market, the incompatibility of combining the demands of child rearing and full-time employment – as if a tradi-tional division of labour adopted because of such structures beyond their control were therefore exempted from any possible inequality. Many also deploy a variety of gendering but apparently gender-neutral devices to maintain a counterfactual sense of equality ('she happens to be better at cooking', 'he doesn't enjoy cooking as much'). Others continue to make explicit reference to traditional beliefs about manhood and womanhood, sometimes disavowing that this is how life should always be organised, but accepting that it works for them (for example, 'It's how I/he/she was brought up' – see other examples in Brannen and Moss 1991; Hochschild 1990; Mansfield and Collard 1988). This is not to deny the significance of a sense of equality for a sense of intimacy among many couples. There is a general taken-for-granted assumption that a good relationship will be equal and intimate. Rather it is to suggest that creative energy is deployed in disguising inequality, not in undermining it (Bittman and Lovejoy 1993).

Mutual self-disclosure is the basis of intimacy in 'the pure relationship', but empirical evidence suggests this is not the sole or necessarily the ascendant type of intimacy between couples. Love and care expressed through actions is a very different dimension of intimacy from 'knowing', the mutual disclosure of the 'pure relationship', but it continues to loom large in how many couples view their relationship. For couples who live together, the time, money and effort each devotes to their household often symbolises love and care for each other. A common traditional rhetoric which couples can and have drawn on when over-looking everyday differences in power and privilege is the visualisation of their relationship in terms of complementary gifts – the man's wage as his expression of care for his partner and his family, and the woman's matching gift of house-work as expressing her tender loving care (Chea 1988; Morgan 1991). Many dual-worker households continue to use a slightly modified version of this theme by talking down the woman's wage as supplementary rather than the main earn-ings and talking up the man's typically relatively limited contributions to domestic work (Brannen and Moss 1991; Hochschild 1990). Tactics also include minimising the significance of men's lack of practical involvement in the household or child care and maximising the significance of their role as an emotional support (although discontent is then the consequence when emotional support is perceived as weak). Expressions of interest, concern and reassurance, 'emotional work', can compensate for a lack of practical assistance. Visualising their relationship as rebalanced in these ways centres on an intimacy that is somewhat removed from the 'pure relationship'. Love and care as expressed by a more practical doing and giving is as much the crux of their relationship as a process of mutually discovering and enjoying each other.

Couples who achieve a more objective equality are not necessarily any closer to a 'pure relationship'. Empirical research identifies a minority of couples who make painstaking efforts to achieve relatively equal contributions to a joint project of a household. In an Australian study, Goodnow and Bowes (1994) discuss heterosexual couples who have been recruited *because* they do things differently. . . . Goodnow and Bowes suggest that their respondents were not of a wholly different mind set from more traditional couples but rather that they focused on the same dimensions of love and care. It was not their assumption that a loving couple would mutually care for each other in practical ways which was distinctive but their thorough analysis of the who, when, where and why of how this was done fairly. . . .

. . . While starting from their own situation, their rules of fairness seek universal principles and are not tied to or derived from knowledge of each other's unique qualities. In focusing intense dialogue on practical arrangements and abstract rules, the couple create projects that inevitably add to the institutionalised frame-work over and above their relationship. Hence they stand outside of the ideal-typical pure relationship which seeks to bracket off distractions from the intensity of the relationship itself.

Giddens suggests that high rates of dissolution among couples reflect the fragility of the 'pure relationships', which require the psychological balancing act of sustaining mutual trust while knowing the relationship is only 'good until further notice'. However, it seems more plausible to see the fragility of heterosexual couples as a consequence of the tension between strengthening cultural emphasis on intimacy, equality and mutuality in relationships and the structural supports of gender inequalities, which make these ideals difficult to attain. Studies such as Brannen and Moss (1991), Hochschild (1990) and Mansfield and Collard (1988) document how collaborative effort can produce a sense of being equal and inti-mate, in spite of inequalities. What is important is not an intense process of mutual self-disclosure and exploration but a shared repertoire of cover stories, taboos and self-dishonesty. However, inequalities and asymmetries in parenting, domestic divisions of labour and 'emotion work' sometimes breed simmering discontent which defies the desire to feel equal and intimate. Drawing on Hochschild's work, Duncombe and Marsden (1993) talk of women 'deep acting' in order to maintain a sense that their relationship is 'ever so happy', but sometimes 'deep acting' gives way to more critically aware and cynical 'shallow acting'. Diane Vaughan (1986) suggests that uncoupling begins with a secret, one partner's unspoken but nurtured feeling of discomfort with the relationship. She theorises the process of uncoupling as the converse of constructing a sense of self and shared world-view through the marriage dialogue described by Berger and Kellner (1964). Interestingly, her respondents' stories of uncoupling show that while the disaffected partner withdraws from the relationship, the other partner often has no sense of loss until the secret is dramatically announced. Couples did not seem to be seeking to inhabit 'pure relationships' in any of these studies but rather relationships which were intended to last, which couples worked to institutionalise *and* wanted to feel equal and intimate.

Same-sex couples, and particularly lesbians, are identified by Giddens as in the vanguard of developing 'pure relationships' and hence as having a high incidence of relationship breakdown. There is a body of work which suggests that same-sex couples, and particularly lesbians, tend to have and to see themselves as having more equal relationships than heterosexual couples (Dunne 1997; Kurdek 1993; Weeks *et al.* 1998; Weston 1991) and that, moreover, lesbian relationships are particularly characterised by high levels of intimacy and communication (Dunne 1997: 201). However, the empirical evidence does not convince me that either lesbians or gay men typically have 'pure relationships', although Weeks and his colleagues sometimes use the term. Some research indicates that lesbians are wary of treating their partner as the sole source of intimacy but rather carefully maintain a supportive network, a 'chosen family' of friends, ex lovers and kin (Heaphy *et al.* 1998; Weston 1991). Scrutiny of the 'ground rules' Christian gay couples construct reveals a range of practical devices to protect their relationship, including an understood tactical silence about casual sexual encounters outside the relationship (Yip 1997). As yet the evidence on which to assess the relative fragility of same-sex relationships is rather sparse and tends to stress similarities to heterosexuals rather than difference (Kurdek 1991). Moreover, there are reasons, other than 'the pure relationship', why same-sex relationships may be vulnerable to breakdown. It is clear that if same-sex couples do manage to securely maintain a long-term relationship they do so despite a wider social fabric which is relatively hostile to its institutionalisation.

References

Backett, K. (1982) *Mothers and Fathers*. London: Macmillan.

Berger, P. and Kneller, H. (1964) 'Marriage and the construction of reality', *Diogenes*, reprinted in M. Anderson (ed.) *The Sociology of the Family*. Harmondsworth: Penguin, 1980.

Bittman, M. and Lovejoy, F. (1993) 'Domestic power: negotiating an unequal division of labour within a framework of equality', *Australian and New Zealand Journal of Sociology*, 29: 302–21.

Brannen, J. and Moss, P. (1991) *Managing Mothers: Dual Earner Households after Maternity Leave*. London: Unwin Hyamn.

Burgess, E. W. and Locke, H. J. (1945) *The Family: From Institution to Companionship*. New York: American Book Company.

Busfield, J. (1996) *Men, Women and Madness: Understanding Gender and Mental Disorder*. London: Macmillan.

Cheal, D. (1988) *The Gift Economy*. London: Routledge.

Dobash, R. E. and Dobash, R. (1992) *Women, Violence and Social Change*. London: Routledge.

Duncombe, J. and Marsden, D. (1993) 'Love and intimacy: the gender division of emotion and "emotion work"', *Sociology*, 27: 221–41.

Duncombe, J. and Marsden, D. (1995) '"Workaholics" and "whingeing women": theorising intimacy and emotion work: the last frontier of gender inequality?' *Sociological Review*, 43: 150–69.

Duncombe, J. and Marsden, D. (1996) 'Whose orgasm is it anyway? "Sex work" in long-term heterosexual couple relationships', in J. Weeks and J. Holland (eds). *Sexual Cultures: Communities, Values and Intimacy*. New York: St Martin's Press.

Dunne, G. (1997) *Lesbian Lifestyles: Women's Work and the Politics of Sexuality*. London: Macmillan.

Giddens, A. (1992). *The Transformation of Intimacy: Sexuality, Love and Eroticism in Modern Societies*. Cambridge: Polity.

Goodnow, J. and Bowes, J. (1994) *Men, Women and Household Work*. Melbourne: Oxford University Press.

Heaphy, B., Weeks, J. and Donovan, C. (1998) '"That's like my life": researching stories of non-heterosexual relationships', *Sexualities*, 1: 453–70.

Hochschild, A. (1990) *The Second Shift: Working Parents and the Revolution at Home*. London: Piatkus.

Holland, J., Ramazanoglu, C., Scott, S., Sharpe, S. and Thomson, R. (1991) *Pressure, Resistance, Empowerment: Young Women and the Negotiation of Safer Sex*. London: Tufnell Press.

Holland, J., Ramazanoglu, C. and Sharpe, S. (1993) *Wimp or Gladiator: Contradictions in the Acquisition of Masculine Sexuality*. London: Tufnell Press.

Holland, J., Ramazanoglu, C. and Sharpe, S. (1994) 'Power and desire: the embodiment of female sexuality', *Feminist Review*, 46: 21–38.

Holland, J., Ramazanoglu, C., Sharpe, S. and Thomson, R. (1998) *The Male in the Head: Young People, Heterosexuality and Power*. London: Tufnell Press.

Jackson, S. and Scott, S. (1997) 'Gut reactions to matters of the heart: reflections on rationality, irrationality and sexuality', *Sociological Review*, 45: 551–75.

Jamieson, L. (1987) 'Theories of family development and the experience of being brought up', *Sociology*, 21: 591–607.

Kinsey, A. (1948) *Sexual Behaviour in the Human Male*. Philadelphia: Saunders.

Kinsey, A. (1953) *Sexual Behaviour in the Human Female*. Philadelphia: Saunders.

Kurdek, L. (1991) 'The dissolution of gay and lesbian couples', *Journal of Social and Personal Relationships*, 8: 265–78.

Kurdek, L. (1993) 'The allocation of household labour in gay, lesbian, and heterosexual married couples', *Journal of Social Issues*, 49: 127–40.

Laumann, E., Michael R., Michaels, S. and Gagnon, J. (1994) *The Social Organization of Sexuality*. Chicago: University of Chicago Press.

McRobbie, A. (1991) *Feminism and Youth Culture: From 'Jackie' to 'Just Seventeen'*. Basingstoke: Macmillan.

McRobbie, A. (1994) *Postmodernism and Popular Culture*. London: Routledge.

McRobbie, A. (1995) '*More!* New sexualities in girls' and women's magazines' in J. Curran *et al.* (eds), *Cultural Studies and Communication*. London: Edward Arnold.

Mansfield, P. and Collard, J. (1988) *The Beginning of the Rest of your Life: A Portrait of Newly-wed Marriage*. London: Macmillan.

Morgan, D. (1991) 'Ideologies of marriage and family life', in D. Clark (ed.), *Marriage, Domestic Life and Social Change: Writings for Jacqueline Burgoyne (1944–88)*. London: Routledge.

Morgan, D. (1992) 'Marriage and society', in J. Lewis, D. Clark and D. Morgan, *Whom God hath joined Together: The Work of Marriage Guidance*. London: Tavistock/ Routledge.

Morgan, D. (1996) *Family Connections: An Introduction to Family Studies*. Cambridge: Polity.

Morris, L. (1990) *The Workings of the Household*. Cambridge: Polity.

Pahl, J. (1989) *Money and Marriage*. London: Macmillan.

Silver, A. (1997) '"Two different sorts of commerce", or, Friendship and stranger-ship in civil society', in J. Weintraub and K. Kumar (eds) *Public and Private in Thought and Practice: Perspectives on the Grand Dichotomy*. Chicago: University of Chicago Press.

Thompson, L. and Walker, A. (1989) 'Gender in families: women and men in marriage, work, and parenthood', *Journal of Marriage and the Family*, 51: 845–71.

Thomson, R. and Scott, S. (1991) *Learning about Sex: Young Women and the Social Construction of Sexual Identity*. London: Tufnell Press.

Tolman, D. L. (1994) 'Doing desire: adolescent girls' struggle for/with sexuality', *Gender and Society*, 8: 324–42.

VanEvery, J. (1995) *Heterosexual Women changing the Family: Refusing to be a 'Wife'*. London: Taylor & Francis.

Vaughan, D. (1986) *Uncoupling: Turning Points in Intimate Relationships*. Oxford: Oxford University Press.

Vogler, C. (1994) 'Money in the household', in M. Anderson, F. Bechhofer and J. Gershuny (eds) *The Social and Political Economy of the Household*. Oxford: Oxford University Press.

Weeks, J. (1995) *Invented Moralities: Sexual Values in an Age of Uncertainty*. Cambridge: Polity.

Weeks, J., Donovan, C. and Heaphy, B. (1998) 'Everyday experiments: narratives of non-heterosexual relationships' in E. Silva and C. Smart (eds) *The 'New' Family?* London: Sage.

Wellings, K., Field, J., Johnson, A. M. and Wadsworth, J. (1994) *Sexual Behaviour in Britain: The National Survey of Sexual Attitudes and Lifestyles*. London: Penguin.

Weston, K. (1991) *Families we Choose: Lesbians, Gays, Kinship*. New York: Columbia University Press.

Wight, D. (1994) 'Boys' thoughts and talk about sex in a working-class locality of Glasgow', *Sociological Review*, 42: 702–37.

Wight, D. (1996) 'Beyond the predatory male: the diversity of young Glaswegian men's discourses to describe heterosexual relationships', in L. Adkins and

V. Merchant (eds) *Sexualizing the Social: Power and the Organizing of Sexuality*. London: Macmillan.

Yip, A. K. T. (1997) 'Gay male Christian couples and sexual exclusivity', *Sociology*, 31: 289–306.

PART FIVE

Becoming gendered

INTRODUCTION

WHEN FEMINIST SOCIOLOGISTS BEGAN to investigate the processes by which we become gendered the dominant paradigm was that of socialisation, drawing on existing sociological and psychological work (see, for example, Oakley 1972). Such accounts focused almost exclusively on childhood and assumed that the human infant was born an empty vessel into which social norms and values were poured. These were seen to be internalised by children as they learnt their social roles. Since gender roles were ascribed at birth and expectations were attached to them almost immediately the accommodation to them was seen as near total, producing an 'oversocialised' view of gendered individuals. Individuals were seen as passively programmed to accept an inevitable gendered fate, which allowed no room for understanding how we might renegotiate or resist dominant definitions of gender. Thus exceptions could be explained only as pathological or deviant, as biological aberrations or as a failure of the socialisation process.

Feminists began to contest this view from the late 1970s onwards. After all, if socialisation into conventional femininity had been so effective, feminism could not have existed. Stanley and Wise (Chapter 34) were among the first to offer a detailed critical analysis of the assumptions underlying the socialisation paradigm and to point to the dangers for feminists of buying in to this model – as many still did into the early 1980s. Those who were critical of socialisation increasingly look to alternative explanatory frameworks. Bronwyn Davies (1989 and Chapter 35) draws on poststructuralism to account for the ways in which pre-school children actively position themselves as gendered. While children face the relatively intractable fact of gender division itself, which constrains them to locate themselves and others on one side or the other, this nonetheless entails active processes of interpretation and negotiation. Moreover small children play with different ways of being feminine or masculine and play at crossing the gender divide. Barrie Thorne, drawing on interpretive sociology, presents a picture which illustrates that the active negotiation of gender continues among older children at elementary and junior high schools in the United States (1993 and Chapter 36). Where previous research had emphasised the divergence between boys' and girls' cultures, Thorne's data reveal greater fluidity and complexity, allowing differing constructions of gender and more varied patterns of gendered social interaction.

The meanings of masculinity and femininity are not fixed. Not only do we individually negotiate our own sense of ourselves as gendered, but ideas about gender vary across social and cultural settings. The dominant definitions of normal masculinity and femininity have been shaped largely by white Western middle class and heterosexual views of the world. Hence other forms of femininity and masculinity have often been seen as deviant. For example young Black people are often seen as problematic because they do not conform to White middle class values. Heidi Mirza (Chapter 37) illustrates the specificity of Black young womanhood. The young Black women in her sample conformed neither to the values of White working class femininity nor to stereotypes of Black women, but were attempting to forge for themselves a sense of autonomous and independent womanhood. Beverley Skeggs, in contrast, considers why White working class women might want to make a personal investment in heterosexual femininity and how this is implicated in a struggle to maintain respectability (Chapter 38).

Gender is closely interrelated with sexuality. As we begin to negotiate sexual encounters they can reinforce, challenge or modify our sense of ourselves as masculine or feminine. Normative masculinity and femininity are defined in part through active heterosexuality, which in turn is shaped by gendered difference. Hence first heterosexual experiences are often marked by complexity and anxiety resulting from the divergent understandings and expectations of young men and women. First sex has different meanings for men and women, as Janet Holland and her colleagues show (Chapter 39). For young men it is an initiation into manhood, a confirmation of their masculinity, whereas for young women it carries no such status and can entail a risk to reputation. Femininity is confirmed by sexual attractiveness rather than sexual activity *per se*. The equation of gender identity with heterosexuality – the idea that a real man must have sex with women and a real woman must desire men – makes becoming sexual a more difficult transition for young lesbians and gay men. They are open to discrimination and bullying for not conforming to heterosexuality and frequently their gender is called into question. Heterosexuals do not need to explain 'how they got that way' – it is simply taken for granted. Lesbians and gay men on the other hand are frequently called upon to account for their very existence. Vera Whisman (Chapter 40) analyses the stories lesbians and gay men tell about themselves and the ways in which they construct their past biographies in terms of their current understanding of their sexual identities. These accounts were gendered, not only in relation to the differences between gay men and lesbians, but also in the ways in which lesbianism and homosexuality were associated with cross-gender identification.

Not everyone stays firmly within the gender category to which they are assigned in infancy. There are a number of ways in which gender boundaries can be crossed or exceeded, from occasional cross-dressing to full reconstruction as another sex. Richard Ekins (Chapter 41) offers an account of cross-dressing and sex changing as complex interactional processes and performances through which gender is produced. This an area which has received a great deal of academic attention, precisely because it renders visible what normally passes unnoticed – that gender is constantly under construction and that this requires considerable interpretative work.

REFERENCES

Crawford, J., Kippax, S., Onyx, J., Gault, U. and Benton, P. (1998) *Emotion and Gender: Constructing Meaning from Memory*. London: Sage.

Davies, Bronwyn (1989) *Frogs and Snails and Feminist Tales*. Sydney: Allen & Unwin.

Haug, F. (1987) *Female Sexualization*. London: Verso.

Holland, J., Ramazanoglu, C., Sharpe, S. and Thomson, R. (1998) *The Male in the Head*. London: Tufnell Press.

Jackson, S. (1998) 'Telling stories: narrative, memory and experience in feminist theory and research', in C. Griffin, K. Henwood and A. Phoenix (eds) *Standpoints and Differences*. London: Sage.

Oakley, A. (1972) *Sex, Gender and Society*. London: Temple Smith.

Plummer, K. (1995) *Telling Sexual Stories: Power, Change and Social Worlds*. London: Routledge.

Scott, S. and Scott, S. (2000) 'Our mother's daughters: autobiographical inheritance through stories of gender and class', in T. Cosslett, C. Lurry and P. Summerfield (eds) *Feminism and Autobiography: Texts Theories, Methods*. London: Routledge.

Thorne, B. (1993) Gender Play: *Girls and Boys in School*. Buckingham: Open University Press.

KEY QUESTIONS

- What are the problems with the socialisation paradigm?
- To what extent do boys and girls grow up in different worlds?
- To what extent must we understand biography in order to understand gender?
- Are gender, sex and sexuality inextricably interrelated?

Chapter 34

Liz Stanley and Sue Wise

WHAT'S WRONG WITH SOCIALISATION?

This extract outlines mainstream and feminist uses of the concept of socialisation and goes on to provide a critique of this approach to understanding how we become gendered.

From *Breaking Out*, London: Routledge (1983).

'SOCIALIZATION', BRIEFLY, IS THAT process by which children are transformed into social beings who have taken on particular norms and values, and know what kinds of behaviours are expected of them. Most feminist writers seem to see socialization as a kind of 'self-fulfilling prophecy': a self-perpetuating system which goes on from generation to generation. But the main focus of feminist concern is not this entire process, but rather that part of it which is seen to be particularly important in women's oppression – sex role socialization. Sex role, or often gender role, socialization is that bit of the process by which children come to be not only social beings, but either 'feminine' or 'masculine' ones. And here, of course, 'femininity' and 'masculinity' – gender – involve clusters of attributes and behaviours seen, within particular societies, to be appropriate for females and males respectively.

What is seen as the 'content' of this process – norms, values, behaviours and so forth – is also seen as a content which derives from the needs of 'the system' we earlier referred to. It is the perpetuation of *capitalism* or *patriarchy* which requires that people should behave, think and *be* in these particular ways, the argument goes. Closely connected is the idea that the demands and requirements of the system translated through an ideology of family life constitute reality. Whether family life is experienced as the embodiment of love and support, or as a destructive hell, is neither here nor there: its *reality* is its particular function within 'the system'. Embedded within ideas about the family are a further two concepts: 'socialization' and 'gender role'. We shall now go on to examine, in the form of composite descriptions, some important although general aspects of feminist thinking about these concepts.

Most feminists argue that at birth all children are assigned a gender which is based on the appearance of their genitals. Gender is then inculcated, at first by their mothers differentiating between children of different sexes through their behaviours towards them. Most feminists also argue that mothers respond differently towards their children on the basis of preconceptions about what biological sex differences are supposed to exist; and these differences include touching, soothing and differential ideas about the autonomy (or lack of it) of boy and girl children.

Some feminists believe that the direction of personality, more specifically its femininity or masculinity, is set in the very earliest interactions between an infant and its parents, more particularly its mother.

Women who believe this suggest that the universal mothering role of women differentially affects boys and girls. For girls there is a universal internalization of certain features of the relationship between them and their mothers; and 'Through this process the individual characteristics of society are reproduced' (Sharpe 1976: 74). The mother/daughter relationship is based on a mutual interaction in which each identifies with the other. However, the mother/son relationship is seen as quite different, because a mother is described as stressing the opposition between herself and her son.

These early processes may be described as unconscious or conscious in nature; whichever, they are seen as the prime determinants of later interactions within the family and as the basis of adult personality. Both interpretations recognize the existence of conscious socialization behaviours, and usually draw on the work of Ruth Hartley in order to describe these (Hartley 1966). One consequence is that 'learning gender' here isn't seen as verbal or disciplinary in nature, but rather as 'kinaesthetic'. Kinaesthetic processes involve, in essence, a number of ways in which children are directly manipulated into 'being socialized'.

The effects of these processes, this argument suggests, is that by the age of four children know their sex identity and are also aware of the find distinctions of gender. And the extent to which they are sexually stereotyped is seen as directly affected by parental behaviours. In other words, the more parents treat their children in sexually differentiated ways, for example in exposing them to particular kinds of toys, the more it is believed that a child will reflect such stereotypes. . . .

Basic concepts in feminist descriptions of the processes involved in 'learning gender' include 'imitation', 'identification' and 'internalization'. Children *imitate* the behaviours of those people they identify with. They tend to *identify* with one or other of their parents and usually their fathers, although for girls a sexually differentiated form of identification is later brought about through the internalization of outside pressures. This particular interpretation of *internalization* suggests a direct and in many cases one-to-one relationship between what children are presented with and what they later enact.

One exceedingly interesting point about feminist ideas about 'socialization' and 'role' which we hope will have been detected by readers is the very great emphasis placed on the part that *mothers* play in socialization and thus in women's oppression. We're told that it is *mothers* who are involved in the earlier unconscious stages of socialization; and that it is *mothers* who are primarily involved in effecting the kinaesthetic processes. *Mothers* treat little boys and little girls differently, and so it is they who produce sexually stereotyped children and adults. Blaming the victim?

. . . [A]mazing agreement about these aspects of 'the family' exists among feminists. We believe that two things account for this, the second much more important than the first. The first is the common use of sources. By and large most feminist writings on this subject seem to rely on the same research, carried out mainly by non-feminists, and now rather dated research at that. The second is that this great unity in thinking derives from the adoption of what is basically the same model of socialization.

This model is one in which the processes of socialization are seen as those by which 'social structures' are internalized by children. Parents are seen as a kind of funnel through which stereotyped behaviours of all kinds are presented to children who then obligingly internalize them. There is a great reliance on the concept of 'internalization': 'gender' as systemized behaviours and attributes derives from this. Some accounts, we should point out, do state that an enormous variety of behaviours and attitudes exist in the real world, even in relation to gender-associated phenomena. But, in spite of this, all such complexities are left behind as of no great importance. This model stresses the paramount importance of generalities, stereotypes and the common processes of socialization, and portrays variations and differences as theoretically unimportant.

We shall go on to argue that this model is one which feminists have taken over and used, practically unchanged, from mono-causal structural approaches within the social sciences. . . .

'Socialization' as a feminist form of functionalism?

We now move away from describing feminist writings on socialization and role through composite pictures, generalizations. Instead we focus on the work of two people who have written about socialization, sex role or gender role socialization in particular. One of these people is a feminist and the other most decidedly not. However, we look at the work of both to suggest that both feminist and non-feminist accounts utilize the same basic model of the processes involved in socialization.

The feminist work on socialization we examine is that of Helen Weinreich; and we do so in order to look at some of its strengths and also some of what we feel to be its limitations (Weinreich 1978). We haven't chosen it because we particularly wish to criticize it. Indeed, rather the reverse. We see Helen Weinreich's examination of socialization as much more complex and highly developed than those of other feminists because it includes within it, in a complex and complementary way, a number of different ideas and concepts which are usually used as opposites, as mutually exclusive, in other accounts of socialization. The reason we've chosen to discuss it is precisely because it includes the strengths of other accounts and excludes many of their weaknesses. It will become clear later that the substance of our feelings about its limitations stems from the *kind* of approach adopted, its basic model of socialization, and indeed the notion of socialization itself; and not more specific features of it.

Socialization, Weinreich suggests, is concerned with the 'transmission' of behaviours, roles, attributes and beliefs to the next generation and has three key facets. The first focuses on internalization through direct proscription, example and expectation. The second emphasizes the part played by 'socializing agents' (primarily but not exclusively the family), who hold stereotypical beliefs about sex-appropriate characteristics which are reflected in their socialization practices. The third points out that many aspects of socialization are particularly concerned with sex roles and these are mainly cultural in origin although 'undoubtedly', Weinreich feels, some are biologically based. . . .

. . . Weinreich outlines a number of the problems which arise from sex-role socialization. She suggests that such problems are experienced by both females and males, although they may occur at different stages and in different ways. She also discusses the conflict that exists between the covert and overt demands which are made of children, using, as an important example of this, the conflicting demands made on girls within the educational system.

The decidedly non-feminist work on socialization that we now look at is that of Talcott Parsons, one of the key figures involved in the development of functionalist theory. We're particularly interested in his work on socialization because we think that a comparison of feminist work with that of a key figure within functionalism, one of the main targets of feminist criticisms, is particularly illuminating.

Parsons's account of the relationship between socialization and family structure borrows heavily from Freudian terminology, although he uses this in an idiosyncratic way (Parsons 1956a, b, c, d; Parsons and Bales 1956). Taking the Freudian concepts of the id, the ego and the super-ego, Parsons relates them to his own belief that there are four key phases of socialization which occur within the family. And so, in order to relate Freudian ideas to his own, he develops and adds on to them the concept of 'identity'. As with most other accounts of socialization, Parsons too emphasizes the crucial importance of 'primary socialization', that aspect of it which occurs in early childhood. And it is because of this that he is so concerned with the processes involved in sex role identification.

A key concept in the Parsonian scheme is that of 'role differentiation'. Parsons maintains that different roles *must* exist in the relationship between spouses, and that the development of sex-role identification in childhood mirrors the different roles which exist between a child's parents. The 'instrumental' role involves 'universalistic norms' of various kinds and is concerned with the relationship between the family unit and the outside world. The 'expressive' role involves 'particularistic norms' and is concerned with the nexus of relationships within the family. There are no prizes for guessing that Parsons identifies the instrumental role with males and the expressive role with females.

In summary, then, Parsons sees the processes of socialization as intimately concerned with the internalization of sets of *reciprocal* expectations which exist between the child and others. In many ways this is a 'learning theory', in which the child takes over specific behaviours of various kinds. But Parsons also uses the idea of identification, and the existence of 'identificands' within the family. And as well as this he retains some allegiance to an 'action' perspective in which the individual is seen to be active in construing and 'making' their own social reality. A result is that Parsons sees the child as itself active in the entire process. It is the child who makes choices and then enacts these, rather than being merely passive in a process of simple internalization.

We feel that there are a number of important ways in which Parsons's and Weinreich's accounts are similar. These include their common complementary use of facets of each of the existing socialization theories, their common adoption of a bi-polar notion of gender role, and their common belief that the sex role socialization they describe is essential to 'the system' that each depicts. . . .

We believe that the main difference between Parson's and Weinreich's work is the moral assessment that each makes of what they describe. Parsons believes that what he describes exists in the real world, that the continued existence of this is necessary for the perpetuation of the *status quo*, and that this is essential and desirable. Weinreich believes that what she describes exists in the real world but, in marked contrast to Parsons, she objects to what exists on moral grounds She doesn't agree that it is good or necessary that males and females should be differentially treated, and she believes that this ought to be changed. But there is an important difference here which we have glossed over. Parsons explains socialization as the product of society – of society's needs and requirements; and Weinreich explains society as the product of socialization. So it might be more accurate to emphasize not only the moral difference between them, but also that they use rather different types of explanation, in terms of what explains what. But in spite of this we feel that in most important respects their ideas are very similar indeed.

'Socialization theory' exists in feminist and non-feminist varieties, but in important ways these are varieties of the *same* theory – the 'socialization model'. We believe that the socialization model is 'psychologistic'. It suggests that there exists *within* the child various innate processes. It postulates a pre-formed and almost autonomously unfolding ego which develops independently of the social. We say 'almost' because it also identifies the existence of parental, and especially mothering, socialization practices which act as 'stimulus', so encouraging this 'response'. Apart from this, it sees what happens in social reality 'outside' of the child as independent of these processes and irrelevant to them. . . .

To us, the socialization model also seems overly deterministic. It presents us with what has been referred to as an over-socialized conception of people within a too deterministic view of social reality (Wrong 1961). People are presented as totally passive and totally malleable and entirely determined by 'society'. There are, of course, some variants within this model which recognize that 'exceptions' exist and that all individuals aren't entirely programmed in this way. However, more often than not these are accounted for by simply saying that 'proper socialization' has failed to take place.

In explaining 'exceptions' these variants aren't adopting probabilistic statements rather than claiming universality. If they did so they would be less objectionable. Instead we see them as both claiming universality and at the same time recognizing that universality doesn't exist. They have their cake and eat it too because they quite simply reject any notion that the existence of 'exceptions' might be important, something for theory to explain.

. . . What feminists who adopt the socialization model seem unwilling to confront is that this model embodies the values of power divisions of sexist society. Conform and you're acceptable; dare to be different and you must be a freak of some kind, are the ideas this model enshrines and perpetuates.

That we've described the socialization model as both psychologistic and presenting an over-socialized view might seem contradictory. After all, 'psychologistic' suggests the natural unfolding of innate processes already 'in' the child, and 'over-socialized' quite the opposite – that the child is totally malleable. We agree: these *are* contradictory things to say. However, we believe that this is a contradiction which exists within the socialization model and not just in our description of it. Although we recognize this contradiction exists, we don't feel that most of the people who adopt the socialization model do. They seem quite happy saying both that gender is psychologically innate *and* that gender stereotyping is dependent on 'agents of socialization'.

The socialization model is also reificatory. By this we mean it suggests that 'the social system' somehow 'demands' that certain things should occur. Within this 'the family' is the means of ensuring that these demands are fulfilled. Such an approach sees social systems existing over, above, and beyond the collection of individuals and artefacts which compose them. It sees the whole as more than the sum of its parts. . . .

We believe that the most important criticism to be made of the socialization model is that it is 'non-reflexive'. By this we mean that it explains obviously 'mal-socialized' or 'un-socialized' people as mistakes within the system, and feminist adoptions of this model let such labels and categorizations stand. The basic dichotomy we've identified within this model is one which sees *feminism*, along with lesbians, 'effeminate' men, career women, and a myriad of other people, as 'mistakes' whose existence can't be explained except by reference to 'mal-socialization'. That the feminists who use this model don't confront or seem to notice this issue comes, we believe, from their take-over of it in a practically unchanged form. They merely add women into it rather than critically focusing on the premises of the model itself. . . .

References

Hartley, R. (1966) 'A developmental view of female sex-role identification', in B. Biddle and E. Thomas (eds) *Role Theory*. New York: Wiley.

Parsons, T. (1956a) 'The American family: its relationship to personality and the social structure', in T. Parsons and R. Bales (eds) *Family: Socialization and Interaction Process*. London: Routledge.

Parsons, T. (1956b) 'Family structure and the socialization of the child', in T. Parsons and R. Bales (eds) *Family: Socialization and Interaction Process*. London: Routledge.

Parsons, T. (1956c) 'The organization of personality as a system of action', in T. Parsons and R. Bales (eds) *Family: Socialization and Interaction Process*. London: Routledge.

Parsons, T. (1956d) 'The mechanisms of personality functioning with special reference to socialization', in T. Parsons and R. Bales (eds) *Family: Socialization and Interaction Process*. London: Routledge.

Parsons, T. and Bales, R. (eds) (1956) *Family: Socialization and Interaction Process*. London: Routledge.

Sharpe, S. (1976) *Just like a Girl*. Harmondsworth: Penguin.

Weinreich, H. (1978) 'Sex-role socialization', in J. Chetwynd and O. Hartnett (eds) *The Sex Role System*. London: Routledge.

Wrong, D. (1961) 'The oversocialized conception of man in modern sociology', *American Sociological Review*, 26: 183–93.

Chapter 35

Bronwyn Davies

BECOMING MALE OR FEMALE

Bronwyn Davies outlines one alternative to conventional models of socialisation: a poststructuralist approach to gender in which gender dualism is understood as discursively constituted but all-pervasive. Children, she argues, are constrained to locate themselves on one or other side of the binary divide but nonetheless actively construct their own understanding of ways of being boys or girls.

From *Frogs and Snails and Feminist Tales*. Sydney: Allen & Unwin (1989).

In order to become recognisable and acceptable members of the society they are born into, children must learn to think with and act in terms of the accepted, known linguistic forms. This is not just a skill they must acquire in order to communicate, but an acquisition of the means by which they constitute themselves as persons in relation to others in the social world. In learning the language they learn to constitute themselves and others as unitary beings, as capable of coherent thought, as gendered, and as one who is in particular kinds of relation to others. Language is both a resource and a constraint. It makes social and personal being possible but it also limits the available forms of being to those which make sense within the terms provided by the language. . . .

Adults require children to adopt their linguistic practices, not just for the child's own benefit but as a way of confirming the rightness of the world as they understand it. Until children have accepted the terms of reference embedded in the language, they are potentially a disruptive force, undermining 'what adults claim is "obvious" and "known" to "everybody"' (Waksler 1986: 74).

Part of what is 'obvious and known to everybody' is that people are either male or female. In learning the discursive practices of their society children learn that they must be socially identifiable as one or the other, even though there is very little if any observable physical difference in most social situations. Dress, hairstyle, speech patterns and content, choice of activity – all become key signifiers that can be used in successfully positioning oneself as a girl or a boy.

Correct positioning is facilitated by the interactive others each child encounters and by the discursive practices they learn in which bipolar maleness and femaleness are embedded. I once gave a toy car to a three-year-old girl as a symbolic refusal of the gender order. She unwrapped the present, looked at my quizzically and said, 'It's really a boys' toy, but don't worry, I can handle it,' at one and the same time reconstituting the gender order that I was attempting to break down, and taking care, as girls should, not to hurt my feelings too much at having my error pointed out to me. A similar gesture with a three-year-old boy, when I gave him a music box, simply resulted in a sulky refusal to interact with me or the music box – how can one, he may well have asked, interact with adults who refuse to co-operate with the establishment of one's correct gendered positioning?

Of course taking oneself up as a boy or a girl is not a unitary process. How one 'does' masculinity or femininity with one's parents, say, may differ profoundly from how one 'does' masculinity with one's friends, or from one friend to another.
. . .

Much of the adult world is not consciously taught to children, is not contained in the *content* of their talk, but is embedded in he language, in the discursive practices and the social and narrative structures through which the child is constituted as a person, as a child and as a male or female. Poststructuralist theory allows us to recognise that what children learn through the process of interacting in the everyday world is not a unitary, non contradictory language and practice – and it is not a unitary identity that is created through those practices, as the example of the boys in the yellow raincoats makes clear. Rather, children learn to see and understand in terms of the multiple positionings and forms of discourse that are available to them. More, they learn the forms of desire and of power and powerlessness that are embedded in and made possible by the various discursive practices through which they position themselves and the positioned.

Children (like adults) may be positioned in many ways during any one day, sometimes powerful and sometimes powerless. At the same time, and contrary to much of our experience, a consistent thread running through our discursive practices is the idea of each person as unitary, coherent, non-contradictory and as fixed in certain ways (cf. Harré 1985). One of these assumed points of fixity is sex/gender.

Sex-role socialisation theory

Being male or female sometimes seems to be taken on more enthusiastically by children than adults expect – one quite often hears parents saying with some regret or puzzlement that their daughter is a real little girl and insists on wearing pretty dresses, or that their son just *is* heavily masculine and aggressive, and was so right from the beginning, despite their discouragement. They claim that they have tried to teach their boys to be gentle and their girls to be assertive, and yet they have turned out like any other boy or girl. Perhaps it is genetic, after all, they say. How else to explain how the supposedly all-powerful parent has had so little influence?

This puzzlement derives to a large extent from the commonsense but inaccurate theories most of us have about the relationship between the individual and the social structure. The commonly used terms 'socialisation' and 'sex roles' are part of the linguistic paraphernalia that misleads us. As well, the conceptual division of the person into the biological self (sex) and the social self (gender) . . . aids in the confusion that is involved here.

In sex-role socialisation theory the biological basis of sexual difference is assumed, and the 'roles' that children are taught by adults are a superficial social dressing laid over the 'real' biological difference. There is, in these two beliefs, a profound confusion about what a person really is, and about how she/he becomes so.

Within the sex-role socialisation mode of the world the child is taught her or his sex role by, usually, one central adult, but is also 'pressed' into maintenance of that role by a multitude of others (peers, media, etc.). There is no room in this model for the child as active agent, the child as theorist, recognising for him or herself the way the social world is organised. Nor is there acknowledgement of the child as implicated in the construction and maintenance of the social world through the very act of recognising it and through learning its discursive practices. . . .

Researchers working within the socialisation model are at risk of getting caught up in doing simplistic research to show the ways in which adults are at fault in *causing* narrow stereotypical behaviours in children . . . But a straightforward causal link is impossible to demonstrate, given the complexity of the social word, the multiple and contradictory nature of social reality, and the fact of simultaneous accommodations and resistances.

When this direct causal link cannot be demonstrated the second string of socialisation theory is called on. Using the conceptual division between sex and gender, we appeal to the biological as the 'real' cause of the child's behaviour and thus fall into a form of biological determinism. . . .

An assumption of poststructuralist theory is that maleness and femaleness do not have to be discursively structured in the way that they currently are. Genitals do not have to be linked to feminine or masculine subjectivities unless we constitute them that way. Children can take up a range of both masculine and feminine positionings if they have access to discourse that renders that non-problematic. Within poststructuralist theory the individual is not longer seen as a unitary, unproblematically sexed being, but rather as a shifting nexus of possibilities. In a world not polarised around a female/male dualism, these possibilities would not be limited by one's reproductive sexual capacity, but would be linked instead to the range of potential positionings each individual person was capable of or interested in taking up.

The process of positioning oneself as male or female

The position that I will explore . . . is that sex and gender are at one and the same time elements of the social structure, and something created by individuals and within individuals as they learn the discursive practices through which that social structure is created and maintained. Social structure is not separate from the individuals who make it up. It is not a 'thing' that can be imposed on individuals. It nevertheless has material force. Individuals cannot float free from social structure. They can choose to act on and transform structures, but structures must always be recognised as constraining individual and social action.

. . . These are not simply an external constraint . . . they provide the conceptual framework, the psychic patterns, the emotions through which individuals position themselves as male or female and through with they privately experience themselves in relation to the social world. As well, they provide the vehicle through which others will recognise that positioning as legitimate, as meaningful, as providing the right to claim personhood. The development and practice of new forms of discourse, then, is not a simple matter of choice, but involves grappling with both subjective and social/structural constraints.

Masculinity and femininity are not inherent properties of individuals, then, they are inherent or structural properties of our society: that is, they both condition and arise from social action. Each of us, as members of society, takes on board as our own the 'knowledge' of sex and of gender as they are socially constituted. As children learn to discursive practices of their society, they learn to position themselves correctly as male or female, since that is what is required of them to have a recognisable identity within the existing social order (Davies 1987). Not to do so, in fact, to resist, is to be perceived as a social failure (Haug 1987; Walkerdine and Lucey 1989). Positioning oneself as male or female is done through the discursive practice and through the subject positionings which are available within those practices, in much the same way and through the same practices that the positioning of 'child' and 'adult' are made available.

Take, for example, a situation in which I, as adult, say to you, as child, 'Good girl.' The major import of this is not that *I* choose to reward *you* for being a particular kind of girl and thus press you into a particular social mould, but that my use of the particular category 'good girl' in this particular situation creates and sustains both the gendered and the adultist elements of the social structure. By using a particular linguistic form I engage in the discursive practice which constitutes you as child, me as adult and your behaviour as praiseworthy and as relevant to your female genderedness. Through hearing me as speaking coherently in relation to the action you have just performed, you see one of the ways in which the concepts of femaleness and virtue are linked by adults within the discursive practices of the society.

Children as well as adults are all members of a society which celebrates hegemonic (dominant, powerful) masculinity. Hegemonic masculinity is an *idea* of masculinity (as well as something practised by some men) that we generally refer to when we go along with those generalisations that make all men not only superior in terms of strength and power to women, but also *opposite* to women. Similarly, when we think of women who are the 'oppressed other' to such men we evoke a housebound mother of small children. All the rest of the men and women (which includes most women for most of their lives) somehow slip from our minds while we do this conceptual work to sustain the polarity. . . . The essential point at this stage is that no one individual stamps another individual in the mould of the society. Rather, the society provides, through its structures, its language and its interactive forms, possible ways of being, of thinking, of seeing (cf. Davies 1983; Garnica 1979). Out of the multitude of conflicting and often contradictory possibilities, each person struggles to achieve themselves as a unitary, rational being whose existence is separate from others, and yet makes sense to those others. In learning the discursive practices we learn the categories, the relations between categories, and the fine conceptual and interactive detail with which to take up our personhood, and with which to interpret who we are in relation to others. Positioning oneself as person within the terms made available within a particular social order also creates and sustains that social order.

Positioning oneself as male or female is not just a conceptual process. It is also a *physical* process. Each child's body takes on the knowledge of maleness or femaleness through its practices. The most obvious, and apparently superficial, form of bodily practice that distinguishes male from female is dress and hairstyle. Many of the practices that are handed to children by adults, such as dress, serve to mark children such that their gender is emphasised and made a predominant feature of their appearance. Joanne, one of the children I encountered in the second stage of the study, tended to wear tracksuits all the time, at least during winter, these being much more suitable than dresses for the kind of activity she enjoyed. But she found that she was so constantly mistaken for a boy that she had to tie her hair up in a distinctively girlish top knot in order to avoid being so mistaken. She found people's inability to see that she was female distressing, presumably because she took it as a signal of her failure to be correctly gendered. She was, on several occasions, at pains to point out to me that she did own several dresses.

But the wearing of dresses is more than symbolic. It is an essential part of the process through which girls learn the meaning of being girls. Jackson comments:

> Sexual modesty is considered a specifically feminine virtue, so any signs of immodesty in girls are condemned most forcefully. In fact, girls are often so well schooled that they are even reluctant to reveal their bodies to other girls . . . These problems are intensified by girls' clothing: if we teach children that it is indecent to reveal their underwear, and then proceed to dress half of them in skirts, we are placing that half at a distinct disadvantage. (1982: 98–9)

Bruce comments on teachers finding 'many examples such as little girls being "punished" by the attitudes of others for behaviour such as hanging up side down from monkey bars and showing their knickers . . .' (1985: 52). Adams and Walkerdine (1986) found that dresses were central to boys' definitions of girls, and the Goldmans reported little boys being quite negative about the idea of being a girl on this basis: '7 year old boy: Boys wear trousers every day and girls usually wear dresses. People can pull them up and see their pants' (Goldman and Goldman 1982: 176). Thus dresses mark the femaleness of their wearers but they also act as part of the process whereby femaleness becomes inscribed in girls' bodies . . .

The process of bodily inscription works from the idea to the reality: what one is able to be is constrained by the idea of what one might be, and this is particularly the case in the division between male and females. Wex (1979) and Haug (1987), for example, have shown that girls are taught to sit in quite unnatural and submissive postures, with knees always together. Boys, in contrast, are free to sit more naturally with knees apart and they look dominant and assertive in doing so. Girls who sit in 'male' postures are not seen as assertive and dominant but as sexually provocative and 'available'. How we hold our bodies and how we interpret that holding depends on which gender we have been ascribed and what is counted as allowable within the frame of the gender one is taken to have (cf. also Herzberger and Tennen 1985). . . .

There are a number of items of dress that are used by pre-school children to mark their sex, such marking being a symbolic means of maintaining the sexes as [clearly] distinct. Generally, skirts, ribbons, shawls, handbags, prams and dollies signify femaleness, and guns, trousers, waistcoats, coats, superhero capes and uniforms such as firefighters' uniforms signify maleness. These gendered symbols were closely associated by the children whom I studied with what they defined as male and female behaviour, so much so that they would cross-dress in order to achieve the behaviour they associated with the form of dress. When I first arrived at one of the pre-schools to carry out my observations there, I noticed several boys who were occasionally to be seen running around wearing a skirt from the dressing-up cupboard. On one occasion I saw a boy, whom I have called Geoffrey, in a black velvet skirt fighting furiously with another boy just near the home corner:

> Two boys start aggressive wrestling and punching. Geoffrey, the bigger of the two, seems to be getting the worst of it. He is dressed in a black velvet skirt. He starts to cry and shouts at the smaller boy, 'You're yucky! You made me [unclear]!' He stands up and takes the skirt off angrily and throws it on the ground. He kicks the smaller boy, saying, 'Now I've got more pants on!' The smaller boy starts to cry, no longer willing to fight back, he cowers away from Geoffrey's kicking. Once he has kicked him several times Geoffrey walks away, seemingly satisfied and no longer tearful. The black velvet skirt is left lying on the ground. . . .

The skirts and trousers are more than superficial dressing. Not only can they construct and sexualise girls, they can act as powerful signifiers of masculine and feminine ways of being. They appear to have a symbolic weight of perhaps equal if not greater significance for the children than the symbolic forms encoded in language.

There were also incidents in which girls dressed in 'male' clothes, or, rather, used male symbols to achieve a masculine form of action. These were less frequent. On one such occasion Catherine, a pretty girl who was always dressed in 'feminine' clothes and often to be found in the 'home corner', needed to get her dolly back from George, who had stolen it from her:

> Catherine is dressing her dolly in the home corner. A small boy, John, who often plays with the girls in the home corner is 'ironing' the dolls' clothes. There is a new toy box in the home corner and Geoffrey comes in and jumps into it.

CATHERINE: (to Geoffrey) You be the father.

GEOFFREY: I'm not the father, I'm the fireman.

JOHN: I'm ironing this jumper.

CATHERINE: No, I'm just putting this doll here.
               (They co-operatively dress the doll.)

GEORGE: (skipping into the room and singing) I'm going to get a dolly, dolly
               dolly, dolly dolly. Oh, a toy box! A toy box! (He picks up a dolly.)
               A dolly for me. I want a dolly like that!

CATHERINE: No, it's my doll!
               (George goes off and bangs a cupboard door.)

JOHN: We'd better ring your mum.
               (George comes back in, grabs Catherine's doll and runs off with it.
               She is on the verge of tears. John hands her the phone, then offers
               her dolls' clothes to put on another doll, attempting with the phone
               call and the suggestion of another doll to maintain their play,
               weaving in the theft to the storyline, so as not to disrupt it.)

CATHERINE: No, that boy took it!
               (John resumes ironing and Catherine wanders off, presumably to
               see if she can get her doll. She comes back without it.)

JOHN: Here you are, they're already ironed.
               (Catherine, ignoring John, goes decisively to the dress-up cupboard
               and puts on a man's waistcoat. She tucks the waistcoat into the
               dress-up skirt that she already has on, and marches out. This time
               she returns victorious with the dolly under her arm. She immedi-
               ately takes off the waistcoat and drops it on the floor. She is now
               very busy and happy.)

CATHERINE: Where are the stockings? (red tights for the doll) . . .

Thus, as we discursively position ourselves as male or female, it can be argued,
our physical being will follow suit. The knowledge of oneself as male or female,
encoded in one's body, makes possible, or precludes, certain forms of relationship with others and with the landscape. How one understands what one's body
can or cannot do immediately affects the way one's body relates to the environment. That is, the idea of femaleness and the adoption of practices relevant to the
idea has a material effect on the child's body. One's sex is thus *inscribed* in one's
body through the activities associated with one's *ascribed* sex (cf. Gross 1986a;
Haug 1987).

An excellent analysis of this difference in bodily inscription is undertaken by
Young (1980). Young cites the work of Strauss on the different ways that very
young boys and girls throw balls. Strauss says:

> The girl of five does not make any use of lateral space. She does not
> stretch her arm sideward; she does not twist her trunk; she does not
> move her legs, which remain side by side. All she does in preparation
> for throwing is to lift her right arm forward to the horizontal and to
> bend the forearm backward in a pronate position . . . The ball is released
> without force, speed or accurate aim . . . A boy of the same age, when
> preparing to throw, stretches his right arm sideward and backward;

supinates the forearm; twists, turns and bends his trunk; and moves his right foot backward. From this stance, he can support his throwing almost with the full strength of his total motorium . . . The ball leaves the hand with considerable acceleration; it moves towards its goal in a long flat curve.

(Strauss 1966: 157–8)

Young analyses the difference between these two forms of throwing in terms of the 'inhibited intentionality' that comes with learning to see oneself primarily as the object of another's gaze, and the learned sense of fragility that comes with being female. She concludes that lack of practice is only one aspect of the problems:

> The modalities of feminine bodily existence are not merely privative, however, and thus their source is not merely lack of practice, though this is certainly an important element. There is a specific positive style of feminine body comportment and movement, which is learned as the girl comes to understand that she is a girl . . . In assuming herself as a girl, she takes herself up as fragile . . . The more a girl assumes her status as feminine, the more she takes herself to be fragile and immobile, and the more she actively enacts her own body inhibition . . . At the root of these modalities . . . is the fact that the woman lives her body as *object* as well as subject – An essential part of the situation of being a woman is that of living the ever present possibility that one will be gazed upon as a mere body, as shape and flesh that presents itself as the potential object of another subject's intentions and manipulations, rather than as a living manifestation of action and intention.

(Young 1980: 153–4)

The *idea* of bipolar maleness/femaleness is something which itself has material force. This is evidenced by the continuing work each person engages in to achieve and sustain their gendered identity, and by the fact that when they fail to do so, they perceive themselves, and are perceived by others, as failing as an individual, rather than perceiving the linguistic structures in which the dualism is embedded as a fault. One of the ways in which the idea of bipolarity functions is to reduce the *actual diversity* (non-polarity) of individual behaviour to a bipolar model. This can involve ignoring or not seeing 'deviations' or actually managing to construe behaviour or categories of behaviour as bipolar, even though they would appear to lend themselves more readily to a non-polar perception. . . .

Several of the children with whom I parked in the first stage of the study showed a remarkable capacity to keep the idea of the dualism intact by ignoring individual deviations, or managing to construe those deviations as somehow fitting into the bipolar system. The following episode, for example, took place during a reading of the story *Jesse's Dream Skirt*. In this story Jesse has a dream that he has a beautiful multi-coloured skirt. In the morning his mother makes him the skirt out of her old dresses and he insists on wearing it to pre-school. Jesse is teased by the others but the teacher persuades them that it is all right for Jesse to dress in this way. Chonny was very angry at the thought of a boy choosing to wear a skirt or a dress:

B.D.:   Do you ever wear a dress?

CHONNY: (Shakes head.)

B.D.:   What about Daddy? Does Daddy sometimes wrap himself up in a dress?

CHONNY: No. My mum.

B.D.:   Your mum does. But sometimes doesn't Dad wrap himself around with a skirt? (pointing to a picture of a man in a sarong, knowing that his father wore sarongs, but not using the word 'sarong', suspecting that it is not part of Chonny's vocabulary)

CHONNY: No.

B.D.:   Doesn't he? (doubtful tone of voice)

CHONNY: Man's don't have some!

B.D.:   Don't they? Well this boy does, doesn't he? (pointing at Jesse) And these men here do, all these different men, a priest and this Greek person (pointing at pictures in the front of the book)

CHONNY: Um (unclear)

B.D.:   This boy's dressing up in his mum's clothes.

CHONNY: Sometimes big girls do that.

B.D.:   Big girls? Do boys ever try on their mother's dresses?

CHONNY: No.

B.D.:   Well, this boy does.

CHONNY: I don't, either.

B.D.:   Right.

CHONNY: I do have pants.

B.D.:   Why don't boys try on dresses? Don't they think/

CHONNY: They don't have some. (said with finality)

Later, when I took him home, he burst out to his Malay father that I had read him this stupid story about a boy who wore a dress. Interestingly, his father had a friend visiting who was wearing a sarong, and thus looking very like the men pictured at the front of the book, but this cut no ice with Chonny. The fact that his father and his father's friend observably wore what could be called dresses needed to be ignored, or construed as not fitting into the category of 'dress' in order to maintain not only the symbolic boundaries of the categories male and female, but their exclusiveness from each other.

Another [boy] . . . at one of the pre-schools I observed also managed the same feat in relation to strength as a defining feature of males. He told me that because he was a boy he was stronger than girls, and gave as an example the fact that he helped his sister, who was weak, over puddles. Shortly afterwards one of the girls of the same age hitched herself up on to a fairly high window sill behind her in order to sit on it. Hamid made a feeble attempt to do the same thing, then whinged for me to lift him up too, knowing that he did not have the strength and agility to match the girl's feat. Once up, however, he continued in his domineering manner, utterly unshaken by this contrary evidence to his earlier assertion.

Each child must get its gender right, not only for itself to be seen as normal and acceptable within the terms of the culture, but it must get it right for others who will be interpreting themselves in relation to it as other. To the extent that it is a competent member of society, it can be seen to be competently constructing the gendered world, achieving the practices, the ways of knowing and of being that make sense within the narrative/interactive structures of the society it lives in. That achievement in turn is treated to a large extent as a *natural* expression of maleness or femaleness, such interpretations being aided by the association in our culture of the body with that which is natural.

Once having taken on the bodily, emotional and cognitive patterns which give substance to the dominance/subordinance forms of gender relations, it is difficult for individuals to imagine any alternative to that social structure. In turn, the apparent facticity of two opposite genders renders those behaviours, thoughts and emotions which are involved in stepping outside the dominant (male) and subordinate (female) patterns appear as incompetence, even immorality. The failure to be 'correctly' gendered is perceived as a moral blot on one's identity, since that which is believed to be is, and generally takes on the weight of a moral imperative – there are, we believe, two opposite sexes, therefore that is the way the world *ought* to be.

References

Adams, C. and Walkerdine V. (1986) *Investigating Gender in the Primary School: Activity Based Inset Materials for Primary Teachers*. London: Inner London Education Authority.

Bruce, W. (1985) 'The implications of stereotyping in the first years of school', *Australian Journal of Early Childhood*, 10 (2).

Davies, B. (1987) 'The accomplishment of genderedness in preschool-aged children', in A. Pollard (ed.) *Children and their Primary Schools*. London: Falmer Press.

Davies, D. (1983) *Towards Non-sexist Language*. Melbourne: FAUSA.

Garnica, O. (1979) '"The boys have muscles and the girls have sexy legs": adult–child speech and the use of generic person labels', in O. Garnica and M. King, *Language, Children and Society: The Effect of Social Factors on Children Learning to Communicate*. Oxford: Pergamon Press.

Goldman, R. and Goldman, J. (1982) *Children's Sexual Thinking*. London: Routledge.

Gross, E. (1986) 'What is feminist theory?' in C. Patemen and E. Gross (eds) *Feminist Challenges: Social and Political Theory*. Sydney: Allen & Unwin.

Harré, R. (1985) *Social Being*. Oxford: Blackwell.

Haug, F. (1987) *Female Sexualization*. London: Verso.

Herzberger, S. and Tennen, H. (1985) '"Snips and snails and puppy-dog tails": gender of agent, recipient and observer as determinants of perceptions of discipline', *Sex Roles*, 12 (7–8).

Jackson, S. (1982) *Childhood and Sexuality*. Oxford: Blackwell.

Waksler, F. (1986) 'Studying children: phenomenological insights', *Human Studies*, 9.

Walkerdine, V. and Lucey, H. (1989) *Democracy in the Kitchen*. London: Virago.

Wex, M. (1979) *Let's take back our space: female and male body language as a result of patriarchal structures*, Berlin: Frauenliteraturverlag Hermine Fees.

Young, I. M. (1980) 'Throwing like a girl: a phenomenology of body comportment, mortality and spirituality', *Human Studies*, 3.

Chapter 36

Barrie Thorne

DO GIRLS AND BOYS HAVE DIFFERENT CULTURES?

Much of the literature on girls and boys growing up assumes that they inhabit, in school and play, separate, gendered cultures. Similar presuppositions inform much popular advice literature on relations between adult women and men. In this account, based on ethnographic work in North American schools, Barrie Thorne contests the 'separate cultures' thesis. The separate cultures thesis assumes that boys roam in large groups whose ethos is based on hierarchy, competitiveness, team games and sports, toughness and aggression. Girls, on the other hand, are assumed to socialise primarily through shifting alliances of 'best friends', to engage in co-operative rather than competitive play, to value emotional and physical intimacy and to prefer 'nice' behaviour to 'meanness' and 'toughness'. All this seems very stereotyped, yet much existing research data appears to support the idea of a sharp gender divide between the social worlds of girls and boys. However, as Barrie Thorne demonstrates, there are considerable biases built into this work and the gendered worlds children inhabit are far more complex, shifting and fluid than the separate cultures thesis would indicate.

From *Gender Play*, Buckingham: Open University Press (1993).

A FAMILIAR STORY LINE runs through the literature on gender and the social relations of children. The story opens by emphasizing patterns of mutual avoidance between boys and girls and then asserts that this daily separation results in, and is perpetuated by, deep and dichotomous gender differences. Groups of girls and groups of boys have contrasting ways of bonding and expressing antagonism and conflict; they act upon different values and pursue divergent goals; in many ways they live in separate worlds The story often concludes by drawing lessons for adults.[1] For example, in one popularized version, Deborah Tannen argues that because they grew up in the gender-separated worlds of childhood, adult men and women are locked into patterns of miscommunication, with women repeatedly seeking intimacy, while men are preoccupied with marking status.[2]

Reading the social science literature and sorting through my own observations, I have circled around and around this influential portrayal. The separate-and-different-worlds story is seductive. It gives full weight to the fact that girls and boys often *do* separate in daily interactions, especially when they create more lasting groups and friendships. The marking of boundaries between groups of boys and groups of girls . . . further drives the genders apart and creates spaces in which they can build and teach different cultures. And when I, like other observers, have compared the dynamics of groups of girls with those of groups of boys, I have been struck by apparent differences.

Furthermore, boys and girls – the 'native informants' – sometimes use different rhetorics to describe their same-gender relationships: boys talk about 'buddies', 'teams', and 'being tough', whereas girls more often use a language of 'best friends' and 'being nice'. And when girls and boys come together, they occasionally comment on experiences of gender difference. When a troupe of Ashton sixth-grade girls grabbed a football from the on-going play of a group of boys, the aide tried to reason with the warring parties by asking the boys, 'Why can't the girls play football with you?' The boys hotly replied, 'They don't do it our way. They can't tackle; when we tackle 'em, they cry.' A similar episode emerged on the Oceanside playground when a group of girls vied with a group of boys for use of a foursquare court. The yard duty tried to resolve the dispute by suggesting that the girls and boys join into one game. This time the girls protested, saying, 'They don't play our way.' One of the girls later explained, 'The boys slam the ball, and we don't.'

In short, much of what has been observed about girls and boys, especially in the relationships they create apart from the surveillance of adults, can be fitted into the model of 'different worlds or cultures'. But as I've tried to line up that model with my own empirical observations and with the research literature, I have found so many exceptions and qualifications, so many incidents that spill beyond and fuzzy up the edges, and so many conceptual ambiguities, that I have come to question the model's basic assumptions. . . .

Problems with the different-cultures approach

The central themes of the different-cultures portrayal – large versus small, public versus private, hierarchy versus connection – operate like well worn grooves on a dirt road; when a new study is geared up, the wheels of description and analysis slide into the contrastive themes and move right along. This path may be compelling because it evokes experience; adults have seen groups of boys insulting and challenging one another and girls negotiating who is 'best friends' with whom. These patterns may also resonate with childhood memories. . . .

But does the evocative power of these themes come solely from the force of reality, or in part from deep-seated cultural beliefs about 'the nature' of girls compared with boys? Because the portrayal skirts around stereotypes (e.g. boys are tough, girls are nice), and because the contrastive grooves by no means cover all the pathways of experience, we should view the different-cultures approach with a degree of skepticism.

I will now give voice to the questions, to the array of 'but what about . . .?'s that kept popping up as I tried to fit my own observations into the dualistic framework. When I searched through my fieldnotes to see how they related to patterns put forward in the literature, I found that much of the supportive evidence came from my observations of the most popular kids in Miss Bailey's classroom. This tips off one central problem with the separate-and-different-worlds literature: not everyone has had an equal hand in painting the picture of what boys and girls are 'like'. Furthermore, because it is based on dichotomies, the different-cultures approach exaggerates gender difference and neglects within-gender variation, including crosscutting sources of division and commonality like social class and ethnicity. These facts seriously undermine the tidy set of contrasts that build up the different-cultures view, and they raise the challenge of how to grasp complex patterns of difference, and commonality, without perpetuating stereotypes.

Whose experiences are represented?

In an early phase of my project, when I largely accepted the different-cultures framework, I went through my fieldnotes on Miss Bailey's fourth to fifth-grade class and tried to compare the dynamics of boys' groups with those of girls. During this search I felt like an explorer shining a flashlight on selected parts of a dark cave. Guided by prior expectations (e.g. that boys would move in larger, more hierarchical, and girls in smaller, more intimate groups), I could indeed light up those patterns in my fieldnotes. But the light mostly hovered around the 'popular kids' – the group of six or seven boys (and one girl) who deferred to John as their leader, and, to a lesser degree, the dyads and triads that maneuvered around Kathryn, the most popular girl in the class. I am not alone: *a skew toward the most visible and dominant – and a silencing and marginalization of the others – can be found in much of the research on gender relations among children and youth.*

John's group was visible in part because it was the largest and most stable clique in the classroom . . . Members of the group shared food, maneuvered to sit together, and called one another 'buddies'; they routinely played team sports (soccer, baseball, and basketball, depending on the season) and talked about their games in the interstices of the school day. (Here lies a striking 'but what about?' The group that seemed to anchor the boys' world included a girl, Jessie . . . [S]he acted out what has been called 'boys' culture' more dramatically than did many other boys in the classroom, and she was also part of a shifting alliance among girls. Not irrelevantly, she was the only African-American student in the classroom.)

John's group not only was large but also included the most popular boys in the classroom. Kathryn shared this source of visibility since she was by far the most popular girl. The lives of the popular often become public drama, and Kathryn's break-ups and renewed affiliations with Jessie and Judy drew attention and even participation, as gossips and messengers, from the rest of the class. . . . Kathryn also got more than her share of attention in my fieldnotes; socially constructed contours of visibility skew ethnographic reports.

The 'Big Man bias' in research on boys. What about the other boys? Apart from John's group, they did not hang out in large, bonded 'gangs', 'flocks', or 'teams', as the literature claims boys do. Matt, Roger, Eddie, and Don were sociable and regularly played team sports, so they could be seen in large groups heading to and from the soccer or baseball fields. But they were not part of a stable clique. Others were loners, including Joel, who was overweight, afraid of sports, and brought extra food and fancy toys from home to gain momentary attention; Neil, who was shy and physically unco-ordinated; and Bert, who was slow on the uptake and at the bottom of the class in academic performance. Miguel and Alejandro, the recent immigrants from Mexico, hung out on the playground with a group of Spanish-speaking boys and girls who played zone dodgeball day after day. Their mixed-gender experiences are, of course, totally obscured by the different-cultures approach, which assumes virtually total separation between boys and girls.

The relationships of four of the boys – Jeremy, Scott, Bill, and Don – fit the 'dyad into triad' description better than relationships among any girls in the classroom, except for Kathryn, Jessie, and Judy.[3] Jeremy, who had a creative imagination, spun fantasy worlds with one other boy at a time . . .

The identity of Jeremy's adventuring partner shifted between Scott and Bill via a 'break up' process often claimed to be typical of girls. The boy on the outs would sometimes sulk and talk about the other two behind their backs. When Scott was excluded, he would activate a long-standing affiliation with Don; when Bill was on the outs, he went solo. Over the course of the school year I saw each of the shifting pairs – Jeremy and Bill; Jeremy and Scott; Scott and Don – celebrate themselves as 'best buddies'. . . . The overall pattern fit the shifting alliances claimed to typify girls' social relations, but *boys* were the protagonists.

In short, when I mold my data into shapes provided by the literature characterizing boys' social relations (in this case, the claim that boys are organized into large, hierarchical groups), I have to ignore or distort the experiences of more than half the boys in Miss Bailey's classroom. And I am not alone. The literature on 'the boys' world' suffers from a 'Big Man bias' akin to the skew found in anthropological research that equates male elites with men in general.[4] In many observational studies of children in pre-schools and early elementary school, large, bonded groups of boys who are physically assertive, engage in 'tough talk', and actively devalue girls' anchor descriptions of 'the boys' world' and themes of masculinity. Other kinds of boys may be mentioned, but not as the core of the gender story.[5]

By fourth grade, as in Miss Bailey's classroom, the Big Men are defined not only by physical self-assertion and group bonds, but also by their athletic skill. In the United States, ethnographers typically detail the social relations of older boys from the vantage point of a clique of popular athletes: 'Don's group' in Robert Everhart's study of a junior high; 'the athletic group' in Philip Cusick's ethnography of a high school; in a participant-observation study of Little League baseball teams, Gary Alan Fine chose the 'leaders' as his chief informants.[6] I detect a kind of yearning in these books; when they went back to scenes from their earlier lives, the authors couldn't resist hanging out at the top. Cusick writes about his efforts to shake off male 'isolates': 'I was there to do a study not to be a friend to those who had no friends.'[7]

British sociologists and anthropologists have done pioneering ethnographic research in schools and on 'youth culture' more generally. This literature also has a systematic bias, but because Marxist assumptions guide the British researchers, the 'Big Men' who get attention are the ones – again bonded in larger groups – who are working-class, flamboyantly masculine, and resisting dominant class structures. *Learning to Labor*, an ethnography done in a vocational high school in England, is the classic of this genre. The author, Paul Willis, focuses on 'the lads', a group who created an oppositional culture of aggression and joking tied to the working-class masculine subculture of factory workers. The lads' subculture, different from that of more conforming boys (whom the lads called the 'ear 'oles'), ironically helped reproduce their eventual position in the working class. We have yet to see an ethnography written from the experiences of more 'conformist' working-class boys like the 'ear 'oles'.[8] . . .

In *Making the Difference*, a pathbreaking ethnography of class and gender relations among secondary school students in Australia, R. W. Connell and his colleagues argue that there are multiple masculinities, some hegemonic and others submerged or marginalized; the patterns are contradictory and continually negotiated. The authors also point to varied forms of femininity, ranging from the 'emphasized' (a term they have chosen because masculinity claims ultimate hegemony over femininity) to less visible forms.[9] Connell and his colleagues observe that although powerfully symbolic, 'hegemonic masculinity' and 'emphasized femininity' are not necessarily the most common patterns. This useful approach pries open unitary notions of masculinity and femininity and raises the question of why and how some forms come to be seen as masculinity and femininity in general. . . .

By junior high and high school, named cliques, or 'groups', as kids call them, consolidate; some are same-gender and others include both girls and boys. Joyce Canaan, an anthropologist who did extensive participant observation in the middle school and high school of a suburban US community, found that from sixth to eighth grade, kids' social relations became increasingly hierarchical. Middle-school girls and boys enacted a three-tiered ranking system: 'popular' (with two 'cool' subgroups, 'jocks' and 'freaks'), 'middle', and 'low' ('scums', 'wimps', and 'fags' – the latter two terms used for boys; 'brains', including both boys and girls, had an ambiguous status). Students more often labeled and talked about the 'popular' than other groups. Canaan found that over the course of high school the group system became more open and ambiguous; it was both present and not present as kids manipulated contradictory values.[10] Research of this kind helps challenge overly coherent and monolithic portayals of 'boys' culture' versus 'girls' culture'. . . .

What about girls? The different-cultures portrayal is as problematic for girls as it is for boys, although in both cases the conventional picture does illuminate some recurring patterns. Among the girls in Miss Bailey's classroom there were no large, bonded groups of the sort that John led.[11] And there indeed were 'tense triangles' and shifting alliances, notably the axis of Kathryn, Jessie, and Judy. Judy also had strong ties to Connie, and Jessie bridged to John's group. Another shifting threesome, rife with conflict, encompassed Nancy, Jessica, and Shelly. Shelly was also friends with Lenore from the other fourth-grade classroom; together they formed the core of a wandering playground troupe. Sheila and Tracy, another pair, often hung out together, especially during baseball season when they journeyed across the playground to seek entry into the boys' games. Neera, Beth, Rosie, and Rita didn't seem to have close friends, at least not at school. As with the more isolated boys, their experiences spill beyond the generalizations.

The conventional emphasis on friendship pairs and shifting alliances masks not only the experience of those without intense affiliations, but also the complex range of girls' interactions. In some activities girls interact in large groups. For example, the playground troupes . . . sometimes included as many as five or six girls, and shifting groups of six to eight girls often played on the bars, talking, doing tricks, and sometimes lining up in a row to twirl their bodies in unison. Although games of jump rope and foursquare involved only three or four active players at any one time, other girls lined up waiting for a turn and joined in the general and often contentious disputes about whether a given player was out.

Drawing on a detailed study of fourth- and fifth-grade girls on a school play-ground, Linda Hughes has challenged the depiction of foursquare as a simple, turn-taking type of play. She notes that within the formal rules of the game, the focus of Lever's generalizations about turn-taking, there may be varied ways of playing. (When the Oceanside girls said that boys 'slammed the ball' and didn't play foursquare 'our way', they recognized this point.) Hughes found – and, alerted by her insights, I could also see this in my observations – that in their playing of foursquare, girls created 'complex, large-group activity', elaborating a complicated structure of rules.[12] These patterns cannot be grasped if one adheres to Lever's contrast between the play of boys (large-scale, competitive, with complex rules) and that of girls (small-scale, co-operative, with a simple structure).[13] Girls, and not just boys, sometimes play in larger groups and negotiate and argue about rules.[14] In short, *separate-worlds dichotomies gloss the fact that interaction varies by activity and context.*[15]

This point is also central to Goodwin's research in an urban neighborhood. The girls who used collaborative language like 'let's' and 'we gotta' when they were engaged in the shared task of making rings out of bottles, shifted to hierarchical interaction, repeatedly giving and obeying direct commands, when they played house.[16] And while these girls used more mitigated and indirect (e.g. gossip) forms of conflict among themselves, they used aggravated verbal forms, including insults, when they argued with boys.[17] Other researchers have also found that African-American girls, as well as boys, tend to be skilled in direct verbal conflict, and several studies also report insult exchanges among white working-class girls who value 'being tough'.[18] *Generalizations about 'girls' culture come primarily from research done with girls who are class-privileged and whit; the experiences of girls of other class, race, and ethnic backgrounds tend to be marginalized.*

My own fieldnotes contain enough instances of girls using insults, threats, and physical fighting to make me uncomfortable with the assertion that these behaviors are somehow distinctively 'male'. Girls directly insulted boys . . . and occasionally they insulted one another. . . .

. . . [A]s Miss Bailey's class was gathering by the classroom door at the end of recess, Matt Yelled, 'You faggot!' at Nancy. Nancy, who was taller and bigger, ran after and knocked Matt down, pulled at his hair while she kicked him hard, and then walked away with a triumphant look on her face. Matt crumpled over and sobbed, 'She pulled my hair.' A group gathered round, discussing how 'a girl beat him up'.

Nancy was white, Jessie, who was Black, also didn't shrink from physical fights with boys; in fact, it was widely acknowledged that she could beat up any boy in the school. Both Nancy and Jessie were skilled at insulting and threatening ('Shut up or I'll punch you out'). It's true that these two girls were relatively exceptional compared with others in Miss Bailey's class. But either by ignoring the occasions when girls hurled insults, made threats, and got into serious physical fights, or by rendering them as forms of gender deviance, the different-cultures framework diverts us from examining important sources of complexity.

What does it mean to have different cultures?

As the difficulties multiply, I find myself wanting to return to fundamentals: what does it *mean* to claim, as Deborah Tannen does, that 'boys and girls grow up in what are essentially different cultures?'[19] . . .

Assertions about gender differences in actual behavior refer, at best, to *average* differences between girls and boys, or between groups of girls and groups of boys. The issue of relative frequency appears in words like 'on average', 'more than', and 'trend to' that sprinkle through the contrastive rhetoric of different-worlds stories. Since qualitative researchers generally avoid careful counting, our 'tend to's and 'more often's are, at best, general impressions or perhaps 'quasi statistics' gleaned from counting up descriptions in fieldnotes. But some of the evidence cited in the different-cultures literature comes from quantitative studies. The patterns are instructive.

For example, in a widely cited study of sex differences in rough-and-tumble play, Janet DiPietro coded observations of pre-school girls and boys at play. Comparing boys and girls as groups, she found an unusually large difference: 15 to 20 per cent of boys scored higher than any of the girls on the measure of rough-and-tumble play.[20] Nonetheless, as Carol Jacklin has observed, in this study '80 to 85 per cent of the boys remain indistinguishable from 80 to 85 per cent of the girls'.[21] Rough and-tumble play may be a 'sex-related difference', but it is *not* a dichotomous difference, since the behavior of most of the boys and girls overlapped.

Other studies show not only commonalities between girls and boys, taken as a whole, but also complex variation within and across those groups. For example, Elliott Medrich and his colleagues interviewed 764 children from different racial/ethnic backgrounds about how they spent their time outside school.[22] Forty-five per cent of the boys and 26 per cent of the girls reported playing team sports (note the sizable overlaps between boys and girls who did, and boys and girls who did not, play team sports). There was no gender difference in the median number of reported close friends (three), but African-American girls and boys reported more friends than either whites or those of other ethnic backgrounds. For all racial-ethnic groups and for both genders, being involved in team sports correlated with reporting more friends. African-American boys had the highest rates of sports participation, and number of friends, and African-American girls had higher rates than white girls. It is a serious distortion to reduce this complex variation into dichotomous claims, like 'boys play team sports and girls engage in turn-taking play' or 'boys organize into large groups and girls into dyads and triads'.[23]

In these studies, as in other statistically based research on sex/gender differences, *within-gender variation is greater than differences between boys and girls taken as groups.* Although the variation may be dutifully reported, the point gets lost when the conclusions and secondary reports fall into the binary language of 'boys versus girls'. . . . These problems seriously qualify general assertions that boys have a different 'culture' than girls, if 'culture' is taken to mean clearly differentiated patterns of behavior.

Claims that boys and girls have different cultures sometimes seem to refer not to externally observable behavior, like the amount of rough-and-tumble play, but to the *symbolic dimension of experience* – patterns of meaning, stereotypes, beliefs, ideologies, metaphor, discourses. (Each of these concepts has a different twist, but they cluster at the symbolic level. Note also that in daily experience 'behavior' and 'meanings' are not easily separable; human conduct is always infused with meanings.) As feminist scholars have thoroughly demonstrated, gendered meanings are deeply embedded in many of the discourses we draw on to make sense of the world. As Valerie Walkerdine has written, femininity and masculinity are powerful fictions or ideas, 'imbued with fantasy and lived as fact'.[24] The discourses of 'girls are nice' and 'boys are tough' enter kids' experiences, but so do other, sometimes contradictory discourses, like the argument of a boy who insisted that boys could be 'nice', or the talk of girls who value being 'tough'.

An ambiguous mixing of the symbolic with claims about differences in behavior can be found in Carol Gilligan's research on gender and moral reasoning. After close and respectful listening to girls and, to a lesser degree, boys as they discussed moral problems, Gilligan concluded that girls have a 'different voice', emphasizing relationships and care, in contrast with boys' preoccupation with individual rights and abstract principles of justice.[25] There is some ambiguity about what Gilligan intends to claim. In some statements she seems to be arguing that there are actual empirical gender differences in modes of moral reasoning, but the evidence for this has been much contested.[26] In her more recent work, however, Gilligan acknowledges that the same individual (male or female) may use both voices, mixing them as 'contrapuntal' themes.[27] The voices may be gendered nonetheless because themes of 'connection and care' are historically and symbolically associated with girls and women, and 'rights and justice' with boys and men.

Once they are identified, systems of meaning – for example, the belief that caring and connection are 'feminine' – can be studied in the context of social action. In her research on girls playing foursquare, Hughes pressed beyond the imagery of girls as co-operative and seeking intimacy by situating girls' talk about 'being nice' within their ongoing interaction. She found that the girls 'competed in a co-operative mode', using a language of 'being friends' and 'being nice' while aggressively getting others out so their friends could enter the game. The girls did not seem to experience 'nice' and 'mean' as sharply dichotomous; they maneuvered their rhetoric (associated with symbolic notions of femininity) and expressed nuances through mixed phrases like 'nice-mean' and 'not really mean'.[28]

In a related vein, Amy Sheldon, who analyzed conversations among pre-schoolers, describes the girls as using a 'double-voice style' that enmeshed or masked self-assertion within an orientation to relationships and maintaining group harmony. In interacting with one another, girls tried to avoid the appearance of hierarchy and overt conflict, but much else – conflict, self-assertion, sometimes aggression – went on beneath the surface. Sheldon found that boys sometimes used this double-voice style, although she argues that it is more often a feature of girls' talk because they are constrained by gender prescriptions to display themselves as egalitarian and harmonious.[29]

Sensitivity to gender meanings within varied social contexts and practices may enrich our understanding of boys as well as girls. In an interpretive study of the sex talk of a group of boys in a London secondary school, Julian wood observes that 'masculinity has at its heart not unproblematic strength but often weaknesses, self-doubt, and confusion'. The outward face may be brash and full of 'presence', or the promise of power, but the inward face is often the reverse.[30]

In short, a given piece of social interaction may be simultaneously co-operative and competitive, self-assertive and oriented to others, and brash and vulnerable.

And these qualities do not sharply divide by gender. This subtlety and complexity become lost when analysis proceeds through a series of gender-linked contrasts (e.g. competitive versus co-operative, agency versus communion), and when varied dimensions of gender are compressed into static dualisms. . . .

. . . [T]he contrastive framework has outlived its usefulness, as has the gender ideology that it builds on and perpetuates. The view of gender as difference and binary opposition has been used to buttress male domination and to perpetuate related ideologics like the division between public and private.[31] A sense of the whole, and of the texture and dynamism of interaction, become lost when collapsed into dualisms like large versus small, hierarchical versus intimate, agency versus communion, and competitive versus co-operative. (The portrayals often sound like a Victorian world of 'separate spheres', writ small and contemporary.)

Furthermore, by relying on a series of contrasts to depict the whole, the approach of girls' culture versus boys' culture exaggerates the coherence of same-gender interaction. Terms like 'culture' and 'subculture' are too often used to reify contrastive images; as R. W. Connell argues, these terms suggest a place which people inhabit rather than an 'aspect of what they do'.[32] We need, instead, to develop concepts that will help us grasp the diversity, overlap, contradictions, and ambiguities in the larger cultural fields in which gender relations, and the dynamics of power, are constructed.[33]

If the separate-cultures story has lost its narrative force, how can we grasp the gendered nature of kid's social relations? To move our research wagons out of the dualistic rut, we can, first of all, try to *start with a sense of the whole rather than with an assumption of gender as separation and difference.* If we begin by assuming different cultures, separate spheres, or contrastive differences, we will also end with a sharp sense of dichotomy rather than attending to multiple differences and sources of commonality.

One way to grasp this complexity is by *examining gender in context* rather than fixing binary abstractions like 'boys emphasize status, and girls emphasize intimacy'. Instead we should ask 'Which boys or girls, where, when, under what circumstances?' As I have shown throughout this book, the organization and meanings of gender vary from schools to neighborhoods to families, and from classroom to playground to lunchroom settings. Some situations, like cross-gender chasing and invasions, evoke a sense of gender as dualism, but other situations undermine and spread out that view. Furthermore, gender takes shape in complex interaction with other social divisions and grounds of inequality, such as age, class, race, ethnicity, and religion. As Joan Scott suggests, we should 'treat the opposition between male and female as problematic rather than known, as something contextually defined, repeatedly constructed'.[34] An emphasis on social context shifts analysis from fixing abstract and binary differences to examining the social relations in which multiple differences are constructed and given meaning.

Notes

1   There have been several widely circulated versions of this argument. (a) Janet Lever emphasizes sex differences in the play of fifth-graders and argues that because they more often engage in team sports, males have a later advantage in the world of occupations and organizations. See Lever, J. 'Sex differences in the complexity of children's play and games', *American Sociological Review*, 43 (1978): 471–483 and 'Sex

differences in the games children play', *Social Problems*, 23 (1976): 478–487. Carol Gilligan uses Lever's work to support her claim that in the process of moral reasoning, girls use a voice of connection and care that is different from boys' emphasis on abstract rules. See Gilligan, C. *In a Different Voice: Psychological Theory and Women's Development*. Cambridge, Mass: Harvard University Press, 1982. (2) Daniel N. Maltz and Ruth A. Borker ('A cultural approach to male–female miscommunication, in J. A. Gumperz (ed.) *Language and Social Identity*. New York: Cambridge University Press, 1983) claim that there are different patterns of talk in all-girl and in all-boy groups, leading to miscommunication between adult women and men; Deborah Tannen's popular book, *You Just Don't Understand: Women and Men in Conversation* (New York: Morrow, 1990) elaborates this basic thesis (for criticisms, see Henley and Kramarae, 'Gender, power, and miscommunication' in N. Coupland, H. Giles & J. M. Wiesman (eds) *Miscommunication and Problematic Talk*. Newbury Park, CA: Sage Publications, 1991). (3) Eleanor E. Maccoby argues that gender-separated groups teach different forms of prosocial and antisocial behavior ('Social groupings in childhood: their relationship to prosocial and antisocial behavior in boys and girls' in D. Olweus, J. Black and M. Radke-Yarrow (eds) *Development of Antisocial and Prosocial Behaviour*. San Diego: Academic Press, 1985).

Collaborating with Zella Luria, I have also followed this story line, arguing that groups of girls and groups of boys teach different sexual scripts, leading to tangles in the more overtly heterosexual experiences of adolescents, with girls emphasizing intimacy and romance, while boys are oriented more to active sexuality. Some of our analysis is included in this chapter, although with serious caveats. See Barrie Thorne and Zella Luria, 'Sexuality and gender in children's daily worlds' *Social Problems*, 33 (1986): 176–190.

2   Tannen, *You Just Don't Understand*.

3   In a study of primary school children in Australia, Bronwyn Davies (*Life in the Classroom and Playground*. Boston: Routledge and Kegan Paul, 1982) also describes group of boys as well as several groups of girls who maneuvered between 'best friends' and 'contingency friends'. She notes that the availability of a contingency friend heightens one's bargaining power over a best friend. Davies does not locate the analysis within the rubric of gender difference.

4   The term and the observation about anthropology come from Sherry B. Ortner, 'The founding of the first Sherpa nunnery and the problem of "women" as an analytic category' in V. Patraka & L. Tilly (eds) *Feminist Re-Visions*. Ann Arbor, MI: University of Michigan Women's Studies Programme, 1984.

5   For example, see Carole Joffe ('As the twig is bent' in J. Stacey, S. Bereaud & J. Daniels (eds) *And Jill Came Tumbling After*. New York: Dell, 1984) on the 'masculine subculture' of four boys in a preschool; Vivian Gussin Paley (*Boys and Girls: Superheroes in the Doll Corner*. Chicago: University of Chicago Press, 1984) on 'the superhero clique' in a kindergarten; and Raphaela Best (*We've All Got Scars* Bloomington, IN: Indiana University Press, 1983) on 'the Tent Club', a dominant male group that continued from first through second grade.

6   Everhart, R. *Reading, Writing, and Resistance*. Boston: Routledge and Kegan Paul, 1983, and Cusick, P. *Inside High School*. New York: Holt, Rinehart & Winston, 1973; Fine, G.A. *With the Boys*. Chicago: University of Chicago Press, 1987.

7   Cusick, P. *Inside High School*, p. 168.

8   AnnMarie Wolpe similarly observes that British ethnographies of schooling include little about 'the ordinary boy who goes through school doing minimal work, but

not necessarily domineering or sexually harassing' (*Within School Walls: The Role of Discipline, Sexuality and the Curriculum.* London: Routledge, 1988, p. 92).

9   Connell, R.W. *et al.*, *Making the Difference.* Boston: Allen & Unwin, 1982. On the conceptual pluralizing of masculinities and femininities, also see Connell, *Gender and Power.* Stanford, CA: Stanford University Press, 1987.

10   Canaan, J. 'A comparative analysis of American suburban middle class, middle school, and high school teenage cliques' in G. Spindler & L. Spindler (eds) *Interpretative Ethnography of Education.* Hillsdale, NJ: Lawrence Erlbaum, 1987. Michael Messner ('Masculinities and athletic careers', *Gender and Society*, 3 (1989): 71–88, p. 82) quotes an African-American man from a lower-class background who recalled that in junior high 'you either got identified as an athlete, a thug, or a bookworm'.

In an insightful ethnography of a largely white high school in the Detroit area, Penelope Eckert traces the dynamic opposition between two categories that dominated the social life of the school. The Jocks, with a middle-class orientation, controlled school athletics and other adult-sponsored activities. The more working-class Burnouts were estranged from the school and rebelled against its authority. Girls and boys were in both categories, and, significantly, the majority of students fell in between. See Eckert, P. *Jocks and Burnouts: Social Categories and Identity in the High School.* New York: Teachers College Press, 1989.

11   On the other hand, in an observational study in a British classroom of twelve and thirteen-year-olds, Robert J. Meyenn ('School girls' peer groups' in P. Wood (ed.) *Pupil Strategies.* London: Croom Helm, 1980) found that groups and not pairs were the dominant form of social organization. He identified four distinct groups of varying sizes and with different patterns of behavior: the 'PE' girls (nine members, physically mature and noisy, who 'rough-and-tumbled' more than the boys); the 'science lab girls' (four members; popular and liked by teachers); the 'nice girls' (five members; unobtrusive and less physically mature); and the 'quiet girls' (four girls who were socially uncertain). Groups maneuvered to be together throughout the school day, and members gave one another help and support. Meyenn writes the girls found it 'inconceivable to just have one best friend', although there were patterns of 'breaking friends' internal to each group (p. 115).

12   Linda Hughes, '"But that's not *really* mean": competing in a co-operative mode', *Sex Roles*, 19 (1988): 669–687, p. 684.

13   Lever, 'Sex differences in the complexity of children's play and games'.

14   For a detailed analysis of arguments about rules during the playing of another turn-taking 'girls'' game, see Marjorie Harness Goodwin, 'The serious side of jump rope: conversational practices and social organization in the frame of "play"', *Journal of American Folklore*, 98 (1985): 315–330.

15   Luria, Z. and Herzog, E.W. ('Sorting gender out in a children's museum', *Gender and Society*, 5 (1991): 224–232) also found that context makes a difference in the organization of same-gender groups. On a class field trip to a children's museum, elementary school boys clustered in much smaller groups than one typically sees on school playgrounds.

16   Goodwin, *He Said, She Said: Talk as Social Organisation among Black Children,* Bloomington IN: Indiana University Press (1991).

17   Ibid., and Marjorie Harness Goodwin and Charles Goodwin, 'Children's arguing' in S. Phillips, S. Steele & C. Tanz (eds) *Language, Gender and Sex in Comparative Perspective.* New York: Cambridge University Press, 1987.

18   For a review of literature and a description of insult exchanges among white working-class girls in a junior high cafeteria, see Donna Eder, 'Serious and playful disputes: variation in conflict talk among female adolescents' in A. D. Grimshaw (ed.) *Conflict Talk*. New York: Cambridge University Press, 1990.

19   Tannen, *You Just Don't Understand*, p. 18.

20   J. A. DiPieto, 'Rough and tumble play: a function of gender' *Developmental Psychology*, 17 (1981): 50–58.

21   Jacklin, 'Methodological issues in the study of sex-related differences' *Developmental Review*, 1 (1981): 226–273.

22   Medrich *et al.*, *The Serious Business of Growing Up*. Berkeley: University of California Press, 1982.

23   In a careful review of empirical research, Nancy Karweit and Stephen Hansell ('Sex differences in adolescent relationships: friendship and status' in J. Levy Epstein & N. Karweit (eds) *Friends in School*. New York: Academic Press, 1983) conclude that the conventional view that boys have larger friendship groups than girls is overdrawn. Some studies find that, up to age seven, boys are either situated in smaller groups than girls, or that there are no gender differences. The research literature does suggest that the *average* size of friendship groups fits the conventional depiction from age seven to adolescence, but patterns vary by setting, such as type of classroom, and by type of activity, for example, participation in team sports. Findings are mixed for junior high and high school.

24   Walkerdine, V. *Schoolgirl Fictions*. New York: Verso, 1990; also see Davies, B. *Frogs and Snails and Feminist Tales*. Boston: Allen & Unwin, 1989.

25   Gilligan, *In a Different Voice*.

26   For example, see Linda K. Kerber *et al.*, 'On *In a Different Voice*: An Interdisciplinary Forum' *Signs*, 11 (1986): 9–39. For a critical discussion of Gilligan's recent research on girls entering adolescence and its neglect of race, ethnicity, and social class as they interact with gender, see Judith Stacey, 'On resistance, ambivalence, and feminist theory' *Michigan Quarterly Review*, 29 (1990): 537–546.

27   Carol Gilligan *et al.* (eds) *Making Connections: The Relational Worlds of Adolescent Girls at Emma Willard School*. Troy, NY: Emma Willard School, 1989.

28   Hughes, '"But that's not *really* mean"'.

29   Amy Sheldon, 'Conflict talk: sociolinguistic challenges to self-assertion and how young girls meet them' *Merrill-Palmer Quarterly*, 38 (1992): 95–117.

30   Julian Wood, 'Groping towards sexism: boys' "sex talk"' in A. McRobbie & M. Nava (eds) *Gender and Generation*. London: Macmillan, 1984, pp. 60–1.

31   Judith Shapiro, 'Gender totemism', in R. R. Randolph, D. M. Schneider and May N. Diaz (eds) *Dialectics and Gender: Anthropological Approaches*. Boulder CO: Westview Press, 1988, pp. 1–19.

32   R. W. Connell, *Which Way is Up: Essays on Class, Sex and Culture*. Boston MA: Allen & Unwin, 1983, p. 226.

33   M. H. Goodwin, *He Said, She Said*. Goodwin resists the temptation to chalk up her findings as 'children's culture', 'gender culture' and/or 'African-American culture'. Instead she asks how participants assemble and interpret activities through telling stories and gossip. Starting with activities rather than an assumption of binary gender difference led her to discover both differences and commonalities between boys and girls.

34   J. W. Scott, *Gender and the Politics of History*. New York: Columbia University Press, 1988, p. 49.

Chapter 37

Heidi Mirza

REDEFINING BLACK
WOMANHOOD

Based on research on young Black British women on the point of leaving school, Heidi Mirza challenges some of the myths surrounding Black womanhood. These young women came from working class backgrounds, but their sense of themselves as Black women fitted neither the 'culture of femininity' thesis, which has been used to explain White female underachievement (McRobbie, *Feminisms and Youth Culture*, 1991), nor with a view of Black femininity as constructed through a female-centred family structure. Rather, she suggests, 'there is a specific form of black femininity among young black women, characterised by relative autonomy between the sexes' (1992: 147) This, she argues, explains the differences between the young Black and White women in her sample, especially the more ambitious career aspirations and greater desire for independence expressed by the former.

From *Young Female and Black*, London: Routledge (1992).

Work and womanhood: the West Indian British experience

ALTHOUGH A GENERAL DESIRE for economic dependency prevailed among the young white working-class women in the sample, there was no evidence that this cultural orientation existed among the black working-class women who were interviewed. Whereas *all* of the black girls responded positively to the prospect of having a full-time career upon leaving school, only 80 per cent of their white female peers said they would. Young black women of all abilities and social backgrounds, with a wide variety of career aspirations, reiterated time and time again their commitment to full-time work and their desire for economic independence. Evidence of this positive ideological orientation was clear in the data:

> I would like just like to be an independent lady. Not dependent on any
> one, especially a man.
>
> (Joy, aged sixteen; aspiration: legal assistant)

> I don't want to rely on anyone. What I want is a good job, as I would
> like my life to be as comfortable as possible, and have a nice environ-
> ment to live in so my children can grow up with everything they
> require.
>
> (Laurie, aged sixteen; aspiration: journalist)

On the basis of this evidence alone there is little justification for adopting an analytical framework that emphasises the centrality of an oppressive form of femininity,
which the prevailing theories on the black female experience clearly do.

The key to why this situation of positive orientation and commitment to work
should prevail was provided by the girls themselves. The statements they made
showed that they expected to work just as their sisters, mothers, aunts and grandmothers had done for generations before them. However, and this is the important
point, they expected to do so without the encumbrance of male dissent. This mean
that the young women did not regard their male relationships, whether within the
institution of marriage or not, as inhibiting their right to work in any way.[1] It was
not uncommon to find among the girls in the study statements such as these:

> My sister has moved out, got a nice little flat to herself . . . having
> your own place . . . a little job, not getting married, just having your
> boyfriend . . . well, living together . . . no . . . well, popping round
> to see you . . . that what I'd like.
>
> (Debra, aged sixteen; aspiration: designer)

. . . When interviewed on the subject of marriage and women's work, the young
black women in the study agreed that women should work regardless of child-
rearing responsibilities. . . .

. . . It was commonplace to find bold and positive statements such as this: 'If
I don't work I'll go mad. . . . You've got to make something of yourself because
in the end no one cares.'

This did not mean, as Riley (1985: 69) seems to suggest in her analysis of
similar types of statements, that young black girls were pursuing a course of aggressive assertion of their femininity (which in the case of black girls is interpreted as
female dominance) at the expense of all else, especially permanent male relationships. Nor, as Fuller (9182: 96) suggests, was this the manifestation of a 'going it
alone' strategy.

In my opinion what the girls were articulating was a much more subtle ideological orientation than either of these two authors suggest. Unlike their white
peers, who had evidently been inculcated in the dominant ideology that women
only take on major economic roles when circumstances prevent their menfolk from
doing so, the black girls held no such belief about the marginality of their economic
participation and about commitment to the family. Providing for the children and
the household was regarded as a joint responsibility, as the following statement

illustrates: 'I think it is important for a woman and man to work, to both provide for your family is an important thing to do' (Karen, aged sixteen: aspiration: computer programmer).

The West Indian boys in the study had no objections to their future partners working.[2] They were in full support of their womenfolk being gainfully employed, as the following statements illustrate:

> My mum, she's a cook and she looks after me and my brother. . . . I think if I got married, I don't see no difference, I don't see it any other way really.
>
> (Davis, aged sixteen; aspiration: armed forces)

> Any woman of mine's got to see about herself anyway, it ain't gonna bother me, but I ain't keeping no woman, that's for sure.
>
> (Maurice, aged sixteen; aspiration: electrician) . . .

The boyfriend of one of the young black women in the study, Anita, who at the age of 16 became pregnant, had a distinctly supportive and encouraging attitude to her moving ahead in her career, as he explained:

> A woman must can and must do all she can . . . but I's believe having children is very important . . . it's good to have kids young and enjoy yourself. . . . You don't have to take time out to do it or stop nothing. . . . Of course she will be set back though, and we have discussed this, I told her to not to stop school, exams are important . . . she can go on to college, you know, yeah, but she got to have 'O' levels or she set right back and she'll have to start from the beginning, I told her not to stop.
>
> (Winston, aged twenty-three; games supervisor at the local sports centre)

The issue of relative economic and social autonomy between the sexes should not be confused with the matter of the sharing of domestic labour or the permanency of male/female relationships, as is so often the case. That West Indian men do not equally participate in household tasks is well documented, as is the tendency towards instability of consensual relationships (Justus 1985; Moses 1985; Powell 1986). These facts, however, do not affect the matter of joint responsibility towards consanguineal offspring or children within a consensual relationship. Relationships which have joint responsibility towards the household, within the context of relative autonomy between the sexes, are a common feature of West Indian life (Sutton and Makiesky-Barrow 1977: 311–12; Dann 1987: 25–30; Thorogood 1987; Barrow 1988; Mohammed (1988).[3] . . .

The young black women in the study did express a cautious yet positive approach to marriage and relationships:

> Eventually I'd want to get married, but you should be like best friends and live together [another girl shouts out, 'You mean platonic'. All laugh].

> Well, things have changed now . . . you can have kids but you don't have to be married. . . . My brother's been together for twelve years and got four kids and they just got married. The girls were the brides-maids and the boy's a pageboy.

> The thing that worries me about marriage, right, is that the fact you are stuck with that one person for life . . . because a lot of girls rush 'this is the one for me, this is the one for me', and all that, and rush into it.

> I'll get married when I'm thirty or thirty-five in the future, after I've done something for myself.

In the study there was no evidence that black men were considered marginal in the lives of young black women. Of West Indian households in the study, to which the girls belonged, 79 per cent had both a male and female adult sharing the parenting role (for white girls 90 per cent belonged to two-parent families). Of the 11 per cent who had only one parent present, 2 per cent were male-headed households, a feature not found among the white families in the study.

Despite the acknowledgement that men in their lives could in the future pose problems, the young black women in the study frequently spoke positively about men and their attitudes. They did so drawing on their own experience and relationships with men, in particular their fathers, male guardians, brothers and uncles. . . .

Studies in America (Moynihan 1965 in Rainwater and Yancey 1967), the Caribbean (Smith 1962) and in Britain (Foner 1979) have persistently attributed the relatively high proportion of black women in the economy to the absence of a male provider or his inability to fulfil his role. This pathological explanation of the black family – that has come about from the belief that it is 'culturally stripped', essentially a hybrid of Western culture (Frazier 1966; Little 1978) – has failed to acknowledge that black culture has evolved an essentially egalitarian ideology with regard to work, an ideology that, as Sutton and Makiesky-Barrow (1977: 323) observe, 'emphasises the effectiveness of the individual regardless of gender'. This argument is supported by the evidence that the proportion of black women in the labour market relative to their white female counterparts is far greater, a fact that is true for the United Kingdom and the United States.

The argument that high black male unemployment determines increased black female labour-market participation cannot be upheld; it is a theory based more on a 'commonsense' assumption than fact. Black male unemployment is no higher than black female unemployment. (In the twenty-five to thirty-five age group in the UK, 17 per cent of black women are unemployed, as are 18 per cent of black men. In other age ranges the proportion is even greater for black females; see Brown 1984: 190.) The fact that males and females are concentrated in different sectors of the labour market and so have access to different employment (and educational) prospects is not a consequence of choice but rather due to the dynamics of a sexually segregated labour market (see Farley and Bianchi 1985).

The study revealed a notable lack of sexual distinctions about work among second-generation West Indian young people. Many girls said that they did not see any difference between themselves and their male counterparts in terms of their capacity to work and the type of work they were capable of.

> I think men and women have the same opportunities, it is just up to you to take it.

> Of course women should do the same jobs that men do. If they feel you can't . . . them stupid. . . . Who's to say anyway, it makes me sick it does.

> Men should do the jobs women do and women the jobs that men do. There's nothing wrong with men midwives, I think all men should find out what it is like to have a child, it's the nearest they can get to it.

Young black women living in the West Indies expressed a similar point of view with regard to women's work, as one girl illustrated when she stated: 'I think what is good for a woman is good for a man, there's no difference between men and women when it comes to work.'

Further evidence of this trend to refuse to regard certain types of work as the sole preserve of men was shown in the results of the study. Black girls were far more likely to express their desire to do non-gendered work than their white female peers.

This ideological position regarding work expectations cannot be the outcome of a 'female-orientated' tradition (Phizacklea 1982). If it were a female-centred ideology, then it would be difficult to account for the obvious preoccupation many young black girls had for, as one Trinidadian girl explained: 'the need for emotional support and strength from a man, you like to feel he rules, even if he don't'.

The young black women in the study, both in the West Indies and in Britain, often commented on the desire for male companionship. This, and the fact that many women treat men as 'guests in the house' (Justus 1985), has been interpreted as evidence of a male centred ideology in the West Indian family structure. The description of the black family as having a male-centred ideology is based largely on the evidence of black male non-participation in the domestic sphere.[4]

It is important to note at this point that there seems to be a contradictory state of affairs with regard to research on the status of the woman in the black family, which can result in a great deal of confusion. On the one hand, it has been argued that what exists is a matrifocal, female-dominated structure (Fuller 1982), and on the other hand the family ideological orientation is often described as 'male-centred' (Justus 1985; Moses 1985).

These two fundamentally divergent theoretical interpretations of the ideological dynamics of the black family have evolved as a consequence of the confused interpretation of the two essentially different aspects of family life: relative autonomy between the sexes and male non-participation in domestic affairs. In effect what we are observing in this study is an ideological orientation governed, not by male bias or female bias, but by the notion of relative economic and social autonomy between the sexes.

Conclusion: the cultural context of gender

The evidence presented here suggests that the cultural construction of femininity among African Caribbean women fundamentally differs from the forms of femininity found among their white peers, and indeed their white migrant peers. Thus the theoretical arguments about the way in which gender disadvantage is reproduced become inappropriate in the black context. What the young black women in the study were expressing was essentially an ideology that emphasised the relative autonomy of both the male and female roles.

Ironically, the dynamic that has produced this equality between the sexes within the black social structure has been the external imposition of oppression and brutality. African Caribbean societies in the Caribbean and in industrialised capitalist settings have not simply replicated the Western pattern of sexual stratification.

Like their parents and grandparents, the young black women in the study had not adopted the dominant Eurocentric ideology: an ideology in which gender is regarded as the basis for the opposition of roles and values. These young black women had, instead, a very different concept of masculinity and femininity [from] their white peers. In the black female definition, as their statements revealed, few distinctions were made between male and female abilities and attributes with regard to work and the labour market. As to why this particular definition of masculinity and femininity should result in greater female participation in the labour market is explained by Sutton and Makiesky-Barrow, who write:

> The distinct qualities of masculine and feminine sexual and reproductive abilities are not viewed by either sex as a basis for different male and female social capacities. And unlike the self-limiting negative sexual identities the Euro-American women have had to struggle with, female identity in Endeavour [a town in Barbados] is associated with highly valued cultural attributes. Because the women are assumed to be bright, strong and competent, nothing in the definitions of appropriate sex role behaviour systematically excludes them from areas of economic and social achievement.
>
> (1977: 320)

Notes

1   While socialist feminists have argued that for white women marriage is a 'psychologically and materially oppressive institution' (Barrett and McIntosh 1982), they state that, for the West Indian, marriage is 'no more than a prestige-conferring act' (Phizacklea 1982: 100; see also Sharpe 1987: 234). The suggestion is that black people 'mimic' the social institutions of the dominant white society. The effect of this widely held racist assumption has been that marriage, the family and male relationships in the West Indian context are dismissed as unimportant in the lives of black women. Caribbean feminists provide evidence to the contrary (Powell 1986).

2   Eggleston et al. (1986: 95) show African Caribbean boys to be the least likely of all ethnic and white groups to want their wives to stay at home upon having

a child. Similarly, research in the United States has shown that black husbands have a 'permissive' attitude to their wives working (Landry and Jendrek 1978).

3   It is also a common feature of black American life. The literature on the black condition in the United States describes what *in essence* are male/female relationships of relative autonomy and independence between the sexes (Billingsley 1968; Gutman 1976; Ladner 1985; Stack 1974, 1985; Jones 1986; Wilson 1978). However, such relationships are often misunderstood and deemed 'pathological' and thus negative.

4   Sutton and Makiesky-Barrow (1977: 317) suggest that while much of the literature on sex roles views the domestic sphere as an area of confinement that is associated with women and their dependent status, for the slave population, the domestic area was the one area of life that for both sexes was associated with human freedom and autonomy. See also Mathurin Mair (1986); Wiltshire Brodber (1988); Bush (1990).

References

Barret, M. and McIntosh, M. (1982) *The Antisocial Family*. London:Verso.

Barrow, C. (1988) 'Anthropology, women and the family in the Caribbean', in P. Mohammed and C. Shepherd (eds) *Gender in Caribbean Development*. Trinidad: University of the West Indies.

Billingsley, A. (1968) *Black Families in White America*. Englewood Cliffs NJ: Prentice-Hall.

Brown, C. (1984) *Black and White in Britain: The Third PSI Survey*. London: Heinemann.

Bush, B. (1990) *Slave Women in Caribbean Society, 1650–1838*. London: James Currey.

Dann, G. (1987) *The Barbadian Male: Sexual Attitudes and Practice*. London: Macmillan.

Eggleston, J., Dunn, D., Anajali, M. and Wright, C. (1986) *Education for Some: the Educational and Vocational Experiences of 15–18 year old Members of Minority Ethnic Groups*. Stoke on Trent: Trentham.

Farley, R. and Bianchi, S. M. (1985) 'Social class polarisation: is it occurring among the Blacks?' *Research in Race and Ethnic Relations*, 4: 1–31.

Foner, N. (1979) *Jamaica Farewell! Jamaican Migrants in London*. London: Routledge.

Frazier, E. F. (1966) *The Negro Family in the United States*. Chicago: University of Chicago Press.

Fuller, M. (1982) 'Young, female and black', in E. Cashmore and B. Troyna (eds) *Black Youth in Crisis*. London: Allen & Unwin.

Gutman, H. (1976) *The Black Family in Slavery and Freedom, 1750–1925*. New York: Vintage Books.

Jones, J. (1986) *Labour of Love, Labour of Sorrow*. New York: Vintage Books.

Justus, I. B. (1985) 'Women's role in West Indian society', in F. C. Steady (ed.) *The Black Woman Cross-culturally*. Cambridge MA: Schenkman.

Ladner, J. A. (1985) 'Racism and tradition: black womanhood in historical perspective', in F. C. Steady (ed.) *The Black Woman Cross-culturally*. Cambridge MA: Schenkman.

Landry, B. and Jendrek, M. (1978) 'The employment of wives from black middle-class families', *Journal of Marriage and the Family* 3 (November).

Little, A. (1978) 'Schools and race', in *Five Views of Multi-cultural Britain*. London: Commission for Racial Equality.

Mathurin Mair, L. (1986) 'Women Field Workers in Jamaica under Slavery', the Elsa Goveia Memorial Lecture, Mona: Department of History, University of the West Indies.

Mohammed, P. (1988) 'The Caribbean family revisited', in P. Mohammed and C. Shepherd (eds) *Gender in Caribbean Development*. Trinidad: University of the West Indies.

Moses, Y. T. (1985) 'Female status, the family and male dominance in a West Indian community', in F. C. Steady (ed.) *The Black Woman Cross-culturally*. Cambridge MA: Schenkman.

Phizacklea, A. (1982) 'Migrant women and wage labour: the case of West Indian women in Britain', in J. West (ed.) *Work, Women and the Labour Market*. London: Routledge.

Powell, D. (1986) 'Caribbean Women and their Response to Familial Experiences' in *Social and Economic Studies* 35 (2), special issue *Women in the Caribbean* I, Bridgetown: Institute of Social and Economic Research, University of the West Indies.

Rainwater, L. and Yancy, W. L. (1967) *The Moynihan Report and the Politics of Controversy*. Cambridge MA: MIT Press.

Riley, K. (1985) 'Black girls speak for themselves', in G. Weiner (ed.) *Just a Bunch of Girls*. Milton Keynes: Open University Press.

Sharpe, S. (1987) *Just like a Girl: How Girls learn to be Women*, second edition. Harmondsworth: Penguin.

Smith, M. G. (1962) *West Indian Family Structure*. Seattle: University of Washington Press.

Stack, C. B. (1974) *All our Kin: Strategies for Survival in a Black Community*. New York: Harper & Row.

Stack, C. B. (1985) 'Sex roles and survival strategies in the urban black community' in F. C. Steady (ed.) *The Black Woman Cross-culturally*. Cambridge MA: Schenken.

Sutton, C. and Makiesky-Barrow, S. (1977) 'Social inequality and sexual status in Barbados', in A. Schegal (ed.) *Sexual Stratification: A Cross-cultural View*. New York: Columbia University Press.

Thorogood (1987) 'Race, class and gender: the politics of housework', in J. Brannen and G. Wilson (eds) *Give and Take in Families*. London: Allen & Unwin.

Wilson, W. J. (1978) *The Declining Significance of Race*. Chicago: University of Chicago Press.

Wiltshire-Brodber, R. (1988) 'Gender, race and class in the Caribbean', in P. Mohammed and C. Shepard (eds) *Gender in Caribbean Development*, Women and Development Studies project, St Augustine: University of the West Indies.

Chapter 38

Beverley Skeggs

AMBIVALENT FEMININITIES

This extract is from an ethnographic study, based on both interviews and participant observation, with groups of young women in the north of England. Beverley
Skeggs sets out to explain how women simultaneously inhabit the social and cultural
positions of class, gender and sexuality and the particular issues which this raises
for working class women in a world which gives status to middle class values.

From *Formations of Class and Gender*, London: Sage (1997).

Femininity is the process through which women are gendered and become specific
sorts of women. The process of becoming feminine, Smith (1988) argues, occurs
in the spaces of textually mediated discourse, in the *dialectic* between the active
creating subject and the organization of her activity in and by texts, produced in
the interests of a wider global market.[1] The ability to engage in this dialectic is a
matter of social positioning and access to texts. Being, becoming, practising and
doing femininity are very different things for women of different classes, races,
ages and nations. If subjectivity is produced through experience (as suggested earlier
by de Lauretis 1984 and Scott 1991) we can see how becoming respectable proceeds
through the experience of textually mediated femininity. . . .

. . . Poovey (1984) charts how the emergence of femininity as an ideal was
produced through textuality in the eighteenth century. The femininity produced
had an affinity with the habitus of the upper classes, of ease, restraint, calm and
luxurious decoration. It was produced as a sign of difference from other women.
Conduct books and magazines encapsulated this habius with the concept of the
'lady' which equated conduct with appearance. This ideal of the lady continued
to be reproduced into the nineteenth century where both textual and visual technologies operated as a strong marker for the development of gendered notions of

sexual propriety (Nead 1988; Pollock 1989; Lury 1993). Through the development of textually mediated feminine ideal the visual became the site where values were allocated to groups of women and the construction of appearance as a sign of value became established. White middle-class femininity was defined as the ideal . . . but also as the most passive and dependent of femininities. It was always coded as respectable.

By the end of the nineteenth century femininity had become established as a (middle-) classed sign, a sign of a particular form of womanhood. It was, Walkerdine ((1989) argues, a projection of male fantasy. Femininity was seen to be the *property* of middle-class women who could *prove* themselves to be respectable through their appearance and conduct. Because femininity developed as a classed sign it became imbued with different amounts of power, as Ware (1992) has shown. White middle-class women could use their proximity to the sign of femininity to construct distinctions between themselves and others. Investments in the ideal of femininity enabled them to gain access to limited status and moral superiority. It was their desire for value that led them to evaluate others. Their take-up of their positioning and their display of it through appearance enabled them to judge those who were lacking in femininity, hence respectability. This generated struggles over respectable appearance and conduct. Hall (1979) shows how middle and upper-class women, in the name of evangelicalism, would visit the houses of the poor in an attempt to redeem them from themselves, that is, from themselves as a sign of dangerous, disruptive sexual women.

Working-class women were coded as inherently healthy, hardy and robust (whilst also, paradoxically, as a source of infection and disease) against the physical frailty of middle-class women. They were also involved in forms of labour that prevented femininity from ever being a possibility. For working-class women femininity was never a given (as was sexuality); they were not automatically positioned by it in the same way as middle and upper-class White women. Femininity was always something which did not designate them precisely. Working-class women – both Black and White – were coded as the sexual and deviant other against which femininity was defined (Gilman 1992). Ware (1992) shows how the categories of White middle-class womanhood were constructed against those of potentially dangerous Black women. And Davis (1995) notes how African-American women have, as a result of these different significations, historically forged models of womanhood that continually and dramatically challenge prevailing notions of femininity.

The distance that is drawn between the sexual and the feminine was drawn onto the bodies of working-class women. . . . It is more difficult for working-class women to make a bodily submission to ideas about herself, for herself and her body is of a different class, within a different cultural and material economy. This is why when they do try on femininity they often feel it is the wrong size. It was designed for someone with a different bodily shape.[2] This is not just metaphoric play: White working-class bodies are generally smaller, less healthy and live shorter lives (Black Report 1982; Bourke 1994). Moreover, the White female working-class body is often represented as out of control, in excess, such as that of *Roseanne*. Rowe (1995) argues that working-class women have often been associated with the lower unruly order of bodily functions such as that of expulsion and leakage (and reproduction) which signified lack of discipline and vulgarity. And, as Bourdieu (1986) shows, working-class women are considered to be distanced from having 'taste'. . . .

. . . Femininity requires the display of classed dispositions, of forms of conduct and behaviour, different forms of cultural capital, which are not part of their cultural baggage: they are unlikely to display 'divine composure', which include the components of femininity as silent, static, invisible and composed (Cixous 1980). Working-class women's relationship to femininity has always been produced through recourse to vulgarity. It is in the desire to avoid being positioned by the vulgar, pathological, tasteless and sexual, in order to prove their respectability, that the women of the study make investments in femininity. Even though they are positioned at a distance from femininity, investments in the forms of femininity to which they have access enable a movement away from the sexual; they offer routes into respectability, but not without incurring costs and implicating women in circuits of exchange. To do femininity they have to both appear and *be* feminine.

The division between the sexual and the feminine was most carefully coded at the level of conduct where appearance became the signifier of conduct; to look was *to be*. Appearance and conduct became markers of respectability, although these had to be coded in the correct way: too much concentration on appearance was seen to be a sign of female deviancy, as Lury (1993) notes: no good girl can afford to appear bad.[3] . . .

. . . The body, as a social product, is, Bourdieu (1986) argues, the only tangible manifestation of the person. The sign-bearing, sign-wearing body is also a producer of signs which are physically marked by the relationship to the body (differences in bearing, posture, movement and use of space).[4] Just as we are born with access to different amounts of economic, social, cultural and symbolic capital we are also born with a physical body which may or may not fit into the sign systems which define what it is to be attractive. Physical attractiveness may as a form of capital (corporeal capital) but, as Bourdieu notes, this is often a class privilege: in France physical advantages are disproportionately allocated to the upper middle classes through selective breeding and healthy diet.[5] Some people will be born with physical advantages (while others may feel they have to spend time, money and emotion trying to appear as attractive). Unattractiveness has little tradable value in the marriage and labour markets. Concern with appearance was a preoccupation for most of the women when they were younger . . .

When they were young, the women were dependent upon their mothers and/or fathers for clothing. This dependence many saw to be the ultimate sign of immaturity and so took part-time jobs to buy clothes and make-up. As well as desiring to be seen to be attractive they also wanted to be independent and be able to construct their appearance for themselves:

> I hate going out with our mam. She wants me to wear the most ridicu-
> lous things you've ever seen. You know like flowery dresses and court
> shoes. She's obsessed, she's obsessed with pink. She'd have me looking

like a fucking fairy if she had her way. I mean can you imagine me in flowery dresses, really old fashioned. I tell you. I said to her, I said last week, I said I've had enough. I said, I don't want nothing. It's not like you could trade it in or anything. It's ridiculous, who does she think I am? She's seen me in my clothes, she lives with me for Christ's sakes. She's just stupid.

(Yvonne 1982)

Here appearance and, more importantly, the autonomy to construct one's appearance is a site of contestation between the projections of mother and daughter over who they think 'she' is. The acrimony between mothers and daughters was often fought out through clothes. A substantial number of mothers wanted to influence their daughters' appearance. They did so when they controlled the finance (but usually not without battles) and the first sign of independence was often made through clothes. (This was financially a lot easier than leaving home.) Mothers wanted their daughters to appear to be respectable[6] and this meant displaying the right amount and type of femininity.[7] For Yvonne, however, her mother's desire for feminine clothing signals a refusal to recognize her as an independent women with her own tastes and attitudes. For Yvonne constructing her physical appearance is displaying independence and constructing a sense of who she thinks she is. Yvonne does not know herself as feminine and accordingly rejects all feminine signs of appearance.

To construct a sense of autonomy through clothing a particular form of consumer knowledge is required. The women had to know what to buy, where from, how to wear it, what to wear it with and on what occasions to wear it. The legacies of knowing one's place through clothing informed their 'choice'. The women had learnt the distinctions between style and fashion, between looking good and looking tarty, between looking feminine and looking sexy. The women's knowledge of femininity was not just absorbed directly from the traditional textual sources of femininity (such as magazines, advertising, etc.), rather, it was an amalgam of this and local knowledge. Textually mediated femininity was put into practice and effect through local interpretation. Looking good involved a substantial amount of labour but also collective discussion.[8] Clothes were nearly always bought with friends and preparing for the purchase by trying on hundreds of clothes was a regular recreational pursuit and a site of pleasure and often hilarity. The Saturday shopping expedition was looked forward to as much as the Friday and Saturday night trying-on sessions. Clothes were highly valued; they were invested in as a source of cultural capital, one of the few alternatives they had.[9]

Female competence, however, was required to make the 'right' decisions. Looking good involved dedication, commitment, labour, knowledge, friendship and being in an all-female group. It is validated and made a site of anxiety through the multitude of women's magazines and adverts which play on the fear of not looking good. This is where the local became an important site for challenging the representations which were produced at national/global levels. There was a clear awareness that certain clothes were not for them. However, local interpretation could also invoke hierarchies of corporeal and cultural capital, as the following conversation demonstrates between Rose and Jean (1986):

ROSE: Now look at Sandra, she's clueless. I wouldn't be seen dead out with her.
             I think her mum must buy all her clothes from a catalogue.

JEAN: And it must be a 1975 catalogue.

ROSE: No, not 1975, that'd make her trendy.

JEAN: Did you see her in that tracksuit last week? It was pink, for goodness'
             sake, and she looked like a sack of potatoes. Well, she's a disgrace to the
             female race. I mean, just look at it.

These distinctions drawn by Rose and Jean at a local level are not a form of system-atizing difference, rather, they are representative of the multitude of distinctions drawn daily. Even for those who draw the distinctions, who are skilled at doing femininity through fashion, their cultural capital can only be increased at a local level. It is unlikely that they can convert their competencies into a form of authority, into symbolic capital. Yet this does mean that they do not position middle-class women as the surveillant other (as they did with caring). Style is not seen to be something that middle-class women are seen to know anything about. It is seen to be a working-class competence. The practice of looking good should not be dismissed as a trivial activity. It was central to the women's sense of self: their interpretations, labour, display and performance.[10] It is a site of pleasure and fear; it is a 'structure of feeling' (Williams 1961, 1977) which makes them feel good and bad about themselves. It enables them to share interests and intimacy with friends, generate admiration and signal desirability, but it also induces the fear of getting behind or not having the right knowledge, of getting it wrong. The act of construction was as significant as the final appearance. They operated with a long list of textually mediated cannots which were based around respectability and fashion, such as 'you can't wear jeans and high heels' and 'you can't wear white stiletto shoes and mini-skirts'. It is indicative that these cannots are frequently invoked as 'cans' in representations of working-class women.

    The women distinguish between being looked at in 'admiration' and looked at as a 'sexual object'. There is a complex interplay between being made to recog-nize oneself as a certain type of person (sexual clothing signifies those who have no respectability) and being given external validation for not looking bad. These distinctions inform the ambivalences about themselves and their relationship to femininity. Feeling good, through looking good, offers momentary respite, provides valuing and offsets any potential positionings by degradation. Putting oneself together to make a feminine performance is where aesthetic creation, skill and pleasure combine together. This is often done on a collective basis:

    We all get dressed up for a Friday night on the town, it takes hours, we all go round to Maureen's house, her mam's dead good and that, and we bring all our stuff, and then we try each other's things on and have a laugh. Like I always like to try Anna's stuff 'cos she's a bit outlandish, I'd never wear stuff like that. We help to put each other's make-up on, apart from Anna, who does her own, and we just mess around. We have music playing all the time, Anna's brother gets all the new records so she steals them from him and we have a dance, then about four hours later we're ready to go. It makes you feel good, being all dressed up, it doesn't matter what happens, you just feel good, feel special, instead of the same old boring you that you are at college.

(Kate 1983)

They learn to 'pass' as feminine together. The final product from these Friday or Saturday night sessions, which were a regular occurrence, may look like femininity but, in the production of it, raucousness, rudeness, outrageousness and challenge to femininity occur. They may have the physical appearance of femininity but their performance, their conduct is definitely not feminine. In becoming physically feminine their look contradicts their performance. When they spill into the pub and the club a lasting pleasure can ensue, based on secret jokes and camaraderie.[11] They have constructed themselves collectively and display their localized competencies. For many men it seemed there was nothing more intimidating than this loud, laughing, together group of women. They *appear* as terrifying. They were claiming their right to their pleasure and social space. Their appearance made it even more disturbing, for they looked the part of the traditional feminine young woman, yet all their behaviour suggested otherwise.[12] Their feminine performance proves that they are precisely that which they are not.

. . . Not only is the ideal of femininity a bourgeois sign but the attempts to subvert femininity are locked within the same range of projections. The women of the research are able to mimic femininity but their mimicry is often not recognized as such; it is often read as a display of feminity.[13] Or, even worse, their fabrication is seen as a display of the authentically sexual and thus pathologized. Even when they are not making feminine performances they may be identified by others as doing so. They do take on, at times, the appearance of femininity, but they also take it off and they rarely identify as feminine. They do not have a possessive relation to femininity. This generates a temporality to the sign of femininity. The sign cannot guarantee a take-up. It will not be and cannot be constantly occupied. For, as Riley (1987) notes, women have to recognize themselves as the term: they may not. Whereas they felt positioned by class they do not feel similarly positioned as feminine. They do not see it as something which is part of them. It is not fundamental to their subjective constructions. However, it can be used tactically to have a good time.

Going out gave them a reason for dressing up, it gave them something to plan for and look forward to. They rarely dressed up when they did not have to; femininity was often done as part of an 'occasion'. The planning that went into preparation for parties was enormous and took over as the main topic of conversation for weeks in advance. Going out was a hedonistic highlight. Femininity was performed in preparation but it had many more meanings beyond the traditional. As Anne notes:

You know what I really miss about having children is that I never go out with the girls any more. We've all got kids and it would involve lots of organizing and really that would lose it. We're too old now but I used to love it, it was really wild. I can't really explain why it was so good, but we were all together and we all just wanted to have a good time. We used to drink when we got older but at first it was just pure adrenalin. It really was that exciting. We'd all look forward to it every week and we'd take piles of clothes to try on. It was all about experimenting and seeing what you could get away with [laugh]. We were really close. I used to feel it was a bit of a let-down sometimes when we went out. Mind you it was a laugh taking the piss out of all the jerks who'd make comments and that . . . No, no it wasn't about men at all, they were irrelevant. Some would try and schmoose their way in but they were soon out. No, it was different from pulling nights. It was about us. you know, I really do regret it, it has such good memories. In fact it was the best part of my life. Now it's all worries. Then we thought we were free. We just enjoyed ourselves.

(Anne 1992)

Anne's lament at her lost youth suggests that the dressing up, the signifying of heterosexuality, are more about friendships, hedonism, irresponsibility and intimate solidarity. The putting on of femininity is experienced as a form of camaraderie in which she is made to feel good about herself. This collective putting on is about women being close, safe and self-indulgent . . .

Appearance is simultaneously and across time a site for pleasure and strength but also a site of anxiety, regulation and surveillance. The feeling of looking good can also be lost if it is not continually externally validated, as Janet suggests:

During the holidays I get dead fed up, you know, we live miles from nowhere so I hardly see anybody unless I can get a lift back somehow and what I hate most is that I just doss around, sometimes I don't even bother to get dressed and you know if you do that for a week when you don't see nobody you start to wonder who you are and then it's really unnerving when you come back to college because you wonder if you still exist and you don't know what to wear and you feel as if everybody has been doing things and you've been on another planet.

(Janet 1983)

In this sense, femininity is very much a public performance dependent upon validation by others. Appearances, as Kate, Pam and Janet suggest, are more than just surfaces. They are intimately linked to valuations of oneself, to knowing oneself and to being an accepted part of a group. They do not recognize themselves by the category of femininity but their appearance (amongst other practices) is central to how they know themselves. This suggests that women are not feminine by default but that femininity is a carefully constructed appearance and/or form of conduct that can be displayed. It is a knowing construction, publicly performed. . . .

Feminine constructions had appropriate times and places. Spending obvious amounts of time with make-up just to go to work or college was seen to be embarrassing and inappropriate, but spending the same amount of time preparing to go out is expected. One woman who was always perfectly put together whilst at college came in for a lot of verbal abuse:

Have you seen all that make-up, it's like inches thick, and the heels, you'd think she were at a night club or something, it's ridiculous, it

> must take her ages to get ready on a morning and she totters around
> looking like a fucking Barbie doll. Just no shame. I think it's really sad,
> like there's no one here to impress, why bother, it's just stupid. She
> looks a real idiot.
>
> (Therese 1983)

Connie's problem is defined through inappropriateness. She also wears clothes that signify sexuality (such as short skirts and stretch jeans which emphasize her body) without any coding through fashion. Therese thinks she should feel ashamed to appear as she does. Basically, Connie just doesn't have the right feminine cultural knowledge to code herself carefully rather than to display herself explicitly. Connie would be the perfect visual example of femininity; she looks very similar to a Barbie doll. She may be an accurate imitation but she is not admired or even thought desirable. She is seen to be only appearance, lacking in substance. Femininity is not an aspiration, but something which is struggled with to gain some value and to ameliorate invalidation. It is a performance not considered to be necessary all the time. Those who appear and behave as feminine across all contexts have very little value: their performance is considered unnecessary. . . .

To not invest at all in femininity is seen to jeopardize others' investments. It is also seen as a lack of collusion with the feminine. Those who do not bother make the others self-conscious of their investments. They are resented but also represent a state of being that some of the women desire:

> You know in a way it'd be good not to have to worry about the way
> you looked. You know, not care if your skirt's tucked into your knickers
> and that, no really it'd be a bit more relaxing. I said to my mum the
> other day, why do we bother with all this. It was having my bikini line
> waxed that did it. It was unbelievable. Pain. God. I thought I was going
> to die. I felt for sick for ages afterwards and I said to her when she
> asked me why I wasn't eating, I said why do we do it? It'd be freedom
> not to care.
>
> (Cindy 1984)

Cindy evokes a sense of being caught up in something which is beyond her control. She knows that she is part of something that produces submission, even pain, but she cannot see a way out, the risks may be too great: cultural stigmatization in her local situation; a challenge to all her friends who collude in femininity; a sign of difference; the loss of potential future emotional and economic security. To challenge femininity can invoke costs, but that does not mean challenges cannot be made:

> I used to shave my legs all the time, so much so that they nearly grew a
> beard. I was really paranoid and then I remember reading this article and
> I thought why am I so concerned, you know in the winter they're not
> exactly on public display and nobody sees them. Well my mum teases
> me about them and that can be a bit cruel at times, but she's hairy too,
> that's where I get it from. So I got to thinking about it and it's daft. We
> start to worry about our hairy legs like it matters. I do them in the

summer now but that's all. They keep me warm in the winter. But sometimes I look at them and think ugh – ugly or what and then I think I like hairy legs on men so why is it so ingrained? To be honest I do think my legs look terrible, look, don't laugh . . . [*I didn't*] I just can't seem to convince myself otherwise. I wish I could.

(Karen 1988)

Karen has begun the long process of change but feels her rebellion as an aesthetic challenge. She has learnt from long contact with the texts of femininity that things should look a particular way. Bartky (1990) argues that the disciplinary practices on the body are part of the processes by which the ideal body of femininity – and hence the feminine body subject – is constructed; in doing this they produce a 'practised and subjected' body, that is, a body in which an inferior status has been inscribed. But, as Cindy's and Karen's comments suggest, there is a reflexivity about the regimes of the body. Femininity is not desired; rather, it is seen as a structuring inconvenience, something which is difficult for them to avoid completely. Distance can be drawn form disciplinary practices. They were able to be far more critical of the incitements for feminine appearance than they were of incitements to be a caring person, although similar systems of self-monitoring and surveillance are established. Caring worked at an intimate level of subjectivity, as quality of being, whereas femininity was less immediate, intimate or important. They were implicated in it but it was not seen to produce the same rewards, although the sanctions may be worse. . . .

. . . [F]or working-class women the sexual has to be disavowed. Glamour, however, is a way of holding together sexuality and respectability, but it is difficult to achieve. Pearce (1995) argues that glamour is always read as 'degrading' unless 'protected' and defended by other marks of middle-class respectability (such as education or wealth).[14] The women have to negotiate being glamorous and desirable – to which they all aspire – whilst not being marked as rough and common. Whilst the women were keen not to be associated with the sexual, they also knew that carefully coded displays of sexuality could generate value . . . They knew that their sexuality had a value that could be traded in their local circuits of exchange. This value was based on a conglomeration of variables, including: physically corresponding to dominant ideals of femininity; wearing locally designated appropriate clothing; limiting their sexual activity to avoid a reputation; not being aggressive, vulgar or domineering. These could all be negotiated through glamour. The women had to carefully code, display and conduct themselves to generate value. Glamour is the mechanism by which the marks of middle-class respectability are transposed onto the sexual body, a way in which recognition of value is achieved. . . .

. . . Whereas other forms of femininity are not experienced as subjectivity, the recognition of oneself as glamorous serves to engender as identification, enabling femininity to operate as a disposition *and* a form of cultural capital, even if only momentarily and always tied to performance. It is the attitude that makes the difference. It gives agency, strength and worth back to women and is not restricted to youth. They do glamour with style. Glamour is about a performance of femininity *with* strength:

> Yea I get glammed up, we all do. You have to be up for it though.
> There's no point if you're not in the mood or feeling down. You've
> got to feel you're invincible. Whistles, comments, chat-ups the lot,
> you've just got to look down your nose at them. I know when I look
> good. I make sure others do too.
>
> (Angela 1992)

Glamour is a way of transcending the banalities of femininity which render women
as passive objects, as signs of appearance without agency, as something which has
to be done. This shows how femininity is fragmented in which some facets can be
re-enacted with vision, pleasure and attitude in a way more appropriate to those
for whom it was not designed. Femininity may be textually mediated, an artifice,
a masquerade, a performance but through glamour it is also experienced as a
temporary 'way of being'. To be feminine, as Butler (1990) argues, is a mode of
enacting and re-enacting of received gender norms which surface as so many styles
of the flesh. Glamour is one of the areas, one of the styles of the flesh, in which
pleasure can be gained. Glamour enables the projection of desirability.

All of the women were concerned to be seen as desirable. To be fancied was
a validation of themselves.[15] To be desirable operated in many ways. Alongside
the regulatory heterosexual aspects of desirability – whose standards, who moni-
tors and who does the desiring – it was a way in which their feminine cultural
capital was confirmed as worth having. Desirability was a legitimation of the value
of performing femininity. Being desirable gave confidence but, more importantly,
it enabled one not to be seen as inadequate, undesirable and not belonging. . . .

. . . Here men are necessary for the confirmation of desirability. For Michelle,
male confirmation of desirability is essential for her sense of being, her subjectivity. Note that real men are not wanted but rather the knowledge that one is
heterosexually desirable is considered necessary for emotional security. Their sense
of themselves as desirable is surveilled through images of (heterosexual) desirability
– Michelle believes only thinness is desirable. Michelle and Clare believe that male
approval is cultural approval. Yet, although not articulated here, it is only certain
males who are designated as worthy of giving approval. Underpinning desirability
is an implicit sexual market where exchanges are governed by estimations of relative value. The 'right' men have to do the desiring. They believe that male approval
will give them cultural validation. This desire for male legitimation can be taken
to extremes in which other women are rendered invisible. Even the friends who
can make them feel good cannot confirm their desirability, as Diane notes with
regret:

> Yea, I was thinking about Rose and she's really lovely and all that but
> she's also very stupid. She'll sleep with anyone just to be able to say
> 'Look at me I'm really fanciable'. It's pathetic. Really, I mean, I think
> sleeping with any old oik makes her look less fanciable, like she looks
> sad and desperate, like she'll have anything. It's really embarrassing.
> I've said to her 'Why do you do it?' and she's come over all superior,
> like as if shagging jerks somehow makes her more fanciable than the
> rest of us. Has she no self-respect? She's admitted that she doesn't even

enjoy it much. I mean how many one-night stands are up to much
. . . Why some idiot saying shag me makes her feel better than me
saying she looks great is beyond me. I mean it makes dickheads seem
more valuable than me, her best mate, than all of us.

(Diane 1988)

Diane is obviously angry (and to some extent jealous) that she has become redundant in this part of her friend's life. Diane cannot understand why Rose, who is
very good-looking, would want to have sex with men who Diane does not rate
or believe hold equal value. Diane values herself and Rose far more highly than
the men they come into contact with. She interprets Rose's lack of valuing herself
as desperateness. Rose sees it differently:

It's about having a laugh. And you do have a laugh. It's no big deal.
It's just not serious. It makes me feel good. Even if the sex isn't always
brilliant it's still fun . . . No, no, I'm not desperate to get laid . . . I
don't know what it's about . . . It's not deep and meaningful. It's just
some men are a real good laugh and they can make you feel good. You
know, they can make you feel that all the effort was worth while.

(Rose 1988)

Rose wants some payback for her investments in femininity and these manifest
themselves through desirability. To be physically confirmed as desirable is the
confirmation that the performance of femininity has worked, that it was worth
while. Here femininity becomes the ultimate legitimator of masculinity (even
though pleasure and fun were gained in the performance); it offers to masculinity
the power to impose standards, make evaluations and confirm validity. . . .

Some women feel capable of finding male approval when they feel they
require it:

I feel more confident now with the kids, I don't need anybody. They're
just trouble. I'm more of a flirt now, I like a laugh. I like playing and
walking away, that's what I like. My looks are my best asset. I go out,
pull a fella, he'll say I'll ring tomorrow and you can say no and walk
away. They're just not worth the bother. I wouldn't trust anybody
with my children. The children having somebody is most important. If
someone was really good with the kids and I didn't really like him,
well I'd make a go of it. If I fancied someone and he wasn't interested
in children, he'd go.

(Angela 1992)

For Angela, aware of the trading value of physical attractiveness, confirmation of
desirability is set against the needs of her children. She also feels confident in her
physical appearance and powerful enough to attract and use men for her purposes.
This confidence is a product of a long hard struggle against the bad behaviour of
her ex-husband. Angela has had male validation and knows from her experience
that it is not worth much.

Being single was experienced as feeling continually monitored by the local cultures of which they are a part, in which to be without a man is seen to be inadequate and undesirable. The feeling of inadequacy testifies to the power and pervasiveness of heterosexuality. Not all women felt culturally annihilated without a man and positions between desperation and indifference were occupied at different times. If they did not have any other external forms of validation (such as work, children) the need for confirmation grew greater. This was because the cultural stigma of being single in working-class cultures increased as they grew older. Women also found that at work they would be passed over for promotion and responsible jobs if they were not married. Fears of being 'left on the shelf' continued throughout the research. Age also meant they had fewer culturally validated ways of meeting potential partners and the numbers of friends to go out with decreased (as the friends were married). Hatred of 'playing the field' or 'being part of the meat market' (their terms) was a strong incentive to settle for inadequate partners.

. . . Not to be in a relationship with somebody is experienced as cultural exclusion. . . . Couple culture (especially heterosexual) makes it difficult for single women to occupy public space and for them to feel as valid as married women. Desirability is not their only concern, it is being given the same social value as those who are in relationships. This is why many women invest in men, not just for economic reasons but for cultural validation. Some of these men provide sustenance and safety. Some, of course, do not. Male partners can enable the construction of confidence generated from cultural validation, otherwise unavailable. The concept of femininity is only partially adequate to encapsulate the experiences by which the women of the study occupied the category 'woman'. It is always over-layered with other categorizations such as class and race. Historically this is because working-class women (Black and White) have been positioned against femininity with the sexual. They were precisely what femininity was not. However, to claim respectability, disavowal of the sexual is necessary and constructions, displays and performances of feminine appearance and conduct are seen as necessary. The women are positioned at a distance from femininity but claim proximity to it. This ambivalent positioning informed their responses. The women made feminine performances appropriate to the situations they were in. These could be made across a range of sites, with differing value and potential (often produced through institutionalization (in the sexual division of labour; the legal system; the education system). These were not masquerades employed to generate distance (that was already guaranteed) but tactical deployments of forms of femininity which protected their investments and gained cultural approval and validations. Their attempts to 'pass' as feminine were always in jeopardy of being read by others as representative of authentic femininity. To not make these performances would have seriously endangered their bids for respectability. Their awareness of their positioning by default as sexual, vulgar, tarty, pathological and without value meant that they felt they had to continually prove that they were different.

. . . They usually 'did' femininity when they thought it was necessary. They did not feel others had the power to judge their appearance, other than through respectability – so style and fashion (although ultimately coded by respectability) were also spaces where fun could be had, pleasure taken, validation given but also distinctions drawn. They did, however, feel economically compelled to appear feminine. They made investments in femininity because they had few other alternatives available to accrue cultural and economic resources. The consequences of not investing in femininity produced a range of responses from desperation to loneliness, few of which were experienced as positive. Femininity provided a cultural resource through which they could try to put a floor on their circumstances. To avoid jeopardizing their investments they sometimes colluded in its production. The investments that could be made were age and place-specific, informed by textual mediations. They saw femininity as a structural inconvenience which was difficult to avoid. Femininity is not something that can be seen simply as physical appearance. It is an institutionalized sign that also operates as a form of cultural capital. McCall (1992) asks if gendered forms of cultural capital can ever function as profitable capital. Rarely, I would argue; they are more likely to operate as halts on losses. It is these processes of investment and experience that operated as a disincentive to the take-up of feminism . . .

Their forays into femininity were immensely contradictory. Femininity offered a space for hedonism, autonomy, camaraderie, pleasure and fun whilst simultaneously regulating and generating insecurities. The women simulated and dissimulated but did not recognize themselves as feminine. They felt most comfortable with glamour because it enabled them to hold femininity and sexuality together in respectable performances and generate value in local circuits of exchange. It also provided a space for them to operate with attitude. This meant glamour could work at the level of subjectivity, whilst other forms of femininity were recognized to be the property of others. However, glamorous performances could be compromised by the desire to be seen and legitimated as desirable.

This suggests that femininity may indeed be an uninhabitable category, reproduced by White working-class women through necessity rather than volition, though their deployment of different forms of femininity. The women's performances did not engender identification because they did not recognize themselves addressed by the classed category of femininity. They do not know themselves as feminine. Aspects of femininity are, however, something which they have learnt to perform and from which they can sometimes take pleasure. . . .

Notes

1   Texts do not necessarily pre-date interpretation; they may be the encoding of forms of behaviour not previously produced as texts. Texts, however, are always produced with interests in mind (Venn 1992) and, as Said (1984) argues, the relations of power and authority are what makes the production of texts possible.

2   This is made most obvious when larger or older women try and do femininity. Roseanne and Dawn French expose the ridiculousness of femininity in their magazine spreads in *Vanity Fair*. Thanks, Celia, for this example.

3   Earlier in the seventeenth century dressing outside of one's class was legislated against (Creed 1995).

4   See the 1975 radical feminist film *Take it like a Man Ma'am* (dirs. Melle Knudsen, Elizabeth Rygard and Li Vilstrup), which brilliantly visualizes these points.

5   By producing a table Bourdieu (1986: table 20, pp. 203–5) argues that working-class women are less likely to enter one of the occupations which most strictly demand conformity to the dominant notions of beauty and are less aware of the 'market' value of beauty. My research does not confirm his findings. The women of the study were acutely aware of the value of physical appearance. It was a site of significant investment.

6   This should not be surprising when we think of the pressures on the mothers themselves to display their respectability through appearance.

7   Jackie Stacey, in personal correspondence, notes how middle-class girls are discouraged by their mothers to display too much femininity. They have to display femininity with 'taste' and without sexuality.

8   It is likely that the labour can decrease when others can be paid to do it for you. Beauticians, who are most likely to be drawn from the working or lower middle classes, have converted their feminine cultural capital to gain employment. They then service, mainly, middle-class women. This investment in feminine labour is not highly socially or economically valued.

9   They had few other pursuits in which to invest, having not been educated in the cultural capitals of middle-class leisure pursuits (see Savage et al. 1992).

10   Nor should dressing up as a means of generating collective identity and camaraderie be seen to be restricted to heterosexual women. See Blackman and Perry (1990) and Creed (1995).

11   O'Neill (1993) notes how these 'nights out with the girls' are a site for the pleasure of many women. The form differs depending on class, age, region, etc.

12   See also Thomson and Henderson (1994) on fag hags.

13   Middle-class women learn to mimic also, but it is unlikely that working-class women will be used as a legitimate source of their mimicry unless they want to mimic femininity with sexuality, thus reproducing working-class women as the site of the sexual.

14   She notes how Princess Diana is never referred to as 'tarty' although she carries all the signs (from personal communication).

15   Desirability is an issue within both the institution of heterosexuality and in lesbian cultures.

References

Bartky, S. L. (1990) *Femininity and Domination: Studies in the Phenomenology of Oppression*, London: Routledge.

The Black Report (1982) *Inequalities in Health*, ed. P. Townsend and N. Davison. Harmondsworth: Penguin.

Blackman, I. and Perry, K. (1990) 'Skirting the issue: lesbian fashion for the 1990s', *Feminist Review*, 34: 67–79.

Bourdieu, P. (1986) *Distinction: A Social Critique of the Judgement of Taste*. London: Routledge.

Bourke, J. (1994) *Working-class Cultures in Britain, 1890–1960*. London: Routledge.

Butler, J. (1990) *Gender Trouble: Feminism and the Subversion of Identity*, London: Routledge.

Cixous, H. (1980) 'The laugh of Medusa', trans. K. Cohen and P. Cohen, in E. Marks and I. de Courtivon (eds) *New French Feminisms*. Brighton: Harvester.

Creed, B. (1995) 'Lesbian bodies: tribades, tomboys and tarts', in E. Grosz and E. Probyn (eds) *Sexy Bodies: The Strange Carnalities of Feminism*. London: Routledge.

Davis, A. Y. (1995) '"I used to be your sweet mama": ideology, sexuality and domesticity in the blues of Gertrude "Ma" Rainey and Bessie Smith', in E. Grosz and E. Probyn (eds) *Sexy Bodies: The Strange Carnalities of Feminism*. London: Routledge.

De Lauretis, T. (1984) *Alice Doesn't: Feminism, Semiotics, Cinema*. London: Routledge.

Gilman, S. L. (1992) 'Black bodies, white bodies: towards an iconography of female sexuality in late nineteenth-century art, medicine and literature', in J. Donald and A. Rattansi (eds) *'Race', Culture and Difference*. London: Sage.

Hall, C. (1979) 'The early formation of Victorian domestic ideology', in S. Burman (ed.) *Fit World for Women*. London: Croom Helm.

Lury, C. (1993) *Cultural Rights: Technology, Legality and Personality*. London: Routledge.

McCall, L. (1992) 'Does gender fit? Bourdieu, feminism and conceptions of social order', *Theory and Society*, 21: 837–67.

Nead, L. (1988) *Myths of Sexuality: Representations of Women in Victorian Britain*. Oxford: Blackwell.

O'Neill, G. (1993) *A Night Out with the Girls: Women having a Good Time*. London: Women's Press.

Pollock, G. (1989) *Vision and Difference: Femininity, Feminism and the Histories of Art*. London: Routledge.

Poovey, M. (1984) *The Proper Lady and the Woman Writer: Ideology as Style in the Works of Mary Wollstonecraft, Mary Shelley and Jane Austen*. Chicago: University of Chicago Press.

Riley, D. (1987) 'Does sex have a history? Women and feminism', *New Formations*, 1 (1): 35–45.

Rowe, K. (1995) *The Unruly Woman: Gender and the Genres of Laughter*. Austin TX: University of Texas Press.

Said, E. (1984) *The World, the Text and the Critic*. London: Faber.

Savage, M., Barlow, J., Dickens, P. and Fielding, T. (1992) *Property, Bureaucracy and Culture in Middle-Class Formation in Contemporary Britain*. London: Routledge.

Scott, J. (1992) 'Experience', in J. Butler and J. Scott (eds) *Feminists Theorise the Political*. London: Routledge.

Smith, D. E. (1988) 'Femininity as discourse', in L. G. Roman, L. K. Christian-Smith and E. Ellsworth (eds) *Becoming Feminine: The Politics of Popular Culture*. Lewes: Falmer Press.

Thomson, R. and Henderson, S. (1994) 'Faghag: Thinking Sexual Identity as Process', paper given to the British Sociological Association conference 'Sexualities in Context', Preston, March.

Venn, C. (1992) 'Subjectivity, ideology and difference: recovering otherness', *New Formations*, 16: 40–61.

Walkerdine, V. (1989) 'Femininity as performance', *Oxford Review of Education*, 15 (3): 267–79.

Ware, V. (1992) *Beyond the Pale: White Women, Racism and History*. London Verso.

Williams, R. (1961) *Culture and Society, 1780–1950*. Harmondsworth: Penguin.

Williams, R. (1977) *Marxism and Literature*, Oxford: Oxford University Press.

Chapter 39

Janet Holland, Caroline Ramazanoglu and Rachel Thomson

IN THE SAME BOAT?

This piece draws on data from the Women Risk and AIDS and Men Risk and AIDS projects, based on interviews, about sex and sexuality, with 150 young women and fifty young men. The authors show that, as a result of very different starting points and expectations when they first engage in heterosexual intercourse, young men and young women are not 'in the same boat'.

From D. Richardson (ed.) *Theorizing Heterosexuality*, Buckingham: Open University Press (1996).

> Q: How was it [with] both of you being virgins? Was it all right the first time? I mean, sometimes it's a bit problematic.
>
> A: No, it was funny. I mean, you've got to get rid of your embarrassment and you're both in the same boat. You both know, and it's just a laugh isn't it? It's not a . . . I didn't find it, like, a nerve-racking experience like a lot of people do. I just sort of took it as it comes. If it doesn't work the first time you have another go. You laugh about it.
>
> > (Young man, aged eighteen at the time of first heterosexual intercourse, white/Asian ethnicity, middle class)

Feminism and heterosexuality

YOUNG PEOPLE ON THE BRINK of heterosexual intercourse are in the same boat in that they have to take the same step from inexperience of intercourse to experience (although not necessarily with an inexperienced partner). . . .

. . . In analysing the interview accounts, we have taken first heterosexual intercourse to be a critically gendered moment in the development of heterosexuality.
The young people in our studies told differing stories of becoming sexually experienced and of what rocks the boat, but in this chapter we consider their accounts
of their first heterosexual experiences of sexual intercourse as one way of making
institutionalised heterosexuality visible.[1]

The moment of 'first sex' is not the only constitutive moment of heterosexuality. Becoming heterosexual occurs at differing levels of social activity, from
the most grounded meeting of bodies to the most abstracted level of institutionalisation. Sexuality is simultaneously both variable bodily states, desires and physical
practices, and also culturally variable understandings of this embodiment and associated identities and social practices. Sexuality is embodied in the sense that it
entails bodily activity; there is a physical aspect to sexual desire, gender and reproduction.[2] Heterosexuality is grounded in this bodily sexuality, but it cannot be
understood independently of the variable beliefs, values, ideologies, discourses,
identities and social relationships through which people become socially heterosexual and practice heterosexuality. Heterosexuality is lived in distinctive lifestyles
(especially those tied to marriage/household arrangements) and in discourses of
masculinity/femininity, normality/abnormality. . . .

. . . [W]e make the case that heterosexual 'first sex' is an induction into adult
masculinity for young men, within which the woman, whether sexually experienced herself or not, plays an ambiguous role. We are arguing that heterosexuality
is not a balanced (or even unbalanced) institutionalisation of masculinity-and-
femininity, it is masculinity. We take young people's accounts to support our
claim that first heterosex is a double construction: the young woman is under
pressure first to consent to the constitution of adult heterosexuality as the construction of masculinity, and then to fit herself to this construction. Within this
construction of masculinity, young women must find ways of existing and making
sense of themselves and their 'otherness'. Sexual intercourse with men becomes
something for them to manage as best they can. This construction of adult
heterosexuality as masculinity offers within it limiting identities of both masculinity and femininity. Femininity is constructed from within heterosexuality
and on male territory, yet this territory can only exist with female consent and
collusion.

It is not difficult to document the gendering of 'normal sexuality' from young
people's accounts of their first sexual experiences. First intercourse is generally a
consciously critical moment for young people whether they are actively seeking sexual intercourse, allowing the intercourse to happen, or having it thrust upon them.[3]
But, we argue here, it is also part of a much more general, and less visible, process
of induction into the dominance of masculine norms and meanings as 'natural'.
Significantly, most young women arrive at their first experience of heterosexual
intercourse already constituted as 'woman'. From the moment that puberty is
marked by first menstruation, they are conscious of what it means to be a woman
and the attendant requirements to discipline their bodily unruliness (Prendergast
1995; see also Martin 1987). Yet, for young men in most Western cultures, puberty
has no such exact marker, and 'first sex' is the key act by which they become a man.
As a result, their sexual agency is expressed through 'doing' rather than 'being'. . . .

Young people in our studies recognised a range of activities as sexual, but also showed how tightly the space for discussion of sexuality has been closed. 'Proper sex' was widely defined as a specific version of heterosexual intercourse in which the man's penis penetrates the woman's vagina; it starts with his arousal and finishes with his climax. 'First sex' in this embodied but fragmented guise is the young man's moment. There is no equivalent definition of the 'sex act' in terms of female agency, action or desire; her orgasm is his production. This is shown by the absence in public discourses of sexuality of positive conceptions of active female sexuality, positive female desire or performance; an absence that clearly characterised most of our interviews with young women (Holland *et al.* 1992b). The female heterosexual subject is absent – except as the feminine object of men's desire, the sexual deviant or the sexless mother (see also Bland 1994; Jackson 1996; Smart 1996). . . .

. . . [W]e suggest that the subordination of female sexual agency can be identified at the moment of first heterosexual intercourse. Yet the salvaging of such agency is not merely a question of resistance. Young women are not simply victims of heterosexuality, but the moment of 'first sex' is currently constructed in such a way that much resistance can safely be accommodated. Young people arrive at the moment of 'first sex' in ways that mean the subsequent division of sexual labour into her 'being' and his 'doing' appears inevitable.

How was it for him?

. . . First intercourse for young men was a challenge that could threaten their successful achievement of manhood. Their potency was at stake, they did not necessarily know what to do with their bodies, and there was a good deal of concern about doing it right. But in these positive accounts, the main point was to *do* it – a masculine performance in which they were the star player. This element of performance was clearly recognised by young women:

> A: And I suppose he must have been on a right high, you know, just, you know, broke someone's virginity – a sixteen year old girl.
>   (Young woman, aged nineteen, ESW,[4] working class)

The issue of 'how was it for her?' is largely irrelevant to the young men's accounts, unless they are actively subverting 'normal' masculinity. Their inexperience as adult males was rectified by the act of intercourse, and this in itself constituted pleasure:

> A: Yeah, it was quite a good experience. I thought I'd done alright, like – never doing it before. I was quite pleased really.
>   (Young man, aged eighteen, ESW, working class)

> A: I mean it's the old saying, 'you enter the bed a boy and you leave it a man' or words to that effect. I felt the same, I didn't alter physically, but I felt different after that first time. I did definitely feel different.
>   (Young man, aged nineteen, ESW, working class) . . .

If a young man can produce apparent pleasure in his partner, this is the icing on the cake, and confirms his own performance as a positive one:

A: I didn't really know what to expect – but it went quite well. And sort of what made it really nice was afterwards she –
Q: Yeah? [laughs]
A: My ego just went WHOOMPH, you know.
                              (Young man, aged eighteen, ESW, middle class)

Some young men were more reluctant to define their first experiences in terms of achievement of manhood, especially if they later regretted not having their first experience with someone they loved, but they still framed the experience in a conception of performance:

A: It was in the back of a friend's car, it was so tacky. We went to a club to meet some girls, and we met them and that was that really. [Later in the interview] It was a big deal, I remember feeling 'Wow!' afterwards, but it wasn't really a good deal – it wasn't 'I'm in love!' or whatever.
                              (Young man, aged seventeen, 'other'
                                        ethnicity, middle class) . . .

These accounts are characterised by an awareness of intercourse as performance that is completely missing from the young women's interviews. There is a marked sense of agency in the young men's reflections on their performance, and their accounts are also more embodied than those of the young women. Embodiment was explicit in anxieties about getting and maintaining an erection and reaching orgasm during penetration, when nervous and unsure of themselves. The young men obliquely defined the power of the female partner as a threat to their performance of masculinity in three main ways: she could refuse his advances, 'I thought God, she's going to say, 'Forget it!'"'; she could be more knowing than the man, through prior experience or, most threateningly, she could ridicule and publicise his failure to perform as expected:

Q: Did you feel confident?
A: No, I felt bloody nervous. I thought, what if I don't get a hard-on? It all goes to pot.
                              (Young man, aged nineteen, ESW, working class)

Q: Is there a sort of feeling do you think amongst men to think they have to be good at sex?
A: I think so, yes, especially if you have seen the girl about and stuff like that, and like you know she is going to open her mouth to everyone else if you are not good, so yes, you have to perform quite well, if you know the girl like, and you have seen her about.
                              (Young man, aged sixteen, African
                                        Caribbean, working class)

Yet this threat is not sourced in the female sexual partner, nor in a critical femininity, but in the male peer group, the men's world that he is entering through this initiation. This sense of threat made young men very reluctant to explore women's pleasure. They did not usually know how to access it, except through their own bravura performance, and any expression of lack of pleasure on the woman's part could undermine the man's achievement. The important thing for a young man was to do it right, and hope the woman, or other women, would come back for more. . . .

The constitution of the moment of first heterosex as a moment of agency and achievement for the young man can be partly explained by what leads to it. There were some differences here in how first intercourse came about. In some of their accounts of relationships with women, young men reported first intercourse being achieved through a war of attrition in which he progressively worked towards sexual access, leaving the young woman with little space other than to say yes or no:

A: So anyway, we sat up until about two o'clock, we were in the launderette, I managed to persuade her to have sex.

Q: I mean how did you persuade her? How did that work?

A: It was very grinding. I had to grind her down, 'Come on now, you know you want it, go on.' Eventually I pissed her off so much she said yes.

Q: What, to shut you up?

A: Yes. But anyways she said, 'Right, condoms.' I runs over to the toilets, she says, 'God, you're eager.' She said, 'When was the last time you had it?' I said I hadn't. She went 'Oh, no!' like this. I thought, God, she's going to say 'Forget it!' We got back to the launderette, did it in the launderette.

(Young man, aged nineteen, ESW, working class)

In this approach to male achievement, women are explicitly targeted to meet a male 'need', and female resistance is not only expected but may be a prerequisite of his agency. One young man described how he had felt himself under pressure to put pressure on a girl in order to initiate himself into manhood. . . .

In young men's accounts of first experiences of intercourse, there were examples where the construction of male and female as respectively active and passive was absent. Significantly, these examples arose where, whether through circumstance or endeavour, the definition of what constituted 'first sex' was broad enough to dissipate anxieties about male performance. Usually these were couples in an established relationship who felt able to communicate with each other about the timing of sexual intercourse, to negotiate the experience openly and so to offer some resistance to conventions of masculinity and femininity.

A young man who did not have intercourse until he was eighteen commented that this had left an unresolved tension in his relationships, but that it was useful in terms of what he was able to learn about sex before embarking on intercourse:

A: When you do go out with someone you are not having sex with you happen to learn a great deal about the workings of the female body which I think has helped me a great deal. I think other than just blindly closing your eyes and having sex, I just couldn't do that, so I actually learned a great deal about what a woman enjoys and wants to get out of sexual things in general.

(Young man, aged nineteen, ESW, working class)

Another commented on his first experience being both good and bad – he succeeded in achieving manhood, but the quality of the experience was limited. He had learned the difference by getting to know a subsequent sexual partner well:

Q: Are you sort of worried about your performance and things like that, getting it right?

A: Yes, it's all the time it's on your mind, because it's also like with someone you don't know, you don't know whether they are appreciating what you are doing or not, so it's sort of hard as well to know what to do. Whereas with my girlfriend Sara, it was different because we knew each other well enough to say, 'Do you like this? Do you like that?' It was easy. But the first time it was good, but it was bad.

(Young man, aged sixteen, ESW, middle class)

Although first intercourse was generally viewed as the establishment of male performance, there was also some resistance to the constraints imposed by conventions of masculinity. Accounts of first intercourse showed considerable variation in the kinds of relationship established between the sexual partners. Where there is a more negotiated relationship, or the influence of feminism (particularly from mothers), then there could be more awareness of the possibility of differences between male and female experience.

The dominance of masculine meaning, and the surveillance of the male peer group, in the construction of heterosexual identity is most acute where sexual encounters are impersonal and transitory. Intimacy, friendship and an equality of inexperience make space within which individual subjectivities can be expressly 'in the same boat'. However, the excerpt at the beginning of this chapter is not typical of the young men's accounts. Being able to laugh together at inexperience, rather than her having the power to laugh at him; exploring desires together, rather than her being expected to service him, requires some initial deconstruction of heterosexual pressures. The extent and problems of effective resistance to heterosexuality seemed clearer in the responses from young women.

How was it for her?

When we compare men's and women's accounts of their first experiences of intercourse, the claim that they are all in the same boat becomes more confused. While young men's accounts are varied, the very general acceptance of first intercourse as a positive step to manhood have no equivalent in the young women's accounts.

Conceptions of first intercourse as about women's pleasure, performance or achievement of adult status are strikingly absent, and the women's accounts are generally much more disembodied and distanced from the experience than those of the young men. For young women, sexual intercourse within a masculine construction of heterosexuality presents specific risks. As she takes him into her body for his pleasure, she confronts problems of how to manage this experience in terms of successful femininity, protect both her body and her reputation, and make sense of the experience for herself. It is not then surprising that young women's accounts of first intercourse seemed more varied and contradictory than those of young men.

In contrast to the young men, young women do not seem to embark on their first experiences of sexual intercourse with the idea of becoming women. In the heterosexual/masculine boat, young women do not gain womanhood through sexual intercourse so much as offer their virginity to men. Drawing on the work of Shirley Prendergast on menstruation (Prendergast 1995), we argue that young women's conceptions of 'now I am a woman' are formed at puberty (and confirmed by pregnancy). It is in the management of first menstruation that a young woman begins to become aware of what it is to be a woman, with its attendant requirements to discipline and conceal her bodily unruliness. Through this discipline she develops a sense of negative power, built upon ideas and experiences of bodily constraint and control (Holland et al. 1994a).

. . . Unless they were directly influenced by feminism, these young women were not generally aware of heterosexuality as anything other than the natural order of things. This put them under considerable pressure to accept the male domination of the entire process of 'first sex' as natural, and not to rock the boat.

Offering their bodies to men gives young women a range of problems which it is often difficult for them to articulate. Since 'first sex' is not primarily initiation into womanhood, it can be a moment of considerable ambivalence for young women. In most of their accounts, there is a sense of awareness that 'sex' is what is happening for their male partner. 'First sex' can then be the price of keeping a social relationship with a boyfriend:

> A: I didn't really want it. He provoked me into it, you know . . . it was like a one-off. You know, I didn't want it really, I just wanted someone to love at that time. He just wanted a bit of – you know.
>
> (Young woman, aged nineteen, ESW, middle class)

Many young women faced a good deal of uncertainty in knowing how to develop the loving relationships they desired, while also having to manage young men's expectations. Young women are positioned within masculinity in such a way that there is always the possibility of force, or other pressure beneath the surface. . . .

A more general problem for young women came from the construction of first intercourse as the man's moment, leaving women to cope with first experiences that did not match their expectations of love, romance, or the earth moving:

A: I was fourteen. It was complete infatuation, you know, like amaze-
ment – these people *like* us, or whatever, and I slept with this
boy then. I just didn't feel anything. I didn't think, 'Oh, it's really
– or whatever, I just sort of thought, 'Oh, great,' and I sort of
felt – I wasn't very happy about it afterwards I sort of felt dirty.
I think partly because I was so young, and I was infatuated with
this person, and he turned out to be so ordinary.
(Young woman, aged seventeen, ESW, middle class)

The range of young women's responses reflects different approaches to the
problems of managing their lack of agency. His achievement of manhood is her
loss of autonomy. One way of claiming agency was through defining first intercourse as the young woman giving the man something valuable:

A: Well, just – losing your virginity for them – it's just, I don't
know it just seems important to me personally.
(Young woman, aged seventeen, ESW, working class) . . .

Further variation in women's management of first intercourse occurs because
young women reported a number of possible ways of accepting sexual experience
while offering some resistance to male domination of its meaning. These strategies, which are echoed in the young men's accounts of 'pushy partners', tend to
be associated with the disruption of the chronology of diminishing resistance to
sex over time, for example, by rushing into it:

Q: Do you think you made the right decision the first time?
A: No. I suppose I wanted to just get it over and done with – I
didn't want to rush into it, just because he was there, and I'd
been going out with him anyway. I didn't like him. I just finished
with him. I hated it. It's not great the first time. Never,
(Young woman, aged eighteen, ESW, working class) . . .

Young women's varied approaches to first intercourse signal the absence of
female agency, power and pleasure within masculinity/heterosexuality. Women
had varying strategies of acceptance of, or resistance to, intercourse as his performance, but the main way in which these absences could be accommodated was by
situating first intercourse within a social relationship with a boyfriend. They made
sense of this accommodation through the acceptance of a careful chronology. There
is a clear sense, which is not found so clearly in the young men's responses, that
there is a right moment, a point at which the woman is ready for what comes
next, so that intercourse is part of a 'natural progression' in a relationship:

A: That was like my first sexual relationship, and I could have done
it beforehand, but I chose not to. I don't know – I don't know.
To a certain extent you feel that you ought to wait till you feel
ready and I felt I could do that, I was just lucky I suppose . . .

it was just the right thing to do at that time. That explains it, really. There's a sort of natural progression.

(Young woman, aged twenty, ESW, middle class)

A: I don't know if either of us was that keen, really. I don't know if he – I think – I don't think he was eager to have it, but it was – it was something there that we was going to do together and then it was time. The time came and we did it. It wasn't 'Oh quick! Let's have it now!' It was just – it just came naturally, really.

(Young woman, aged eighteen, African Caribbean, middle class)

This chronology could also relieve young men from the pressure to prove their manhood. Where young women expect men to demand intercourse, which they can then either accept or resist, it could be up to the man to respect this sense of timing, and to allow space for a relationship to develop before he made his move:

A: We was going out for nine months. He waited for about five months. I really got to like him.
Q: Was it your decision to do it or was he hassling you?
A: No, he's so shy, you see, he's nice looking and – so, he made the first move. I was shocked because lads sometimes wait about a week and then jump in your knickers.

(Young woman, aged seventeen, African Caribbean, working class)

Ros Coward (1984) has argued that female heterosexuality is constructed so that women are positioned in ways that only enable them to choose between 'yes' and 'no'. Perhaps, through their acceptance of a careful chronology, young women are also attempting agency, learning from their established experience in resisting young men's sexual advances. By accepting that men will be making advances, and that these advances do not have to be accepted, they can manage their sexuality by refusing intercourse:

A: There was one boy that just pushed me a bit too far, and I got rid of him as well, because I thought, 'Well, I don't need this. What right have you to push yourself on me?' And that was on the first night.

(Young woman, aged eighteen, ESW, middle class)

Yet if the time somehow is right, then they can find that their agency is simply ceded to the male partner to define the sexual situation, and they lose the right to say no:

Q: Do you feel in relationships in the past you've been able to make decisions?

> A: Yeah, but not sexually, because he's the first one I've slept with – but we really do make equal decisions apart from that one.
>
> > (Young woman, aged sixteen, African
> > Caribbean, middle class)

By adopting different strategies of acceptance and resistance, young women can position themselves within first heterosex encounters with differing degrees of power, thereby challenging the symbolic meaning of the moment. However, with little or no previous experience to draw on as to the nature of female sexual pleasure, it is difficult for them to be constituted as agents rather than objects; they have no boat of their own. . . .

Positive, empowered experiences of first heterosex were, in contrast to the accounts of young men, rare among our female respondents. The constraints of first sexual experience for women were widely recognised. Making the experience a positive one depended on transforming conventional male behaviour into practices in which he was detached from his peer group, and communication about female desires was possible. One young woman illustrates this: with the benefit of age and experience she was able to revisit 'first sex' by having a relationship with a male virgin, inducting him into her own tailor-made version of heterosexuality:

> A: The bloke I am actually going out with is about three years younger than I am and we can talk for hours and we get on really well. And he hadn't actually had a sexual experience before that . . . and it was like such a reversal of positions. He had got all these ideals about having sex before marriage and it was only going to be with someone he really cared about or had been married or whatever. And it just sort of developed because we became very close and he changed his ideas about it. So I was like the experienced one although I had only done it about four or five times. So the way I used to ask questions, I used to love talking about it, and he was actually doing that and it was just working it out within ourselves. And because he had no sort of ideals about it, it was a lot more – he was a lot more thoughtful of me as well which is why it is very different.
>
> > (Young woman, aged twenty-one, ESW,
> > middle class)

What is strikingly lacking in most of the women's accounts of first intercourse is this sense of either partner being 'thoughtful of me'.

These young women's varied accounts of their experiences of 'first sex' indicate their strategies for managing masculinity. Heterosexual intercourse is not only differently experienced by men and women: it is socially different. For a young man, achieving intercourse is an empowering moment of symbolic and physical importance, whereby through a physical performance, his identity as a man and, therefore, a competent sexual actor is confirmed. The passage from inexperience for the young woman is far more ambiguous and contradictory. Despite various possibilities for (re-)claiming it, first intercourse is not really her moment. Yet she has an important role to play in 'being heterosexual', through her part in constituting heterosexuality through intercourse, and managing the interaction. It is only through access to her body that the boy can achieve manhood. Through her participation in his performance she is inducted to the world of heterosexual sexuality, where she must learn to play by the masculine rules of the game, or take the consequences of resistance.

Within this game, her sexual identity, subjectivity and desire are silent. To succeed as a woman, and to be rewarded, she must become proficient in supporting and satisfying masculine values and needs. Negotiation of the rules of the game is not merely a matter for the woman and her sexual partner: reward and sanction are rather held by the wider peer group, and exercised through social mechanisms such as 'reputation' (Holland et al. 1996).

How was it for you?

Young people's accounts of their first sexual experiences go some way towards making the process of achieving heterosexual sexual identities visible, and offer some insight into the constitution of heterosexuality as masculinity. Making heterosexuality visible is difficult, since its power as 'the natural order of things' hinders both its actors and the social theorist in extricating contested meanings from the apparent certainties of first intercourse. Young people are all in the same boat, in that heterosexuality turns out to be masculinity only thinly disguised, but from a feminist perspective they are not in the same boat, in that heterosexuality could be otherwise. . . .

It is possible that a key to female empowerment may lie in resisting the institutionalisation of intercourse as *the* sexual act. It is this social construction of intercourse that locks together the languages and practices of male agent and female object, the fear and bravado of male performance and the absence of female sexual agency. Lucy Bland's observation, that the identification of 'sex' with heterosexual intercourse may have hindered the possibilities of our thinking on sexuality (Bland 1994), could also offer some optimism for the future possibilities of reworking the languages and practices of being heterosexual.

Notes

1   Since sexuality cannot be taken as fixed and universal, our generalisations are limited, and definitions need to be qualified. Our analysis should apply fairly generally to English-speaking cultures and to much of Europe, but the nature of extent of variation, across time, cultures and social divisions is not established.
2   We do not have space here to develop and qualify this contentious claim but have argued the point elsewhere (Holland et al. 1994a; Ramazanoglu 1995).
3   In exploring these issues we are not considering here cases where young women have been forcibly penetrated by men, or have their first experiences of intercourse under direct social or physical pressure. We have discussed pressured sex in Holland et al. (1992a).

4   'ESW' indicates 'English/Scottish/Welsh', which was used in our purposive sample as a category of ethnic origin.

References

Bland, L. (1994) 'The shock of the *Freewoman* journal', in J. Weeks and J. Holland (eds) *Sexual Cultures: Communities, Values and Intimacy*. London: Macmillan.

Coward, R. (1984) *Female Desire: Women's Sexuality Today*. London: Collins/Paladin.

Holland, J., Ramazanoglu, C., Sharpe, S. and Thomson, R. (1992a) 'Pleasure, pressure and power: some contradictions of gendered sexuality', *Sociological Review*, 40 (4): 645–74.

Holland, J., Ramazanoglu, C., Scott, S., Sharpe, S. and Thomson, R. (1992b) 'Pressure, resistance, empowerment: young women and the negotiation of safer sex', in P. Aggleton, P. Davies and G. Hart (eds) *AIDS: Rights, Risk and Reason*. London: Falmer Press.

Holland, J., Ramazanoglu, C., Sharpe, S. and Thomson, R. (1996) 'Reputations: journeying into gendered power relations', in J. Weeks and J. Holland (eds) *Sexual Cultures: Communities, Values, Intimacy*. London: Macmillan.

Holland, J. Ramazanoglu, C., Sharpe, S., Thomson, R. *et al*. (1994) 'Power and desire: the embodiment of female sexuality', *Feminist Review*, 46: 22–38.

Jackson, S. (1996) 'Heterosexuality as a problem for feminist theory', in L. Adkins and V. Merchant (eds) *Sexualising the Social: Power and the Organisation of Sexuality*. London: Macmillan.

Martin, E. (1987) *The Woman in the Body*. Milton Keynes: Open University Press.

Prendergast, S. (1995) 'With gender on my mind: menstruation and embodiment at adolescence', in J. Holland and M. Blair with S. Sheldon (eds) *Debates and Issues in Feminist Research and Pedagogy*. Clevedon: Multilingual Matters in Association with the Open University.

Ramazanoglu, C. (1995) 'Back to basics: heterosexuality, biology and why men stay on top', in M. Maynard and J. Purvis (eds) *(Hetero)sexual politics*. London: Taylor & Francis.

Smart, C. (1996) 'Desperately seeking post-heterosexual woman', in J. Holland and L. Adkins (eds) *Sex, Sensibility and the Gendered Body*. London: Macmillan.

Chapter 40

Vera Whisman

CHOOSING A STORY

Vera Whisman's study of lesbian and gay life histories and identities explores the different understandings of the origins of lesbianism and homosexuality. She found three different accounts or 'stories' in circulation: those who saw their sexuality as 'determined' as 'born that way', those who said they chose to be lesbian or gay, and those who offered 'mixed' accounts in which sexual orientation was assumed to be inborn but sexual preference – recognising and acting on that orientation – entailed choice. The last was the dominant account, especially among gay men. Of the thirty-three gay men in the sample, four gave 'determined' accounts, six gave 'chosen' accounts and twenty-two gave 'mixed' accounts. Of the thirty-nine lesbians, four offered 'determined', twelve 'chosen' and twenty-three 'mixed' accounts. These were reflections not simply of life experience but of the ways in which that experience was retrospectively constructed, drawing on available cultural resources. Whisman's analysis suggests that the sexual self is a narrative reconstruction.

From *Queer by Choice*, New York: Routledge (1996).

Determined and chosen accounts

THE LESBIANS AND GAY MEN who use the 'determined' account and those who use the 'chosen' account are distinguished by more than just their beliefs about the source of their sexual preferences; for the most part these different accounts reflect very different life experiences. Perhaps the central differentiating experience is continuity: 'determined'-account respondents recall an unbroken sense that they were homosexual from an early age, while those who offer the 'chosen' account do not claim this continuity of identity.[1] The 'chosen'-account group also has more heterosexual experience and fewer members who recall childhood gender nonconformity. A few respondents present exceptions to these patterns, but generally these two groups' accounts reflect their experiences in a logical way.

I invited respondents to begin telling me their stories by asking, 'Could you tell me how you came to decide that you are gay/a lesbian?' a wording I had chosen to avoid limiting respondents to the essentialist language of knowledge and discovery. But it was a wording soundly rejected by most of the nine individuals who offered the 'determined' account, in favor of language that referred more directly to an underlying orientation.

> I don't think I ever decided. It just sort of happened. It's not a deci-sion anybody makes, you're just born that way.
>
> (Dan Bartlett)

Whether or not they resisted using the term 'decide', 'determined'-account respon-dents answered my query with some version of the statement 'I always knew.' With only one exception, all of them made it clear that their homosexuality was continuous; they became aware of it at or before puberty, and they never self-identified as anything but homosexual. Although they never changed identities, and never experienced a momentous discovery, there certainly were turning points where their awareness intensified and their identities crystallized. Many recall learning a word – 'gay', 'homosexual', 'lesbian', 'faggot' – and recognizing them-selves in it. . . . But it was their understanding that changed, not their feelings. These respondents describe a continuous knowledge of an underlying homosexual orientation.

> I had known since the time I was four years old that I was gay. I always had these sexual feelings toward men. And I figures that maybe it was a normal thing to do, to be that way. I've always felt that way.
>
> (Eric Lehman)

. . . Most believe they were born gay.

> I think I've been gay from birth. And I've never had a heterosexual experience. And I've never had the desire to have one, so I guess you could say I'm gay to the full extent.
>
> (Malcolm Wilson)

Only one of the 'determined'-account respondents did not experience contin-uity in his homosexuality. His story is somewhat unusual, for although he did not always know he was gay, he does not recall an onset of awareness. He reconciles these two somewhat contradictory claims by using the concept of 'drift'. Dan Bartlett, a fifty-one-year-old architect from a white, Protestant, and upper-class Manhattan family, describes a process that was slow but inevitable.

> V.W.:   So do you remember when you first said to yourself, 'I'm gay'?
>
> D.B.:   I don't think I ever did. You don't say that. I think it was probably when I was twenty years old, when I had my first big affair.
>
> V.W.:   That was a turning point?
>
> D.B.:   Yeah, but it was never anything momentous. Just sort of happened. It's not something I ever thought about. It just seemed very natural to just sort of slide into it. I was also having sex with women, and up until I was about twenty, I didn't think of myself as anything but having a good time. I never thought of myself as either one or the other.

Dan's ability to 'slide', to be sexually active for a period of years without self-labeling, is unusual, as he is well aware. . . . Although Dan's story departs from the others', he did not choose to be gay, he means he never exercised any choices; he drifted into a gay life without experiencing the lifelong sense of sexual difference to which the other 'determined'-account respondents refer. Dan demonstrates the absence of choice in one sense – the actual exercise of choice – while the other 'determined' respondents define choice differently – as the existence of other viable options (see Card 1995).

In contrast, nearly all the eighteen respondents who offered the 'chosen' account experienced a discontinuity between their gay and pre-gay selves. They initially identified as heterosexual, then changed to a gay or lesbian identity in their teens or twenties.[2] Most now embrace their discontinuous pasts, and avoid defining their previous identities as false.

> V.W.:   So while you were going through this [coming-out] process, did you find yourself looking back at your past in a different way?
>
> P.J.:   You mean, was I in love with my gym teacher? (*We laugh.*) Not a lot. I mean it explained some things in terms of dealing with boys, I guess, when I was a teenager and stuff. But a lot of that was just fucked-up stuff that happens when you're a teenager, and you have to deal with boys. I think that heterosexual – girls that feel pretty heterosexual, or that eventually end up claiming that identity, or whatever, probably had the same experiences, you know?
>
> (Pearl Johnson) . . .

> V.W.:   Do you remember looking back on earlier years of your life and seeing them differently?
>
> V.B.:   Not entirely, but to some extent. It wasn't as if I was always having terrible relationships with men. I did have good experiences, you know, really nice ones. But I felt like there was much more to what I was experiencing with women.
>
> V.W.:   So you didn't feel like your life up to then had been all wrong or something like that?
>
> V.B.:   No.
>
> (Virginia Bradford)

. . . Having selected the 'chosen' account, these respondents do not present evidence of early homosexuality; they pass up the opportunity to attribute such meaning to their pasts. But there are two exceptional cases that are counterintuitive, two respondents who simultaneously claim to have chosen their homosexuality and to have always been aware of it.

Henry Yount, the one man of the 'chosen' group who claims a continuous knowledge of his homosexuality, is a forty-five-year-old white man, originally from rural Pennsylvania, who works as a freelance copy-editor. He belongs to a small group in New York City that studies and practises the ideas of a gay psychiatrist who claimed that homosexuality is a choice (Rosenfels 1971). . . . Henry explains his position with certainty:

> It was as a result of running into this group that I began to take my homosexuality much more seriously. I began to think a lot about choice, and why we're not permitted to see it as a choice, and why it's not talked about as a choice. If you ask most homosexuals, they'll say, 'No, I didn't have a choice. I was born this way.'

But in spite of taking this position, Henry tells a story of 'always knowing'.

> I've been sexually attracted to my peers beginning around age ten. There was actual incidents. I of course saw that as some kind of deviation that would pass, or something like that. I remember specifically when I was thirteen, fourteen, all the boys who were involved in this activity kind of moving away from it, and me wondering why that wasn't happening to me.

The two strands of his narrative exist alongside one another. He explains the apparent contradiction by maintaining that, in a homophobic and heterosexist context, we make choices without being aware of them. While, as we will see below, many 'mixed'-account respondents claim that they were 'always gay but unaware of it', Henry reverses the terms, claiming that he chose to be gay but was unaware of doing so, having made an 'unconscious choice'. . . .

Tina Fiore, the one 'chosen' lesbian who claims continuous awareness, is a forty-year-old white woman from a working-class background who currently works as a retail clerk. After twenty years identifying and living as a lesbian, she is considering becoming involved with a man. She adamantly resists claiming that her lesbian history was inauthentic or mistaken, just as the other 'chosen' respondents resist making that claim about their heterosexual experience.

> V.W.: So what do you currently think of as your sexual identity? Do you still think of yourselves as a lesbian, or –?
>
> T.F.: I was thinking about that last night. I think that if I were to say, 'No, I'm not a lesbian,' then that would be sort of like saying that none of it was real. That my relationships were not real to me, and that's not true. I think that it doesn't matter to me anymore? I think that I'm just more, um, interested in who I feel is more compatible.

As with the other 'chosen' lesbians, Tina's claims of choice allows her to embrace and explain the changes and discontinuities in her life course. But, unlike the others, she tells a story about 'always knowing' alongside a story about being bisexual, and exercising various choices.

> v.w.:   When did you first start thinking of yourself as a lesbian?
>
> t.f.:   Oh, God. Actually, the truth is, when I was in third grade, I had a dream about one of my teachers. I loved this woman so much (*chuckles*). I can always remember feeling that I wanted to be with a woman. Always felt that. Even when I dated guys, I always knew in the back of my mind that it was a woman I wanted to be with. When the opportunity finally came, I took it. And I always knew it would come, and I always knew I would take it.
>
> v.w.:   So could you have chosen not to take it?
>
> t.f.:   I could have, but I also felt that if I didn't like it, that I could always walk away from it. I didn't feel that it was anything I had to commit myself to. . . .

That her story is currently under revision shows through this narrative. The claim that she always knew she was attracted to women is fleshed out with detailed childhood memories – a crush on a teacher, what she felt when she was dating boys. Her claims that she always felt she could go either way is worded more vaguely and lacks supportive detail. Tina seems to be revising her opinions as well, as illustrated in the following quotation. She initially asserts that people are born with their sexual preferences, and then backs away from that statement, step by step, until she arrives at an opinion that is in accord with her current situation.

> v.w.:   Do you think that people are born with their sexual prefer-ence?
>
> t.f.:   I do. I think that if they're not born with it – maybe we're not born with much of anything, except your flesh – but it happens months after birth. I really believe that. I really believe that we see and hear and smell and taste all these things, and as an infant you can decide what you like and don't like. Even though at that time they're just sensations, but they really form the basis of choices as adolescents.
>
> v.w.:   So do you think that's something that's set then, once that happens in the first year or so?
>
> t.f.:   Set? I think if you're unlucky they become set. I don't think that it's that good to – I wouldn't want to think that things are set. I think that you know intuitively the atmosphere of the rest of the life you would like to have. But I don't think it's healthy to say, 'This is the way it's going to be, no matter what.' 'Cause then you don't question what you're about.

Tina's unusual pattern – claiming both continuity and a 'chosen' account – is part of her unusual life history, and part of a story that seems to be currently under revision. . . . Generally, the women who offer the 'chosen' account tell a fairly consistent story, one that does not feature some underlying sexual orientation of which they 'always knew'.

Nearly all of the 'determined'-account respondents report that other recognized them as homosexual, or as 'different', early on, a report which none of the 'chosen' respondents makes.

> I've sat down and talked to my brothers, and my brothers have said that they knew something was wrong when I was a child. Something was different about me. When given a choice of dolls or trucks I went to the trucks. It's just the way I've always been, I never thought about being any other way. I think I was born gay, I say it from the get-go. I think it was meant for me to be this way.
>
> (Sandie Martin)

> I was seven years old, and I came home crying because the other boys called me a sissy. And my mother said – and to this day, I'm so grateful to my mother for saying this – she said, 'Well, that's just the way you are, so there's no need to cry about it. You just have to be the way you are and every time they say that, you say, "Yes, I am, and that's the way I am; there's nothing I can do about it, and I don't care."' And I said, 'Well, I guess that's it.' And every time they said that I said, 'Yes, I am,' and they went, 'Oh.' And they never called me that again because they said, 'We're not getting the reaction anymore.' At that time, I needed what she said. I credit that with a lot of my sort of self-fulfillment as a gay man to this day.
>
> (Malcolm Wilson)

As Sandie's and Malcolm's quotations suggest, when 'determined'-account respondents say they or others 'always knew', they often are referring to an early awareness that they were less feminine than other girls, or less masculine than other boys. Here respondents invoke the well established commonsense belief that sissy boys, and to a less predictable extent tomboy girls, will mature into homosexual adults. . . . Of the 'determined' group, only Dan and Terry have no such memories of childhood gender nonconformity. . . .

The 'chosen'-account group was least likely to recall childhood gender nonconformity. Of the men, only Brian identifies as a childhood sissy.

> I had been persecuted by schoolmates in a perhaps typical way for a sissy boy, bad at sports. And you know, called 'faggot' and all that.
>
> (Brian Polaski)

Even though he owns to having been a sissy boy, he does not treat it as an indicator of underlying homosexuality . . . A few of the 'chosen' lesbians indicate that they were tomboys, and like Brian . . . they do not see their history of gender nonconformity as indicative of early homosexuality. If anything, they see it as an indication of an inchoate childhood feminism.

> I know I definitely never fell into what the media represented as young
> girls. Though I came from a middle-class family, I always felt that I
> was different. Which in retrospect everybody thinks that they're
> different. And I always preferred to play with boys and I couldn't stand
> to be around girls. Because I wore pants and most little girls wore
> dresses, and they didn't like to do the thins that I liked to do, more
> active types of things. And girls made me feel sort of inadequate, because
> they were a certain way and I felt I should be that way. I didn't want
> to be that way, as much as I felt I should be that way.
>
> (Sara Pritchard)

. . . [T]he 'determined' group has less heterosexual experience than the others;
just half of these respondents report any at all. Some recall that they enjoyed
heterosexual sex,[3] but less than with a partner of their own gender.

> I actually liked girls. I was having a good time, and enjoying sex with
> women as well. Not as much as men, but I guess there was a period,
> actually, at about eighteen, nineteen, when there were more girls than
> boys.
>
> (Dan Bartett)

> I've had sexual relationships with men, but the feeling wasn't there,
> the heart, caring wasn't there. Sex was good but that was about it.
>
> (Sandie Martin)

Others report that they never liked it.

> I had a girlfriend for a short time in high school, because she really
> desperately wanted it. We had sex but that wasn't very successful.
>
> (Brent McKenna)

> I dated a man when I was fourteen, fifteen years old. Because I started
> to feel, 'Well, maybe I am the only one. And maybe there is some-
> thing wrong with me. And maybe if I date everybody in my family will
> get off my back about when am I gonna start dating.' So I dated a man.
> From the first time he kissed me to the last time he kissed me, it didn't
> feel right. I couldn't kiss him. I tried to get myself to be sexual with
> him, and it was a fight. So I stopped.
>
> (Justine DiAngelo)

As Sandie's quotation suggests, what was missing from heterosexual sex was
often as much emotional as physical. Only one respondent in the 'determined'
group has ever been involved in a meaningful heterosexual relationship; Dan dated
a woman for two years in college. . . . [N]one of those who used the 'determined'
account ever thought of themselves as bisexual, even for a short time. . . .

Those who offer the 'chosen' account have more heterosexual experience than
those who offer the 'determined' account. All of the 'chosen' men, and all but

two of the 'chosen' women, have sexual experience with at least one person of the other gender. Nearly all say that their heterosexual experiences were enjoyable, but usually less so than their homosexual ones.

> I was involved on and off with the same woman for eighteen years. And she was better in bed than eighty-five per cent of the guys I've ever been with. But with men, a small percent of them, the emotion has been so great that I would not care to settle for anything else.
>
> (Edward Porter)

> I had been with men sexually, and I had been with women sexually. Speaking of mere sexuality, I enjoyed both. It was emotionally that I nowhere felt the same at all with men as I did with women.
>
> (Lois Hayes) . . .

'Chosen'-account respondents were also more likely than others to have been emotionally involved in a heterosexual relationship. Three women and two men had been married, or had lived with a heterosexual partner for a year or more. . . .

. . . [T]hree men and four women of the 'chosen'-account group see themselves as 'basically bisexual', and ground their 'chosen' account on that claim. The rest ground their 'chosen' account on something other than bisexuality, but nonetheless are more likely than 'determined' or 'mixed' respondents to believe that they have some bisexual potential. Many felt that they could be bisexual if they really wanted to. . . .

For men especially, the year 1969 marks the divide between two major cohorts, the pre- and post-Stonewall generations.[4] Although their ages range from thirty to sixty-three, all but one of the men of the 'determined'-account group are from the pre-Stonewall cohort. They came out young; the median age at which 'determined'-account respondents first took on a gay identity is fourteen, compared to twenty for the 'chosen' group. All but one of the 'chosen' group first took on a gay identity after 1969.

Very few of the women I interviewed came out before 1969, but Stonewall had less immediate effect on lesbians' than gay men's lives. The year 1980, which saw the first stirrings of the lesbian sexual revolution and the beginnings of lesbian-feminism's cultural decline, is probably more historically important. But cohort differences were slight between the 'determined' and 'chosen' lesbians. . . . The two groups are, however, distinguished by the ages at which they came out. Where 'determined'-account respondents typically 'grew up gay' (the median age at which they came out is twelve), 'chosen'-account respondents tended to come out as young adults (median age: twenty).

Because 'determined'-account respondents usually adopted a gay identity when they were children, they came out in relatively isolated contexts – they knew no lesbians or gay men, and sought out information that might explain their feelings. The feminists who offer a 'chosen' account, by contrast, became lesbians in a feminist atmosphere that supported their decisions. They were meeting, usually for the first time, other women who were lesbians, and other women who were questioning and changing their sexuality. . . . They discovered not only that lesbianism exists, but that it could offer them an entirely new way to understand their lives and their sexualities. . . . Most of the 'chosen' lesbians who came out in a feminist context remain actively involved in lesbian community life, frequently taking part in lesbian gatherings in public space, including social, cultural, and political events, meetings, and the like.

Unlike these women, the 'chosen'-account men, and the 'chosen'-account women who claim an underlying bisexual orientation, came out in relatively isolated contexts. Only Diane Rivera, whose mother had many lesbian and gay friends, came out in a setting that acknowledged the viability of a homosexual way of being. Today, most of them remain fairly isolated, with few or no lesbian and gay friends, and little contact with any gay community life.[5]

> When I first came out, I didn't feel especially that I'd come home. I felt as alien in the gay environment as I did in most environments at the time. It's never really changed that much; I still feel alienated.
>
> (Rick Gross)

Although they have had many sexual partners, half of the 'chosen' gay men have never been involved in a serious romantic relationship with another man, unlike the overwhelming majority of the men in the 'determined' and 'mixed' account groups. The bisexual 'chosen' lesbians, following a pattern more typical of women, have had lovers or are currently in a relationship, but are not a part of a public lesbian or gay community life. . . .

Coming out in an isolated context does not necessarily mean one will remain there. Although all of the 'determined'-account men came out on their own, today all are very involved in gay community life; as a group they are among the most socially and politically active people I interviewed. Most of the 'determined'-account lesbians, on the other hand, have remained relatively isolated, living private coupled lives . . . Table 1 summarizes the various ways that 'chosen' and 'determined' respondents are and have been isolated from an integrated into gay and lesbian community life.

In some ways 'chosen' and 'determined' respondents' experiences are radically different: 'determined' respondents 'grew up gay', identifying in some way as homosexual continuously from an early age, while 'chosen' respondents did not. 'Chosen' respondents were considerably more likely than those who offer the 'determined' account to have experienced heterosexual relationships and sexual encounters, and less likely to report that their childhood behavior crossed gender

Table 1 Coming out context by current integration into lesbian/gay community life

Came out in	Currently isolated	Currently integrated
Isolated context	'Chosen' men 'Determined' women Bisexual 'chosen' women	'Determined' men
Integrated context		Feminist 'chosen' women

boundaries. 'Determined'-account respondents do not consider themselves bisexual and never did, while 'chosen'-account respondents – even those who do not see themselves as 'basically bisexual' – once identified as bisexual, or believe they could develop a bisexual orientation if they wanted to. 'Determined' and 'chosen'-account respondents' relationships to lesbian and gay community life, however, compare in more complicated ways that differ by gender (a topic that will be addressed again below).

'Determined' and 'chosen' accounts seem to reflect very different experiences, sometimes diverging early in respondents' lives. Many would conclude that they represent different underlying orientations, following an argument that would go something like this: respondents who offer the 'determined' account do so because they actually were born gay or became so very early on. They are exclusively and unalterably homosexual. Those who offer the 'chosen' account, on the other hand, are probably bisexually oriented, whether they know it or not, and the various stories they tell are just different ways of representing that. These two groups are truly different types of people, whose biologies or histories have left them with different internal configurations of sexual desire. My research is not designed to test such a hypothesis – if it could be tested at all – but I am generally disinclined to privilege such a 'professional diagnosis' of an individual's sexuality over her own sense of it. What I will show is that the rest of the individuals I interviewed – the largest group, those using the dominant account – exhibit a much more complex relationship between experience and account, 'underlying reality' and its 'representations', and are more resistant to a facile judgment that they are distinguished by some shared underlying orientation.

The mixed account

Like those who use the 'determined' account, many of the 'mixed'-account respondents resisted my use of the term 'decide'. . . . Many of these respondents, like nearly all the 'determined' group, had experienced continuous awareness of homosexual feelings. As Al and Gary puts it, they 'always knew'.

But not all 'mixed'-account respondents experienced such continuity; some can recall a period before they were gay or lesbian – or, as they put it, before they *knew* they were. A few of these respondents who experienced discontinuity recall that their homoerotic feelings appeared after some years of feeling relatively asexual. . . .

> I knew when I was very young that I did not want to get married and did not want to have children, but I thought that I was going to be a nun. So I thought that I didn't want to get married and didn't want to have children because I was going to be a nun. It was very simple. Then, when I was nineteen I became friends with a woman who was a lesbian, but I didn't even know what it *was*. I had no idea that this existed, and I was fascinated to understand this. . . . [Later] I sat in the seminary library and said, 'I think I'm gay.'
>
> (Katie Lee)

Most experienced discontinuity by changing from a heterosexual to a gay identity. Their earliest sexual feelings were heteroerotic; these were supplemented or
replaced by desires for members of their own gender. . . .

Whether they were previously heterosexual or previously asexual, many
'mixed'-account respondents experienced a discontinuity in their sexualities. For
the majority of such respondents, this separated their lives before and after
becoming gay or recognizing their homosexuality. But for two women, the discontinuity was more complicated: both grew up with some awareness of sexual interest
in women but later become involved in serious relationships with men, and came
to believe that they were no longer homosexual. This changed their sexual self-
concepts. Years later, sexual desire toward women returned. So far they have
come out, returned to straight life, and then come out again. Their accounts explain
this rupture in what they otherwise see as a consistent lifelong sexual preference.
Neither dismisses her heterosexual relationship entirely, but each portrays it as an
aberration, and her return to lesbianism as inevitable. . . .

> C.S.:   I went through a very weird time of falling for the wrong
>   women. I got very, very fed up with everything, and that's
>   how I met John. I was twenty-eight when we started living
>   together.
> V.W.:   So as the relationship went on, did you still think of yourself
>   as a lesbian?
> C.S.:   No. I also didn't think of myself as — I think I thought of myself
>   as nothing, sexwise. I was living with a man who was like my
>   father. He was like the father I always wanted. . . .
> V.W.:   Did you ever think of yourself as bisexual?
> C.W.:   Yes. When I first met John. Because I liked him, I liked him
>   a lot. After that period of where I couldn't find anybody and
>   I was falling for all the wrong people, that's when I thought,
>   'Maybe it's not the wrong people, that's when I thought,
>   'Maybe it's not the wrong people, maybe I'm with the wrong
>   sex. Maybe I really should be with a man. Maybe I should give
>   it a try.' That's what I think John was all about, was giving it
>   a try. In giving it a try, we developed a very strong relation-
>   ship.
>   (Cathy Saunders)

The other respondents experienced a simpler form of discontinuity, between their
pre-gay and gay selves.

Table 2 summarizes the three account-groups' experiences of continuity and
discontinuity. As we have already seen, 'determined'-account respondents generally 'always knew', while 'chosen'-account respondents have a discontinuous history
of sexual self-understanding. The 'mixed'-account group is divided, with a decided
gender difference: Most of the women's homosexuality has been discontinuous,
while most of the men experienced continuity.

Continuity/discontinuity is a dichotomous variable not only as I operationalize

Table 2 Account type by continuous awareness of homosexuality

Gay men[a]	Continuity	Discontinuity	Total
No choice	4	1	5
Partial choice	15	7	22
Total choice	1	5	6
Total	20	13	33
Lesbians[b]			
No choice	4	0	4
Partial choice	6	17	23
Total choice	1	11	12
Total	11	28	39

Notes

a   Chi-square 6.18, dof = 2, $p < 0.05$. Because this sample is not randomly selected, I am not using this statistic to estimate probability, but simply as a convenient device for determining which relationships I will treat as noteworthy.

b   Chi-square 12.55, dof - 2. $p < 0.01$

it but as respondents use it as well. Many of those who report continuity asserted early in the interview that they 'always knew', frequently using those very words. Others were just as quick to explain that they 'didn't find out until later'.[6]

Respondents of the 'mixed' group who experienced discontinuity between their former and current sexualities treated that as a problem to be explained. . . . They were as likely as those who were continuously homosexual to believe that they were born gay. . . .

All of the 'mixed' respondents who experienced discontinuity explained it the same way, by invoking an underlying, continuous and previously unknown homosexual orientation: They were always homosexual but didn't always know it. None believe they became homosexual at the same time that they discovered it. They gather evidence for this belief via retrospective interpretation (Schur 1979), a re-reading of their pre homosexual pasts in terms of their present sexual identities.[7]

> v.w.:   Could you tell me how you came to decide that you're a lesbian?
>
> k.h.:   It was a fairly gradual process. Retrospectively, there were probably earlier indications of it, but the time I was really conscious was probably in my freshman year of college. It was just something that I had been missing that I just thought, 'Oh, why didn't I think of that before?'
>
> (Kate Hargrave)

> I think – I mean, in retrospect – I feel that I always was a lesbian. But
> I've only been out four or five years. It was this gradual process. I went
> to Catholic school for thirteen years, let me say that (*laughs*).
>
> (Karen McNally)

Many of these 'mixed'-group respondents actively performed this recasting of
the past as part of their coming out.

> When I came out I looked back on the types of games I liked to play
> as a child, or the kind of toys I wanted to have, or what my goals
> were. And I think I probably saw them differently.
>
> (Cindy Schwarz) . . .

> D.R.:   The year after I graduated from high school, this woman I was
>   going with said, 'Do you think you might be gay?' And without
>   even thinking about it, I said, 'Yeah.' It was that simple, and
>   then I just like took the ball and ran.
> V.W.:   Had you been thinking about it before she asked that?
> D.R.:   No.
> V.W.:   Did you surprise yourself, answering that way?
> D.R.:   No. It was like immediately I went through my whole life, and
>   took a whole inventory of like where that fit, where it fit into
>   my life.
>
> (Dwight Russell, 'mixed')

Their accounts must square a relatively late onset of 'awareness' with a claim
to a sexual orientation that was determined early on. As such, these respondents
explain the discontinuity so as to explain it away, allowing them to claim that they
were, in fact, always gay. Some use the language of denial and repression to explain
away their pre-homosexual pasts:

> I think I discovered something that I'd been hiding from myself. And
> I feel like I was discovering something that I knew since I was twelve
> years old. But I just never wanted to face up to it.
>
> (Sharon Halpern, 'mixed') . . .

The most notable feature of these explanations is that half the women mention
their early ignorance of lesbian existence. The discovery of lesbianism (usually
through meeting women who identified as lesbians) was an important feature of
these stories of discontinuity. It wasn't just that they could now put a name
on their homosexuality, or that they could now see that there were others like
them. Rather, the feelings came up only after these women discovered the possibility of lesbianism; the experience is much like that of many 'chosen' lesbians,
but interpreted differently. In the 'chosen' account, involvement with feminism
enabled the respondent to become a lesbian. In the 'mixed' account, as illustrated
in the quotations below, feminism enabled the respondent to realize she already
was one.

When I was nineteen I became friends with a woman who was a lesbian, but I didn't even know what it *was*. I had no idea that this existed, and I was fascinated to understand this. I decided to do a sociology paper on female homosexuality so I started reading everything I could. And as I was reading stuff like *Lesbian/Woman* and *Our Bodies, Ourselves*, I started to think that that was me. I could relate to it, several of the things that people said. And it got me real scared.

(Katie Lee, 'mixed')

When I was in high school National Gay Task Force came and did a spiel. This was in '69, '70. And they were all excited about being gay and I didn't know what that was all about. Now I realize that was really like a seed, early, very early on. And later, in grad school, I learned that one of my sister's best friends was a lesbian. She lived in a notorious lesbian house at college and I went to visit. I stayed with them. And they were real nice women, I thought. And I thought, 'Oh, gosh, I'm attracted to them, too.'

(Ruth Chang, 'mixed')

Almost none of the men were unaware of male homosexuality in a parallel fashion; their stories of discontinuity are stories of denial and repression.

Finally, one woman's story of continuity involves the repudiation of her earlier, 'chosen' account. Suzie Gluck, a thirty-five-year-old Jewish woman from Brooklyn, came out in a feminist context, and at that time would have sounded much like the women I interviewed who gave the feminist 'chosen' account. But over time, Suzie replaced that account with a 'mixed' one.

Well, it felt I think initially like a choice I was making. But then, the more time went on, it felt like something I was really discovering about myself. I thought at the time that I didn't want to be straight, that I wanted to be a lesbian. But looking back I realize now that it was really more accepting who I was.

In the seventeen years between her coming out and the time of our interview, Suzie had earned a master's degree in social work and embarked on a career as a therapist serving a lesbian and gay clientele. Both endeavours would increase her exposure to the dominant account and its logic.

Although the 'mixed'-respondents' coming-out stories differ, with some 'always knowing' of their homosexuality and some 'discovering' it late on, those who experienced discontinuity cast their stories to minimize that difference. Their actual experiences of discontinuity are similar to those of the 'chosen'-account respondents, but these respondents elect to use a 'mixed' account, which aligns them with people who were continuously aware. Although they cannot themselves claim to have 'always known', they do claim that the underlying reality of a homosexual orientation was 'always there'. The discontinuity, then, is for them only in the state of knowing. The state of being, conceived as an entirely separate realm, is continuous. 'Mixed'-account respondents' experiences of continuity and discontinuity do not fall some-where between those of the 'determined' and 'chosen' groups, nor do they combine them. The respondents who offer the 'mixed' account recall continuity (like the 'determined' group) or discontinuity (like the 'chosen' group). Their experiences overlap the other two account groups, but they use an account that covers both kinds of experience, uniting them under the umbrella of a single account.

A similar pattern occurs in the distribution of all sorts of experiences among the 'mixed'-account respondents. Some resemble those who offer the 'determined' account, while others resemble those who offer the 'chosen' account. The 'mixed' group includes, for example, individuals whose childhood gender conduct ranges from gender-crossing to gender-typical. About half the men of the 'mixed'-account group identified their childhood gender conduct as being like other boys their age. . . .

The other half of the 'mixed' men said that as children they were 'effeminate' or 'sissy'. Most of these men treated that as an early sign of homosexual orientation.

> It was clearly from a real early stage. I was sort of a sissy boy, not particularly athletic. So in the way that kids knew things, I knew it just in myself. Then as my mind started kicking, around then or something, I remember reading books about homosexuality.
>
> (Al Davis)

> Being gay had been part of my subconscious being all my life. Being five years old, and not knowing what these crushes on these other boys were, and wishing I would wake up in the morning and be a girl.
>
> (Dwight Russell)

When these men recall a childhood of gender-crossing behavior, they are recalling the gap between their behavior and the local class- and ethnicity-specific expectations for heterosexual males. Their behavior may have conformed nicely to local expectations for homosexual males. . . .

Unlike the term 'sissy', the assignation 'tomboy' is not entirely insulting. The young girl who aspires to boyish pursuits earns a begrudged respect, for those pursuits are considered superior by boys and girls alike (see Schur, 1984). Although, like the men, about half of the 'mixed'-account women engaged in gender-crossing behavior as children, there is a qualitative difference in the meaning assigned to it. Some claim childhood tomboyism as early evidence of homosexual orientation.

> In grade school I suppose I was the stereotypical model, in the sense that I was very athletic, played tackle football with the boys, and all that sort of thing. I enjoyed that more than doing what girls did at that age. Everyone called me a tomboy.
>
> (Kate Hargrove)

But claiming a tomboy past is also claiming evidence of characteristics that are valued in many lesbian communities: physical activity and athleticism, independence, and a rejection or disregard for the typical expectations of femininity. . . .

Half the women who offer the 'mixed' account point out that they were tomboys, but not all use that information to indicate their innate sexual orientation. Some talk about it the same way the 'chosen'-account lesbians do, the way it is presented in the classical lesbian novel of the 1970s, *Rubyfruit Jungle*: as an early and intuitive understanding that much of what femininity expresses is submission.

Just over half the 'mixed'-account men told of some sexual experience with women, while nearly all the 'mixed'-account women had experienced some heterosexual sex. But equivalent behavior cannot be taken to carry equivalent meanings for men and women. These women's heterosexual experience may be unrelated to their accounts of choice because, for women, heterosexual experience itself is often not fully chosen. While we could assume that the gay men of the 'mixed' group in some way wanted their heterosexual experiences – even if they wanted them only in response to pressure to behave heterosexually, as was often the case – we cannot make the same assumption of the 'mixed'-account lesbians. Certainly, some of the encounters related above took place because the woman desired the man sexually. Others occurred because she wanted the experience itself, perhaps to attempt to prove to herself or to others that she was straight. But some also certainly merely went along, participating in sexual encounters they would not have initiated. And even in a group of this size, some were coerced or forced. Cindy Schwartz's experience is illustrative:

> He pursued me, and once I was up in his room in the dorm and we got really drunk and he ended up having sex. And I didn't want to be having sex. So I woke up in the middle of the night and realized I wasn't home, and just got up and went downstairs to my room.

So due to the current construction of heterosexuality as male-dominated, heterosexual experience is nearly a constant among these lesbians. (Other researchers have also found high levels of heterosexual experience among lesbians. See Bell and Winberg 1978; Blumstein and Schwartz 1983.)

Both the men and women of the 'mixed' account group were likely to have been romantically involved in a heterosexual relationship than to have experienced sex, with more women than men recalling such relationships. Most 'mixed'-account women had been emotionally involved with a man, and about half of the 'mixed'-account men had been involved with a woman. Some of those relationships had been serious; two men and five women had been married or long-term cohabitators. Both of the men knew they were gay before they married, and both told their wives. . . .

Two of the married women, Cathy Saunders and Celia Daugherty . . . also had identified themselves as lesbians before they married, but had come to believe they were no longer. The remaining three women did not think of themselves as gay when they married or moved in with a man. Cindy Schwartz, a white thirty-two-year-old artist from Massachusetts who works as a carpenter, was married for five years.

> I met him in a class, and I was really attracted to him. So I pursued him, really. I had to work really hard on him, because I wasn't his usual type. We moved in together, and got married in about a year.

Another two women, one each from the 'mixed' and 'chosen' groups, were involved with a man at the time of the interview. They account for these anomalous relationships in surprising terms. Leah Rosenthal, a twenty-one-year-old manager of a family business, was married when we met, having wed to fulfill the expectations of her very strict Orthodox Jewish parents.

> When I first started thinking I was a lesbian, I thought, 'Maybe I'm just afraid to get married.' But now I'm married, and I am sure I prefer women. My therapist says that lesbianism is childish, that it's immature, and I sort of agree. But I don't care. I told him, 'Then I'll stay a child.'

Leah is frightened by the prospect of being alienated from her family and her religious community; nonetheless, she does see her relationship with her husband as at odds with what she really wants, which is to be with women.[8]

In contrast, Kate Hargrove, a twenty-seven-old magazine editor from a white, working-class Catholic family, is currently involved in a voluntary relationship with a man. Although compulsory heterosexuality is certainly a reality that diminishes the extent to which Kate's relationship with a man can be called a choice, her situation is quite different from Leah's: Kate's family did not directly pressure her to enter this relationship, and in fact are unaware of it. She came out eight years ago, and her current heterosexual involvement does not seem to alter her lesbian identity.

> I met him through friends and he is perfectly aware of my background, but we just get along very well and it's very comfortable. And I don't think it's ever going to – I *know* that it's not going to ever be anything that will have the emotional significance that a relationship with a woman could have for me. I think we basically have a very nice friendship that also has this other sexual element at the moment and I think eventually we'll have to lose that and go back to a friendship. There was a point at which I thought perhaps it might develop more than it had, but I think if that was going to happen it would already have happened.

Leah, who is in a marriage that she entered under rather coercive circumstances, thinks of herself as lesbian by choice, while Kate, who is involved in a heterosexual relationship that she chose, considers her lesbianism to be an innate, unchosen orientation. Commonsense reasoning would predict the opposite: Leah is a real lesbian, whose current circumstances are at odds with her true identity. Kate, on the other hand, must really be bisexual, since she chose her heterosexual affiliation more freely. Apparently, there are reasons for claiming to have chosen or not chosen to be a lesbian that surpass the fit between that claim and one's personal history.

But Leah and Kate are exceptional; most discuss their (past) relationships with men in ways that are consistent with their identity account. In the examples below, Cathy Saunders, whose account is of the 'mixed' type, explains her ten-year heterosexual relationship in terms of her lesbianism. Sarah Pritchard, of the 'chosen' group, does not offer such an explanation, allowing the apparent contradiction between that experience and her current lesbianism to stand.

> That's what John was all about, was giving it a try. In giving it a try, we developed a very strong relationship.
>
> (Cathy Saunders, 'mixed')

> When we split, it was not for lack of love. I just had to get out on my own.
>
> (Sara Pritchard, 'chosen')

In general, 'chosen'-account respondents tend to embrace the contradiction between their past heterosexual experience and their current lesbian identities, and 'mixed'-account respondents tend to explain it in a way that supports a belief in a continuous underlying homosexual orientation.

A final note on the gender of sexual partners: Barbara Linders, a white twenty-five-year-old artist who works in a bookstore, is currently in a serious relationship with a pre-operative male-to-female transsexual. They clearly consider themselves a lesbian couple, and have been hurt and surprised when they have been rejected by individual lesbians and lesbian organizations. To Barbara, who offers the 'mixed' account, her lover *is* a woman in every sense that matters:

> V.W.: Did you ever think of yourself as bisexual?
> B.L.: No, I never could really picture myself being with a man. My lover's a different case; it doesn't really matter what her body's like. I really think she's woman inside, and that makes a difference.

Most respondents, and the structure of the interview itself, take the gender distinction between men and women for granted, and we shared an implicit definition of whom we included in the term 'woman'. Barbara's relationship brings up questions that are beyond the scope of this study, but it does highlight the fact that one may define an erotic relationship between a 'biological female' and a 'biological male' as lesbian.

Perhaps not surprisingly, given the relatively high incidence of heterosexual experience, significant minorities of both the men and women of the 'mixed' group report that they had once considered themselves bisexual. For some, that bisexual identification was a very brief stage . . .

. . . Others considered themselves bisexual for years:

> I think originally I thought I was bisexual. Actually, it was hard for me to accept the word 'lesbian'. It wasn't being with a woman that scared me, it was the not being with men. . . . I think at one point when I was sixteen, I walked into my shrink's office and said, 'Listen, I'm not bisexual. I'm definitely gay.'
>
> (Paula Weiss)

A few respondents of the 'mixed' group, two women and two men, identify themselves as bisexual, at the same time that they describe themselves as gay or lesbian.

> I would say that I'm probably bisexual, but more of a lesbian, and I definitely like to identify myself as a lesbian, and not as bisexual.
>
> (Sharon Halpern)

> In a way I still think of myself as bisexual, but I definitely consider myself gay. I don't think there's a lot of support on either side for being bisexual. That's really lacking. But I have made a commitment to my relationship at present, and it's important to me within this relationship to consider myself gay.
>
> (Dwight Russell)

A few more express that in some way they are gay without being exclusively homosexual, although they do not use the word bisexual . . .

> V.W.: Did you ever think of yourself as bisexual?
> B.F.: No, although I have a son, and I've been with many women. I totally accepted my homosexuality at a very young age, and in addition to that, I knew that I could also have sex with women.
>
> (Billy Fine) . . .

When members of the 'mixed'-account group speak of bisexuality as a temporary and incorrect self-concept, they maintain the existence of a consistent and true homosexual orientation even in the face of their sometimes considerable heterosexual experience. Some of those who offer the 'chosen' account had less heterosexual experience than some of the 'mixed' group. 'Mixed' and 'chosen'-respondents' experiences with bisexual identification overlap; some of the 'mixed' respondents embrace an underlying bisexuality, while a few 'chosen' respondents relegate the concept to their pasts. Clearly, feeling that one is at least somewhat sexually and/or emotionally attracted toward the other gender does not necessarily lead one to claim the 'chosen' account. But it does seem to be difficult to believe that one exercised complete choice in the absence of any heterosexual attraction in the present or past; all the respondents who describe this pattern offer either the 'determined' or the 'mixed' account.

A pattern emerges whereby the 'mixed' group's range of experiences, behaviors, and self-concepts overlap those of the 'chosen' and 'determined' groups. Some grew up gay; others became homosexual later, experiencing a discovery. Some were typically gendered; others were tomboys and sissies; some had extensive heterosexual experience, some little or none. Some never thought of themselves as bisexual, some once did, and a few still do.

Over half of the 'mixed'-account women came out over the course of the 1980s, at a median age of twenty. The vast majority of the 'mixed'-account men are part of the post-Stonewall generation; they came out at a median age of nineteen. A good number came out in earlier years, and at younger ages. Most are involved in gay and/or lesbian community life, though some lead very private lives, and a few are isolated from other gay men and lesbians. Some of the 'mixed' group came out in relatively isolated contexts; most of these adopted a gay identity as children, and most are men. Half of the women came out after first getting to know other lesbians, and a very few came out in a feminist context, but did not end up adopting a 'chosen' account, as did most of the women who came out in the context of the women's movement. . . .

Choosing a story

Respondents' accounts do not merely recount their experiences; they are stories told to fit those experiences into a coherent, conventionalized story. The largest group of respondents, those who use the 'mixed' account to speak for themselves and others, is an amalgam of individuals whose personal histories of love, sex, and gender differ profoundly. Many 'mixed'-account respondents always knew they were gay, never thought they were or could be bisexual, have little heterosexual experience, and were seen as atypical children for their gender; they *could* use the 'determined' account, but they don't. Other 'mixed' respondents changed their identity from heterosexual to homosexual, thought of themselves as bisexual (or perhaps still do), have a good deal of heterosexual experience, which they may have enjoyed, and were not considered tomboys or sissies; they *could* tell their stories using the 'chosen' account, but they do not. Most respondents, whatever their experience, utilize the 'mixed' account. As the dominant account, it assimilates alternatives; there is no experience it cannot be used to explain. That is, in fact, the point of its appeal.

The 'chosen' and 'determined' accounts are less robust; if this sample included only those who use one of these two accounts, my conclusions about the relationship between experience and account would be different, for the two groups are distinguished on nearly every measure: heterosexual experience, bisexual iden tification, childhood gender behavior, age at coming out. But these are not the only two account types, so the pattern is more complex. For example, though nearly all 'determined' respondents recall continuous awareness of their homosexuality, the reverse is not true; not all respondents who recall continuity offer the 'determined' account. Similarly, while nearly everyone who offers the 'chosen' account experienced discontinuity, not everyone with a discontinuous identity history offers the 'chosen' account. Most respondents, whatever their experience of identity continuity, use the 'mixed' account. Respondents want to use it, and so they are willing to do the cognitive and emotional work to fit their experience to its contours.

Nowhere is this more evident than when many 'mixed'-account respondents retrospectively interpret their pasts in order to create narrative continuity in the face of a discontinuous history. 'I was always gay but didn't know it' is a recognizable claim that is consistent with commonsense understandings of sexual orientation. Its user is welcomed under the umbrella of the dominant account. . . .

For most respondents, accounts mark their similarity to others, not their distance from them. This is particularly so for respondents who use the 'mixed' account, for they tell not only a shared story but in fact the only story, the one that explains how it is for everyone. By using the 'mixed' account in one's personal narrative, an individual both draws upon and contributes to a collective discourse that is a piece of the process of sexuality formation. Like Omi and Winant's concept of 'racial formation', sexual formation is 'the historical process by which [sexual] categories are created, inhabited, transformed, and destroyed' (1994: 55). Accounts are the site of a dynamic interaction between collective and individual social processes that create homosexuality – and by extension heterosexuality – as categories.

The collective account also aims to neutralize stigma and argue for legitimacy. It portrays homosexuality as an essential and immutable characteristic, and at the same time recognizes the political importance of choosing to come out – to one's self, to friends and family, to a public. We do not choose to be gay, but we can, do, and must choose to come out. The account tells the story of a collective strategy. That strategy was the brainchild of the post-Stonewall generation, for whom 'Come out, come out, wherever you are' was an imperative. And among the men in this sample it is those respondents who came out before 1969 who are most likely to hold to an account other than the dominant one. The men who use the dominant account, on the other hand, nearly all came out after Stonewall, and are generally well integrated into gay community life.

That community life was relatively sex-segregated throughout the 1970s, due as much to the explosive growth of urban gay male ghettoes (Levine 1979) as to the separatism of lesbian-feminism. As such, gay male and lesbian identity accounts may have converged less in the 1970s than they did a decade later. Among the 'mixed'-account lesbians in this sample, two-thirds came out during the 1980s, the years when joint gay-lesbian organizations multiplied under the pressure of AIDS and the right-wing backlash, and when lesbian-feminism lost its central place in lesbian culture (Stein 1992).

The 'determined'-account group is so small in this sample that it is difficult to analyze. The men who offer this account are well integrated into gay community life, and tend to be older and wealthier than the men who use the 'mixed' account. But like the 'mixed'-account men, they assume that theirs is the account that speaks for everyone. In their eyes, their account is the dominant account, and clearly the distinction between the 'determined' and 'mixed' accounts is slight compared to the gulf dividing the 'chosen' account from the other two. The 'determined'-account women, on the other hand, do not assume that theirs is the dominant account. Because 'chosen' accounts are more viable, and more common, for lesbians than for gay men, these women must be aware that they don't speak for everyone.

The four women whose 'chosen' account was based on an underlying bisexual orientation resembled the 'chosen'-account men in their tendency to be only tangentially connected to lesbian community life; they offer an account that, at the time these interviews took place, lacked the authority of a collective experience. Since that time many women and men have asserted a bisexual identity and have successfully pressed for recognition in lesbian and gay-movement organizations, particularly on college campuses. As we have seen, many 'chosen' and 'mixed' respondents told me that their underlying, basic, or technical orientations were bisexual; perhaps some of them today identify as bisexual rather than lesbian or gay. But such an outcome is by no means certain, for I do not see these individuals as bisexuals waiting for the chance to speak the truth. Identities have proliferated, not simply become more and more accurate.

If, in 1988, the bisexual version of the 'chosen' account remained an individual story, the feminist 'chosen' account was clearly a collective one; all of the women who use it came out in a feminist context of one sort or another. (I do not posit that exposure to feminism 'produces' lesbian-feminists; a few 'mixed'-account respondents also came out in a feminist context but do not use the 'chosen' account.) The feminist context was the immediate source of their account, but the questions remain of why they ever were drawn to it, why they ever made it work for them.

I have identified some of the interpretive work that those who use the 'mixed' account perform to make their experiences fit it. What do the lesbian-feminists who use a 'chosen' account do to maintain it as truth? This process is less visible than the 'mixed'-account respondents' process. Although some of the 'chosen'-account respondents are selectively interpreting their pasts when they make a point of stating that they had enjoyed sex with men (a few offer this information within their first statements in the interview), they never reinterpret their pasts to reach this point.

I have thus far left the feminist 'chosen' account relatively intact, giving the appearance of assumed truth. I have certainly paid more attention to the dominant account, not to claim that it is false, but to determine why it is the preferred truth among many possible ones. The alternative accounts, on the other hand, already appear to be untrue, and those who use them are already seen as false lesbians. . . . [T]he lesbian-feminist 'chosen' account . . . distinguishes lesbians from gay men and provides a political link to heterosexual women, providing good reason – aside from accuracy – to utilize this account.

While many 'mixed'-account respondents have life histories that could easily fit a 'determined' account, and many have histories that could easily fit a 'chosen' account, gender complicates the picture. If the women who use the 'mixed' account were to use another, most would best fit their stories to a 'chosen' account. And if the 'mixed'-account men were to switch accounts, it would most likely be to a 'determined' account. Put another way, those variables that tend to differentiate 'determined' from 'chosen'-account respondents also tend to differentiate the gay men from the lesbians. In both pairings, the latter group is more likely to have experienced discontinuity of sexual identity, and to have more heterosexual experience. So the 'mixed' account assimilates not only varying experiences but different genders as well; it creates the appearance of similarity between lesbians and gay men. Walt Richardson describes that appearance perfectly:

Gay men and lesbians are simply two sides of exactly the same coin.
(Walt Richardson)

It's a similarity that is central to the representation of homosexuality as a sexual orientation that floats free from gender rather than a gender inversion. As Chauncey (1982–83) has persuasively argued, the 'homosexuality' concept fully replaced the 'gender inversion' concept only when it was eventually applied to women as well as men. But applying it to women requires the retrospective interpretation of their pasts, a vigorous effort made less often by men. So it is women who perform the lion's share of the cognitive and emotional labor that keeps the dominant account in place. . . . [T]he dominant account does more for and requires less of men than of women.

Notes

1   Ponse (1978) distinguishes between lesbians whose identity history is continuous, whom she calls 'primary', and those whose identity histories are discontinuous. The latter characterizes the lesbians whose identities Ponse terms 'elective', a term which tends to conflate choice and continuity. Here I am building on Ponse's insights by distinguishing between these.

2   The process of taking on a heterosexual identity is not parallel to the process of taking on a lesbian or gay identity. Most people who identify as straight never 'decided' on that identity, or 'discovered' that orientation, or 'admitted' those desires. It is entirely possible to adopt a heterosexual identity as a default, simply by allowing the nearly universal assumption of heterosexuality to settle upon one.

3   I allowed respondents to define 'sexual experience' for themselves. When they talked about heterosexual experience, they were nearly always referring to intercourse, which is the act that 'counts' as sex in the popular conception.

4   A third cohort, those men who came out after the beginning of the AIDS epidemic, has now passed its first decade. At the time of these interviews, it was nascent.

5   I use the term 'gay community life' instead of 'gay community' to underline the point that there are many communities, and many ways to be involved in them.

6   Among lesbians the distinction between those who 'grew up gay' and those who didn't is commonly recognized. One researcher demonstrates that this form of difference is live enough to be a significant piece of relationship dynamics, and she even suggests that continuous and discontinuous lesbians tend to be drawn to one another (Burch 1993).

7   Ponse (1978) calls the process 'biographical reconstruction'.

8   It was clearly a difficult time for her, and I have often wondered where she is now. After our interview, we talked casually for a while and I told her that I, too, had come out when I was married and that everything had eventually worked out. She rose immediately from her chair and bolted from the room, scarcely saying goodbye. I did not hear from her again.

References

Bell, A. P. and Weinberg, M. S. (1978) *Homosexualities*. New York: Simon & Schuster.
Blumstein, P. and Schwartz, P. (1983) 'American couples', *Urban Life*, 5: 79–98.
Card, C. (1995) *Lesbian Choices*. New York: Columbia University Press.

Chauncey, G. (1982–3) 'From sexual inversion to homosexuality: medicine and the changing conceptualisation of female deviance', *Salmagundi*, 58–9: 114–46.

Levine, M. (1979) 'Gay ghetto', in M. Levine (ed.) *Gay Men: The Sociology of Male Homosexuality*. New York: Harper Colophon.

Omi, M. and Winant, H. (1994) *Racial Formation in the United States*. New York: Routledge.

Ponse, B. (1978) *Identities in the Lesbian World: The Social Construction of Self*. Westport CT: Greenwood Press.

Rosenfels, P. (1971) *Homosexuality: The Psychology of the Creative Process*. New York: Ninth Street Center.

Schur, E. (1979) *Interpreting Deviance*. New York: Harper & Row.

Schur, E. (1984) *Labelling Women Deviant*. Englewood Cliffs NJ: Prentice-Hall.

Stein, A. (1992) 'Sisters and queers: the decentering of lesbian feminism', *Socialist Review*, 22: 33–55.

Chapter 41

Richard Ekins

THE CAREER PATH OF THE MALE FEMALER

Here Richard Ekins uses a grounded theory to analyse the crossing of gender boundaries from male to female. This approach focuses on the themes which emerge from his ethnographic data. It enables Ekins to explore the complex interactional and interpretive processes entailed in 'male femaling'.

From R. Ekins and D. King (eds) *Blending Genders: Social Aspects of Cross-dressing and Sex Changing*, London: Routledge (1966).

MALE FEMALING TAKES PLACE in three major modes: body femaling, erotic femaling and gender femaling. These are broadly comparable with facets of sex, sexuality and gender, respectively, where 'sex' refers to the biological and physiological aspects of the division of humans into male and female; 'sexuality' to 'those' matters pertaining to the potential arousability and engorgement of the genitals' (Plummer 1979: 53); and 'gender' to the socio-cultural correlates of the division of the sexes.

Body femaling refers to the desires and practices of femalers to female their bodies. This might include desired, actual or simulated changes in both primary and secondary characteristics of 'sex'. Thus it would include chromosomal change (not presently possible), gonadal, hormonal, morphological and neural change, at one level (Money 1969); and change to facial hair, body hair, scalp hair, vocal chords, skeletal shape and musculature, at another level (Lukacs 1978).

Erotic femaling refers to femaling which is intended to, or has the effect of, arousing sexual desire or excitement. Although the term might be stretched to include femaling that is intended to arouse, or that does arouse, sexual desire or excitement in others, the particular feature of erotic femaling in cross-dressers is that the desire, or excitement, is aroused in the femaler himself by his own femaling and/or through the awareness of others of his own erotic femaling.

Gender femaling refers to the manifold ways in which femalers adopt the behaviors, emotions and cognitions socio-culturally associated with being female. Gender femaling need not be associated with erotic femaling.

In the process of femaling, persons (bodies, selves and identities), actions, events, and objects (clothes and the paraphernalia of femininity) are variously implicated. They are, or become over time, in varying degrees and with varying degrees of interconnectedness, sexed, sexualised and/or gendered . . . Thus, in body femaling, for example, the characteristics of the genetic female's (sexed) body are taken on by the genetic male's body which becomes correspondingly sexed as female whereas in erotic femaling the gendered object 'petticoat' may become eroticized (sexualized). Again, in gender femaling the gendered mannerism sitting down in 'ladylike fashion' may be adopted by the gender femaler as a facet of his gendered presentation of self (Goffman 1969, 1979). This is an exceedingly complex business, the components of which may be best illustrated with reference to the major phases in an ideal-typical career path of the male femaler that emerged from my analysis of the staged (Glaser 1978: 97–100) male femalings of over 200 informants. The analysis reports the results of field work carried out in major British cities and life-history work with selected male cross-dressers and sex-changers, both since 1980.

Phase one: beginning femaling

In this first phase of femaling the emphasis is upon initial femaling behaviors – deviancy theorists would call primary deviance.

An incident of cross-dressing occurs. It might occur by chance. It might be encouraged by others. It might take place in childhood, adolescence or adulthood. It might be more or less charged with affect. The cross-dressing incident, which I take to include the context and accompanying feelings and cognitions, may evoke varying degrees of certainty about its meaning. It could be remembered, re-experienced, or reconstructed as primarily erotic or sexual, especially when originally accompanied by perceived sexual excitement and arousal. It could be remembered, re-experienced or reconstructed in terms of fascination, sensuousness, mystery or awe. Further, the experience may be conceptualized in terms of the tactile, the visual or the olfactory, or any combination of them, and with varying degrees of focus and precision.

. . . In terms of the interrelations between sex, sexuality and gender, the feature of this phase is undifferentiated. There is undifferentiation because in this phase the untoward incident is dismissed, not taken seriously, or is seen as a temporary aberration and no subtle distinctions are made. There is also undifferentiation because the individual lacks not only the conceptual wherewithal, but also a sense of purpose, direction and volition, and, indeed, the means to gain them through interaction with others or relevant literature.

As likely as not, he will simply and inchoately conceive the incident in terms of 'something to do with sex'. Possibilities include variants of: 'I wish I was the girl' . . . 'I wish these clothes were part of my world. I wish I could be part of this world' . . . Where the erotic looms large, beginning femaling might be seen in terms of the sexual . . . with the relations between the sexual and sex and gender obscure at this stage.

. . . [T]ypically 'normality' reinstates itself after the incident. Nevertheless, thenceforth the meaning of female objects – clothes, for example – may well be different . . . pondered on and invested with new meaning. Likewise, new self-concepts will be rendered more or less negotiable, though typically, in this phase, the reinvolvement within the meaning frames of 'normal' everyday life, following the cross-dressing incident, are such as to leave 'normal' self-concept and world more or less intact.

Phase two: fantasying femaling

Fantasying femaling will frequently arise in tandem with 'doing femaling' (phase three), but in this phase the stress is on the elaboration of fantasies involving femaling. The fantasies may be more or less elaborate, scripted, adapted from incidents in 'real' life, innovative and imaginative. They might entail nothing more than fantasying the feel and texture of an imagined petticoat as implicated within a femaling episode . . . They might involve an elaborate script in which the boy child is taken shopping by his mother, has chosen for him all sorts of 'feminine' finery, and lives 'happily ever after' as an accepted girl child in the family.

In terms of sex, sexuality and gender and their interrelations, a number of possibilities arise. There may be quite unambiguous fantasies of being a girl or woman . . . A common boyhood variant is fantasying 'waking up in the morning as a girl'. Many femalers who later conceptualize themselves as transsexuals and who are conceptualized as primary transsexuals within the psychiatric-medical literature (Person and Ovesey 1974a) recall variations on this theme. For others, the fantasy femaling takes on a gender stress. . . . [T]he emphasis is upon romantic fantasies relating to such things as dreamy dresses, ribbons, doll play, and the like. For still others, the emphasis is upon masturbatory fantasy cross-dressing in a range of variations.

There is a tendency in this phase for fantasies initially to cluster around certain themes, which develop only slowly. They may have a body/sex, gender, or erotic/sexual core, which may then be fuelled by one or other mode.

. . . As with 'beginning femaling', there is a tendency for the meaning frames (Goffman 1974) of everyday life to reassert themselves when the incident of daydreaming or masturbation is over. However, in the case of erotic fantasy femaling, gendered objects are increasingly invested with potential affect, to form material for future masturbatory scripts. . . . Alternatively, there may be an increasing fascination with 'the world of women' . . . with varying degrees of volition. As regards self and world, body femalers may become so preoccupied with their fantasying that their self-concepts as males become increasingly under threat; gender femalers, likewise, in more dreamy a fashion. More typically, however, there will be merely what might be termed incipient 'dual worlding'. An embryonic world will be constituted within which a femaling self and femaling related objects and practices are emerging, but which at this stage, the fantasying femaler keeps separate from his everyday world, thus keeping the latter more or less 'normal' and enabling its development more or less boundaried from the incipient female world.

Phase three: doing femaling

Although fantasying femaling is frequently accompanied by partial cross-dressing, doing femaling includes more 'serious' cross-dressing and acting out aspects of fantasy body femaling. The body femaler may, for instance, depilate parts of his body periodically. He may experiment with hiding his male genitalia ('tucking') and producing a simulated vulva. With, or just as likely without, body femaling variants, the gender femaler may well build up private collections of clothes and may experiment with more complete dressing using make-up, jewellery and accessories. All of these may, or may not, be built into masturbatory routines (erotic femaling), which may become more protracted.

In terms of sex, sexuality and gender, and their interrelations, it is as though the femaler is developing along clustered lines, without really quite knowing what he is doing. Cross-dressing is likely to play a major part in this phase whether the clusters follow sex, sexuality or gender patterns, but typically the femaler is not sure of the differences or where precisely he stands with regard to them. In this phase femalers become more knowledgeable about the gendered world of girls and women, about what dresses they like, about styles and so forth, this, in itself, giving pleasure. Others may place the emphasis upon increasingly elaborate masturbatory routines. Others may become more preoccupied with aspects of their morphology.

As regards the interrelations between the constitution of self and world . . . this is likely to be the period of particular personal confusion and of vacillation. Not only is the femaler 'betwixt and between' two worlds, but he has no clear notion of what he is doing or its likely outcome. His 'everyday' meanings in respect of his self and world are increasingly threatened by his developing 'doing femaling', but he is still not advanced in his conceptualisation of what he is doing and what it means. . . .

As 'doing femaling' becomes more frequent, the tendency to seek to 'explain' it may well become more pressing. The search for meaning is incipient. But unless the femaler chances upon, for example, media coverage of 'people like me', or comes across 'explanations' by others in scientific texts, he may well continue to think, as many do in this phase, that 'I am the only one in the world,' 'I am a freak,' 'I don't know why I do this,' 'Where will it all end?'

Phase four: constituting femaling

This phase marks the period where the femaler begins to constitute the meaning of his activities in a more serious and sustained way. As femaling experiences and activities increase many femalers are drawn increasingly to 'explain' themselves,

to 'make sense' of themselves and their activities and to work out where femaling fits with the rest of their lives.

A number of possibilities are typical of this phase. The femaler may seek
professional guidance – a 'cure' – having constituted himself as, for example, a
pervert in need of help. He may in rare cases construct his own definition of the
situation without access to literature or subculture. More typically, he will have
chanced upon media references to 'people called transvestites (or transsexuals)',
with whom he can identify. Many femalers, either through contact with subcultural literature or through their reading of the 'scientific' literature, begin to
constitute a pesonalised transvestite or transsexual self-concept within a world of
femaling, which is refined as they compare themselves with self-proclaimed transvestites and transsexuals they may meet in the subculture. Some definitions of the
situation will be adopted 'ready made' as it were. Others are seen as inapplicable.
More typically, the newly confronted constitutions are moulded to fit the particular self-concepts and understandings of self and femaling that the femaler has
constituted thus far.

It is in this phase that meanings begin to crystallize around particular 'namings'
(Strauss 1977: 15–30), often quite discriminating namings having to do with psychiatric-medical conceptualisations as they have been absorbed into the subculture.
Frequently, much thought and careful consideration is directed towards 'finding
the label that fits'. Some come to label themselves as a 'true transsexual'; others
as a 'TV (transvestite) with TS (transsexual) tendencies'; others as a 'middle-of-
the-road transvestite'; while others, as 'primarily fetishistic'.

Having adopted a label, meanings can now be ordered and understood. Once
the femaler has sorted out *what* he is . . . beginnings can be made towards understanding who he is . . . The emphasis in 'constituting femaling' does, however,
tend to be on conceptualizations of self and identity. Once the label has been
adopted, past identities are typically reinterpreted in the light of the newly discovered 'condition' . . .

Phase five: consolidating femaling

This stage marks the period where a more full-blown constitution of femaling self
and world is established. This will provide the individual with a more or less
comprehensive and coherent framework within which to consolidate or develop
his femaling self and world, and will also provide him with the means to relate
these systematically to his 'everyday', non-femaling world, where this remains, as
it normally will.

The consolidation may be centred around body femaling, erotic femaling or
gender femaling, with the emphasis upon the corresponding features and facets of
sex, sexuality or gender. Various combinations over time are possible, but, typically, having constituted self and world, 'consolidating' sees reconstructions of
pasts, consolidations of presents and moves made towards intended futures, clus-
tering around 'chosen' foci.

Thus, a consolidating body femaler having come to see that 'really' 'she' was
transsexual all along (sexed identity), takes stock of 'herself' and embarks upon a

programme of appropriate body feminisation, which may be seen as culminating in 'the op.', now defined in terms of becoming as near as is possible and practicable to what 'she' should have been all along. 'She' now dresses as a woman, because 'she' *is* a woman. Her presentation of self is herself. . . . 'She' is not merely expressing parts of 'herself', or play-acting. Thus, the meanings of what might have been conceptualised in terms of gender or sexuality are now redefined and may take on different career paths of their own, all, in a sense, as adjuncts to the major focus of 'her' femaling. As regards gender issues, 'she' develops 'her' personal style much as a genetic girl would have done – the difference being that 'she' is starting rather late, has to do it rather quickly, and is likely to be hampered by residues of 'her' maleness. As regards 'her' sexuality, as hormonal treatment continues, 'she' loses what male sexuality 'she' has, and is, in effect, desexualizing 'her' old sexuality concurrent with the construction of a new sex and sexuality.

The erotic femaler, having now consolidated his femaling around the erotic/sexual, may look to new ways to develop his erotic femaling. He may build up collections of subcultural literature and exotic paraphernalia. He may experiment with a view to finding what most 'turns him on'. He may begin to conceptualize what 'turns him on' in a fairly fine-tuned way. His female style may take on sado-masochistic variants which would normally be considered fetishistic and which may take increasingly bizarre forms, for he is not so much interested in the subtleties of femininity as with his personal sexual excitement. The role and meaning of body and gender femaling are redefined and clarified accordingly. Serious and sustained body femaling has no appeal at all. It would entail the loss of his eroticism and his pleasure-giving penis. Likewise, orthodox gender femaling may come to be seen as having prissy, drab or effete connotations.

Another approach lies in the developing of subcultural contacts that will lead to a conscious celebration of the erotic. Erotic femalers may advertise for partners in subcultural magazines . . . They may provide the magazines with photographs, personal details and accounts of some of their sexual exploits carried out with other 'TVs' (transvestites) or 'TV punters' (apparent 'straights' who fancy and hang around TVs and TSs) met through the magazine. Many erotic femalers build up something of a cult following through this procedure. Some may get further excitement from being paid for their services. In this case the erotic femaler gets maximum sexual excitement by becoming the stereotypical erotic female, the 'sexy hooker'. . . .

The gender femaler, on the other hand, tends to move in the opposite direction. Residual fetishisms may erode. Now his fascination with the whole world of the feminine knows no bounds. He wants to look like and behave like a 'real' woman (as he sees women), not some stereotypical male fantasy of one. This may entail the steady development of his femme self with 'her' own personality, tastes and enthusiasms. Many will model themselves on admired 'RGs' (real girls; others will study deportment, voice production, fashion, make-up and the like.

Body femaling and erotic femaling are now redefined in terms of the gender foci. It is not necessarily true that there is no body femaling. In fantasy there may be much of it. Similarly, the gender femaler may adopt every bit of the sex-role paraphernalia his ingenuity can dream up. He may, for instance, insert tampons in his fantasied vagina (rectum), or occasionally 'go on the pill'. But he does these things 'because that is what RGs do', not because he thinks he is one, or is becoming one, or because of any very obvious erotic kick he gets out of doing it. ('That wouldn't be feminine'.)

Typically, his relationship with the erotic is likely to be ambiguous. While there are gender femalers who are asexual, or who increasingly become so and who female for 'reasons of tranquillity' or even aesthetic reasons, the eroticism is more likely, perhaps, to be attenuated and dispersed, and may indeed become increasingly so. We might say eroticism is adjuncted to gender femaling in these cases. For some, with increased gender fine-tuning an ever-increasing number of objects in the world of women become mildly eroticized. But, at the same time, their own sexuality becomes increasingly genderized. This can lead to a distaste for sexuality except as expressed in gender form. Sexual intercourse, for example, is fantasied in terms of gender femaling role-play. Another possibility is that past gender femalings which were not erotic femalings at the time, come to form material for erotic scripts in subsequent episodes of fantasy femaling . . .

. . . Grounded theory work with cross-dressers and sex-changers enables the ordering of a mass of what Herbert Blumer would have called 'intimate detail' (Anselm Strauss, personal communication, 1944). In particular, consideration of this detail in terms of the basic social process of 'male femaling' has a number of advantages. It enables the proper respect to be paid to the processual and emergent nature of much cross-dressing and sex-changing phenomena. It facilitates the generation of a number of categories which highlight facets of male femaling hitherto unstudied. Finally, it provides the framework for a rigorous examination of the various shifting interrelations between human sex, sexuality and gender which feature in a phased male femaling career path. All too often these complex interrelations are conflated or ignored. . . .

References

Glaser, B. (1978) *Theoretical Sensitivity Advances in the Methodology of Grounded Theory*. Mill Valley CA: Sociology Press.

Goffman, E. (1969) *The Presentation of Self in Everyday Life*. Harmondsworth: Penguin.

Goffman, I. (1979) *Gender Advertisements*. London: Macmillan.

Lukacs, M. (1978) *Let me Die a Woman: The Why and How of Sex Change Operations*. New York: Rearguard Productions.

Money, J. (1969) 'Sex reassignment as related to hermaphroditism and transsexualism', in R. Green and J. Money (eds) *Transsexualism and Sex Reassignment*. Baltimore MD: Johns Hopkins University Press.

Person, E. S. and Ovesey, L. (1974a) 'The transsexual syndrome in males' I, *American Journal of Psychotherapy*, 28: 4–20.

Person, E. S. and Ovesey, L. (1974b) 'The transsexual syndrome in males' II, *American Journal of Psychotherapy*, 28: 174–93.

Plummer, K. (1979) *Symbolic Interactionism and Sexual Differentiation: An Empirical Investigation*. Final report on grant HR 4043 to the UK Social Science Research Council.

Strauss, A. L. (1977) *Mirrors and Masks*. London: Martin Robertson.

PART SIX

Gendered embodiment

INTRODUCTION

U NTIL RELATIVELY RECENTLY BODIES were seen, even by sociologists, as simply the biological form which human social actors happened to
inhabit. This bracketing off of the body has its historical roots in a dualistic tradition of thought which stressed the pre-eminence of rational, civilising qualities of
mind over the brute 'nature' of the body. This philosophy also associated men with
mind and rationality and women with the body and nature, a negative association
which prompted feminists to examine these assumptions more closely (Ortner 1974;
Sydie 1987). Thinking about gender also inspired feminists to think about the
ways in which women's bodies had been defined, constructed and regulated. Once
feminists moved beyond seeing 'sex' as biological and gender as social, it became
possible to ask how gender shaped the ways we think about bodily biological differences (see the main introduction and Part One).

Whereas men's bodies were regarded as quite unproblematic, women have long
been seen as at the mercy of their unruly bodies. A recent manifestation of this
is premenstrual tension/syndrome, a 'diagnosis' which enables women to be seen
as emotionally and intellectually problematic as a result of their bodily processes
(see Chapter 42). While some women have welcomed this medicalisation as a
recognition of their problems, it is double-edged as it can also serve to invalidate
women's justified anger and frustration ('It's just that time of the month'). Medical
and biological science is never gender-neutral, but always looks at bodily processes
through a gendered lens. A very clear example of this is provided by Emily Martin
(Chapter 42) in her discussion of the anthropomorphic representation of the egg
and the sperm in medical textbooks.

Representations of the body have not been shaped by gender in isolation, but

by all distinctions which render certain bodies as other in relation to the dominant White male. In the context of nineteenth-century imperialism the bodies of
Black women were defined as even more aberrant than those of White women, as
simultaneously exotic and debased, as less evolved and thus closer to animal nature
(see Chapter 43). Working-class women, of whatever culture, and particularly prostitutes, were defined in similar terms.

As well as criticising the all-pervasive pathologisation of women's bodies, feminists have called for the problematisation of men's bodies. One of the men to
respond to this challenge, in the early 1980s, was Emmanuel Reynaud, who drew
attention to the mind/body split as a means by which patriarchal power is retained
(Chapter 44). This strategy is not without its costs for men in that it distances
them from the sensuous potential of their own bodies, permitting physicality only
as an expression of virile athleticism. Some similar themes were later taken up
by David Morgan (Chapter 45), who invites us to consider men and women as
equally embodied and to explore the varied forms of bodily action and display
open to men in differing social contexts. He also draws attention to changing styles
of masculinity which are emerging as men's bodies become more commodified and
aestheticised.

Both men and women can now work on their bodies in order to bring about
bodily change. Traditionally this body work has been thought of as gender-differ-
entiated, with men seeking strength and performance and women pursuing aesthetic
perfection. These boundaries are becoming less fixed and even where bodily self-
improvement follows gendered lines, the conditions under which it occurs are
changing. An obvious example is cosmetic surgery, which offers possibilities of
bodily transformation which would once have been unimaginable. It is hardly
surprising that cosmetic surgeons find most of their clientele among women. It
can be seen as simply the latest in a long line of pressures on women to endure
pain in the pursuit of 'beauty' – another patriarchal strategy for reducing women
to their bodies. However, as Kathy Davis (Chapter 46) reveals, women undergoing
cosmetic surgery cannot simply be seen as passive victims chasing an unrealisable
ideal of beauty. Rather many of them are seeking to correct perceived abnormalities in order to be 'just ordinary'. In this context women should be understood
as exercising embodied agency in the pursuit of a more positive sense of self. Davis
is certainly not denying the ways in which gendered power is enacted on women's
bodies in the process of such transformations, but asks us to consider the contradictions of bodily management which women experience.

Women body builders are also engaged in managing both bodily transformation and the contradictions entailed in maintaining femininity. Mansfield and
McGinn (Chapter 47) alert us to the constraints under which women enter physical pursuits once reserved for men. Building muscle produces a body which could
challenge conventional ideals of femininity, but on the competitive circuit this
threat is contained by the requirement that women should develop only appropriate muscularity and retain markers of femininity – such as long hair and make-
up. In the absence of these constrains the 'built' female body could potentially
subvert ideas about the bodily fixity of gender. Another form of embodiment which

challenges the strict division of male and female is that entailed in drag and camp performance. This entails something other than men pretending to be or parodying women, rather it depends upon a complex interplay of inner and outer gender. Esther Newton's analysis of these practices (see Chapter 48) was a key influence on Judith Butler's now famous discussion of drag as dramatising the construction of gender (Butler 1990).

Having a male or a female body is frequently taken for granted as a 'natural' marker of gender. Susanne Kessler's study (Chapter 49) questions the ways the bodies of the intersexed are literally made to conform to gender dimorphism. Despite appearances to the contrary not all babies are born clearly male or female. There are a variety of genital, hormonal and chromosomal variations which are associated with the conditions identified as intersexed. Such is the social pressure to assign gender that the birth of such a child is treated as a serious medical emergency and every effort is made to render the child either male or female as fast as possible and with maximum secrecy (see Kessler 1998; Fausto-Sterling 2000). Once a decision has been made, conformity is imposed upon the child through surgery and, later, hormonal treatment. Here gender is quite literally socially constructed.

REFERENCES AND FURTHER READING

Backett-Milburn, K. and Mackie, L. (eds) (2001) *Gender and Sexualities*. Basingstoke: Macmillan.

Butler, J. (1990) *Gender Trouble*. New York: Routledge.

Fausto-Sterling, A. (2000) *Sexing the Body*. New York: Basic Books.

Jacobus, M., Fox Keller, E. and Shuttleworth, S. (1990) *Body/Politics: Women and the Discourses of Science*. New York: Routledge

Jagger, A. and Bordo, S. (1989) *Gender/Body/Knowledge: Feminist Reconstructions of Being and Knowing*. New Brunswick N.J: Rutgers University Press.

Kessler, S. (1998) *Lessons from the Intersexed*. New Brunswick NJ: Rutgers University Press.

McSween, M. (1993) *The Anorexic Body*. London: Routledge.

Ortner, S. (1974) 'Is female to male as nature is to culture?' in M. Z. Rosaldo and L. Lamphere (eds) *Women, Culture and Society*. Stanford CA: Stanford University Press.

Sydie, R. A. (1987) *Natural Women/Cultured Men: A Feminist Perspective on Sociological Theory*. Milton Keynes: Open University Press.

KEY QUESTIONS

- Why have women historically been thought of as more embodied than men? With what consequences?
- To what extent are bodies carriers of class and 'race' as well as gender?
- Why and how are women and men encouraged to treat their bodies as a project to be worked on?
- How are bodies made male or female?

Chapter 42

Sophie Laws

SEEING RED

Sophie Laws challenges the medicalisation of premenstrual tension, arguing that it is a socially constructed 'syndrome' which reduces women to their bodies and denies the real problems in women's lives.

From 'Who needs PMT?' in S. Laws, V. Hey and A. Eagan, *Seeing Red: The Politics of Premenstrual Tension*, London: Hutchinson (1985).

PMT has made me nervous for some time. As a women's health worker, other women used often to ask me what I thought about it, and I never knew what to say. As a feminist, I try to understand my life in new ways, refusing to accept male-centred ways of thinking which deny or distort my own experience. I find I have contradictory and confusing feelings about the menstrual cycle, and there seems to be little feminist work to look to. In 1981 I began a research project on the social aspects of menstruation. Almost as soon as I had begun that work, two cases came to court where women were offering PMT as a defence against criminal charges. This forced me to think again about PMT.

The press coverage of those cases . . . shocked me and led me to read further – I turned first to the popular advice books, as they appeared to be offering a more feminist view. I was appalled at the ideas about women I actually found there. I tried to compare their assertions to what the medical and scientific 'experts' say. And I talked with other women about what I found there.

This chapter is my attempt to make sense of what is said about PMT from a radical feminist point of view. . . .

. . . Over the last few years there has been a good deal of debate about premenstrual tension in this country, and not just within the medical profession. It has often been said that this public discussion is good for women, breaking down a

taboo, bringing us medical help. At last, women's problems are being taken seriously by doctors. But are they? Does the medical definition of PMT[1] actually
describe correctly what women are feeling?

There tend to be two sides to the argument. Either women aren't really much
affected by their menstrual cycles and just use them as excuses for bad behaviour;
or some, perhaps most, menstruating women suffer a time of illness each month
during which time they are not responsible for their actions. Both these views are
anti-woman. We need not accept that these are the only choices we have.

So how can we understand the ways in which our menstrual cycles affect our
lives? I suggest that we must begin by looking carefully at what we are being
offered as a description of our experiences, and at where it comes from. We must
begin to see this as a *political* issue.

We must ask in whose interests is it that PMT is becoming accepted as a
medical condition? Have its promoters really discovered new truths about female
biology? What evidence is there that hormones can *control* human behaviour in the
way that is claimed? How does the idea of PMT encourage us to see women in
general? Should we necessarily see cyclic change as in itself a bad thing? And are
the 'symptoms' of PMT signs of sickness or could they be reasonable reactions to
the world?

In this chapter I am not proposing new 'truths' about women's experience of
their menstrual cycles. All I am hoping to do here is undertake a work of critique:
to lay bare a piece of male ideology and to challenge the 'scientific' evidence used
to support it.

. . . Feminists have always recognized the political importance of the health
and control of women's bodies. However, it is not always at all obvious which
approaches to women's health will turn out to be most positive for women. There
seems to be a deep conflict between the need for us to control our bodies, especially our fertility, and the need of our bodies to be left alone. While we remain
in many ways dependent on the medical profession and bound by existing medical
knowledge it is extremely difficult to work out where our control of our bodies
ends and their control of us begins. Many of us have found ourselves longing for
freedom from our bodies (an aspiration which is encouraged by the male view of
women as defective men), and unable to conceive of women becoming free *in* our
bodies. . . .

The menstrual cycle has now been transformed by the medical profession into
something only experts can tell us about. Women are supposed to be at the mercy
of it, and our hopes for release depend upon doctors gaining a full understanding
and finally control of it. The medical description of the menstrual cycle is taught
to women, rather than women's own versions of their experiences being listened
to: if you deviate from their norm, you need treatment. PMT is part of this medical
model, not an idea which came from women.

PMT is not only an imposed category. It provides a survival strategy for
women. If unacceptable parts of one's personality can be labelled PMT and regarded
as the results of a pitiable hormonal imbalance, one can retail one's hold on a self-
definition as a good woman. Now, at the societal level, PMT may become a possible
legal defence. Some women I spoke to about these cases said, 'Oh, great, next
time I get into trouble I'll make sure I'm premenstrual.' From the judge's point

of view, then, they need not believe that *women* are ever violent, aggressive, anti-social but that women with PMT are. And women can use this to deny responsibility for their actions. This may be necessary or even useful in dealing with an unjust legal system, but the wider consequences are alarming. . . .

Katharina Dalton and other PMT doctors have received a lot of favourable publicity as champions of womankind – yet it seems to me that what they actually defend is the ideal of the traditionally feminine woman. They use statistics to blame women for a most extraordinary range of acts of disruption and violence. Judy Lever's book, for example, contains allegations that PMT causes increased criminal offences, baby battering and accidents to children, attacks on husbands, suicide attempts, heavy drinking, accidents in the home, at work, on the road, broken marriages – even wife battering: 'his wife provokes him by her own violent behaviour when suffering from PMT' (Lever 1980: 69). This is a fairly standard list for the PMT literature, though items drop in and out of it between different authors. For instance, although a lessened interest in sex is sometimes included in the symptom list, Dalton wrote recently that:

> Among PMS women, increased libido is occasionally noticed in the premenstruum, a fact recorded by Israel back in 1938. All too often it is this nymphomaniac urge in adolescents which is responsible for young girls running away from home, or custody, only to be found wandering in the park or following the boys. These girls can be helped, and their criminal career abruptly ended, with hormone therapy.
>
> (Dalton 1982a)

Yet the doctors maintain at the same time that women are innocent, misunderstood victims of their hormones. PMT patients want to be *nice*:

> Then suddenly her irritability ends. She is once more her usual sweet-tempered and placid self, or she may be filled with guilt and remorse at the problems her actions have caused. One woman said, 'I wish others would realize that it wasn't the true me who caused all this.'
>
> (Dalton 1969: 62)

> Another pleads, 'If only you could give me something so that I'm not so spiteful against my fiancé, whom I really do love.'
>
> (Ibid.: 111)

The advertisement used in medical journals for Cyclogest (progesterone pessaries) also illustrates with plodding clarity this imagery of Good woman *v.* Bad woman. The photograph shows two versions of one woman: one in a black round-necked tee shirt with untidy hair and a sad expression, the second with shining hair, a shining smile and a white V-neck blouse.

PMT can be used to completely invalidate a woman's feelings. Dalton cites with sympathy a marriage guidance counsellor who 'arranges to see both partners eight days after they quarrel: in this way he hopes that the woman will have safely passed through both her premenstruum and her menstruation before the time of the interview' (ibid.: 112). This man then simply refuses to contemplate women's feelings at this time – he declares them invalid and places them outside the range of what must be dealt with in repairing the marital relationship.

I think that many women will recognize this situation, where a man feels that he can ignore what you say if you are premenstrual at the time you say it. A man who is spoken to angrily by a woman can at any time quietly comfort himself with the idea that she's only upset because of her hormones. PMT, of course, only covers women who menstruate: anger in older women can be put down to the menopause, in pregnant women to their state of pregnancy, in adolescent women to their adolescence, in women who don't have period or whose periods are irregular to their hormonal peculiarity. It's a pretty complete system, and each part of it supports all the others!

Miriam Stoppard would like us to do the undermining for ourselves: 'You may even confess during the bad times that you know you are behaving improperly. If not, admit to your loss of control when you feel well again' (Stoppard 1982). According to Dalton, men are well pleased with her treatments: 'Many a husband has commented after the first course of injections that his wife is now more like the woman he knew at their marriage' (Dalton 1969: 73). How pleasant to be able to attribute any problem in a marriage to the wife's illness! The husband need not even consider whether there could be any *other* reasons why his wife might have changed since they married. . . .

. . . The PMT advice books written for the popular market put their position very clearly, and form the most straightforward statement of the PMT ideology of the last few years. These are not, of course, 'pure' sources, in the sense that they do not try to make consistent arguments, and often give no evidence at all for the statements they make. The newspaper articles may, for all I know, misquote their interviewees. The point is that this is where most women will derive their impressions about what PMT is supposed to be. These kinds of writings have an influence which is to some degree independent of the scientific 'proofs' they use to back themselves up. . . .

These books put forward a most alarming list of dreadful things women do during the premenstrual phase. From the panicky tone of the writing, one would think that violent crime committed by women was *the* social problem of our times. And yet when we look at the figures for offenders found guilty of the kinds of offences the PMT books talk about – murder, manslaughter, infanticide, other violence against the person, sexual offences and criminal damage – the picture is rather different. In 1982, of the 81,000 found guilty of these crimes, only 6,700 were women. Among these women, the most common offence was 'violence against the person' short of killing – but there were still nine times more men than women in this category (*Social Trends* 1984). And of course we know too that the vast majority of acts of violence to women by men – wife battering and rape – never even come to court, as they are regarded as private, domestic matters.

Books like these tend to simplify in blinding ways. Each gives some descriptions of menstrual taboos and restrictions, which are listed all together and described as belonging to some past time or to uncivilized societies. Then 'science' is invoked to explain these supposedly incomprehensible things:

In those days people thought there was something magic or evil about menstrual blood. Now we know that it's chemistry that's doing the damage. We're clumsy and accident-prone because the chemical balance of our bodies is upset.

(Kingston 1980: 63) . . .

A Birmingham gynaecologist who runs a PMT clinic . . . advocates the use of a drug still in the experimental stage which stops the cycle altogether:

'Some women are disturbed by not having periods, they think it is unnatural,' says Dr Parsons. 'But if you are talking about what Mother Nature intended, it is for women to get pregnant with her first period and spend the rest of her life bearing children until she dies at 40. PMT is unnatural, so is the menopause.'

(Sarah Pepper, *Coventry Evening Telegraph*, 4 May 1982)

This is quite a common medical attitude towards PMT. The fantasy of the 'natural woman' it relies upon is most alarming. . . .

. . . Since the recent publicity about PMT, women have been going to doctors in large numbers complaining of it. Much of the thrust of the pro-PMT lobby's argument is that women *want* it to be defined as a medical problem. All the doctors who are studying PMT refer to huge responses from women whenever they appear in the media discussing it. They take this as evidence that it is a real medical problem 'out there'.

It is clear that women want acceptance of the reality of the cyclic change they know they experience; but need we accept that PMT as a 'syndrome' exists because of this? Clearly what is called PMT refers to real experiences. What we must bring into question is the whole category – how we are being taught to describe cyclic changes we notice, and *why*: who benefits from this kind of description? It is difficult to think beyond the categories we are accustomed to using. Let me explain why I think we should make the effort: why I believe that it is possible for us to rethink PMT.

Most of the time, if someone came round asking us in detail about our health, most of us would have something or other we could complain to them about. Surveys have found that at any given time up to 90 per cent of the adult population is aware of the presence of some symptom which, if it was taken to a doctor, would be considered 'clinically serious' (e.g. Pearse and Crocker 1949; Siegel 1963). Thus a state of illness, in one sense, appears to be statistically the norm. And yet most of the time we don't see ourselves as ill.

'Being ill', then, is a social process, which we may or may not decide to enter into when we experience some feeling which could be called a symptom. The actions which follow from (or, rather, constitute) a decision to 'be ill' – stopping work, going to the doctor, and so on – clearly do not follow automatically from feeling a pain, or suspecting some bodily malfunction.

So one must examine not why people who have symptoms do not take any action but rather why some people do, and why they do so at the time that they do. I. K. Zola undertook a study exploring this question in 1966, looking at people attending the out-patients clinic of the General Eye and Ear Hospital in Boston, Massachusetts (see also Zola 1973). What is interesting about this survey, for our purposes here, is that it focused on complaints which medical science places in an entirely 'physical' category – these people could be diagnosed as having good solid identifiable illnesses. While the medical profession certainly believes that people present them with complaints which they cannot categorize tidily at times which are arbitrary or which relate more to their social lives than to their physical condition, this study shows that this in fact applies to all kinds of illness. To say that because of some social event in her life a person decides that some problem with her vision, for instance, is an illness requiring treatment is not to say that she does not have a problem with her sight or that this problem should be consigned to the 'psychosomatic' category.

Zola concluded that attendance at the hospital had nothing to do with the seriousness of the symptom the person was suffering, but arose from the constraints of their social situations. Whether or not a person went along depended largely on the 'fit or lack of fit' of their symptom with cultural expectations. (He was looking at differences between cultural groups in the area and it seemed, for example, that those of Irish origin would regard different parts of the body as important than would those of Italian origin.)

Zola suggested that several kinds of social events would tend to encourage a person to define their symptom as part of an illness. Some unrelated interpersonal crisis in their lives had occurred to a large proportion of the patients interviewed. If their symptom interfered in some way with their social relationships, or with their work, they would be likely to seek treatment. Another person actively encouraging them could also be crucial.

So, in the premenstrual time, women's experiences of discomfort or sadness, etc., have to be organized into a syndrome and socially accepted as a medical problem before the woman can be said to 'have PMT'. It is interesting that most human cultures do not seem to recognize anything equivalent to premenstrual tension: Janiger *et al.* (1972) searched anthropological records and found that they 'revealed many items pertaining to cultural myths, taboos and superstitions associated with menstruation but no report of premenstrual distress as such'.

The presence of a symptom as such does not necessarily lead us to define or treat ourselves as ill. A great number of other factors come into play in this decision. This is why it can make sense to talk about the creation and the history of premenstrual tension. We can accept that women are affected by our menstrual cycles in various ways, and that some of these effects may be unpleasant, without necessarily saying that we are therefore suffering from an illness and in need of treatment. We can choose whether or not to label the feelings we have premenstrually as signs of illness, but that choice is not necessarily made individually: cultural definitions, doctors and individual men may take that choice out of our hands. So our understandings of health and illness are not only social but *political*: that is, they relate to power. Ideas about 'female troubles', especially affect and are affected by the ways in which women as a group are seen in a culture.

Of course, particular feelings we may have may be decidedly unpleasant: painful breasts would be the most common example of that kind. I am not suggesting that women should indulge in wishful thinking to avoid this fact. But what we do about them, how and if we treat them, depends on socially constructed definitions. Hilary Allen (1984) illustrates this point by suggesting that we might

> pose the category of 'pre-breakfast syndrome' in which to lump together all the various complaints which could ever, in any individual, be shown to appear regularly in the first hours after waking and then to subside. These could include such diverse problems as habitual hangover, morning sickness, smoker's cough, lethargy or excitability, reduced or increased libido, irritability, intellectual impairment and numerous others. . . .

It is interesting that in one recent survey of women attending St Thomas's Hospital's PMT clinic, when women were asked which symptoms they experienced, 'loss of libido' was the second most commonly reported 'symptom' (Taylor and James 1979). It came level with irritability and second only to depression. Cyclic change in sexual energies is defined as a symptom of sickness only in a culture which expects women to be sexually responsive to men at all times. Where health equals constant sexual availability, appealing to illness definitions may be a woman's only way out of unwanted sex.

Women do, certainly, suffer various kinds of pain as a result of their menstrual cycles: for many women period pain is a far more serious problem that PMT. But period pain is mainly a problem for the woman herself – it is not socially disruptive. If women taking time off work can be induced to lie about the reason for it, the problem can be made to disappear – unlike the 'symptoms' of PMT. The excitement about PMT results from 'the fact that the symptoms often spill over to affect not just the woman but also her family, her marriage and her working life' (Cooper 1977).

Ronald Taylor, who is Professor of Obstetrics and Gynaecology at St Thomas's Hospital, London, writes: 'I have known of no other condition in which so many husbands take time off to accompany their wives to the first Clinic visit' (Women's Health Concern n.d.). If you consider the range of painful and distressing conditions that a consultant in gynaecology would see, it does look rather as though men have some particular interest in wanting their wives' 'PMT' treated.

We do, then, have a certain amount of choice about whether or not we accept PMT as a description of our experiences of cyclic change. Feminists have raised similar questions in relation to the menopause, and to pregnancy, which doctors tend to treat as states of illness. We should think about the consequences of defining a large proportion of otherwise well women as ill because of unpleasant feelings during part of their menstrual cycle. To assert the reality of these feelings – yes, this is essential – but to decide that they are abnormal and to be stamped out . . . that is another matter.

. . . So we can see that PMT can be looked at as a construction, an idea, rather than as a 'discovery' of something already there. It is then important to see that PMT, as an idea, has a history which goes back further than its present phase of publicity. . . .

. . . Basic ideas about PMT have not changed a great deal since it was first described, which was, as far as I know, by Frank in 1931. But the idea has become more sophisticated, and now that treatment with hormones is a possibility, doctors can feel that they have more to offer if they diagnose it. From the start PMT was a very vague concept: over the years doctors have claimed over 150 symptoms to be associated with a premenstrual syndrome (Moos 1968).

I took to collecting symptoms myself, to amuse myself while I ploughed through the medical literature on PMT. The resulting list goes as follows, in no special order.

weeping
tantrums
quarrels
depression
asthma
vertigo
migraine
headache
backache
epileptic fits
pain
herpes
rhinitis (runny nose)
urticaria (patches of itchy skin)
suicide
lethargy
irritability
dizziness
palpitations
bloated feelings in the abdomen and breasts
swelling in the fingers and legs
increased sexual desire
drowsiness
increased thirst or appetite
aggression
oliguia (producing too little urine)
increase in weight
spontaneous subcutaneous haemorrhages (bleeding under the skin)
tightness of the clothing
stiffness of the hands
fever
ulcerative stomatitis (mouth ulcers)
transient nymphomania

pain in the breasts
emotional instability
aching in the thighs
menstrual irregularity
nausea and vomiting
pruritis vulvae (inflamed vulva)
sciatica
pains in the shoulder, knees, feet, neck
apathy
tiredness
phobic panic attacks
anger
sleeplessness
diarrhoea
constipation
feelings of intimacy
paranoid ideas
obsessive compulsive behaviour
impatience
metatarsalgia (pain in the bones of the feet)
bad breath
labial elephantiasis (extreme enlargement of the lips of the vulva)
a sense of internal shaking
feelings of well-being
apprehension
fretfulness
sluggishness
sudden outbursts of emotion
irritated eyes
reduction in hearing or temporary deafness
bleeding from the nose

crushing chest pain
rectal pressure
feeling of pressure in the bladder
hair falling out
muscle weakness
aching and cramping
pain, swelling and stiffness of joints
difficulty thinking in a rational way
forgetfulness
hypersensitivity to sounds, sight and touch
stimulus overload
sinusitis
glaucoma
tension
fainting
exhaustion
upper respiratory tract infections
tonsillitis
acne
styes
boils
hypoglycaemia (low blood sugar)
hoarsenes
amnesia
postural hypotension (low blood pressure on standing up suddenly)
clumsiness
alcoholism
violence
lack of concentration
illogical reactions
feelings of worthlessness

The emphasis which has been placed on different 'symptoms' has changed somewhat, with different authors taking an interest in different 'symptoms'. For instance, as we have seen, while two early writers said that PMT patients had nymphomania (Israel 1938; Gray 1941), women today are often treated for 'loss of libido'. The symptoms of PMT seem to be pretty flexible, perhaps depending more on what is inconvenient behaviour than on anything else. . . .

. . . All menstruating women experience cyclic change of many kinds – Southam and Gonzaga (1965) describe changes in nearly every system of the body. It is clear that some women feel these changes more intensely than others, but these changes still constitute part of a woman's being, and are not signs of sickness. Women do not have times of normality (mid-cycle) followed by times of illness (PMT and menstruation), when their hormones suddenly overcome them – the menstrual cycle forms a continuum of change, physical, mental and social. If these changes are to be examined, one must look at the positive as well as the negative changes. . . .

If we are to respect ourselves as women we have to own all our states of being as parts of ourselves, even, and perhaps especially, the painful ones. If we are angry or sad before our periods, there is anger or sadness in us, and there are reasons for it. The menstrual cycle does not impose extraneous problems on a woman – it is part of her. A newspaper report about an American PMT doctor's new book tells of 'a husband's monthly heart-rending ordeal of holding his wife down on the bed until her suicidal urges have passed' (*Daily Gleaner* 1983). Are we really to believe that there is no problem in this woman's life except PMT?

There is no denying that many women feel worse premenstrually than they do during the rest of their cycles. Could it not be that 'PMT sufferers' should be seen as saving up the bad feelings of the whole month and feeling them intensely during the premenstrual period, rather than as having extra misery directly created by their hormones? This seems to be a more acceptable view of the menstrual cycle than one which implies that if it did not exist women would be calm, cheerful and placid at all times.

One of the recurrent images of women used in pornography shows the woman's body divided up, sectioned off into bits. The PMT theory of a woman's body is that her hormones are somehow separate from her and affect her as if from outside herself. It is frighteningly easy for us to imagine ourselves separated from our hormones. It seems easier for us to imagine being human without our femaleness than it is for a man to imagine himself without his maleness!

Many women's lives are very difficult. The word 'stress' seems totally inadequate to describe the circumstances in which women are expected to live. And women's pain is rarely taken seriously by those who are supposed to 'help'. PMT has seemed to offer a way of getting one's troubles listened to; it enables a medical solution to be found which avoids us being labelled as neurotic or inadequate. But ultimately it dehumanizes us to be forever looking inside ourselves for the cause of our problems.

The question should not be: do I have PMT? It should be: why have the changes I am used to going through with my menstrual cycle become intolerable to me? It is important to pay attention to what exactly it is that we feel when we say we feel 'premenstrual', rather than just to try to suppress the 'worst' of it.

What is it that we find we can't bear at those times? If women, together, seek the answers to these questions, I would guess that we will find much that we have in common, as well as many individual differences. And what we have in common may perhaps be due more to our shared social oppression than to our biology.

In suggesting that women's feelings during their premenstrual times are valid, I do not mean that such feelings are necessarily more true than those of other times of the month, or that they should necessarily be acted upon. Maybe we could better learn to live with the knowledge that our emotional states are affected by the menstrual cycle if we could do away with the assumption that that makes us inferior to men, and makes those emotions less valid than men's.

Perhaps the most stubborn problem of PMT is the feeling of being out of control of one's emotions. Keeping track of your cycle so as to be forewarned can make this easier to cope with, certainly. But how much are we really in control the rest of the time? The interplay of mind and body is complex and is a matter of continual change – things do look different at 3.00 a.m. than they do in mid-afternoon. We expect to have to adjust to certain changes in our bodies. That the particular kind of change we find hardest to tolerate is the one which is felt only by women is hardly surprising in a society where women are regarded as a lower form of life.

And what sort of control does a medical solution give us? Accepting the medical model of PMT implies that women cannot live their lives without medical help. We are disabled when our ability to allow for our own physical changes is denied.

PMT is a political construct. When a woman is said to have PMT, her distress or anger is invalidated. It is part of our oppression as women that if we are feeling bad we are encouraged to blame that feeling on our female bodies. The way some people use it, PMT has become a word which describes female badness, unreliability, inferiority. PMT is medical invention and will not be useful to us in attempting to find new, positive ways of seeing our bodies.

We do need to learn about our bodies, and finding out about our menstrual cycles is one part of that. But only through a process of collective self-discovery by women can we discover what we need to know. It is very dangerous for us to feel that we must depend upon the medical profession to tell us the 'objective' truth about ourselves, because that profession is riddled with anti-woman prejudice.

Why menstruating women's lives should involve cyclic change, and often unpleasant or painful feelings which recur cyclically, is a philosophical and political problem for us all. It is not a problem which we can safely hand over to doctors to deal with.

Note

1   Some doctors have recently taken to using the term 'premenstrual syndrome' (PMS) instead of premenstrual tension, claiming that this is a more accurate scientific term. When something gets a bad name, one tactic is to change the name rather than the thing – Long Kesh, the prison in Northern Ireland, becomes the Maze: Windscale, the nuclear power station in Cumbria, becomes Sellafield. I prefer to use the term 'premenstrual tension' because it is the one most people recognize.

References

Hilary Allen, 'At the mercy of her hormones: premenstrual tension and the law', *M/f*, no. 9 (1984): 19–44.

Wendy Cooper, 'A lay view of premenstrual syndrome', *Current Medical Research and Opinion*, 4, supp. 4 (1977): 5–8.

Daily Gleaner, 'Book reports on women's syndrome' (quoting Ronald Norris, *Premenstrual Syndrome*), 6 October 1983, p. 7 (Fredericton, USA).

K. Dalton, *The Menstrual Cycle*. Penguin, Harmondsworth (1969).

K. Dalton, 'What is this premenstrual syndrome?' *Journal of the Royal College of General Practitioners*, 32 (December 1982): 717–23.

K. Dalton, 'Legal implications of premenstrual syndrome', *World Medicine*, 17 April 1982, pp. 93–4.

R. T. Frank, 'The hormonal cause of premenstrual syndrome', *Arch. Neurol. and Psychiatry*, 26 (1931): 1053–7.

L. A. Gray, 'Use of progesterone in nervous tension states', *Southern Medical Journal*, 34 (1941): 104.

S. L. Israel, 'Premenstrual tension', *Journal of the American Medical Association*, 110 (1938): 1721.

Oscar Janiger, Ralph Riffenburgh and Ronald Kersh, 'Cross-cultural study of premenstrual symptoms', *Psychosomatics*, 13 (1972): 226–35.

Beryl Kingston, *Lifting the Curse*. London: Ebury Press (1980).

Judy Lever, *PMT: the unrecognised illness*. London: New English Library (1980).

R. H. Moos, 'The development of the Menstrual Distress Questionnaire', *Psychosomatic Medicine*, 3, 30 (1968): 853.

I. H. Pearse and L. H. Crocker, *The Peckham Experiment*. London: Allen & Unwin.

G. S. Siegel, *Periodic Health Examinations: Abstracts from the literature*, Public Health Service Publication no. 1010. Washington DC: US Government Printing Office (1963).

Social Trends 1984. London: HMSO (1984).

A. L. Southam and F. P. Gonzaga, 'Systemic changes during the menstrual cycle', *American Journal of Obstetrics and Gynecology*, 91 (1965): 142–65.

Miriam Stoppard, *Everywoman's Lifeguard*. London: Macdonald (1982).

R. W. Taylor and C. E. James, 'The clinician's view of patients with the premenstrual syndrome', *Current Medical Research and Opinion*, 6, supp. 5 (1979): 46–51.

Women's Health Concern, *Premenstrual Syndrome* (pamphlet). London: self-published (n.d.).

I. K. Zola, 'Pathways to the doctor: from person to patient', *Social Science and Medicine*, 7 (1973).

Chapter 43

Emily Martin

THE EGG AND THE SPERM

Emily Martin analyses the ways in which medicine portrays the reproductive process and shows how such 'knowledge' is constructed and rooted in stereotypical assumptions about gender.

From *Signs* 16 (3) 1991.

. . .

IN THE COURSE OF MY RESEARCH I realized that the picture of egg and sperm drawn in popular as well as scientific accounts of reproductive biology relies on stereotypes central to our cultural definitions of male and female. The stereotypes imply not only that female biological processes are less worthy than their male counterparts but also that women are less worthy than men. Part of my goal in writing this article is to shine a bright light on the gender stereotypes hidden within the scientific language of biology. Exposed in such a light, I hope they will lose much of their power to harm us.

Egg and sperm: a scientific fairy tale

At a fundamental level, all major scientific textbooks depict male and female reproductive organs as systems for the production of valuable substances, such as eggs and sperm.[1] In the case of women, the monthly cycle is described as being designed to produce eggs and prepare a suitable place for them to be fertilized and grown – all to the end of making babies. But the enthusiasm ends there. By extolling the female cycle as a productive enterprise, menstruation must necessarily be viewed as a failure. Medical texts describe menstruation as the 'debris' of the uterine lining, the result of necrosis, or death of tissue. The descriptions imply that a system has gone awry, making products of no use, not to specification, unsalable, wasted, scrap. An illustration in a widely used medical text shows menstruation as a chaotic disintegration of form, complementing the many texts that describe it as 'ceasing', 'dying', 'losing', 'denuding', 'expelling'.[2]

Male reproductive physiology is evaluated quite differently. One of the texts that sees menstruation as failed production employs a sort of breathless prose when it describes the maturation of sperm: 'The mechanisms which guide the remarkable cellular transformation from spermatid to mature sperm remain uncertain. . . . Perhaps the most amazing characteristic of spermatogenesis is its sheer magnitude: the normal human male may manufacture several hundred million sperm per day.'[3] . . . None of these texts expresses such intense enthusiasm for any female processes. It is surely no accident that the 'remarkable' process of making sperm involves precisely what, in the medical view, menstruation does not: production of something deemed valuable.[4]

One could argue that menstruation and spermatogenesis are not analogous processes and, therefore, should not be expected to elicit the same kind of response. The proper female analogy to spermatogenesis, biologically, is ovulation. Yet ovulation does not merit enthusiasm in these texts either. Textbook descriptions stress that all of the ovarian follicles containing ova are already present at birth. Far from being *produced*, as sperm are, they merely sit on the shelf, slowly degenerating and aging like overstocked inventory: 'At birth, normal human ovaries contain an estimated one million follicles [each], and no new ones appear after birth. Thus, in marked contrast to the male, the newborn female already has all the germ cells she will ever have. Only a few, perhaps 400, are destined to reach full maturity during her active productive life. All the others degenerate at some point in their development so that few, if any, remain by the time she reaches menopause at approximately fifty years of age.'[5] Note the 'marked contrast' that this description sets up between male and female: the male, who continuously produces fresh germ cells, and the female, who has stockpiled germ cells by birth and is faced with their degeneration. . . .

To avoid the negative connotations that some people associate with the female reproductive system, scientists could begin to describe male and female processes as homologous. They might credit females with 'producing' mature ova one at a time, as they're needed each month, and describe males as having to face problems of degenerating germ cells. This degeneration would occur throughout life among spermatogonia, the undifferentiated germ cells in the testes that are the long-lived, dormant precursors of sperm.

. . . In a section heading for *Molecular Biology of the Cell*, a best-selling text, we are told that 'Oogenesis is wasteful.' The text goes on to emphasize that of the seven million oogonia, or egg germ cells, in the female embryo, most degenerate in the ovary. Of those that do go on to become oocytes, or eggs, many also degenerate, so that at birth only two million eggs remain in the ovaries. Degeneration continues throughout a woman's life: by puberty 300,000 eggs remain, and only a few are present by menopause. 'During the 40 or so years of a woman's reproductive life, only 400 to 500 eggs will have been released,' the authors write. 'All the rest will have degenerated. It is still a mystery why so many eggs are formed only to die in the ovaries.'[6]

The real mystery is why the male's vast production of sperm is not seen as wasteful.[7] Assuming that a man 'produces' 100 million (10^8) sperm per day (a conservative estimate) during an average reproductive life of sixty years, he would produce well over two trillion sperm in his lifetime. . . . Assuming two or three offspring, for every baby a woman produces, she wastes only around two hundred eggs. For every baby a man produces, he wastes more than one trillion (10^{12}) sperm.

How is it that positive images are denied to the bodies of women? A look at language – in this case, scientific language – provides the first clue. Take the egg and the sperm.[8] It is remarkable how 'femininely' the egg behaves and how 'masculinely' the sperm.[9] The egg is seen as large and passive.[10] It does not *move* or *journey*, but passively 'is transported', 'is swept',[11] or even 'drifts'[12] along the fallopian tube. In utter contrast, sperm are small, 'streamlined',[13] and invariably active. They 'deliver' their genes to the egg, 'activate the developmental program of the egg',[14] and have a 'velocity' that is often remarked upon.[15] Their tails are 'strong' and efficiently powered.[16] Together with the forces of ejaculation, they can 'propel the semen into the deepest recesses of the vagina'.[17] For this they need 'energy', 'fuel',[18] so that with a 'whiplashlike motion and strong lurches'[19] they can 'burrow through the egg coat'[20] and 'penetrate' it.[21]

. . . Gerald Schatten and Helen Schatten liken the egg's role to that of Sleeping Beauty: 'a dormant bride awaiting her mate's magic kiss, which instills the spirit that brings her to life'.[22] Sperm, by contrast, have a 'mission',[23] which is to 'move through the female genital tract in quest of the ovum'.[24] One popular account has it that the sperm carry out a 'perilous journey' into the 'warm darkness', where some fall away 'exhausted'. 'Survivors' 'assault' the egg, the successful candidates 'surrounding the prize'.[25] Part of the urgency of this journey, in more scientific terms, is that 'once released from the supportive environment of the ovary, an egg will die within hours unless rescued by a sperm.'[26] The wording stresses the fragility and dependency of the egg, even though the same text acknowledges elsewhere that sperm also live for only a few hours.[27] . . .

The more common picture – egg as damsel in distress, shielded only by her sacred garments; sperm as heroic warrior to the rescue – cannot be proved to be dictated by the biology of these events. While the 'facts' of biology may not *always* be constructed in cultural terms, I would argue that in this case they are. The degree of metaphorical content in these descriptions, the extent to which differences between egg and sperm are emphasized, and the parallels between cultural stereotypes of male and female behavior and the character of egg and sperm all point to this conclusion.

New research, old imagery

As new understandings of egg and sperm emerge, textbook gender imagery is being revised. But the new research, far from escaping the stereotypical representations of egg and sperm, simply replicates elements of textbook gender imagery in a different form. . . .

In this recent investigation, the researchers began to ask questions about the mechanical force of the sperm's tail. (The lab's goal was to develop a contraceptive that worked topically on sperm.) They discovered, to their great surprise, that the forward thrust of sperm is extremely weak, which contradicts the assumption that sperm are forceful penetrators.[28] Rather than thrusting forward, the sperm's head was now seen to move mostly back and forth. The sideways motion of the sperm's tail makes the head move sideways with a force that is ten times stronger than its forward movement. So even if the overall force of the sperm were strong enough to mechanically break the zona, most of its force would be directed sideways rather than forward. In fact, its strongest tendency, by tenfold, is to escape by attempting to pry itself off the egg. Sperm, then, must be exceptionally efficient at *escaping* from any cell surface they contract. And the surface of the egg must be designed to trap the sperm and prevent their escape. Otherwise, few if any sperm would reach the egg. . . .

Although this new version of the saga of the egg and the sperm broke through cultural expectations, the researchers who made the discovery continued to write papers and abstracts as if the sperm were the active party who attacks, binds, penetrates, and enters the egg. The only difference was that sperm were now seen as performing these actions weakly.[29] Not until August 1987, more than three years after the findings described above, did these researchers reconceptualize the process to give the egg a more active role. They began to describe the zona as an aggressive sperm catcher, covered with adhesive molecules that can capture a sperm with a single bond and clasp it to the zona's surface.[30] . . .

. . . [A]nother researcher has recently made discoveries that seem to point to a more interactive view of the relationship of egg and sperm. This work, which Paul Wassarman conducted on the sperm and eggs of mice, focuses on identifying the specific molecules in the egg coat (the zona pellucida) that are involved in egg/sperm interaction. At first glance, his descriptions seem to fit the model of an egalitarian relationship. Male and female gametes 'recognize one another', and 'interactions . . . take place between sperm and egg'.[31] But the article in *Scientific American* in which those descriptions appear begins with a vignette that presages the dominant motif of their presentation: 'It has been more than a century since Hermann Fol, a Swiss zoologist, peered into his microscope and became the first person to see a sperm penetrate an egg, fertilize it and form the first cell of a new embryo.'[32] This portrayal of the sperm as the active party – the one that *penetrates* and *fertilizes* the egg and *produces* the embryo – is not cited as an example of an earlier, now outmoded view. . . .

The imagery of sperm as aggressor is particularly startling in this case: the main discovery being reported is isolation of a particular molecule *on the egg coat* that plays an important role in fertilization! Wassarman's choice of language sustains the picture. He calls the molecule that has been isolated ZP3, a 'sperm receptor'. By allocating the passive, waiting role to the egg, Wassarman can continue to describe the sperm as the actor, the one that makes it all happen: 'The basic process begins when many sperm first attach loosely and then bind tenaciously to receptors on the surface of the egg's thick outer coat, the zona pellucida. Each sperm, which has a large number of egg-binding proteins on its surface, binds to many sperm receptors on the egg. More specifically, a site on each of the egg-binding proteins fits a complementary site on a sperm receptor, much as a key fits a lock.'[33] With the sperm designated as the 'key' and the egg the 'lock', it is obvious which one acts and which one is acted upon. Could this imagery not be reversed, letting the sperm (the lock) wait until the egg produces the key? Or could we speak of two halves of a locket matching, and regard the matching itself as the action that initiates the fertilization? . . .

Social implications: thinking beyond

. . . [T]hese revisionist accounts of egg and sperm cannot seem to escape the hierarchical imagery of older accounts. Even though each new account gives the egg a larger and more active role, taken together they bring into play another cultural stereotype: woman as a dangerous and aggressive threat. In the Johns Hopkins lab's revised model, the egg ends up as the female aggressor who 'captures and tethers' the sperm with her sticky zona, rather like a spider lying in wait in her web.[34] The Schatten lab has the egg's nucleus 'interrupt' the sperm's dive with a 'sudden and swift' rush by which she 'clasps the sperm and guides its nucleus to the center'.[35] Wassarman's description of the surface of the egg 'covered with thousands of plasma membrane-bound projections, called microvilli' that reach out and clasp the sperm adds to the spiderlike imagery.[36]

These images grant the egg an active role but at the cost of appearing disturbingly aggressive. Images of woman as dangerous and aggressive, the *femme fatale* who victimizes men, are widespread in Western literature and culture.[37] More specific is the connection of spider imagery with the idea of an engulfing, devouring mother.[38] New data did not lead scientists to eliminate gender stereotypes in their descriptions of egg and sperm. Instead, scientists simply began to describe egg and sperm in different, but no less damaging, terms. . . .

Further research would show us exactly what social effects are being wrought from the biological imagery of egg and sperm. At the very least, the imagery keeps alive some of the hoariest old stereotypes about weak damsels in distress and their strong male rescuers. That these stereotypes are being written in at the level of the *cell* constitutes a powerful move to make them seem so natural as to be beyond alteration.

The stereotypical imagery might also encourage people to imagine that what results from the interaction of egg and sperm – a fertilized egg – is the result of deliberate 'human' action at the cellular level. Whatever the intentions of the human couple, in this microscopic 'culture' a cellular 'bride' (or *femme fatale*) and a cellular 'groom' (her victim) make a cellular baby. Rosalind Petchesky points out that through visual representations such as sonograms, we are given '*images* of younger and younger, and tinier and tinier, fetuses being "saved".' This leads to 'the point of visibility being "pushed back" *indefinitely*'.[39] Endowing egg and sperm with intentional action, a key aspect of personhood in our culture, lays the foundation for the point of viability being pushed back to the moment of fertilization. This will likely lead to greater acceptance of technological developments and new forms of scrutiny and manipulation, for the benefit of these inner 'persons': court-ordered restrictions on a pregnant woman's activities in order to protect her fetus, fetal surgery, amniocentesis, and rescinding of abortionrights, to name but a few examples.[40]

Even if we succeed in substituting more egalitarian, interactive metaphors to describe the activities of egg and sperm, and manage to avoid the pitfalls of cybernetic models, we would still be guilty of endowing cellular entities with personhood. More crucial, then, than what *kinds* of personalities we bestow on cells is the very fact that we are doing it at all. This process could ultimately have the most disturbing social consequences.

One clear feminist challenge is to wake up sleeping metaphors in science, particularly those involved in descriptions of the egg and the sperm. Although the literary convention is to call such metaphors 'dead', they are not so much dead as sleeping, hidden within the scientific content of texts – and all the more powerful for it.[41] Waking up such metaphors, by becoming aware of when we are projecting cultural imagery on to what we study, will improve our ability to investigate and understand nature. Waking up such metaphors, by becoming aware of their implications, will rob them of their power to naturalize our social conventions about gender.

Notes

1   The textbooks I consulted are the main ones used in classes for undergraduate premedical students or medical students (or those held on reserve in the library for these classes) during the past few years at Johns Hopkins University. These texts are widely used at other universities in the country as well.

2   Arthur C. Guyton, *Physiology of the Human Body*, sixth edition (Philadelphia: Saunders College Publishing, 1984), 624.

3   Arthur J. Vander, James H. Sherman, and Dorothy S. Luciano, *Human Physiology: The Mechanisms of Body Function*, third edition (New York: McGraw-Hill, 1980), 483–4.

4   For elaboration, see Emily Martin, *The Woman in the Body: A Cultural Analysis of Reproduction* (Boston: Beacon, 1987), 27–53.

5   Vander *et al.*, 568.

6   Bruce Alberts *et al.*, *Molecular Biology of the Cell* (New York: Garland, 1983), 795.

7   In her essay 'Have only men evolved?' (in *Discovering Reality: Feminist Perspectives on Epistemology, Metaphysics, Methodology, and Philosophy of Science*, ed. Sandra Harding and Merrill B. Hintikka, Dordrecht: Reidel, 1983, 45–69, especially 60–1), Ruth Hubbard points out that sociobiologists have said the female invests more energy than the male in the production of her large gametes, claiming that this explains why the female provides parental care. Hubbard questions whether it 'really takes more "energy" to generate the one or relatively few eggs than the large excess of sperms required to achieve fertilization'. For further critique of how the greater size of eggs is interpreted in sociobiology, see Donna Haraway, 'Investment strategies for the evolving portfolio of primate females', in *Body/Politics*, ed. Mary Jacobus, Evelyn Fox Keller, and Sally Shuttleworth (New York: Routledge, 1990), 155–6.

8   The sources I used for this article provide compelling information on interactions among sperm. Lack of space prevents me from taking up this theme here,

but the elements include competition, hierarchy, and sacrifice. For a newspaper report, see Malcolm W. Browne, 'Some thoughts on self sacrifice', *New York Times* (July 5, 1988), C6. For a literary rendition, see John Barth, 'Night-sea journey', in his *Lost in the Funhouse* (Garden City NY: Doubleday, 1968), 3–13.

9   See Carol Delaney, 'The meaning of paternity and the virgin birth debate', *Man* 21, 3 (1986): 494–513. She discusses the differences between this scientific view that women contribute genetic material to the fetus and the claim of long-standing Western folk theories that the origin and identity of the fetus comes from the male, as in the metaphor of planting a seed in soil.

10   For a suggested direct link between human behavior and purportedly passive eggs and active sperm, see Erik H. Erikson, 'Inner and outer space: reflections on womanhood', *Daedalus* 93, 2 (1964): 582–606, especially 591.

11   Guyton (n. 2 above), 619; and Mountcastle (n. 5 above), 1609.

12   Jonathan Miller and David Pelham, *The Facts of Life* (New York: Viking Penguin, 1984), 5.

13   Alberts *et al.*, 796.

14   Ibid., 796.

15   See, e.g., William F. Ganong, *Review of Medical Physiology*, seventh edition (Los Altos CA: Lange Medical Publications, 1975), 322.

16   Alberts *et al.* (n. 6 above), 796.

17   Guyton, 615.

18   Solomon (n. 6 above), 683.

19   Vander *et al.* (n. 3 above), fourth edition (1985), 580.

20   Alberts *et al.*, 796.

21   All biology texts quoted above use the word 'penetrate'.

22   Gerald Schatten and Helen Schatten, 'The energetic egg', *Medical World News* 23 (January 23, 1984): 51–3, especially 51.

23   Alberts *et al.*, 796.

24   Guyton (n. 2 above), 613.

25   Miller and Pelham (n. 12 above), 7.

26   Alberts *et al.* (n. 6 above), 804.

27   Ibid., 801.

28   Far less is known about the physiology of sperm than comparable female substances, which some feminists claim is no accident. Greater scientific scrutiny of female production has long enabled the burden of birth control to be placed on women. In this case, the researchers' discovery did not depend on development of any new technology. The experiments made use of glass pipettes, a manometer, and a simple microscope, all of which have been available for more than one hundred years.

29   Jay Baltz and Richard A. Cone, 'What force is needed to tether a sperm?' (abstract for Society for the Study of Reproduction, 1985), and 'Flagellar torque on the head determines the force needed to tether a sperm' (abstract for Biophysical Society, 1986).

30   Jay M. Baltz, David F. Katz, and Richard A. Cone, 'The Mechanics of the sperm–egg interaction at the zona pellucida', *Biophysical Journal* 54, 4 (1988): 643–54. Lab members were somewhat familiar with work on metaphors in the biology of female production. Richard Cone, who runs the lab, is my husband, and he talked with them about my earlier research on the subject from time to time. Even though my current research focuses on biological imagery and I heard

about the lab's work from my husband every day, I myself did not recognize the role of imagery in the sperm research until many weeks after the period of research and writing I describe. Therefore, I assume that any awareness the lab members may have had about how underlying metaphor might be guiding this particular research was fairly inchoate.

31 Paul M. Wassarman, 'Fertilization in mammals', *Scientific American* 259, 6 (1988): 78–84, especially 78, 84.

32 Ibid., 78.

33 Ibid., 78.

34 Baltz *et al.* (n. 30 above), 643, 650.

35 Schatten and Schatten, 53.

36 Wassarman, 'The Biology and chemistry of fertilization', 557.

37 Mary Ellman, *Thinking about Women* (New York: Harcourt Brace Jovanovich, 1968), 140; Nina Auerbach, *Woman and the Demon* (Cambridge MA: Harvard University Press, 1982), especially 186.

38 Kenneth Alan Adams, 'Arachnophobia: love American style', *Journal of Psychoanalytic Anthropology* 4, 2 (1981): 157–97.

39 Rosalind Petchesky, 'Fetal images: the power of visual culture in the politics of reproduction'' *Feminist Studies* 13, 2 (1987): 263–92, especially 272.

40 Rita Arditti, Renate Klein, and Shelley Minden, *Test Tube Women* (London: Pandora, 1984); Ellen Goodman, 'Whose right to life?' *Baltimore Sun* (November 17, 1987); Tamar Lewin, 'Courts acting to force care of the unborn', *New York Times* (November 23, 1987), A1 and B10; Susan Irwin and Brigitte Jordan, 'Knowledge, practice, and power: court ordered Cesarean sections', *Medical Anthropology Quarterly* 1, 3 (1987): 319–34.

41 Thanks to Elizabeth Fee and David Spain, who in February 1989 and April 1989, respectively, made points related to this.

Chapter 44

Sander Gilman

BLACK BODIES, WHITE BODIES
Toward an iconography of female sexuality
in the late nineteenth century

Sander Gilman argues that the representation of individuals in art is frequently
'iconographic' in character, in which specific individuals come to represent particular classes of people. This is particularly evident where that class of people is
perceived as 'other', where their differences from 'normal' (White, male) humanity
are emphasised, where human diversity is selectively reduced to specific mythical
icons. In the article from which this reading is taken, Gilman explores the construction of female sexuality in art, literature and medicine. The extracts chosen focus
on the conventions underlying medical representations of the linkage between two
icons, the 'Hottentot' (representing Black female sexuality) and the prostitute
(representing 'pathological' forms of White female sexuality).

From Henry Louis Gates Jnr (ed.) *Race, Writing and Difference*, Chicago,
University of Chicago Press (1986).

. . .

O**NE EXCELLENT EXAMPLE OF** the conventions of human diversity captured in the iconography of the nineteenth century is the linkage of
two seemingly unrelated female images – the icon of the Hottentot female and
the icon of the prostitute. In the course of the nineteenth century, the female
Hottentot comes to represent the black female *in nuce*, and the prostitute to represent the sexualized woman. Both of these categories represent the creation of
classes which correspondingly represent very specific qualities. While the number
of terms describing the various categories of the prostitute expanded substantially
during the nineteenth century, all were used to label the sexualized woman.
Likewise, while many groups of African blacks were known to Europeans in the

nineteenth century, the Hottentot remained representative of the essence of the black, especially the black female. Both concepts fulfilled an iconographic function in the perception and the representation of the world. How these two concepts were associated provides a case study for the investigation of patterns of conventions, without any limitation on the 'value' of one pattern over another. . . .

. . . By the eighteenth century, the sexuality of the black, both male and female, becomes an icon for deviant sexuality in general . . .

Buffon commented on the lascivious, apelike sexual appetite of the black, introducing a commonplace of early travel literature into a 'scientific' context.[1] He stated that this animal-like sexual appetite went so far as to lead black women to copulate with apes. The black female thus comes to serve as an icon for black sexuality in general. . . . [I]n this view of mankind, the black occupied the antithetical position to the white on the scale of humanity. This polygenetic view was applied to all aspects of mankind, including sexuality and beauty. The antithesis of European sexual *mores* and beauty is embodied in the black, and the essential black, the lowest rung on the great chain of being, is the Hottentot. The physical appearance of the Hottentot is, indeed, the central nineteenth-century icon for sexual difference between the European and the black . . .

. . . To meet [nineteenth-century] scientific standards, a paradigm was needed which would technically place both the sexuality and the beauty of the black in a an antithetical position to that of the white. This paradigm would have to be rooted in some type of unique and observable physical difference; they found that difference in the distinction they drew between the pathological and the normal in the medical model. . . . [T]he medical model assumes the polygenetic difference between the races.[2]

. . . J. J. Virey . . . was the author of the study of race standard in the early nineteenth century and also contributed a major essay (the only one on a specific racial group) to the widely cited *Dictionnaire des sciences médicales* [*Dictionary of medical sciences*] (1819).[3] In this essay, Virey summarized his (and his contemporaries') views on the sexual nature of black females in terms of acceptable medical discourse. According to him, their 'voluptuousness' is 'developed to a degree of lascivity unknown in our climate, for their sexual organs are much more developed than those of whites'. Elsewhere, Virey cites the Hottentot woman as the epitome of this sexual lasciviousness and stresses the relationship between her physiology and her physiognomy (her 'hideous form' and her 'horribly flattened nose'). His central proof is a discussion of the unique structure of the Hottentot female's sexual parts, the description of which he takes from the anatomical studies published by his contemporary, Georges Cuvier.[4] According to Cuvier, the black female looks different. Her physiognomy, her skin color, the form of her genitalia label her as inherently different. In the nineteenth century, the black female was widely perceived as possessing not only a 'primitive' sexual appetite but also the external signs of this temperament – 'primitive' genitalia. Eighteenth-century travelers to southern Africa, such as François Le Vaillant and John Barrow, had described the so-called Hottentot apron, a hypertrophy of the labia and nymphae caused by the manipulation of the genitalia and serving as a sign of beauty among certain tribes, including the Hottentots and Bushmen as well as tribes in Basutoland and Dahomey.[5]

The exhibition in 1810 of Saartjie Baartman, also called Sarah Bartmann or Saat-Jee and known as the 'Hottentot Venus', caused a public scandal in a London inflamed by the issue of the abolition of slavery, since she was exhibited 'to the public in a manner offensive to decency. She . . . does exhibit all the shape and frame of her body as if naked'. The state's objection was as much to her lewdness as to her status as an indentured black. In France her presentation was similar. Sarah Bartmann was not the only African to be so displayed: in 1829 a nude Hottentot woman, also called 'the Hottentot Venus', was the prize attraction at a ball given by the Duchess Du Barry in Paris. A contemporary print emphasized her physical difference from the observers portrayed.[6] After more than five years of exhibition in Europe, Sarah Bartmann died in Paris in 1815 at the age of twenty-five. An autopsy was performed on her which was first written up by Henri de Blainville in 1816 and then, in its most famous version, by Cuvier in 1817.[7] Reprinted at least twice during the next decade, Cuvier's description reflected de Blainville's two intentions: the comparison of a female of the 'lowest' human species with the highest ape (the orangutan) and the description of the anomalies of the Hottentot's 'organ of generation'. It is important to note that Sarah Bartmann was exhibited not to show her genitalia but rather to present another anomaly which the European audience (and pathologists such as de Blainville and Cuvier) found riveting. This was the steatopygia, or protruding buttocks, the other physical characteristic of the Hottentot female which captured the eye of early European travelers. Thus the figure of Sarah Bartmann was reduced to her sexual parts. The audience which had paid to see her buttocks and had fantasized about the uniqueness of her genitalia when she was alive could, after her death and dissection, examine both, for Cuvier presented to 'the Academy the genital organs of this woman prepared in a way so as to allow one to see the nature of the labia'.[8]

Sarah Bartmann's sexual parts, her genitalia and her buttocks, serve as the central image for the black female throughout the nineteenth century. And the model of de Blainville's and Cuvier's descriptions, which center on the detailed presentation of the sexual parts of the black, dominates all medical description of the black during the nineteenth century. To an extent, this reflects the general nineteenth-century understanding of female sexuality as pathological: the female genitalia were of interest partly as examples of the various pathologies which could befall them but also because the female genitalia came to define the female for the nineteenth century. . . . [W]hen one turns to the autopsies of Hottentot females in the nineteenth century, their description centres about the sexual parts. . . . These presentations of Hottentot or Bushman women all focus on the presentation of the genitalia and buttocks. Flower, the editor of the *Journal of Anatomy and Physiology*, included his dissection study in the opening volume of that framed journal. His ideological intent was clear. He wished to provide data 'relating to the unity or plurality of mankind'. His description begins with a detailed presentation of the form and size of the buttocks and concludes with his portrayal of the 'remarkable development of the labia minoria, or nymphae, which is so general a characteristic of the Hottentot and Bushman race'. These were 'sufficiently well marked to distinguish these parts at once from those of any of the ordinary varieties of the human species'. The polygenetic argument is the ideological basis for all the dissections of these women. If their sexual parts could be shown to be inherently different, this would be a sufficient sign that the blacks were a separate (and, needless to say, lower) race, as different from the European as the proverbial orangutan. Similar arguments had been made about the nature of all blacks' (and not just Hottentots') genitalia, but almost always concerning the female. . . . In comparison, when one turns to the description of the autopsies of black males from approximately the same period, the absence of any discussion of the male genitalia whatsoever is striking. For example, William Turner, in his three dissections of male blacks in 1878, 1879, and 1896, makes no mention at all of the genitalia.[9] The uniqueness of the genitalia and buttocks of the black is thus associated primarily with the female and is taken to be a sign solely of an anomalous *female* sexuality.

By mid-century the image of the genitalia of the Hottentot had assumed a certain set of implications. The central view is that these anomalies are inherent, biological variations rather than adaptions. In Theodor Billroth's standard handbook of gynecology, a detailed presentation of the 'Hottentot apron' is part of the discussion of errors in development of the female genitalia (*Entwicklungsfehler*). By 1877 it was a commonplace that the Hottentot's anomalous sexual form was similar to other errors in the development of the labia. The author of this section links this malformation with the overdevelopment of the clitoris, which he sees as leading to those 'excesses' which 'are called "lesbian love"'. The concupiscence of the black is thus associated also with the sexuality of the lesbian.[10] In addition, the idea of a congenital error incorporates the disease model applied to the deformation of the labia in the Hottentot, for the model of degeneracy presumes some acquired pathology in one generation which is the direct cause of the stigmata of degeneracy in the next. . . .

At this point, an aside might help explain both the association of the genitalia, a primary sexual characteristic, and the buttocks, a secondary sexual characteristic, in their role as the semantic signs of 'primitive' sexual appetite and activity. Havelock Ellis . . . believed that there is an absolute scale of beauty which is totally objective and which ranges from the European to the black. Thus men of the lower races, according to Ellis, admire European women more than their own, and women of lower races attempt to whiten themselves with face powder. Ellis then proceeded to list the secondary sexual characteristics which comprise this ideal of beauty, rejecting the 'naked sexual organ[s]' as not 'aesthetically beautiful' since it is 'fundamentally necessary' that they 'retain their primitive characteristics'. Only people 'in a low state of culture' perceive the 'naked sexual organs as objects of attraction'.[11] The list of secondary sexual characteristics which Ellis then gives as the signs of a cultured (that is, not primitive) perception of the body – the vocabulary of aesthetically pleasing signs – begins with the buttocks. This is, of course, a nineteenth-century fascination with the buttocks as a displacement for the genitalia. Ellis gives it the quality of a higher regard for the beautiful. His discussions of the buttocks ranks the races by size of the female pelvis . . . Darwin himself, who held similar views as to the objective nature of human beauty, saw the pelvis as a 'primary [rather] than as a secondary . . . character' and the buttocks of the Hottentot as a somewhat comic sign of the primitive, grotesque nature of the black female.[12]

When the Victorians saw the female black, they saw her in terms of her buttocks and saw represented by the buttocks all the anomalies of her genitalia. In a mid-century erotic caricature of the Hottentot Venus, a white male observer views her through a telescope, unable to see anything but her buttocks.[13] This fascination with the uniqueness of the sexual parts of the black focuses on the buttocks over and over again. . . .

In the nineteenth century, the prostitute is perceived as the essential sexualized female. She is perceived as the embodiment of sexuality and of all that is associated with sexuality – disease as well as passion.[14] Within the large and detailed literature concerning prostitution written during the nineteenth century (most of which documents the need for legal controls and draws on the medical model as perceived by public health officials), the physiognomy and physiology of the prostitute are analyzed in detail. We can begin with the most widely read early nineteenth-century work on prostitution, that of A. J. B. Parent-Duchatelet, who provides a documentation of the anthropology of the prostitute in his study of prostitution in Paris (1836).[15] . . . He presents his readers with a statistical description of the physical types of the prostitutes, the nature of their voices, the color of their hair and eyes, their physical anomalies, and their sexual profile in relation to childbearing and disease. Parent-Duchatelet's descriptions range from the detailed to the anecdotal. His discussion of the *embonpoint* of the prostitute begins his litany of external signs. Prostitutes have a 'peculiar plumpness' which is attributed to 'the great number of hot baths which the major part of these woman take' – or perhaps to their lassitude, since they rise at ten or eleven in the morning, 'leading an animal life'. They are fat as prisoners are fat, from simple confinement. As an English commentator noted, 'the grossest and stoutest of these women are to be found amongst the lowest and most disgusting classes of prostitutes'.[16] These are the Hottentots on the scale of the sexualized female.

When Parent-Duchatelet considers the sexual parts of the prostitutes, he provides two sets of information which merge to become part of the myth of the physical anthropology of the prostitute. The prostitute's sexual parts are in no way directly affected by her profession. . . . While he does not see the genitalia of the prostitute altering, he does observe that prostitutes were subject to specific pathologies of their genitalia. They are especially prone to tumors 'of the great labia . . . which commence with a little pus and tumefy at each menstrual period' (*P*, p. 49). He identifies the central pathology of the prostitute in the following manner: 'Nothing is more frequent in prostitutes than common abscesses in the thickness of the labia majora' (*P*, p. 50). Parent-Duchatelet's two views – first, that there is no adaption of the sexual organ and, second, that the sexual organ is especially prone to labial tumors and abscesses – merge in the image of the prostitute as developing, through illness, an altered appearance of the genitalia.

From the Parent-Duchatelet's description of the physical appearance of the prostitute (a catalog which reappears in most nineteenth-century studies of prostitutes, such as Josef Schrank's study of the prostitutes of Vienna), it is but a small step to the use of such catalogs of stigmata as a means of categorizing those women who have, as Freud states, 'an aptitude for prostitution' (*SE*, 7:191).[17] The major work of nineteenth-century physical anthropology, public health, and pathology to undertake this was written by Pauline Tarnowsky. . . . Her categories remain those of Parent-Duchatelet. She describes the excessive weight of prostitutes, their hair and eye color; she provides anthropometric measurements of skull size, a catalog of their family background (as with Parent-Duchatelet, most are the children of alcoholics), and their level of fecundity (extremely low) as well as the signs of their degeneration. These signs deal with the abnormalities of the face: asymmetry of features, misshapen noses, overdevelopment of the parietal region of the skull, and the appearance of the so-called Darwin's ear. All of these signs are the signs of the lower end of the scale of beauty, the end dominated by the Hottentot. All of these signs point to the 'primitive' nature of the prostitute's physiognomy, for stigmata such as Darwin's ear (the simplification of the convolutes of the ear shell and the absence of a lobe) are a sign of the atavistic female.

In a later paper, Tarnowsky provided a scale of appearance of the prostitute, in an analysis of the 'physiognomy of the Russian prostitute'. At the upper end of the scale is the 'Russian Helen'. Here, classical aesthetics are introduced as the measure of the appearance of the sexualized female. A bit further on is one who is 'very handsome in spite of her hard expression'. Indeed, the first fifteen prostitutes on her scale 'might pass on the street for beauties'. But hidden even within these seeming beauties are the stigmata of criminal degeneration: black, thick hair; a strong jaw; a hard, spent glance. . . .

. . . Change over time affects the physiognomy of the prostitute just as it does her genitalia, which become more and more diseased as she ages. For Tarnowsky, the appearance of the prostitute and her sexual identity are preestablished by heredity. What is most striking is that as the prostitute ages, she begins to appear more and more mannish. The link between the physical anomalies of the Hottentot and those of the lesbian appear in Billroth's Handbuch der Frauenkrankheiten (Handbook of gynecologial diseases); here, the link is between two further models of sexual deviancy, the prostitute and the lesbian. Both are seen as possessing the physical signs which set them apart from the normal.

The paper in which Tarnowsky undertook her documentation of the appearance of the prostitute is repeated word for word in the major late nineteenth-century study of prostitution This study of the criminal woman, subtitled The Prostitute and the Normal Woman, written by Cesare Lombroso and his son-in-law, Guillaume Ferrero, was published in 1893.[18] Lombroso accepts Tarnowsky's entire manner of seeing the prostitute and articulates one further subtext of central importance in the perception of the sexualized woman in the nineteenth century. Thus subtext becomes apparent only by examining the plates in his study. Two of the plates deal with the image of the Hottentot female and illustrate the 'Hottentot apron' and the steatopygia. Lombroso accepts Parent-Duchatelet's image of the fat prostitute and sees her as similar to women living in asylums and to the Hottentot female. He regards the anomalies of the prostitute's labia as atavistic throwbacks to the Hottentot, if not the Chimpanzee. Lombroso deems the prostitute to be an atavistic subclass of woman, and he applies the lower of the polygenetic argument to the image of the Hottentot to support his views. Lombroso's text, in its offhanded use of the analogy between the Hottentot and the prostitute, simply articulates in images a view which had been present throughout the late nineteenth century. . . . Ferrero, Lombroso's coauthor, described prostitution as the rule in primitive societies and placed the Bushman at the nadir of the scale of primitive lasciviousness: adultery has no meaning for them, he asserted, nor does virginity; the poverty of their mental universe can be seen in the fact that they have but one word for 'girl, woman, or wife'.[19] The primitive is the black, and the qualities of blackness, or at least of the black female, are those of the prostitute. The work of a student of Lombroso's, Abele de Blasio, makes this grotesquely evident: he published a series of case studies on steatopygia in prostitutes in which he perceives the prostitute as being, quite literally, the Hottentot.[20]

The perception of the prostitute in the late nineteenth century thus merged with the perception of the black. Both categories are those of outsiders, but what does this amalgamation imply in terms of the perception of both groups? It is a commonplace that the primitive was associated with unbridled sexuality. . . . Blacks, if both G. W. F. Hegel and Arthur Schopenhauer are to be believed, remained at this most primitive stage, and their presence in the contemporary world served as an indicator of how far mankind had come in establishing control over his world and himself. The loss of control was marked by a regression into this dark past – a degeneracy into the primitive expression of emotions in the form of either madness or unrestrained sexuality. Such a loss of control was, of course, viewed as pathological and thus fell into the domain of the medical model. . . .

The 'white *man's* burden' thus becomes his sexuality and its control, and it is this which is transferred into the need to control the sexuality of the Other, the Other as sexualized female. The colonial mentality which sees 'natives' as needing control is easily transferred to 'woman' – but woman as exemplified by the caste of the prostitute. . . .

Notes

1   See John Herbert Eddy, Jr, 'Buffon, Organic Change, and the Races of Man' (Ph.D. dissertation, University of Oklahoma, 1977), p. 709. See also Paul Alfred Erickson, 'The Origins of Physical Anthropology' (Ph.D. dissertation, University of Connectucut, 1974) and Werner Krauss, *Zur Anthropologie des achtzehnten Jahrhunderts: Die Frühgeschichte der Menschheit im Blickpunkt der Aufklärung*, ed. Hans Kortum and Christa Gohrisch (Munich, 1979).

2   See William F. Bynum, 'The great chain of being after forty years: an appraisal', *History of Science*, 13 (1975): 1–28, and 'Time's Noblest Offspring: The Problem of Man in British Natural Historical Sciences' (Ph.D. dissertation, Cambridge, 1974).

3   See J. J. Virey, 'Nègre,' *Dictionnaire des sciences médicales*, forty-one volumes (Paris, 1819), 35: 398–403.

4   See Virey, *Histoire naturelle du genre humaine*, two volumes (Paris, 1824), 2: 151.

5   See George M. Gould and Walter L. Pyle, *Anomalies and Curiosities of Medicine* (Philadelphia, 1901), p. 307, and Eugen Holländer, *Aeskulap und Venus. Eine Kultur- und Sittengeschichte im Spiegel des Arztes* (Berlin, 1928). Much material on the indebtedness of the early pathologists to the reports of travelers to Africa can be found in the accounts of the autopsies I will discuss below.
One indication of the power which the image of the Hottentot still possessed in the late nineteenth century can be found in George Eliot, *Daniel Deronda*, ed. Barbara Hardy (1876; Harmondsworth, 1967). On its surface the novel is a

hymn to racial harmony and an attack on British middle-class bigotry. Eliot's liberal agenda is nowhere better articulated than in the ironic debate concerning the nature of the black in which the eponymous hero of the novel defends black sexuality (see p. 376). This position is attributed to the hero not a half-dozen pages after the authorial voice of the narrator introduced the description of this very figure with the comparison: 'And one man differs from another, as we all differ from the Bosjesman' (p. 370). Eliot's comment is quite in keeping with the underlying understanding of race in the novel. For just as Deronda is fated to marry a Jewess and thus avoid the taint of race mixing, so too is the Bushman, a Hottentot surrogate in the nineteenth century, isolated from the rest of mankind. The ability of Europeans to hold simultaneously a polygenetic view of race and a liberal ideology is evident as far back as Voltaire. But in Eliot's novel the Jew is contrasted to the Hottentot, and, as we have seen, it is the Hottentot who serves as the icon of pathologically corrupted sexuality. Can Eliot be drawing a line between outsiders such as the Jew or the sexualized female in Western society and the Hottentot? The Hottentot comes to serve as the sexualized Other on to whom Eliot projects the opprobrium with which she herself was labeled. For Eliot, the Hottentot remains beyond the pale; even in the most whiggish text, the Hottentot remains the essential Other.

6   Paul Edwards and James Walvin, *Black Personalities in the Era of the Slave Trade* (Baton Rouge (LA, 1983), pp. 173, 175. A print of the 1829 ball in Paris with the nude 'Hottentot Venus' is reproduced in *Illustrierte Geschichte der Medizin*, ed. Richard Toellner, nine volumes (Salzburg, 1980), 4: 1319; this is a German reworking of Jacques Vie *et al.*, *Histoire de la médicine*, eight volumes (Paris, 1977).

7   See Henri de Blainville, 'Sur une femme de la race hottentote', *Bulletin des sciences par la société philomatique de Paris* (1816): 183–90. This early version of the autopsy seems to be unknown to William B. Cohen, *The French Encounter with Africans: White Response to Blacks, 1530–1880* (Bloomington IN, 1980), especially pp. 239–45. See also Stephen Jay Gould, 'The Hottentot Venus', *Natural History* 91 (1982): 20 7.

8   Georges Cuvier, 'Extraits d'observations faites sur la cadavre d'une femme connue à Paris et à Londres sous le non de Vénus Hottentote', *Memoires du Museum d'histoire naturelle* 3 (1817): 259–74; reprinted with plates in Geoffrey Saint-Hilaire and Frédéric Cuvier, *Histoire naturelle des mammiferes avec des figures originales*, two volumes (Paris, 1824), 1: 1–23. The substance of the autopsy is reprinted again by Flourens in the *Journal complémentaire du dictionnaire des sciences médicales* 4 (1819): 145–9, and by Jules Cloquet, *Manuel d'anatomie de l'homme descriptive du corps humaine* (Paris, 1825), plate 278. Cuvier's presentation of the 'Hottentot Venus' forms the major signifier for the image of the Hottentot as sexual primitive in the nineteenth century.

9   See William Turner, 'Notes on the dissection of a Negro', *Journal of Anatomy and Physiology* 13 (1878): 382–6; 'Notes on the dissection of a second Negro', *Journal of Anatomy and Physiology* 14 (1879): 244–8; and 'Notes on the dissection of a third Negro', *Journal of Anatomy and Physiology* 31 (1896): 624–6. This was not merely a British anomaly. Jefferies Wyman reports the dissection of a black suicide (originally published in *Proceedings of the Boston Society of Natural History*, 2 April 1862 and 16 December 1863) and does not refer to the genitalia of the male Hottentot at all; see *Anthropological Review* 3 (1865): 330–5.

10   H. Hildebrandt, *Die Krankheiten der äusseren weiblichen Genitalien*, in *Handbuch der Frauenkrankheiten 3*, ed. Theodor Billroth, three volumes (Stuttgart, 1885–86), pp. 11–12. See also Thomas Power Lowry (ed.) *The Classic Clitoris: Historic Contributions to Scientific Sexuality* (Chicago, 1978).

11   Havelock Ellis, *Studies in the Psychology of Sex*, vol. 4, *Sexual Selection in Man* (Philadelphia, 1920), p. 158 . . .

12   Charles Darwin, *The Descent of Man and Selection in Relation to Sex* (Princeton NJ, 1981), 2: 317, and see 2: 345–6.

13   See John Grand-Carteret, *Die Erotik in der Französischen Karikatur*, trans. Cary von Karwarth and Adolf Neumann (Vienna, 1909), p. 195.

14   The best study of the image of the prostitute is Alain Corbin, *Les Filles de noce: misère sexuelle et prostitution (dix-neuvième et vingtième siècles)* (Paris, 1978). On the black prostitute, see Khalid Kishtainy, *The Prostitute in Progressive Literature* (London, 1982), pp. 74–84. On the iconography associated with the pictorial representation of the prostitute in nineteenth-century art, see Hess and Nochlin, *Woman as Sex Object*; Nochlin, 'Lost and Found: once more the fallen woman', *Art Bulletin* 60 (March 1978): 139–53; and Lynda Nead, 'Seduction, prostitution, suicide: *On the Brink* by Alfred Elmore', *Art History* 5 (September 1982): 310–22. On the special status of medical representations of female sexuality, see the eighteenth-century wax models of female anatomy in the Museo della Specola, Florence, and reproduced in Mario Bucci, *Anatomia come arte* (Florence, 1969), especially plate 8.

15   See A. J. B. Parent-Duchatelet, *De la prostitution dans la ville de Paris*, two volumes (Paris, 1836). 1: 193–244.

16   Parent-Duchatelet, *On Prostitution in the City of Paris* (London, 1840), p. 38; all further references to this work, abbreviated *P*, will be included in the text. It is exactly the passages on the physiognomy and appearance of the prostitute which this anonymous translator presents to his English audience as the essence of Parent-Duchatelet's work.

17   See my 'Freud and the prostitute: male stereotypes of female sexuality in *fin de siècle* Vienna', *Journal of the American Academy of Psychoanalysis* 9 (1981): 337–60. [SE, Standard Edition.]

18   See Cesare Lombroso and Guillaume Ferrero, *La donna deliquente: la prostituta e la donna normale* (Turin, 1893), especially pp. 349–50, 361–62, and 38.

19   See Ferrero, 'L'atavisme de la prostitution', *Révue scientifique* (1892): 136–41.

20   See A. de Blasio, 'Staetopigia in prostitute', *Archivio di psichiatria* 26 (1905): 257–64.

Chapter 45

Emmanuel Reynaud

MANLY AESTHETICS

In this extract from his scathing critique of masculinity, Emmanuel Reynaud illustrates the ways in which men impose standards of 'beauty' on women's bodies while denying their own embodiment.

From *Holy Virility*, London: Pluto Press (1983).

Manly aesthetics

THE WAY MAN TREATS his physical appearance and imposes feminine aesthetics on women is a good illustration of his attitude towards the body. It can be seen from clothes and from fashion in general, where virility and femininity express their different functions, heightening anatomical differences, increasing women's dependence and stressing anything that seems to represent human strength in the man.

Man identifies woman with nature and treats her accordingly: he tames and cultivates her. Just as he turns forests into fields and gardens, so he makes women into housewives and models. As woman is supposed to hold the key to all the dark and disturbing mysteries of the body, man seeks to give her a reassuring and seductive image. She represents the fear and disgust he feels for the flesh; by moulding her according to his own interests, he is trying to give her a reassuring form. And so when a woman takes off her pinafore she must be 'beautiful'; it is out of the question for her to be natural – she is supposed to be natural enough as it is. She must wear make-up, be deodorised, perfumed, shave her legs and armpits, put on stockings, high heels, show her legs, emphasise her breasts, pull in her stomach, paint her nails, dye her hair, tame her hairstyle, pierce her ears, reduce her appetite and, without making a single clumsy gesture, or uttering one word too many, she must seem happy, dainty and original.

By imposing femininity on women, man not only establishes his power and creates objects which are pleasant to behold, he also aims to produce, out of the restrictions and discomfort that women suffer, the inverted image of his own freedom and independence (the example used is one of fashion and dress, but we could also speak of mutilation, various forms of physical, intellectual and sexual violence, limiting or forbidding contraception and abortion, etc.): the more man restricts the freedom and well-being of a woman through her body, the more he feels he is in control of his own body and certain of his pleasures. He is not dependent, as she is, on the fickleness of looks, on the flimsiness of a girdle or the precariousness of a stiletto heel; flabby, paunchy, bald or spotty, what does it matter? What is important for a man is what is in his head and his strength: he is not fallow flesh to be enhanced, but a mind, lord and master of his body. Make no mistake about it: the stronger sex is certainly not the fair sex!

One of the main purposes of clothing is to differentiate the sexes. The wearing of trousers is obligatory for Western men and French law even forbids a man to wear a skirt or a dress outside carnival time; on the other hand, it is only recently that women have started wearing trousers. In France it was generally forbidden in high schools before 1968, and, even today, a woman who has to take an examination, or go to a job interview, is advised not to wear trousers. She must show her legs and make her vagina accessible, whereas a man does not have to reveal his calves or offer easy access to his penis. One does not trifle with the accessories of the difference between the sexes; that is why, a few years ago, the Thai army radio, accusing the police of being 'soft' in the upholding of law and order, gave the following advice: 'The police chiefs ought to get a new uniform and swap their trousers for skirts.'[1]

The attitudes of the two sexes towards clothes are also completely different. Woman, supposed to exist only as a body, is expected to 'embellish' it, and 'personalise' it, to dress with a certain originality – to the extent that the same dress worn by two different women can transform a party into a disaster. Man, on the other hand, need not worry so much about his appearance, as it is of secondary importance to his mind or muscles; if he does pay any attention to his clothes it is to ensure that they symbolise his strength or conceal his flesh.

Mostly man seeks to let his body blend into uniformity and to use dress as the symbol of his power. This ambitious project is usually realised in the army, which is the last stage in the initiation into the joys of virility. The minute he reports to army camp, man is greeted with the barber's clippers and a uniform: not a hair must be out of place, no colour must clash; and, when they are all at attention, it must look like there is only one head. The purpose of military uniform is not only to standardise, it also symbolises strength and the exercise of power. The material and the colours, the boots and the clothes themselves – fatigues, battledress, parka, etc. – everything is designed for efficiency in battle. Of course, in civilian life, man is not this military caricature; even so, the colours he prefers are neutral and dull – grey, beige, dark brown, navy blue – and there is not much variety in style: he traditionally sports suit and tie, or for everyday wear, different variations of the eternal shapeless jacket, baggy trousers and heavy, uncomfortable shoes.

Still, it seems recently that a new outfit – jeans, bomber jacket and running shoes – has become increasingly popular. The colours are usually less sad but they remain pure – red, black, green, blue – and the clothing is tighter-fitting. Apart from the ease and mobility it offers, this dress has the advantage of looking sporty, evoking strength and physical prowess. That is no doubt one of the main reasons for its success. Rather than comfort, he looks for an expression of his power in his clothes and accessories. Once again, the army is the best example of the masculine approach: the only touches which individualise the uniform are the stripes and decorations; these are so highly esteemed that leaders like Brezhnev, Bokassa or Amin Dada used to cover their chests with medals. And when man does not have, or no longer has, the opportunity of sticking decorations all over himself, he can still fall back on wearing a black leather jacket, or a president-style suit: anything will do to symbolise power.

Masculine elegance provides a good example of the way man asserts himself through standardisation and through control over his body. A distinguished or smart outfit is neither complicated nor very varied: it consists of a two- or three-piece suit in a (very) dark colour, black or dark-coloured shoes, a pale shirt, white, more often than not, dull socks and underwear. To round off, the whole effect, a long thin band of material called a 'tie' is knotted under the chin. If the rest is not particularly comfortable the tie is downright unpleasant. To understand its presence, it must be remembered that the neck is a crucial point; the link between the head and the rest of the body – in short, in masculine imagery, it is the dividing line between the flesh and the mind. Therefore it is of utmost importance to draw attention to the boundary, and to try and eliminate the risk of a link being made, a garrotte is placed between the two. Thus, the tie is reassuring; just observe a man straightening his tie after a tricky situation – whew! that's better – he seems able to breathe again: his neck is tightly gripped, he is no more than a head suspended in the air.

As Charles Reich points out in *The Greening of America* 'Sitting across from a man in a business suit, it is as if he did not have a body at all, just a face and a voice.' That is precisely the effect sought by the well groomed man: but the face must not reveal a hint of sensuality, it must be nothing more than a receptacle for the brain. His face must not express a trace of innocence or neglect, and so he is clean-shaven and his hair is closely cropped; a humiliation which is sometimes inflicted on women, but for the man it is the confirmation of his power. As one general said, at a time when there was a slight wave of protest in the French army: 'You will not ride twice in a tank with long hair!'

It seems that over the last few years, a new attitude towards masculine aesthetics has developed. Some of the people in charge are worried – will it be possible to tell men from women, is man becoming effeminate? So far it is not too serious; in the 1960s young people simply refused to camouflage their corporality under a white shirt or submit to the barber's razor: a rejection of the clean-cut close shave. Masculine hair was worn much longer, clothes became less drab and more comfortable, and, to the rhythm of rock music, masculine aesthetics took a step forward.

From the Beatles, who caused a scandal for setting the trend for 'long' hair, to David Bowie and Lou Reed, who went in for transvestism, including Mick

Jagger and the Californian rock groups at the end of the 1960s, man's image has undergone some changes. But in spite of appearances (and not forgetting the backlash that has taken place since – macho fashion: tie, close-cropped hair, black leather, pointed boots, etc.) virility has remained intact. To the classic insult 'With your long hair you look like a woman' the answer was, for example, very rarely 'That's true. It's good – why don't you try it?' but rather 'That doesn't mean anything, I'm still a man, I am, mate.' And, if the balance of power and the tension were sufficient, this altercation could easily end in a fight. Moreover, to avoid any ambiguity or error, long hair was quickly accompanied by irrefutable proof or virility: sideburns, beard or moustache – clear emblems – and often heavy boots, leather jacket and a mean expression were added for good measure.

Similarly, the beauty industry, sensing the change, began a long-term offensive aimed at men. Since their favourite field, woman's body, was almost totally colonised – from the most 'intimate' parts to the most 'feminine' days – they could only maintain their expansion rate by using imagination and extending their market to include products for men. From the beginning, it was a matter of not being too ambitious, and gradually easing men on from shaving products towards deodorants and perfumes. The principal line of attack was first of all to rid perfume of its exclusively feminine character so that it could become a new attribute of virility. Not a simple task, and the advertisers used kid gloves to put over the message – 'Don't worry, if you wear perfume, you won't become sensual and desirable but sporty and elegant, virile and refined. You will smell clean and tough, you won't become a woman; on the contrary, you'll be even more of a man.' Everything has been used, from the most virile-sounding names – Brut, Victor, Mandate – to the most varied male images – from Don Juan to Henry Cooper. With slogans like 'the great smell of Brut', the path has been cleared, man has picked up the scent.

Over the last few years stylishness has become a new facet of virility, which now tends to adopt the more flexible name of 'masculinity'. Perfume and elegance, once the prerogative of the aristocrat and the bourgeois, have been democratised on the body of the trendy young executive. The man who knows how 'to live' nowadays is increasingly elegant, he has exchanged his plain white pants and vest for red, yellow or striped ones, his suits have got a little lighter and are cut to follow the contours of his body, his hair is longer and more attention is paid to the style. What is more, he invariably leaves in his wake a fresh and discreet smell, the product of various syntheses of modern chemistry.

The market has kept pace. Boutiques for 'him' are opening and prospering everywhere; small local barbers with their clippers are being replaced, little by little, by much more sophisticated hairdressing salons; and on street corners, advertisements of half-naked men showing off the colours of their new underpants can be seen. But here the advertisers become very cautious again, they know that they must not go too far; in France in 1967 an advertisement showing the blurred silhouette of a naked man in semi-darkness caused an outcry, and since then too much masculine nudity has been avoided. It is a matter of not confusing the genders: the body which is plastered naked over walls, photographed from every angle and in every position, is that of the woman – on the rare posters where man exposes his flesh, not only is he wearing underpants but he keeps his running shoes on or

wears a grimace of physical exertion; and if by chance he risks a slightly suggestive pose, then it is balanced by *The Times* in his hand.

The beauty industry is cautious in its approach; for them, it is not a matter
of questioning the sex categories but of exploiting them to the utmost and using
any means available to play on the frustrations these categories bring about. Thus
the mechanisms for exploiting women through femininity have been highly polished
and the dividends pay off regularly; as for man, the offensive is barely under
way when already a new masculinity is rising over the horizon and it seems clear
that to sell him 'a right to beauty', when he is bogged down in the uniformity
of his dress and hatred for his body, will prove to be an excellent prospect to
exploit. . . .

Note

1   *Le Monde*, August 1975, pp. 10–11.

Chapter 46

David Morgan

YOU TOO CAN HAVE A BODY LIKE MINE

David Morgan surveys the sociological literature on the body and challenges the overemphasis on women's embodiment. In turning to men's bodies he analyses the ways in which they are managed so that men appear to be the embodiment of rationality and civilisation.

From S. Scott and D. H. J. Morgan (eds) *Body Matters: Essays on the Sociology of the Body*, London: Falmer (1993).

IF, IN GENERAL, THE SOCIOLOGY of the body is a relatively late arrival on the scene, the sociology of the male body would seem to be even more of a newcomer. . . . This concentration on women's bodies is clearly apparent in that area of sociology most directly concerned with bodily matters, the sociology of health and illness. This is not simply a greater representation of issues dealing with women – childbirth, menstruation, eating disorders and so on – but the greater likelihood of a more gendered discussion where women are the subject of the research in question. . . .

. . . An emphasis upon women and their bodies was clearly an important and necessary part of the feminist critique as women became increasingly aware of the various ways in which patriarchy entailed various forms of control over their bodies (Freund 1983: 24). Martin, for example, noted how, for the women in her sample, a central image was one of separation from self and body (Martin 1987: 77). None of this should be ignored or marginalized, nevertheless, it might be argued that one of the paradoxical consequences of this feminist critique has been the relative underemphasis on men and their bodies, thereby leaving some aspects of the exercise of men's power unexamined.

If it be the case that, at least superficially, women tend to be more embodied and men less embodied in social scientific, popular and feminist writings and representations, various reasons might readily be provided for such a bias. Very generally, it may be seen as part of a wider problem which has only recently begun to be rectified, namely one where women are more likely to be problematized than men. Wherever women are the subject of examination, directly or indirectly – whether it be health studies, cultural studies, the sociology of work and industry or criminology – the analysis tends to be more gendered than similar treatments where men are the research subjects. A greater emphasis upon women's bodies may, therefore, be part of this more general tendency. Further, a. greater tendency to write and speak of women and their bodies may be seen as reflecting the well-known ideological equation between women/men and nature/culture (Ortner 1974; Sydie 1987).

It might also be added that where 'issues of men and their bodies do come under sociological examination, the consequences are often limited and disappointing. Thus accounts with strong sociobiological overtones of body language or bodily abuse in discussion of young men and aggro, for example (Marsh 1978), tend to present a relatively unproblematic and depoliticized equation of masculinity and violence. These kinds of emphases are, or were, sometimes to be found in writings associated with men's studies or more critical accounts of men and masculinity. Here, a somewhat one-dimensional picture of men and their bodies emerges, one over-concerned with hardness, aggression and heterosexual performance, a kind of 'over-phallusized picture of man' (examples in various degrees: Easthope 1986; Hoch 1979, Reynaud 1983).

This chapter can only begin to suggest some of the complexities involved in considering men, masculinities and their bodies, in the hope that they may provide a research agenda for more detailed work. Contrary to what might seem to have been argued up to now, I begin with the argument that, in modern society at least, men and ideas of masculinity are both embodied and non-bodied. Clearly, bodily differences are taken as major magnifiers of differences between men and women, and these physical differences are often read, in complex ways, as being the very source of essential differences between the masculine and the feminine. The popular linkages between penis and strength, hardness and action are well known and have been the subject of critical deconstruction and satirical comment. Similarly, in many versions of popular masculine speech, to have balls is to have courage, nerve and to be, in a Goffmanesque sense, a man of action (Goffman 1967).

Yet, just as it would be wrong to accept uncritically the idea that women are the more embodied gender, so it would be misleading to see men as straightforwardly more embodied than women. Many images of men in sport, at war and in doing sex are highly embodied or, to be more exact, we are encouraged to read these representations in this way. Pictures of stockbrokers, bishops or dons might not seem as embodied as images of sportsmen or warriors, but if we fail to see their bodies in these cases this may be because of a prior framework of understanding that links men, bodies and action.

Moreover, many ways of understanding or constructing men and masculinity would seem to go to some lengths to exclude considerations of bodies. This is, of course, another variation on the nature/culture divide, especially where this shades into the mind/body distinction. Men, in this model, are reasonable, more clearly identified with rational activities, and are less emotional. This is not to say that men do not have emotions or feelings but rather that, within certain cultures at least, they are less likely to express these feelings in overt, visible and unambiguously embodied ways. Representations of the male body often seek to deny that body. The classic men's suit hides or minimizes the shape of the body (Byrde 1979) and, even in the supposed age of the new man. men are less likely to be described as wearing figure-hugging clothes. Clearly, of course, such representations of the male body are subject to very wide cultural and historical variation.

Hence, divisions between men and women cannot simply be expressed in terms of degrees of embodiment. In some constructions it is the man who is more embodied, where women may be seen as the more spiritual or refined. In other cases, as we have seen, it is women who are more clearly embodied. Further, degrees and kinds of embodiment signify differences between men as well as differences between women and men. Some men have more balls than other men; some men are coarser, more overtly physical, than others.

Beyond dichotomies

. . . [I]t is instructive to consider some of the ambiguities in connection with the more bodily aspects of the constructed differences between men and women. At first, the matter seems to be straightforward. Men's power is exercised in the public arena and this power frequently, one might say always, takes on a bodily form. This is closely linked to the occupation and the use of space:

> To be an adult male is distinctly to occupy space, to have a physical presence in the world.
>
> (Connell 1983:19)

Hooligans, subjects of popular fears and moral panics through the centuries (Pearson 1983), are groups of, for the most part, young men occupying public space in a particularly loud and aggressive manner. The verb 'to swagger' dealing with a particular kind of male performance in public space could rarely be applied to women. Men, as women sometimes complain, take up more space on public transport, and men's bodies predominate in public parades representing state power or military might. Whether by right or by force, men come to occupy public space in a distinctly embodied fashion.

Yet this is not the whole story. Often men in public space are, officially or unofficially, uniformed as soldiers, policemen, clergy or stockbrokers. The nature of uniform is, among other things, to divert attention away from the particularities and idiosyncrasies of specific bodies and to focus on generalized public roles and statuses. The disciplining of a body of men is at the expense of individual bodies. This is not to say that, for a wide range of societies, men do not tend to occupy public spaces with greater frequency and often greater freedom than women. However, the ways in which men occupy public space and the degrees to which such presences are licensed or circumscribed do vary considerably. Further, the claims to public spaces may be the subject of conflict and contestation between men and women, as we see in the debates around sexual harassment.

Rather than explore a whole range of other dichotomies and their interconnections with issues of gender and embodiment . . . I shall here develop one particular theme in order to highlight issues of complexity and ambiguity. This is, what I describe as the 'embodiment of reason'. . . . [A] major axis around which these issues are organized is between mind and body. This is not the place to explore complex philosophical issues but simply to raise some sociological themes. Whatever the complex term 'mind' signifies, it clearly overlaps with several other widely used terms such as 'thinking' or 'reason'. These terms have clear gender connotations in that they are more readily associated with men than with women in central ideological constructions. What is less readily appreciated is that they also have bodily connotations, despite the apparent location of the realms of thought, reason and mind in some trans-bodily space.

This is not simply a question of the obvious point that thinking is associated with a bodily organ, the brain. Let us consider Rodin's often reproduced (and parodied) statue, 'The Thinker'. Firstly, it is almost certainly no accident that the figure is a male figure, it is by no means certain if the statue would work if it depicted a woman in an identical pose. Further, it is clearly a matter of some importance that it is not any old male body that is being depicted. An obese figure or a skeletal figure would be as inappropriate as would be a female figure. Secondly, the figure clearly represents a special kind of unity of mind and body. The figure is not simply thinking: he can be said to be actively doing thinking.

Thinking, therefore, can be understood as being a particularly embodied way of being in the world. In so far as intellectual labour is woven into wider patterns of the sexual division of labour, then to do thinking is to occupy a particularly distinctive and often privileged place in space, public or private. The thinker allows for no interruptions from the mundane world of domestic responsibilities or small children. Yet obligations are placed upon the thinker to be seen doing thinking, to occupy space in a particular watchful or concentrating manner. Certain props, extensions of the body, may help, such as the book-lined study, thick-rimmed spectacles or a pipe, but the body has to be deployed in a way to legitimate the title of thinker.

Doing thinking also points out differences between men. Popular stereotypes locate the business of thinking in particular physical types such as eggheads and pointy-heads, and these popular images reflect wider patterns of the social division of labour between mental labour and manual labour. Although such stereotypes often associate the former with the lack of any kind of physicality, it can again be seen that the distinction in reality deals with different bodily ways of being in the world. Thinking, being reasonable, doing rationality, are all closely interconnected and are all socially distributed not simply between women and men but between different classes of status groups of men. These bodily contrasts are given dramatic expression in conventional depictions of industrial disputes. On the one side we have the mass meeting where individual bodies merge into a body of men; on the other side we have more identifiable individuals moving in and out of offices. On the one side the embodiment of feelings, on the other side the embodiment of rationality and efficiency. The analyses of media representations of industrial disputes have perhaps had less to say than they might have about the bodily codes around which such conflicts are constructed.

Men, power and bodies

The processes whereby women's bodies have, generally, been more problematized than those of men or, to put it another way, whereby women have been constructed as being more embodied than men, is clearly not a simple error or oversight. Intellectual blind spots generally have social and political roots, and issues to do with men and their bodies provide no exceptions to this rule. Here, as elsewhere, we are in the simplest terms dealing with systems of patriarchy or male power. However this troublesome word might be understood, one deeprooted and long-term feature of systems of patriarchal domination is the fact that men are not routinely required to reflect upon their positions as men in society or to consider themselves as gendered or embodied subjects. Throughout history, it is the relatively powerless who find themselves reflecting upon their identity in society and upon those social structural features that contribute to their minority, subordinate or marginal status within a given society. Only under certain situations of crisis do the relatively powerful find themselves engaging in similar processes of self-reflection.

It has frequently been argued that our present times constitute one such period of crisis for men and masculinity (see Morgan 1992). What we need to do here is to explore the relationships between issues of power and issues of embodied gender. We should not assume that the connections between men's bodies and systems of patriarchal power (and other power) are identical in all societies. Further comparative discussion is clearly necessary. However, confining our discussion to modern societies, one clear point of departure is, as has already been indicated, the Weberian theme of rationality (Seidler 1989). Where social systems come to be dominated by themes of rationality and where such themes become, covertly at least, to be identified with men, then issues of the body together with the associated issues of the emotions come to be marginalized. In many cases and in a variety of ways this has entailed being identified with women. This is not to say that bodies are inherently non-rational, but simply that the processes whereby rational systems develop tend, symbolically and often practically, to locate the source of that rationality outside the body in realms of pure thought, abstract reason or systems of logic, or, within but not of the body, in the realm of the mind. In the circle of men, power and rationality, men become less and women become more embodied. . . . Women 'do not simply come to an understanding of their lives as being significantly embodied in many ways, but also come to understand the systems of control and domination over their bodies (Freund 1983: 24). . . .

. . . There are intimate connections between issues of men's bodies and issues or men's power, and it has been the challenging of the latter that has led to the problematization of the former. Clearly, there are no difficulties in making the connections between patriarchal power and men's bodies. Popular or pornographic representations of the erect and thrusting penis; imperial representations of a glorious past or socialist representations of a glorious future; popular scientific discourses around body language: all these and many more features of modern culture make these equations without effort. The domination of men over other men, over women and over children (and indeed over animals and nature) are expressed in bodily terms, directly as well as indirectly. In his useful typology of body-use in action, Frank distinguishes between the Disciplined, the Dominating, the Mirroring and the Communicative Body (Frank 1991). While issues of gender and masculinity are not absent from these other three types, the links are most clearly expressed in his discussion of the Dominating Body:

> . . . it is impossible to consider the dominating body without also questioning the construction of the masculine body.
>
> (Frank 1991: 69)

Without going into the details of Frank's analysis (which at times leans towards essentialism) some general points may be made about the dominating body and masculinity. In the first place, while the most dramatic examples of the dominating body come from war and physical violence (Frank deals with Theweleit's analysis of fascist power at some length) such examples do not exhaust the range of possibilities. Dominance may be established in the board room as well as on the battlefield and, as studies of proxemics maintain, such dominance can be expressed in terms of bodily posture and sitting as well as through the more overtly physical deployments of the body. The discussion about the connections between power, rationality and masculinity underlines this point. Linked to this consideration is the continuing need to stress that such discussions of dominance should not be interpreted in straightforwardly biological or deterministic terms. It is not the possession of a penis which provides the basis for male dominance over women. Rather it is systems of patriarchy which enable the penis to be represented or understood in ways that express domination. Thirdly, it is clear that the dominations that are being discussed do not simply refer to dominations of men over women. We are also dealing with dominations of men over other men, and the possible and complex links between these and other patterns of domination.

It is especially important, when exploring the relationships between gender, bodies and domination, to avoid too simplified an account of the interconnections. The links between them are the outcome of complex and diverse historical and social processes rather than determinate laws. . . . In much of the recent men's literature, I find accounts of penis anxiety on the part of young men. They are supposed to be routinely concerned about the length of their penis and to engage in covert or overt comparisons with other young men. . . .

. . . Erections are a source of embarrassment and humour not simply because they draw attention to the penis, something that is normally kept well out of the public gaze in most Western cultural situations, but because they are seen, rightly or wrongly, as an outer signifier of inner thoughts and desires. While all kinds of stimuli (not all of these sexual by any means) might produce erections, the meanings given to such an event are primarily sexual. What is particularly disturbing about such events is their apparently arbitrary and unpredictable character. In short, the erection has an irrationality about it which contrasts markedly with Western, and especially middle-class, one might assume, themes of control and predictability. The erection is a jester in the wings of the civilizing process. . . .

Sites of bodily power

. . . A recognition of the multiplicity and diversity of sites where men, bodies and power converge should serve, yet again, as a warning against any kind of essentialism. While some sites are more obviously embodied than others (at least for a given culture) embodiment is a feature of all sites, certainly in those sites where gender and power interact. To illustrate this, I take a site where, to the superficial observer, issues of bodies and physicality would seem to be at their minimum, namely that of angling. I must be a little more specific here. While deep-sea fishing as a sport and fishing as an occupation have very strong associations with conventional constructions of masculinity, these considerations would seem to be at their minimum when contemplating the solitary figures on the banks of many English rivers or canals. Here there would seem to be no Hemingwayesque battle between Man and Nature and no collective camaraderie in the face of danger and uncertainty. Putting aside any of the more obvious and reductionist phallic connotations of the fishing rod or the emphasis upon the size of the catch, where are the bodies? Where is the masculinity?

In the absence of any specific research on this topic, what follows is simply suggestive. In the first place, angling very obviously takes place in the public space, even though the activity itself might seem to be highly privatized. An unproblematic occupation of a piece of public space, which appears to be so characteristic of leisure angling, is part of a wider phenomenon, the clear gender divide when it comes to the deployment of bodies in public or open spaces. Part of the reason why there appear to be so few women anglers is simply to do with expectations about the occupation of public space, free from sexual, or other, harassment.[1]

In the second place, angling is very obviously the deployment of a set of skills which, in common with all such skills, are to do with the control and deployment of the body. The fact that these skills are linked. directly and symbolically, with strong masculine traditions is also a matter of some significance. However, in keeping with some earlier observations in this chapter, I should emphasize the theme of control, the emphasis upon the development of particular sensitivities and the deployment of watchful patience, rather than the obvious deployment of brute strength.

Finally, angling has clear associations with what Goffman calls 'action', that is, with situations where outcomes are problematic and consequential (Goffman 1967). Action in this sense, as I have recorded elsewhere (Morgan 1990), has strong gendered, indeed masculine, connotations. Matters are more complex in the present example. The author of *The Complete Angler* or the *Contemplative Men's Recreation* (Walton 1983) argued that angling represented the meeting point of action and contemplation, locating the activity in well established but highly, if covertly, gendered philosophical debates. Hence, even in something like angling, the interplays between bodies and gender, and hence also power, are a complex and overdetermined phenomenon.

We may perhaps conclude, therefore, that there are no social sites or arenas which are unembodied just as there are no sites that are ungendered and that, in such sites, gender, power and bodies interact. This is not, of course, the same as saying that all sites are equally or similarly gendered or embodied. In order to begin to explore the nature of variations in embodied locations, we may first consider the extent to which, in a given culture, bodily deployment or display is licensed, permitted or required. Following the arguments of Elias about the associations between the civilizing process and bodily control (Elias 1978) both in terms of the internal and external controls, we may argue that certain forms of bodily expression or deployment are, in modern society, licensed or legitimated, but only for particular times and particular spaces. This is especially true where physical violence is concerned. The overlapping arenas of war and sport (especially physical contact sports such as boxing) are clear examples where particular kinds of bodily conduct are licensed or even required. Such conduct would be liable to negative sanctions were it to take place outside these arenas.

Yet we should not confine such arenas to those involving the deployment of physical violence. The world of fashion, for example, may often be an arena where certain kinds of display are permitted which might be the subject of negative or satirical comment were they to take place away from the catwalks. Thus the captions on one article on men's fashions read:

> Cowboy-style chaps over blue denim
> Macho man with feathered knickers
> A gaucho look, along with white gloves
> Chinese ideographs on a streamlined silhouette
> (All from *The European* 18–20 January 1991)

Similar observations may be made, perhaps more strongly, about the world of male strippers (Barham 1985).

Thus there are certain arenas where bodily deployment and display on the part of men may clearly be permitted. Overlapping with these are those arenas where bodily performance will be required. The distinctions here are often matters of degree. For example, there are certain work contexts where it would seem obvious that bodily skill and deployment will be required: policing, deep-sea fishing, extractive industries, etc. Even here, however, it is often difficult to distinguish between those features of bodily deployment which are strictly required by the work and those which are part of a masculine occupational context. Less obvious, perhaps, are the more private arenas where more particular expectations are made in terms of bodily performance. Chief among these must be those sites associated with sexuality where, conventionally, physical expectations come to the fore. While sexual advice, from manuals, magazines or therapists, will now routinely bracket the physical and the emotional, the emphasis will still tend to be around genital sex and intercourse. Conversely, sexual dysfunction (itself often seen as a signifier of relational or emotional problems) is conventionally understood in terms of such indicators as failure to achieve erection, failure to achieve orgasm or premature ejaculation . . .

It may be suggested that we are dealing here with contexts, often ceremonial contexts, where the generalized social body clearly takes precedence over the individual physical body. This is presumably why the soldier who faints on parade will be the object of censure or discipline. While such situations clearly impose their constraints on both women and men (one might think of the long periods of grooming and corseting that must have preceded ceremonial events in the upper-class season in late Victorian England) it is likely that, generally speaking, the expectations of bodily control fall more heavily upon men than women. This is partly because men are more likely to occupy centre stage on ceremonial and public occasions than women, and partly because, in the last two centuries at least, the formal dress of British men has tended away from the physical body and very much towards the social body.

It is possible, therefore, to think of a kind of continuum running from those situations where bodily deployment is both required and legitimated to those where it is neither required nor approved. Between these two extremes there are some more ambiguous situations. There are sites where bodily action is clearly required although not necessarily approved (arm wrestling, for example) or approved but not necessarily required (recreational walks). The ambiguities in this area reflect the complexities of a modern society, the multiplicities of overlapping reference groups or fields of meaning and the struggles and negotiations around the legitimacy or otherwise of different forms of embodied activities.

The point of this analysis is, as has already been stressed, not to provide a list of particular sites where embodiment, masculinities and power meet, but rather to suggest some of the principles upon which such sites might be constructed. To use another metaphor, the aim is not so much to point to a particular spot on a map but to suggest some rules by which this, and similar, maps might be constructed and read. One set of rules or principles, therefore, has been to do with the degree to which bodily deployment is required or is legitimated. Another set of principles might be to do with the ever-problematic distinction between the public and the private. There is, as has been stressed elsewhere, need for caution here partly because of the ambiguities built into the opposition itself and partly because such oppositions are in part ideological constructions which are used and called upon in difficult circumstances. Here I am arguing that just as social situations may be described as being more or less embodied, so they may also be described as being more or less open to the scrutiny of others. Such scrutiny may be direct or indirect or potential or actual. Thus speaking on a soapbox in Hyde Park is a public act, whether or not it attracts an audience. Putting these two sets of principles together or cross-cutting the two continually shows the various ways in which social contexts may be more or less embodied and more or less public. Thus a football match is both embodied and public while the training for such a match may well be equally embodied but much less public. Similarly (and putting to one side for a moment the approaches of Foucault and popular understandings of permissiveness) sexual intercourse is both embodied and private.

Hence, while in modern society there are clearly certain sites where embodiment, gender and power meet, the aim of this section has not been to provide a list of such sites, but to argue that all sites are in principle open to such analysis, and to provide a provisional guide to some of the investigative strategies that might be adopted in explaining such sites. To return to our solitary angler: he is both public and private and his activities, while embodied, are as much to do with bodily control and the art that conceals art as with more overt bodily display or deployment. And in his own rather unspectacular way he exercises power, not only power over nature but also the power to define his time and his space.

Types of men's bodies

Just as we should beware of seeking to provide a list of sites where embodiment and gendered power meet (with the implication that such a list provides a set of fixed or essential locations) so too we should be wary of establishing a typology of men's bodies. Assuming that we are not interested in simple physical descriptions of men's bodies (although the meanings given to such classifications may well be of interest) we are left with accounts which either provide for a plurality of masculinities and their bodily signifiers or concomitants or, more contentiously, with accounts which argue for embodiment being strongly or weakly associated with types of masculinities. In other, simpler, words, some bodies may be seen as more masculine than others.

Something of this kind of assumption appears to inform Frank's typology of body use in action (Frank 1991). As already noted, he draws up a typology around the words 'Disciplined', 'Dominating', 'Mirroring' and 'Communicating'. In so far as issues of gender, especially masculinity, enter into the discussion, it is around the second of these terms, 'Dominating'. It is likely that such a linkage is drawing upon commonsensical notions of masculinity or upon the more overt and obvious manifestations of embodied masculine power. Yet it is likely that issues of masculinity arise in all four although in different ways and to different degrees. Put another way, all four types of body use in action may be seen as being gendered.

After 'Dominating', the next type of body use in action which is most obviously associated with masculinity is probably 'Disciplined'. Here the medium which Frank cites is 'regimentation', something with clear associations with the military and with religious orders. The former has strong masculine connotations, of course, while the latter applies to both men and women. While the disciplined body can be strongly associated with some aspects of femininity (Frank instances the example of fasting) it is clear that this is a theme strongly associated with the developments of masculinities, especially within the early and middle stages of capitalism.

As has already been noted, the Dominating body, where the medium is that of force, is most closely associated with masculinity in many societies. However, it would be misleading to suggest that the Dominating body was anchored firmly and exclusively to men and to masculinity. Woman can and do use force and exercise domination, over children, over other women, and sometimes over men. Such instances are certainly less frequent for women than for men, although in many cases it would seem that the difference is not so much one of whether women are capable or not of exercising force, but the wider frameworks of meaning within which the exercise of force by women is conventionally understood.

The other two types of body use in action would seem to have much stronger feminine connotations in modern society. The Mirroring body, where the medium is consumption, would seem to have stronger feminine associations, since the wider gender division of labour tends to allocate the consumption function, generally speaking, to women rather than to men. Further, women are more likely to be directly involved in the commodification of their bodies, in the presentation of their bodies as objects of consumption. Again, there is nothing inevitable about this and recent research has provided plenty of examples of the ways in which the links between consumption and the male body, develop in modern society (e.g. Featherstone 1991). In the case of the Communicative body, where the medium is that of recognition, Frank argues that in present times we have only hints as to what this may mean. Certainly, his account of this type of body (using the illustrations of dance) does have strong feminine connotations, with the stress on the mutual interplay between dyadic other-relatedness and self-recognition. Yet, while perhaps the strongest intimations in modern society come from relations between or involving women, there are also hints of the Communicative body in relationships between men, sometimes under the most extreme of circumstances in the face of danger or at time of battle.

The purpose of this elaboration of Frank's types is partly to continue the exploration in terms of gender, which Frank himself began, but mainly to make the more general point that while certain types of body or bodily use in action have, in present cultures at least, strong masculine connotations, this is by no means inevitable. Indeed, if certain modes of bodily use readily conjure up images of men (such as Dominating) this may be because such understandings are ready to hand, deeply embedded in the culture. In contrast, an approach which stresses a plurality of masculinities will also allow for a range of bodily uses to be associated with men, some less obvious than others. This seems to suggest a cafeteria model of masculinities, whereby it is claimed that there are a variety of forms of available masculinities within modern society and that men may choose from these masculinities more or less at will. This is, of course, a model which is in keeping with some aspects of the postmodern debate as applied to issues of gender. Somewhat more structured, and more sociologically appealing, is the model suggested by Connell (and adopted by many writers on men and masculinities) whereby certain masculinities are seen as more dominant or hegemonic than others within any particular society (Connell 1987). Thus, generally speaking, the warrior is more hegemonic than the wimp. While there is clearly value in arguing for a hierarchy, rather than a simple plurality, of masculinities, the relationships between hegemony, embodiment and gender are by no means straightforward.

As an illustration of some of these complexities, I shall consider a distinction which derives from Bakhtin and which has been used by Stallybrass and White and, to a lesser extent, by Featherstone (Bakhtin 1984; Featherstone 1991: 79; Stallybrass and White 1986). This is a distinction between the grotesque body and the classical body. Generally speaking and with some simplification, classical bodies are controlled, in conformity with dominant (in this case European, Western?) aesthetic standards, and are constructed as being much closer to culture or to the civilized. In contrast, the grotesque body is uncontrolled, unappealing according to dominant aesthetic standards, and constructed as being much closer to nature. Almost, one might say, the distinction is close to that between the sacred and the profane. There are clear, historically located, class connotations to this distinction, the classical body being much closer to models prevailing amongst the aristocracy or the court society, while the grotesque body is more likely to be represented as a member of the peasant or the lower classes. Such bodies were also identified with particular spatial sites. In eighteenth-century England, classical bodies were more associated with the coffee houses, the grotesque bodies with taverns (Stallybrass and White 1986). . . .

In a more industrial society the boundaries become less clear and it may be suggested that the contrasts between the classical and the grotesque are of reduced significance. Nevertheless, their variations as models of masculinity still persist and still have their significance. In the face of the disciplines of capitalism and bureaucracy, the classical body becomes the rational body but the grotesque body still, at least symbolically, tends to be associated with the working or the lower classes. Yet today, as in former times, the grotesque body is by no means wholly stigmatized. Beer-bellied, prone to fits of violence or uncontrollable mirth and licking any of the conventional signs of self-discipline, the grotesque body can serve as a warning to society as a whole. This is certainly the case in some public health advertisements, highlighting the links between beer drinking, smoking, lack of exercise and chip eating with a proneness to heart complaints. Yet, at the same time, the grotesque body's symbolic closeness to natural instincts, its apparent rejection of the conventional limitations of a proper time or place may be a source of admiration, an ironic comment on the 'unnaturalness' of respectable or civilized society. The symbol of this covert celebration of naturalness may be the fart or the belch which, instead of being disguised or apologized for, is acknowledged as a source of pleasure or relief. . . .

It should be stressed that the grotesque and the classical or rational bodies (at whatever social level) have particular if different relations to masculine power. The grotesque body represents the symbolic power of the natural, a capacity for violence and sheer physical domination, highlighting the potential fragility of respectable society. In reversal of the conventional equation, it is a man's apparent unmediated links with nature, in all its earthiness and unpredictability, that provide the power of the grotesque body. Respectable, cultured society in this context becomes feminine or effeminate. The classical or rational body represents the power that resides in control, control over self and control over others. The aesthetic order of the classical body both mirrors and is a metaphor for the social order.

It may be suggested further that there are relationships, often covert, between the two manifestations of bodily power. The power of the controlled classical body, through the very emphasis upon control and discipline suggests a capacity for violence which the classical body shares, although less obviously, with the grotesque body. The rituals of Officers' Messes or all-male colleges symbolize the subterranean links between the two types. And similarly, although this is perhaps less well explored, the power of the grotesque body derives in part from the licence it is accorded by the classical body. Upper and middle-class patronage of bohemian society may be one example of this. At the very least, the grotesque body may serve as an abiding warning to respectable society as to what may happen if matters are allowed to get out of control.

It is not being claimed that this contrast between the classical (or rational) and grotesque body exhausts the range of types of male bodies which may be called upon in any given society. Rather, the contrast can be seen as representing one major theme around which modes of embodied masculinities can be analysed . It is designed to serve as a reminder that there are many ways, just as there are many sites, where gender and bodily power interact.

Conclusion: men, bodies and social change

It has been one of the main themes of this chapter that, while there has been relatively more scholarly and other attention paid to women's than to men's bodies, it cannot be maintained that women are more embodied than men. Nor, indeed, can the reverse be argued. The relationships between men and women and embodiment are different in character rather than degree, and the difference lies in the complex triangular relationships between gender, embodiment and power rather than in any straightforward physiological determination.

Another consequence of a more sociological approach to the study of men's bodies is to focus on the variations between men, on masculinities in the plural, as well as upon the variations between women and men. Again, such differences cannot be reduced to any straightforward differences in terms of physical strength, weight or height. Rather, these differences are to be sought, firstly in the different sites within which masculinities are constructed and reproduced. These sites are not, as might be understood in a more functional model, to be seen as fixed places or institutions but rather as shifting points of convergence around a variety of themes, such as those to do with the public and the private or in terms of the degree of legitimacy accorded to bodily action or display. Within many societies, some sites emerge with considerable frequency, such as those to do with war and sport. Yet even here, the strong linkages between gender, power and bodies are undergoing change and facing challenge.

In the second place, the differences between men can be seen in terms of the variety and the hierarchies of masculinities within a particular society. Over-use of the term 'hegemonic masculinities' might suggest that these are relatively straightforward, perhaps even fixed, hierarchies. However, even a brief consideration of the ideal-typical contrast between the classical and the grotesque bodied suggests that the relationship may be more complex. However, it may be said that the sheer physicality of the grotesque body loses out, in the long run, to the control of the rational or classical body.

One major historical theme has not been so much the shift from nature to culture or from the embodied to the less embodied. Rather, the emphasis may be better formulated in terms of a greater degree of control over bodies, both internally and externally. This, of course, is a major strand in the analysis of the civilizing process. The complexities of these controls cannot be explored in detail at this point: they include not only the well known processes of societal rationalization and bureaucratization but also a greater degree of surveillance, particularly in the processes generally defined as medicalization. Clearly, these processes affect women as well as men and often more directly, although it may be suggested that these processes have a peculiar significance in the lives and experiences of men, given the strong historical links that may be made between masculinities, rationality and the growth of scientific discourses. It is this greater degree of emphasis upon issues of control and discipline that might have led, misleadingly, to the belief that men were less embodied than women.

These long-term historical processes, much oversimplified in the context of a brief essay, do not proceed with an inexorable logic detached from human critique or praxis. Thus, in recent years, very often directly or indirectly as a consequence of the women's movements, some men have begun to look critically at certain bodily aspects of men's behaviour and men's lives in general. At least four aspects of this critique may be noted:

1. *The oppressing body*. More critical account of men and masculinities, that is, those accounts which take the feminist critique as their main point of departure, have looked at the male body as a site for the oppression of women. There have been several manifestations of this, including critiques of conventional models of male sexuality (both heterosexual and homosexual), searching examinations of men and sexual violence, and more general critiques of the role of men's violence, against both women and men, as one of the institutions or mechanisms of patriarchy (see, for example, Hearn 1987). Considerable attention has been paid to issues of pornography which, while overtly dealing with the objectification and commodification of women's bodies, simultaneously construct simple and essentialist models of men's desires and embodied sexualities. The common definition of a pornographic book as being one which is read with one hand reflects the way in which men's bodies are constructed through pornography. Another illustration is to do with all aspects of sexual harassment and the way in which, in certain contexts such as public places at night, men's bodies are perceived as potential threats to women. It may be argued that these discussions of the various embodied ways in which men's oppression of women operates has tended to focus upon the details of individual cases while failing to bring them together in a thoroughgoing theoretical analysis of the links between embodiment and power in men's routine and everyday practices.

2. *The body as a site for the emotions*. It is by now a commonplace that men have difficulty in expressing their feelings and their emotions. Sometimes this understanding is linked to a general feminist-inspired and historically-based critique while elsewhere it might be simply part of a diffuse therapeutic understanding of the self and personal identity in modern society. The lack on the part of men is sometimes understood to be an inability or a deeply structured unwillingness to verbalize feelings, but it may also include a critique of a failure to give non-verbal, more embodied expression to one's emotions. The common phrase 'to get in touch with one's feelings' has significantly embodied connotations. The paradigmatic example of the bodily expression of emotion is, of course, the ability to shed tears or to weep in public. It is as if, in the face of a lot of comparative historical and anthropological evidence, the shedding of tears were the guarantee of authenticity, the embodiment of a true self.

3. *The body and fraternity*. Part of the contemporary search for male identity is an exploration of the positive aspects of being a man. This search may be more or less directly anti-feminist or it may be, more ambiguously, a response to a perceived lack in comparison with the more overt expressions of sisterhood that

feminism has been seen as emphasizing. Positive virtues of masculinity are perceived to be in fraternity and male bonding, the direct expression of which may be in uninhibited bodily contact or a collective sharing of bodily experiences:

> We were chanting and sweating and screaming and hollering. It was fun and uplifting because it involved prayers and a lot of affirmation. People talked about pain.
>
> (Account of men's weekend retreat, *Newsweek*, 24 June 1991)

4. *The healthy body*. Concerns about the body are scarcely new, nor are they confined to men. However, there are some signs that recent concerns do have some overt links with a critical understanding of men's routine practices. In the first place, a simple recognition of the male body as a site for concern may be a relative novelty:

> The sum of my knowledge about the male body, its structure and functioning was the fact that I had one. It worked very satisfactorily for me, performed most of the tasks that were required of it and without too much difficulty. It never seriously bothered me, and consequently, I never seriously bothered about it.
>
> (Lewis 1978: ix)

Further, this recognition may contribute towards a critique of some routine manifestations of the 'grotesque body' in terms of consumption and everyday lifestyle: drinking, eating conventional masculine foods and failing to subject oneself to the disciplines of regular exercise.

It should not be imagined that this list exhausts the various ways in which reassessments of men's bodies have been taking place in recent years. We might, for example, wish to add to this list some modern version of the more traditional dandified body, a theme much emphasized in some recent men's magazines. Further, it should be stressed that these various modes of problematizing men's bodies do not necessarily add up to a coherent or widespread critical understanding, of men and their bodies. Certainly, we should not see them in terms of any straightforward linear progressive model. While there have been critiques of both the apparent inhibitions of the classical or the rational body and the apparent excesses of the grotesque body, theories of postmodernity have called into question any idea of progressive development and might instead seem to suggest that the classical and the grotesque bodies are being placed alongside or mixed with bodies based upon consumption and commodification:

> Postmodernity then is no longer an age in which bodies produce commodities, but where commodities produce bodies . . .
>
> (Faurschou 1988: 82)

Again, this process is not one that is confined to men, and indeed, it has been one in which women have often predominated. However, a growing emphasis on men's fashions and the proliferation of non-pornographic men's magazines certainly points to the elaboration of consumption-led masculinities. The healthy body, the stylish body and the athletic body become part of a range of bodies that are available in commodified form. Even some apparently traditional heroic models of men's bodies, in the films of Arnold Schwarzenegger for example, tend to be ironic parodies of the traditionally heroic.

Here too, it would be wrong to read too much into the signs. A little bit of unease with the grotesque body here or a bit of a critique of the classical body there, mixed up with a few men's magazines, hardly adds up to a total transformation or even a fully articulated critique. However, it is clear that some kinds of changes are taking place and that the links between embodiment and power and gender are being loosened, perhaps even as a consequence of being recognized as links.

Note

1   By way of illustration, consider a recent edition of a publication called *The Complete Angler's Guide* (no. 5 (3), July/August 1991). Here there were some forty-seven photographs featuring humans, the most common picture being that of a man holding his catch. These forty-seven pictures contained seventy-seven men, three women and five who were probably men. The three identifiable women were instructive. One was the writer's daughter in an article about a family angling holiday ('Erica and Heather walked off to the village just down the road to get some groceries . . .'). A second was on a page dealing with 'Pollution-free game' and the third was part of a husband-and-wife angling team.

References

Bakhtin, M. (1984/1965) *Rabelais and his World*. Bloomington, IN, Indiana University Press.

Barham, S. B. (1985) 'The phallus and the man: an analysis of male striptease', in L. Manderson (ed.) *Australian Ways*. Sydney: Allen & Unwin.

Byrde, P. (1979) *The Male Image: Men's Fashion in Britain, 1300–1700*. London: Batsford.

Connell, R. W. (1983) *Which Way is Up? Essays on Class, Sex and Culture*. Sydney: Allen & Unwin.

Connell, R. W. (1987) *Gender and Power*. Cambridge: Polity.

Easthope, A. (1986) *What a Man's Gotta Do: The Masculine Myth in Popular Culture*. London: Paladin.

Elias, N. (1978/1939) *The Civilizing Process, vol. 1, The History of Manners*. New York: Urizen.

Faurschou, G. (1988) 'Fashion and the cultural logic of postmodernity', in A. Kroker, and M. Kroker (eds) *Body Invaders: Sexuality and the Postmodern Condition*. Basingstoke: Macmillan.

Featherstone, M. (1991) *Consumer Culture and Postmodernism*. London: Sage.

Frank, A. W. (1991) 'For a sociology of the body: an analytical review', in M. Featherstone, M. Hepworth and B. S. Turner (eds) *The Body: Social Processes and Cultural Theory*. London: Sage.

Freund, P. E. S. (1983) *The Civilised Body: Social Domination, Control and Health*. Philadelphia: Temple University Press.

Goffman, E. (1967) 'Where the action is', in E. Goffman, *Interaction Ritual*. New York: Doubleday Anchor.

Hearn, J. (1987) *The Gender of Oppression: Men, Masculinity and the Critique of Marxism*. Brighton: Wheatsheaf.

Hoch, P. (1979) *White Hero, Black Beast*. London: Pluto.

Lewis, A. A. (1978) *The Male: His Body, His Sex*. New York: Doubleday Anchor.

Marsh, P. (1978) *Aggro: The Illusion of Violence*. London: Dent.

Martin, E. (1989/1987) *The Woman in the Body*. Milton Keynes: Open University Press.

Morgan, D. (1990) ' "No more heroes"? Masculinity, violence and the civilizing process', in L. Jameson and H. Corr (eds) *State, Private Life and Political Change*. Basingstoke: Macmillan.

Morgan, D. (1992) *Discovering Men*. London: Routledge.

Ortner, S. (1974) 'Is female to male as nature is to culture?' in M. Z. Rosaldo and L. Lamphere (eds) *Women, Culture and Society*. Stanford, CA: Stanford University Press.

Pearson, G. (1983) *Hooligan: A History of Respectable Fears*. London: Macmillan.

Reynaud, E. (1983) *Holy Virility: The Social Construction of Masculinity*. London: Pluto.

Seidler, V. (1989) *Rediscovering Masculinity: Reason, Language and Sexuality*. London: Routledge.

Stallybrass, P. and White, A. (1986) *The Politics and Poetics of Transgression*, London: Methuen.

Sydie, R. A. (1987) *Natural Women/Cultured Men: A Feminist Perspective on Sociological Theory*. Milton Keynes: Open University Press.

Walton, I. (1983) *The Compleat Angler, 1653–1676*, ed. J. Bevan, Oxford: Clarendon Press.

Chapter 47

Kathy Davis

FROM OBJECTIFIED BODY TO EMBODIED SUBJECT

Drawing on empirical research, Kathy Davis explores the meanings of cosmetic surgery for the women who undergo it. In so doing she challenges simplistic accounts of women's pursuit of beauty and suggests a more complex understanding of women's agency.

From S. Wilkinson (ed.) *Feminist Social Psychologies*, Buckingham: Open University Press, (1996)

COSMETIC SURGERY BELONGS TO the growing arsenal of techniques and technologies for body improvement and beautification which are part of the cultural landscape of late modernity. Women, who are numerically and ideologically the primary objects of these practices, have a long tradition of enduring pain 'for the sake of beauty'. From the practices of foot binding in ancient China to chemical face peeling and collagen-inflated lips in Southern California, women have been prepared to go to great lengths to meet cultural ideals of feminine shape and countenance.

The recent cosmetic surgery craze seems to be just one more expression – albeit a particularly dramatic and dangerous one – of what has been called the feminine 'beauty system' (MacCannell and MacCannell 1987). This system includes an enormous complex of cultural beauty practices drawn upon by individual women in order to meet the contemporary requirements of feminine appearance. It is one of the central ways that Western femininity is produced and regulated. Symbolically, Woman as sex is idealized as the incarnation of physical beauty, while most ordinary women are rendered 'drab, ugly, loathsome or fearful bodies' (Young 1990a: 123).

Feminist scholars have tended to cast a critical eye on women's involvement with 'the beauty system' (Wolf 1991). Originally, beauty was described in terms of suffering and oppression. Women were presented as the victims of beauty norms and of the ideology of feminine inferiority which they sustain. The beauty system was compared to the 'military-industrial complex' and decried as a 'major artic-ulation of capitalist patriarchy' (Bartky 1990: 39–40). By linking the beauty practices of individual women to the structural constraints of the beauty system, a convincing case was made for treating beauty as an essential ingredient of the social subordination of women – an ideal way to keep women in line by lulling them into believing that they could gain control over their lives through continued vigilance over their bodies. . . .

If feminists have had reason to be sceptical of the more mundane practices of the beauty system, it is not surprising that they are even more critical of the prac-tice of cosmetic surgery. Cosmetic surgery goes beyond the more routine procedures of body improvement and maintenance, such as leg waxing, make-up and dieting. Along with the pain and costs, it often involves serious side effects and the not infrequent chance of permanent maiming should the operation fail to achieve the desired result. With its expanding arsenal of techniques for reshaping and remaking the body, cosmetic surgery seems to be the site *par excellence* for disciplining and normalizing the female body – for, literally, 'cutting women down to size'.

Within feminist scholarship, it is difficult to view the woman who has cosmetic surgery as an agent who – at least to some extent – actively and knowledgeably gives shape to her life, albeit under circumstances which are not of her own making. Whether blinded by consumer capitalism, oppressed by patriarchal ideologies, or inscribed within the discourses of femininity, the woman who opts for the 'surgical fix' marches to the beat of a hegemonic system – a system which polices, constrains and inferiorizes her. If she plays the beauty game, she can only do so as 'cultural dope' (Garfinkel 1967) – as duped victim of false consciousness or as normalized object of disciplinary regimes.

While I share this critical assessment of the feminine beauty system and the cultural discourses and practices which inferiorize the female body, it is my contention that it is only part of the story. Moreover, in the case of cosmetic surgery, it is a story which may miss the point altogether. It is my contention that considerably more than beauty is at stake when women place their bodies under the surgeon's knife. Understanding why women have cosmetic surgery requires taking a closer look at how women themselves make sense of their decision in the light of their embodied experiences before and after surgery.

Surgical stories

This chapter is based on my research on women's narratives about cosmetic surgery (Davis 1995). . . . My inquiry spanned a period of several years. I conducted narra-tive interviews (see, for example, Sarbin 1986; Gergen and Gergen 1988, 1993; Shotter and Gergen 1989; Stanley 1990) with women who had already had, or were planning to have, some kind of cosmetic surgery. In some cases, I was able to talk to women both before and after their operation. The interviews were conducted in my home, or the woman's home and, later, in a clinical setting.

I spoke with women who had undergone many kinds of surgery: from a relatively simple ear correction or a breast augmentation to – in the most extreme case – having the whole face reconstructed. My interest being in surgery 'for looks', I did not talk to women who had reconstructive surgery as a result of trauma, illness or a congenital birth defect.

Since the research was conducted in the Netherlands, where cosmetic surgery was – until recently – included in the national health care package, the recipients came from a variety of socioeconomic backgrounds. Some were professional women or academics, others were cashiers or home helps, and some were full-time housewives and mothers. Some were married, some single, some heterosexual, some lesbian. Some were feminists, others were not. They ranged in age from a seventeen-year-old schoolgirl whose mother took her in for a breast augmentation (a bit like the ritual of buying the first bra) to a successful middle-aged businesswoman seeking a face-lift in order to 'fit into the corporate culture'.

These women told me about their history of suffering because of their appearance, how they decided to have their bodies altered surgically, their experiences with the operation itself, and their assessments of the outcome of the surgery. While their stories involved highly varied experiences of embodiment as well as different routes towards deciding to have cosmetic surgery, the act of having their bodies altered surgically invariably constituted a biographical 'turning point' (Denzin 1989) – a point from which they could look back at the past to make sense of their decision and forward to the future in order to anticipate what it would mean for them. Their stories were organized in such a way that cosmetic surgery could be viewed as an understandable and, indeed, unavoidable course of action in the light of their particular biographical circumstances.

Being ordinary

None of the women I spoke with had cosmetic surgery for the reasons many of us think they do – that is, having their bodies altered so that they could become more beautiful. Indeed, most displayed a noted reluctance to connect their particular problem to beauty and even went to great lengths to assure me that it had nothing to do with a desire to be more beautiful. This point was driven home in different ways.

Some women assured me that they were not particularly interested in how they looked. 'It was never *my* ambition to be Miss World' or '*I* don't have to be some sex bomb' were frequently heard remarks. They would make disparaging comments about other women who were preoccupied with physical attractiveness. For example, a woman who had her breasts 'lifted' after her second pregnancy explained that she found face-lifts ridiculous because 'wrinkles just go along with getting older'. A face-lift candidate, on the other hand, expressed disbelief that any woman could even consider having her breasts augmented: 'Breasts just don't make that much difference; it's not like your face. That's really important.'

Other women acknowledged that beauty did matter to them and that they, too, worried about how they looked ('What woman doesn't?'). They would produce lengthy lists of their own 'beauty problems'. For example, a woman who had a breast augmentation might complain that she had 'never liked the wrinkles on her face' or had always been much too thin ('a real beanpole'). A face-lift candidate would sigh that she 'would give anything for bigger breasts' or 'really hated having such hairy legs'. Others admitted that they would love to have different bodies — bigger breasts, fewer wrinkles, slimmer thighs. However, they would 'never consider cosmetic surgery for something like that'.

For the most part, the women I spoke with insisted that their reasons for having cosmetic surgery were of another order. In their case, one, and only one, part of their body — this nose or these ears, breasts or hips — was perceived as being too different, too abnormal, too out-of-the-ordinary to be endured. They didn't feel 'at home' in their bodies; this particular body part just didn't 'belong' to the rest of their body or to the person they felt they were. As one woman who had a breast reduction explained: 'I know a lot of people think big breasts are sexy, but I'm just not that kind of person. I'm basically a small-breasted type. That's just who I am.' In short, women who have cosmetic surgery want to be ordinary. They were not primarily concerned with becoming more beautiful; they just wanted to be 'like everyone else'.

Ironically, I did not necessarily share these women's conviction that they were physically abnormal or different. Their dissatisfaction had, in fact, little to do with intersubjective standards for acceptable or 'normal' feminine appearance. For example, when I spoke with women who were contemplating having cosmetic surgery, I rarely noticed the 'offending' body part, let alone understood why it required surgical alteration. From their stories, I could not help but notice that they were generally able to acquire jobs, find partners, produce families and, in general, lead fairly ordinary lives despite their problems with their appearance. In other words, their appearance and the circumstances of their lives did not seem noticeably different from those of women who do not have cosmetic surgery.

While women's bodily imperfections were often invisible to me, their pain was not. As they told me about the devastating effects their appearance had on their sexuality, their relationships, their feelings about themselves and their ability to move about in the world, their distress and anguish were utterly convincing. Despite the differences in the specific circumstances which led to a woman's decision to have cosmetic surgery, the experience of suffering was the common feature of their stories. Thus, cosmetic surgery was presented as the only way to alleviate suffering which had passed beyond what any woman should 'normally' have to endure. It was an extra-ordinary solution for an extra-ordinary problem.

. . . Cosmetic surgery is not the answer to women's problems with their appearance. A new body does not automatically provide a brand new self. Contrary to media promises of an exciting new life in the fast lanes, the women I spoke with described their lives after surgery as still constrained by the mundane problems and worries that were there prior to the surgery. Nevertheless, they indicated that there had been a transformation. This transformation required a long and often painful process of renegotiating their relationship to their bodies as well as their sense of self. . . .

Embodied subjects?

Cosmetic surgery is a cultural product of late modernity. It can only emerge as a 'solution' to women's problems with their appearance in a culture where the surgical alteration of the body is both readily available and socially acceptable (Bordo 1993). It requires a culture with an unshakable conviction in the technological 'fix' — the endless makability and remakability of ourselves through our bodies. It requires a culture with a dualistic conception of body and mind, in which surgery enables us to enact our intention upon our bodies. And, last but not least, it requires a culture where gender/power relations are typically enacted in and through women's bodies — that is, a culture in which women must negotiate their identities vis-à-vis their appearance.

In her phenomenology of female body experience, the feminist political theorist Iris Young (1990b) has argued that the 'typical' contradiction of feminine embodiment in Western highly industrialized societies is the tension between the female subject as embodied agent and the female body as object. On the one hand, a woman is the person whose body it is, the subject who enacts her projects and aims through her body. Like men, women experience their bodies as vehicles for enacting their desires or reaching out in the world. On the other hand, women are objectified bodies. In a gendered social order, they are socially defined through their bodies. Under constant critical surveillance by others, women begin to experience their own bodies at a distance. They view themselves as the objects of the intentions and manipulations of others.

Given this tension in women's bodily experience, it is hardly surprising that many women have difficulties feeling at ease, let alone at home, in their bodies. The body is both the site of their entrapment and the vehicle for expressing and controlling who they are. Although the objectification of the female body is part and parcel of the situation of most Western women and accounts for a shared sense of bodily alienation, women are also agents — that is, knowledgeable and active subjects who attempt to overcome their alienation, to act upon the world themselves instead of being acted upon by others. They may not be able to 'transcend' their bodies as the male subject presumably can,[1] but, as subjects, neither can they ever be entirely satisfied with a rendition of themselves as nothing but a body. Women must, therefore, live a contradiction. As Young (1990b: 144) puts it: 'As human she is a free subject who participates in transcendence, but her situation as a woman denies her that subjectivity and transcendence.'

It is in the context of this disempowering tension of feminine embodiment — the objectification of women as 'just bodies' and the desire of the female subject to act upon the world — that cosmetic surgery must be located.

In conclusion, cosmetic surgery is not simply the expression of the cultural constraints of femininity, nor is it a straightforward expression of women's oppression or of the normalization of the female body through the beauty system. Cosmetic surgery can enable some women to alleviate unbearable suffering, reappropriate formerly hated bodies, and re-enter the mundane world of femininity where beauty problems are routine and — at least to some extent — manageable. It is not a magical solution. Nor does it resolve the problems of feminine embodiment, let alone provide the path to liberation. Cosmetic surgery does, however, allow the individual woman to renegotiate her relationship to her body and, in so doing, construct a different sense of self. In a gendered social order where women's possibilities for action are limited, and more often than not ambivalent, cosmetic surgery can, paradoxically, provide an avenue towards becoming an embodied subject rather than remaining an objectified body.

Note

1   Obviously, men never fully transcend their bodies. The notion of the disembodied masculine subject – the mind without a body – is, like the objectified female body – the body without a mind – a fiction and has been amply criticized in feminist theory (see, for example, Bordo 1986; Code 1991).

References

Bartky, Sandra (1990) *Feminity and Domination. Studies in the Phenomenology of Oppression*. New York: Routledge.

Bordo, Susan (1986) 'The Cartesian masculination of thought', *Signs*, 11: 439–56.

Bordo, Susan (1993) *Unbearable Weight. Feminism, Western Culture, and the Body*. Berkeley CA: University of California Press.

Code, Lorraine (1991) *What Can She Know? Feminist Theory and the Construction of Knowledge*. Ithaca NY and London: Cornell University Press.

Davis, Kathy (1995) *Reshaping the Female Body. The Dilemma of Cosmetic Surgery*. New York: Routledge.

Denzin, Norman K. (1989) *Interpretive Biography*. Newbury Park CA: Sage.

Garfinkel, Harold (1967) *Studies in Ethnomethodology*. Englewood Cliffs NJ: Prentice-Hall; Cambridge: Polity.

Gergen, Kenneth J. and Gergen, Mary M. (1988) 'Narrative and the self as relationship', in L. Berkowitz (ed.) *Advances in Experimental Social Psychology*, vol. 21. New York: Academic Press.

Gergen, Mary M. and Gergen, Kenneth J. (1993) 'Narratives and the gendered body in popular autobiography', in R. Josselyn and A. Leiblich (eds) *The Narrative Study of Lives*. London: Sage.

MacCannell, Dean and MacCannell, Juliet Flower (1987) 'The beauty system', in Nancy Armstrong and Leonard Tennenhouse (eds) *The Ideology of Conduct*. New York: Methuen.

Sarbin, Theodore (ed.) (1986) *Narrative Psychology*. New York: Praeger.

Shotter, John and Gergen, Kenneth (eds) (1989) *Texts of Identity*. London: Sage.

Stanley, Liz (ed.) (1990) *Feminist Praxis: Research, Theory and Epistemology in Feminist Sociology*. London: Routledge.

Wolf, Naomi (1991) *The Beauty Myth: How Images of Beauty are used against Women*. New York: Morrow.

Young, Iris Marion (1990a) *Justice and the Politics of Difference*. Princeton NJ: Princeton University Press.

Young, Iris Marion (1990b) *Throwing like a Girl and other Essays in Feminist Philosophy and Social Theory*. Bloomington and Indianapolis IN: Indiana University Press.

Chapter 48

Alan Mansfield and
Barbara McGinn

PUMPING IRONY

This discussion of women body builders illustrates the contradictions entailed in this pursuit, showing that women are permitted to transform their bodies only within gendered limits.

From A. Mansfield and B. McGinn 'Pumping irony: the muscular and the feminine', in S. Scott and D. H. J. Morgan, *Body Matters: Essays on the Sociology of the Body*, London: Falmer (1993).

. . .

T HERE IS AN EXPLICIT politic to our inquiry into the transmogrification of the flesh. At some level our paper is part of a larger inquiry concerned with the way in which gender structures the social world. We are concerned at some level with the relation between masculinity and violence. No account of bodybuilding, particularly one concerned to speak of women, could ignore the connection between musclepower and manpower. More specifically, however, what we want to focus on in this paper is the number of levels in which the experience of women bodybuilders and women's bodybuilding reflects the irony of the connections between powerful muscularity and (potentially) violent masculinity. What we are examining then is the socialization of women into the world of bodybuilding, seeing, in common with other sociologists, socialization as a process of 'making safe'.

Bodybuilding as we would wish to use the term applies to something more specific than simply using weights in a gym, and it is important at this point to explain just what is being talked about when the term 'bodybuilder' is used. We do not want to discuss powerlifters and weightlifters (those who train to competitively lift maximum amount of weight, and whose physiques are developed as a by-product of this activity), not because they are uninteresting but simply because their inclusion would dissipate the focus of the paper.[1] Nor are we looking specifically at those people who use gyms and health clubs for what they might describe as keeping fit or 'body toning', although it is clear that these discourses are important and do intersect with those of bodybuilding.[2] The bodybuilder can be described as a person who deliberately cultivates an increase in mass and strength of the skeletal muscles (hypertrophy) by means of the lifting and pushing of weight.[3] The aim is to produce a body which fulfils certain criteria in terms of muscular size, shape, definition and tone. Success in achieving these aims on the part of an individual athlete is measured by means of physique contest ranging from the professional competitions such as Ms Olympia to those held in local gyms. This is not to suggest that all bodybuilders by definition enter competitions, because most do not, but simply to point out that a definitional structure exists in the sport which powerfully influences what happens in the gym. It is interesting to note that whilst there are many men who bodybuild seriously without any idea of ever competing, it seems that there is a much higher proportion of women bodybuilders who see competition as an important part of the activity. This suggests that there is a significant difference in the meaning that bodybuilding has for men and for women.

Another distinction may usefully be made here, and that is between what has been called the 'chromed-up health spa' (Francis 1989: 23) and the 'hard core' gym. Certainly over the last ten to fifteen years there has been a rapid expansion and growth of health clubs commonly associated with meeting the exercise needs of middle class professionals. Bodybuilders are actively discouraged from using this type of institution by the deliberate exclusion of certain aspects of the technology necessary to carry out the activity from the facilities on offer. It is often the case that the weights available are simply not heavy enough to meet the needs of a bodybuilder. The ambience created by bodybuilding is not one which is valued by health clubs.[4] A gym, on the other hand, whilst of course not being used exclusively by muscle 'freaks', can best be described for our purposes as being situated within a discourse which makes the 'outlandish' body possible.[5]

Bordo, writing primarily about dieting, notes some interesting connections between the slender body and the muscled body. Her argument is basically that the anorexic body and the muscled body are on a continuum, and although superficially very different images, are united against 'a common platoon of enemies: the soft, the loose; unsolid, excess flesh' (Bordo 1990: 90). Both dieting and bodybuilding are seen as powerful panoptic technologies producing self-monitoring 'docile' bodies. Bordo argues:

> increasingly, the size and shape of the body has come to operate as a marker of personal, internal order (or disorder) – as a symbol for the state of the soul
>
> (Bordo 1990: 94)

She also notes, however, something of the gendered nature of these normalizing practices. She argues, in relation to bulimia and anorexia, that a focus on the pathology of these phenomena obscures the function of the technologies of diet and body management as a central means in the production of gender. As she concludes. 'no *body* can escape either the imprint of culture or its' gendered meanings' (Bordo 1990: 109, our emphasis). Bordo's argument is generally very convincing: there certainly are a number of connections to be made, notably in the way the body is objectified in both the discourses of dieting and those of bodybuilding.

Bodybuilding is about developing individual body parts into a symmetrical, well balanced whole, but is important to note that although symmetry and proportion, that is, the way muscles and muscle groupings relate to each other, are crucial things for the bodybuilder's body, the discourse of bodybuilding produces a structure of fragmentation and objectification of the body. Basic and isolation exercises allow the bodybuilder to experience individual muscles and groups of muscles. Carol Mock, for example, talks about training her arms: 'I loved training my arms. Watching my biceps and triceps literally explode, really turned me on' (Bradford 1990: 28). Robin Parker talks about training her calves: 'I think that calves are an outrageously sexy body part. I have been able to put a lot more size on them in the past year. I love to train them and I love to watch them grow' (Nixon, 1990: 27). One of the problems, however, is that Bordo's work is weaker and less specific in relation to bodybuilding. This becomes clear in her discussion of the changed meanings in the muscled body where she talks about muscles 'developed to extremes' (Bordo 1990: 94) and in her difficulty in explaining the obvious pleasure in their bodies experienced by the women quoted above.

The failure to specify whether one is talking about the users of health spas or gyms has led to a great deal of confusion when discussing women's bodybuilding, and generally in relation to issues of women, the body, and social power. Contrary to what some writers, even in bodybuilding magazines, would suggest, there is a great deal of difference between two kinds of female hard body image. The currency of body maintenance techniques and the proliferation of health clubs is part of an acceptable hard body image such as that of Madonna, Elle McPherson (better known 'simply as Elle the Body', *Cleo*, November 1990: 104) or indeed the woman in the advertisement for *The Joy of Cooking* which Bordo (1990: 108) mistakenly suggests is that of a bodybuilder. There is, however, another hard body image which appears to be potentially more threatening: the image of the female bodybuilder, an image which goes far beyond that of the 'more athletic woman of today'. This image is clearly not safe enough for consumption yet, even (or should it be especially) in the market of fitness products. It is interesting to note that Reebok refused to sponsor a women's bodybuilding contest because 'they only liked the way three or four of the girls looked' whilst being happy to attach their corporate image to the UK National Aerobic Championships 1990 (*Musclemag*, July 1990: 104). Much of the second part of our paper is devoted to a discussion of the ways in which the bodybuilding community, which would include contests, judges, sponsors, bodybuilding magazines, regulating bodies, and women and men bodybuilders themselves, make safe the figure of the woman bodybuilder. Women bodybuilders themselves could be said to be at the forefront of this process, being more aware than anyone of what their bodies mean. This process of making safe for social, cultural and economic consumption should be understood as a process which occurs in many different ways on many different levels.

Pumping iron too!

Women's bodybuilding in its current manifestation dates from the 1970s when women (particularly in the United States) began to push for a place for women in the sport which radically changed the status quo. Prior to this time, the only contests available to women were little more than 'bathing beauty' contests, albeit organized by bodybuilding organizations. The other place for women in the sport, the gym itself, also had to be 'taken' and the last ten years have seen unprecedented numbers of women working out with weights in gyms which were previously exclusively male. We should also mention at this juncture that there are, of course, other significant sites of this struggle, more generally, the mass media and the public sphere and more particularly, for our purposes here, in bodybuilding magazines. There are women's bodybuilding magazines, women's bodybuilding is covered in 'men's' bodybuilding magazines (that is, those directed at men, and those directed at 'bodybuilders'). Further, other magazines occasionally deal with women's bodybuilding.[6] A discussion of magazine representation raises many issues to do with the commercial organization of publishing, histories and conventions of representation and so forth. We cannot in this article focus in sufficient detail on these matters, but we do make some comments about the relation between such matters and the issues we are concerned with. Representations of women's bodybuilding and women bodybuilders in magazines are very complex and contradictory, but it is precisely these contradictions which are evident in the judging of female bodybuilding competitions and in discussions of the ideal female bodybuilder's body. Constantly in the variety of discourse available, it is women bodybuilders, like others of their sex in other spheres, who carry manifestly the contradictions (and often penalties) of their gender. This is clear, for example, in the doubly transgressive nature of bodybuilding for women as opposed to men.

Increasing numbers of women have, however, been using weights and gyms, and a number of these women have become serious competitive bodybuilders. In an editorial in *Muscle and Fitness* Joe Weider ('the master-blaster, trainer of champions for over half a century') makes the point that women have invaded this traditionally masculine territory with 'their own form of muscular development'. He argues,

> it has given woman the opportunity to claim her equality. Her initial struggle for superiority has given way to pure love for her activity. And muscle becomes cut-glass through which we see the heightened qualities that make her so essential to our existence.

Weider concludes with the statement that

> WOMEN'S BODYBUILDING IS ONE OF THE STRONGEST EXPRESSIONS TO COME OUT OF THE FEMINIST MOVEMENT.
>
> (Weider 1990: 6)

One of the more well-known commentaries on women bodybuilders is, of course, the film *Pumping Iron II: The Women* which, as Annette Kuhn notes, was hailed by some as *the* feminist film of the year. The narrative of the film concerns a body-building championship held in 1984. The action, then, is set around who will win the contest, the 'shapely' Rachel McLish or the Australian power-lifter turned bodybuilder, Bev Francis. To cut a long story short, Carla Dunlap wins, and Bev Francis is placed well down the line in eighth position. All three of these women are muscular. What is important is that Bev Francis's position reflects the judges' point of view that she has muscles which are 'too masculine'. Francis clearly has more and bigger muscles than anyone else in the competition, and what is perhaps even more important, these muscles are also in different places from those of her competitors. Dunlap wins the competition because her body is judged to be some-where between that of McLish and Francis. It is not our purpose to comment here on the film's resolution of the plot, something of a compromise, Kuhn suggests. It is, however, important to point out the wider parameters of the debate the film sets up as they are crucial to our aims in this paper.

In '*Pumping Iron II*' the contest, particularly between Francis and McLish, is also a contest over definitions of women's bodies and what they do or should look like. Most simply, then, this concerns what is the ideal shape or look for a female bodybuilder. More broadly, however, this involves questions of women's and men's bodies generally and how they differ from each other, but also the question of who controls these images, and the locations of their enactment and reproduction. It is the 'transgressive' nature of female bodybuilders, that is, women with pronounced musculature, cut-glass muscle as Joe Weider would have it, which becomes the focus. When does muscle on a woman become 'too much', that is, masculine'? What is the relationship between muscularity and femininity, and how is this affected by the relationship between muscularity and masculinity? What happens when there is the 'threat'/possibility of muscularity equalling femininity? Our concern is to examine the ways in which this irony, these contradictions are negotiated. This involves an account of hegemonic struggle within the discourse and discursive practices of bodybuilding. Our account is thus put forward as an attempt to sketch out, albeit briefly, an account of power, resistance and social change. How will women's bodybuilding alter the sexual formation? How does the sexual formation manage or make safe women's bodybuilding? How can/do women bodybuilders resist or subvert this process? . . .

. . . [H]uman beings get defined as either male or female and from these defi-nitions flow a succession of others dependent upon this primary difference. The film *Pumping Iron II* (and in our analysis women's bodybuilding generally) high-lights something of what is going on in this process. The irony is then that bodybuilding unavoidably suggests a purposive and active production of the body. The enormous amount of hard work over a long period needed to produce the sculpted body cannot be ignored. Women's bodybuilding unavoidably raises ques-tions about both the naturalness of the body *and* the meanings centred via the body upon sexual difference.

Kuhn notes that muscles already do of course carry a great deal of cultural meaning, most significantly in those meanings centred upon the givenness of sexual difference, where of course they are heavily coded as masculine. Any investiga-tion of women bodybuilders then must also be investigation of bodybuilding *per se*. The matter is quite complex, being classed and raced as well as gendered, but some male bodybuilders can encounter a certain social approbation for their pumped highly vascular physiques. Even on men muscles are given and natural only up to a point. Of concern to us at the moment is the greater degree of social approbation incurred by muscular women and the vastly different points of transgression for men and women. We develop the point below, but for now we can note that if muscles are 'natural' and the body 'given', then there is a double transgression involved in female bodybuilding . . .

Weights and measures: working the edge

We would now like to turn our attention to the ideal of the women bodybuilders' body and the ways in which the interplay between the muscularity/masculinity fusion and notions of femininity are managed, particularly through the judging of women's bodybuilding contests. The proposition that the body is not an historical given demands an investigation of the discourses which produce the 'built' body of our text. This body, however, as has been pointed out above, is significantly gendered. The discourses involved in bodybuilding address the problem posed by the deviant and dangerous muscled female body by a differential construction of acceptable form between men and women.

Much has been written in recent years about the ways in which the idealized women's body has shifted from the 'womanly' ideal most lately seen in the 1950s to the androgynous (or more accurately boyish) look of the past thirty years or so. Bordo claims that both the extreme thinness of the 1960s and the more 'athletic' look of the 1980s can be encompassed within a discourse of androgynous slenderness which is marked by a rejection of

> The most literal symbolic form of maternal femininity . . . represented by the nineteenth-century 'hourglass' figure, emphasising breasts and hips – the markers of reproductive femaleness – against a wasp waist.
> (Bordo 1990: 104)

When looking at something as radically challenging to conventional notions of the gendered body as female bodybuilding the superficiality of this shift is pointed up. Doris Barrilleaux, who has been involved in the bodybuilding world for over thirty years, explains what is at stake as women bodybuilders begin to exhibit extreme muscularity:

> I think it may ruin the sport . . . A lot of women tell me they don't want to look that (more muscular). I like the athletic look . . . broad shoulders but small waists . . . I like the hourglass look. The V-shape is traditional to the male.
> (Bugg 1989: 51)

When the crunch comes, the masculine counterpoint is an archetypal feminine unrelated to any notions of boyishness. Recognizable markers of femininity were needed, the very breasts, hips and waist of the maternal woman, accompanied by hair and make-up styles which add up to a notion of idealized woman-hood, which can in no sense be described as androgynous. Bev Francis, one of the key figures of *Pumping Iron II*, was, told to 'get feminine or get out of women's bodybuilding' (Pearl 1989: 75). What Ross (1990: 45) refers to as the 'extreme emphasis on marketability' (of women's bodybuilding) has led Cory Everson to engage in a different kind of body work.

> Cory's biceps aren't getting any bigger but her breasts are. That's okay, the implants are enhancing her femininity and marketability.
>
> (Teagan, cited Pearl 1989: 73)

If the apotheosis of bodybuilding is winning at physique contests, then we have a very simple method of enforcement of the notion of the correct body for a woman. If a woman does not conform to this standard she cannot win. Women's body-building has been the site of struggle over the construction (in both senses) of its proponents' flesh. The judging of female physique contests brings together all the ambivalences about women and muscularity and these have been expressed in the controversies which have raged within and about women's bodybuilding since the late 1970s. Responses have ranged from condescending patronage to outright hostility, but as Pearl suggests, 'as the sport has grown, issues have been raised about just how far women should be allowed to build and about judging criteria' (Pearl 1989: 72). The use of the term 'allowed' here is noteworthy, suggesting that the muscular woman is threatening and needs in some way to be controlled and contained.

There is evident confusion (on the part of contestants, audiences and judges) over the judging criteria in women's contests. It is clear that bodybuilding, for women at least, is not just about being 'allowed to gain as much muscle as is humanly possible whilst at the same time retaining good symmetry and a healthy condition' (Pearl 1989: 72). An article on Dorothy Herndon, a relative newcomer on the competitive scene, exemplifies this;

> Her quest for size . . . has been the biggest drawback in her compet-itive career. In 1986 Dorothy's massive upper body turned heads, but managed only twelfth place position at the USA. In 1987 an even bigger Dorothy sat crying in the audience as she watched the top fifteen vie for the title − she hadn't even been placed in the running.
>
> (Dayton 1990: 46) . . .

It would be difficult to find a more powerful commentary on the way in which the woman bodybuilder constructs her body to fulfil the twin constraints of aesthetic and safe femininity than the career of Bev Francis, and the changes she has made to her body in order to become a successful bodybuilder. Over the years her waist and hips have become more slender, and the proportions of her body have changed to become more symmetrical, the development of her leg muscles has been toned down, she has brought out the 'detail' of her musculature rather than concen-trating on pure size or mass, she uses make-up and nail polish and has grown, lightened and curled her hair.

It seems that the one criterion for success about which there is no ambiguity in women's bodybuilding is the necessity to adopt the soft touch. It is these traditional markers of the feminine which have been adopted by women as a counterbalance to their musculature. Mandy Tanny, also commenting on the 1989 Ms Olympia, in which, as Everson explained above, the more heavily muscled women were successful, enthuses,

> Instead of the usual racehorse lineup . . . the whole presentation was like a muscular beauty pageant, and the audience loved it.
>
> (Tanny 1990: 128)

It is as though, when pushing at the limits of gender identity, lipstick and blonde locks are as necessary for the woman bodybuilder as they are for the female impersonator. There are a wide variety of styles of dress and personal presentation available to Western women of the late twentieth century to the extent that the notion of female-to-male cross-dressing has become almost meaningless. However, in the same way as it is necessary for the extreme gender markers of the hyperfeminine to be adopted by the male cross-dressers in order to make it clear that they wish to be recognized as 'women', so too is it necessary for women bodybuilders.[7] It is the adoption of the caricature features of femininity which allows a recognition of the familiar, the non-threatening. So long as women remain powerless, it is acceptable for them to ape the boys wearing their jeans and haircuts, but any incursions into the 'strict territory of a special kind of man' (Lyon and Kent Hall 1981: 2) requires, in the words of Cory Everson, that these women 'act and speak like ladies' (*Musclemag*, July 1990: 103). It seems that the female muscled body is so dangerous that the proclamation of gender must be made very loudly indeed.

These strategies for asserting gender should be viewed as falling within a discourse which holds 'woman' to be 'non-man', which produces the masculine as 'given' and the feminine as 'other'. Male gender is taken for granted, or occluded altogether as being unproblematic, not a subject for viewing or examination, whilst women are visible firstly as women and only then as (gendered) bodybuilders.

> As far as judging goes, many a judge has told me that they hate judging women and find it most difficult. One in fact openly admitted that he did not like women bodybuilders and could never get used to women having so much muscle, much preferring his women to be 'soft and cuddly'.
>
> (Pearl 1989: 72)

Conclusion: the battle of the bulges

. . . We have taken bodybuilding to be a limit case of the trainable body, a physical body which is situated within a pattern of social power which both enables and directs its production in a particular form in a definite historical moment. This social power, we have argued, is expressed through powerful panoptic techniques of self-monitoring, where 'the word' is, literally, 'made flesh', and the state of the physical body comes to operate as a symbol for the health, and thus the worth of, the 'soul'.

The body of the woman bodybuilder, then, becomes the site (sight) of the intersection of the discourses of bodybuilding and of gender. Because muscularity has been coded as a fundamentally masculine attribute, its adoption by women has offered a threat and a challenge to notions of both the feminine *and* the masculine. It seems that the possibility of the equation of muscularity with femininity is, in both senses, unspeakable.

Ros Coward, in a discussion of women and dieting, puts this another way:

> A large woman who is not apologising for her size is certainly not a figure to invite the dominant meanings which our culture attaches to femininity. She is impressive in ways that our culture's notion of the feminine cannot tolerate.
>
> (Coward 1984: 41)

Fat is equated with the libidinous, female sexually mature body, and thus with lack of control. Coward suggests that women suffer for this by adopting a masochistic, punitive attitude to their bodies. Paradoxically, women bodybuilders, through exerting extreme self-control, fragmentation and objectification of their bodies, achieve the 'impressive' body, which takes up more space than is proper for a woman. The irony is that the fruits of self-control become, in this case, highly visible, not to be viewed without discomfort. Yet women bodybuilders speak of their bodies with pleasure, rather than the self-hatred of the discourse of dieting, enabled by the valorization of moral worth displayed as a physical attribute, so noticeable in the 'body age' of the 1980s and 1990s. However, as Bordo suggests, this correct management of desire, what she terms ' "virile" capacity for self-management' (Bordo 1990: 101) is equated with accepted notions of masculinity. Women have adopted physical attributes strongly coded as masculine, by the use of regimens of self-management which are themselves so coded. The doubly transgressive position of the woman bodybuilder comments ironically on this masculinity.

In the early 1980s, Robert Mapplethorpe photographed Lisa Lyons' muscular arm wearing a lace glove, for its subversive and mocking effects on received notions of masculinity and femininity. This juxtaposition of masculine and feminine attributes on the bodies of muscular women has become a commonplace image in the bodybuilding world, even, we have suggested, necessary and desirable for the process of making the body 'safe'. This contradictory coding does, however, remain subversive. In drawing attention to the very power it aims to soften, it pumps the ironies of gender relations . . .

Notes

1   Bev Francis makes the difference between powerlifting and bodybuilding clear. In powerlifting the aim is to lift the heaviest possible weight, and you try to use

as much of your body as you can to achieve this aim, concentrating on the weight and not on the muscles or groups of muscles being used. This is a completely different method of training from that used by bodybuilders. As Bev Francis states, 'I try to isolate the movement so that the rest of my body is completely still. I try to feel the muscle through the entire movement' (Francis 1989: 11–13).

2   We do not have space to elaborate the complex positioning of bodybuilding within and across other fitness discourses, but our analysis thus far shows this positioning to be gendered, dynamic and tied in significant ways to both the current 'fitness craze' (an obsession with the 'hard body') and wider social developments of the 1980s and 1990s. The many new magazines on fitness and 'superfitness', for example *Excel*, reveal many of these developments.

3   The materials presented in this essay exclude one whole section of our writing on the specifics of bodybuilding discourse, a section entitled 'From calves to cows'. Exigencies of space prohibit extended commentary on hypertrophy and hyperplasia (the latter being an increase in the actual number of muscle cells) or the techniques of blitzing, flushing, muscle confusion, giant sets, angle training and so forth.

4   This point, we feel, needs further research and discussion, but may well be connected with the gendered nature of panoptic technologies which form the conclusion to our paper.

5   This distancing between a 'hard body' image and bodybuilder's body can be seen in the more public and media-oriented representatives of gym bodies. Advertising, for example in Britain, America and Australia, has a current fascination with bodybuilding images and paraphernalia. The international magazine on superfitness referred to above, *Excel*, is a good example. Again this process is gendered: the bodybuilding men represented have quite large muscles but are seldom 'pumped' and vascular, while the women represented are athletic but seldom bodybuilders (even more rarely 'pumped' or vascular). Bodybuilders are as unwelcome in magazines and advertisements as they are in health clubs. Nonetheless, at all of these sites the potential of bodybuilding is being mobilized, even if in a 'controlled' form.

6   The September 1989 edition of *20/20* magazine had an article on female bodybuilders entitled 'Broad smoulders'. Even the title of this article seems to support our thesis on the making safe of women bodybuilders. It produces a conjunction of a hyperfeminine attribute (smouldering looks) to make unambiguous attributes which are either masculine, potentially masculine or ambiguous (broad shoulders).

7   It is interesting to note that powerful women in another sphere, that of business, are similarly enjoined not to mix short hair with shoulder pads.

References

Bordo, S. (1990) 'Reading the slender body', in M. Jacobs (ed.) *Body/Politics: Women and the Discourses of Science*. London: Routledge.

Bradford, R. (1990) 'Carol Mock: body business', *Female Bodybuilding and Weight Training*, 28–9. New York: Starlog.

Bugg, L. (1989) 'Doris Barrilleaux, the world's sexiest grandmother', *Bodybuilding Monthly*, 12 (9): 50–1.

Cheshire, C. and Lewis, J. (1985) *Body Chic*. London, Pelham Books.

Coward, R. (1984) *Female Desire: Women's Sexuality Today*. London: Paladin.

Dayton, L. (1990) 'Dorothy Herndon: bodybuilding with passion', *Female Bodybuilding and Weight Training*, 21: 44–6.

Francis, B. with Reynolds, W. (1989) *Bev Francis' Power Bodybuilding*. New York: Sterling.

Lyon, L. and Kent Hall, D. (1981) *Lisa Lyon's Body Magic*. London: Bantam.

Nixon, D. (1990) 'Robin Parker: bodybuilding as an artform', *Female bodybuilding and Weight Training*, 21: 26–7.

Pearl, R. 91989) 'Woman and men judges', *Bodybuilding Monthly*, 12 (8): 72–5.

Pumping Iron II – The Women. (US 1985) directed by George Butler, British Distributor, Blue Dolphin, Video Distributor, Virgin.

Ross, D. (1990) 'Vascularity', *Super Fitness Excel*, 1 (1): 45–7.

Tanny, M. (1990) 'Cory's closest win', *Muscle and Fitness*, 51 (4): 126–38.

Weider, J. (1990) 'Those wonderful female bodybuilders', *Muscle and Fitness*, 51 (7): 6.

Chapter 49

Esther Newton

DRAG AND CAMP

This extract is taken from Esther Newton's classic ethnography of the world of drag queens in the United States in the 1960s – in the days before Gay Liberation and feminism. In drawing out the key elements of drag and camp performances and distinguishing between them. Newton analyses how both play with gender in innovative ways; neither entails a simple unproblematic imitation of the feminine.

From *Mother Camp: Female Impersonators in America*, Chicago: University of Chicago Press (1972).

. . .

THE ROLE OF THE FEMALE impersonator is directly related to both the drag queen and camp roles in the homosexual subculture.. In gay life, the two roles are strongly associated. In homosexual terminology, a drag queen is a homosexual male who often, or habitually, dresses in female attire. (A drag butch is a lesbian who often, or habitually, dresses in male attire.) Drag and camp are the most representative and widely used symbols of homosexuality in the English-speaking world.

The principal opposition around which the gay world revolves is masculine/feminine. There are a number of ways of presenting this opposition through one's own person, where it becomes also an opposition of 'inside' = 'outside' or 'underneath' = 'outside'. Ultimately, all drag symbolism opposes the 'inner' or 'real' self (subjective self) to the 'outer' self (social self). For the great majority of homosexuals, the social self is often a calculated respectability and the subjective or real self is stigmatized. The 'inner' = 'outer' opposition is almost parallel to 'back' = 'front'. In fact, the social self is usually described as 'front' and social relationships (especially with women) designed to support the veracity of the 'front' are called 'cover'. The 'front' = 'back' opposition also has a direct tie-in with the body: 'front' = 'face'; 'back' = 'ass'.

There are two different levels on which the oppositions call be played out. One is *within* the sartorial system[1] itself, that is, wearing feminine clothing 'underneath' and masculine clothing 'outside'. (This method seems to be used more by heterosexual transvestites.) It symbolizes that the visible, social, masculine clothing is a costume, which in turn symbolizes that the entire sex-role behavior is a role – an act. Conversely, stage impersonators sometimes wear jockey shorts underneath full stage drag, symbolizing that the feminine clothing is a costume.

A second 'internal' method is to mix sex-role referents *within* the visible sartorial system. This generally involves some 'outside' item from the feminine sartorial system such as earrings, lipstick, high-heeled shoes, a necklace, etc., worn *with* masculine clothing. This kind of opposition is used very frequently in informal camping by homosexuals. The feminine item stands out so glaringly by incongruity that it 'undermines' the masculine system and proclaims that the inner identification is feminine.[2] When this method is used on stage, it is called 'working with (feminine) pieces'. The performer generally works in a tuxedo or business suit and a woman's large hat and earrings.

The second level poses an opposition between a one sex-role sartorial system and the 'self', whose identity has to be indicated in some other way. Thus when impersonators are performing, the oppositional play is between 'appearance', which is female, and 'reality' or essence which is male. One way to do this is to show that the appearance is an illusion; for instance, a standard impersonation maneuver is to pull out one 'breast' and show it to the audience. A more drastic step is taking off the wig. Strippers actually routinize the progression from 'outside' to 'inside' visually, by starting in a full stripping costume and ending by taking off the bra and showing the audience the flat chest. Another method is to demonstrate 'maleness' verbally or vocally by suddenly dropping the vocal level or by sonic direct reference. One impersonator routinely tells the audience. 'Have a ball. I have two.' (But genitals must *never* be seen.) Another tells unruly members of the audience that he will 'put on my men's clothes and beat you up'. . . .

. . . The effect of the drag system is to wrench . . . sex roles loose from that which supposedly determines them, that is, genital sex. Gay people know that sex-typed behavior can be achieved, contrary to what is popularly believed They know that the possession of one type of genital equipment by no means guarantees the 'naturally appropriate' behavior.

Thus drag in the homosexual subculture symbolizes two somewhat conflicting statements concerning the sex-role system. The first statement symbolized by drag is that the sex-role system really is natural: therefore homosexuals are unnatural (typical responses: 'I am physically abnormal'; 'I can't help it, I was born with the wrong hormone balance'; 'I am really a woman who was born with the wrong equipment'; I am psychologically sick').

The second symbolic statement of drag questions the 'naturalness' of the sex-role system *in toto*; if sex-role behavior can be achieved by the 'wrong' sex, it logically follows that it is in reality also achieved, not inherited, by the 'right' sex. Anthropologists say that sex-role behavior is learned. The gay world, via drag, says that sex-role behavior is an appearance; it is 'outside'. It can be manipulated at will.

Drag symbolizes both these assertions in a very complex way. At the simplest level, drag signifies that the person wearing it is a homosexual, that he is a male who is behaving in a specifically inappropriate way, that he is a male who places himself as a woman in relation to other men. In this sense it signifies stigma. At the most complex, it is a double inversion that says 'appearance is an illusion'. Drag says, 'My "outside" appearance is feminine, but my essence "inside" [the body] is masculine.' At the same time it symbolizes the opposite inversion: 'My appearance "outside" [my body, my gender] is masculine but my essence "inside" [myself] is feminine.'

In the context of the homosexual subculture, all professional female impersonators are 'drag queens'. Drag is always worn for performance in any case; the female impersonator has simply professionalized this subcultural role. Among themselves, and in conversation with other homosexuals, female impersonators usually call themselves and are called drag queens. In the same way, their performances are referred to by themselves and others as drag shows. . . .

The camp

While all female impersonators are drag queens in the gay world, by no means are all of them 'camps'. Both the drag queen and the camp are expressive performing roles, and both specialize in transformation. But the drag queen is concerned with masculine/feminine transformation, while the camp is concerned with what might be called a philosophy of transformations and incongruity. Certainly the two roles are intimately related, since to be a feminine man is by definition incongruous. But strictly speaking, the drag queen simply expresses the incongruity while the camp actually uses it to achieve a higher synthesis. To the extent that a drag queen does this, he is called 'campy'. The drag queen role is emotionally charged and connotes low status for most homosexuals because it bears the visible stigma of homosexuality; camps, however, are found at all status levels in the homosexual subculture and are very often the center of primary group organization.[3] . . .

Camp is not a thing. Most broadly it signifies a *relationship* between things, people, and activities or qualities, and homosexuality. In this sense, 'camp taste', for instance, is synonymous with homosexual taste. Informants stressed that even between individuals there is very little agreement on what is camp because camp is in the eye of the beholder, that is, different homosexuals like different things, and because of the spontaneity and individuality of camp, camp taste is always changing. . . .

While camp is in the eye of the homosexual beholder, it is assumed that there is an underlying unity of perspective among homosexuals that gives any particular campy thing its special flavor. It is possible to discern strong themes in any particular campy thing or event. The three that seemed most recurrent and characteristic to me were *incongruity*, *theatricality*, and *humor*. All three are intimately related to the homosexual situation and strategy. Incongruity is the subject matter of camp, theatricality its style, and humor its strategy.

Camp usually depends on the perception or creation of *incongruous juxtapositions*. Either way, the homosexual 'creates' the camp, by pointing out the incongruity or by devising it. For instance, one informant said that the campiest thing he had seen recently was a Midwestern football player in high drag at a Hallowe'en ball. He pointed out that the football player was seriously trying to be a lady, and so his intent was not camp, but that the *effect* to the observer was campy. (The informant went on to say that it would have been even campier if the football player had been picked up by the police and had his picture published in the paper the next day.) This is an example of unintentional camp, in that the campy person or thing does not perceive the incongruity.

Created camp also depends on transformations and juxtapositions, but here the effect is intentional. The most concrete examples can be seen in the apartments of campy queens, for instance in the idea of growing plants in the toilet tank. One queen said that *TV Guide* had described a little Mexican horse statue as campy. He said there was nothing campy about this at all, but if you put a nude cut-out of Bette Davis on it, it would be campy. Masculine/feminine juxtapositions are, of course, the most characteristic kind of camp, but any very incongruous contrast can be campy. For instance, juxtapositions of high and low status, youth and old age, profane and sacred functions or symbols, cheap and expensive articles are frequently used for camp purposes. Objects or people are often said to be campy, but the camp inheres not in the person or thing itself but in the tension between that person or thing and the context or association. For instance, I was told by impersonators that a homosexual clothes designer made himself a beautiful Hallowe'en ball gown. After the ball he sold it to a wealthy society lady. It was said that when he wore it, it was very campy, but when she wore it, it was just an expensive gown, unless she had run around her ball saying she was really not herself but her faggot dress designer.

The nexus of this perception by incongruity lies in the basic homosexual experience, that is, squarely on the moral deviation. One informant said, 'Camp is all based on homosexual thought. It is all based on the idea of two men or two women in bed. It's incongruous and it's funny.' If moral deviation is the locus of the perception of incongruity, it is more specifically role deviation and role manipulation that are at the core of the second property of camp, *theatricality*.

Camp is theatrical in three interlocking ways. First of all, camp is style. Importance tends to shift from what a thing *is* to how it *looks*, from *what* is done to *how* it is done. It has been remarked that homosexuals excel in the decorative arts. The kind of incongruities that are campy are very often created by adornment or stylization of a well defined thing or symbol. But the emphasis on style goes further than this in that camp is also exaggerated, consciously 'stagey' specifically theatrical. This is especially true of *the* camp, who is definitely a performer.

The second aspect of theatricality in camp is its dramatic form. Camp, like drag, always involves a performer or performers and an audience. This is its structure. It is only stretching the point a little to say that, even in unintentional camp, this interaction is maintained. In the case of the football player, his behavior was transformed by his audience into a performance. In many cases of unintentional camp, the camp performs to his audience by commenting on the behavior or appearance of 'the scene', which is then described as 'campy'. In intentional camp, the structure of performer and audience is almost always clearly defined. This point will be elaborated below.

Third, camp is suffused with the perception of 'being as playing a role' and 'life as theatre'.[4] It is at this point that drag and camp merge and augment each other. I was led to an appreciation of this while reading Parker Tyler's appraisal of Greta Garbo.[5] Garbo is generally regarded in the homosexual community as 'high camp'. Tyler stated that ' "Drag acts," I believe, are not confined to the declassed sexes. Garbo "got in drag" whenever she took some heavy glamour part, whenever she melted in or out of a man's arms, whenever she simply let that heavenly-flexed neck . . . bear the weight of her thrown-back head.'[6] He concludes, 'How resplendent seems the art of acting! It is all *impersonation*, whether the sex underneath is true or not.'[7]

We have to take the long way around to get at the real relationship between Garbo and camp. The homosexual is stigmatized, but his stigma can be hidden. In Goffman's terminology, information about his stigma can be managed. Therefore, of crucial importance to homosexuals themselves and to non-homosexuals is whether the stigma is displayed so that one is immediately recognizable or is hidden so that he can pass to the world at large as a respectable citizen. The covert half (conceptually, not necessarily numerically) of the homosexual community is engaged in 'impersonating' respectable citizenry, at least some of the time. What is being impersonated?

The stigma essentially lies in being less than a man and in doing something that is unnatural (wrong) for a man to do. Surrounding this essence is a halo effect: violation of culturally standardized canons of taste, behavior, speech, and so on, rigorously associated (prescribed) with the male role (e.g. fanciful or decorative clothing styles, 'effeminate' speech and manner, expressed disinterest in women as sexual objects, expressed interest in men as sexual objects, unseemly concern with personal appearance, etc.). The covert homosexual must therefore do two things: first, he must conceal the fact that he sleeps with men. But concealing this *fact* is far less difficult than his second problem, which is controlling the *halo effect* or signals that would announce that he sleeps with men. The covert homosexual must in fact impersonate a *man*, that is, he must *appear* to the 'straight' world to be fulfilling (or not violating) all the requisites of the male role as defined by the 'straight' world.

The immediate relationship between Tyler's point about Garbo and camp/drag is this: if Garbo playing women is drag, then homosexuals 'passing' are playing men; they are in drag. This is the larger implication of drag/camp. In fact, gay people often use the word 'drag' in this broader sense, even to include role playing which most people simply take for granted: role playing in school, at the office, at parties, and so on. In fact, all of life is role and theatre – appearance.

But granted that all acting is impersonation, what moved Tyler to designate Garbo's acting specifically as 'drag'? Drag means, first of all, role playing. The way in which it defines role playing contains its implicit attitude. The word 'drag' attaches specifically to the outward, visible appurtenances of a role. In the type case, sex role, drag primarily refers to the wearing apparel and accessories that designate a human being as male or female, when it is worn by the opposite sex. By focusing on the outward appearance of role, drag implies that sex role and, by extension, role in general is something superficial, which can be manipulated, put on and off again at will. The drag concept implies *distance* between the actor and the role or 'act'. But drag also means 'costume'. This theatrical referent is the key to the attitude toward role playing embodied in drag as camp. Role playing is *play*; it is an act or show. The necessity to play at life, living role after superficial role, should not be the cause of bitterness or despair. Most of the sex role and other impersonations that male homosexuals do are done with ease, grace, and especially humor. The actor should throw himself into it; he should put on a good show; he should view the whole experience as fun, as a camp.[8]

The double stance toward role, putting on a good show while indicating distance (showing that it is a show), is the heart of drag as camp. Garbo's acting was thought to be 'drag' because it was considered markedly androgynous, and because she played (even overplayed) the role of *femme fatale* with style. No man (in her movies) and very few audiences (judging by her success) could resist her allure. And yet most of the men she seduced were her victims because she was only playing at love – only acting. This is made quite explicit in the film *Mata Hari*, in which Garbo the spy seduces men to get information from them.

The third quality of camp is its *humor*. Camp is for fun; the aim of camp is to make an audience laugh. In fact, it is a *system* of humor. Camp humor is a system of laughing at one's incongruous position instead of crying.[9] That is, the humor does not cover up, it transforms. I saw the reverse transformation – from laughter to pathos – often enough, and it is axiomatic among the impersonators that when the camp cannot laugh, he dissolves into a maudlin bundle of self-pity.

One of the most confounding aspects of my interaction with the impersonators was their tendency to laugh at situations that to me were horrifying or tragic. I was amazed, for instance, when one impersonator described to me as 'very campy' the scene in *Whatever Happened to Baby Jane* in which Bette Davis served Joan Crawford a rat, or the scene in which Bette Davis makes her 'comeback' in the parlor with the piano player.

Of course, not all impersonators and not all homosexuals are campy. The camp is a homosexual wit and clown; his campy productions and performances are a continuous creative strategy for dealing with the homosexual situation, and, in the process, defining a positive homosexual identity. As one performer summed it up for me, 'Homosexuality is a way of life that is against all ways of life, including nature's. And no one is more aware of it than the homosexual. The camp accepts his role as a homosexual and flaunts his homosexuality. He makes the other homosexuals laugh; he makes life a little brighter for them. And he builds a bridge to the straight people by getting them to laugh with him.' . . .

Notes

1   This concept was developed and suggested to me by Julian Pitt-Rivers.
2   Even one feminine item ruins the integrity of the masculine system; the male loses his caste honor. The superordinate role in a hierarchy is more fragile than the subordinate. Manhood must be achieved and, once achieved, guarded and protected.

3   The role of the 'pretty boy' is also a very positive one, and in some ways the camp is an alternative for those who are not pretty. However, the pretty boy is subject to the depredations of aging, which in the subculture is thought to set in at thirty (at the latest). Because the camp depends in inventiveness and wit rather than on physical beauty, he is ageless.

4   Sontag, 'Notes on "camp"', *Parisian Review* (Fall 1964): 515–30, at p. 529.

5   Parker Tyler, 'The Garbo image;, in *The Films of Greta Garbo*, ed. Michael Conway, Dion McGregor, and Mark Ricci (New York: Citadel Press, n.d.), pp. 9–31.

6   Tyler, 'The Garbo image', p. 12.

7   Ibid., p. 28.

8   It is clear to me now how camp undercuts rage and therefore rebellion by ridiculing serious and concentrated bitterness.

9   It would be worth while to compare camp humor with the humor systems of other oppressed people (Eastern European Jewish, Negro, etc.).

Chapter 50

Susanne J. Kessler

DEFINING AND PRODUCING GENITALS

The medical management of intersex has much to teach us about the social construction of gendered bodies. These extracts from Susanne Kessler's study show how cultural preconceptions about gendered genitals affect the decisions that doctors take about babies' gender. These preconceptions and the decisions based on them are in turn used to justify surgical alteration of genitals that do not match cultural ideals of 'proper' male and female bodies.

From *Lessons from the Intersexed*, New Brunswick NJ: Rutgers University Press (1998).

. . .

OBSTETRICIANS DO NOT STAND at the delivery table with ruler in hand, comparing the genitals they see with a table of values.[1] They seem to know ambiguity when they see it. In the medical literature on intersexuality, where physicians communicate their findings and their assumptions, the phrase 'ambiguous genitals' is used freely with no apparent need to define what 'ambiguous' means in this context. One could say that ambiguous genitals are described ambiguously. It is not uncommon to read statements likes 'Their [intersexed] external genitals look much more like a clitoris and labia than a penis or scrotum.'[2] One surgeon writes, without further specification, that the tip of the phallus should be the 'expected size for the patient's age.'[3] Another states that the need for surgery 'must be judged on the basis of the size of the shaft and glans of the clitoris in relation to the size of the patient and the interrelationship of the labia, mons veneris, and pubis.'[4]

One way to interpret this vagueness is that the ambiguity is so obvious that a physician who has seen scores of genitals has no need to validate the obvious. But the nonmedical reader is left wondering to what extent genitals must be ambiguous before they are seen to be in need of 'correction'. There are, of course, normative data on genital size, shape, and location,[5] but I will delay a discussion of specifications in order to consider the meaning of genital variations for physicians, as projected through their justifications for surgery and their descriptions of aberrant genitals.

Genital intolerance

Physicians describe all genital surgery on intersexed infants as necessary. Yet there are at least three categories of distinguishable genital surgery:

1   that which is *lifesaving* – for example, a urethra is rerouted so that the infant can pass urine out of his or her body,
2   that which *improves the quality of life* – for example, the urethral opening is redesigned so that a child can eventually urinate without spraying urine on the toilet seat; and
3   that which is *aesthetic* – for example, the small penis is augmented so that the (eventual) man will feel that he looks more manly.

Nowhere in the medical literature on intersexuality are these different motivations alluded to.[6] In fact, although variant genitals rarely pose a threat to the child's life, the postdelivery situation is referred to as a 'neonatal psychosexual emergency', seeming to require life-saving intervention.[7]

Few arguments are put forth in defense of performing surgery on intersexed infants. When pressed for a reason, physicians assert that 'normal' genitals will maximize the child's social adjustment and acceptance by the families. [. . .] Current attitudes about variant genitals are embedded (not too deeply) in medical reports and offer insight into the late-twentieth-century medical management of intersexuality. Feelings about larger-than-typical clitorises are illustrated by these representative quotations (my emphasis):

> The excision of a hypertrophied clitoris is to be preferred over allowing a *disfiguring and embarrassing* phallic structure to remain.[8]
> The anatomic *derangements* [were] surgically corrected. . . . Surgical techniques . . . remedy the *deformed* external genitals . . . [E]ven patients who suffered from major clitoral *overgrowth* have responded well. . . . [P]atients born with *obtrusive* clitoromegaly have been encountered. . . . [N]ine females had persistent phallic enlargement that was *embarrassing* or *offensive* and incompatible with satisfactory feminine presentation or adjustment. [After] surgery no prepubertal girl . . . described *troublesome* or painful erections.[9]
> Female babies born with an *ungainly* masculine enlargement of the clitoris evoke grave concern in their parents. . . . [The new clitoroplasty technique] allow[s] erection without cosmetic *offense*.[10]

Failure to [reduce the glans and shaft] will leave a button of *unsightly tissue*.[11]

[Another surgeon] has suggested . . . total elimination of the *offending* shaft of the clitoris.[12]

[A particular surgical technique] can be included as part of the procedure when the size of the glans is *challenging* to a feminine cosmetic result.[13]

These descriptions suggest not only that there is a size and malformation problem but that there is an aesthetic and moral violation. The language is emotional. Researchers seem disgusted. The early items on the list suggest that the large clitoris is imperfect and ugly. The later items suggest more of a personal affront. Perhaps the last item says it most transparently: the clitoris is "challenging".[14]

A social psychologist should ask: How were embarrassment and offense displayed? if the clitoris is troubling, offending, and embarrassing, who exactly is troubled, offended, and embarrassed and why? Not only are these questions not answered by intersex specialists, they are not even asked. A comment from an intersexed adult woman about her childhood is a relevant counterpoint: "I experienced the behavior of virtually everyone towards me as absolutely dishonest, embarrassing." Her comment reminds us that objects in the world (even non-normative organs) are not embarrassing; rather, people's reactions to them are. Another intersexual woman's "uncorrected" clitoris was described by her sexual partner as "easy to find."[15] Whether a clitoris is easy to find is arguably of some importance in sexual interactions, but it is not a criterion that physicians use for determining the suitable size for a clitoris.

An unexceptional quotation about the clitoris further substantiates the physicians' attitude:

The clitoris is not essential for *adequate* sexual function and sexual *gratification* . . . but its preservation would seem to be *desirable* if achieved while maintaining *satisfactory* appearance and function. . . . Yet the clitoris clearly has a relation to erotic stimulation and to sexual gratification and its presence is desirable, even in patients with intersexed anomalies if that presence does not interfere with *cosmetic, psychological, social and sexual* adjustment.[16] [my emphases]

Using my emphases as a guide, the alert reader should have some questions about the above quotation: Is 'adequate sexual function' the same as 'gratification'? If not, then which refers to the ability to orgasm? Why is the presence of the clitoris only desirable if it maintains a satisfactory appearance (whatever that is) and does not interfere? Lastly, how are the four different adjustments assessed and ranked, and is the order accidental?

Compared to language describing the larger-than-average clitoris, the language describing the small penis is less emotional but no less laden with value judgments. Common descriptors for the small penis are 'short, buried, and anomalous'. Sometimes there is a discussion about whether the microphallus is normally proportioned or whether it has a *'feminine stigmata* typical of intersexuality' indicative of *'arrested (feminine) development'*[17] (my emphases).

The emotionality in the case of the small penis is reserved for the child 'who cannot be a boy with this insignificant organ. . . . They *must* be raised as females. . . . They are *doomed* to life as a male without a penis.'[18] This last quotation suggests that if the penis is small enough, some physicians treat it as though it does not actually exist. Given its size, it does not qualify as a penis, and therefore the child does not qualify as a boy. 'Experience has shown that the most *heartbreaking* maladjustment attends those patients who have been raised as males in the vain hope that the penis will grow to a more masculine appearance and size "at a later date"'[19] (my emphases).

Physicians do not question whether a large clitoris ill prepares a girl for the female role. The emphasis is more on its ugliness. In contrast, physicians' descriptions of the micropenis are tied quite explicitly to gender role (my emphases): 'Is the size of the phallus . . . *adequate* to support a male sex assignment? [If not], those patients [regardless of genotype] are *unsuited* for the masculine role.'[20] A ten-year-old boy (with a microphallus) considering sex change was given testosterone ointment, after which he *'reaffirmed his allegiance to things masculine'.*[21] The sexual identification of the patients by their parents 'seemed less ambiguous following [testosterone] treatment, and the parents encouraged *more appropriate male behavior* in the patients following treatment.'[22] . . .

Defining the penis and clitoris[23]

Before pursuing the issue of ambiguity, some details about genital specifications must be discussed. Most neonate penises range between 2.8 cm and 4.5 cm in length and 0.9 cm and 1.3 cm in width.[24] The median length is about 3.5 cm.[25] Although there is some discussion in the literature about how penile measurements should be made (flaccid, stretched, or erect), the consensus is that flaccid penile lengths vary too much and therefore are not a reliable measure, and that there is a correlation between the fully stretched penis and the erect length.[26]

Standards for penile diameter or circumference also depend on whether the penis is measured relaxed, erect, or stretched. Because penile diameter is not a reliable measure, the definition of normal size is based on length, not width, although the two are correlated. Usually, the shorter the penis, the smaller the diameter of the shaft and the shorter the overall body length.[27] One researcher is exceptionally clear about why it is necessary to have genital norms: 'There is no need to stress the importance of having mean values and [a] range of measurements of normal genitals in the newborn infant. These can be most helpful in those cases in which the infant is suspected of having genitals of abnormal size.'[28]

When is a penis too small? . . .

In general, medical standards permit infant penises as small as 2.5 cm (about one inch) to mark maleness, but usually not smaller. One influential and highly published surgeon writes that she is concerned about penises that are smaller than 2.0 cm at birth, and she reassigns the infant to the female gender if the phallus (no longer a penis) is less than 1.5 cm long and 0.7 cm wide. She believes that a male infant needs a penis of a certain size in order to be accepted by family and peers. Yet she believes that infants with a form of pseudohermaphroditism known as 5-alpha-reductase deficiency should be raised as males, in spite of the fact that their penises are not 'male-like' at birth and will not become 'male-like' until puberty.[29] Clearly, to accept a small penis in this case, it is only necessary that the physician and the family expect that the infant will eventually have a penis of the proper size. If the parents of children with 5-alpha-reductase deficiency are capable of ignoring the materiality of their child's genitals in the anticipation of ones that more customarily match the child's gender assignment, why could not *most* parents? . . .

In spite of one writer saying, 'The size of an enlarged clitoris . . . cannot be stated in exact measurements,'[30] there are published norms for the clitorises of fetuses, infants, and adults.[31] This was not always so. A 1916 medical text gives size ranges for the penis and testicle, but not for the clitoris.[32] Tables of normative clitoral values appeared only in the late 1980s, more than forty years after similar values for penile sizes.[33] In one contemporary report, the clitoral length of eighty-two neonates ranged from 0.2 cm to 0.85 cm and the clitoral width ranged from 0.2 cm to 0.6 cm.[34] Some researchers factor length and width to compute a 'clitoral index'.[35] A clitoral index comparison of 'normal' infants and those with a form of intersexuality called congenital adrenal hyperplasia (CAH) noted measurements over nine times greater among the infants with CAH.[36]

How big must a clitoris be before physicians decide it is too large? In one study, infant clitorises that were reduced ranged from 1.5 cm to 3.5 cm prior to surgery.[37] In spite of there being a table of standards, physicians are more likely to refer to the average clitoris in food terminology, such as a pea or small bean.[38] In general, medical standards do not allow clitorises larger than 0.9 cm (about ⅜ in.). Figure 1 indicates standard clitoral and penile lengths for infants, revealing that intermediate area of phallic length that neither females nor males are permitted to have.

Not all pediatric surgeons who treat the intersexed are aware that there are published guidelines for clitoral size. One physician who has operated on intersexed infants for over twenty years was not – he told an interviewer that 'overall appearance is most important'.[39] We can only speculate about whether greater

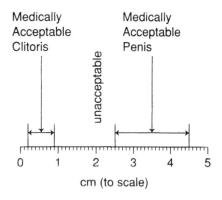

Figure 2 Ranges of medically acceptable infant clitoral and penile lengths

dissemination of information about the normal range for clitoral size would increase or decrease the number of clitoral reductions. Some have argued that universal standards would permit more 'consistent guidelines for gender assignment',[40] but it seems likely that if clitoral sizes are publicized and treated as guidelines, even more surgeries will be performed. Perhaps without a standardized set of ranges, physicians have been accepting more variability. . . .

Unlike the reluctance of medical personnel to wait and see if the girl 'grows into' her clitoris, nature is more likely to be permitted to run its course in terms of the labia. For example, if the prepuce adheres to the clitoris of a small child, this is not considered to be of clinical significance, since it is assumed that separation will occur spontaneously with androgen production at puberty. 'An attempt to strip the prepuce from the underlying tissues is not only meddlesome but painful.'[41]

Despite the fact that the degree of labia/scrotal fusion is an important criterion for determining that genitals are ambiguous, there is scant discussion in the medical literature of how 'normal' labia and scrotum ought to look. Unlike the relatively narrow standards for clitoral size, labial variation seems to be more permissible.[42] Texts say that the labia should not be completely fused, but a minor degree of posterior fusion is tolerable, and the labia majora are not required to completely cover the minora. Even a hundred years ago, medical texts acknowledged labia variability: The extension backward of the labia minora varies very much. In some women they go back to the middle line, so as to form a complete ring inside of that formed by the labia majora. In others they do not even reach the level of the meatus urinarius.'[43]

Looking at genitals with expectations

Ambiguity is at least partially determined by factors such as who is looking, why they are looking, and how hard they are looking. Intersex specialists warn against jumping to conclusions about what is there and what is not.[44] For example, physicians are cautioned about using testosterone in 'treating [an] infant or young boy with a normal-size penis which *appears* [my emphasis] small because it is partially buried in the prepubic fat pad'.[45]

How hard one 'looks' at genitals and what one 'sees' is not constrained by the optic nerve but by ideology. Given gender socialization, boys probably look at each others' genitals more than girls do. This is not because boys' genitals are objectively more obvious than girls' but because 'male' genitals have a different sociological import.[46]

Not all parts of 'male' genitals are equally important. The cultural meaning of the penis so overshadows the scrotum (fused or not and filled or not) as a gender marker that scrotal 'imperfection' is generally irrelevant. A writer who interviewed Roger Gorski, a physician/researcher at the University of California, Los Angeles, reported that Gorski showed him a close-up photograph of a child's genitals and asked, 'What sex is it?' The writer, seeing a penis 'plain as day', said confidently that it was a boy. 'Gorski's eyebrows shot up. "Where are the testicles?" he asked. I looked closer. Oops.'[47] Gorski was using the photograph to show

how the genitals of a genetic female with CAH can be affected, but the example illustrates as well how the average (nonmedical) person, even one who is interviewing a doctor about genitals and gender, can accept a missing scrotum as reasonable.

What one sees when one looks at a clitoris betrays as much about the viewer's assumptions as about the clitoris. One urologist, who was adamant about the need to reduce a girl's larger-than-typical clitoris, told a reporter that he worried about the effects on her when the girl's parents and caregivers saw her spend her early life with *'a big huge phallus in the lower end of the abdomen'*.[48] Readers will recall that this 'enormity' is likely to be about an inch in length. The atypical clitoris, as it is photographed for medical texts (brightly lit in a tight 'close-up', with the labia held wide apart), is more conspicuous than it might otherwise seem – certainly more than it is in almost all real-life circumstances.

The fact that 'looking' matters is supported by the invention of a surgical technique that involves recessing the enlarged clitoris beneath the labia so that it can no longer be seen. One problem with this technique is that the 'buried' clitoris swells during sexual arousal and produces a painful erection. At what cost is the clitoris required to be an internal organ? In older drawings of the female organs, the clitoris is portrayed as internal, like the bladder, uterus, and cervix.[49] More recent sketches treat it as an external part of the genitals.[50] Clitorises are not protruding more than they used to. Rather, public discussions of female sexuality in the last thirty years have helped evolve a public meaning for the clitoris.

Labia, in contrast, do not (yet) have much of a public role in Western cultures. The less delineated and meaningful a body part is, the more variability is tolerated. . . .

Notes

1   There are grading schemes for describing phenotypic features of external genitals: for example, the Prader stage classification for congenital adrenal hyperplasia (referred to in Ursula Kuhnle, Monika Bullinger, and H. P. Schwarz, 'The quality of life in adult female patients with congenital adrenal hyperplasia: a comprehensive study of the impact of genital malformations and chronic disease on female patients' life', *European Journal of Pediatrics* 154, 1995: 708–16) and a comparable system developed by Quigley and French for androgen-insensitivity syndrome (Charmian Quigley and Frank French, 'Androgen receptor defects: historical, clinical and molecular perspectives', *Endocrine Reviews* 16 (3), 1995: 271–321). These kinds of systems, though, are used to grade levels of intersex severity after the physician has already determined, through commonsense reasoning, that this is a case of genital 'ambiguity'. The scales are not used in the delivery room.

2   Jared Diamond, 'Turning a man', *Discover* 13, 6 (June 1992): 74.

3   John K. Lattimer, 'Relocation and recession of the enlarged clitoris with preservation of the glans: an alternative to amputation', *Journal of Urology* 81, 1 (1961): 113.

4   Judson G. Randolph and Wellington Hung, 'Reduction clitoroplasty in females with hypertrophied clitoris', *Journal of Pediatric Surgery* 5, 2 (April 1970): 224.

5   See, for example, William A. Schonfeld and Gilbert W. Beebe, 'Normal growth and variation in the male genitalia from birth to maturity', *Journal of Urology* 48 (1942): 759–77.

6   Surgeons are taught as part of their general training to distinguish degrees of urgency, from those conditions requiring immediate attention to those where surgery is elective (C. I. Clark and S. Snooks, 'Objectives of basic surgical training', *British Journal of Hospital Medicine* 50, 1993: 477–9). It seems as if, once intersex becomes the topic, those distinctions become obscure.

7   Barbara C. McGillivray, 'The newborn with ambiguous genitalia', *Seminars in Perinatology* 16, 6 (1992): 365. See also Domeena C. Renshaw, 'Sexual birth defects: telling the parents', *Resident and Staff Physician* 39, 2 (February 1993): 87–9.

8   Robert E. Gross, Judson Randolph, and John F. Crigler Jr, 'Clitorectomy for sexual abnormalities: indications and technique', *Surgery* (February 1966): 300. The authors of this report also refer to girls in need of clitoral surgery as having 'grossly enlarged' clitorises (*ibid.*, 301).

9   Judson Randolph, Wellington Hung, and Mary Colaianni Rathlev, 'Clitoroplasty for females born with ambiguous genitalia: a long-term study of thirty-seven patients', *Journal of Pediatric Surgery* 16, 6 (December 1981): 882, 883, 885, 886, and 887.

10 Kurt Newman, Judson Randolph, and Kathryn Anderson, 'The surgical management of infants and children with ambiguous genitalia', *Ann. Surg.* 215, 6 (June 1992): 651.

11 Stanley J. Kogan, Paul Smey, and Selwyn B. Levitt, 'Subtunical total reduction clitoroplasty: a safe modification of existing techniques', *Journal of Urology* 130 (October 1983): 748.

12 Randolph and Hung, 'Reduction clitoroplasty in females with hypertrophied clitoris', 230.

13 Lawrence E. Allen, B. E. Hardy, and B. M. Churchill, 'The surgical management of the enlarged clitoris', *Journal of Urology* 128 (August 1982): 352.

14 Julia Epstein makes a similar point about how emotionally charged the language of intersexuality is in her excellent historical analysis 'Either/or – neither/both'.

15 Private communication from Cheryl Chase, 3 December 1994.

16 Randolph and Hung, 'Reduction clitoroplasty in females with hypertrophied clitoris', 230.

17 Frank Hinman Jr, 'Microphallus: characteristics and choice of treatment from a study of twenty cases', *Journal of Urology* 107 (March 1972): 499.

18 Newman, Randolph, and Anderson, 'The surgical management of infants and children', 650.

19 *Ibid.*, 650.

20 *Ibid.*, 645.

21 *Ibid.*

22 Robert D. Guthrie, David W. Smith, and C. Benjamin Graham, 'Testosterone treatment for micropenis during early childhood', *Journal of Pediatrics* 83, 2 (1973): 250.

23 In spite of the female genitals being at least as complex as the male genitals, specifications of the former have historically been limited. For example, a 1916 medical text devotes forty-three pages to a discussion of the anatomy and physiology of the male sexual organ but only ten to the female (Winfield Scott Hall, *Sexual*

Knowledge, Philadelphia: John C. Winston Co., 1916). Sarah Hardy, in her review of Roger Short's comprehensive analysis of sexual selection and genital selection in humans and great apes, points out that he allocates twenty sections of the paper to the male genitals with scarcely a mention of female genitals (Sarah Hardy, *The Woman that never Evolved*, Cambridge MA: Harvard University Press, 1981). The most recent edition of *Dorland's Illustrated Medical Dictionary* (twenty-eighth edition, Philadelphia: W. B. Saunders, 1997, 341 and 1253) uses nine lines to define the penis but only three for the clitoris. One of the lines defining the clitoris reads 'Homologous with the penis in the male,' and one of the lines defining the penis reads 'Homologous with the clitoris in the female,' the latter being absent from the twenty-third edition of the dictionary, published forty years earlier. In so far as dictionaries reflect changes in the culture, an incipient symmetry between 'female' and 'male' genitals is confirmation that genital features can be recast over time, giving hope to those of us trying to reconceptualize intersexed genitals.

24   Kenneth W. Feldman and David W. Smith, 'Fetal phallic growth and penile standards for newborn male infants', *Journal of Pediatrics* 86, 3 (March 1975): 395–8.

25   E. Flateau, 'Penile size in the newborn infant', Letters to the editor, *Journal of Pediatrics* 87, 4 (October 1995): 663–4; Schonfeld and Beebe.

26   Peter A. Lee *et al.*

27   Hinman; Flateau.

28   Flateau, 664. John Money and colleagues discuss the discrepancy in data on norms for adult penile length. John Money, Gregory K. Lehne, and Frantz Pierre-Jerome, 'Micropenis: adult follow-up and comparison of size against new norms', *Journal of Sex and Marital Therapy* 10, 2 (1984): 105–14. Although there are published standards for infant and adult stretched penises, norms for adult erect penises are more difficult to locate in the medical literature. Sex researcher Leonore Tiefer claims that 'the assumption that everyone knows what a normal erection is is central to the universalization and reification that supports both medicalization and phallocentrism. . . . The symbolic need for a universal phallus has prevented examination of the range of real erections' (Tiefer, 'The medicalization of impotence', 365). On the other hand, organizations whose members are extremely interested in penile size publish norms, have standards for membership, and give advice on how to reliably measure the adult penis (*Measuring up*, a magazine published by the Hung Jury, a social organization for men with penises at least eight inches long, as measured erect from the base). In the words of one researcher, 'The true physiological length of the penis is its erect length' (Schonfeld and Beebe, 761).

29   Donahoe.

30   Gross, Randolph, and Crigler, 307.

31   The average adult clitoris, including the glans, body, and crura, is about an inch long. Although the growth of the clitoris does not receive the same degree of cultural attention as the growth of the penis, the clitoris, like all the female's other body parts, grows throughout her life. There are moderate increases through puberty. Kumud Sane and Ora Hirsch Pescovitz, 'The clitoral index: a determination of clitoral size in normal girls and in girls with abnormal sexual development', *Journal of Pediatrics* 120, 2 part 1 (February 1992): 264–6. In geriatric patients the average clitoral index is about 30 mm and may exceed 80 mm. John W. Huffman, 'Some facts about the clitoris', *Postgraduate Medicine* 60, 5 (November 1976): 245–7.

456 SUSANNE J. KESSLER

32   Hall.
33   Ellen Hyun-ju Lee, 'Producing Sex: An Interdisciplinary Perspective on Sex Assignment Decisions for Intersexuals', unpublished senior thesis, Brown University, April 1994.
34   Sharon E. Oberfeld et al., 'Clitoral size in full-term infants', American Journal of Perinatology 6, 4 (October 1989): 453–4.
35   Sane and Pescovitz; Huffman.
36   Sane and Pescovitz.
37   A. Sotiropoulos et al., 'Long-term assessment of genital reconstruction in female pseudohermaphrodites', Journal of Urology 115 (May 1976): 599–601.
38   This is particularly true in literature directed to the lay person. See, for example, M. J. Exner, The Sexual Side of Marriage (New York: W. W. Norton, 1932).
39   Ellen Hvun-ju Lee, 59.
40   Ibid., 32.
41   Huffman, 245.
42   The hymen, like the labia, is described in its variability, with a focus on individual differences of thickness and completeness. It is also interesting to note that the hymen is the only part of the female genitals described as tough. Kenneth M. Walker, Preparation for Marriage (New York: W. W. Norton, 1933), and Henry J. Garriques, A Textbook of the Diseases of Women (Philadelphia: W. B. Saunders, 1894).
43   Garriques, 37.
44   Hinman. The same could be said about adult genitals: 'Extremely fleshy women may be so plump that the clitoris cannot be seen within the inner lips' (L. T. Woodward, Sophisticated Sex Techniques in Marriage, New York: Lancer Books, 1968).
45   Guthrie, Smith, and Graham, 251.
46   Kessler and McKenna.
47   Chandler Burr, 'Homosexuality and biology', Atlantic Monthly (March 1993): 59.
48   'Is early vaginal reconstruction wrong for some intersex girls?' Urology Times (February 1997): 12.
49   John H. Holzaepfel, Marriage Manual (Pamphlet), 1959; Hall.
50   Robert Crooks and Karla Baur, Our Sexuality, sixth edition (Pacific Grove CA: Brooks-Cole, 1996).

Index

CPSIA information can be obtained at www.ICGtesting.com
Printed in the USA
BVOW062356180712

295599BV00005B/3/P